Literature and Globalization

'[I] wonder how we have managed without such a text'.
Rita Raley, USBC, USA

'Globalization' has had a huge impact on thinking across the humanities, redefining the understanding of fields such as communication, culture, politics, and literature.

This groundbreaking reader is the first to chart significant moments in the emergence of contemporary thinking about globalization and explore their significance for, and impact on, literary studies. The book's three parts look in turn at:

- an overview of globalization theory and influential works in the field
- the impact of globalization on literature and our understanding of the 'literary'
- how issues in globalization can be used to read specific literary texts.

Containing essays by leading critics including Arjun Appadurai, Jacques Derrida, Simon Gikandi, Ursula K. Heise, Graham Huggan, Franco Moretti, Bruce Robbins and Anna Tsing, this volume outlines the relationship between globalization and literature, offering a key sourcebook for and introduction to an exciting, emerging field.

Liam Connell is Senior Lecturer in English at the University of Winchester and has published in journals including ARIEL and Interventions and in the collections *Globalisation and its Discontents* (2006) and *Global Babel* (2007).

Nicky Marsh is Senior Lecturer in English at the University of Southampton and her publications include *Gender and Democracy in Contemporary American Poetry* (2007), *Teaching Modernist Poetry* (ed. with Peter Middleton, 2010), *Money, Speculation and Finance in Contemporary British Fiction* (2007).

Routledge Literature Readers

Also available
The History of Reading

For further information on this series visit: www.routledgeliterature.com/books/
series

Literature and Globalization

A Reader

Edited by

Liam Connell and Nicky Marsh

Routledge
Taylor & Francis Group

LONDON AND NEW YORK

First edition published 2011
by Routledge
2 Park Square, Milton Park, Abingdon, Oxon OX14 4RN

Simultaneously published in the USA and Canada
by Routledge
270 Madison Avenue, New York, NY 10016

Routledge is an imprint of the Taylor & Francis Group, an informa business

Typeset in Perpetua by
RefineCatch Limited, Bungay, Suffolk
Printed and bound in Great Britain by
The MPG Books Group

British Library Cataloguing in Publication Data
A catalogue record for this book is available from the British Library

Library of Congress Cataloging in Publication Data
Literature and globalization : a reader / edited by Liam Connell and Nicky Marsh. – 1st ed.
p. cm.
Includes bibliographical references and index.
1. Literature and globalization.   2. Globalization in literature.   3. Globalization.   I. Connell, Liam.
II. Marsh, Nicky.
PN56.G55L57 2010
809'.933552–dc22

2010008758

ISBN 10: 0-415-49667-5 (hbk)
ISBN 10: 0-415-49668-3 (pbk)

ISBN 13: 978-0-415-49667-4 (hbk)
ISBN 13: 978-0-415-49668-1 (pbk)

Contents

Acknowledgements

The publisher and the editors would like to thank the following for permission to reprint material under copyright:

From David Harvey, 'Time-Space Compression and the Postmodern Condition' from *The Condition of Postmodernity* (London: Blackwell, 1990), pp.284–5 and pp.291–307. Reproduced by permission of the publisher.

From Anthony Giddens, 'The Globalising of Modernity' from *The Consequences of Modernity* (London: Polity, 1990), pp.70–78. Reproduced by permission of Polity Press and Stanford University Press. Copyright © 1990 by the Board of Trustees of the Leland Stanford Jr. University.

From Roland Robertson, 'The Universalism-Particularism Issue', from *Globalization: Social Theory and Global Culture* (London: Sage, 1992), p. 97 and pp.100–105. Reproduced by permission of the of SAGE Publications, London, Los Angeles, New Delhi and Singapore.

Arjun Appadurai 'Disjuncture and Difference' From *Modernity at Large: Cultural Dimensions of Globalization* (Minnesota: University of Minnesota Press, 1996), 31–40, 41–43. © 1996 Regents of the University of Minnesota.

From J.K. Gibson-Graham, 'Querying Globalization', from *The End of Capitalism (as we knew it): A Feminist Critique of Political Economy* (Oxford: Blackwell, 1996), pp.120–124 and pp.134–147. Reproduced by permission of the publisher.

Anna Tsing, 'The Global Situation', *Cultural Anthropology* 15. 3 (2000), 327–328, 330–334, 336–342, 345–347, 351–360. Reproduced by permission of the American Anthropological Association from *Cultural Anthropology* Volume 15 (3), pp. 327–360, 2000. Not for sale or further reproduction.

Arif Dirlik, 'Modernity as history: post-revolutionary China, globalization and the question of modernity', *Social History*, 27.1 January (2002), 16–39 [16–18, 20–22, 23, 36–37]. Reprinted with permission of Taylor and Francis.

George Yudice, 'Free Trade and Culture (Chapter 8) excerpt,' from *The Expediency of Culture*, pp. 214–221. Copyright, 2003, Duke University Press. All rights reserved. Used by permission of the publisher.

Angus Cameron and Ronen Palan, 'Performative Discourse and Social Form'. Reproduced by permission of SAGE Publications, London, Los Angeles, New Delhi and Singapore, from *The Imagined Economies of Globalization* (© Angus Cameron and Ronan Palan 2004) pp. 54–68.

Antonio Negri and Michael Hardt, 'The Multitude Against Empire'. Reprinted by permission of the publisher from EMPIRE by Michael Hardt and Antonio Negri, pp. 393–400, Cambridge, Mass.: Harvard University Press, Copyright 2000 by the President and Fellows of Harvard College.

Franco Moretti, 'Conjectures on World Literature', *New Left Review,* 1 (2000), 54–64. Reproduced by permission of the publisher.

Paul Jay, 'Beyond Discipline? Globalization and the Future of English'.[32–36, 42–44] Reprinted by permission of the Modern Language Association from *PMLA,* 116 (2001), pp.32–47. © 2001 The Modern Language Association of America.

Simon Gikandi, 'Globalization and the Claims of Postcoloniality,' in *South Atlantic Quarterly*, Volume 100, no. 3, 627–658 [627–633, 636, 638–640, 643–658]. Copyright 2002, Duke University Press. All rights reserved. Used by permission of the publisher.

Jacques Derrida, 'Globalization, Peace, and Cosmopolitanism', from *Negotiations: Interventions and Interviews 1971–2002* by Jacques Derrida and translated by Elizabeth Rottenberg. Used by permission of Stanford University Press. [372–386] Copyright © 2002 by the Board of Trustees of the Leland Standford Jr. University.

From Masao Miyoshi, 'Turn to the Planet: Literature, Diversity, and Totality' from *Globalization and the Humanities* ed. By David Leiwei Li (Hong Kong: Hong Kong University Press, 2004), pp.19–35, [19–26, 32–35]. Reproduced by permission of the publisher.

Emily Apter, '"Untranslatable" Algeria: The Politics of Linguicide'. pp. 97–105. From APTER, EMILY; *The Translation Zone: a New Comparative Literature*, Princeton University Press 2006. Reprinted by permission of Princeton University Press.

Ursula K. Heise, 'Deterritorialization and Eco-Cosmopolitanism', from *Sense of Place and Sense of Planet: The Environmental Imagination of the Global* (Oxford: Oxford University Press, 2008), pp. 50–62. Reproduced by permission of the publisher.

From Huggan, Graham. Greening Postcolonialism: Ecocritical Perspectives. Modern Fiction Studies 50:3 (2004), 703–709, 719–732. © 2004 Purdue Research Foundation. Reprinted with permission of The Johns Hopkins University Press.

Pablo Mukerhjee 'Surfing the Second Wave: Amitav Ghosh's *The Hungry Tide*', *New Formations* 59 (Lawrence and Wishart 2006), 144–157. Reproduced by permission of the publisher.

Tratner, Michael. 'Derrida's Debt to Milton Friedman'. *New Literary History* 34:4 (2003), 791–806. © 2004 New Literary History, The University of Virginia. Reprinted with permission of The Johns Hopkins University Press.

Tim Woods, 'Giving and Receiving: Nurudin Farah's *Gifts* or the Postcolonial Logic of Third World Aid'. *The Journal of Commonwealth Literature*, 38 (2003), pp. 91–112. Reproduced by permission of of SAGE Publications, London, Los Angeles, New Delhi and Singapore.

Challakere, Padmaja. Aesthetics of Globalization in Contemporary Fiction: The Function of the fall of the Berlin Wall in Zadie Smith's *White Teeth* (2000), Nicholas Royle's *Counterparts* (1996), and Philip Hensher's *Pleasured* (1998). *Theory & Event* 10:1 (2007), 1–36 [1–23 and 32–36]. © 2007 Padmaja Challakere and The Johns Hopkins University Press. Reprinted with permission of The Johns Hopkins University Press.

Rita Raley 'eEMPIRES'. From *Cultural Critique* 57.1 (2004): 111, 115–37. © 2004 Regents of the University of Minnesota.

Fredric Jameson, 'Fear and Loathing in Globalization', *New Left Review* 23 (2003), pp.105–114. Reproduced by permission of New Left Review.

From Sieg, Katrin. 'Indians: The Globalized Woman on the Community Stage'. *Theatre Journal* 55:2 (2003), 291–302, 308–331. © 2003 The Johns Hopkins University Press. Reprinted with permission of The Johns Hopkins University Press.

Bruce Robbins, '*The Sweatshop Sublime*'. Reprinted by permission of the Modern Language Association from *PMLA* 117:1 (January 2002), 84–97. © 2002 The Modern Language Association of America.

Joseph Medley and Lorrayne A Carroll, 'The Hungry Ghost: IMF Policy, Capitalist Transformation and Laboring Bodies in Southeast Asia'. From: *Postcolonialism Meets Economics*, ed. by S Charusheela and Eiman Zein-Elabdin (© 2004 Joseph Medley and Lorrayne Carroll), pp. 145–164. Reproduced by permission of Taylor & Francis Books UK.

Neville Hoad 'An Elegy for African Cosmopolitanism: Phaswane Mpe's Welcome to Our Hillbrow' From *African Intimacies: Race, Homosexuality, and Globalization* (Minnesota: University of Minnesota Press, 2007), 113–27. © 2007 Regents of the University of Minnesota.

Lee, Sue-Im. 'We are Not the World: Global Village, Universalism, and Karen Tei Yamashita's *Tropic of Orange*'. Modern Fiction Studies 53:3 (2007), 501–527. © 2007 Purdue Research Foundation. Reprinted with permission of The Johns Hopkins University Press.

Peter J. Kalliney 'East African Literature and the Politics of Global Reading', *Research in African Literatures* 39:1 (2008), pp.1–23. Reproduced by permission of the publisher.

Suman Gupta 'Movements and Protests.' From *Globalization and Literature* (Cambridge: Polity, 2009), pp.13–31. Reproduced by permission of the publisher.

Every effort has been made to trace and contact copyright holders. The publishers would be pleased to hear from any copyright holders not acknowledged here, so that this acknowledgement page may be amended at the earliest opportunity.

We would also like to acknowledge the support of the University of Southampton and the University of Winchester. We would like to thank colleagues in both institutions for long-standing conversations, notably Mick Jardine, Peter Middleton, Stephen Marton and Sujala Singh. Special thanks go to Mandy Bloomfield and Stephanie Jones.

Introduction

THIS *READER* CONTRIBUTES TO THE WORK of framing, narrating and recording some of the varied ways in which literary studies has approached the heterogeneous discourses of globalization. It has three main, inter-related, aims: it is intended to introduce the student of literature to a selection of theoretical readings from a range of disciplines that have tried to understand the ramifications of the varied discourses of globalization; it reviews the multivalent ways in which different aspects of literary studies have sought to accommodate, critique and engage with these perspectives; and it offers a range of sustained readings of literary and cultural texts that explore some of the possibilities for implementing these perspectives as critical practice.

This tripartite structure obviously seeks to frame the field of globalization and literature in particular ways, and it seeks to do so somewhat more instrumentally than the several significant collections on globalization and culture to date (see, for example, Jameson and Miyoshi 1998; Cruz and Manalansan 2002; Kumar 2003; Saussy 2006; Dayal and Murphy 2007; Krishnaswamy and Hawley 2008).[1] Our focus is both broader (attempting to provide a general overview of the theorization of globalization in literature's cognate disciplines) and more restricted (focusing predominantly upon how the term globalization has reshaped literary studies as a discipline and how it has led critics to read specific literary texts). The *Reader* aims to provide students of contemporary literature with a set of well-developed theoretical questions and a series of case-studies that provide possible ways of answering them.

One of the primary difficulties in assigning meaning to contemporary modes of globalization is that the term has been consistently deployed to name quite different things and that a great deal of its energy derives from the potent and inevitable slippage between these varied meanings. Additionally, of course, there is an important and still unresolved debate regarding its relationship to alternative, earlier and concurrent, models of transnationalism.[2] We want to briefly separate out the three

prevalent uses of the term that concern us most before describing how our deployment of the term seeks to understand the connections between these different
meanings.[3]

First, most obviously, the word globalization has been used to identify a set of
broad socio-economic changes that began to occur in some geographical locations in
the early 1970s and gathered a triumphant pace following the end of the Cold War.
These changes are frequently associated with neoliberalism and include the deregulated expansion of speculative capital; rapid technological development, especially in
communicative technology; the transnationalization of production and the weakening
of labour movements; the reforming of some international trade agreements and
an increasing multinationalization of some corporations. Linked to this has been
an increased role for multilateral inter-governmental organizations such as the G5,
G8 and G20 groupings, the World Trade Organization, the European Union and
the United Nations in the legislative and regulatory structures of contemporary
governance.

Attempts to understand the political, social and experiential implications of
these changes have underpinned what we can think of as a second use of the term
globalization, as it refers to the increasingly large and multidisciplinary body of
intellectual work that Part 1 of the *Reader* gestures towards. It is possible to begin
to list some of the theoretical concepts and intellectual frames synonymous with this
work. Studies of globalization have explored the implications of the disarticulation of
politics from space and place known as 'deterritorialization' or 'disembedding'. The
dialectical intermingling of the 'local' and the 'global', the pervasive interpenetration
of these two dichotomous axes of globalization, has been described using the neologism of the 'glocal'. The constantly shifting topologies and movements of technology,
people and money that globalization involves have been described using the language
of 'scapes' and 'flows'. Our connections with people in ever more remote locations
have produced a social 'distanciation' while, at the same time, improved travel networks seem to banish distance through the 'compression' of space.

Yet, as this critical work often readily foregrounds, it is clearly impossible and
undesirable to suggest that either these changes, or the theorization of their effects,
are stable, self-evident or universal: the forms, prevalence, timing and locations of
these broad shifts are characterized only by an overwhelming heterogeneity. The
banking crisis that in the UK began in 2007, with the collapse of the Northern Rock
bank was swiftly attributed to the vertiginous reach of a globally integrated financial
industry,[4] whereas it actually seemed to demonstrate how profoundly socially, geographically and historically stratified the financial sector really is. Hence a third use
of the term globalization refers to the rhetoric, narratives and images that have
sought to constitute globalization as a unifying discourse for globality, a language of
unity and inclusion, albeit one that is frequently predicated upon creating and
denying difference and exclusion.

The discourses of globalization that seek to assign a coherent meaning to the
widely disparate experiences of contemporary politics are remarkably powerful,
remarkably diverse, and remarkably ubiquitous. The language of the globe has been
seized upon as a code for political agency not only by politicians, corporations, NGOs
and political activists but by consumers, advertisers, theologians, film makers and
environmentalists. To take the last example, in 2009 we have witnessed ExxonMobil

position itself as the solution to a twin challenge of 'global energy demand' and 'global environmental challenge'; we have seen the release of a biopic about Rachel Carson's 'love for the natural world and her fight to defend it', and in Copenhagen we saw the bitter failure of the international community to agree upon a response to the global problem of climate change.

Yet the implications of this assumption of global unity or coherence are profoundly diverse. In their crudest forms the languages of globalization are deeply divided and deeply divisive. They represent globalization as the celebrated bringer of the 'general prosperity based on free trade' that the international order must protect at all costs (The Economist 2007) and as a damning indictment of the powerful perversions of social relations wrought by advanced capital (Kaplinsky 2005). Yet a brief glance at some of the recurring debates that have characterized this discursive terrain complicates this schema, resisting the political spectrums of left and right as much as the moral Manichaeism of good and bad. The suggestions that globalization produces a form of homogenizing integration, or the development of certain universal ideals, for example, are familiar and politically enduring but also endlessly contested. Former libertarian neo-conservatives such as the political philosopher John Gray damn the universalizing impulse of globalization as the last remnant of a failed Utopian Enlightenment (Gray 2004), whereas radical critics such as Noam Chomsky retain the term despite its 'propagandist' status, precisely because it holds out the possibility of an international integration outside of the neo-liberal agenda: 'the most enthusiastic proponents of globalization', Chomsky argues with only partial irony, 'are those who meet at the World Social Forum' (2006). It is hardly surprising that some of the most popularized discourses for globalization are those that enact, in order to win, the idea of globalization as contest. This performance is variously repeated, from Samuel Huntington's contentious 'The Clash of Civilizations' (1993), to the opposition of modernity and tradition in Thomas Friedman's *The Lexus and the Olive Tree* (1999), to George Monbiot's opposition of the 'global dictatorship of vested interests' and 'activists in poor nations' in *The Age of Consent* (2003). For those most actively engaged in proselytizing and effecting these discourses, of course, they are represented as, simply, entirely self-evident and the axis of contest lies elsewhere: as Tony Blair told the Labour Party Conference in September 2005, 'I hear people say we have to stop and debate globalization. You might as well debate whether autumn should follow summer. They're not debating it in China and India' (2005).

Blair is right, at least, in suggesting that we can ill afford to simply reject the notion of globalization: although his Eurocentric point of closure is our point of entry into this debate. Our concern is with the heterogeneity and motivated contingency of the discourses of globalization that have become vital not only to the contemporary academy but to a vast array of social, cultural and political constituencies. The notion that a central component of globalization is the ability to define its implications, effects and terminologies has obvious attractions to literary scholars, for whom language and culture have long been an integral constituent of the political. Accordingly, our concern in this collection is with understanding how the varied discourses of globalization have represented and narrated the radically uneven and heterogeneous effects of the enormous economic, political and cultural shifts that have taken place in the last four decades. In particular, this involves trying to understand how the analyses of globalization developed in other political, cultural and intellectual realms can be made meaningful within the discipline of literary studies. This is motivated not by the desire to ensure that the discipline of literary studies remains abreast of developments in cognizant fields but by the conviction that literary studies – which, according to Arjun Appadurai, has seized the 'high ground' of contemporary thought (1996, 51) – has much to offer an analysis of the discourses of globalization.

Notes

1   As well as these collections there are a number of journal issues devoted to questions of globalization and literature. These inlcude *American Literary History* (2006) 18(3), *Comparative Literature* (2001) 53(4), *Contemporary Literature* (2006) 47(4), *Concentric: Literary and Cultural Studies* (2005) 31(2), *Modern Fiction Studies* (2002) 48(1), *New Literary History* (2008) 39(3), *PMLA* (2001) 116(1), *Public Culture* (2001) 13(1), *symploke* (2001) 9(1–2), *South Atlantic Quarterly* (2001) 100(3) and see also the journal *The Global South* since 2007.

2   The question of whether globalization resembles or is differentiable from imperialism has commanded considerable attention (for instance Saul 2003; Dallmayr 2005; Kiely 2005; Gopal and Lazarus 2006; Hoogvelt 2006). Similarly, considerable work has been done on the relationships between Islam and globalization, which suggests a range of different engagements with, and interpretations of the contemporary lines of international connection (see, for example, Mohammadi 2002; Pasha 2004).

3   Other definitions of globalization are, of course, possible. For instance, Martin Albrow has argued that globalization represents a distinct epoch, reinstating historical periodicity in opposition to modernity's insistence upon its endless vista as perpetual, and familiar, present (1996). There are obvious overlaps, here, with Frederic Jameon's periodization of globalization as *late* capitalism (1991).

4   In April 2008 Gordon Brown, for example, used the word 'global' no less than four times in a single statement on the crisis (Sawer 2008).

PART 1

Theorizing globalization

THIS FIRST PART OUTLINES SOME OF THE key theoretical gestures that have helped shape the emerging, multidisciplinary conversations about the significance, the remit and the forms of contemporary models of globalization. These excerpts have not been chosen in order to critique or create any single or representative impression of globalization studies and our bibliography indicates a much fuller reading list, which includes the work of those influential theorists who are absent from this very brief cross-section of many fields.[1] Our selection seeks to introduce the literary student to some of the central debates in this field, while gesturing, also, to the extent to which these debates are still contested. We have also tried to give space to some emerging voices within this area, as well as to more canonical figures, and to signal the development of more recent issues for globalization studies. Our specific interest in literary and cultural texts has also guided this selection, so that we have consciously attempted to prioritize writing which is most relevant to the specific concerns of the literary critic and to the issues that that we identify in the following two parts.

An originary point of critical thinking for these theoretical questions is neither easy nor useful. Although the academic study of contemporary globalization has well-recognized and significant forerunners, such as Marshall McLuhan's notion of the global village and Immanuel Wallerstein's analysis of world systems, we have chosen to begin with the influential, interdisciplinary and far-reaching work of David Harvey. Harvey's work was focused on the disorientations of a phenomenon characterized by its capacity to collapse the relations of time and space and his early accounts of this paradigm highlighted two issues that were to be formative to the conceptual explanations of globalization. Firstly, Harvey was closely attuned to the dialectical energies of the thing he was attempting to describe, and he is everywhere conscious of the fact that globalization contained within it its own contradictions. In our selected extract, for example, he notes that 'localism and nationalism' are both strengthened by the international impetus of 'flexible accumulation'; that the 'greater the ephemerality', the greater the desire for 'some kind of eternal truth'; and that the 'highly unified global space economy of capital flows' produces 'fragmentation, insecurity' and 'uneven development'. Secondly, and as importantly, Harvey was concerned with how the 'distinctive material basis' he ascribes to the economic shifts associated with globalization gave rise to 'distinctive systems of interpretation and representation'. For Harvey, the dematerialization of money that occurred after the failing of Bretton Woods in the early 1970s was central to the diminishment of referentiality that was to be widely associated with the postmodern for much of the following decade. As capitalism's primary 'value system' becomes 'dematerialized', so cultural texts seem to mirror 'the dissolution of the material *representations* of value'.

These elegantly suggestive characteristics of globalization, the capacity to absorb its own contradictions and to be made coherent by a mode of representation commensurate with the crisis it produces, became the central preoccupation of initial theorists of globalization. As our first tranche of essays suggests, this dynamic of contradiction and synthesis was used to reveal that some of the most troubling characteristics assigned to globalization are all formed through the potential for their own negation. Widely heralded features of globalization, including the diminishment of the sovereignty of the nation-state, the emergence of a homogenizing capitalist culture and the ascendancy of a single version of European and American modernity all appear simultaneously to be manifestly apparent and also substantially exaggerated. Yet, as our broader selection of essays demonstrates, a consensus about such canonical assumptions also needs to be contextualized and critically engaged with. This has specifically involved a direct critique of the inevitability that discussions regarding globalization often afford its totalizing reach over both culture and economics.

The tensions that constitute the discourses of globalization produced both a distinctive language for understanding the contemporary moment and a reassessment of the political foundations of modernity. Anthony Giddens' emphasis on the reflexive practices of 'disembedding' offered a social and markedly less political view of the disarticulation of time and space than that described by Harvey. Yet Giddens' delineation of the four 'dimensions' of globalization nonetheless emphasizes what he dubs the ' "push and pull" between opposing tendencies' of globalization, noting, for example, that concerted action between states, or between states and international corporations, could just as effectively bolster as diminish state sovereignty. For Roland Robertson the dialectical movement between the local and the global, or between the particular and the universal, is the very core of globalization, captured in the neologism of the 'glocal'. A parallel dynamic, as Robertson himself notes, is at work in Arjun Appadurai's analysis of the disjuncture 'between cultural homogenization and cultural heterogenization' that runs through the processes of globalization. For Appadurai these dynamics require a fluid and irregular schema and his attention to 'global cultural flows' indicates an analysis not of 'objectively given relations that look the same from every angle of vision' but of 'deeply perspectival constructs, inflected by the historical, linguistic, and political situatedness of different sorts of actors'.

For later critics these ambivalent energies were taken to suggest the possibility of reviewing and expanding the very political framing of globalization. For Arif

Dirlik these processes of contradiction and reversal are integral to the 'EuroAmerican' origins of 'capitalist modernity' that 'in its globalization, has had to interiorize cultural difference as part of its very constitution'. Yet the apparent historicization of Eurocentric modernity that follows from this, as it emerges 'not as the end of history' but as one model of modernity 'no less provincial in its claims than any of its competitors', suggests no kind of political emancipation. Rather, the apparent abandonment of Eurocentricism in favour of the 'recognition of cultural diversity takes place on the common grounds of a globalized capitalism' that 'serves also as the motor force in the universalizing of institutional structures fundamental to its functioning, as well as of the technologies and values of development, production and consumption'. In the celebratedly controversial work of Negri and Hardt the political implications of these relations of production and consumption in a new dialectical moment are made centre stage. For Michael Hardt and Antonio Negri, the totalizing and expansive energy of Empire has resulted in the deterritorialization of the proletarian, 'the dialectic between productive forces and the system of domination no longer have a determinate place' (p. 209). Yet this negation of geographical place becomes the core of Negri and Hardt's vision of subversion, as they posit that it is through 'circulation' that 'the multitude reappropriates space and constitutes itself as an active subject' capable of reclaiming an already existing global citizenship.

For theorist J.K. Gibson-Graham, such attempts to negotiate or reappropriate the apparently totalizing languages of global discourse are fraught, as they privilege the inevitable and invasive properties of globalization over an analysis capable of critiquing this assumption of 'unboundedness [. . .] Having set the signifier free from the referent, theorists of the global economy are loath to think about the effects of seepage, porosity, uncontrollability, that is, to feminize economic identity'. Hence Gibson-Graham cautions against being too easily 'bedazzled by images of the superior morphology of global capitalism' and urge us to imagine, instead, the 'renewed viability of noncapitalist globalization', to pay attention to the already existing but under-represented alternatives.

The differences between these essays highlight that the discourses of globalization are ongoing and contested, informed as much by the desire to identify resistance and fragmentation as by the desire to analyse the potency of its apparently universalizing sweep. Integral to this is the awareness of the productive authority of the discourses of globalization that constitute rather than merely describe a set of powerful social and economic conditions. Harvey's attention to the aesthetics of the postmodern found a different but equally influential form in Giddens' emphasis upon the reflexivity of late modernity, and this emphasis upon the formative power of representation was to be given an explicit, centrality by many of the theorists who followed in their wake. The dialectical relationship of globalization which concerns us most in this part is that which exists between globalization's economic and discursive forms, between what we once may have been able to deem its material base and its cultural superstructure.

The primacy of this relationship between the cultural and the economic has been given a variety of emphases. In its most obvious, and perhaps weaker, form, culture is recognized to be a profoundly significant component of the economic rather than a narrative fig leaf for what occurs beneath. Roland Robertson, for example, distances himself from the clear assertion of causality suggested by Fredric Jameson (the 'production of culture is directed by the "logic" of "late" capitalism') whilst acknowledging the necessary 'interpenetration' of culture and economy. Yet Robertson also presents this interpenetration as more than a reassertion of the commodity aesthetic, as he argues that globalization 'refers both to the compression of the world and the intensification of consciousness of the world as a whole' (1992, 8). It is the significance of this 'consciousness', the formative power that we can assign to our imaginative comprehension of globality, that provided a point of particular intellectual and critical purchase for theorists as varied as Arjun Appadurai, J.K. Gibson-Graham, Ronan Palan and Angus Cameron. 'The imagination', Appadurai states, 'is now central to all forms of agency, is itself a social fact, and is the key component of the new global order'. Although other critics are much less quixotically optimistic than Appadurai about the subversive agency stored in the imaginative constructions of the global, they do acknowledge that, as the 'prevailing narratives of political action and engagement are changing through the production of the particular imagery of globalization', then 'cultural theories and literary criticism may be of much greater use' for reading these possibilities than is 'normally acknowledged' outside of these disciplines (Cameron and Palan 2004, 4).

Yet, of course, the dyadic movement between culture and economy can easily collapse into itself and it is too easy to assume that the former always offers a privileged respite from, or insight into, the latter. This much is made apparent in George Yúdice and Anna Tsing's explorations of the specificity of this relationship in different sites in the local/global terrain. Yúdice makes it clear that the all-important cultural texts for globalization are themselves subject to its pervasive power imbalances and that the rolling out of intellectual property law, for example, under the inauspicious rubric of free trade fails to recognize the 'forms of labor' at the 'heart of indigenous knowledge and cultural forms' and perpetuates the 'asymmetry in capital accumulation between developed and developing countries and native peoples'. Anna Tsing's work on the fantasies of globalization projected onto Indonesia offers a different but equally critical account of the role of 'popular thinking about the pleasures and dangers of international finance and associated dreams of globalization' (2000, 117). Tsing is usefully sceptical regarding the tenacious power of the fantasies of 'globalism' that can easily draw critics into 'its rhetoric until we take its claims for true descriptions'. Indeed, we could do worse in any attempt to position our work within the discourses of globalization than heeding Tsing's note of caution, as she urges us to 'scale back the epochal claims' of globalization studies in order to 'pay close attention to ideologies of scale, that is, cultural claims about locality, regionality, and globality; about stasis and circulation; and about networks and strategies of proliferation'.

Note

1   These might include (Wallerstein 1974; Wallerstein 1984; Ohmae 1990; Ahmad 1992; Huntington 1993; Miyoshi 1993; Albrow 1996; Sassen 1996; Brennan 1997; Bauman 1998; Spivak 1998; Held, McGrew, et al. 1999; Hirst and Thompson 1999; Klein 1999; Tomlinson 1999; Sassen 2000; Held and McGrew 2002; Sassen 2002; Spivak 2003; Klein 2005; Chakrabarty 2008)

Chapter 1

David Harvey

TIME–SPACE COMPRESSION AND THE POSTMODERN CONDITION

From *The Condition of Postmodernity* Oxford: Blackwell, 1990, pp. 284–85 and pp. 291–307.

HOW HAVE THE USES AND MEANINGS OF SPACE and time shifted with the transition from Fordism to flexible accumulation? I want to suggest that we have been experiencing, these last two decades, an intense phase of time–space compression that has had a disorienting and disruptive impact upon political–economic practices, the balance of class power, as well as upon cultural and social life. While historical analogies are always dangerous, I think it no accident that post-modern sensibility evidences strong sympathies for certain of the confused political, cultural, and philosophical movements that occurred at the beginning of this century (in Vienna for example) when the sense of time–space compression was also pecu-liarly strong. I also note the revival of interest in geopolitical theory since around 1970, the aesthetics of place, and a revived willingness (even in social theory) to open the problem of spatiality to a general reconsideration (see, e.g., Gregory and Urry 1985; Soja 1988).

The transition to flexible accumulation was in part accomplished through the rapid deployment of new organizational forms and new technologies in production. Though the latter may have originated in the pursuit of military superiority, their application had everything to do with bypassing the rigidities of Fordism and accelerating turnover time as a solution to the grumbling problems of Fordism–Keynesianism that erupted into open crisis in 1973. Speed-up was achieved in production by organizational shifts towards vertical disintegration – sub-contracting, outsourcing, etc. – that reversed the Fordist tendency towards vertical integration and produced an increasing roundaboutness in production even in the face of increasing financial centralization. Other organizational shifts – such as the 'just-in-time' delivery system that reduces stock inventories – when coupled with the new technologies of electronic control, small-batch production, etc., all reduced turn-over times in many sectors of production (electronics, machine tools, automobiles, construction, clothing, etc.). For the labourers this all implied an intensification (speed-up) in labour processes and an acceleration in the de-skilling and re-skilling required to meet new labour needs. . . .

Accelerating turnover time in production entails parallel accelerations in exchange and consumption. Improved systems of communication and information flow, coupled with rationalizations in techniques of distribution (packaging, inventory control, containerization, market feed-back, etc.), made it possible to circulate commodities through the market system with greater speed. Electronic banking and plastic money were some of the innovations that improved the speed of the inverse flow of money. Financial services and markets (aided by computerized trading) likewise speeded up, so as to make, as the saying has it, 'twenty-four hours a very long time' in global stock markets.

Of the many developments in the arena of consumption, two stand out as being of particular importance. The mobilization of fashion in mass (as opposed to elite) markets provided a means to accelerate the pace of consumption not only in clothing, ornament, and decoration but also across a wide swathe of life-styles and recreational activities (leisure and sporting habits, pop music styles, video and children's games, and the like). A second trend was a shift away from the consumption of goods and into the consumption of services – not only personal, business, educational, and health services, but also into entertainments, spectacles, happenings, and distractions. The 'lifetime' of such services (a visit to a museum, going to a rock concert or movie, attending lectures or health clubs), though hard to estimate, is far shorter than that of an automobile or washing machine. If there are limits to the accumulation and turnover of physical goods (even counting the famous six thousand pairs of shoes of Imelda Marcos), then it makes sense for capitalists to turn to the provision of very ephemeral services in consumption. This quest may lie at the root of the rapid capitalist penetration, noted by Mandel and Jameson, of many sectors of cultural production from the mid-1960s onwards.

[. . .]

Baudrillard (1986), never afraid to exaggerate, considers the United States as a society so given over to speed, motion, cinematic images, and technological fixes as to have created a crisis of explanatory logic. It represents, he suggests, 'the triumph of effect over cause, of instantaneity over time as depth, the triumph of surface and of pure objectivization over the depth of desire'. This, of course, is the kind of environment in which deconstructionism can flourish. If it is impossible to say anything of solidity and permanence in the midst of this ephemeral and fragmented world, then why not join in the [language] game? Everything, from novel writing and philosophizing to the experience of labouring or making a home, has to face the challenge of accelerating turnover time and the rapid write-off of traditional and historically acquired values. The temporary contract in everything, as Lyotard remarks, then becomes the hallmark of postmodern living.

But, as so often happens, the plunge into the maelstrom of ephemerality has provoked an explosion of opposed sentiments and tendencies. To begin with, all sorts of technical means arise to guard against future shocks. Firms sub-contract or resort to flexible hiring practices to discount the potential unemployment costs of future market shifts. Futures markets in everything, from corn and pork bellies to currencies and government debt, coupled with the 'securitization' of all kinds of temporary and floating debts, illustrate techniques for discounting the future into the present. Insurance hedges of all kinds against future volatility become much more widely available.

Deeper questions of meaning and interpretation also arise. The greater the ephemerality, the more pressing the need to discover or manufacture some kind of eternal truth that might lie therein. The religious revival that has become much stronger since the late sixties, and the search for authenticity and authority in politics (with all of its accoutrements of nationalism and localism and of admiration for those charismatic and 'protean' individuals with their Nietzschian 'will to power') are cases in point. The revival of interest in basic institutions (such as the family and community), and the search for historical roots are all signs of a search for more secure moorings and longer-lasting values in a shifting world. Rochberg-Halton (1986, 173), in a sample study of North Chicago residents in 1977, finds, for example, that the objects actually valued in the home were not the 'pecuniary trophies' of a materialist culture which acted as 'reliable indices of one's socio-economic class, age, gender and so on', but the artefacts that embodied 'ties to loved ones and kin, valued experiences and activities, and memories of significant life events and people'. Photographs, particular objects (like a piano, a clock, a chair), and events (the playing of a record of a piece of music, the singing of a song) become the focus of a contemplative memory, and hence a generator of a sense of self that lies outside the sensory overloading of consumerist culture and fashion. The home becomes a private museum to guard against the ravages of time—space compression. At the very time, furthermore, that postmodernism proclaims the 'death of the author' and the rise of anti-auratic art in the public realm, the art market becomes ever more conscious of the monopoly power of the artist's signature and of questions of authenticity and forgery (no matter that the Rauschenberg is itself a mere reproduction montage). It is, perhaps, appropriate that the postmodernist developer building, as solid as the pink granite of Philip Johnson's AT & T building, should be debt-financed, built on the basis of fictitious capital, and architecturally conceived of, at least on the outside, more in the spirit of fiction than of function.

The spatial adjustments have been no less traumatic. The satellite communications systems deployed since the early 1970s have rendered the unit cost and time of communication invariant with respect to distance. It costs the same to communicate over 500 miles as it does over 5,000 via satellite. Air freight rates on commodities have likewise come down dramatically, while containerization has reduced the cost of bulk sea and road transport. It is now possible for a large multinational corporation like Texas Instruments to operate plants with simultaneous decision-making with respect to financial, market, input costs, quality control, and labour process conditions in more than fifty different locations across the globe (Dicken 1986, 110–13). Mass television ownership coupled with satellite communication makes it possible to experience a rush of images from different spaces almost simultaneously, collapsing the world's spaces into a series of images on a television screen. The whole world can watch the Olympic Games, the World Cup, the fall of a dictator, a political summit, a deadly tragedy . . . while mass tourism, films made in spectacular locations, make a wide range of simulated or vicarious experiences of what the world contains available to many people. The image of places and spaces becomes as open to production and ephemeral use as any other.

We have, in short, witnessed another fierce round in that process of annihilation of space through time that has always lain at the center of capitalism's dynamic. . . . Marshall McLuhan described how he thought the 'global village' had now become a communications reality in the mid-1960s:

> After three thousand years of explosion, by means of fragmentary and mechanical technologies, the Western World is imploding. During the mechanical ages we had extended our bodies in space. Today, after more than a century of electronic technology, we have extended our central nervous system itself in a global embrace, abolishing both space and time as far as our planet is concerned.

In recent years a whole spate of writing has taken this idea on board and tried to explore, as for example Virilio (1980) does in his *Esthétique de la disparition*, the cultural consequences of the supposed disappearance of time and space as materialized and tangible dimensions to social life.

But the collapse of spatial barriers does not mean that the significance of space is decreasing. Not for the first time in capitalism's history, we find the evidence pointing to the converse thesis. Heightened competition under conditions of crisis has coerced capitalists into paying much closer attention to relative locational advantages, precisely because diminishing spatial barriers give capitalists the power to exploit minute spatial differentiations to good effect. Small differences in what the space contains in the way of labour supplies, resources, infrastructures, and the like become of increased significance. Superior command over space becomes an even more important weapon in class struggle. It becomes one of the means to enforce speed-up and the redefinition of skills on recalcitrant work forces. Geographical mobility and decentralization are used against a union power which traditionally concentrated in the factories of mass production. Capital flight, deindustrialization of some regions, and the industrialization of others, the destruction of traditional working-class communities as power bases in class struggle, become leitmotifs of spatial transformation under more flexible conditions of accumulation (Martin and Rowthorn 1986; Bluestone and Harrison 1982; Harrison and Bluestone 1988).

As spatial barriers diminish so we become much more sensitized to what the world's spaces contain. Flexible accumulation typically exploits a wide range of seemingly contingent geographical circumstances, and reconstitutes them as structured internal elements of its own encompassing logic. For example, geographical differentiations in the mode and strengths of labour control together with variations in the quality as well as the quantity of labour power assume a much greater significance in corporate locational strategies. New industrial ensembles arise, sometimes out of almost nothing (as the various silicon valleys and glens) but more often on the basis of some pre-existing mix of skills and resources. The 'Third Italy' (Emilia-Romagna) builds upon a peculiar mix of co-operative entrepreneurialism, artisan labour, and local communist administrations anxious to generate employment, and inserts its clothing products with incredible success into a highly competitive world economy. Flanders attracts outside capital on the basis of a dispersed, flexible, and reasonably skilled labour supply with a deep hostility to unionism and socialism. Los Angeles imports the highly successful patriarchal labour systems of South-East Asia through mass immigration, while the celebrated paternalistic labour control system of the Japanese and Taiwanese is imported into California and South Wales. The story in each case is different, making it appear as if the uniqueness of this or that geographical circumstance matters more than ever before. Yet it does so, ironically, only because of the collapse of spatial barriers.

While labour control is always central, there are many other aspects of geographical organization that have risen to a new prominence under conditions of more flexible accumulation. The need for accurate information and speedy communication has emphasized the role of so-called 'world cities' in the financial and corporate system (centres equipped with teleports, airports, fixed communication links, as well as a wide array of financial, legal, business, and infrastructural services). The diminution of spatial barriers results in the reaffirmation and realignment of hierarchy within what is now a global urban system. The local availability of material resources of special qualities, or even at marginally lower costs, starts to be ever more important, as do local variations in market taste that are today more easily exploited under conditions of small-batch production and flexible design. Local differences in entrepreneurial ability, venture capital, scientific and technical know-how, social attitudes, also enter in, while the local networks of influence and power, the accumulation strategies of local ruling elites (as opposed to nation state policies) also become more deeply implicated in the regime of flexible accumulation.

But this then raises another dimension to the changing role of spatiality in contemporary society. If capitalists become increasingly sensitive to the spatially differentiated qualities of which the world's geography is composed, then it is possible for the peoples and powers that command those spaces to alter them in such a way as to be more rather than less attractive to highly mobile capital. Local ruling elites can, for example, implement strategies of local labour control, of skill enhancement, of infrastructural provision, of tax policy, state regulation, and so on, in order to attract development within their particular space. The qualities of place stand thereby to be emphasized in the midst of the increasing abstractions of space. The active production of places with special qualities becomes an important stake in spatial competition between localities, cities, regions, and nations. Corporatist forms of governance can flourish in such spaces, and themselves take on entrepreneurial roles in the production of favourable business climates and other special qualities. And it is in this context that we can better situate the striving . . . for cities to forge a distinctive image and to create an atmosphere of place and tradition that will act as a lure to both capital and people 'of the right sort' (i.e. wealthy and influential). Heightened inter-place competition should lead to the production of more variegated spaces within the increasing homogeneity of international exchange. But to the degree that this competition opens up cities to systems of accumulation, it ends up producing what Boyer (1988) calls a 'recursive' and 'serial' monotony, 'producing from already known patterns or molds places almost identical in ambience from city to city: New York's South Street Seaport, Boston's Quincy Market, Baltimore's Harbor Place'.

We thus approach the central paradox: the less important the spatial barriers, the greater the sensitivity of capital to the variations of place within space, and the greater the incentive for places to be differentiated in ways attractive to capital. The result has been the production of fragmentation, insecurity, and ephemeral uneven development within a highly unified global space economy of capital flows. The historic tension within capitalism between centralization and decentralization is now being worked out in new ways. Extraordinary decentralization and proliferation of industrial production ends up putting Benetton or Laura Ashley products in almost every serially produced shopping mall in the advanced capitalist world. Plainly, the new round of time—space compression is fraught with as many dangers as it offers possibilities for survival of particular places or for a solution to the overaccumulation problem.

The geography of devaluation through deindustrialization, rising local unemployment, fiscal retrenchment, write-offs of local assets, and the like, is indeed a sorry picture. But we can at least see its logic within the frame of the search for a solution to the overaccumulation problem through the push into flexible and more mobile systems of accumulation. But there are also a priori reasons to suspect (as well as some material evidence to support the idea) that regions of maximum churning and fragmentation are also regions that seem best set to survive the traumas of devaluation in the long run. There is more than a hint that a little devaluation now is better than massive devaluation later in the scramble for local survival in the world of severely constrained opportunities for positive growth. Reindustrializing and restructuring cannot be accomplished without deindustrializing and devaluing first.

None of these shifts in the experience of space and time would make the sense or have the impact they do without a radical shift in the manner in which value gets represented as money. Though long dominant, money has never been a clear or unambiguous representation of value, and on occasion it becomes so muddled as to become itself a major source of insecurity and uncertainty. Under the terms of the postwar settlement, the question of world money was put on a fairly stable basis. The US dollar became the medium of world trade, technically backed by a fixed convertibility into gold, and backed politically and economically by the overwhelming power of the US productive apparatus. The space of the US production system became, in effect, the guarantor of international value. But, as we have seen, one of the signals of the breakdown of the Fordist–Keynesian system was the breakdown of the Bretton Woods agreement, of convertibility of US dollars to gold, and the shift to a global system of floating exchange rates. The breakdown in part occurred because of the shifting dimensionalities of space and time generated out of capital accumulation. Rising indebtedness (particularly within the United States), and fiercer international competition from the reconstructed spaces of the world economy under conditions of growing accumulation, had much to do with undermining the power of the US economy to operate as an exclusive guarantor of world money.

The effects have been legion. The question of how value should now get represented, what form money should take, and the meaning that can be put upon the various forms of money available to us, has never been far from the surface of recent concerns. Since 1973, money has been 'de-materialized' in the sense that it no longer has a formal or tangible link to precious metals (though the latter have continued to play a role as one potential form of money among many others), or for that matter to any other tangible commodity. Nor does it rely exclusively upon productive activity within a particular space. The world has come to rely, for the first time in its history, upon immaterial forms of money – i.e. money of account assessed quantitatively in numbers of some designated currency (dollars, yen, Deutsch Marks, sterling, etc.). Exchange rates between the different currencies of the world have also been extremely volatile. Fortunes could be lost or made simply by holding the right currency during the right phases. The question of which currency I hold is directly linked to which place I put my faith in. That may have something to do with the competitive economic position and power of different national systems. That power, given the flexibility of accumulation over space, is itself a rapidly shifting magnitude. The effect is to render the spaces that underpin the determination of value as unstable as value itself. This problem is compounded by the way that speculative shifts bypass actual economic power and performance, and then trigger self-fulfilling expectations. The de-linking of the financial system from active production and from any material monetary base calls into question the reliability of the basic mechanism whereby value is supposed to be represented.

These difficulties have been most powerfully present in the process of devaluation of money, the measure of value, through inflation. The steady inflation rates of the Fordist – Keynesian era (usually in the 3 per cent range, and rarely above 5 per cent) gave way from 1969 onwards, and then accelerated in all the major capitalist countries during the 1970s into double-digit rates. Worse still, inflation became highly unstable, between as well as within countries, leaving everyone in doubt as to what the true value (the buying power) of a particular money might be in the near future. Money consequently became useless as a means of storing value for any length of time (the real rate of interest, measured as the money rate of interest minus the rate of inflation, was negative for several years during the 1970s, so dispossessing savers of the value they were seeking to store). Alternative means had to be found to store value effectively. And so began the vast inflation in certain kinds of asset prices – collectibles, art objects, antiques, houses, and the like. Buying a Degas or Van Gogh in 1973 would surely outstrip almost any other kind of investment in terms of capital gain. Indeed it can be argued that the growth of the art market (with its concern for authorial signature) and the strong commercialization of cultural production since around 1970 have had a lot to do with the search to find alternative means to store value under conditions where the usual money forms were deficient. Commodity and general price inflation, though to some degree brought under control in the advanced capitalist countries during the 1980s, has by no means diminished as a problem. It is rampant in countries like Mexico, Argentina, Brazil, and Israel (all with recent rates in hundreds of per cent), and the prospect of generalized inflation looms in the advanced capitalist countries, where it is in any case arguable that the inflation of asset prices (housing, works of art, antiques, etc.) has taken over where commodity and labour market inflation left off in the early 1980s.

The breakdown of money as a secure means of representing value has itself created a crisis of representation in advanced capitalism. It has also been reinforced by, and added its very considerable weight to, the problems of time—space compression which we earlier identified. The rapidity with which currency markets fluctuate across the world's spaces, the extraordinary power of money capital flow in what is now a global stock and financial market, and the volatility of what the purchasing power of money might represent, define, as it were, a high point of that highly problematic intersection of money, time, and space as interlocking elements of social power in the political economy of postmodernity.

It is, furthermore, not hard to see how all of this might create a more general crisis of representation. The central value system, to which capitalism has always appealed to validate and gauge its actions, is dematerialized and shifting, time horizons are collapsing, and it is hard to tell exactly what space we are in when it comes to assessing causes and effects, meanings or values. The intriguing exhibition at the Pompidou Centre in 1985 on 'The Immaterial' (an exhibition for which none other than Lyotard acted as one of the consultants) was perhaps a mirror image of the dissolution of the material representations of value under conditions of more flexible accumulation, and of the confusions as to what it might mean to say, with Paul Virilio, that time and space have disappeared as meaningful dimensions to human thought and action.

There are, I would submit, more tangible and material ways than this to go about assessing the significance of space and time for the condition of postmodernity. It should be possible to consider how, for example, the changing experience of space, time, and money has formed a distinctive material basis for the rise of distinctive systems of interpretation and representation, as well as opening a path through which the aestheticization of politics might once more reassert itself. If we view culture as that complex of signs and significations (including language) that mesh into codes of transmission of social values and meanings, then we can at least begin upon the task of unravelling its complexities under present-day conditions by recognizing that money and commodities are themselves the primary bearers of cultural codes. Since money and commodities are entirely bound up with the circulation of capital, it follows that cultural forms are firmly rooted in the daily circulation process of capital. It is, therefore, with the daily experience of money and the commodity that we should begin, no matter if special commodities or even whole sign systems may be extracted from the common herd and made the basis of 'high' culture or that specialized 'imaging' which we have already had cause to comment upon.

The annihilation of space through time has radically changed the commodity mix that enters into daily reproduction. Innumerable local food systems have been reorganized through their incorporation into global commodity exchange. French cheeses, for example, virtually unavailable except in a few gourmet stores in large cities in 1970, are now widely sold across the United States. And if this is thought a somewhat elite example, the case of beer consumption suggests that the internationalization of a product, that traditional location theory always taught should be highly market-oriented, is now complete. Baltimore was essentially a one-beer town (locally brewed) in 1970, but first the regional beers from places like Milwaukee and Denver, and then Canadian and Mexican beers followed by European, Australian, Chinese, Polish, etc. beers became cheaper. Formerly exotic foods became commonplace while popular local delicacies (in the Baltimore case, blue crabs and oysters) that were once relatively inexpensive jumped in price as they too became integrated into long-distance trading.

The market place has always been an 'emporium of styles' (to quote Raban's phrase) but the food market, just to take one example, now looks very different from what it was twenty years ago. Kenyan haricot beans, Californian celery and avocados, North African potatoes, Canadian apples, and Chilean grapes all sit side by side in a British supermarket. This variety also makes for a proliferation of culinary styles, even among the relatively poor. Such styles have always migrated, of course, usually following the migration streams of different groups before diffusing slowly through urban cultures. The new waves of immigrants (such as the Vietnamese, Koreans, Filipinos, Central Americans, etc. that have added to the older groups of Japanese, Chinese, Chicanos, and all the European ethnic groups that have also found their culinary heritage can be revived for fun and profit) make a typical United States city such as New York, Los Angeles, or San Francisco (where the last census showed the majority of the population to be made up of minorities) as much an emporium of culinary styles as it is an emporium of the world's commodities. But here, too, there has been an acceleration, because culinary styles have moved faster than the immigration streams. It did not take a large French immigration to the United States to send the croissant rapidly spreading across America to challenge the traditional doughnut, nor did it take a large immigration of Americans to Europe to bring fast-food hamburgers to nearly all medium-sized European cities. Chinese takeaways, Italian pizza-parlours (run by a US chain), Middle Eastern felafel stalls, Japanese sushi bars . . . the list is now endless in the Western world.

The whole world's cuisine is now assembled in one place in almost exactly the same way that the world's geographical complexity is nightly reduced to a series of images on a static television screen. This same phenomenon is exploited in entertainment palaces like Epcot and Disneyworld; it becomes possible, as the US commercials put it, 'to experience the Old World for a day without actually having to go there'. The general implication is that through the experience of everything from food, to culinary habits, music, television, entertainment, and cinema, it is now possible to experience the world's geography vicariously, as a simulacrum. The interweaving of simulacra in daily life brings together different worlds (of commodities) in the same space and time. But it does so in such a way as to conceal almost perfectly any trace of origin, of the labour processes that produced them, or of the social relations implicated in their production.

The simulacra can in turn become the reality. Baudrillard (1986) in *L'Amérique* even goes so far, somewhat exaggeratedly in my view, to suggest that US reality is now constructed as a giant screen: 'the cinema is everywhere, most of all in the city, incessant and marvellous film and scenario'. Places portrayed in a certain way, particularly if they have the capacity to attract tourists, may begin to 'dress themselves up' as the fantasy images prescribe. Mediaeval castles offer mediaeval weekends (food, dress, but not of course the primitive heating arrangements). Vicarious participation in these various worlds has real effects on the ways in which these worlds get ordered. Jencks (1984, 127) proposes that the architect should be an active participant in this:

> Any middle class urbanite in any large city from Teheran to Tokyo is bound to have a well-stocked, indeed over-stocked 'image bank' that is continually restuffed by travel and magazines. His *musée imaginaire* may mirror the pot-pourri of the producers but it is nonetheless natural to his way of life. Barring some kind of totalitarian reduction in the heterogeneity of production and consumption, it seems to be desirable that architects learn to use this inevitable heterogeneity of languages. Besides, it is quite enjoyable. Why, if one can afford to live in different ages and cultures, restrict oneself to the present, the locale? Eclecticism is the natural evolution of a culture with choice.

Much the same can be said of popular music styles. Commenting on how collage and eclecticism have recently come to dominate, Chambers (1987) goes on to show how oppositional and subcultural musics like reggae, Afro-American and Afro-Hispanic have taken their place 'in the museum of fixed symbolic structures' to form a flexible collage of 'the already seen, the already worn, the already played, the already heard'. A strong sense of 'the Other' is replaced, he suggests, by a weak sense of 'the others'. The loose hanging together of divergent street cultures in the fragmented spaces of the contemporary city re-emphasizes the contingent and accidental aspects of this 'otherness' in daily life. This same sensibility exists in postmodern fiction. It is, says McHale (1987), concerned with 'ontologies', with a potential as well as an actual plurality of universes, forming an eclectic and 'anarchic landscape of worlds in the plural'. Dazed and distracted characters wander through these worlds without a clear sense of location, wondering, 'Which world am I in and which of my personalities do I deploy?' Our postmodern ontological landscape, suggests McHale, 'is unprecedented in human history – at least in the degree of its pluralism'. Spaces of very different worlds seem to collapse upon each other, much as the world's commodities are assembled in the supermarket and all manner of sub-cultures get juxtaposed in the contemporary city. Disruptive spatiality triumphs over the coherence of perspective and narrative in postmodern fiction, in exactly the same way that imported beers coexist with local brews, local employment collapses under the weight of foreign competition, and all the divergent spaces of the world are assembled nightly as a collage of images upon the television screen.

There seem to be two divergent sociological effects of all of this in daily thought and action. The first suggests taking advantage of all of the divergent possibilities, much as Jencks recommends, and cultivating a whole series of simulacra as milieux of escape, fantasy, and distraction:

> All around us – on advertisement hoardings, bookshelves, record covers, television screens – these miniature escape fantasies present themselves. This, it seems, is how we are destined to live, as split personalities in which the private life is disturbed by the promise of escape routes to another reality.
>
> (Cohen and Taylor 1978, quoted in McHale, 1987, 38)

From this standpoint I think we have to accept McHale's argument that postmodern fiction is mimetic of something, much as I have argued that the emphasis upon ephemerality, collage, fragmentation, and dispersal in philosophical and social thought mimics the conditions of flexible accumulation. And it should not be surprising either to see how all of this fits in with the emergence since 1970 of a fragmented politics of divergent special and regional interest groups.

But it is exactly at this point that we encounter the opposite reaction that can best be summed up as the search for personal or collective identity, the search for secure moorings in a shifting world. Place-identity, in this collage of superimposed spatial images that implode in upon us, becomes an important issue, because everyone occupies a space of individuation (a body, a room, a home, a shaping community, a nation), and how we individuate ourselves shapes identity. Furthermore, if no one 'knows their place' in this shifting collage world, then how can a secure social order be fashioned or sustained?

There are two elements within this problem that deserve close consideration. First, the capacity of most social movements to command place better than space puts a strong emphasis upon the potential connection between place and social identity. This is manifest in political action. The defensiveness of municipal socialism, the insistence on working-class community, the localization of the fight against capital, become central features of working-class struggle within an overall patterning of uneven geographical development. The consequent dilemmas of socialist or working-class movements in the face of a universalizing capitalism are shared by other oppositional groups – racial minorities, colonized peoples, women, etc. – who are relatively empowered to organize in place but disempowered when it comes to organizing over space. In clinging, often of necessity, to a place-bound identity, however, such oppositional movements become a part of the very fragmentation which a mobile capitalism and flexible accumulation can feed upon. 'Regional resistances', the struggle for local autonomy, place-bound organization, may be excellent bases for political action, but they cannot bear the burden of radical historical change alone. 'Think globally and act locally' was the revolutionary slogan of the 1960s. It bears repeating.

The assertion of any place-bound identity has to rest at some point on the motivational power of tradition. It is difficult, however, to maintain any sense of historical continuity in the face of all the flux and ephemerality of flexible accumulation. The irony is that tradition is now often preserved by being commodified and marketed as such. The search for roots ends up at worst being produced and marketed as an image, as a simulacrum or pastiche (imitation communities constructed to evoke images of some folksy past, the fabric of traditional working-class communities being taken over by an urban gentry). The photograph, the document, the view, and the reproduction become history precisely because they are so overwhelmingly present. The problem, of course, is that none of these are immune from tampering or downright faking for present purposes. At best, historical tradition is reorganized as a museum culture, not necessarily of high modernist art, but of local history, of local production, of how things once upon a time were made, sold, consumed, and integrated into a long-lost and often romanticized daily life (one from which all trace of oppressive social relations may be expunged). Through the presentation of a partially illusory past it becomes possible to signify something of local identity and perhaps to do it profitably.

The second reaction to the internationalism of modernism lies in the search to construct place and its meanings qualitatively. Capitalist hegemony over space puts the aesthetics of place very much back on the agenda. But this, as we have seen, meshes only too well with the idea of spatial differentiations as lures for a peripatetic capital that values the option of mobility very highly. Isn't this place better than that place, not only for the operations of capital but also for living in, consuming well, and feeling secure in a shifting world? The construction of such places, the fashioning of some localized aesthetic image, allows the construction of some limited and limiting sense of identity in the midst of a collage of imploding spatialities.

The tension in these oppositions is clear enough but it is hard to appreciate their intellectual and political ramifications. Here, for example, is Foucault (1984, 253) addressing the issue from his own perspective:

Space is fundamental in any form of communal life; space is fundamental in any exercise of power. . . . I recall having been invited in 1966, by a group of architects, to do a study of space, of something that I called at the time 'heterotopias', those singular spaces to be found in some given social spaces whose functions are different or even the opposite of others. The architects worked on this, and at the end of the study someone spoke up – a Sartrean psychologist – who firebombed me, saying that *space* is reactionary and capitalist but *history* and *becoming* are revolutionary. This absurd discourse was not at all unusual at the time. Today everyone would be convulsed with laughter at such a pronouncement, but not then.

The proposition the Sartrean critic offers is, though crude and oppositional, nowhere near as laughable as Foucault avers. On the other hand, postmodernist sentiment definitely leans towards Foucault's position. Whereas modernism looked upon the spaces of the city, for example, as 'an epiphenomenon of social functions', post-modernism 'tends to disengage urban space from its dependence on functions, and to see it as an autonomous formal system' incorporating 'rhetorical and artistic strategies, which are independent of any simple historical determinism' (Colquhoun 1985). It is precisely this disengagement that permits Foucault to deploy spatial metaphors so extensively in his studies of power. Spatial imagery, liberated from its roots in any social determination, becomes a means to depict the forces of social determination. It is a short step, however, from Foucault's metaphors to reinforcement of a political ideology that sees place and *Being* with all its associated aesthetic qualities as a proper basis for social action. Geopolitics and the Heideggerian trap come not too far behind. Jameson (1988, 351), for his part, views the

> spatial peculiarities of post-modernism as symptoms and expressions of a new and historically original dilemma, one that involves our insertion as individual subjects into a multidimensional set of radically discontinuous realities, whose frames range from the still surviving spaces of bourgeois private life all the way to the unimaginable decentering of global capital-ism itself. Not even Einsteinian relativity, or the multiple subjective worlds of the older modernists, is capable of giving any adequate figur-ation to this process, which in lived experience makes itself felt by the so-called death of the subject, or, more exactly, the fragmented and schizophrenic decentering and dispersion of this last. . . . And although you may not have realized it, I am talking about practical politics here: since the crisis of socialist internationalism, and the enormous strategic and tactical difficulties of coordinating local and grassroots or neighbor-hood political actions with national or international ones, such urgent political dilemmas are all immediately functions of the enormously complex new international space I have in mind.

Jameson exaggerates somewhat with respect to the uniqueness and newness of this experience. Stressful though the current condition undoubtedly is, it is qualitatively similar to that which led to Renaissance and various modernist reconceptualizations of space and time. Nevertheless, the dilemmas which Jameson depicts are exact and capture the drift of postmodern sensibility as to the meaning of space in contempor-ary political and cultural as well as economic life. If, however, we have lost the modernist faith in becoming, as Foucault's Sartrean critic argued, is there any way out except via the reactionary politics of an aestheticized spatiality? Are we sadly destined to end up on the track that Sitte began with, in his turn to Wagnerian mythology as support for his assertion of the primacy of place and community in a world of changing spaces? Worse still, if aesthetic production has now been so thoroughly commodified and thereby become really subsumed within a political economy of cultural production, how can we possibly stop that circle closing onto a produced, and hence all too easily manipulated, aestheticization of a globally mediatized politics?

This should alert us to the acute geopolitical dangers that attach to the rapidity of time—space compression in recent years. The transition from Fordism to flexible accumulation, such as it has been, ought to imply a transition in our mental maps, political attitudes, and political institutions. But political thinking does not necessarily undergo such easy transformations, and is in any case subject to the contradictory pressures that derive from spatial integration and differentiation. There is an omnipresent danger that our mental maps will not match current realities. The serious diminution of the power of individual nation states over fiscal and monetary policies, for example, has not been matched by any parallel shift towards an internationalization of politics. Indeed, there are abundant signs that localism and nationalism have become stronger precisely because of the quest for the security that place always offers in the midst of all the shifting that flexible accumulation implies. The resurgence of geopolitics and of faith in charismatic politics (Thatcher's Falklands War, Reagan's invasion of Grenada) fits only too well with a world that is increasingly nourished intellectually and politically by a vast flux of ephemeral images.

Time—space compression always exacts its toll on our capacity to grapple with the realities unfolding around us. Under stress, for example, it becomes harder and harder to react accurately to events. The erroneous identification of an Iranian airbus, ascending within an established commercial flight corridor, with a fighter-bomber descending towards a targeted US warship – an incident that resulted in many civilian deaths – is typical of the way that reality gets created rather than interpreted under conditions of stress and time—space compression. The parallel with Kern's account of the outbreak of World War I . . . is instructive. If 'seasoned negotiators cracked under the pressure of tense confrontations and sleepless nights, agonizing over the probable disastrous consequences of their snap judgements and hasty actions', then how much more difficult must decision-making now be? The difference this time is that there is not even time to agonize. And the problems are not confined to the realms of political and military decision-making, for the world's financial markets are on the boil in ways that make a snap judgement here, an unconsidered word there, and a gut reaction somewhere else the slip that can unravel the whole skein of fictitious capital formation and of interdependency.

The conditions of postmodern time—space compression exaggerate in many respects the dilemmas that have from time to time beset capitalist procedures of modernization in the past (1848 and the phase just before the First World War spring particularly to mind). While the economic, cultural, and political responses may not be exactly new, the range of those responses differs in certain important respects from those which have occurred before. The intensity of time—space compression in Western capitalism since the 1960s, with all of its congruent features of excessive ephemerality and fragmentation in the political and private as well as in the social realm, does seem to indicate an experiential context that makes the condition of postmodernity somewhat special. But by putting this condition into its historical context, as part of a history of successive waves of time—space compression generated out of the pressures of capital accumulation with its perpetual search to annihilate space through time and reduce turnover time, we can at least pull the condition of postmodernity into the range of a condition accessible to historical materialist analysis and interpretation. . . .

Chapter 2

Anthony Giddens

THE GLOBALISING OF MODERNITY

From *The Consequences of Modernity* London: Polity, 1990, p. 63 and pp. 70–78

MODERNITY IS INHERENTLY GLOBALISING – this is evident in some of the most basic characteristics of modern institutions, including particularly their disembeddedness and reflexivity. But what exactly is globalisation, and how might we best conceptualise the phenomenon? [. . .]

If we consider the present day, in what sense can world economic organisation be said to be dominated by capitalistic economic mechanisms? A number of considerations are relevant to answering this question. The main centres of power in the world economy are capitalist states – states in which capitalist economic enterprise (with the class relations that this implies) is the chief form of production. The domestic and international economic policies of these states involve many forms of regulation of economic activity, but, as noted, their institutional organisation maintains an 'insulation' of the economic from the political. This allows wide scope for the global activities of business corporations, which always have a home base within a particular state but may develop many other regional involvements elsewhere.

Business firms, especially the transnational corporations, may wield immense economic power, and have the capacity to influence political policies in their home bases and elsewhere. The biggest transnational companies today have budgets larger than those of all but a few nations. But there are some key respects in which their power cannot rival that of states – especially important here are the factors of territoriality and control of the means of violence. There is no area on the earth's surface, with the partial exception of the polar regions, which is not claimed as the legitimate sphere of control of one state or another. All modern states have a more or less successful monopoly of control of the means of violence within their own territories. No matter how great their economic power, industrial corporations are not military organisations (as some of them were during the colonial period), and they cannot establish themselves as political/legal entities which rule a given territorial area.

If nation-states are the principal 'actors' within the global political order, corporations are the dominant agents within the world economy. In their trading relations with one another, and with states and consumers, companies (manufactur-ing corporations, financial firms, and banks) depend upon production for profit. Hence the spread of their influence brings in its train a global extension of commod-ity markets, including money markets. However, even in its beginnings, the capitalist world economy was never just a market for the trading of goods and services. It involved, and involves today, the commodifying of labour power in class relations which separate workers from control of their means of production. This process, of course, is fraught with implications for global inequalities.

All nation-states, capitalist and state socialist, within the 'developed' sectors of the world, are primarily reliant upon industrial production for the generation of the wealth upon which their tax revenues are based. The socialist countries form something of an enclave within the capitalist world economy as a whole, industry being more directly subject to political imperatives. These states are scarcely post-capitalist, but the influence of capitalistic markets upon the distribution of goods and labour power is substantially muted. The pursuit of growth by both Western and East European societies inevitably pushes economic interests to the forefront of the policies which states pursue in the international arena. But it is surely plain to all, save those under the sway of historical materialism, that the material involvements of nation-states are not governed purely by economic considerations, real or per-ceived. The influence of any particular state within the global political order is strongly conditioned by the level of its wealth (and the connection between this and military strength). However, states derive their power from their sovereign capabil-ities, as Hans J. Morgenthau emphasises (1960). They do not operate as economic machines, but as 'actors' jealous of their territorial rights, concerned with the fostering of national cultures, and having strategic geopolitical involvements with other states or alliances of states.

The nation-state system has long participated in that reflexivity characteristic of modernity as a whole. The very existence of sovereignty should be understood as something that is reflexively monitored, for reasons already indicated. Sovereignty is linked to the replacement of 'frontiers' by 'borders' in the early development of the nation-state system: autonomy inside the territory claimed by the state is sanctioned by the recognition of borders by other states. As noted, this is one of the major factors distinguishing the nation-state system from systems of states in the pre-modern era, where few reflexively ordered relations of this kind existed and where the notion of 'international relations' made no sense.

One aspect of the dialectical nature of globalisation is the 'push and pull' between tendencies towards centralisation inherent in the reflexivity of the system of states on the one hand and the sovereignty of particular states on the other. Thus, concerted action between countries in some respects diminishes the indi-vidual sovereignty of the nations involved, yet by combining their power in other ways, it increases their influence within the state system. The same is true of the early congresses which, in conjunction with war, defined and redefined states' borders – and of truly global agencies such as the United Nations. The global influence of the U.N. (still decisively limited by the fact that it is not territorial and does not have significant access to the means of violence) is not purchased solely by means of a diminution of the sovereignty of nation-states – things are more complicated than this. An obvious example is that of the 'new nations' – autonomous nation-states set up in erstwhile colonised areas. Armed struggle against the colonising countries was very generally a major factor in persuading the colonisers to retreat. But discussion in the U.N. played a key role in setting up ex-colonial areas as states with internationally recognised borders. However weak some of the new nations may be economically and militarily, their emergence *as* nation-states (or, in many cases, 'state-nations') marks a net gain in terms of sovereignty, as compared to their previous circumstances.

The third dimension of globalisation is the world military order. In specifying its nature, we have to analyse the connections between the industrialisation of war, the flow of weaponry and techniques of military organisation from some parts of the world to others, and the alliances which states build with one another. Military alliances do not necessarily compromise the monopoly over the means of violence held by a state within its territories, although in some circumstances they certainly can do so.

In tracing the overlaps between military power and the sovereignty of states, we find the same push-and-pull between opposing tendencies noted previously. In the current period, the two most militarily developed states, the United States and the Soviet Union, have built a bipolar system of military alliances of truly global scope. The countries involved in these alliances necessarily accept limitations over their opportunities to forge independent military strategies externally. They may also forfeit complete monopoly of military control within their own territories, in so far as American or Soviet forces stationed there take their orders from abroad. Yet, as a result of the massive destructive power of modern weaponry, almost all states possess military strength far in excess of that of even the largest of pre-modern civilisations. Many economically weak Third World countries are militarily power-ful. In an important sense there is no 'Third World' in respect of weaponry, only a 'First World', since most countries maintain stocks of technologically advanced armaments and have modernised the military in a thoroughgoing way. Even the possession of nuclear weaponry is not confined to the economically advanced states.

The globalising of military power obviously is not confined to weaponry and alliances between the armed forces of different states – it also concerns war itself. Two world wars attest to the way in which local conflicts became matters of global involvement. In both wars, the participants were drawn from virtually all regions (although the Second World War was a more truly worldwide phenomenon). In an era of nuclear weaponry, the industrialisation of war has proceeded to a point at which [. . .] the obsolescence of Clausewitz's main doctrine has become apparent to everyone. [. . .] The only point of holding nuclear weapons – apart from their possible symbolic value in world politics – is to deter others from using them.

[. . .]

The fourth dimension of globalisation concerns industrial development. The most obvious aspect of this is the expansion of the global division of labour, which includes the differentiations between more and less industrialised areas in the world. Modern industry is intrinsically based on divisions of labour, not only on the level of job tasks but on that of regional specialisation in terms of type of industry, skills, and the production of raw materials. There has undoubtedly taken place a major expan-sion of global interdependence in the division of labour since the Second World War. This has helped to bring about shifts in the worldwide distribution of production, including the deindustrialisation of some regions in the developed countries and the emergence of the 'Newly Industrialising Countries' in the Third World. It has also undoubtedly served to reduce the internal economic hegemony of many states, particularly those with a high level of industrialisation. It is more difficult for the capitalist countries to manage their economies than formerly was the case, given accelerating global economic interdependence. This is almost certainly one of the major reasons for the declining impact of Keynesian economic policies, as applied at the level of the national economy, in current times.

One of the main features of the globalising implications of industrialism is the worldwide diffusion of machine technologies. The impact of industrialism is plainly not limited to the sphere of production, but affects many aspects of day-to-day life, as well as influencing the generic character of human interaction with the material environment.

Even in states which remain primarily agricultural, modern technology is often applied in such a way as to alter substantially preexisting relations between human social organisation and the environment. This is true, for example, of the use of fertilisers or other artificial farming methods, the introduction of modern farming machinery, and so forth. The diffusion of industrialism has created 'one world' in a more negative and threatening sense than that just mentioned – a world in which there are actual or potential ecological changes of a harmful sort that affect everyone on the planet. Yet industrialism has also decisively conditioned our very sense of living in 'one world'. For one of the most important effects of industrialism has been the transformation of technologies of communication.

This comment leads on to a further and quite fundamental aspect of globalisation, which lies behind each of the various institutional dimensions that have been mentioned and which might be referred to as cultural globalisation. Mechanised technologies of communication have dramatically influenced all aspects of globalisation since the first introduction of mechanical printing into Europe. They form an essential element of the reflexivity of modernity and of the discontinuities which have torn the modern away from the traditional.

The globalising impact of media was noted by numerous authors during the period of the early growth of mass circulation newspapers. Thus one commentator in 1892 wrote that, as a result of modern newspapers, the inhabitant of a local village has a broader understanding of contemporary events than the prime minister of a hundred years before. The villager who reads a paper 'interests himself simultaneously in the issue of a revolution in Chile, a bush-war in East Africa, a massacre in North China, a famine in Russia' (Nordau 1968 [1892], 39).

The point here is not that people are contingently aware of many events, from all over the world, of which previously they would have remained ignorant. It is that the global extension of the institutions of modernity would be impossible were it not for the pooling of knowledge which is represented by the 'news'. This is perhaps less obvious on the level of general cultural awareness than in more specific contexts. For example, the global money markets of today involve direct and simultaneous access to pooled information on the part of individuals spatially widely separated from one another.

Chapter 3

Roland Robertson

THE UNIVERSALISM–PARTICULARISM ISSUE

From *Globalization: Social Theory and Global Culture* London: Sage, 1992, p. 97 and pp. 100–105

The nationalisms of the modern world are not the triumphant civilizations of yore. They are the ambiguous expression of the demand both for . . . assimilation into the universal . . . and *simultaneously* for . . . adhering to the particular, the reinvention of differences. Indeed, it is universalism through particularism, and particularism through universalism.

(Wallerstein 1984, 166–67)

Modern societies are characterized less by what they have in common or by their structure with regard to well-defined universal exigencies, than by the fact of their *involvement in the issue of universalization*. . . . The need, even the urgency, for 'universal reference' has never been felt so strongly as in our time. . . . The process of modernization is . . . the challenge hurled at groups closed in by their own contingencies and particularities to form themselves into an open ensemble of interlocutors and partners . . .

(Bourricaud 1987, 21, emphasis [Robertson])

Like nostalgia, diversity is not what it used to be; and the sealing of lives into separate railway carriages to produce cultural renewal or the spacing of them out with contrast effects to free up moral energies are romantic dreams, not undangerous. . . . [M]oral issues stemming from cultural diversity . . . that used to arise . . . mainly between societies . . . now increasingly arise within them. . . . The day when the American city was the main model of cultural fragmentation and ethnic tumbling is quite gone.

(Geertz 1986, 114–15)

[. . .]

MUCH HAS BEEN WRITTEN ABOUT UNIVERSALITY and universalism in recent years. On the one hand, those ideas have been looked upon with skepticism by communitarians, who are generally resistant to the claim that there can be viable bodies of universalistic ethics and morals. On the other hand, universalism has been rejected by many poststructuralist and postmodernist theorists. Such rejection constitutes a vital feature of the critique of foundationalism. At the same time, much has been written about particularity and particularism, difference, locality and, of course, community. A primary concern of the present chapter is to bring these two sets of interests – which are usually counterposed – into alignment.

[. . .]

My own argument involves the attempt to preserve direct attention *both* to particularity and difference *and* to universality and homogeneity. It rests largely on the thesis that we are, in the late twentieth century, witnesses to – and participants in – a massive, twofold process involving *the interpenetration of the universalization of particularism and the particularization of universalism*, a claim that I will flesh out in reference to the three quotations with which I began this chapter.

Speaking specifically of recent nationalism – which is, in a number of respects, paradigmatic of contemporary particularism – Wallerstein insists, in my view correctly, on the simultaneity of particularism and universalism. However, I do not think he goes far enough in addressing the issue of their direct interpenetration, a shortfall which can be largely attributed to Wallerstein's (1984, 167) adamance in grounding the relationship between them in 'the genius and the contradiction of capitalist civilization'. While I think there is much to the view that capitalism *amplifies* and is bound up with 'the ambiguous expression of the demand both for assimilation into the universal and for . . . adhering to the particular', I do not agree with the implication that the problematic of the interplay of the particular and the universal is unique to capitalism. Indeed, I would claim that the differential spread of capitalism can partly be explained *in terms of its accommodation to* the historical 'working out' of that problematic. Nor do I agree with the argument that we can, in an explanatory sense, trace the contemporary connection between the two dispositions directly to late twentieth-century capitalism (in whatever way that may be defined). Rather, I would argue that the consumerist global capitalism of our time is wrapped into the increasingly thematized particular–universal relationship in terms of the connection between globewide, universalistic supply and particularistic demand. The contemporary *market* thus involves the increasing *interpenetration* of culture and economy: which is not the same as arguing, as Jameson (1984) tends to do, that the production of culture is *directed by* the 'logic' of 'late' capitalism. More specifically, the contemporary capitalist creation of consumers frequently involves the tailoring of products to increasingly specialized regional, societal, ethnic, class and gender markets – so called 'micro-marketing'.

Wallerstein (1984, 167) also argues that 'capitalist civilization . . . as it hurtles towards its undoing . . . becomes in the interim stronger and stronger'. This is undoubtedly both a more sophisticated and a 'safer' point of view than that of another prominent advocate of world-systems analysis, namely Christopher Chase-Dunn, who had the misfortune to have the following statement published in late 1989: 'The revolutions in the Soviet Union and the People's Republic of China have increased our collective knowledge about how to build socialism despite their only partial successes and their obvious failures. Their existence widens the space available for other experiments with socialism' (1989, 342). The difference between Wallerstein and Chase-Dunn is important, because it illustrates the contrast between sophisticated and simplistic forms of world-systems analysis. Whereas the apparent collapse of much of communistic socialism in 1989 (and subsequently) surely came as a great disappointment to utopian members of that school of thought, there is nothing about 1989 and its aftermath which should embarrass 'true Wallersteinians'. In fact there is a crucial sense in which Wallerstein predicted the collapse of in-one-country 'socialism'.

Bourricaud, although less specific in that he does not indicate a 'driving mechanism', comes closer to the mark in suggesting that there has emerged a globewide circumstance involving the spatial and temporal compression of the world, which increasingly constrains multitudes of groups and individuals to face each other in what he calls an 'open ensemble of interlocutors and partners'. This is what gives rise to *the issue* of 'universalization' and also accentuates *the issue* of particularization. Bourricaud draws attention to a critical matter which must surely lie at the center of any discussion of globalization and culture – namely, the ideational and practical aspects of interaction and communication between collective and individual actors on the global scene. This is an aspect of global 'reality construction' which has been almost continuously neglected. However, Bourricaud does not go far enough. Missing from his formulation is concern with *the terms* in which interaction between different particularisms may occur. To him the issue of universalization is apparently a more or less purely contingent matter arising from the problem of 'how to get along' in a compressed world, and thus has little or no cultural autonomy; although, in all fairness, it should be said that Bourricaud is mainly trying to move us away from the purely logical or ideal solutions to the problem of world order which some of the more philosophically minded anthropologists and sociologists have offered in recent years in the face of sharp cultural discontinuities, in particular Louis Dumont (1983). [. . .]

I am emphasizing two main points with respect to the interesting ways in which Wallerstein and Bourricaud have raised the universalism–particularism issue. First, I am arguing that the issue is a basic feature of the human condition, which was given substantial and extremely consequential historical thematization with the rise of the great religiocultural traditions during what Karl Jaspers (1953) called the Axial Age. Those traditions were, in large part, developed precisely around what has come to be called the universalism–particularism theme and their significance in that regard has continued into our time. A major example of great contemporary relevance, which I have already mentioned, has to do with the way in which Japan acquired the substantive theme of universality through its encounters with and modifications, along nativistic lines, of Confucianism and Mahayana Buddhism. Japan's crystallization of a form of 'universalistic particularism' since its first encounter with China has resulted in its acquiring paradigmatic, global significance with respect to the handling of the universalism–particularism issue. Specifically, its paradigmatic status is inherent in its very long and successful history of selective incorporation and syncretization of ideas from other cultures in such a way as to particularize the universal and, so to say, return the product of that process to the world as a uniquely Japanese contribution to the universal. [. . .]

Second, I am arguing that in more recent world history the universalism–particularism issue has come to constitute something like a global-cultural form, a major axis of the structuration of the world as a whole. Rather than simply viewing the theme of universalism as having to do with principles which can and should be applied to all, and that of particularism as referring to that which can and should be applied only 'locally', I suggest that the two have become tied together as part of a globewide nexus. They have become united in terms of the universality of the experience and, increasingly, *the expectation of* particularity, on the one hand, and the experience and, increasingly, the *expectation of* universality, on the other. The latter – the particularization of universalism – involves the idea of the universal being given global-human concreteness; while the former – the universalization of particularism – involves the extensive diffusion of the idea that there is virtually no limit to particularity, to uniqueness, to difference, and to otherness. (One aspect of the latter tendency is conveyed by Jean Baudrillard's (1988, 41) aphorism concerning our present condition: 'It is never too late to revive your origins'.)

I suggest that along these lines we may best consider contemporary globalization in its most general sense as a form of institutionalization of the two-fold process involving the universalization of particularism and the particularization of universalism. *Resistance* to contemporary globalization – as, for example, some consider to be involved on the more radical side of the general Islamic movement – would thus be regarded as opposition not merely to the world as one, homogenized system but also – and, I believe, more relevantly – to the conception of the world as a series of culturally equal, relativized, entities or ways of life. The first aspect could well be regarded as a form of anti-modernity, while the second could fruitfully be seen as a form of anti-postmodernity. Put another way, it is around the universalism–particularism axis of globalization that *the discontents of globality* manifest themselves in reference to new, globalized variations on the oldish themes of *Gesellschaft* and *Gemeinschaft*. The *Gemeinschaft-Gesellschaft* theme has been a primary focus for the critique of modernity (most directly in Germany). It is now increasingly interwoven with the discourse of globality in the sense that it has been 'upgraded' so as to refer to the general relationship between the particular and the communal, on the one hand, and the universal and the impersonal, on the other. This issue is closely related to what Arjun Appadurai (1990, 5) calls 'the tension between cultural homogenization and cultural heterogenization', which he regards as 'the central problem of today's global interactions'.

Appadurai (1990, 17) argues that 'the central feature of global culture today is the politics of the mutual effort of sameness and difference to cannibalize one another and thus to proclaim their successful hijacking of the twin Enlightenment ideas of the triumphantly universal and the resiliently particular'. This evocative interpretation is, it should be noted, connected by Appadurai (1990, 20) to his suggestion that 'the theory of global cultural interactions . . . will have to move into something like a human version of the theory that some scientists are calling "chaos" theory'. While this cannot be the place for an adequate discussion of this complex issue, it should be said that Appadurai's advocacy of a *chaos*-theoretic approach to global culture – which he sees more specifically in terms of a 'disjunctive' series of 'scapes' (ethnoscapes, technoscapes, finanscapes, mediascapes and ideoscapes) – clearly involves rejection of the idea of the global institutionalization of the relationship between universalized particularism and particularized universalism.

While not denying the fruitfulness of Appadurai's ideas about the existence of empirically disjunctive relationships between different cultural 'scapes' at the global level, I do insist upon the general structuring significance of the particular–universal connection – its crystallization as 'the elemental form of global life'. Some of my differences with Appadurai may arise from his suggestion that the Enlightenment ideas of universalism and particularism were necessarily incongruent. My own interpretation is that they were basically complementary. As Anthony Smith has written of the late eighteenth century, '[A]t the root of the "national ideal" is a certain vision of the world. . . . According to this vision mankind is "really" and "naturally" divided into distinct . . . nations. Each nation . . . has its peculiar contribution to make to the whole, the family of nations'. (1979, 2) [. . .] Or, to put it more incisively, *the idea* of nationalism (or particularism) develops *only* in tandem with internationalism. This way of looking at the issue is compatible with Simon Schama's (1991) analysis of the origins in the West of the association between land and homeland. We now, of course, tend to take such an association for granted but, as Schama (1991, 13) points out, 'for much of Western history [it] was not at all axiomatic'. Schama traces the beginning of the association, at least in image making, to the later years of the European Renaissance in northern Europe and in the Netherlands. That period and region witnessed the development of landscape as an autonomous form, rather than as a supplement to sacred or classical narratives. Schama (1991:13) is interested in 'the moment of alternation from the universal to the particular, from world to home'. His specific point is that images in Dutch painting involved a differentiation of 'visual parochialism' from a wider universalistic and imperialistic culture.

Finally, as far as fleshing out in relation to my introductory quotations is concerned, the citation from Geertz reminds us strongly of the fact that globalization is not simply a matter of societies, regions and civilizations being squeezed together in various problematic ways but also of this occurring with increasing intensity *inside* nationally constituted societies. Nowadays, to quote further from Geertz (1986, 112), 'foreignness does not start at the water's edge but at the skin's . . . the wogs begin long before Calais'. Published in 1986, Geertz's suggestions have since acquired poignant relevance to current trends in Central and Eastern Europe and the former Soviet Union, for in those areas the problems of old ethnic identity are being played out within the context of increasing global thematization of ethnicity-*within-*humankind, although there are undoubtedly elements of relatively raw atavism involved.

Geertz's observations press us, *inter alia*, to take seriously into account the position of *individuals* in the globalization process. There has been a marked tendency in many discussions of the world-system, world society or whatever, to ignore individuals – more precisely, the contemporary construction of individualism – for the apparent reason that globalization of alleged necessity refers to very large-scale matters, in contrast to the 'small-scale' status of individuals. This bow in the direction of the textbook wisdom which distinguishes microsociological from macrosociological approaches in terms of naive conceptions of scale and complexity is, I believe, misplaced. I insist that individuals are as much a part of the globalization process as any other basic category of social-theoretical discourse. I have argued that there are four elemental points of reference for any discussion of contemporary globalization – national *societies*; *individual selves*; *the world system of societies* (international relations); and *humankind*. My general argument in making this set of distinctions is that globalization increasingly involves thematization of these four elements of the global-human condition or field (rather than the world-system). Any given element is constrained by the other three. For example, individuals as such are increasingly constrained by being members of societies, members of an increasingly thematized and endangered human species and greatly affected by the vicissitudes of international relations. Thus late twentieth-century globalization involves the institutionalization of both the universalization of particularism and the particularization of universalism and can be more specifically indicated as consisting in the interpenetrating processes of societalization, individualization, the consolidation of the international system of societies, and the concretization of the sense of humankind.

Returning directly to the individual, my primary claim is that globalization has involved and continues to involve the *institutionalized construction* of the individual. Even more specifically, we must recognize that world-political culture has led to a globewide institutionalization of 'the life course' — which has, John Meyer (1987, 243–44) maintains, two dimensions: 'aspects of the person that enter into rationalized social organization' and 'the public celebration of . . . the "private" or subjective individual'. Much of that has been and continues to be mediated by state structures, but international *non*-governmental organizations have also increasingly mediated and promoted individualism in the areas of education, human rights, the rights of women, health, and so on. In sum, the globewide encouragement of individualism in association with increasing polyethnicity and multiculturality — themselves encouraged by large migrations and 'diasporations' — has been crucial in the move towards the circumstance of 'foreignness' described so well by Geertz. At the same time, what Meyer calls the celebration of subjective identity *relative to* involvement in 'rationalized social organization' has played a major part in the virtually globewide establishment of various 'minority' forms of personal and collective identification — among which gender has been of particular significance. This has a considerable bearing on the question raised earlier about identity, particularly personal identity, in the current condition of late twentieth-century life.

Chapter 4

Arjun Appadurai

DISJUNCTURE AND DIFFERENCE

From *Modernity at Large: Cultural Dimensions of Globalization* Minneapolis: University of Minnesota Press, 1996, pp. 31–40 and pp. 41–43

[. . .]

THE IMAGE, THE IMAGINED, THE IMAGINARY – these are all terms that direct us to something critical and new in global cultural processes: *the imagination as a social practice*. No longer mere fantasy (opium for the masses whose real work is elsewhere), no longer simple escape (from a world defined principally by more concrete purposes and structures), no longer elite pastime (thus not relevant to the lives of ordinary people), and no longer mere contemplation (irrelevant for new forms of desire and subjectivity), the imagination has become an organized field of social practices, a form of work (in the sense of both labor and culturally organized practice), and a form of negotiation between sites of agency (individuals) and globally defined fields of possibility. This unleashing of the imagination links the play of pastiche (in some settings) to the terror and coercion of states and their competitors. The imagination is now central to all forms of agency, is itself a social fact, and is the key component of the new global order. But to make this claim meaningful, we must address some other issues.

[. . .]

The central problem of today's global interactions is the tension between cultural homogenization and cultural heterogenization. A vast array of empirical facts could be brought to bear on the side of the homogenization argument, and much of it has come from the left end of the spectrum of media studies (Schiller 1976; Hamelink 1983; Mattelart 1983), and some from other perspectives (Gans 1985; Iyer 1988). Most often, the homogenization argument subspeciates into either an argument about Americanization or an argument about commoditization, and very often the two arguments are closely linked. What these arguments fail to consider is that at least as rapidly as forces from various metropolises are brought into new societies they tend to become indigenized in one or another way: this is true of music and housing styles as much as it is true of science and terrorism, spectacles and constitutions. The dynamics of such indigenization have just begun to be explored systematically (Barber 1987; Hannerz 1987; Feld 1988; Ivy 1988; Hannerz 1989; Nicoll 1989; Yoshimoto 1989), and much more needs to be done. But it is worth noticing that for the people of Irian Jaya, Indonesianization may be more worrisome than Americanization, as Japanization may be for Koreans, Indianization for Sri Lankans, Vietnamization for the Cambodians, and Russianization for the people of Soviet Armenia and the Baltic republics. Such a list of alternative fears to Americanization could be greatly expanded, but it is not a shapeless inventory: for polities of smaller scale, there is always a fear of cultural absorption by polities of larger scale, especially those that are nearby. One man's imagined community is another man's political prison.

This scalar dynamic, which has widespread global manifestations, is also tied to the relationship between nations and states. For the moment let us note that the simplification of these many forces (and fears) of homogenization can also be exploited by nation-states in relation to their own minorities, by posing global commoditization (or capitalism, or some other such external enemy) as more real than the threat of its own hegemonic strategies.

The new global cultural economy has to be seen as a complex, overlapping, disjunctive order that cannot any longer be understood in terms of existing center-periphery models (even those that might account for multiple centers and peripheries). Nor is it susceptible to simple models of push and pull (in terms of migration theory), or of surpluses and deficits (as in traditional models of balance of trade), or of consumers and producers (as in most neo-Marxist theories of development). Even the most complex and flexible theories of global development that have come out of the Marxist tradition (Wallerstein 1974; Mandel 1978; Amin 1980; Wolf 1982) are inadequately quirky and have failed to come to terms with what Scott Lash and John Urry have called disorganized capitalism (1987). The complexity of the current global economy has to do with certain fundamental disjunctures between economy, culture, and politics that we have only begun to theorize.[1]

I propose that an elementary framework for exploring such disjunctures is to look at the relationship among five dimensions of global cultural flows that can be termed (a) *ethnoscapes*, (b) *mediascapes*, (c) *technoscapes*, (d) *financescapes*, and (e) *ideoscapes*. [. . .] The suffix-*scape* allows us to point to the fluid, irregular shapes of these landscapes, shapes that characterize international capital as deeply as they do international clothing styles. These terms with the common suffix-*scape* also indicate that these are not objectively given relations that look the same from every angle of vision but, rather, that they are deeply perspectival constructs, inflected by the historical, linguistic, and political situatedness of different sorts of actors: nation-states, multinationals, diasporic communities, as well as subnational groupings and movements (whether religious, political, or economic), and even intimate face-to-face groups, such as villages, neighborhoods, and families. Indeed, the individual actor is the last locus of this perspectival set of landscapes, for these landscapes are eventually navigated by agents who both experience and constitute larger formations, in part from their own sense of what these landscapes offer.

These landscapes thus are the building blocks of what (extending Benedict Anderson) I would like to call *imagined worlds*, that is, the multiple worlds that are constituted by the historically situated imaginations of persons and groups spread around the globe. An important fact of the world we live in today is that many persons on the globe live in such imagined worlds (and not just in imagined communities) and thus are able to contest and sometimes even subvert the imagined worlds of the official mind and of the entrepreneurial mentality that surround them.

By *ethnoscape*, I mean the landscape of persons who constitute the shifting world in which we live: tourists, immigrants, refugees, exiles, guest workers, and other moving groups and individuals constitute an essential feature of the world and appear to affect the politics of (and between) nations to a hitherto unprecedented degree. This is not to say that there are no relatively stable communities and networks of kinship, friendship, work, and leisure, as well as of birth, residence, and other filial forms. But it is to say that the warp of these stabilities is everywhere shot through with the woof of human motion, as more persons and groups deal with the realities of having to move or the fantasies of wanting to move. What is more, both these realities and fantasies now function on larger scales, as men and women from villages in India think not just of moving to Poona or Madras but of moving to Dubai and Houston, and refugees from Sri Lanka find themselves in South India as well as in Switzerland, just as the Hmong are driven to London as well as to Philadelphia. And as international capital shifts its needs, as production and technology generate different needs, as nation-states shift their policies on refugee populations, these moving groups can never afford to let their imaginations rest too long, even if they wish to.

By *technoscape*, I mean the global configuration, also ever fluid, of technology and the fact that technology, both high and low, both mechanical and informational, now moves at high speeds across various kinds of previously impervious boundaries. Many countries now are the roots of multinational enterprise: a huge steel complex in Libya may involve interests from India, China, Russia, and Japan, providing different components of new technological configurations. The odd distribution of technologies, and thus the peculiarities of these technoscapes, are increasingly driven not by any obvious economies of scale, of political control, or of market rationality but by increasingly complex relationships among money flows, political possibilities, and the availability of both un- and highly skilled labor. So, while India exports waiters and chauffeurs to Dubai and Sharjah, it also exports software engineers to the United States – indentured briefly to Tata-Burroughs or the World Bank, then laundered through the State Department to become wealthy resident aliens, who are in turn objects of seductive messages to invest their money and know-how in federal and state projects in India.

The global economy can still be described in terms of traditional indicators (as the World Bank continues to do) and studied in terms of traditional comparisons (as in Project Link at the University of Pennsylvania), but the complicated technoscapes (and the shifting ethnoscapes) that underlie these indicators and comparisons are further out of the reach of the queen of social sciences than ever before. How is one to make a meaningful comparison of wages in Japan and the United States or of real-estate costs in New York and Tokyo, without taking sophisticated account of the very complex fiscal and investment flows that link the two economies through a global grid of currency speculation and capital transfer?

Thus it is useful to speak as well of *financescapes*, as the disposition of global capital is now a more mysterious, rapid, and difficult landscape to follow than ever before, as currency markets, national stock exchanges, and commodity speculations move megamonies through national turnstiles at blinding speed, with vast, absolute implications for small differences in percentage points and time units. But the critical point is that the global relationship among ethnoscapes, technoscapes, and financescapes is deeply disjunctive and profoundly unpredictable because each of these landscapes is subject to its own constraints and incentives (some political, some informational, and some technoenvironmental), at the same time as each acts as a constraint and a parameter for movements in the others. Thus, even an elementary model of global political economy must take into account the deeply disjunctive relationships among human movement, technological flow, and financial transfers.

Further refracting these disjunctures (which hardly form a simple, mechanical global infrastructure in any case) are what I call *mediascapes* and *ideoscapes*, which are closely related landscapes of images. *Mediascapes* refer both to the distribution of the electronic capabilities to produce and disseminate information (newspapers, magazines, television stations, and film-production studios), which are now available to a growing number of private and public interests throughout the world, and to the images of the world created by these media. These images involve many complicated inflections, depending on their mode (documentary or entertainment), their hardware (electronic or preelectronic), their audiences (local, national, or transnational), and the interests of those who own and control them. What is most important about these mediascapes is that they provide (especially in their television, film, and cassette forms) large and complex repertoires of images, narratives, and ethnoscapes to viewers throughout the world, in which the world of commodities and the world of news and politics are profoundly mixed. What this means is that many audiences around the world experience the media themselves as a complicated and interconnected repertoire of print, celluloid, electronic screens, and billboards. The lines between the realistic and the fictional landscapes they see are blurred, so that the farther away these audiences are from the direct experiences of metropolitan life, the more likely they are to construct imagined worlds that are chimerical, aesthetic, even fantastic objects, particularly if assessed by the criteria of some other perspective, some other imagined world.

Mediascapes, whether produced by private or state interests, tend to be image-centered, narrative-based accounts of strips of reality, and what they offer to those who experience and transform them is a series of elements (such as characters, plots, and textual forms) out of which scripts can be formed of imagined lives, their own as well as those of others living in other places. These scripts can and do get disaggregated into complex sets of metaphors by which people live (Lakoff and Johnson 1980) as they help to constitute narratives of the Other and protonarratives of possible lives, fantasies that could become prolegomena to the desire for acquisition and movement.

Ideoscapes are also concatenations of images, but they are often directly political and frequently have to do with the ideologies of states and the counterideologies of movements explicitly oriented to capturing state power or a piece of it. These ideoscapes are composed of elements of the Enlightenment worldview, which consists of a chain of ideas, terms, and images, including *freedom*, *welfare*, *rights*, *sovereignty*, *representation*, and the master term *democracy*. The master narrative of the Enlightenment (and its many variants in Britain, France, and the United States) was constructed with a certain internal logic and presupposed a certain relationship between reading, representation, and the public sphere. (For the dynamics of this process in the early history of the United States, see Warner 1990.) But the diaspora of these terms and images across the world, especially since the nineteenth century, has loosened the internal coherence that held them together in a Euro-American master narrative and provided instead a loosely structured synopticon of politics, in which different nation-states, as part of their evolution, have organized their political cultures around different keywords (e.g., Williams 1976).

As a result of the differential diaspora of these keywords, the political narratives that govern communication between elites and followers in different parts of the world involve problems of both a semantic and pragmatic nature: semantic to the extent that words (and their lexical equivalents) require careful translation from context to context in their global movements, and pragmatic to the extent that the use of these words by political actors and their audiences may be subject to very different sets of contextual conventions that mediate their translation into public politics. Such conventions are not only matters of the nature of political rhetoric: for example, what does the aging Chinese leadership mean when it refers to the dangers of hooliganism? What does the South Korean leadership mean when it speaks of discipline as the key to democratic industrial growth?

These conventions also involve the far more subtle question of what sets of communicative genres are valued in what way (newspapers versus cinema, for example) and what sorts of pragmatic genre conventions govern the collective readings of different kinds of text. So, while an Indian audience may be attentive to the resonances of a political speech in terms of some keywords and phrases reminiscent of Hindi cinema, a Korean audience may respond to the subtle codings of Buddhist or neo-Confucian rhetoric encoded in a political document. The very relationship of reading to hearing and seeing may vary in important ways that determine the morphology of these different ideoscapes as they shape themselves in different national and transnational contexts. This globally variable synaesthesia has hardly even been noted, but it demands urgent analysis. Thus *democracy* has clearly become a master term, with powerful echoes from Haiti and Poland to the former Soviet Union and China, but it sits at the center of a variety of ideoscapes, composed of distinctive pragmatic configurations of rough translations of other central terms from the vocabulary of the Enlightenment. This creates ever new terminological kaleidoscopes, as states (and the groups that seek to capture them) seek to pacify populations whose own ethnoscapes are in motion and whose mediascapes may create severe problems for the ideoscapes with which they are presented. The fluidity of ideoscapes is complicated in particular by the growing diasporas (both voluntary and involuntary) of intellectuals who continuously inject new meaning-streams into the discourse of democracy in different parts of the world.

This extended terminological discussion of the five terms I have coined sets the basis for a tentative formulation about the conditions under which current global flows occur: they occur in and through the growing disjunctures among ethnoscapes, technoscapes, financescapes, mediascapes, and ideoscapes. This formulation, the core of my model of global cultural flow, needs some explanation. First, people, machinery, money, images, and ideas now follow increasingly nonisomorphic paths; of course, at all periods in human history, there have been some disjunctures in the flows of these things, but the sheer speed, scale, and volume of each of these flows are now so great that the disjunctures have become central to the politics of global culture. The Japanese are notoriously hospitable to ideas and are stereotyped as inclined to export (all) and import (some) goods, but they are also notoriously closed to immigration, like the Swiss, the Swedes, and the Saudis. Yet the Swiss and the Saudis accept populations of guest workers, thus creating labor diasporas of

Turks, Italians, and other circum-Mediterranean groups. Some such guest-worker groups maintain continuous contact with their home nations, like the Turks, but others, like high-level South Asian migrants, tend to desire lives in their new homes, raising anew the problem of reproduction in a deterritorialized context.

Deterritorialization, in general, is one of the central forces of the modern world because it brings laboring populations into the lower-class sectors and spaces of relatively wealthy societies, while sometimes creating exaggerated and intensified senses of criticism or attachment to politics in the home state. Deterritorialization, whether of Hindus, Sikhs, Palestinians, or Ukrainians, is now at the core of a variety of global fundamentalisms, including Islamic and Hindu fundamentalism. In the Hindu case, for example, it is clear that the overseas movement of Indians has been exploited by a variety of interests both within and outside India to create a complicated network of finances and religious identifications, by which the problem of cultural reproduction for Hindus abroad has become tied to the politics of Hindu fundamentalism at home.

At the same time, deterritorialization creates new markets for film companies, art impresarios, and travel agencies, which thrive on the need of the deterritorialized population for contact with its homeland. Naturally, these invented homelands, which constitute the mediascapes of deterritorialized groups, can often become sufficiently fantastic and one-sided that they provide the material for new ideoscapes in which ethnic conflicts can begin to erupt. The creation of Khalistan, an invented homeland of the deterritorialized Sikh population of England, Canada, and the United States, is one example of the bloody potential in such mediascapes as they interact with the internal colonialisms of the nation-state (e.g., Hechter 1975). The West Bank, Namibia, and Eritrea are other theaters for the enactment of the bloody negotiation between existing nation-states and various deterritorialized groupings.

It is in the fertile ground of deterritorialization, in which money, commodities, and persons are involved in ceaselessly chasing each other around the world, that the mediascapes and ideoscapes of the modern world find their fractured and fragmented counterpart. For the ideas and images produced by mass media often are only partial guides to the goods and experiences that deterritorialized populations transfer to one another. In Mira Nair's brilliant film *India Cabaret*, we see the multiple loops of this fractured deterritorialization as young women, barely competent in Bombay's metropolitan glitz, come to seek their fortunes as cabaret dancers and prostitutes in Bombay, entertaining men in clubs with dance formats derived wholly from the prurient dance sequences of Hindi films. These scenes in turn cater to ideas about Western and foreign women and their looseness, while they provide tawdry career alibis for these women. Some of these women come from Kerala, where cabaret clubs and the pornographic film industry have blossomed, partly in response to the purses and tastes of Keralites returned from the Middle East, where their diasporic lives away from women distort their very sense of what the relations between men and women might be. These tragedies of displacement could certainly be replayed in a more detailed analysis of the relations between the Japanese and German sex tours to Thailand and the tragedies of the sex trade in Bangkok, and in other similar loops that tie together fantasies about the Other, the conveniences and seductions of travel, the economics of global trade, and the brutal mobility fantasies that dominate gender politics in many parts of Asia and the world at large.

While far more could be said about the cultural politics of deterritorialization and the larger sociology of displacement that it expresses, it is appropriate at this juncture to bring in the role of the nation-state in the disjunctive global economy of culture today. The relationship between states and nations is everywhere an embattled one. It is possible to say that in many societies the nation and the state have become one another's projects. That is, while nations (or more properly groups with ideas about nationhood) seek to capture or co-opt states and state power, states simultaneously seek to capture and monopolize ideas about nationhood (Baruah 1986; Chatterjee 1986; Nandy 1989). In general, separatist transnational movements, including those that have included terror in their methods, exemplify nations in search of states. Sikhs, Tamil Sri Lankans, Basques, Moros, Quebecois – each of these represents imagined communities that seek to create states of their own or carve pieces out of existing states. States, on the other hand, are everywhere seeking to monopolize the moral resources of community, either by flatly claiming perfect coevality between nation and state, or by systematically museumizing and representing all the groups within them in a variety of heritage politics that seems remarkably uniform throughout the world (Herzfeld 1982; Handler 1988; McQueen 1988).

Here, national and international mediascapes are exploited by nation-states to pacify separatists or even the potential fissiparousness of all ideas of difference. Typically, contemporary nation-states do this by exercising taxonomic control over difference, by creating various kinds of international spectacle to domesticate difference, and by seducing small groups with the fantasy of self-display on some sort of global or cosmopolitan stage. One important new feature of global cultural politics, tied to the disjunctive relationships among the various landscapes discussed earlier, is that state and nation are at each other's throats, and the hyphen that links them is now less an icon of conjuncture than an index of disjuncture. This disjunctive relationship between nation and state has two levels: at the level of any given nation-state, it means that there is a battle of the imagination, with state and nation seeking to cannibalize one another. Here is the seedbed of brutal separatisms – majoritarianisms that seem to have appeared from nowhere and microidentities that have become political projects within the nation-state. At another level, this disjunctive relationship is deeply entangled with global disjunctures: ideas of nationhood appear to be steadily increasing in scale and regularly crossing existing state boundaries, sometimes, as with the Kurds, because previous identities stretched across vast national spaces or, as with the Tamils in Sri Lanka, the dormant threads of a transnational diaspora have been activated to ignite the micropolitics of a nation-state.

[. . .]

Returning then to the ethnoscapes with which I began, the central paradox of ethnic politics in today's world is that primordia (whether of language or skin color or neighborhood or kinship) have become globalized. That is, sentiments, whose greatest force is in their ability to ignite intimacy into a political state and turn locality into a staging ground for identity, have become spread over vast and irregular spaces as groups move yet stay linked to one another through sophisticated media capabilities. This is not to deny that such primordia are often the product of invented traditions (Hobsbawm and Ranger 1983) or retrospective affiliations, but to emphasize that because of the disjunctive and unstable interplay of commerce, media, national policies, and consumer fantasies, ethnicity, once a genie contained in the bottle of some sort of locality (however large), has now become a global force, forever slipping in and through the cracks between states and borders.

But the relationship between the cultural and economic levels of this new set of global disjunctures is not a simple one-way street in which the terms of global cultural politics are set wholly by, or confined wholly within, the vicissitudes of international flows of technology, labor, and finance, demanding only a modest modification of existing neo-Marxist models of uneven development and state formation. There is a deeper change, itself driven by the disjunctures among all the landscapes I have discussed and constituted by their continuously fluid and uncertain interplay, that concerns the relationship between production and consumption in today's global economy. Here, I begin with Marx's famous (and often mined) view of the fetishism of the commodity and suggest that this fetishism has been replaced in the world at large (now seeing the world as one large, interactive system, composed of many complex subsystems) by two mutually supportive descendants, the first of which I call production fetishism and the second, the fetishism of the consumer.

By *production fetishism* I mean an illusion created by contemporary transnational production loci that masks translocal capital, transnational earning flows, global management, and often faraway workers (engaged in various kinds of high-tech putting-out operations) in the idiom and spectacle of local (sometimes even worker) control, national productivity, and territorial sovereignty. To the extent that various kinds of free-trade zones have become the models for production at large, especially of high-tech commodities, production has itself become a fetish, obscuring not social relations as such but the relations of production, which are increasingly transnational. The locality (both in the sense of the local factory or site of production and in the extended sense of the nation-state) becomes a fetish that disguises the globally dispersed forces that actually drive the production process. This generates alienation (in Marx's sense) twice intensified, for its social sense is now compounded by a complicated spatial dynamic that is increasingly global.

As for the *fetishism of the consumer*, I mean to indicate here that the consumer has been transformed through commodity flows (and the mediascapes, especially of advertising, that accompany them) into a sign, both in Baudrillard's sense of a simulacrum that only asymptotically approaches the form of a real social agent, and in the sense of a mask for the real seat of agency, which is not the consumer but the producer and the many forces that constitute production. Global advertising is the key technology for the worldwide dissemination of a plethora of creative and culturally well-chosen ideas of consumer agency. These images of agency are increasingly distortions of a world of merchandising so subtle that the consumer is consistently helped to believe that he or she is an actor, where in fact he or she is at best a chooser.

The globalization of culture is not the same as its homogenization, but globalization involves the use of a variety of instruments of homogenization (armaments, advertising techniques, language hegemonies, and clothing styles) that are absorbed into local political and cultural economies, only to be repatriated as heterogeneous dialogues of national sovereignty, free enterprise, and fundamentalism in which the state plays an increasingly delicate role: too much openness to global flows, and the nation-state is threatened by revolt, as in the China syndrome; too little, and the state exits the international stage, as Burma, Albania, and North Korea in various ways have done. In general, the state has become the arbitrageur of this *repatriation of difference* (in the form of goods, signs, slogans, and styles). But this repatriation or export of the designs and commodities of difference continuously exacerbates the internal politics of majoritarianism and homogenization, which is most frequently played out in debates over heritage.

Thus the central feature of global culture today is the politics of the mutual effort of sameness and difference to cannibalize one another and thereby proclaim their successful hijacking of the twin Enlightenment ideas of the triumphantly universal and the resiliently particular. This mutual cannibalization shows its ugly face in riots, refugee flows, state-sponsored torture, and ethnocide (with or without state support). Its brighter side is in the expansion of many individual horizons of hope and fantasy, in the global spread of oral rehydration therapy and other low-tech instruments of well-being, in the susceptibility even of South Africa to the force of global opinion, in the inability of the Polish state to repress its own working classes, and in the growth of a wide range of progressive, transnational alliances. Examples of both sorts could be multiplied. The critical point is that both sides of the coin of global cultural process today are products of the infinitely varied mutual contest of sameness and difference on a stage characterized by radical disjunctures between different sorts of global flows and the uncertain landscapes created in and through these disjunctures.

Note

1   One major exception is Fredric Jameson, whose work on the relationship between post-modernism and late capitalism has in many ways inspired this essay. The debate between Jameson and Aijaz Ahmad in *Social Text*, however, shows that the creation of a globalizing Marxist narrative in cultural matters is difficult territory indeed (Jameson 1986; Ahmad 1987). [. . .]

Chapter 5

J. K. Gibson-Graham

QUERYING GLOBALIZATION

From *The End of Capitalism (as we knew it): A Feminist Critique of Political Economy* Oxford: Blackwell, 1996, pp. 120–24 and pp. 134–43 and pp. 145–46

IT WAS AN ARTICLE ON RAPE BY SHARON MARCUS that first 'drove home' to me the force of globalization. The force of it as a discourse, that is, as a language of domination, a tightly scripted narrative of differential power. What I mean by 'globalization' is that set of processes by which the world is rapidly being integrated into one economic space via increased international trade, the internationalization of production and financial markets, the internationalization of a commodity culture promoted by an increasingly networked global telecommunications system. A forceful visual image of this present and future domain is the photograph of Spaceship Earth which is increasingly used to advertise the operating compass of global banks or businesses, promoting the message that 'we' all live in one economic world. [. . .]

Heralded as a 'reality' by both the right and the left, globalization is greeted on the one hand with celebration and admiration, on the other with foreboding and dismay. This chapter focuses initially upon left discussions in which globalization is represented as the penetration (or imminent penetration) of capitalism into all processes of production, circulation and consumption, not only of commodities but also of meaning: [. . .]

> The distinctive mark of late capitalism, underpinning its multinational global reach, is its ability to fuse and obliterate the boundaries of production and consumption through the *pervasive domination* of all levels of consumer culture and everyday life.
> (Deshpande and Kurtz 1994, 35 emphasis [Gibson-Graham])

> Multinational capital formation . . . no longer makes its claims through direct colonial subjugation of the subject, but rather by the hyperextension of interpellative discourses and representations generated with and from a specifically new form of capital *domination*. Thus, it is important

> to recognize that *domination* occurs intensively at the levels of discourse, representation, and subjectivity.
>
> (Smith 1988, 138 emphasis [Gibson-Graham])

> the prodigious new expansion of multinational capital ends up *penetrating* and colonizing those very precapitalist enclaves (Nature and the Unconscious) which offered extraterritorial and Archimedean footholds for critical effectivity.
>
> (Jameson 1991, 49 emphasis [Gibson-Graham])

Fueled by the 'fall of socialism' in 1989, references are rampant to the inevitability of capitalist penetration and the naturalness of capitalist domination. The dynamic image of penetration and domination is linked to a vision of the world as already or about to be wholly capitalist – that is, a world 'rightfully owned' by capitalism.

It was in the light of this pervasive discourse of capitalist penetration and of assertions that the Kingdom of Capitalism is *here* and *now* that Marcus's argument about rape spoke to me so directly. Marcus challenges the inevitability of the claim that rape is one of the 'real, clear facts of women's lives' (1992, 385). She draws attention to a 'language of rape' which assumes that 'rape has always already occurred and women are always either already raped or already rapable' (386). Reading her analysis of the positioning of women in the language of rape, I found myself replacing her object of study with my own – rape became *globalization*, men became *capitalism* or its agent the *multinational corporation* (*MNC*), and women became *capitalism's 'other'* – including economies or regions that are not wholly capitalist, non-commodified exchanges or commodities that are not produced by capitalist production, and cultural practices that are conducted outside the economy.

When Marcus expressed her concern that feminist activism to make rape visible in communities had also produced a politics of fear and subjection, I thought of the industry activism I had participated in that had generated a knowledge of globalization and capital flight, and the way in which a politics of fear and subjection had emerged from it. When she made reference to the ways in which women limit their activities – for example, avoiding or thinking twice about being out in public spaces alone or in the evening, for fear of being accused of 'asking for' rape – my mind turned to the way in which workers have limited their demands for higher wages or improved working conditions, given the knowledge about capital mobility and the operations of the MNC, for fear that they might be 'asking for' capital abandonment. [. . .]

But how, Marcus prompted me to ask, was this message of fear conveyed by analyses of globalization? How had globalization become normalized so as to preclude strategies of real opposition, as in Marcus's view the normalization of rape has hindered feminist strategies for real and active resistance within the rape event itself? Within the discourse of globalization fear of capital flight and subjection to heightened exploitation are positioned as legitimate responses to the so-called 'realities' of globalization [. . .] – just as fear of violation, and passivity or paralysis in the face of violence become legitimate responses to the 'realities' of rape. As Marcus notes, '(w)e are taught the following fallacy – that we can best avoid getting hurt by letting someone hurt us' (395). She argues that unquestioned acceptance of rape as a fact of life limits the political efficacy of feminist actions that could be taken to prevent it. Accepting men's capacity to rape as a self-explanatory 'fact' encourages activism in the areas of litigation and reparation 'after the fact', rather than in the form of direct challenges to the victim role prescribed by the 'rape script'.

Parallels can be drawn here with the 1970s industrial activism that accompanied the widespread acceptance of capitalist globalization as a 'fact'. Some unions within national labor movements were tempted into aggressive bids for their piece of the action – a role in the World Car plan, for example. Others accepted globalization by pressing for state assistance to regions hardest hit by capital flight. Rather hollow-sounding calls for the 'international workers of the world' to unite were revived; but while the polemic was inspirational for a time (in a nineteenth-century kind of way) efforts to realize such a movement were largely thwarted by the discursive positioning of capital's globalization as a more powerful force than labor's internationalism. [. . .]

In her suspicion of claims about 'reality' and the unmediated nature of women's 'experience', indeed, in her refusal to recognize 'rape as the real fact of our lives' (388), Marcus is led to explore the construction of rape as a linguistic artifact and

> to ask how the violence of rape is enabled by narratives, complexes and institutions which derive their strength not from outright, immutable, unbeatable force but rather from their power to structure our lives as . . . cultural scripts.
>
> (388–89)

A language shapes the rape script – 'the verbal and physical interactions of a woman and her would-be assailant' – permitting the would-be rapist to constitute feelings of power and causing the woman to experience corresponding feelings of terror and paralysis. But the language also 'enables people to experience themselves as speaking, acting, embodied subjects' (390), offering the potential for new words, different feelings and unexpected actions to emerge. By invoking the metaphor of a language, something that has rules of grammar but rules that can be used to say many different things, Marcus suggests that we might begin to imagine an alternative script of rape (387).

I could see in Marcus's project the contours of an argument very similar to the one I was constructing to challenge the dominant discourse of capitalist globalization. And what began as a simple game of seeing how far the comparisons and analogies between rape and globalization might take me ultimately developed into a rather complex form of play – the project of reading the globalization literature through the lens of poststructuralist feminist and queer writings about bodies, sexuality and gender. In pursuing this project I hoped to gain some purchase on globalization discourse, to become more active in the face of it, less prey to its ability to map a social terrain in which I and others are relatively powerless and inconsequential.

[. . .]

Inscribing sexual/economic identity

Rewriting the script of gendered violence so that women are no longer subjects of fear and objects of violence but become subjects of violence (and therefore capable of real opposition) in their own right is enabled by discussions and evidence that challenge the unquestioned capability of male bodies to rape, and that question their superior strength and the impossibility of resistance. Stories of resistance, of cases where women averted rape or fought back, provide empowering images that might help women to 'rewrite' the standard rape script. But Marcus is concerned to go beyond the tactics of reversal and individual empowerment. This leads her to another kind of interest in the metaphor of a script.

One of the powerful things about rape in our culture is that it represents an important inscription of female sexual identity. Marcus argues that we should

> view rape not as the invasion of female inner space, but as the forced *creation* of female sexuality as a violated inner space. The horror of rape is not that it steals something from us but that it *makes* us into things to be taken . . . The most deep-rooted upheaval of rape culture would revise the idea of female sexuality as an object, as property, and as inner space.
> (399 emphasis [Gibson-Graham]) [. . .]

The rape act draws its legitimacy (and therefore the illegitimacy of resistance) from a very powerful discourse about the female body and female and male sexuality. Thus the subject position of victim for the woman is not created merely by the strength and violence of the rapist but also by the discourse of female sexual identity that the rape script draws upon in its enactment:

> Rape *engenders* a sexualized female body defined as a wound, a body excluded from subject–subject violence, from the ability to engage in a fair fight. Rapists do not beat women at the game of violence, but aim to exclude us from playing it altogether.
> (397 emphasis [Gibson-Graham])

In Marcus's view, the creation of alternatives to the standard rape script is predicated upon a significant revision of the very powerful discourses of sexual identity that constitute the enabling background of all rape events:

> New cultural productions and reinscriptions of our bodies and our geographies can help us begin to revise the grammar of violence and to represent ourselves in militant new ways.
> (400)

The feminist project of rewriting and reinscribing the female body and sexuality has born[e] much theoretical fruit in recent years, prompted especially by the work of French philosophers Irigaray, Kristeva, and Cixous. Marcus's challenge and encouragement to marry this rethinking with strategizing a new (poststructuralist) feminist politics of rape prevention has prompted me to further thoughts about globalization and the politics of economic transformation. In particular, they have led me to consider how a rewriting of the male body and sexuality might affect views of capitalism and its globalizing capacities:

> Men still have everything to say about their sexuality, and everything to write. For what they have said so far, for the most part, stems from

the opposition activity/passivity, from the power relation between a fantasized obligatory virility meant to invade, to colonize, and the consequential phantasm of woman as a 'dark continent' to penetrate and 'pacify'.

(Cixous 1980, 247)

Feminist theorists have generated many new representations to replace that of the vacant, dark continent of female sexuality. However, as Grosz remarks, the particularities of the male body that might prompt us to challenge its naturalized hard and impermeable qualities have largely remained unanalyzed and unrepresented (Grosz 1994, 198). Discussion of bodily fluids, for example, is rarely allowed to break down the solidity and boundedness of the male body:

> Seminal fluid is understood primarily as what it makes, what it achieves, a causal agent and thus a thing, a solid: its fluidity, its potential seepage, the element in it that is uncontrollable, its spread, its formlessness, is perpetually displaced in discourse onto its properties, its capacity to fertilize, to father, to produce an object.
>
> (Grosz 1994, 199)

Grosz's suggestive words offer a brief glimpse of how we might differently conceive of the body of capitalism, viewing it as open, as penetrable, as weeping or draining away instead of as hard and contained, penetrating, and inevitably overpowering. Consider the seminal fluid of capitalism – finance capital (or money) – which has more traditionally been represented as the lifeblood of the economic system whose free circulation ensures health and growth of the capitalist body. . . . As seminal fluid, however, it periodically breaks its bounds, unleashing uncontrollable gushes of capital that flow every which way, including into self-destruction. One such spectacle of bodily excess, a wet dream that stained markets around the globe, occurred in October 1987, when stock markets across the world crashed, vaporizing millions of dollars in immaterial wealth (Wark 1994b, 169). The 1987 crash was for many the bursting of a bubble of irrationality, 'a suitable ending, fit for a moral fable, where the speculators finally got their just deserts' (Wark 1994b, 171–72). But the growth of activity on international financial markets represents an interestingly contradictory aspect of the globalization script.

One of the key features of globalization has been the complete reorganization of the global financial system since the mid-1970s:

> The formation of a global stock market, of global commodity (even debt) futures markets, of currency and interest rate swaps, together with an accelerated geographical mobility of funds, meant, for the first time, the formation of a single world market for money and credit supply.
>
> (Harvey 1990, 161)

On the one hand this growth has been seen to facilitate the rapid internationalization of capitalist production, and the consolidation of the power of finance capital is seen to represent the 'supreme and most abstract expression' of capital (Hilferding quoted in Daly 1991, 84). On the other, this growth has unleashed money from its role as a means of circulation and allowed the rampant proliferation of global credit:

> Now detached from its necessity to abide by the laws of capital accumulation the finance sector oversees and facilitates capital movement into speculation, mergers, acquisitions – 'financial gamesmanship'.
>
> (Harrison and Bluestone 1988, 54)

Money has become

> a kind of free-floating signifier detached from the real processes to which it once referred. Through options, swaps and futures, money is traded for money. Indeed since much of what is exchanged as commodities are future monetary transactions, so what is traded in no sense exists.
>
> (Lash and Urry 1994, 292)

The globalization of credit and financial markets has created an 'opening' for capital to transcend its own limits:

> The economy is an ensemble of movements and flows, mostly tied more or less to the physical space of fixed assets that persist in time. The financial vector is a dynamic development that seeks to escape from commitment to such permanence.
>
> (Wark 1994b, 176) [. . .]

For those interested in historical periodizations of capitalism, this development signifies the demise of capitalism in its 'second nature' (Debord 1983), when the productive base anchored the movements of credit and money. [. . .] Today, the whole relation between signifier, signified and referent has been ruptured thereby unleashing capitalism's 'third nature', 'the spectacle' (Debord 1983), 'the enchanted world' (Lipietz 1985) in which the 'economic real' is buried under the trade of risk, information, image, futures, to be revealed only in momentary displays such as occurred when stock markets crashed in October 1987 (Wark 1994b). At such orgasmic moments the body of capitalism undergoes a spasm of uncontrollability and unboundedness, to be brought back to itself and recontained within its own limits during the little death that follows:

> Capital pushes the development of the [finance] vector so hard and fast that it bursts through its own limit, as it did in October 1987. Like a meltdown, the crash was an accident programmed in advance to happen as the system pushed against its own limits . . . In attempting to increase its power over itself and the world via the vector, capital encounters obstacles within itself . . . Third nature is both the means by which capital extends itself, and the symptom of its inability to do so . . . The event [the crash] is a privileged moment in which to see third nature for what it really is, stripped of its myths and kitchen gods.
>
> (Wark 1994b, 192 [brackets by Gibson-Graham])

Globalization, it seems, has set money free of the 'real economy' and allowed capital to seep if not spurt from the productive system, but the implications of this unboundedness, this fluidity, for the identity of capitalism remain . . . unexplored. Having set the signifier free from the referent, theorists of the global economy are loath to think about the effects of seepage, porosity, uncontrollability, that is, to feminize economic identity (Grosz 1994, 203). The global economy may have been opened up by international financial markets, but nothing 'other' comes into or out of this opening. It would seem that the homophobia that pervades economic theorizing places a taboo on such thinking: [. . .]

> Part of the process of phallicizing the male body, of subordinating the rest of the body to the valorized functioning of the penis, with the culmination of sexual activities occurring ideally at least, in sexual penetration and male orgasm, involves the constitution of the sealed-up, impermeable body. Perhaps it is not after all flow in itself that a certain phallicized masculinity abhors but the idea that flow moves or can move in two-way or indeterminable directions that elicits horror, the possibility of being not only an active agent in the transmission of flow but also a passive receptacle.
>
> (Grosz 1994, 200–201)

How might we confront the economic 'unthinkable', engendering a vision of the global economy as penetrable by noncapitalist economic forms? Perhaps the very same financial system that is represented as both the agent of seepage and the agent of capital's assertion of identity might yield a further surplus of effects. Perhaps we might see the proliferation of credit and deregulation of financial markets as creating opportunities for the growth of noncapitalist class relations as well as capitalist ones. The huge expansion of consumer credit (including credit card financing with large maximum limits, home equity loans, and a variety of other instruments almost forced upon 'consumers') is often assumed to promote personal indebtedness associated with a culture of consumption. Yet, given the growth in self-employment and of home-based industries – some of which is associated with the downsizing and streamlining of capitalist firms – it is clear that much of what is seen as consumer credit is actually (or also) producer credit, in other words it is used to buy means of production (including computers and other equipment) and other inputs into the production process of self-employed workers. Historically such loans have been notoriously difficult to obtain from traditional financial institutions like local and regional banks, but with the growth of new international credit markets they have become quite instantaneous and straightforward. This has contributed to an increase in small businesses that are sites of noncapitalist class processes of individual and collective surplus appropriation (as well as providing a source of credit to small capitalist firms). The financial sector can be seen, then, as an *opening* in the body of capitalism, one that not only allows capital to seep out but that enables noncapitalism to invade.

The script of globalization need not draw solely upon an image of the body of capitalism as hard, thrusting and powerful. Other images are available, and while we cannot expect the champions of globalization to express pleasure in leakage, unboundedness and invasion, it is important to draw upon such representations in

creating an anticapitalist imaginary and fashioning a politics of economic transformation. If the identity of capitalism is fluid, able to penetrate and be penetrated, then
the process of globalization need not constitute or inscribe 'economic development'
as inevitably *capitalist* development. Globalization might be seen as liberating a
variety of different economic development paths. In fact, the script of globalization
may already (without explicit instances of opposition) be engendering economic
differences. [. . .]

Marcus encourages a rejection of the fixed sexual identity that is *inscribed* upon
the body of women by the rape script. Given that this identity is rooted in a
dominant discourse of heterosexuality (in which the bodies of men and women are
distinguished by rigid and fixed gender differences and in which male and female
behavior can only be understood in terms of opposition, complementarity or sup-
plementarity), one of the implications of Marcus's argument is that rape (along with
marriage) is a recognized and accepted (if not acceptable) practice of heterosexuality. Challenging the legitimacy our culture implicitly grants to rape becomes, in this
formulation, a challenge to heteronormativity itself.

My desire to reject globalization as the inevitable inscription of capitalism
prompts me to take Marcus's implication one step further and to explore the ways in
which discourses of homosexuality might liberate alternative scripts or inscriptions
of sexual/economic identity:

> many gay men . . . are prepared not only to send out but also to receive
> flow and in this process to assert other bodily regions than those singled
> out by the phallic function. A body that is permeable, that transmits in a
> circuit, that opens itself up rather than seals itself off, that is prepared to
> respond as well as to initiate, that does not revile its masculinity . . . or
> virilize it . . . would involve a quite radical rethinking of male sexual
> morphology.
>
> (Grosz 1994, 201)

Queering globalization/'the universality of intercourse'

Rethinking capitalist morphology in order to liberate economic development from
the hegemonic grasp of capitalist identity is indeed a radical project. Yet resources
for such a project are already available in the domain of social theory, especially
within queer theory, where a rethinking of sexual morphology is taking place. For
queer theorists, sexual identity is not automatically derived from certain organs or
practices or genders but is instead a space of transitivity (Sedgwick 1993, xii):

> one of the things that 'queer' can refer to [is] the open mesh of possi-
> bilities, gaps, overlaps, dissonances and resonances, lapses and excesses
> of meaning when the constituent elements of anyone's gender, of any-
> one's sexuality aren't made (or *can't be* made) to signify monolithically.
>
> (Sedgwick 1993, 8 [emphasis in Gibson-Graham])

Sedgwick's evocation of the way in which things are supposed to 'come together' at
certain social sites – she speaks of the family, for example, where a surname, a

building, a legal entity, blood relationships, a unit in a community of worship, a system of companionship and caring, a sexual dyad, the prime site of economic and cultural consumption, and a mechanism to produce, care for, and acculturate children [. . .] are 'meant to line up perfectly with each other' (6) – captures the oppressiveness of familiar identity-constituting/policing discourses and provides a glimpse of the productiveness of fracturing and highlighting dissonances in seemingly univocal formations. Through its challenges to such consolidities of correspondences and alignments, queer theory has encouraged me to attempt to rupture monolithic representations of capitalism and capitalist social formations.

One key conflation or 'coming together' that participates in constituting a capitalist monolith is the familiar association of capitalism with 'commodification' and 'the market'. When it is problematized, which is not very often, the presumed overlap between markets, commodities and capitalism will often be understood as the product of a capitalist tendency to foster what Marx calls 'the universality of intercourse' (1973, 540). This tendency is central to the representation of the capitalist body as inherently capable of invading, appropriating and destroying:

> while capital must on one side strive to tear down every spatial barrier to intercourse, i.e. to exchange, and conquer the whole earth for its market, it strives on the other side to annihilate this space with time, i.e. to reduce to a minimum the time spent in motion from one place to another . . . There appears here the universalizing tendency of capital, which distinguishes it from all previous stages of production.
>
> (Marx 1973, 539–40)

> When the 'market' is invoked today, nearly fifty years after the construction of the post-war order, the main referent must be to the world market – to the markets for goods and services, capital (or 'loci of production'), money and credit. The world market is the site of economic reproduction of the global capital relation, as well as of the political organization of hegemony. An opening to the world market is thus synonymous with integration into the global process of economic reproduction and a historically determined system of hegemony.
>
> (Altvater 1993, 80–81) [. . .]

In discussions of the bodily interactions (that is, market transactions) between capitalism and its 'others', the metaphor of infection sometimes joins those of invasion and penetration:

> capital is the virus of abstraction. It enters into any and every social relation, corrupts it, and makes it manufacture more relations of abstraction. It is a form of viral relations which has a double aspect. It turns every qualitative and particular relation into a quantitative and universal one.
>
> (Wark 1994b, xii)

It is perhaps not surprising that capitalism is represented as a body that invades and infects, but is not itself susceptible to invasion or infection. In the shadow of the

AIDs [*sic*] crisis queer theorists have shed light upon the homophobia that pervades social theory (if not the specific heteronormativity of economic theory) (Sedgwick 1993). The infection metaphor suggests an 'immensely productive incoherence' (to use Sedgwick's phrase [1993, xii]) that may help to disrupt the seamlessness of capitalist identity, reconfiguring capitalism's morphology in ways that our earlier rethinking of heterosexual rape and penetration could not.

The locus and agent of universalizing intercourse is 'the market', which continually seeks new arenas/bodies in which to establish a medium, or circuitry, through which contamination by capitalism may flow. Globalization discourse highlights the one-way nature of this contamination and the virtual impossibility of immunity to infection. But markets/circuits cannot control what or who flows through them. The market can, in fact, communicate many diseases, only one of which is capitalist development. Consider as an example the increasingly international labor market, another character in the standard script of globalization. The huge increase in international migration and the establishment of large immigrant 'underclasses' in the metropolitan capitals (world cities) of the global economy since the 1960s is attributed both to economic and political destabilization in 'donor' countries and to the voracious appetite of 'first world' capitalism for cheap labor, particularly in the growing service and low-wage manufacturing industries (Sassen 1988). The loss of labor from source countries is usually portrayed as yet another outcome of the penetration of capitalism, via a process in which 'the market' or 'commodification' has destroyed the traditional, often agricultural, economy and forced people into proletarianization.

When incorporated into a script of globalization, the extraordinary economic diversity of immigrant economies in 'host' countries is subsumed to, or depicted as an 'enclave' within, the capitalist totality, located on a trajectory of homogenization or synthesis with the host society. The noncapitalist nature of immigrant entrepreneurial activity is documented for its cultural interest, but is rarely allowed the autonomy afforded to 'capitalist enterprise'. Yet immigrant economies made up of self-employed and communal family-based enterprises (as well as small capitalist enterprises) operate their own labor and capital markets, often on a global scale (Collins et al. 1995; Waldinger 1986). They maintain complex economic as well as political and cultural connections with other diasporic communities and with their 'home' countries.

Even immigrant workers who may be wage laborers in metropolitan capitalist economies cannot be seen as 'subsumed' in any complete sense. Rouse (1991) documents how Mexican immigrants working as wage laborers in the service industries of US cities manage two distinct ways of life, maintaining small-scale family based farms or commercial operations in Mexico. Money received as wages in the US is siphoned into productive investment in noncapitalist activity in the Mexican economy:

> Aguilillans have come to link proletarian labor with a sustained attachment to the creation of small-scale, family based operations . . . Obliged to live within a transnational space and to make a living by combining quite different forms of class experience, Aguilillans have become skilled exponents of a cultural bifocality that defies reduction to a singular order.
>
> (Rouse 1991, 14–15)

Globalization, it would seem, has not merely created the circuitry for an increased density of international capital flows: 'Just as capitalists have responded to the new forms of economic internationalism by establishing transnational corporations, so workers have responded by creating transnational circuits' (14). Labor flows have also grown, and with them a variety of noncapitalist relations.

This case is a wonderful example of the productive incoherence that can be generated through a metaphor of infection – an infection whose agent is the market (in this instance the international labor market). It challenges the imperial nature of capitalism, depriving capitalism of its role as sole initiator of a spatially and socially expansive economic circuitry of infection. If capitalist globalization is an infection, it can be said to coexist with many other types of infection. Were we not bedazzled by images of the superior morphology of global capitalism, it might be possible to theorize the global integration of noncapitalist economic relations and non-economic relations and to see capitalist globalization as coexisting with, and even facilitating, the renewed viability of noncapitalist globalization.

[. . .]

Conclusion: globalization and its 'other' or globalization as 'other'

> To treat rape simply as one of . . . 'the realities that circumscribe women's lives' can mean to consider rape as terrifyingly unnameable and unrepresentable, a reality that lies beyond our grasp and which we can only experience as grasping and encircling us.
>
> (Marcus 1992, 387)

The discourse of globalization that I have been discussing in this chapter presents capitalism as something that is certainly 'grasping and encircling us'. Against the force of globalization many have focused upon the 'local' (or localization) as its only 'other'. Localization invokes the way in which 'global processes can in a sense be pinned down in certain localities and hence can become the basis for self-sustaining growth in those places' (Lash and Urry 1994, 284). 'As spatial barriers diminish so we become much more sensitized to what the world's spaces contain' (Harvey 1990, 294). Theorists such as Haraway have been concerned to make visible the many and heterogeneous globalized organizations that build alliances across situatednesses and establish 'webs of systematicity' between locales.

But while localization may involve certain resistances to global processes, there is no room for the penetration of globalization/capitalism by the local. Localization, it seems, is not so much 'other' to globalization as contained within it, brought into being by it, indeed part of globalization itself.

Marcus's discussion of the rape script has prompted me to explore the ways in which we might resist and rethink the representation of globalization as the social disciplinarian that polices all economic transactions – forcing them into line, into direct competition and equilibration – and thereby establishes a Kingdom on earth in which the local is humbled. [. . .] Her rethinking of rape has inspired me to imagine the repositioning of subjects in the globalization script, and to think differently about globalization (based upon a differently constituted morphology of capitalist identity) as itself 'other'.

The strategies suggested by Marcus involve first rewriting the globalization script from within, denying the inevitability and 'reality' of MNC power over workers and communities and exploring ways in which the hard and penetrating body of the MNC can be seen as soft, fragile, and vulnerable. Making global capitalism lose its erection becomes a real possibility if we reject the naturalization of power and violence that is conferred upon the MNC by the globalization script. It also becomes possible to challenge the representation of economic penetration as necessarily inducing sterility or causing death in the Third World body economic. [. . .] Both these rewritings attempt to generate a vision of alternative scripts and outcomes for economic transformation without challenging the naturalness of (capitalist) globalization itself.

The second strategy for querying globalization entails identifying the larger discourse of economic identity and development that grants 'reality' and legitimacy to global capitalism, and exploring the inscription by the globalization script of a hegemonic capitalist identity upon the world body economic. Drawing upon feminist retheorizations of sexual identity, the naturalness of capitalist identity as the template of all economic identity can be called into question. We may attempt to make globalization less genital, less phallic, by highlighting various points of excess in its inscriptions – places where the inscription can be seen as uncontrollable or indeterminate, or as potentially inscribing noncapitalist identity.

Finally, the severing of globalization from a fixed capitalist identity is enabled by a queering of economic identity, a breaking apart of the monolithic significations of capitalism (market/commodity/capital) and a liberation of different economic beings and practices. A space can be made for thinking globalization as many, as other to itself, as inscribing different development paths and economic identities. Globalization need not be resisted only through recourse to the local (its other within) but may be redefined discursively, in a process that makes room for a host of alternative scriptings, capable of inscribing a proliferation of economic differences.

[. . .]

Chapter 6

Anna Tsing

THE GLOBAL SITUATION

From *Cultural Anthropology* 15.3 (2000): 327–28, 330–34, 336–42, 345–47, 351–60

CLICK ON WORLDMAKING.INTERCONNECTIONS. Your screen fills with global flows.

Imagine a creek cutting through a hillside. As the water rushes down, it carves rock and moves gravel; it deposits silt on slow turns; it switches courses and breaks earth dams after a sudden storm. As the creek flows, it makes and remakes its channels.

Imagine an internet system, linking up computer users. Or a rush of immigrants across national borders. Or capital investments shuttled to varied offshore locations. These world-making 'flows', too, are not just interconnections but also the recarving of channels and the remapping of the possibilities of geography. Imagine the landscape nourished by the creek. Yet even beyond the creek's 'flows', there are no stable landscape elements: Trees sprout up, transforming meadows into forests; cattle browse on saplings, spreading meadows past forest edges. Nor are forests and meadows the only way to divide up the landscape. Consider the perspective of the earthworm, looking for rich soils, or the weed, able to flourish in both meadow and forest, though only when each meets certain conditions. To tell the story of this landscape requires an appreciation not only of changing landscape elements but also of the partial, tentative, and shifting ability of the storyteller to identify elements at all.

Imagine ethnic groups, corporations, refugees, nongovernmental organizations (NGOs), nation-states, consumers, social movements, media moguls, trade organizations, social scientists, international lawyers, and bankers, all swarming alongside creeks and earthworms to compose the landscape, to define its elements, carve its channels of flow, and establish its units of historical agency. We live in a time of self-consciousness about units and scales: Where shall we draw the boundaries of regions? How are local communities composed? And, most important for this essay, what is this thing we call the globe? [. . .] [I]n the last ten years, talk about the globe has heated up to the point that many commentators imagine a global *era*, a time in which no units or scales count for much except the globe. 'Globalization', the process taking us into that era, has caught up enthusiasts ranging from corporate managers to social activists, from advertisers to cultural theorists.

For many years, the creek makes only gradual changes in the landscape. Then a storm sweeps the flux beyond its accustomed boundaries, shifting every bank and eddy. Trees are uprooted, and what was once on the right side is now on the left. So, too, the social world has shifted around us. Market enthusiasms have replaced communism; national governments prostrate themselves before international finance; social movements market 'culture' on a global scale. How should social scientists analyze these changes? This question is muddied by the fact that social science changes too. 'Global' practices challenge social scientists to internationalize their venues, as North American and European scholars are brought into discussion with scholars from the South. Social science theories no longer take Western genealogies for granted but, rather, require fluency with a wider range of perspectives, from Latin American dependency theories to South Asian subaltern studies. The excitement of this internationalization of scholarship encourages many of us to throw ourselves into endorsements of globalization as a multilayered evolution, drawing us into the future. Sometimes our critical distance seems less useful than our participation. And yet, can we understand either our own involvement or the changing world without our critical skills? This essay argues that we cannot.

Is globalization like modernization?

[. . .]

In this essay, I use . . . three directions of analysis to learn something about social science commitments to the newly emerging significance of a global scale. First, I examine the charisma of social science globalisms. By *globalism*, I refer to endorsements of the importance of the global. I want to know how the idea of the global has worked to excite and inspire social scientists. I pick out a number of elements that add to this charisma and argue for their obfuscating as well as enlivening features.

Second, to see how this charisma produces effects in the world, I examine reading and discussion practices in the field of anthropology, as these produce and reproduce commitments to globalization. As an observer, I try to track the excitement of my students and colleagues; yet, as a participant, I want to argue for a *better* use of the charisma of global frameworks.

Thus, third, I show how questions about global interconnections might be detached from the most problematic globalist commitments to offer a more nuanced and critical analysis of culture and history, including recent shifts that have turned attention to the global. I argue that we can investigate globalist projects and dreams without assuming that they remake the world just as they want. The task of understanding planet-wide interconnections requires locating and specifying globalist projects and dreams, with their contradictory as well as charismatic logics and their messy as well as effective encounters and translations.

Globalization draws our enthusiasm because it helps us imagine interconnection, travel, and sudden transformation. Yet it also draws us inside its rhetoric until we take its claims for true descriptions. In the imagery with which I began, flow is valorized but not the carving of the channel; national and regional units are mapped as the baseline of change without attention to their shifting and contested ability to define the landscape. We lose sight of the coalitions of claimants as well as their partial and shifting claims. We lose touch with the material and institutional components through which powerful and central sites are constructed, from which convincing claims about units and scales can be made. We describe the landscape imagined within these claims rather than the culture and politics of scale making. This essay suggests approaches to the study of the global that seem to me to hold onto the excitement of this endorsement of planetary interconnection without trading our critical stance for globalist wishes and fantasies.

Hurtling through space

To invoke the global at the turn of the second millennium is to call attention to the speed and density of interconnections among people and places. In this imagery, the planet overwhelms us in its rush toward the future; we must either sit on top of it or be swamped and overcome. [. . .] It seems worth hesitating for a moment to consider the difference between this aggressive globe, hurtling through space, and an only slightly earlier fragile planet, floating gently in its cloud cover. This fertile yet vulnerable green planet was conjured by the global environmentalism that emerged in the United States and Europe at the end of the 1960s and blossomed in the 1970s, 1980s, and early 1990s. As Yaakov Garb (1990) has shown, the global environmentalists' globe gained its power from the visual image of the earth first seen in photographs from space in the 1960s; this awe-inspiring image was repeated in many forms and contexts to mobilize sentiment for the kind of nature that most needed our respect, love, and protection. It became possible to imagine this nature as extending across the planet because global environmentalism brought together the universalist morality of 1960s social justice politics and the transboundary expertise of an emergent ecological science (Haas 1992; Taylor and Buttel 1992).[. . .]

[. . .] Beginning most intensely in the 1980s, social movements – including environmentalism, human rights, indigenous rights, and feminist causes – extended themselves through NGOs; they sought to work around the restrictions of nation-states by forging transnational lines of financial, scientific, and political support (Keck and Sikkink 1998). Activists put pressure on their respective governments with these resources; national policies were also pressed to respond to international agreements. The global here is a never-ending process of 'networking' and building lines of support.

It was only at the beginning of the 1990s that the process of 'globalization', as the definitional characteristic of an *era*, became popular in the media and advertising. The triumph of the capitalist marketplace had been proclaimed with the dismantling of the Soviet Union, and enthusiasm ran high for national economic deregulation and privatization in the North and more thorough forms of structural adjustment in the South. In this atmosphere, *globalization* came to mean an endorsement of international free trade and the outlawing of protected or public domestic economies (Chomsky 1998). Yet the term came to encompass much more. Corporate reorganizations required not just markets but also the ability to transfer operations and finances transnationally to find the most profitable conditions; these kinds of corporate transfers, although reaching several decades back, became caught up in the talk of globalization. Furthermore, social commentators reminded the public that the new mobility of labor was tied to capital mobility and global market guarantees (e.g., Schiller, Basch, et al. 1992; Sassen 1998). [. . .]

At the turn of the century, then, globalism is multireferential: part corporate hype and capitalist regulatory agenda, part cultural excitement, part social commentary and protest. Within this shifting agenda, several features attract and engage an expanding audience for imagining the globe: first, its futurism, that is, its ability not only to name an era but to predict its progress; second, its conflations of varied projects through which the populist and the corporate, the scientific and the cultural, the excluded margins and the newly thriving centers, all seem wrapped up in the same energetic movement; and, third, its rhetoric of linkage and circulation as the overcoming of boundaries and restrictions, through which all this excitement appears positive for everyone involved. These elements are worth examining separately.

Futurism

Globalization is a crystal ball that promises to tell us of an almost-but-not-quite-there globality. This is powerful stuff for experts, politicians, and policy makers. Social scientists are particularly caught by the force of this charisma. The rush of prescience returns social science to the period after World War II, when the field charted the development of the new nations of the South and, in the North, the welfare state. Since then, social scientists have been better known – like economists and sociologists – as technicians of the present or – like anthropologists and geographers – as collectors of ancient survivals. Now the opportunity has come to look forward with a new expertise. The crystal ball inspires us to rush anxiously into the future, afraid to be left behind.

The future orientation of this discussion of the global requires the assumption of newness. If global interconnections do not define the contemporary era, setting it off from the past, to examine these interconnections shows us complexity rather than direction. Analysts of globalization force attention to the break that differentiates the present from the past because in the context of that break they can see forward. The assumption of newness has other benefits. It can help us see the distinctiveness of a historical moment. It can inspire a 'bandwagon' effect whereby unexpected and creative alliances among different kinds of analysts may be forged.[1] In this spirit, it can break up too-comfortably established fields, inspiring new forms of discussion. [. . .] However, the assumption of newness can also stifle other lines of inquiry and disallow questions about the construction of the field for which it forms the starting line. In history and anthropology, for example, the idea that global interconnections are *old* has only recently been revitalized, muffled as it was for much of the 20th century by the draw of nationally contained legacies, in history, and functionally contained social worlds, in anthropology; it seems unfortunate to lose this insight so quickly (see Mintz 1998, 123). [. . .]

Perhaps the worst fault of the assumption of global newness is that it erects stereotypes of the past that get in the way of appreciating both the past and the present. This fault has been particularly glaring in the discussion of the nation inspired by talk of globalization. [. . .] In interpreting the defeat of various national attempts to control financial capital, analysts have imagined an unprecedented world-historical defeat of the nation, as if nations, until now, were unquestioned, consistent, and everywhere hegemonic. Yet national control of finance may itself have been a recent, ephemeral product. After World War II, economic regulations emerging from the Bretton-Woods agreement made it possible for nation-states to control domestic financial capital, providing funding for welfare states. An earlier free-flowing internationalization of finance was cut off, as national capitalisms were set in place (Helleiner 1993).

Similarly, political commitment to national territorial boundaries and the importance of regulating population movements across national borders has a par-ticular history. The new nation-states that emerged after World War II in Africa and Asia, for example, developed special concerns for territorial sovereignty to declare their autonomy from the colonial condition; their national histories and geographies stress self-development, not regional and transregional flow.[2] To turn nationalist visions from this period into a description of a homogeneous past seems likely to lead to distortions.

[. . .]

Conflations

Jameson (Jameson 1998) argues that globalization is best understood through the Hegelian dialectic: its ideological logic produces both a dark and a light side. This is a useful reminder that the global developments that we, as social commentators, find promising are often deeply connected to those we find dangerous. But why jump quite so quickly into the assumption that the vast array of transcommunal and transnational ideas and activities around us form a single ideological system? There are some important advantages. Overlaps among ideological projects produce an added intensity all around. When the machinery of corporate and state publicity has converged on a single image, it is doubly hard to avoid the sense of complicity, for better or worse. In analyzing recent developments, it would be silly to argue for autonomous institutional, regional, or political-cause domains. It is clear that the appreciation of synergy among varied globalist projects is at the heart of the new enthusiasm about the globe. My point is that this very search for overlaps, alliances, collaborations, and complicities is one of the most important phenomena we could study. We might look at how particular projects become formulated, how they are tied and transformed in the process, and how they sometimes interrupt each other despite themselves. The 'globalization' that is formed from these hit-and-miss convergences would be considerably more unstable, and more interesting, than the one posited by any single claimant as a world-making system. One step in looking for this kind of globalization must be to recognize that there are varied agendas, practices, and processes that may or may not be deeply interconnected at a given historical moment.

[. . .]

Circulation

Interconnection is everything in the new globalisms. And interconnection is created through circulation. Many things are said to circulate, ranging from people to money; cultures to information; and television programs, to international protocols, to the process called globalization itself. 'Circulation' is in global rhetoric what the 'penetration' of capitalism was in certain kinds of Marxist world-systems theory: the way powerful institutions and ideas spread geographically and come to have an influence in distant places. The difference is significant; where *penetration* always evokes a kind of rape, a forcing of some people's powerful interests onto other people, *circulation* calls forth images of the healthy flow of blood in the body and the stimulating, evenhanded exchange of the marketplace.

Both bodies and markets as models for understanding social process have been much criticized in social theory in the 20th century. Images of society as organically interconnected like a body were important in establishing the social sciences, but they have been largely discredited as disallowing the study of power, meaning, conflict, disjuncture, and historical change. Images of society as a market have had a different kind of lasting power. Caught up in the endorsement of capitalism as an economic system and free trade as its ideal political context, they have been revived and given new authority in celebration of the end of communism and the Cold War. [. . .] Recent endorsements of 'global circulation' as the process for making the future partake in the obfuscations of inequality for which market models are known.

Global circulation is not just a rhetoric of corporate expansion, however. Leftist social commentators often find as much good use for circulation models as capitalist apologists. Circulation is used to discuss the breaking down of oppressive barriers among cultures, races, languages, and nations, including immigration restrictions and segregation policies. Diasporas circulate, bringing the wealth of their cultural heritage to new locations. Authoritarian regimes prevent the circulation of information, inspiring democratic movements to create underground channels of flow. The circulation of film inspires creative viewing practices. Circulation is thus tapped for the endorsement of multicultural enrichment, freedom, mobility, communication, and creative hybridity.

In part, the acceptability of circulation rhetoric among liberal and leftist social scientists derives from a self-conscious rejection of the Marxist emphasis on capitalist production and its consequent deemphasis on market exchange and consumption (e.g., Baudrillard 1975; Appadurai 1986). Leftist critics of corporate globalization point to the importance of marketing and consumption in contemporary corporate strategies for reaching out to new fields of operation (e.g., Jameson 1998); these are topics that need to be discussed. The growth of managerial and service professions (e.g., Sassen 1998; Ong 1999) also calls out to critics to abandon an exclusive analytic focus on factory production to attend to the variety of economic forms of contemporary capitalism.

[. . .] A focus on circulation shows us the movement of people, things, ideas, or institutions, but it does not show us how this movement depends on defining tracks and grounds or scales and units of agency. This blindness may not be inherent in the idea of circulation itself but, rather, may be caused by the kinds of circulations that have delineated the model. For historically layered political reasons, the model has been closed to attention to struggles over the terrain of circulation and the privileging of certain kinds of people as players. We focus on the money – the *ur* object of flow – instead of the social conditions that allow or encourage that flow. If we imagined creeks, perhaps the model would be different; we might notice the channel as well as the water moving.

[. . .]

[. . .] Analysts can also examine the material and institutional infrastructure of movement and pay special attention to the economic coercions and political guarantees that limit or promote circulation. In order to do this, however, we would need to redefine the common distinction between the 'local' and the 'global'. Most commonly, globalist thinkers imagine the local as the stopping point of global circulations. It is the place where global flows are consumed, incorporated, and resisted (Pred and Watts 1992). It is the place where global flows fragment and are transformed into something place bound and particular (Wilson and Dissanayake 1996). But if flow itself always involves making terrain, there can be no territorial distinctions between the 'global' transcending of place and the 'local' making of places. Instead, there is place making – and travel – all around, from New York to New Guinea. [. . .]

[. . .]

Readings in anthropology

Social science globalisms take particular forms in relation to disciplinary reading and discussion practices. They gain their influence not only because they are adopted in the work of articulate practitioners but, equally importantly, because they enter local trajectories of disciplinary momentum. They are rebuilt to speak to disciplinary challenges as these, in turn, are understood in relation to specific social locations of scholarly practice. In the process, social science globalisms pick up regional and disciplinary frameworks and assumptions, even as they throw themselves as objections against others.

Anthropologists do not merely mimic the understandings of globalism of other experts, even as they are influenced by them. No anthropologist I know argues that the global future will be culturally homogeneous; even those anthropologists most wedded to the idea of a new global era imagine this era as characterized by 'local' cultural diversity. Disciplinary concern with cultural diversity overrides the rhetoric of global cultural unification pervasive elsewhere, even though, for those in its sway, globalism still rules: Diversity is generally imagined as forming a reaction or a backdrop to the singular and all-powerful 'global forces' that create a new world. (Globalisms are not themselves regularly regarded as diverse.) Politically progressive anthropologists sometimes show how this kind of circumscribed, reactive, self-consciously 'local' diversity is a form of resistance to the proliferation of globalist capitalism and hypermodernist governmentality; however, the possibility that capitalisms and governmentalities are themselves situated, contradictory, effervescent, or culturally circumscribed is much less explored. Anthropologists who have argued against simplistic models of 'global culture' have also, then, naturalized globalist ideologies of the global.

[. . .]

This 'freeing up' variety of globalism is both exhilarating and problematic. On the one hand, it shows us new dreams and schemes of world making; on the other, as an aspect of its liberatory project, it also turns attention away from the quirky eccentricities of culture and history that have perhaps been U.S. anthropology's most vital contribution to critical thought. In the process, too, anthropologists tend to endorse the globalist dreams of the people they study, and thus we lose the opportunity to address the located specificity of those globalist dreams.

[. . .]

Futurism

U.S. anthropologists come to an endorsement of a singular global future from their interest in the macroeconomic context of cultural diversity. An important part of the disciplinary trajectory away from the study of isolated cultures has been attention to the capitalist world system. Anthropologists have been able to show how even out-of-the-way and exotic cultures respond to capitalism's challenges. This is crucial work. At the same time, risks and dilemmas remain in this analysis: In turning one's gaze to the systemic features of world capitalism, it is easy to lose track of the specificity of particular capitalist niches. In coming to terms with the transnational scope of contemporary finance, marketing, and production, it is easy to endorse globalism as a predictive frame. Indeed, it is in this context that anthropologists most commonly imagine singular global futures. Even as critics, we are caught in the hyperboles imagined by advocates of neoliberalism, structural adjustment, and transnationalization. Particularly in its critical versions, this global future forms part of a narrative of the evolution of capitalism. Furthermore, most anthropologists attracted by this narrative take their model from a single source: David Harvey's *The Condition of Postmodernity* (1990). Within much globalist anthropology, Harvey's book establishes the fact of epochal change, laying the ground for global futurism. Yet I find this a particular, peculiar reading of Harvey, and it is worth considering in its own right: For anthropologists, Harvey provides the evidence for a new era. As readers, they pick out 'flexible specialization' and 'time-space compression' as the characteristics of this new era. [. . .]

Yet, when I turn to Harvey's book, it seems to me that the central argument is that the 'cultural aesthetic' of postmodernism is related to the economic logic of flexible accumulation. The first section of the book reviews modernism and post-modernism as trends in the arts and letters, including architecture and philosophy. This is 'capital C' culture: a genealogy of great men and their ideas. The second section of the book turns to the economic 'regimes of accumulation' of Fordism and post-Fordist 'flexible accumulation'. The book's original idea is to juxtapose these two bodies of literature and to argue that postmodernism mirrors post-Fordism. It takes a certain amount of economic determinism to make this argument, in which Culture acts as a mirror of economic realities. [. . .] But in this gap, space and time come in. For Harvey, the 'experience' of space and time mediates between Culture and the (nonculturally organized) economy.

[. . .]

In this context, it is strange that anthropologists so often pick only 'the acceleration of space-time compression' along with 'flexible accumulation' out of this book. In the process of citation, too, the book's tone changes. Harvey's book is polemical. He ranges over a wide variety of scholarship to criticize postmodern aesthetics. This is not a science experiment but, rather, a book-length essay. Yet somehow Harvey's description of economic evolution comes to have the status of a fact when drawn into globalist anthropology. Harvey brings with him the ability to read economics, a skill few anthropologists have developed. It may be that anthropologists ignore the discussion of aesthetics, thinking they know more about culture than he does, and go for the accumulation strategy and associated space-time requirements because they feel like the macroeconomic facts that are outside of their knowledge base.

The result is that a selection of Harvey's terms is used to build a noncultural and nonsituated futurist framework, 'beyond culture' (Gupta and Ferguson 1992). One set of problems derives from the attempt to make this future global; as anthropologist Michael Kearney admits, Harvey's thesis is 'not dealing with globalization per se' (1995, 551). Indeed, Harvey has a distinct blindness for everything outside dominant Northern Cultures and economies; to make his story applicable to North–South articulations is not impossible, but it is a challenge. Another set of problems seems even more intractable. If we drop Harvey's discussion of aesthetics (as Culture) but still ignore the ethnographic sources through which anthropologists identify culture, just how do we know the shape of space and time? The pared-down Harvey readings preferred by anthropologists have lost even literary and filmic representations of temporal and spatial processes; we are left with economic facts. Without 'Culture' or 'culture', we must assume rapid circulation, fragmentation, compression, and globality; certainly, we cannot consult either popular or official representations, discourses, or cultural practices. Anthropological analysis, which could look at scale-making claims and representations in conjunction with the social processes that support and result from those claims and representations, becomes reduced to building starships on millennial fantasies.

Another way Harvey's work could be used is to scale back its epochal claims to look at some limited but powerful alliances between aesthetics and economics. Harvey's claim that postmodernism and flexible accumulation have something to do with each other could be pursued by locating patterns and players more specifically. This kind of project, however, diminishes the excitement of another globalist reading practice, which I have called 'conflations'. Let me examine how this practice both brings to life and impoverishes the anthropology of global interconnection.

Conflations

Not all anthropological globalism is engaged in understanding the systemics of capitalism; another significant sector attempts to hold onto 'culture' as an anthropological object while showing its increased contemporary mobility and range. In this genre, anthropologists have done exciting work to specify modes of cultural interconnection that tie people in far-flung locales or travel with them across heterogeneous terrains. This work offers the possibility of attention to regionalisms and histories of place making within an appreciation of interconnection. However, to the extent that this work has been harnessed for the search for a singular anthropological globalism, it has blurred the differences among places and perspectives to emphasize the break from past localisms. This anthropological globalism renaturalizes global dreams instead of examining and locating them ethnographically. [. . .]

[. . .]

Circulation

Circulation has a deep genealogy in anthropology. I keep waiting to find an author who takes me through this legacy, perhaps tracing his or her thoughts from French structuralist 'exchange' through global 'flows'. But I have not yet found that author. Instead, it has become easy for anthropologists to talk about global circulations as a sign of everything new and of future making.

Circulations are said to be what we are able to study as global. [. . .]

[. . .]

Newness is defined by increased flow. Because authors and readers focus on the excitement of this newness, there has been almost no discussion about the implied dichotomies here: circulation versus stagnation, new versus old. Does the newness and globality of movement mean that once-immobile 'local' places have recently been transcended by 'global' flow? If analysts must 'move out of local situations' to find circulation, there must be some local folks who are still stuck inside them, being stagnant. These imagined stagnant locals are excluded from the new circulating globality, which leaves them outside, just as progress and modernity were imagined as leaving so many behind. [. . .]

[. . .]

Scale as an object of analysis

Understanding the institutional proliferation of particular globalization projects requires a sense of their cultural specificities as well as the travels and interactions through which these projects are reproduced and taken on in new places. In thinking about where one would begin a globally informed investigation of local and global processes that avoids the pitfalls I have been discussing, I might begin with two analytic principles. First, I would pay close attention to *ideologies* of scale, that is, cultural claims about locality, regionality, and globality; about stasis and circulation; and about networks and strategies of proliferation. I would track rhetorics of scale as well as contests over what will count as relevant scales. Second, I would break down the units of culture and political economy through which we make sense of events and social processes. Instead of looking for world-wrapping evolutionary stages, logics, and epistemes, I would begin by finding what I call 'projects', that is, relatively coherent bundles of ideas and practices as realized in particular times and places. The choice of what counts as a project depends on what one is trying to learn about, but, in each case, to identify projects is to maintain a commitment to localization, even of the biggest world-making dreams and schemes. The various instantiations of capitalism can be regarded as projects; so can progressive social movements, everyday patterns of living, or university-based intellectual programs. Projects are to be traced in relation to particular historical travels from one place to another; they are caught up in local issues of translation and mobilization; although they may be very powerful, we cannot assume their ability to remake nature and society according to their visions. Projects may articulate with each other, creating moments of fabled stability and power (see Tsing 1999; 2000). They may also rub up against each other awkwardly, creating messiness and new possibilities. Through joint attention to ideologies of scale and projects of scale making, it is possible to move into those cracks most neglected by unselfconscious reliance on global futurism, globalist conflation, and global circulation.

[. . .]

Release

Let me return for a moment to the parallels between modernization and globalization. Many anthropologists are able to look at the dreams and schemes of modernization with a critical distance. We need this critical distance, too, in studying globalization. Globalization is a set of projects that require us to imagine space and time in particular ways. These are curious, powerful projects. Anthropologists need not ignore them; we also need not renaturalize them by assuming that the terms they offer us are true.

At this point, some readers may say, 'Why not throw out "the global" completely, since it exists as a fantasy'? My answer is that even fantasies deserve serious engagement. The best legacies of ethnography allow us to take our objects of study seriously even as we examine them critically. To study ghosts ethnographically means to take issues of haunting seriously. If the analyst merely made fun of beliefs in ghosts, the study would be of little use. Several other steps would be needed: a description of ghost beliefs; an examination of the effects of ghost beliefs on social life; and, in the spirit of taking one's informants seriously, a close attention to the questions that ghosts raise, such as the presence of death and its eerie reminders of things gone. In the same spirit, an analyst of globalism cannot merely toss it out as a vacant deception. Instead, an ethnographic study of the global needs careful attention not only to global claims and their effects on social life but also to questions of interconnection, movement, and boundary crossing that globalist spokespeople have brought to the fore. To take globality as an object of study requires both distance and intimate engagement.

Other readers may object that it is important to reify globalization because of the terrible toll it promises to take on cultural diversity and human well-being. Their endorsement of a self-consciously paranoid vision of total transformation involves the choice to glimpse the terrors of the new world order it promises. Yet I would argue that by reproducing this totalizing framework of social change, critics bind themselves within the assumptions and fantasies of those they oppose. If we want to imagine emergent forms of resistance, new possibilities, and the messiness through which the best laid plans may not yet destroy all hope, we need to attune ourselves to the heterogeneity and open-endedness of the world.

This is not, however, an argument for 'local' diversity; if anything, it is an argument for 'global' diversity and the wrongheadedness of imagining diversity – from an unquestioning globalist perspective – as a territorially circumscribed, 'place-based', and antiglobalist phenomenon. (Since when are globalists not place based?) Unlike most anthropologists working on 'global' issues, I have tried to examine some basic assumptions of globalism, using them to form a critical perspective rather than a negative or positive endorsement of projects for making a future imagined as global.

[. . .] The debate about global cultural unification has encouraged anthropologists to agree that we are indeed entering an era properly called global, although that era, according to anthropologists, is characterized by local cultural divergences as much as unification. In the embrace of the argument, the cultural divergence we find must be part of the globalist phenomenon. [. . .]

This is not, I think, a useful place to be stuck. To get out of its grip, analysts need to give up several of the tools and frames we have found most easy to work with, perhaps because they resound so nicely with popular 'common sense', at least in the United States. First, we might stop making a distinction between 'global' *forces* and 'local' *places*. This is a very seductive set of distinctions, promising as it does to give us both focused detail and the big picture, and I find myself slipping into this vocabulary all the time. But it draws us into globalist fantasies by obscuring the ways that the cultural processes of all 'place' making and all 'force' making are *both* local and global, that is, both socially and culturally particular and productive of widely spreading interactions. Through these terms, global 'forces' gain the power to cause a total rupture that takes over the world.

Second, we might learn to investigate new developments without assuming either their universal extension or their fantastic ability to draw all world-making activities into their grasp. International finance, for example, has surely undergone striking and distinctive transformations in the last 30 years. Certainly this has effects everywhere, but what these effects are is unclear. It seems unlikely to me that a single logic of transformation is being produced – or a singular moment of rupture. [. . .]

Third, globalisms themselves need to be interrogated as an interconnected, but not homogeneous, set of projects – with their distinctive cultural commitments and their powerful but limited presence in the world. Critical studies of modernization projects provide some thought-provoking examples of analytic direction here.

Freed up in these ways, it might be possible to attend to global visions without imagining their world hegemony. Outside the thrall of globalization, a more nuanced and surprising appreciation of the making and remaking of geography might yet be possible.

Notes

1   I take the notion of the building of a 'bandwagon' effect from Joan Fujimura's (1988) work on cancer research.

2   This set of post-World War II nationalist commitments was brought to my attention in the insightful comments of Malaysian economist Jomo K. S. at the conference 'Public Intellectuals in Southeast Asia', in Kuala Lumpur, May 1998. As an example, he pointed out that histories in which nationalism in Southeast Asia was stimulated by conversations with overseas Chinese (e.g., Pramoedya 1996) were suppressed by post-World War II Southeast Asian nations.

Chapter 7

Arif Dirlik

MODERNITY AS HISTORY: POST-REVOLUTIONARY CHINA, GLOBALIZATION AND THE QUESTION OF MODERNITY

From *Social History* 27.1 January (2002): 16–39 [16–18, 20–23 and 36–37]

I TAKE UP BELOW A QUESTION THAT IS THROWN up insistently in contemporary discussions of modernity: the meaning for modernity of what one French analyst has described as the 'resurgence of history'. Jean-Marie Guehenno uses the phrase with reference to those who see in the 'resurgence of history' the resurgence of nationalism; a conclusion he deems to be insufficiently radical. As he puts it, '1989 marks the close of an era that began not in 1945 or 1917, but that was institutionalized thanks to the French Revolution, in 1789. It brings an end to the age of the nation-states.' (Guehenno 1995, x).

The resurgence of history is visible in our day in the resurgence of nationalism, but also in the resurgence of claims to history that erode the nation-state both from within and without, that range from localized claims of various kinds to global and civilizational claims. Guehenno's statement concerning the French Revolution suggests also that what is being eroded, ultimately, is not just the nation-state, but the institutions of modernity which he identifies with the nation-state. The irony of it all is that the resurgence of history may also signal the end of history as we have known it. If history itself is 'a sign of the modern', the conceptualization of the past as history, which has become integral to our very existence, is inseparable from the idea of the modern (Koselleck 1985; Dirks 1990). Indeed, claims against the modern are often accompanied by challenges to historical ways of knowing.

The irony points to the many contradictions presented by contemporary discussions of history, modernity and the nation-state. How could the victory of history, as implied by its resurgence, also signal its demise? How is it possible to declare the end of the nation-state or of national identity when nationalism seems to be on the rise everywhere? What does it mean that modernity is in question when there is every sign that it is becoming a global condition? How do we reconcile the pervasiveness of a sense of global fragmentation with the equally pervasive sense that more than ever in the past globality characterizes the human condition?

Questions of this magnitude and complexity do not lend themselves to easy answers, and certainly not the answers of an earlier day that dissolved the contradictions of modernity into the teleologies of either a capitalist or socialist version of modernization. The latter is out of the competition, and where it survives, it appears more and more as a local variant of a globalized capitalism. On the other hand, capitalist modernity, in its globalization, has had to interiorize cultural difference as part of its very constitution; one fundamental consequence of which has been to compromise its identification with EuroAmerican models of modernity, which provided an earlier modernization discourse with its teleological power.

It is this latter development that drives most contemporary efforts to reformulate modernity, which accounts for the prominence of a preoccupation with overcoming the legacy of Eurocentrism. The critique of Eurocentrism is not novel, but it has taken some novel turns over the last two decades which have witnessed a surge of alternative cultural claims on modernity. This is in part due to the retreat of the revolutionary discourse on modernity during the same period. Conflicts over modernity articulated in the post-World War II period through the opposition of socialist and capitalist models of development find expression presently through competing cultural claims on the modern. But this, I think, is only part of the explanation, as those cultural claims which demand the most attentive hearing are those that are empowered by success in the global economy, and/or the ability to influence the configurations of global power; most notably the societies of eastern and south-east Asia, and Islamic societies.

The most important issue raised by 'the resurgence of history' is that modernity may no longer be approached as a dialogue internal to Europe or EuroAmerica, but is a global discourse in which many participate, producing different formulations of the modern as lived and envisaged within their local social environments. This in some ways *is* the fulfilment of modernity, which not only drew all globally into modernity, but promised an open-endedness in doing so. But does the fulfilment of modernity also signal its end, as that same open-endedness is exposed as being conditional upon a pre-determined telos, and others are drawn into the process who do not share in its teleology? If modernity called forth a universal history that would be all-inclusive, the pretension to universality could be sustained only by rendering spatial into temporal difference. Having historicized time, modernity's histories proceeded to suppress or marginalize temporalities that did not accord with the teleologies of modernity, conceived through programmes of economic (capitalism), political (the nation-state) and cultural (science) development, for which the history of modern Europe provided the ultimate frame of reference. Those who joined or were compelled into history were placed in history according to their proximity to the ideal of progress that informed those teleologies. Historical time conceived in terms of the teleologies of modernity excluded both those who lacked history by virtue of being caught up in different temporalities, and those who were handicapped by a surplus of history in their entrapment in tradition.

We witness presently the resurgence of those histories suppressed or marginalized under a regime of modernity that is being progressively eclipsed even as the sign of 'modernity' remains current and authoritative in public and official discourses everywhere. The globalization of modernity issues not in the victory of

Eurocentric modernity but in *its* historicization. The teleologies to which history had been yoked appear now in their historicity; not as the end of history, but as the ideological products of one modality of modernity among possible others that is no less provincial in its claims than any of its competitors, who are equally entitled to make claims upon history. The competition here is radically different from an earlier competition between bourgeois and Marxist modernities. Marxism challenged the claims to universality of a Eurocentric modernity founded upon capitalism, but it did so in the name of a higher universalism that would fulfil the promises of bourgeois modernity that could not be achieved under capitalism. It was, if anything, even more strongly teleological in its assumptions.

Present-day claims on modernity are cultural. To the extent that they express themselves in universalistic terms, the universality is contained within cultural spaces at odds with one another – which is another way of saying that they represent the end of universalism, as they rule out any commonly shared vision of the future. Cultural claims extend even to the political economy of capitalism, arguably the only universal that survives into the present as the dynamic force of globalization, and provides the common terrain in the articulation of cultural conflict.

Too much preoccupation with Eurocentrism distracts attention from the fragmentation of the world in other significant ways. For one thing, Eurocentrism (in its broadest sense, including the practices of everyday life) is no longer external to non-European societies but is part of a global modernity, and challenges to Eurocentrism also create problems in those societies that have long taken modernization as their guiding principle. Also, there is a 'resurgence of history' in those societies as well, where pasts suppressed or marginalized under modernizing regimes demand a hearing of their own, as in the case most importantly of religions or philosophies long relegated to the past as 'backward'. This may be visible most dramatically in the case of the former socialist regimes, but it is a phenomenon that is global, that cuts across East–West, Three Worlds or national divisions; which in turn renders these once conventional divisions problematic as obsolete ideological constructs that are, in the sense of contemporary understandings of global modernity, no longer 'properly' modern.

[. . .]

In its most recent reincarnation modernization discourse seeks to absorb and to contain cultural claims to alternative modernities. This seeming abandonment of its Eurocentric origins to accommodate different cultures of modernity is responsible above all for the ascendancy of the idea of globalization, which perpetrates the goals of modernization but is prepared now to invite into modernity traditions that had been condemned to irrelevance in an earlier modernization discourse as obstacles to progress. I say 'seeming' abandonment, because the recognition of cultural diversity takes place on the common grounds of a globalized capitalism; this may be subject to local variation due to its internalization of different cultural repertoires in economic practices, but serves also as the motor force in the universalizing of institutional structures fundamental to its functioning, as well as of the technologies and values of development, production and consumption. One striking instance of this new mode of universalization can be seen in the array of ethnic representatives as newsreaders on major news channels like CNN and the BBC, whose ethnic/racial difference becomes fetishized as the triumph of multiculturalism while their training in one or another metropolitan school of news elocution and self-presentation – their membership within a global professional class – is obscured. Nevertheless, the accommodation of different cultural claims on modernity represents an important break with past modernization discourse; this does not merely lead to further theoretical differentiation, but calls into question the very possibility of theory as it is fragmented into conflicting cultural spaces. Globalization represents not only a further unification of the world through the agency of capitalism, and its attendant political and cultural institutions, but also an effort to contain new forms of fragmentation.

The victory of modernization discourse, under the circumstances, is but a hollow victory; and modernization discourse owes its survival not to its ability to account for the contemporary world, but to a nostalgic embrace of culturalist assumptions about the world which are in fact no longer sustainable. It is ultimately of little consequence that the discourse may call upon non-western alibis for its legitimation, which it does, and which is less a sign of its validity than of the investment in certain kinds of modernization programmes of global elites who enforce these programmes on vast populations without regard to the complexity of lived local differences. The globalization of the ideology of development – developmentalism, which is what modernization discourse is about ultimately – may serve as empirical evidence of the appeals of modernization only so long as the discourse ignores the ongoing resistance to modernization by portraying as backward any such resistance, and the deployment of power in overcoming it. The reification of culture serves this end by investing the definition of civilizational cultures with those who are well placed by virtue of political power or global cultural capital to define the cultures of multitudes placed physically in nations or civilizations, who differ quite significantly from one another in everyday cultural practices, but whose lives are vulnerable to colonization by the cultural ideals of their leaders, which are shaped more by participation in metropolitan dialogues on culture than by the understanding of those whose lives they would shape.

This is what modernization discourse has been about all along: to enforce a cultural homogeneity that is consistent with a programme of modernization conceived, if not along EuroAmerican lines, then along their functional equivalents. The persistence of such assumptions, and the language in which they are expressed, is at best an effort to contain fragmentation, which for its effectiveness depends not on theoretical or discursive validity, but the exercise of power, which is most clearly evident in the revised geopolitics of Samuel Huntington. . . . It also has a great deal to do with the political economy of a globalized capitalism, which for its own survival depends at once on a valorization of difference, and the convergence of difference into homogeneity through techniques of representation that carefully assign equivalence only to those practices that accord with the logic of ongoing capitalist expansion.

The downgrading of a Eurocentric modernity, accompanied by culturally driven claims on modernity, goes a long way toward explaining the contradictions to which I referred above, and why those contradictions may appear differently to participants in the new dialogue on modernity. On the other hand, too much preoccupation with Eurocentrism or colonialism also disguises fundamental questions of contemporary modernity that cut across so-called cultural divides, especially as the locations of modernity and culture are themselves thrown into question with the reconfigurations of economic and political organization globally. Differences framed in terms of geographical or spatial cultural locations serve above all to conceal the fact that these are the least important differences that may matter in an age of globalization. They are no less anachronistic than the persistence of the Three Worlds idea, which informed an earlier modernization discourse, but they do serve a purpose in the containment of difference.

Ours is a time of reversals, when traditions and ideologies that were assigned by modernization discourse to the dustbin of history have made a comeback with a vengeance, empowered by reconfigurations in global relations, and legitimized by the repudiation of Eurocentrism. A case in point is the Confucian revival in contemporary China. In his seminal work on Chinese modernity published in the early 1960s, *Confucian China and its Modern Fate*, Joseph Levenson argued that Marxist historicism had resolved a problem that had plagued Chinese intellectuals ever since the encounter with the modern West had forced a parochialization of Confucian values from their once universalistic status into the circumscribed endowment of a national past; an endowment, moreover, that was inconsistent with the struggle for modernity. Continued attachment to Confucianism, despite loss of faith in its intellectual validity, represented for Levenson a tension between history and value. Confucianism, necessary as the historical source of a Chinese national identity, had to be overcome if China was to become a nation (Levenson 1968).

While not a Marxist himself, and not particularly sympathetic to the Chinese Revolution, Levenson nevertheless sought to understand the source of the appeals of Marxism; these he found in the ability of Marxist historicism to resolve this fundamental tension in Chinese intellectual life, by relegating Confucianism into the museum, salvaging Confucius for the nation, but also rendering him irrelevant to the living present. As he put it,

> Confucius . . . redeemed from both the class aberration (feudal) of idolization and the class aberration (bourgeois) of destruction, might be kept as a national monument, unworshipped, yet also unshattered. In effect, the disdain of a modern pro-Western *bourgeoisie* for Confucius cancelled out, for the dialecticians, a feudal class's pre-modern devotion. The Communists, driving history to a classless synthetic fulfilment, retired Confucius honorably into the silence of the museum.
>
> (1968, 79)

It may be one of the profound ironies of our times that this situation has been reversed since Levenson wrote his analysis: Confucius has been brought out of the museum once again, while it is the revolution that is on its way to being museumified – not by feudal worshippers of Confucius, but by the bourgeoisie who once disdained Confucius, and the Communist party that remains in power as the beneficiary of that revolution.

Levenson's analysis, and his evaluation of what the revolution had achieved in resolving the tension between the past and the present, was informed by a teleology of modernity; that the claims of the values of ancient civilizations must inevitably be relegated to the past with the victory of modernity as represented by the modern nation. If the pasts of those civilizations have been resurrected once again, it is not only because of the passing of revolutions, but more importantly the questioning of this teleology that has come to the fore as globalization has replaced modernization as a paradigm of contemporary change.

The passing of the Chinese Revolution, as of socialist revolutions in general, may be attributed to their particular failings. Similarly, advocates of the Confucian revival may attribute the revival to the particular virtues inherent in Confucianism. While there may be something to be said for such views, in my view they suffer from a debilitating parochialism that fails to account for a larger historical context where it is not just socialist revolutions that are relegated to the past, but the very idea of revolution, and it is not just the Confucian tradition that is at issue, but the return of traditions in general. [. . .] For all the talk about Asia and Asian values over the last few years, the idea of Asia remains quite problematic, and so do the ideological and cultural sources from which Asian values are to be derived. The most visible competitor to the Confucian revival may be the Islamic revival that has also become visible during this same period; but the period has also witnessed a Hindu revival in India, and right-wing nationalists in Turkey, echoing east Asian nationalists and their EuroAmerican cheerleaders, have resurrected earlier Pan-Turanian utopias to assert that the twenty-first century will be a Turkish century. In other societies in Asia, Buddhism continues to hold sway. It is difficult to avoid an inference that all these revivals, coinciding temporally, are products of the same world situation, though they obviously have local inflections depending on social context and ideological claims.

It is this same situation that prompted Samuel Huntington to conclude that with socialisms out of the way, the major problem of the present was not a problem of conflict between nations but a 'clash of civilizations' (Huntington 1993; 1996a; 1996b). [. . .] It is important to underline two aspects of Huntington's argument here. First, that the civilizations he referred to, while they represented long-standing cultural traditions, were not relics of the past but were products of modernity that were empowered by their claims on modernity. Second, that to impose the values of the modern West on these societies would not only not work, but also represented a kind of imperialism.

[. . .] What is pertinent here is that the argument does indeed resonate with contemporary cultural claims on modernity in many non-western societies. It is also echoed, if with greater circumspection, in recent efforts to revise modernization discourse.

[. . .]

Globalization may be a consequence of the disintegration of universalism, as Bauman suggests, and in turn has opened up spaces for rethinking alternative ways of knowing. On the other hand, it is too easy in the enthusiasm or despair over globalization to overlook the fact that globalization also serves as an agent for spreading the epistemological assumptions of Eurocentrism, which acquire progressively more compelling power as capitalism is globalized. The social sciences and the humanities, as we have known them, are not merely European or American, but are entangled in a social system of which capitalism has been the dynamic formative moment. The globalization of capitalism has given additional force to the ideology of development, or developmentalism, which forces all societies under the threat of extinction to acquire the technologies of knowledge that contribute to this end. These knowledges are no longer just European or American, but are internal to societies world-wide which provide the personnel for the global institutions of capital.

If 'now' has been conjoined to the 'not-yet', as Chakrabarty suggests, that has not meant the end of the universalistic claims of modernity's ways of knowing. The so-called retreat or 'provincialization' of Europe may be a product of the universalization of those knowledges in their appropriation into different social and intellectual universes, which no longer permits or recognizes European or American monopoly over them but feels obliged to recognize their historical origins [. . .].

This is not to suggest that other, non-European traditions may not serve as reservoirs of values and knowledges with which to amend, and enrich, modern ways of knowing; but, for better or worse, that is not the same as taking modernity out of the picture by an act of will, least of all by intellectuals who are better prepared by their education to participate in EuroAmerican dialogues on modernity than to serve as representatives of their so-called cultural traditions. We need to remember also that the present is witness not just to revivals of traditions, but also to an enthusiastic embrace by elites globally of the promises of technological modernity. Even the reassertion of traditions often takes the form of articulating those traditions to the demands of a global capitalism. [. . .] Where there is a stubborn clinging to imagined traditions against the demands of modernity, as in the case for instance of the Taliban in Afghanistan or the Iranian Revolution in its more extreme phases, the result is not acceptance but isolation. On the other hand, those native scholars who have sought to sinicize or islamicize sociology quickly find out that this could not be accomplished without a simultaneous 'sociologization' of Chinese values or of Islam. (Gole 2000: 113; Ma 1985) [. . .] The very process of nativization reveals the impossibility of sustaining reified, holistic notions of those traditions, which have already experienced the transformations of modernity, and themselves come to serve as sites of conflict between different social interests and different visions of the modern.

[. . .]

Chapter 8

George Yúdice

FREE TRADE AND CULTURE

From *The Expediency of Culture: Uses of Culture in the Global Era* Durham and London: Duke University Press, 2003, pp. 214–21

What is free trade, what is free trade under the present condition of society? . . . Whose freedom? It is not the freedom of one individual in relation to another, but the freedom of capital to crush the worker . . . When you have overthrown the few national barriers which still restrict the progress of capital, you will merely have given it complete freedom of action . . . So long as you let the relation of wage labor to capital exist . . . there will always be a class which will exploit and a class which will be exploited . . . The free trade system is destructive. It breaks up old nationalities and pushes the antagonism of the proletariat and the bourgeoisie to the extreme point. It is in this revolutionary sense alone, that I vote in favor of free trade.

Karl Marx, 'On the Question of Free Trade'

NAFTA has the virtue of making integration visible; it certainly did sharpen the contradictions, as the Old Man might have put it. If capital insists on integrating, those who joust with it have to do the same.

'The Philanthropy of Financiers'[. . .]

What does culture have to do with free trade?

FREE TRADE AND CULTURE DO NOT, BY ANY means, have transparent meanings.[1] For example, the qualifier 'free' suggests that government and international accords envision trade as unrestricted. Nothing could be further from reality now or at any time in the past. Free trade is anything but unrestricted; it must be managed, as is evident in the hundreds of protocols, declarations, and articles that constitute trade agreements. The last set of protocols generated by GATT in 1993 consisted of twenty thousand pages weighing over eighteen hundred pounds. Moreover, participating corporations receive subsidies, bailouts, and tax credits from their home government for their 'competitiveness'. Similarly, the term culture is not transparent. Depending on the context – national or local cultural policy;

artistic and academic traditions; anthropological and sociological theory; feminist, racial, (post)colonial, and cultural studies approaches; law and the litigation of discrimination; and, of course, political discourse – the term may refer to the arts; to the media; to the rituals and other practices by which nations or smaller-scale social groups reproduce themselves symbolically; or to the differences by which some groups, usually defined as subaltern, distinguish themselves from (or resist) other, dominant, groups. [. . .] [T]he very notion of innovation as an engine of capital accumulation is often identified with culture; the strategies of global trade are rearticulating all conceptions of culture, even to the point that some of the most economically profitable products and services, say computer software and Internet sites, are treated, respectively, as cultural forms of intellectual property and cultural 'content'. Also examined are strategies for cultural integration in Latin America that, even as they counter the inordinate influence of U.S. and transnational entertainment culture, also increasingly rely on partnerships with private capital and neoliberal policies. Although the relationship between trade and culture is woefully understudied in the United States, it nevertheless has brought about many transformations.

I do not pretend to give hard and fast definitions of these two terms. I approach them, rather, by examining what other issues are being negotiated through the linking of free trade and culture. Culture is invoked, Virginia R. Dominguez has argued, to 'make strategic social and political interventions'. She goes on to recommend displacing studies 'about culture – what belongs, what doesn't belong, what its characteristics are, whose characteristics are being imposed and whose are being excluded – . . . [with] asking what is being accomplished socially, politically, discursively when the concept of culture is invoked to describe, analyze, argue, justify, and theorize' (1992, 21 [brackets by Yúdice]).

It is in this sense that I explore the shift (or the contribution to the shift) that free trade has produced in the arts and notions of citizenship and public culture, particularly the relationship of the state to civil society. What are the state's responsibilities? What are the means available for citizens to participate in shaping opinions and engaging in decision making? How do changes at these levels involve changes in how we understand cultural issues, not just those of national identity but, more fundamentally, how the constitution of community, identity, solidarity, even artistic practices are transformed by new technologies and market values? Free trade has an important role in the redefinition of all of these dimensions.

Beginning in the 1980s, free trade was repackaged as a means to manage a worldwide economic crisis. Economic restructuring became a necessity as a result of a conjuncture of factors. The foreign debt of countries in the southern hemisphere grew to the point of economic crisis (a result in large part of the structural adjustment policies of the IMF and the World Bank under U.S. tutelage), and the rate of profit in the production of goods and services had fallen due to the glut of commodities produced in the reemergent economic powers of Germany and Japan and to innovations in new information and labor-saving technologies. The new president of the World Bank reoriented its poverty-reduction policies by putting greater emphasis on 'rent seeking'. This change made it easier for the Bank to follow the criteria of the IMF, whose approval was needed to make loans. Consequently, both institutions became 'missionaries' that imposed free trade and structural adjustment programs on poor countries that had no choice but to assent (Stiglitz 2002, 13–14).

In this context, free trade means deregulation, that is, the elimination of barriers (tariffs) to trade but also the curtailment of state support of industry (never fully achieved in developed countries), and, most significant, the forsaking of labor protection (more easily achieved), resulting in lower wages and benefits, the reduction of welfare and social services (health care, education), and the rollback of environmental safeguards. These changes not only ensure greater profits for corporations, particularly multinational enterprises, but guarantee that there will be little interference with the conduct of business because the organizations that manage trade (those that negotiate tariffs *and* regulations on production and distribution) are not subject to oversight by any electorate. In effect, GATT, its successor the WTO, NAFTA, the World Bank, the IMF, and others have not been empowered by voters and yet impose their policies virtually unchecked, although there is an emerging antiglobalization movement aimed at the irresponsibility of these institutions.

The repercussions of this restructuring, although presumably generated at the transnational level in trade agreements and structural adjustment policies, are experienced acutely at the local level, as witnessed by the loss of jobs in the United States and the defunding of school systems in Latin America. Immigrants – Mexicans in the United States or Bolivians in Argentina – are often blamed for the problems faced by the working class, as politicians characterize them as a drain on society, making parasitic use of 'undeserved' benefits at the expense of taxpaying citizens (as if immigrants didn't pay taxes). Moreover, they are portrayed as a threat to the national culture. The global economic impact is redirected such that different sectors of society as well as different societies are pitted against each other in the competition for ever scarcer jobs, occluding the sources of the competition (displacements of production in search of ever cheaper labor) in the first place. Such ideological projections have a profound effect on how citizens and other residents understand themselves, their identities.

Transnational corporations manage to have it both ways under WTO ordinances: they can operate more freely across borders at the same time that they are considered local firms in host countries (Dobson 1993). Yet, even as transnational corporations have such an impact on labor issues, they produce very different images of their relationship to diverse workers, consumers, and publics. As I argue below, the hegemony of 'corporate diversity', as the ideological face of global capitalism, is reproduced by the millions of public relations images in which social harmony is achieved through relations of difference. Or it might be more accurate to say that the successful (consumer) society is projected as one in which difference works as the motor of marketing. Market values come to prevail as the services that the Keynesian state had been providing are now privatized. Even in the realm of social provision, difference is also what drives conceptions and practices of 'cultural citizenship', such as making claims for inclusion and participation in specific countries and even transnationally via the 'global civil society' projected in the discourse of NGOs, foundations, and intergovernmental organizations like UNESCO. In UNESCO discourse, 'economic and political rights cannot be realized separately from social and cultural rights' (Pérez de Cuéllar 1996).

We might ask at this point if such notions of cultural citizenship, though important for eliminating the impediments to inclusion, have not, especially when understood through the medium of consumer-oriented representations, obfuscated increasing class difference, which can be measured more or less objectively in terms of income disparity. Katz-Fishman and Scott (1994) report that poverty has been on the increase throughout the 1980s and 1990s, such that the 'polarization of wealth and poverty is greater than at any time since the government has been tracking such data'. A more recent analysis of the 2000 Census data shows that poverty is deepening in the United States as the rich get richer (Bernstein 2000). This is the situation in the United States; in other parts of the world the number of people barely surviving on less than $2 per day increased by 100 million from 1990 to 2000 (World Bank 2000, 29).

In Latin America, the widening income gap is more acute due to the inability of those countries to compete in the global economy. The prevalence of market and consumption values and increasing poverty go together as integral factors in the redefinition of the cultural field. This alarming development is not naturally given but has been produced and thus requires a critical reinterpretation of the relation of citizenship and consumption to capital.

Intellectual property and the redefinition of culture

The rise of market values is an important factor for the redefinition of culture in another sense. As the Europeans have argued, U.S. GATT and WTO negotiators have defined cultural goods such as films, television programs, video and audio recordings, and books as commodities subject to the same kinds of trade conditions as cars and clothing. Consequently, the Europeans contend, such trade arrangements legitimize the colonization of the European imaginary by Hollywood images, not to speak of filling the pockets of the shareholders of transnational entertainment conglomerates with most of the profits generated by films and other audiovisual products. In 1992, for example, Europeans 'exported $250 million to the U.S. while the latter had sales of $4.6 billion in Europe' (Balladur 1993). U.S. audiovisual sales in Europe continue to rise: the 1992 figure for exports had been matched in half the time, by midyear in 1994 ('After GATT Pique' 1994, 16). Globally, sales figures surpass US$12 billion per annum in foreign revenues (Motion Picture Association of America 1999). And when one looks at the sum of revenues from the copyright industries (theatrical films, TV programs, homevideo, DVDs, business software, entertainment software, books, music and sound recordings), that figure rises to US$535.1 billion, or 5.24 percent of the GDP (Motion Picture Association of America 2002).

Culture has become a grab bag into which all kinds of technological innovations are deposited as a means to protect the ownership claims of transnational corporations. The clearest example of this trend is the displacement of the categories to which the concept of 'intellectual property' applies. NAFTA, following the example of GATT, redefined the notion of culture as forms of property that include copyrights, patents, trademarks, plant breeder rights, industrial designs, trade secrets, integrated circuits, geographical indications, encrypted satellite signals, and so on. Furthermore, such intellectual property is protected insofar as it belongs to individuals (including corporations), obviating any recognition of collective rights, particularly the notion that communities generate culture and other forms of intellectual invention, such as seed varieties devised by peasant communities. Instead, according to NAFTA, 'computer programs [are protected] as literary works and databases as compilations' (*North American Free Trade Agreement* 1993, 36, [brackets by Yúdice]). The agreement states that 'intellectual property rights [will be provided adequate and effective protection] on the basis of national treatment', but computer programs are hardly an example of a cultural product that merits evaluation on the basis of national identity.

The Clinton administration's Working Group on Intellectual Property Rights recommended decisions that further redefined culture and enhanced benefits for commercial interests (McKenna 1995, 8). The impact of these decisions contributed to changes in the character of authorship, production, publication, and retransmission; rights were increasingly put in the domain of corporations, with privacy intervened by state and business enterprises. Even human life is increasingly subject to patenting and copyrighting (Dillon 1993, 11), and the rights to the digital reproduction of art and music have largely been acquired by entertainment conglomerates and telecommunications companies rather than the museums or original recording companies that own or owned the works (Powell 1995, 31). The extensive catalogues of national musics are now owned by the five major entertainment conglomerates, thus delinking value from national origin (Yúdice 1999). Noncompliance with intellectual property laws advanced particularly by the United States has already brought threats of punitive trade sanctions. International 'piracy' of U.S. 'culture' (software, books, music, video) reached $8 billion in 1993, rising by more than 50 percent to $12.38 billion in 1998, according to the International Intellectual Property Alliance (Wellman 1999), leading U.S. enterprises to seek greater adherence to copyright and trademark protections. [. . .] Mexico was virtually forced to change its intellectual property laws and to enforce them as of 1994, and China was threatened with a $30 billion sanction to discourage the piracy of trademarked products (Faison 1995a; 1995b; Sanger 1995; Scioliono 1995).

Although there are controversies revolving around the difference between authors' rights and copyright, the global knowledge-based economy nevertheless operates on the basis of the latter, in great part due to U.S. dominance in the organizations that oversee intellectual property rights. The United States and other postindustrial countries have recourse to international law and to the sanctions they can bring to bear on transgressor countries. Developing countries and fourth world indigenous peoples do not have the same clout, despite the drafting of international covenants by their own representatives (International Covenant on the Rights of Indigenous Nations 1994) and UNESCO (Recommendation on Safeguarding Traditional Cultures and Folklore 1989; Chartrand 1999). Western intellectual property law ascribes rights only to those who operate an alteration on a substance from the natural state such that the resulting product is 'non-obvious' (Roht-Arriaza 1996, 18). Consequently, intellectual property law does not recognize the forms of labor, especially immaterial or ritualistic forms such as shamanism, at the heart of indigenous knowledge and cultural forms like rhythms. This difference ensures that the asymmetry in capital accumulation between developed and developing countries and native peoples will become greater. The hegemonic redefinition of culture raises problems for the legal protection of community and other collective practices that generate marketable knowledge (folk remedies, seed varieties) and products (music, crafts) that are not recognized as such by states and transnational corporations, the major brokers in the arena of international law. Particularly in regard to popular music, such as the Afro-Brazilian rhythms of Bahia, controversies have arisen because these cultural forms do not receive the kind of protection from usage (appropriation by pop and rock musicians from the North such as David Byrne and Paul Simon) that is accorded to computer programs. On the other hand, the very notion of what appropriation means has also undergone major redefinition in the recent past, as appropriative practices such as sampling (assimilable to influential postmodern theories of pastiche and parody) have gained currency.

The transnational character of much cultural production and distribution, particularly in music and entertainment, makes it unlikely that the protection of culture can be effectively legislated on the basis of national states (which are already marked by the lack of recognition [protection] of many collective cultural practices, as noted above). As Garnham states, 'An analysis of culture structured around the concept of the cultural industries . . . directs our attention precisely at the dominant private market sector. It sees culture, defined as the production and circulation of symbolic meaning, as a material process of production and exchange, part of, and in significant ways determined by, the wider economic processes of society with which it shares many common forms' (1987, 25). The repercussions for how we understand and relate to the public realm are enormous. Public space, in which cultural forms circulate, is increasingly conditioned by commodified and transnational discourses and ideologies that combine and conflict with local forms in ways that disrupt the coherence of traditional national discourses, particularly those founded on conventional notions of the popular. . . . As García Canclini argues, 'It is not that national culture is extinguished but, rather, that it is converted into a formula for designating the continuity of an unstable historical memory that is now being reconstituted in interaction with transnational cultural referents' (1982, 8). It has become an 'international popular' (Ortiz 1988, 182–206), [. . .] or better yet, a 'transnational popular'. [. . .]

Note

1   I would like to thank Donna Lazarus for research assistance and much initiative in conducting the survey of arts professionals.

Chapter 9

Angus Cameron and Ronen Palan

PERFORMATIVE DISCOURSE AND SOCIAL FORM

From *The Imagined Economies of Globalization* London: Sage, 2004, pp. 54–68.

[. . .]

Globalization and social exclusion as acts of narrative framing

AN INSIGHT INTO THE OPERATION OF FRAMING around and through the concepts of globalization and social exclusion is to be found in the ongoing debate concerning the 'future' of the nation-state – future in inverted commas because the debate emphasizes the imminent demise of the nation-state. Much of the discussion about the meaning of globalization and exclusion is framed precisely within parameters set by our common understanding of what the nation-state has been in the past, is now, and ought to be in the future. Many globalization theorists, for example, are explicit in their belief that the state is about to wither away, or at the very least to undergo fundamental change as a result of the disaggregation of national territory; others reject this prognosis and in fact reject the very concept of globalization as mere hype. They do so largely in defence of the idea of the nation-state, which they claim, with apparently considerable empirical evidence to support their argument, is as lively as ever. The relationship of social exclusion to the state is more ambiguous. At the very least, however, it implies a process of differentiation of the normative space of the state and the creation of an externalized domain which, if it does not threaten the state as a whole, reconstitutes certain core responsibilities of the state with respect to particular groups. In both cases, it is important to note that even when the whole purpose of the debate has been to declare the death of the state, these debates are predicated on the establishment of common frames of reference based firmly on the conventional conception of the territorially bounded nation-state.

To debate the relationship between the state and globalization, in order that these concepts can function properly as descriptors and predictors of the future of the state, they have to be constituted within an epistemological frame whereby both the territorial state and the extra-territorial spaces opened up by globalization and social exclusion can be seen to inhabit the same spatio-temporal plane. Not surprisingly, the easier way of doing this is favoured. Hence, the 'global' system explicitly predicted by the concept of globalization takes a form that is essentially *similar* to but larger than the territorial nation-state; it is routinely accorded a concrete and apparently conventional spatial representation. According to this view, even relative to the largest continental states controlling significant portions of the earth's land mass, globalization implies processes on a larger, planetary scale. Hence, the problem for the state is that an increasing portion of human activities is operating on a geographical scale larger than the state. This sort of spatial essentialism runs through the entire globalization debate and it is taken so much for granted that many fail to notice that it really is not empirically verifiable at all.

To take one plausible argument against this type of naturalized framing of globalization, it is argued that the state is a concrete social organization with its own historical institutions and boundaries, while globalization is no more than a concept; a term used to describe a series of otherwise disconnected processes. Strictly speaking, the relationship between globalization and the state is one between a concrete institutional structure and a descriptive concept; that is to say, since they belong to separate epistemological orders, the extent to which they can interact is questionable. How could a mere concept change an institution as established and enduring, as *real*, as the nation-state? The concept of globalization may be able to say something about the state, but in belonging to a different order of existence cannot affect it directly. Globalization as a concept is therefore presented as external to the concrete reality of the state.

However, as Justin Rosenberg (2002) has pointed out, a curious slippage has taken place within the contemporary debate whereby *theories of globalization*, that is theories that seek to explain the processes that have led to globalization, in other words theories that seek to explain the processes whose aggregate outcome may merit the appellation globalization, have somehow turned into what he calls *globalization theories*, that is theories according to which globalization has itself become the causal factor. Theories that describe social change leading to globalization turn out, all of a sudden, to be theories that explain social change as caused by it. This sort of slippage arises precisely because of the ways in which the nature of the epistemological framing of the debate itself changes. Because of the overwhelming concern with the spatial dimensions of economics and politics in conventional accounts of globalization, it has very rapidly turned from being employed as a speculative and sometimes voluntaristic concept (e.g., Ohmae 1990), to being treated as a spatio-temporal reality, equivalent to, and interacting with, the state (e.g., Giddens 1998).

By the same token, the state itself has also been transformed through these processes of representation. Its territoriality, which has for many years been the inviolable and indivisible basis of the nation-state's sovereign integrity, has become more fragmentary and fluid. In order to occupy the same frame of reference, we can see a process taking place whereby the global has come to be constructed more in terms of the state and the state in terms of the global. These two concepts, which for so long have seemed to be mutually exclusive, suddenly seem to be made of the very same stuff. So long as we do not enquire too closely into the precise nature of that 'stuff' – that we accept it as common sense and natural – the material reality of both is not only secured but becomes mutually constitutive. Globalization has not only become more 'real' ('reality' being articulated as the territorial conventions of the nation-state), reality has also become more global!

Let us be clear, however, that our interest in the minutiae of the construction of the epistemological framing of globalization and social exclusion is not born of a desire to somehow improve or replace this framing with another that is somehow better or more sophisticated. We are not interested in showing the deficiencies of current framing in order to replace them at last with the 'right' framing. Rather, our aim is to be better aware of the complex relationships between certain theoretical and conceptual processes, including the operation of framing of arguments and subsequent policy responses. We want to demonstrate that policy is not reacting passively to 'structural forces' (merely adapting to something that is already existing), but rather that it operates within a context of intervening and intermediating cognitive processes.

Indeed, a similar process of framing can be seen to take place in the context of social exclusion. As we will see, the concept of exclusion is rendered comprehensible in the light of the concept of *inclusion*. And the not too subtle message in the globalization and social exclusion literature is that the space of *inclusion*, though rarely defined explicitly (because it is so natural that it does not need defining), is in most cases understood to be that of the nation-state. However, whilst at one level this seems to confirm the status of the nation-state as the prime organization constituted in and constitutive of social space and, therefore, the provider of welfare and social cohesion, it also denies, or at least fundamentally alters, the role of the state *vis-à-vis* its citizens. By constituting a 'space beyond' the social, the debate on social exclusion, simply by presenting particular categories of the poor as 'the excluded', serves to disaggregate the spatial contiguity of the nation-state in a manner exactly parallel to that of globalization. Again, the territorial integrity of the state is both asserted and rendered more complex as the spatial requirements of the exclusion debate become naturalized. In this case, 'reality' (again the reality of the territorial state) has become more locally exclusive as exclusion has become more locally 'real'.

The nation-state (or, rather, a retrospectively developed 'idea' of the nation-state) serves, as we will see, as the point of departure against which difference can be gauged – a background and counterfoil for our understanding of globalization and social exclusion. The state has become the 'white wall', as Deleuze and Guattari (1987) call it, that provides the very possibility of signification. The surprising centrality of the state, framing the prevailing imageries of globalization – including those who firmly predict the end of the state – is a central component in our interpretation.

Framing time

The frames of reference of the territorial state and those of globalization and exclusion are brought together in order that a specific set of processes can be articulated. They are intended to create a set of common terms through which a story unfolding through *time* can be told. This means that the temporal dimension itself must also be brought into line with the frames of reference of these debates – time itself must be configured to fit with the normative requirements of the unfolding narratives of the globalized and excluded world.

Whatever else it may be, globalization is explicitly a story of temporal change – it posits up front the idea that the world is becoming 'more global'. This teleological aspect of globalization, although it has been noted many times, has not led to much consideration of the way in which time is represented through the concept. Rather, the teleology of globalization has tended to be treated, particularly in Marxist analyses of 'false consciousness', as a convenient fiction used instrumentally to legitimize specific institutional changes brought in by powerful and interested actors. The temporal expectations of globalization are certainly deployed in this way, to justify all manner of specific changes in the nature of economies and societies (Peck 1998), but to reduce the temporal aspects of globalization to these activities misses some of its more profound implications. Specifically, globalization, in combination with social exclusion, represents the opening up of new normative temporal domains – the differentiated velocities of social life anticipated by Virilio (1986), Bauman (2002) and others. How does this come about?

Here, Ricoeur's analysis of the narrative function offers a clue. One of the big mistakes made by conventional historiographers, he argues, is that they view narrative as narrowly 'bound to a strictly chronological order' (1981, 278). If we accept this conception of linear sequential time – which, given that this is the way we experience the passage of time, is not hard to do – then the idea of history as narrative seems to be commonsensical. If time itself is sequential, then the task of the properly disinterested historian or social scientist is to excavate and narrate the 'real' sequences of 'real' history. However, this apparently natural process of strictly sequential, linear temporality has the effect of locking social life into a pre-determined 'structural' unfolding of the system. If this were true then our capacity to influence the future would be reduced to zero – human life would simply be governed by 'blind fate' or an extreme form of structural determinism. Just as knowledge of social reality does not come to us in a ready-made, unmediated manner, so this is also true of social time. The stories we tell ourselves about ourselves (and not by any means only those of historians) are very specifically stories about the passage of time. They tell us what used to be, what will be (quite explicitly in the case of globalization) and, perhaps most importantly of all, how we are moving from the interpreted past to the anticipated future. As Ricoeur argues,

> any narration combines, in varying proportions, two dimensions: a chronological dimension and a non-chronological dimension. The first may be called the 'episodic dimension' of the narrative. Within the art of following a story, this dimension is expressed in the expectation of contingencies which affect the story's development; hence it gives rise to questions such as: and so? And then? What happened next? What was the outcome? Etc.
>
> (1981, 278)

The episodic dimension holds a considerable power over the individual and collective imagination, not least because it seems to correspond to our lived experience of the passage of time. However, as a *narrative account* of the passage of time, any such history is a *representation*; like a 'realist' painting which tries to fool the eye into believing that the painted object is real, narrative seeks to represent historical events in a manner comprehensible to minds trained to think of time as sequential. This suggests, as Nelson Goodman (1978, 20) powerfully put it, that 'reality in a world, like realism in a painting, is largely a matter of habit'. [. . .]

The realist habit of narrating history as episodic sequence is much in evidence in conventional theories of globalization. Such accounts seek to answer precisely the sort of questions that Ricouer poses: 'And so? And then? What happened next? What was the outcome?' However, as the quote above suggests, Ricoeur adds a second non-chronological dimension to the function of the historical narrative which runs counter to the 'logic of the episodic sequence'. He borrows from Louis Mink the notion that any narrative, including historical narratives which claim to merely describe the found world, also constitute[s] a simultaneous process of *configuration* of an entire period. Narrative, Ricoeur claims,

> does not consist simply in adding episodes to one another; it also constructs meaningful totalities out of scattered events. This aspect of the art of narrating is reflected, on the side of following a story, in the attempt to 'grasp together' successive events. The art of narrating, as well as the corresponding art of following a story, therefore require that we are able *to extract a configuration from a succession*.
>
> (1981, 278 emphasis [Ricoeur])

This leads Ricoeur to an important conclusion: 'every narrative can be conceived in terms of the competition between its episodic dimension and its configurational dimension, between sequence and figure' (1981, 278). The narrative is a form of contestation, and any narrative displays complexity far beyond the mere chronological addition of facts. To broaden the argument further, the act of narrating any account of social reality and its development entails simultaneous processes of definition, interpretation and, in the more general sense, exclusion – the story of social reality is not merely 'found' and related, but is actively, if not consciously made. As Ricoeur's editor and translator John Thompson argues, human action may be regarded as a text: 'action, like a text, is a meaningful entity which must be constructed as a whole' (1981, 15).

The competition between the episodic and the configural will play a central role in our own narrative. We will seek to demonstrate that the simple imagery of globalization, as an end point beyond which the world can be reflexively rebuilt, is the product of a far more complex configural narrative than is commonly acknowledged.

Framing space

Just as positivist conceptions of historical fact have been challenged by critical theorists and the hermeneutics tradition, so conventional conceptions of the nature of social space have been critically reappraised. In much the same way that critical historiographers have explored the constructed nature of historical narratives, recent critical geographers and others have responded to [the] fact that such narratives are always presented in *spatial* terms (cf. Crang and Thrift 2000). Furthermore, the spatial framing of historical arguments and the 'visualization' of events is not simply a neutral process independent of the events that are taking place 'out there'. As a consequence the idea that space itself is not the natural, given substance we assume but that it is 'produced' has gained considerable currency in recent years. Space conceived as something actively and discursively produced can no longer be seen, as in conventional mainstream geography, as the passive backdrop against which the events of history are played out (Soja 1988).

The idea that social space has a form distinct from physical space and that it is, moreover, socially reproduced, has been a consistent theme in a growing body of theoretical work in anthropology (e.g., Shapiro 1997; 1999), critical and social geography (Soja 1988; Harvey 1990; Thrift 1996; Keil 1998; Crang and Thrift 2000), literary theory (Berman 1983; Ross 1988; 1995; Moretti 1998) and sociology (Poulantzas 1978; Davis 1990; Lefebvre 1991; Zukin 1993; Castoriadis 1998). [. . .] Although this has its roots in some of the earliest challenges to the spatial ortho-doxies of academic geography, for example in the 'social geography' of the French anarchist and communard Elisée Reclus in the 1870s (Ross 1988), the development of this more critical and constructivist approach to social space is much more recent – dating primarily from the 1970s and a 'reassertion of space in critical social theory' (Soja 1988).

At one level, the production of space refers to something we are less interested in here, namely the creation and transformation of the 'real' spaces of architecture and topography, in which the 'background' of social interaction, the city, the landscape and so on, the apparently neutral and unchanging backdrops to life, are viewed no longer as merely neutral containers but living, dynamic, affective and rich in symbolism. Even the most evident physical barrier, the limits of the earth, is in part a socially constructed limit, best exemplified in the commonsense adage, 'the sky is the limit'. As Paul Virilio has demonstrated, however, we are living in an era in which literally the sky is no longer the limit. For Virilio, the technology that has effectively removed our physical barriers, also serves to remove barriers to the imagination. The limitless sky is for him the harbinger of a different sort of social relationship embedded in a new conception of territory where space, and indeed social reality as a whole, is 'virtualized' and internalized (Virilo 1997; Derian 1998). The task of such hermeneutic approaches to social space, therefore, is to 'read' the rich semiological map, stripped of its 'naturalized' symbolic value.

But the issue of the production of space is not only about providing a more complex description of the landscape or reading of the 'semiotic compasses' of everyday life; to view the world of artefacts and architecture as a form of communi-cation. Such approaches are very important, but of greater significance here is the notion that space generally, and not simply certain spaces, is discursively reproduced. As such, space itself, or *spatiality*, to use Soja's terminology (1989), needs to be understood as a dialectic process that is constituted in and by all social forms, processes and practices.

Perhaps the best known and most influential theorist of socio-spatial produc-tion, the French philosopher Henri Lefebvre, argued that a complex and dialectic spatiality is a fundamental aspect of social reality:

> Social relations, which are concrete abstractions, have no real existence
> save in and through space. *Their underpinning is spatial.* In each particular

case, the connection between this underpinning and the relations it supports calls for analysis. Such an analysis must imply and explain a genesis and constitute a critique of those institutions, substitutions, transpositions, metaphorizations, anaphorizations, and so forth, that have transformed the space under consideration.

(1991, 404 emphasis [Lefebvre])

Social and spatial relationships, Lefebvre claims, are mutually constitutive or, to put it [in] terms of the narrative function outlined above, the social narrative is a spatial narrative. Our capacity to affect, think, imagine, speak, indeed to act in any manner whatsoever in society, is both enabled and bounded by a mental 'map' which is at the same time a spatial map. Such a map includes co-ordinates for the familiar concrete spatial forms that set limits on our physical movement – hard, solid spaces through which we cannot move and liquid, gaseous spaces that we can traverse. And yet, over and above these, it is the spatiality of our metaphors and our knowledge of the spatio-temporal environment that they reproduce, that contribute complexity to the plot and which create rhythms and conclusions. Social relations are, therefore, spatial relations; their concreteness is *ipso facto* spatial; 'their underpinning is spatial', says Lefebvre. This view, in turn, contains a dynamic theory of change: it assumes that spatial forms are never static, and considering that they underpin social relations, it follows that 'social relations' – the principles we can infer by analysis – themselves are undergoing continuous if not constant change.

As this suggests, the production of the spatial environment is subject to a process of 'emplotment' similar to that of the historical narrative proposed by Ricoeur and others. That the former is plotted across space rather than time constitutes a significant difference, but not one that prevents us from applying to spatial narratives the same sort of critique that Ricoeur applies to historical ones. To adapt Ricoeur's terminology, social narratives not only 'extract a configuration from a succession' – succession being a chronological temporal distribution – but also extract a configuration from a spatial distribution. Whereas the tension in the historical narrative is that between chronology and simultaneity – between, in Ricoeur's terms, the episodic and configural function of the narrative – in spatial terms the tension lies between 'territoriality' and simultaneity. Here the simultaneous aspect of spatiality is different, however, in that it refers less directly to temporal simultaneity – things happening at the same time – than to spatial simultaneity – the co-presence, co-extension and overlapping of spatial forms that are expected and/or claimed to be discrete, internally and externally coherent and contiguous. Again, therefore, spatial narratives contain a hidden configural function which stands in tension to the foregrounded territorial function. Describing the landscape also encapsulates it, categorizes it and alters it. Just as, 'the whole novel is present on every page' (Hermann J. Weigand quoted in Mink 1974, 114) – in order that we reach the acceptable conclusion – so we can read the entire spatial order at every point on the social landscape. This does not mean that social space is undifferentiated, rather that the pattern of differentiation is present in all of the various elements of the spatial narrative.

So, for example, as we have already pointed out, conventional readings of the territorial state posit a very strong form of territorial coherence within national borders and a very strong form of territorial rupture at the border. This is reproduced through the languages and practices of law, economics (the 'national economy'), politics, citizenship, 'official' language, culture, sport, religion and so on. Few would defend the idea that these many different spatial forms actually correspond to each other, or to the lines on the map – indeed such an idea is indefensible – but most of us nevertheless act as though this were the case. Indeed because, as in the case of the historical narrative, our spatial experience and expression is grounded in pervasive epistemologies and their institutional expressions which predetermine what constitutes space and how space is to be both read and inhabited, it is extremely difficult to act other than in accordance with prevailing spatial orthodoxies. By the same token, the theories of spatial causality that are contained within such orthodoxies render the reading, let alone transformation, of spatial dynamics very opaque.

For example, Kathleen Kirby shows how the Enlightenment concept of the 'individual', the naturalized 'individual-as-actor' that we take for granted today, is a fundamentally spatial category. [. . .] Or rather, she demonstrates how awareness of the spatial metaphor embedded in certain concepts helps explain a more general problematic of narration of the role of the individual in society.

> [P]roblems with the Enlightenment individual derive it seems from its spatial form. The 'individual' (it has become commonplace to point out), is 'undivided' within itself, and unquestionably separate from other subjects and the external environment as a whole. Graphically, the 'individual' might be pictured as a closed circle: its smooth contours ensure its clear division from its location, as well as assure its internal coherence and coherence and consistency.
>
> (1996, 38)

The implications of such conceptions, she continues, are profound:

> Inside the circle of the rational self all is consistent, co-operating; outside lies a vacuum in which objects appear within their own bubbles, self-sufficient Ego. Will, thought, perception, might be depicted as rays issuing outward from this solitary mind to play over the surface of Objects.
>
> (1996, 38)

This spatial reading of the individual begs a question about the nature of the line of causality that resulted in such a conception of the self-contained, bounded self. Is it the case, for example, that the notion of the modern 'individual' has produced alongside it a 'proper' spatialization within which that particular historical construction of the self can be articulated and can function effectively? Or was it the other way around – did changing conceptualizations of space and concomitant spatial practices (for example, the organization of productive labour into specialist units separate both from each other and from the domestic sphere) impact on the nature of the individual? Neither explanation seems convincing on its own but rather both seem to be simultaneous processes, the one implying and reinforcing the other. Whatever is the case, the epistemological framing of spatial dynamics, such that they appear as and are claimed to be ontologies, only rarely reaches the realm of public debate. It is our contention that the debates on globalization and social exclusion, as fundamentally and unavoidably spatial narratives, provide just such a rare moment – a very open and public narrative re-configuration of socio-spatial form which is re-plotting our basic social maps in ways we simply cannot ignore.

As such, what is interesting about globalization and social exclusion is not that they involve a reconfiguration of spatial form; as implied above, this is immanent to social life. Social space is dynamic and therefore is continuously, if not constantly, reconfigured. Rather, what is important about globalization and exclusion is that the reconfiguration is of such a magnitude, and is taking place at such a pace, that it cannot remain hidden – it is forced out into the open. Since we, as academic commentators, politicians, journalists, economists and ordinary individuals are unaccustomed to dealing with such grand shifts in our basic conceptual framing at the level of explicit discourse, perhaps we should not be so surprised that the resulting attempts to figure out what is going on have tended rather to miss the target. By trying to deal with socio-spatial change at the level of the empirical – which is familiar and comfortable territory to a social science praxis still steeped in the predilections of positivism – we might expect to find silences around matters of epistemology and hermeneutics.

Framing the social

If social life is made possible through the internalization of precognitive 'maps' of the social world, which encapsulate the content and delineate the boundaries of our discursive frames, where do we find them and how are they plotted in the first place? Clearly, conventional cartography presents us with one set of spatial co-ordinates – those most familiar as maps corresponding, however abstractly, to territories. However, for all their apparent groundedness in the physical forms of the landscape, such maps – particularly 'political' maps outlining the boundaries of national and sub-national state spaces – represent not 'real' spaces but political, economic and juridical boundaries imposed by people. As such, the boundaries of political maps are graphic symbols which embody the configural narratives of a prevailing spatio-temporal order.

Whilst conventional maps are those that we recognize most readily and most uncritically, the configurations they contain are also narrated through other media whose mapping function is less obvious. The literary historian Franco Moretti observes that 'literary maps' – in other words, those maps implied and contained within fictional narratives – constitute important elements in the reproduction of spatio-temporal conceptions. Fictional narratives, Moretti argues, contain their own 'geography' which allows the reader to see two things:

> First, they highlight the . . . place-bound nature of literary forms; each of them with its peculiar geometry, its boundaries, its spatial taboos and favourite routes. And then, maps bring to light the *internal* logic of narrative: the semiotic domain around which the plot coalesces and self-organizes. Literary form thus appears as the result of two conflicting, and equally significant forces: one working from the outside, and one from the inside. It is the usual, and at bottom

the only real issue of literary history: society, rhetoric and their interaction.

(1998, 5)

The relationship of the literary novel to the production of space has, therefore, a dual character. On the one hand it serves to 'write' the spatiality of, in the case of Moretti's work, the nation-state, not as it is in any empirical sense, but as it *ought* to be according to the normative predilections of the time, the author and ultimately the reader. The nation-state of the countless 'fictions', novels and social commentaries then merged, in time, with an 'empirical' nation-state constructed in the image of the imaginary one. This is Ricoeur's argument about the merging of fictional and historical narratives.

The novels that Moretti analyses are written within the context of a prevailing and hegemonic spatial imaginary which acts as a constraint, whether the authors or readers are aware of it or not, on the *possible spaces* that can be written. This corresponds to the delimited notion of 'worldmaking' developed by Nelson Good-man and outlined above. We might also add a third dimension to this, which is in fact implied throughout Moretti's subsequent account of the relationship between the modern novel and the nation-state, that the imaginary maps that are produced by literature and the other arts are not socially 'neutral' with regard to their subjects. The depiction of the landscape of England in the eighteenth-century novel was not, therefore, innocent but, as Moretti notes, operated a form of 'literary exclusion' whereby the nation-state was reduced to a small area of central England, highly gendered and entirely divorced from the rest of the UK.

Benedict Anderson's (1991) famous account of the production of 'imagined communities' of the nation-state also examines the significant role played by fictional narratives in contributing to the formation of nationalisms and nation-states. He goes one step further, however, adding 'the census, the map and the museum' to various forms of vernacular and nationalist literature to explain the ways in which the territory of the state also came to delineate, at least in theory, the boundaries of the national culture. But the literary novel, and as Anderson shows, the whole paraphernalia of other communicative technologies, was in the process of producing (or rather affirming) an historically evolving notion of collective identities. These were not necessarily co-extensive with political boundaries, although interesting relationships evolved between the institutions of the state, political ideologies, and these broader 'cultural' socio-spatial formats, to generate between them a complex mapping of the nation-state. Indeed, considering that each nation-state drew on different . . . histories, different novels, operating within different territories, if sharing much in terms of institutional and political innovation, the concept of the nation-state can only be an 'ideal-type'; each nation-state produced a different, if in many ways similar, format. State theory, generally speaking, is interested in commonality, in finding the basic, universal principle. But this 'academic' pursuit is itself a component of the modern way of 'story-telling', its universalizing and homogenizing structure plays precisely the same role. Goodman makes a similar point with respect to the naïve empiricism of the sciences:

Truth, far from being a solemn and severe master, is a docile and obedient servant. The scientist who supposes that he is single-mindedly dedicated to the search for truth deceives himself . . . He seeks system, simplicity, scope; and when satisfied on these scores he tailors truth to fit. He as much decrees as discovers the laws he sets forth, as much designs as discerns the patterns he delineates.

(1978, 18)

The same is, of course, true of the social 'sciences'. This implies that the relationship between concepts of globalization and social exclusion and those social sciences that claim to stand back from them and debate them at a distance is in practice much more intimate. Put another way, could we have thought of globalization or social exclusion, let alone institutionalize them in theory and practice, without the century or so old world of the social sciences?

Globalization as *fās*

How then do we propose to advance our investigation? In his famous study of the role of mythology in human societies, Ernst Cassirer demonstrates how thoroughly high modern Western cultures are drenched with atavistic fears and superstitions (1955). Such mythologies are not merely hangovers from a primitive past that we have yet to eliminate; they are integral to the very fabric of modernism and, by extension, to any and all politics. Myths do not simply play a legitimizing role. Émile Durkheim notes that 'representation is not a simple image or reality, a motionless shadow projected onto us by things. It is rather a force that stirs up around us a whole whirlwind of organic and psychological phenomena' (1984, 53). Representations, the stories we tell ourselves about ourselves and about the world we live in, are guides to action and forces of change in themselves, stimulating and constraining the entire gamut of human emotion, from happiness to despair, from violence to love. Societies are not simple or closed systems, they contain multiple levels and many different narratives. Nevertheless, an overlap between Hankiss' [2001] 'Promethean' and 'Apollonian' [. . .] strategies is achieved at every historical period with the aid of what may be described as a foundational story. These foundational stories, without which social life would be devoid of meaning, have been central to Western philosophy and social theory for centuries.

In Western philosophy, religion, particularly within the Judaeo-Christian tradition, has conventionally provided a source for these myths, claiming originary and divine truths as the basis for social order. As modern philosophy has moved away from religious essentialism, so new secular foundations have been found in, for example, constructions built around ideas of 'human nature', economic 'realism', structural functionalism, psychoanalysis, the 'nation', and so on. In each case, these founding stories are constructed with the aid of differing and often multiple narrative structures, but the presence of such mythologies themselves remains constant. Similarly, contemporary societies also develop their own myths of origin without which they have no picture of themselves.

In *The Practice of Everyday Life*, Michel de Certeau develops an account of human praxis which is founded upon an instituted and formally sanctioned mythic space. He employs the ancient Latin noun *fās* to describe what he calls a 'mystical foundation', without which human action cannot take place. 'The creation of the *fās* – the institution of the foundation', he remarks, 'was conducted by special priests called "fetiāles" who would conduct rituals which would "create the field" necessary for political and military operations' (1984, 124). The establishment of the *fãs*, the socially constructed field or space necessary for political action, has historically not been confined to the Romans. Indeed, we argue that until recently – particularly in northern Europe, north America and other parts of the industrialized world – the 'nation' has played very precisely this role of the *fãs*, serving as a foundational myth in modern society. For all its prevalence, the founding myth of the nation, as demonstrated most famously by Benedict Anderson (1991), does not take a single form across time and space, but comes into being, in part at least, to serve the prevailing interests and powers at work in a given place (Delanty 2000; 2001). In whatever form, however, the nation – particularly when institutionalized as the nation-state – has functioned historically as simultaneously a concept, a praxis, a political programme, a set of institutions and a 'social fact' (in a Durkheimian sense) all rolled into one. Combining all these elements, the concept of the nation 'opens a space and provides a foundation for the operations of the military men, diplomats or merchants who dare to cross the frontiers' (de Certeau 1984, 124).

From such a perspective, the current debate on globalization, which on all sides tries to find a truth *behind* ideology and symbols, is missing a crucial point. Whether one belongs to the 'booster' or 'hypercritic' (Dicken, Peck, et al. 1997) factions that have polarized the debate in recent years, it is not possible to somehow strip the ideology and/or discourse out of globalization, either to demonstrate its 'real' nature, or to refute its existence altogether. Rather, globalization can only be properly understood in the context and as an integral part of an emergent *fãs*, one being deployed skilfully to replace and/or reform that established around the central fiction of the nation. Just like its predecessor, globalization is simultaneously a concept, a praxis, a political programme, (increasingly) a set of institutions and a social fact, all rolled into one. It is for this reason that debates about factuality of globalization have proved to be so fruitless. This is not to suggest that there is no empirical evidence to support the claims made for globalization – far from it, and we will analyse particular aspects of that evidence in subsequent chapters. It is, however, to state that anyone attempting to treat globalization as being only one of these things (as *either* a concept, an ideology, a political programme, an institutional structure, *or* a social fact) at once mis-recognizes its social and political function and, unwittingly, reaffirms its mythology. [. . .]

Although it is all around us, thoroughly infiltrating and shaping the world we inhabit, the narratives that underpin and give force to the concept of globalization as an articulation of a contemporary *fãs* have been largely misunderstood. As a result the power, rhythm, nature and effects of globalization are also misunderstood. Our aim in this book is not to argue that globalization *is* the contemporary *fãs* in any complete sense. That would be to misunderstand the way in which the *fãs* itself functions as a precognitive framework for social identity and praxis and, in so doing, to reduce it to a single set of processes and institutional arrangements, those that have come collectively to be labelled 'globalization'. As Montrose argues: 'a closed and static, singular and homogenous notion of ideology must be succeeded by one that is heterogeneous and unstable, permeable and processual' (quoted in Colebrook 1998, 25). In our description, we emphasize precisely these qualities of globalization as *fãs*, heterogeneity, instability and permeability. We are not even particularly bothered whether the reader will accept the correlation between globalization and de Certeau's notion of the *fās*. Rather, we will ask you to suspend judgement, to accept provisionally that any society, at any time, necessarily operates within some kind of *fās* and that globalization *might* be an integral and very significant part of its contemporary manifestation. We therefore also ask that our argument is judged less on its methodological and theoretical assumptions than on its concrete descriptions and interpretations. We will examine the phenomena of globalization (and by 'phenomena' we refer as much to the conceptual aspects of globalization as we do to its empirical manifestation) as evidence of changes in the contemporary *fās* of Western (post-) industrial societies – changes that are having consequences far beyond the spatial and conceptual limits of those societies. In analysing globalization as part of a history of the production of the contemporary *fās*, we propose a distinctive perspective on changes taking place in the contemporary world and in particular the changing construction of the normative socio-spatial relationships between globalization, nation, state and citizens.

Conclusion

We have argued that our conceptions and perceptions of social reality are framed for and by us in a number of different, but overlapping ways. First, an *a priori* framing, the epistemological plane without which social communication and meaning cannot take place because it is immanent to the social itself, delimits what can and cannot be said and done. For all that this clearly imposes constraints on social knowledge and action, such a plane also provides the foundation upon which debates about knowledge and action can take place at all. We are all bound to occupy such epistemological planes, even if we are aware of their existence and can be reflexive about the limitations on us that they imply. Being reflexive about the existence of gravity does not mean that we can abandon it.

Unlike gravity, however, the epistemological plane is not an external reality, but an internal, social one. As such, whilst we may not be able to escape it, we can at least alter its dimensions; our conceptual foundations change – sometimes, as Thomas Kuhn (1962) most famously observed, quite suddenly – even if we still have to have them in some form or another. The conceptual foundations of the nation-state are, whether we are aware of it or not, being transformed by the related discourses of socio-spatial change that are globalization and social exclusion. As the passions aroused by both concepts and/or processes indicate, the effects of their incorporation into the *fās* of the contemporary nation-state are being keenly felt. However, responding to them effectively presupposes that we understand them for what they are. Resisting a narrative is, after all, a very different thing to resisting a set of concrete institutions – not least because if we mis-recognize the meaning of those institutions, as evidence of the *fās* rather than the *fās* itself, we can end up reinforcing them by reproducing the very narratives on which they are based.

Chapter 10

Antonio Negri and Michael Hardt

THE MULTITUDE AGAINST EMPIRE

From *Empire* Harvard: Harvard University Press, 2005, pp. 393–400

The great masses need a *material religion of the senses* [*eine sinnliche Religion*]. Not only the great masses but also the philosopher needs it. Monotheism of reason and the heart, polytheism of the imagination and art, this is what we need . . . [W]e must have a new mythology, but this mythology must be at the service of ideas. It must be a mythology of *reason*.

> *Das älteste Systemprogramm des deutschen Idealismus*, by Hegel,
> Hölderlin, or Schelling

We do not lack communication, on the contrary we have too much of it. We lack creation. *We lack resistance to the present.*

> Gilles Deleuze and Félix Guattari

IMPERIAL POWER CAN NO LONGER RESOLVE the conflict of social forces through mediatory schemata that displace the terms of conflict. The social conflicts that constitute the political confront one another directly, without mediations of any sort. This is the essential novelty of the imperial situation. Empire creates a greater potential for revolution than did the modern regimes of power because it presents us, alongside the machine of command, with an alternative: the set of all the exploited and the subjugated, a multitude that is directly opposed to Empire, with no mediation between them. At this point, then, as Augustine says, our task is to discuss, to the best of our powers, 'the rise, the development and the destined ends of the two cities . . . which we find . . . interwoven . . . and mingled with one another' (Saint Augustine 1972, 430). Now that we have dealt extensively with Empire, we should focus directly on the multitude and its potential political power.

The two cities

We need to investigate specifically how the multitude can become a *political subject* in the context of Empire. We can certainly recognize the existence of the multitude from the standpoint of the constitution of Empire, but from that perspective the multitude might appear to be generated and sustained by imperial command. In the new postmodern Empire there is no Emperor Caracalla who grants citizenship to all his subjects and thereby forms the multitude as a political subject. The formation of the multitude of exploited and subjugated producers can be read more clearly in the history of twentieth-century revolutions. Between the communist revolutions of 1917 and 1949, the great anti-fascist struggles of the 1930s and 1940s, and the numerous liberation struggles of the 1960s up to those of 1989, the conditions of the citizenship of the multitude were born, spread, and consolidated. Far from being defeated, the revolutions of the twentieth century have each pushed forward and transformed the terms of class conflict, posing the conditions of a new political subjectivity, an insurgent multitude against imperial power. The rhythm that the revolutionary movements have established is the beat of a new *aetas*, a new maturity and metamorphosis of the times.

The constitution of Empire is not the cause but the consequence of the rise of these new powers. It should be no surprise, then, that Empire, despite its efforts, finds it impossible to construct a system of right adequate to the new reality of the globalization of social and economic relations. This impossibility [. . .] is not due to the wide extension of the field of regulation; nor is it simply the result of the difficult passage from the old system of international public law to the new imperial system. This impossibility is explained instead by the revolutionary nature of the multitude, whose struggles have produced Empire as an inversion of its own image and who now represents on this new scene an uncontainable force and an excess of value with respect to every form of right and law.

To confirm this hypothesis, it is sufficient to look at the contemporary development of the multitude and dwell on the vitality of its present expressions. When the multitude works, it produces autonomously and reproduces the entire world of life. Producing and reproducing autonomously mean constructing a new ontological reality. In effect, by working, the multitude produces itself as singularity. It is a singularity that establishes a new place in the non-place of Empire, a singularity that is a reality produced by cooperation, represented by the linguistic community, and developed by the movements of hybridization. The multitude affirms its singularity by inverting the ideological illusion that all humans on the global surfaces of the world market are interchangeable. Standing the ideology of the market on its feet, the multitude promotes through its labor the biopolitical singularizations of groups and sets of humanity, across each and every node of global interchange.

Class struggles and revolutionary processes of the past undermined the political powers of nations and peoples. The revolutionary preamble that has been written from the nineteenth to the twentieth centuries has prepared the new subjective configuration of labor that comes to be realized today. Cooperation and communication throughout the spheres of biopolitical production define a new productive singularity. The multitude is not formed simply by throwing together and mixing nations and peoples indifferently; it is the singular power of a *new city*.

One might object at this point, with good reason, that all this is still not enough to establish the multitude as a properly political subject, nor even less as a subject with the potential to control its own destiny. This objection, however, does not present an insuperable obstacle, because the revolutionary past, and the contemporary cooperative productive capacities through which the anthropological characteristics of the multitude are continually transcribed and reformulated, cannot help revealing a telos, a material affirmation of liberation. In the ancient world Plotinus faced something like this situation:

> 'Let us flee then to the beloved Fatherland': this is the soundest counsel . . . The Fatherland to us is There whence we have come, and There is the Father. What then is our course, what the manner of our flight? This is not a journey for the feet; the feet bring us only from land to land; nor need you think of a coach or ship to carry you away; all this order of things you must set aside and refuse to see: you must close the eyes and call instead upon another vision which is to be waked within you, a vision, the birth-right of all, which few turn to use.
>
> (Plotinus 1956, 63)

This is how ancient mysticism expressed the new telos. The multitude today, how-ever, resides on the imperial surfaces where there is no God the Father and no transcendence. Instead there is our immanent labor. The teleology of the multitude is theurgical; it consists in the possibility of directing technologies and production toward its own joy and its own increase of power. The multitude has no reason to look outside its own history and its own present productive power for the means necessary to lead toward its constitution as a political subject.

A material mythology of reason thus begins to be formed, and it is constructed in the languages, technologies, and all the means that constitute the world of life. It is a material religion of the senses that separates the multitude from every residue of sovereign power and from every 'long arm' of Empire. The mythology of reason is the symbolic and imaginative articulation that allows the ontology of the multitude to express itself as activity and consciousness. The mythology of languages of the multitude interprets the telos of an *earthly city*, torn away by the power of its own destiny from any belonging or subjection to a *city of God*, which has lost all honor and legitimacy. To the metaphysical and transcendent mediations, to the violence and corruption are thus opposed the absolute constitution of labor and cooperation, the earthly city of the multitude.

Endless paths (the right to global citizenship)

The constitution of the multitude appears first as a spatial movement that constitutes the multitude in limitless place. The mobility of commodities, and thus of that special commodity that is labor-power, has been presented by capitalism ever since its birth as the fundamental condition of accumulation. The kinds of movement of individuals, groups, and populations that we find today in Empire, however, cannot be completely subjugated to the laws of capitalist accumulation – at every moment they overflow and shatter the bounds of measure. The movements of the multitude designate new spaces, and its journeys establish new residences. Autonomous movement is what defines the place proper to the multitude. Increasingly less will passports or legal documents be able to regulate our movements across borders. A new geography is established by the multitude as the productive flows of bodies define new rivers and ports. The cities of the earth will become at once great deposits of cooperating humanity and locomotives for circulation, temporary residences and networks of the mass distribution of living humanity.

Through circulation the multitude reappropriates space and constitutes itself as an active subject. When we look closer at how this constitutive process of subjectivity operates, we can see that the new spaces are described by unusual topologies, by subterranean and uncontainable rhizomes — by geographical mythologies that mark the new paths of destiny. These movements often cost terrible suffering, but there is also in them a desire of liberation that is not satiated except by reappropriating new spaces, around which are constructed new freedoms. Everywhere these movements arrive, and all along their paths they determine new forms of life and cooperation — everywhere they create that wealth that parasitic postmodern capitalism would otherwise not know how to suck out of the blood of the proletariat, because increasingly today production takes place in movement and cooperation, in exodus and community. Is it possible to imagine U.S. agriculture and service industries without Mexican migrant labor, or Arab oil without Palestinians and Pakistanis? Moreover, where would the great innovative sectors of immaterial production, from design to fashion, and from electronics to science in Europe, the United States, and Asia, be without the 'illegal labor' of the great masses, mobilized toward the radiant horizons of capitalist wealth and freedom? Mass migrations have become necessary for production. Every path is forged, mapped, and traveled. It seems that the more intensely each is traveled and the more suffering is deposited there, the more each path becomes productive. These paths are what bring . . . the 'earthly city' out of the cloud and confusion that Empire casts over it. This is how the multitude gains the power to affirm its autonomy, traveling and expressing itself through an apparatus of widespread, transversal territorial reappropriation.

Recognizing the potential autonomy of the mobile multitude, however, only points toward the real question. What we need to grasp is how the multitude is organized and redefined as a positive, political power. Up to this point we have been able to describe the potential existence of this political power in merely formal terms. It would be a mistake to stop here, without going on to investigate the mature forms of the consciousness and political organization of the multitude, without recognizing how much is already powerful in these territorial movements of the labor power of Empire. How can we recognize (and reveal) a constituent political tendency within and beyond the spontaneity of the multitude's movements?

This question can be approached initially from the other side by considering the policies of Empire that repress these movements. Empire does not really know how to control these paths and can only try to criminalize those who travel them, even when the movements are required for capitalist production itself. The migration lines of biblical proportions that go from South to North America are obstinately called by the new drug czars 'the cocaine trail'; or rather, the articulations of exodus from North Africa and sub-Saharan Africa are treated by European leaders as 'paths of terrorism'; or rather still, the populations forced to flee across the Indian Ocean are reduced to slavery in 'Arabia félix'; and the list goes on. And yet the flows of population continue. Empire must restrict and isolate the spatial movements of the multitude to stop them from gaining political legitimacy. It is extremely important from this point of view that Empire use its powers to manage and orchestrate the various forces of nationalism and fundamentalism [. . .]. It is no less important, too, that Empire deploy its military and police powers to bring the unruly and rebellious to order (see De Landa 1991). These imperial practices in themselves, however, still do not touch on the political tension that runs throughout the spontaneous movements of the multitude. *All these repressive actions remain essentially external to the multitude and its movements.* Empire can only isolate, divide, and segregate. Imperial capital does indeed attack the movements of the multitude with a tireless determination: it patrols the seas and the borders; within each country it divides and segregates; and in the world of labor it reinforces the cleavages and borderlines of race, gender, language, culture, and so forth. Even then, however, it must be careful not to restrict the productivity of the multitude too much because Empire too depends on this power. The movements of the multitude have to be allowed to extend always wider across the world scene, and the attempts at repressing the multitude are really paradoxical, inverted manifestations of its strength.

This leads us back to our fundamental questions: How can the actions of the multitude become political? How can the multitude organize and concentrate its energies against the repression and incessant territorial segmentations of Empire? The only response that we can give to these questions is that the action of the multitude becomes political primarily when it begins to confront directly and with an adequate consciousness the central repressive operations of Empire. It is a matter of recognizing and engaging the imperial initiatives and not allowing them continually to reestablish order; it is a matter of crossing and breaking down the limits and segmentations that are imposed on the new collective labor power; it is a matter of gathering together these experiences of resistance and wielding them in concert against the nerve centers of imperial command.

This task for the multitude, however, although it is clear at a conceptual level, remains rather abstract. What specific and concrete practices will animate this political project? We cannot say at this point. What we can see nonetheless is a first element of a political program for the global multitude, a first political demand: *global citizenship*. During the 1996 demonstrations for the *sans papiers*, the undocumented aliens residing in France, the banners demanded 'Papiers pour tous!' Residency papers for everyone means in the first place that all should have the full rights of citizenship in the country where they live and work. This is not a utopian or unrealistic political demand. The demand is simply that the juridical status of the population be reformed in step with the real economic transformations of recent years. Capital itself has demanded the increased mobility of labor power and continuous migrations across national boundaries. Capitalist production in the more dominant regions (in Europe, the United States, and Japan, but also in Singapore, Saudi Arabia, and elsewhere) is utterly dependent on the influx of workers from the subordinate regions of the world. Hence the political demand is that the existent fact of capitalist production be recognized juridically and that all workers be given the full rights of citizenship. In effect this political demand insists in postmodernity on the fundamental modern constitutional principle that links right and labor, and thus rewards with citizenship the worker who creates capital.

This demand can also be configured in a more general and more radical way with respect to the postmodern conditions of Empire. If in a first moment the multitude demands that each state recognize juridically the migrations that are necessary to capital, in a second moment it must demand control over the movements themselves. The multitude must be able to decide if, when, and where it moves. It must have the right also to stay still and enjoy one place rather than being forced constantly to be on the move. *The general right to control its own movement is the multitude's ultimate demand for global citizenship.* This demand is radical insofar as it challenges the fundamental apparatus of imperial control over the production and life of the multitude. Global citizenship is the multitude's power to reappropriate control over space and thus to design the new cartography.

[. . .]

PART 2

Literature in the discipline

ONE OF THE CHARACTERISTICS OF LITERARY studies since the 1960s has been a tendency towards self-analysis and critique. From the high point of the so-called 'theory wars' to the more settled consensus that all criticism is necessarily theorized in some way, literary scholars have frequently been exercised about what exactly literary criticism is supposed to do and what it might be for. The proliferation of different kinds of criticism (classically enumerated in university courses on literary theory) has frequently seen scholars defined as certain kinds of critics: Feminist, New Historicist, Marxist, Post-structuralist and so on. This has been matched to a lesser extent by challenges to the idea of literature as a national category. Though degree courses in 'English Literature' are still the norm throughout the English-speaking world, there has been a growing interest in the various different literatures in English. If the idea of a settled canon has been challenged by a number of the approaches to literary study, this has only been intensified by the attention that is now paid to writing in English from places other than England. To talk, then, of English Literature as *a discipline* may be to talk of an object that is rather more settled than the actual practices on the ground. Nevertheless, this does not negate the fact that the idea of globalization, in its various forms, has recently begun to influence the thinking of literary scholars and has begun to suggest future directions that literary criticism may be persuaded, or obliged, to follow.

In Part 3 we provide some examples of attempts by critics to read specific texts through this prism. In this part, however, the essays have been selected because they demonstrate some of the ways that literary scholars have approached the question of how globalization theory might be used to inform the study of literature as whole. As a result the focus is largely on how literary studies as a discipline is reoriented by globalization as a term rather than on specific texts. One notable feature about these contributions is the fact that they have all been published in the decade since 2000 and, therefore, a good decade later than the major theorizations of globalization in

the social sciences. In comparison to other disciplines literary studies has been relatively slow to turn to the question of globalization and it is worth considering why it
might have made this move so belatedly, especially as this helps us to understand the
particular approaches that emerge from the selections below.

One obvious reason why critics have been slow to engage with the theories of
globalization as they were being developed in other disciplines is the fact that literary
studies seemed to possess, in postcolonialism and postmodernism, two prior models
for thinking about transnationalism. The prominence of these critical models for
thinking about contemporary literature, in particular, has perhaps appeared to make
a thorough exploration of globalization seem redundant. This certainly appears to be
the case for the critic Lawrence Grossberg, who has argued that the word globalization now serves as the preferred substitute for postmodernity (O'Brien and Szeman
2001, 606). Similarly, in Fredric Jameson's influential account of postmodernism,
he explicitly states that the relationship between globalisation and the postmodern is
that of base and superstructure (Jameson 1991, 5). For Jameson, the 'ideological
task' of postmodernism is to co-ordinate 'new forms of practice and social and mental habits . . . with the new forms of economic production and organisation thrown up
by the modification of capitalism – the new global division of labor' (xiv). By reading
postmodernism as the cultural expression of globalization it is possible to acknowledge globalization while retaining the existing critical vocabularies of postmodernism which have been established over the last twenty years. Indeed, some of the key
debates that characterized the heterogeneous strands of postmodern thought within
literary studies – the contested status of the commodity aesthetic, the nature of the
distinction between high and low culture, the abstraction of the sign and the fraught
apparent dematerialization of the political, the celebration of the resistance of the
local as a response to a hegemonic universal and an anxiety about an ensuing relativism – find a variety of forms in many of the essays collected in this Reader. Literary
studies' most recent responses to globalization seem to differ from the general
approaches associated with the postmodern in that they have involved an explicit
and direct engagement with the significance of the specific forms, rather than the
assumed alienating effects, of late capitalism. The language of globalization in this
context often suggests both a political engagement with the self-consciously formative discourses of a transnational late capitalist culture and the desire to name what
is either specific or new about that culture.

Postcolonial critics have likewise sought to incorporate the idea of the global
into the existing vocabulary of the field. When Patrick Williams and Laura Chrisman
included Arjun Appadurai's essay 'Global Cultural Economy' (see Chapter 4) in their
early survey of *Colonial Discourse and Post-colonial Theory*, they placed his essay in
a section that was purportedly 'theorising post-coloniality' (Williams and Chrisman
1993). Their assumption seemed to be that globalization merely contributed to postcolonialism's usual vocabulary, offering, at best, a new word to describe ideas such as
neo-colonialism that were already in play. This is especially true when theorists like
Gayatri Spivak have frequently spoken of 'the most serious of *global* questions'
(1987, x, emphasis added) or 'global economics' (218) and yet have been widely
incorporated into disciplinary practices that name themselves postcolonial. In this
vein, it is useful to note how Simon Gikandi's contribution below traces terms
like hybridity in globalization theory as a continuation of postcolonial ways of

interpreting culture. Understood in this way, globalization appears to be merely attendant upon the major narratives of transnational interrelations and history that had already been widely theorized. When globalization is thought of in these terms, it is easy to see why the critical attention that it has received has not substantially altered the shape of the field of study: globalization may offer a new terminology for talking about transnationalism but it does not alter the general structure of language used for such discussions.

The prominence of postcolonialism as a model of literary analysis gained further energy in the early years of the twenty-first century from the revitalization of the terms 'empire' and 'imperialism' as models of transnationalism that could explain globalization. During the early phases of the Anglo-American 'war on terror' commentators on both the left and the right of the political spectrum readily used the term imperialism to try and make sense of the place of the United States in contemporary international relations. The use of such language was fairly widespread and appeared in the popular media as well as political and academic debates. In 2004, for example, the BBC's World Service broadcast a six-part series entitled *The Age of Empire*, which claimed that 'the USA appears both as one of the chief advocates and beneficiaries of globalisation', leading to talk of an 'American empire' (Marcus 2004). Alongside the popular use of the terminology of imperialism, the language of empire gained new currency within academic debates, including within literary studies (see Lazarus 2006). The publication of Michael Hardt and Antonio Negri's *Empire* in 2000 prompted considerable intellectual interest within postcolonial studies (Abu-Manneh 2003; Cooppan 2006). Despite their own attempt to distinguish the theoretical category of Empire from modern imperialism, the debates over *Empire* often offered a new theoretical vitality to the language of imperialism rather than altering the frame of this debate in terms of a novel mode globalization.

It is, however, worth noting that the vocabularies of globalization and postcolonialism are not mutually exclusive and that there is some benefit to thinking about globalization from the perspective of postcolonial criticism. As the selections in this part demonstrate, the attempt to read globalization back into postcolonialism can offer a valuable means of analysing the assumptions that lie behind the terminology of the global. Well-regarded postcolonial scholars have argued that postcolonialism takes on a new significance in the face of contemporary systems of trade and governance which prioritize the international (Loomba, Kaul, et al. 2005). If Arif Dirlik has argued that postcolonialism is a 'product' of 'global capitalism' which throws 'the cover of culture over material relationships' in order to divert criticism of capitalism onto a criticism of Eurocentrism (1994, 347), he has more recently pointed out the potentials, as well as problems, of globalization's shift in the focus from colonialism to a more narrow sense of capitalist modernity (Dirlik 2002). Such claims need not collapse globalization within the colonial, although one strand of postcolonial attention to globalization has been an attempt to make visible the continuities between historical European colonization and contemporary globalization. Such an approach clearly requires a good deal of care. It is one thing to argue that 'a worldly system of exchange' predates globalization (Behdad 2006, 67). Such a claim has been widely asserted by social scientists as well as postcolonial scholars alike. However, what it ignores is that globalization is not simply a 'novel phenomenon' (Behdad 2006, 69) but is also a *discourse of novelty*. If postcolonialism has been helpful for detailing the degree to which globalization draws upon the structures of international engagement that originated in earlier periods of imperialist colonization, it has also helped to show how certain discourses of the global chime with the assumptions that governed a colonialist logic. The ideas of universalism or global-homogenization might be particularly open to this last type of critique. However, while this kind of approach to globalization is obviously attractive for postcolonial scholars it may cloud our awareness of what is distinctive or new about globalization as a way of organizing international inequalities and a mode of narrating transnational interactions. In this respect it is debatable what is gained when Paul Jay reads Edward Said's *Culture and Imperialism* as an exploration of 'literature's facilitation of economic and cultural globalization' rather than an exploration of literature's facilitation of imperialism (see below and Said 1993).

The continuing resilience and value of postcolonialism as mode for analysing contemporary literature is quite evident in the range of selections below. Many of these, in varying ways, employ aspects of postcolonial criticism to shape their understanding of the impact that globalization has had upon the field. In his contribution, Paul Jay makes much of the claim that postcolonial readings of globalization reveal the deep continuities between earlier forms of transnationalism and contemporary global modernity. In his attempt to combine Roland Robertson's view of globalization, as an enduring historical process, with postcolonial literary histories, which demonstrate the enduring contribution of non-western authors to English literature, Jay argues that globalization can transform approaches across the whole of the literary syllabus. His view of globalization is somewhat at odds with the understanding of globalization more widely prevalent in this reader. As Jay points out, the view that globalization refers to recent developments in economics, politics and the discourses of internationalism tends to limit the scope of global literary studies to contemporary literature; a fact that has governed our own choice of essays in Part 3 of this reader. By querying globalization's novelty, Jay tries to transform the study of English literature as a whole, using globalization as a way of opening up the contributions of texts from disparate places to seemingly national literary traditions. Jay's concern then is fundamentally with literary history and, if this suggests that globalization functions principally as a metaphor in his work, he is careful to argue that the relationship of texts to national traditions should be pursued 'in historical and materialist terms'. Moreover, Jay draws on earlier postcolonial criticism to remind us that literature itself contributed to economic and cultural globalization through the systems of value and exchange.

Although the view of globalization that Jay uses is different to that used in most of the essays in this part, it leads him to the somewhat typical conclusion that the yoking of globalization theory and literature will expand the canon of texts open for analysis. This view is repeated in many of the contributions here, notably by Franco Moretti. Anticipating many of the other responses to globalization in this part, Moretti imagines world literature as a structure of connection, of modular repetition, that manifests itself as endless difference rooted in local particularity. His theorization of this concept, then, can be taken to be a literary response to the questions about the interplay between the global and the local that we see occupying so many of the thinkers in Part 1. As with the other calls for an expanded canon that we see in this part, Moretti's essay serves as a challenge to the usual model of literary study which is grounded in national traditions. The continuing centrality of such national models represents a further difficulty facing those scholars trying to map out strategies for linking the study of globalization to the study of literature. To that end, it is interesting to note the disciplinary affiliations of the scholars in this part. Few of the authors whose work is included here can be placed squarely within the study of a particular national literature. Franco Moretti, Masao Miyoshi and Emily Apter all come from the discipline of Comparative Literature and, although their focus is upon specific local literatures, their disciplinary methodologies require them to seek connections between different national traditions. Similarly, although Simon Gikandi works in the department of English at Princeton, his research has mostly been carried out on African and Caribbean Literature from various nations and, in studies such as *The Cambridge History of African and Caribbean Literature*, he necessarily adopts a comparative approach. The preponderance of comparative scholars in this part may be revealing about the continuing influence of the nation as a structure for the study of literature. If, in practice, many scholars working in English Literature departments study literature from many nations, the tendency to organize literature into national groupings remains the dominant model for literary studies. While it may be reductive to read globalization as a phase of post-nationalism, as some theorists have been wont to do, the persistence of national models for literary study has served as an impediment to the engagement with globalization as a critical idea.

It would be wrong, of course, to see globalization purely in terms of the opposition between the global and the national. As Cameron and Palan have pointed out, the conceptual understanding of the nation as the unit of correspondence with the state has had a powerful influence on shaping the ways that globalization has been theorized. In the selections from Apter and Gikandi we can see different ways that this binary has been problematized in recent attempts to bring the study of globalization to bear on the study of literature. For Gikandi, literary studies' prior claim to globalization rests upon the combination of the national with universalism in Leavisite theories of literary value; theories that were widely exported through the colonial university. In Gikandi's reading, Leavis assumed his readers to share assumptions and interpretations that could be either nationally particular or globally universal. The model of literary studies which follows from this proves to be one that is capable of accommodating a transnational notion of Englishness rather than merely a parochial national one. For Gikandi a vivid demonstration of globalization has been the internationalization of archetypes for the nation and its relationship to culture. From a different perspective, Apter points to the way that, despite a growing homogenization of the global book trade, with literature increasingly sold in ways that appear to confirm theories of post-nationalism, certain nationalized identities continue to resist such homogenization by bearing the mark of irreconcilable difference. Her analysis of the question of translatability offers clues to why Algerian writers have struggled to penetrate a 'global canon', indicating that notions of cultural recognition based upon the cultural models of economically dominant nations continue to haunt claims of national obsolescence. What such models serve is actually a concentration of economic and cultural power in 'the mega-houses' of an international publishing industry.

One final reason for the apparent reluctance to abandon the terminology of post-colonialism may be a critical wariness about the dangers of adopting the languages of globalization. If, as we claimed in our general introduction, the languages of globalization are frequently used to bolster neo-liberal capitalism, it is natural to be suspicious that any use of the terminologies of globalization, even a critical one, is likely to be co-opted in the service of these economics. Such caution may lie beneath Jacques Derrida's choice of the term *mondialisation* which is partly an attempt to resist this co-option using the techniques of deconstructive criticism. Gayatri Spivak makes similar claims in *Death of a Discipline* where she proposes 'the planetary' as a substitute for globalization in order to unpick 'the gridwork of electronic capital' with the 'undivided "natural" space' of the planet (Spivak 2003, 72). Such contributions to the debate on globalization are particularly helpful for thinking about the particular contribution of literary studies to a study of globalization, of which we say more in the introduction to Part 3. Derrida is particularly concerned with the question of how to construct global affiliations and contacts without succumbing to the '*homo-hegemonizations*' of Anglo-American globalization. His essay seeks to map out a universalizing 'world contract' which does not reside in the narrow universalism of any particular culture. For him this involves unstinting resistance to contemporary globalization which relies not on '*fact* or techno-scientific knowledge-power' but on its conceptualization as globalization. From here, Derrida argues that 'the most visible and massive' resistance to the imbalances of contemporary globalization 'are linguistic'. The potential for literary criticism, a discipline which is rooted in its attention to the power and unstable qualities of language, is obvious. In slightly different ways, though to similar purpose, the planetary also emerges in Miyoshi's contribution. Here it functions not as a nominal synonym for globalization but rather as a critical imperative for literary studies in the face of impending environmental crisis. For him, this crisis is precisely the product of neo-liberal globalization which is rooted in patently unsustainable patterns of consumption. However, as he argues, it is also evident in the changing critical practices of literary studies which, following the early promptings of postcolonial criticism, moved towards an identitarian politics that is incapable of encompassing the full force of globalization. Sharing some of the early criticisms of postcolonial analysis offered by the likes of Dirlik (1994) and Aijaz Ahmad (1992), Miyoshi calls for a reclaiming of notions of totality that can counter the global economy's assertion of globality. Like other critics here, this is not a call to retreat to the nation state, which he concedes is a 'proven . . . failure'. Instead he suggests that a notion of the 'common bonds to the planet' may serve as a 'true totality that includes everyone in the world'.

Chapter 11

Franco Moretti

CONJECTURES ON WORLD LITERATURE

From *New Left Review* 1 (2000):54–64.

[. . .]

'NOWADAYS, NATIONAL LITERATURE DOESN'T mean much: the age of world literature is beginning, and everybody should contribute to hasten its advent'. This was Goethe, of course, talking to Eckermann in 1827; and these are Marx and Engels, twenty years later, in 1848: 'National one-sidedness and narrow-mindedness become more and more impossible, and from the many national and local literatures, a world literature arises'. *Weltliteratur*: this is what Goethe and Marx have in mind. Not 'comparative', but world literature: the Chinese novel that Goethe was reading at the time of that exchange, or the bourgeoisie of the *Manifesto*, which has 'given a cosmopolitan character to production and consumption in every country'. . . . . comparative literature has not lived up to these beginnings. It's been a much more modest intellectual enterprise, fundamentally limited to Western Europe, and mostly revolving around the river Rhine (German philologists working on French literature). Not much more.

This is my own intellectual formation, and scientific work always has limits. But limits change, and I think it's time we returned to that old ambition of *Weltliteratur*: after all, the literature around us is now unmistakably a planetary system. The question is not really *what* we should do – the question is *how*. What does it mean, studying world literature? How do we do it? I work on West European narrative between 1790 and 1930, and already feel like a charlatan outside of Britain or France. World literature?

Many people have read more and better than I have, of course, but still, we are talking of hundreds of languages and literatures here. Reading 'more' seems hardly to be the solution. Especially because we've just started rediscovering what Margaret Cohen calls the 'great unread'. 'I work on West European narrative, etc. . . . '. Not really, I work on its canonical fraction, which is not even one per cent of published literature. And again, some people have read more, but the point is that there are thirty thousand nineteenth-century British novels out there, forty, fifty, sixty thousand – no one really knows, no one has read them, no one ever will. And then there are French novels, Chinese, Argentinian, American . . . Reading 'more' is always a good thing, but not the solution. [. . .]

Perhaps it's too much, tackling the world and the unread at the same time. But I actually think that it's our greatest chance, because the sheer enormity of the task makes it clear that world literature cannot be literature, bigger; what we are already doing, just more of it. It has to be different. The *categories* have to be different. 'It is not the "actual" interconnection of "things" ', Max Weber wrote, 'but the *conceptual* interconnection of *problems* which define the scope of the various sciences. A new "science" emerges where a new problem is pursued by a new method'. (1949, 68) That's the point: world literature is not an object, it's a *problem*, and a problem that asks for a new critical method: and no one has ever found a method by just reading more texts. That's not how theories come into being; they need a leap, a wager – a hypothesis, to get started.

World literature: one and unequal

I will borrow this initial hypothesis from the world-system school of economic history, for which international capitalism is a system that is simultaneously one, and unequal: with a core, and a periphery (and a semiperiphery) that are bound together in a relationship of growing inequality. One, and unequal: one literature (*Weltliteratur*, singular, as in Goethe and Marx), or perhaps, better, one world literary system (of inter-related literatures); but a system which is different from what Goethe and Marx had hoped for, because it's profoundly unequal. 'Foreign debt is as inevitable in Brazilian letters as in any other field', writes Roberto Schwarz in a splendid essay on 'The Importing of the Novel to Brazil': 'it's not simply an easily dispensable part of the work in which it appears, but a complex feature of it' (1992, 50); and Itamar Even-Zohar, reflecting on Hebrew literature: 'Interference [is] a relationship between literatures, whereby a . . . source literature may become a source of direct or indirect loans [*Importing* of the novel, direct and indirect loans, foreign debt: see how economic metaphors have been subterraneously at work in literary history] – a source of loans for . . . a target literature . . . *There is no symmetry in literary interference. A target literature is, more often than not, interfered with by a source literature which completely ignores it'*. (1990, 54, 62 [brackets by Moretti])

This is what one and unequal means: the destiny of a culture (usually a culture of the periphery, as Montserrat Iglesias Santos (1994, 339) has specified) [. . .] is intersected and altered by another culture (from the core) that 'completely ignores it'. A familiar scenario, this asymmetry in international power – and later I will say more about Schwarz's 'foreign debt' as a complex literary feature. Right now, let me spell out the consequences of taking an explanatory matrix from social history and applying it to literary history.

Distant reading

Writing about comparative social history, Marc Bloch once coined a lovely 'slogan', as he himself called it: 'years of analysis for a day of synthesis' (1928); and if you read Braudel or Wallerstein you immediately see what Bloch had in mind. The text which is strictly Wallerstein's, his 'day of synthesis', occupies one third of a page, one fourth, maybe half; the rest are quotations (fourteen hundred, in the first volume of *The Modern World System*). Years of analysis; other people's analysis, which Wallerstein's page synthesizes into a system.

Now, if we take this model seriously, the study of world literature will somehow have to reproduce this 'page' – which is to say: this relationship between analysis and synthesis – for the literary field. But in that case, literary history will quickly become very different from what it is now: it will become 'second hand': a patchwork of other people's research, *without a single direct textual reading*. Still ambitious, and actually even more so than before (world literature!); but the ambition is now directly proportional *to the distance from the text:* the more ambitious the project, the greater must the distance be.

[. . .] [T]he trouble with close reading (in all of its incarnations, from the new criticism to deconstruction) is that it necessarily depends on an extremely small canon. This may have become an unconscious and invisible premiss by now, but it is an iron one nonetheless: you invest so much in individual texts only if you think that very few of them really matter. Otherwise, it doesn't make sense. And if you want to look beyond the canon (and of course, world literature will do so: it would be absurd if it didn't!) close reading will not do it. It's not designed to do it, it's designed to do the opposite. At bottom, it's a theological exercise – very solemn treatment of very few texts taken very seriously – whereas what we really need is a little pact with the devil: we know how to read texts, now let's learn how not to read them. Distant reading: where distance, let me repeat it, *is a condition of knowledge*: it allows you to focus on units that are much smaller or much larger than the text: devices, themes, tropes – or genres and systems. And if, between the very small and the very large, the text itself disappears, well, it is one of those cases when one can justifiably say, Less is more. If we want to understand the system in its entirety, we must accept losing something. We always pay a price for theoretical knowledge: reality is infinitely rich; concepts are abstract, are poor. But it's precisely this 'poverty' that makes it possible to handle them, and therefore to know. This is why less is actually more. [. . .]

The Western European novel: rule or exception?

Let me give you an example of the conjunction of distant reading and world literature. An example, not a model; and of course my example, based on the field I know (elsewhere, things may be very different). A few years ago, introducing Kojin Karatani's *Origins of Modern Japanese Literature*, Fredric Jameson noticed that in the take-off of the modern Japanese novel, 'the raw material of Japanese social experience and the abstract formal patterns of Western novel construction cannot always be welded together seamlessly'; and he referred in this respect to Masao Miyoshi's *Accomplices of Silence*, and Meenakshi Mukherjee's *Realism and Reality*; a study of the early Indian novel. (Jameson in Kojin 1993, xiii) And it's true, these books return quite often to the complicated 'problems' (Mukherjee's term) arising from the encounter of western form and Japanese or Indian reality.

Now, that the same configuration should occur in such different cultures as India and Japan – this was curious; and it became even more curious when I realized that Roberto Schwarz had independently discovered very much the same pattern in Brazil. So, eventually, I started using these pieces of evidence to reflect on the relationship between markets and forms; and then, without really knowing what I was doing, began to treat Jameson's insight as if it were – one should always be cautious with these claims, but there is really no other way to say it – as if it were a *law of literary evolution*: in cultures that belong to the periphery of the literary system (which means: almost all cultures, inside and outside Europe), the modern novel first arises not as an autonomous development but as a compromise between a western formal influence (usually French or English) and local materials.

This first idea expanded into a little cluster of laws, [. . .] and it was all very interesting, but . . . it was still just an idea; a conjecture that had to be tested, possibly on a large scale, and so I decided to follow the wave of diffusion of the modern novel (roughly: from 1750 to 1950) in the pages of literary history. Gasperetti and Goscilo on late eighteenth-century Eastern Europe (Goscilo in Krasicki 1992, 'Introduction'; Gasperetti 1998, 5); [. . .] Toschi and Martí-López on early nineteenth-century Southern Europe (Toschi 1989, 19; Martí-López 1996); [. . .] Franco and Sommer on mid-century Latin America (Franco 1969, 56; Sommer 1991, 31–32); [. . .] Frieden on the Yiddish novels of the 1860s (1995, x); [. . .] Moosa, Said and Allen on the Arabic novels of the 1870s (Said 1985, 81; Allen 1995, 12; Moosa 1997, 93); [. . .] Evin and Parla on the Turkish novels of the same years (Evin 1983, 10; Parla forthcoming); [. . .] Anderson on the Filipino *Noli Me Tangere*, of 1887 (1991); Zhao and Wang on turn-of-the-century Qing fiction (Zhao 1995, 150; Wang 1997, 5, 19); [. . .] Obiechina, Irele and Quayson on West African novels between the 1920s and the 1950s (Obiechina 1975, 17; Irele 1990, 147; Quayson 1997, 162); [. . .] (plus of course Miyoshi, Mukherjee, Even-Zohar and Schwarz). Four continents, two hundred years, over twenty independent critical studies, and they all agreed: when a culture starts moving towards the modern novel, it's *always* as a compromise between foreign form and local materials. Jameson's 'law' had passed the test – the first test, anyway. [. . .] And actually more than that: it had completely reversed the received historical explanation of these matters: because if the compromise between the foreign and the local is so ubiquitous, then those independent paths that are usually taken to be the rule of the rise of the novel (the Spanish, the French, and especially the British case) – *well, they're not the rule at all, they're the exception*. They come first, yes, but they're not at all typical. The 'typical' rise of the novel is Krasicki, Kemal, Rizal, Maran – not Defoe.

Experiments with history

See the beauty of distant reading plus world literature: they go against the grain of national historiography. And they do so in the form of *an experiment*. You define a unit of analysis (like here, the formal compromise), [. . .] and then follow its metamorphoses in a variety of environments [. . .] – until, ideally, *all* of literary history becomes a long chain of related experiments: a 'dialogue between fact and fancy', as Peter Medawar calls it: 'between what could be true, and what is in fact the case' (quoted in Bird 1993, 5). [. . .] Apt words for this research, in the course of which, as I was reading my fellow historians, it became clear that the encounter of western forms and local reality did indeed produce everywhere a structural compromise – as the law predicted – but also, that the compromise itself was taking rather different forms. At times, especially in the second half of the nineteenth century and in Asia, it tended to be very unstable: [. . .] an 'impossible program', as Miyoshi says of Japan. [. . .] At other times it was not so: at the beginning and at the end of the wave, for instance (Poland, Italy and Spain at one extreme; and West Africa on the other), historians describe novels that had, certainly, their own problems – but not problems arising from the clash of irreconcilable elements. [. . .]

I hadn't expected such a spectrum of outcomes, so at first I was taken aback, and only later realized that this was probably the most valuable finding of them all, because it showed that world literature was indeed a system – but a system *of variations*. The system was one, not uniform. The pressure from the Anglo-French core tried to make it uniform, but it could never fully erase the reality of difference. [. . .] The system was one, not uniform. And, retrospectively, of course it had to be like this: if after 1750 the novel arises just about everywhere as a compromise between West European patterns and local reality – well, local reality was different in the various places, just as western influence was also very uneven: much stronger in Southern Europe around 1800, to return to my example, than in West Africa around 1940. The forces in play kept changing, and so did the compromise that resulted from their interaction. And this, incidentally, opens a fantastic field of inquiry for comparative morphology (the systematic study of how forms vary in space and time, which is also the only reason to keep the adjective 'comparative' in comparative literature) [. . .].

[. . .]

Chapter 12

Paul Jay

BEYOND DISCIPLINE?: GLOBALIZATION AND THE FUTURE OF ENGLISH

From *PMLA* 116 (2001): 32–36, 42–44.

CAN ENGLISH SURVIVE THE GLOBALIZATION of literary studies, and if so, what will it look like? The emergence of what we have come to call global culture, characterized by the rapid circulation of cultural commodities such as books, films, works in electronic media, clothing, and food in a way that seems to overwhelm local cultural forms and practices, has come at the expense of the nation-state's ability to control the formation of national subjectivities and ideologies. The nation-state, to be sure, is alive and well as a political and military entity, and [. . .] critics who predict its imminent demise in the face of globalization are, I think, mistaken. However, it is true that cultural change in nation-states is increasingly beyond their control (with the important exception of fundamentalist states exerting rigid cultural control in the face of Westernization). Culture is now being defined in terms less of national interests than of a shared set of global ones. This shift in the cultural role of the nation-state has profound implications for its institutions, particularly its schools, colleges, and universities. Since the rise of the modern university in the West is directly linked to the development and needs of the nation-state, as a number of critics have recently argued, the globalizing of literary studies portends a remarkable reversal, one that is bound to have a deep effect on the discipline we call English (see Eagleton 1983; Graff 1987; Court 1992; Readings 1996; Miller 1999). [. . .] For in the United States, English has been at the center of a curricular world organized along the lines of a political map, the borders of which have neatly duplicated those between modern nation-states. If the conventional structures of literary study (English, French, Spanish, Italian, German, etc.) have been transparently nationalist, they mirror the aesthetic ideology of literary studies, one that can be traced to the linkage among nation, race, and literature forged in nineteenth-century Europe by writers like Hippolyte-Adolphe Taine and Matthew Arnold. In the United States Ralph Waldo Emerson and Walt Whitman articulated the need for a national literature decades before it became incorporated in the curricula of American universities. As Peter Carafiol and others have demonstrated, the structure of American literary studies in United States universities has always been informed by a broadly nationalist ideal.[1]

While this ideal was based on forging an aesthetic and ideological consensus about culture and identity grounded in a limited set of texts unified around certain themes and values, contemporary criticism has become increasingly preoccupied with difference in ways that undermine the neat, superficial cultural homogeneity informing the study of national literatures. This interest in difference developed simultaneously in the academy and in the streets, driven on the one hand by decon-structive, Marxist, and feminist theories and on the other hand by the civil rights, antiwar, women's, and gay and lesbian movements, which began to emphasize the difference racial and gender distinctions have made in American life. Deconstruction helped lay the theoretical groundwork for thinking differently about the structure and power of literary, political, and cultural discourses and in so doing contributed to the critique of dominant nationalist ideologies in British and United States litera-tures. Perhaps more important, critical theories more explicitly engaged with polit-ical issues and affiliated with social movements dating from the 1960s helped create alliances among writers, critics, and students across national and state boundaries in a way that has systematically diminished the rationale for mapping literary studies with reference to the old paradigm of homogeneous nation-states. Our awareness of the complex ways in which English and American identities have been constructed historically through migration, displacement, colonialism, exile, gender relations, and cultural hybridity has radically restructured our sense of what Paul Gilroy has dubbed the 'roots/routes' of these identities (1993, 19).

With this awareness it has become increasingly difficult to study British or American literature without situating it, and the culture(s) from which it emerged, in transnational histories linked to globalization. At the same time the remarkable explosion of English literature produced outside Britain and the United States has made it clear that this literature is becoming defined less by a nation than by a language, in which authors from a variety of cultural and ethnic backgrounds write. The globalization of English from this point of view is not a theoretical formulation or a political agenda developed by radicals in the humanities to displace the canon. It is a simple fact of contemporary history. English literature is increasingly postnational, whether written by cosmopolitan writers like Salman Rushdie, Derek Walcott, Arundhati Roy, and Nadine Gordimer or by a host of lesser-known writers working in their home countries or in diasporic communities around the world, from Europe and Africa to the Caribbean and North America. I want to argue that we can more effectively reorganize our approach to the study of what we have heretofore treated as national literatures (in our curricula and programs) by emphasizing literature's relation to the historical processes of globalization. Such a step involves rejecting the idea that globalization is a fundamentally contemporary event and recognizing that it has a long history. [. . .]

What is globalization?

To say that English literature is becoming increasingly globalized, that its contem-porary production and consumption no longer take place within discrete national borders but unfold in a complex system of transnational economic and cultural exchanges characterized by the global flow of cultural products and commodities, is not the same thing as describing how the study of literature could or should be globalized. To do that, we need to review the rise of globalization studies as a theoretical discourse and a disciplinary field. For the study of English or of literature in general cannot be globalized without a thorough understanding of the key terms, issues, and debates that have marked the rise of globalization studies, a critical movement that has only recently migrated to the arena of cultural and literary studies. [. . .]

[. . .]

In the light of the argument I want to make in favor of viewing globalization historically (rather than as a specifically postmodern phenomenon), it is important to stress that Wallerstein characterizes his modern world system as the product of a long historical process. Many globalization theorists would say that this trait significantly distinguishes his world system theory from theories of globalization, which often equate globalization with postmodernity and insist that it marks a rupture or break with modernity. But in fact globalization theorists are divided on this question, and it is an important one to consider when we think about the globalization of literary studies. If globalization is fundamentally a contemporary or postmodern phenomenon, then it would seem to offer us a way to rethink the study mainly of recent (and emerging) literatures. But if globalization is a long historical process that has dramatically accelerated in recent years, then the globalization of literary studies cannot restrict itself to this contemporary acceleration. Literature's relation to the processes of globalization as they manifest themselves in a variety of historical periods – indeed, literature's facilitation of economic and cultural globalization – is becoming a potentially important field of study that might get short-circuited if we think of globalization only as a postmodern eruption (see Said 1993). [. . .]

[. . .]

With the differences among Robertson [1992], Giddens [1990] and Harvey [1990] in mind, we can see that the question of what globalization is turns out to be inextricably linked to how it is historicized. Robertson's view of globalization is fundamentally different from Giddens's and Harvey's, and [. . .] each one offers us a different context for thinking about how to globalize literary study. Following Robertson, the globalizing of literary studies would engage literatures and cultures from nearly every period, while if, with Giddens and Harvey, we conceive of globalization as a specifically modern or postmodern phenomenon, we would focus primarily on the literatures of the late nineteenth and the twentieth centuries. Which of these points of view is correct? While the arguments Giddens and Harvey make about the acceleration of globalization in the late twentieth century are important, it seems to me that Robertson's approach is the more accurate one and that it offers wider opportunities for those of us in literary studies interested in the intersection of globalization and literary and cultural production. Although it would be a mistake not to acknowledge that a set of explosive forces unleashed in the last half of the twentieth century have radically revised transnational exchange, it would be an even bigger mistake not to contextualize these changes in a longer historical view of globalization like the one Robertson offers. Globalization can certainly help us map the future of literary studies, but it also provides an important way to rethink our approach to the study of literature across a range of historical periods.

[. . .]

Conclusion: Globalizing literary studies

[. . .] As Susan Stanford Friedman has written, we need to resist 'simplistically universalist and binarist narratives' as we think about globalizing the study of literature; we must undertake the more 'difficult negotiation between insistence on multidirectional flows of power in [a] global context and continued vigilance about specifically western forms of domination' (1998, 6 [brackets by Jay]). This would clearly involve looking at local cultures outside the West not as the passive recipients of mass culture but as sites of transformation or even active resistance. However, this does not mean simply reasserting the autonomy of the local over against the global. The trap here is that we may perpetuate a simple-minded binarism that facilely and uncritically celebrates the local as pure culture opposed to rapacious Westernization. The stress, rather, ought to be on the multidirectionality of cultural flows, on the appropriation and transformation of globalized cultural forms wherever they settle in, with close attention to how those forms are reshaped and sent off again to undergo further transformations elsewhere. This work will take on increasing urgency as globalization accelerates and these processes remake English into something altogether new and more complicated.

We need to continue to reorganize the study of literature in ways that move us beyond the outmoded nationalist paradigm in which we still operate and that highlight how during various periods literature has been caught up in the multidirectional flows Friedman identifies. This does not mean we should abandon the study of literary texts and cultural practices in their relation to the modern nation-state. That study, however, ought to concentrate on the relation in historical and materialist terms. We ought to focus less on identifying what seems inherently English or American in the literatures we teach and write about and more on understanding the functional relation between literature and the nation-state, how literary writing has been theorized and politicized in efforts to define and empower nation-states, especially from the Enlightenment onward. This kind of approach must give primary attention to the historical role literature has had in global systems of cultural exchange and recognize that this exchange has always been multidirectional. With the understanding that globalization is a long historical process, we can usefully complicate our nation-based approach to the study of English, not by dropping the nation-state paradigm but by foregrounding its history and its function *for* the nation-state, insisting that our students come to understand the instrumental role literature has played in the complicated world of transnational political and cultural relations.

[. . .]

Our desire to rethink the connections among literature, nationalism, and cultural identity in the context of ever-expanding transnational relations is only the latest in a series of developments suggesting that *English* has become a confusing descriptive or organizing term for literary study in the United States. *English* more and more simply refers to the language in which the texts we teach and write about are written, and this trend is bound to accelerate as transnational literatures in English proliferate. It might be argued that this is a recent phenomenon, that only in the last quarter of the twentieth century did English begin to undergo the transformations I have been discussing. But as Robertson's approach to globalization suggests, Western literature has been caught up in the transnational flow of commodities and cultures at least since the rise of trade and colonial expansion (George 1996; Gikandi 1996). We need to bring this transnational perspective to how we present the history of literature in the West, moving away from a traditional division of discrete national literatures into ossified literary-historical periods and giving the history of global expansion, trade, and intercultural exchange precedence in our curriculum over the mapping of an essentially aestheticized national character. In this model the older, nationalist paradigm for literary study would cease to stand at the center of the discipline and would become an object of study among others in a field that spent more time teaching its students about the history of the discipline, which after all has shifted remarkably since the late nineteenth century in ways that until recently we kept hidden from our students. Indeed, fostering a more programmatic self-consciousness about the history of the discipline, what Terry Eagleton long ago termed 'the rise of English' (1983, 17–53), can provide one of the best safeguards against the danger that English will end up subordinate to an outworn nationalist paradigm that seeks to colonize world literatures in English. The more we emphasize the historically constructed, politically and culturally interested nature of literary studies, the easier it will be to avoid putting British or United States English at its center and to prevent it from being disconnected from the history of transnational cultural politics. This danger can also be mitigated by a commitment to putting knowledge about the social, cultural, and political history informing global literatures in English ahead of our ingrained impulse to read them through the lens of Western theoretical and critical idioms.

[. . .] Globalization studies in the culturalist mode [. . .] provides a context for studying literary texts and works in other media not simply as aesthetic objects but also as cultural objects caught up in complex systems of transnational and intercultural exchange, appropriation, and transformation. It offers a context, in particular, for dealing with the proliferation of English literatures written in diasporic conditions, literatures that would otherwise be assimilated to a narrow, nationalist paradigm ('Anglo-Indian' or 'Asian American'). The expansion of diasporic English dramatically underscores the sense in which contemporary writing is produced in a postnational, global flow of deterritorialized cultural products appropriated, translated, and recirculated worldwide. Whether we keep working under the increasingly ambiguous concept of English or develop new terms and paradigms to describe what we do, we need to find a way to accommodate the transnational and postnational perspectives of globalization studies in our programs and curricula without subordinating the heterogeneous literatures we deal with to outdated critical paradigms.

[. . .]

Note

1   For critical discussions of the role of nationalism in American literary studies, see Carafiol (1991); G. Jay (1991); Porter (1994); P. Jay (1998). On American literature and globalization, see Buell (1994; 1998).

Chapter 13

Simon Gikandi

GLOBALIZATION AND THE CLAIMS OF POSTCOLONIALITY

From *The South Atlantic Quarterly* 100 (2001): 627–33, 636, 638–40, 643–58

GLOBALIZATION AND *POSTCOLONIALITY* are perhaps two of the most important terms in social and cultural theory today. Since the 1980s, they have functioned as two of the dominant paradigms for explaining the transformation of political and economic relationships in a world that seems to become increasingly interdependent with the passing of time, with boundaries that once defined national cultures becoming fuzzy. The debates on globalization and postcolonialism are now so universal in character, and the literature on these topics is so extensive, that they are difficult to summarize or categorize. And to the extent that it dominates most debates on the nature of society and economy in the social sciences, globalization must be considered one of the constitutive elements of disciplines such as anthropology and sociology. Similarly, it is difficult to conceive an area of literary studies, from medievalism to postmodernism, that is not affected by debates on postcolonial theory and postcoloniality. While diverse writers on globalization and postcolonialism might have differing interpretations of the exact meaning of these categories, or their long-term effect on the institutions of knowledge production in the modern world, they have at least two important things in common: they are concerned with explaining forms of social and cultural organization whose ambition is to transcend the boundaries of the nation-state, and they seek to provide new vistas for understanding cultural flows that can no longer be explained by a homogenous Eurocentric narrative of development and social change. For scholars trying to understand cultural and social production in the new millennium, globalization is attractive both because of its implicit universalism and its ability to reconcile local and global interests. Furthermore, globalization is appealing to social analysts because of what is perceived as its conjunctive and disjunctive form and function. [. . .] the language that enables conjuncture or disjunction – hybridity and cultural transition, for example – comes directly from the grammar book of postcolonial theory. In this sense, one could argue that what makes current theories of globalization different from earlier ones, let's say those associated with modernization in the 1950s and 1960s, is their strategic deployment of postcolonial theory.

Besides their shared cultural grammar, however, the relationship between globalization and postcoloniality is not clear; neither are their respective meanings or implications. Is postcoloniality a consequence of the globalization of culture? Do the key terms in both categories describe a general state of cultural transformation in a world where the authority of the nation-state has collapsed or are they codes for explaining a set of amorphous images and a conflicting set of social conditions? The discourse of globalization is surrounded by a rhetoric of newness, but what exactly are the new vistas that these terms provide analysts of societies and cultures that have acquired a transnational character? Is globalization a real or virtual phenomenon? Where do we locate postcoloniality – in the spaces between and across cultures and traditions or in national states, which, in spite of a certain crisis of legitimacy, still continue to demand affiliation from their citizens and subjects? These questions are made even more urgent by the realization that while we live in a world defined by cultural and economic flows across formally entrenched national boundaries, the world continues to be divided, in stark terms, between its 'developed' and 'underdeveloped' sectors. It is precisely because of the starkness of this division that the discourse of globalization seems to be perpetually caught between two competing narratives, one of celebration, the other of crisis.

From one perspective, globalization appears to be a sign of the coming into being of a cultural world order that questions the imperial cartography that has defined global relations since the early modern period. Globalization constitutes, in this regard, what Appadurai calls 'a complex overlapping, disjunctive order that cannot any longer be understood in terms of existing center-periphery models' (1996, 32). And for those who might argue that globalization is simply the Westernization or Americanization of the world, Appadurai makes a crucial distinction between older forms of modernity, whose goal was the rationalization of the world in Weberian terms, [and] the symbolic economy of a new global culture based on reciprocal rather than nonlinear relationships[.]

[. . .]

Clearly, globalization appeals to advocates of hybridity [. . .] because it seems to harmonize the universal and the particular and, in the process, it seems to open up to a multiplicity of cultural relationships unheard of in the age of empire: for Bhabha, the globalization of social spaces reflects a state of 'unsatisfaction' that, nevertheless, enables the articulation and enunciation of 'a global or transnational imaginary and its "cosmopolitan subjectivities"' (1994, 204); for Pieterse, it is through hybridity that globalization works against 'homogenization, standardization, cultural imperialism, westernization, Americanization' (1998, 76).

Nevertheless, this optimistic and celebratory view of globalization, which is particularly pronounced in postcolonial studies because it uses the lexicon that postcolonial theory makes available to us, is constantly haunted by another form of globalization, one defined by a sense of crisis within the postcolony itself. Unsure how to respond to the failure of the nationalist mandate, which promised modernization outside the tutelage of colonialism, citizens of the postcolony are more likely to seek their global identity by invoking the very logic of Enlightenment that postcolonial theory was supposed to deconstruct. For me, there is no better representation of this *other* desire for globalization within the logic of Enlightenment than the . . .

letter left behind by two Guinean boys whose dead bodies were found in the cargo hold of a plane in Brussels in August 1998[.][1] [. . .] Although the Guinean boys may now appear to be signs of those others who have been left out of the global dream of prosperity, there is no disputing the fact that the globalization that they had in mind when they became stowaways on the European plane was different from that espoused by postcolonial theorists. The boys were neither seeking cultural hybridity nor ontological difference. Their quest was for a modern life in the European sense of the world; their risky journey from Africa was an attempt to escape both poverty and alterity; it was predicated on the belief that their salvation could only come from that Europe which, only two generations earlier, black nationalists such as Jomo Kenyatta and Aimé Césaire had declared to be the major threat to the prosperity and well-being of Africa (Césaire 1955, 24–25; Kenyatta [1938] 1962, 305–6).

Now, my primary interest in this discussion is not to adjudicate between the celebratory narrative of globalization and the more dystopic version represented in the letter by the Guinean boys; it is not even my intention to rationalize the actions of Africans who die seeking the dream of a European identity in very colonial and Eurocentric terms. On the contrary, I am interested in using these contrasting views of globalization to foreground at least three closely related problems, which, I believe, call into question many of the claims motivating the theoretical literature on globalization and its relations to postcoloniality.

The first problem arises from the realization that when social scientists try to differentiate older forms of globalization (located solidly within the discourse of colonialism and modernization) from the new forms structured by hybridity and difference, they often tend to fall back on key words borrowed from postcolonial theory. Although some of these key words – the most prominent are *hybridity* and *difference* – have been popular in literary studies since the 1970s, they have been shunned by empirical social scientists who decry the lack of the conceptual foundations that might make them useful analytical categories (e.g., Robertson 1990, 15–30). At the same time, however, social scientists eager to turn globalization into the site of what Pieterse calls 'conceptual renewal' have found the language of postcolonial theory indispensable to their project (1998, 75). In the first part of my discussion, I will argue that part of the attraction of postcolonial theory to questions of globalization lies precisely in its claim that culture, as a social and conceptual category, has escaped 'the bounded nation-state society' and has thus become the common property of the world (Featherstone 1990, 2). This point is made power-fully by Bhabha when he asserts that the postcolonial perspective represents a critical departure from 'the traditions of sociology of underdevelopment and dependency theory'; as a mode of analysis, postcolonial theory disavows any nationalist or nativist pedagogy that sets up the relations of third world and first world in a binary structure of opposition, recognizing that the social boundaries between first and third worlds are far more complex (1991, 63).

The second problem concerns the rather optimistic claim that the institutions of cultural production provide irrefutable evidence of new global relations. It is important here to note that when advocates of the new global order, most promin-ently Appadurai and Bhabha, talk about globalization, they conceive it almost exclusively in cultural terms; but it is premature to argue that the images and narratives that denote the new global culture are connected to a global structure or that they are disconnected from earlier or older forms of identity. In other words, there is no reason to suppose that the global flow in images has a homological connection to transformations in social or cultural relationships. My interest here, then, is on the disjuncture between the emergence of global images and the global stories of global subjects, like the two Guinean boys, who are not concerned with ideas or images, but are focused on the material experiences of everyday life and survival. Global images have a certain salience for students of culture, especially postmodern culture, but this does not mean that they are a substitute for material experiences. In regard to cultural images, my argument is that we cannot stop at the site of their contemplation; rather, as Mike Featherstone has noted, we 'need to inquire into the grounds, the various generative processes, involving the formation of cultural images and traditions' (1990, 2).

The last problem [. . .] concerns the premature privileging of literary texts – and the institutions that teach them – as the exemplars of globalization. No doubt, the most powerful signs of the new process of globalization come from literary texts and other works of art. For critics looking for the sign of hybridity, heterogeneity, and newness in the new world order, there cannot be a better place to go than Salman Rushdie's *Satanic Verses* or Gabriel García Márquez's *Cien años de soledad*. Such works are now considered world texts because, as Franco Moretti has argued, they have a frame of reference that is 'no longer the nation-state, but a broader entity – a continent, or the world-system as a whole' (1996, 50). Surprisingly, however, no reading of these seminal texts is complete without an engagement with the nation-state, its history, its foundational mythologies, and its quotidian experiences. To the extent that they seek to deconstruct the foundational narrative of the nation, these are world texts; yet they cannot do without the framework of the nation. What needs to be underscored here, then, is the persistence of the nation-state in the very literary works that were supposed to gesture toward a transcendental global culture. I will conclude my discussion by arguing that one of the great ironies of the discourse of globalization is that although English literature has become the most obvious sign of transnationalism, it is continuously haunted by its historical – and disciplinary – location in a particular national *ethos* and *ethnos*. What are we going to do with those older categories – nation, culture, and English – which function as the absent structure that shapes and yet haunts global culture and the idea of literature itself?

[. . .]

[W]hatever reservations we may have about postcolonial theory, we need to recognize that the postcolonial perspective on globalization has been the most salient attempt to question older forms of globalization based on the centrality of the nation and theories of modernization. My claim is that a postcolonial theory of globalization involves a rethinking of the temporality of colonial and national modernity. A key argument in the works of postcolonial scholars such as Appadurai, Bhabha, and Hall is that it is in the process of understanding cultural margins and marking social difference that Eurocentric time and its symbolic economies are dispersed and undone. One of the central ironies of 'the politics of global flows' in the areas of cultural production, claims Appadurai, is that it plays havoc 'with the hegemony of Eurochronology' (1996, 30). In addition, postcolonial theories of globalization insist that this displacement of European time – and modernity in general – takes place in the arena of art, culture or, more appropriately, the imaginary.

[. . .]

[G]lobal culture linked with postmodernism (the subject of postcolonial theory) has brought us to a point where the traditional association between national spaces and cultural practices cannot be sustained: there no longer seems to be a clear relationship between cultural practices and localities. One is as likely to come across Santeria worship in Miami as in Havana. One can watch and enjoy reruns of *Dallas* in Dallas and in the highlands of Kenya. In these circumstances, it doesn't seem to make sense to argue that there is a homological relationship between nations and cultures. Where culture seems to supersede nation, or to be at odds with its claims, then the postcolonial solution sketched above is appealing because, by making *culture* the primary term in the relationship between 'life' and its 'images', it is much easier to have a handle on a world in which social realities and cultural representations seemed to be out of joint. This is how postcolonial theories of globalization come to valorize the image and the imaginary[.]

[. . .]

But the letter from the Guinean boys provides us with another, more problematic narrative of globalization, one driven by impossible dreams and mediated by not simply the new media, but also older narratives about civilization and development. And it is the existence of this other narrative of death and decay, unwittingly tied to Enlightenment and rationality and tormented by the brutal realities of poverty, that seems to suggest that contrary to the optimistic view expressed by Appadurai and others, globalization might, after all, be a discourse of failure and atrophy. In short, there seems to be a powerful disjuncture between the global narratives and images that attract postcolonial critics and another set of narratives and images which do not exactly fit into a theoretical apparatus that seems bent on difference and hybridity. Postcolonial literature is not, of course, deaf to the disjuncture between its performance of a global culture and the persistence of this other, darker, older narrative of poverty, of failed nationalism, of death, that will simply not go away. Postcolonial theorists may have sought to forget the nation in order to become global, but the nation has not forgotten them. One of the most disturbing aspects of the *Satanic Verses*, for example, is the way it seems to call its upbeat rhetoric of globalization into question by privileging a moment of closure associated with forces – *nation* and *patria* – that the novel had ostensibly set out to undo in its search for newness. Why does a 'world' text, one committed to blasphemy and transgression, resort to a romantic closure that affirms the very site of identity that it had set out to undo? In order to answer this question we need to rethink modes of reading and analysis that are focused so much on the familiar tropes of postcolonial theory – globalization, transgression, and hybridity – that they fail to take notice of unfamiliar, but equally powerful, local scenes of being and belonging.

In 'Reading the *Satanic Verses*', Spivak makes two points that are central to the critique of postcolonial theories of globalization that I want to develop in the second part of my discussion: first, she notes that 'the *Satanic Verses*, in spite of all its plurality, has a rather aggressive theme: the postcolonial divided between two identities: migrant and national' (1993, 219). Second, she notes that 'because the migrant as paradigm is a dominant theme in theorizations of postcoloniality, it is easy to overlook Rushdie's resolute effort to represent contemporary India' (1993, 221). In my discussion, I have suggested that postcolonial theories of globalization have been influential in the mapping of global culture because they have appeared to be focused on tropes that speak powerfully to the experience of migration.

The downside to this focus on migrancy and its images, however, is that the national has tended to be negated, although it is indeed one of the enabling conditions of the trope of migration in the first place. I agree with Spivak that Rushdie's resolute effort to represent contemporary India is overlooked in readings of his novel. But the issue I want to pursue here is not why the national and the local is overlooked in postcolonial theories of global culture and its literature, but the larger questions that are elided in the process. Let me frame the problem this way: since stories about dead Africans in cargo holds of European planes cannot be read as stories of hybridity, diaspora, or métissage, they demand a rethinking of the tropes that have dominated the discourse of postcolonial theory in relation to both global culture and nationalism.

[. . .]

Is it possible . . . that we are eager to embrace globalization and its images or fictions because of its amorphous character? This question comes from two directions. From the perspective of the boys from Guinea, who are represented in this discussion as representatives of hundreds of other migrants who die every day trying to get 'there' to be 'like you', the identification with globality is not ethical but material; they do not seek to occupy the interstitial spaces between nations and cultures, but to leave what they consider to be a failed polity for a successful one. From the perspective of an influential group of social scientists, the problem here is not so much the experience of globalization but the way it is represented in postcolonial theory. There are two main complaints here: the first one is that the more the key words in postcolonial theories of globalization, most prominently *hybridity*, become ubiquitous, the more they become diffuse and meaningless (Pieterse 1998, 77). The other complaint is that the emphasis on culture in postcolonial theory hinders the recognition of the global experience as a structural experience (produced out of the complex interaction of politics, economics, the social, and the like). As long as globalization is conceived as a cultural rather than a structural experience, it functions as what Roland Robertson has called 'a site of social theoretical interests, interpretative indulgence, or the display of world-ideological preferences'; considered as an aggregate of local experiences in displacement rather than a structure patterned by causal relationships, the culture of globalization cannot account for 'the global-human condition' (1990, 16, 17). Still, there is no guarantee that a rigorous analysis of social structures will give us any more insights into the immigrants who die in European cargo planes or the sweatshops of New York or Los Angeles, for as Fredric Jameson's acute observation of the chasm between realities and representations has revealed, there is always the possibility that 'the sense people have of themselves and their own moment of history may ultimately have nothing whatsoever to do with its reality' (1991, 281). Is it possible that the citizens of the new diasporic spheres live through experiences that are 'wildly at odds from their own inner experiences and their interior daily life' (1991, 282)?

Ultimately, what is at issue here is not that certain forms of globalization are more compelling than others but that many of the codes we use to explain the global phenomenon can be anterior to the people who live through the transnational experience. Like the legendary subalterns of colonial culture, the majority of the postcolonial subjects who live through the experience of globalization cannot speak. And when they speak, they sometimes speak a language that is alien to their liberal sympathizers or the postcolonial émigré elite. Quite often, close encounters with the new migrants in the West challenge liberal sentiments at the core: What do we do when we discover that the subaltern element in the new diasporas, instead of adopting the cosmopolitanism beloved of the postcolonial elite, continues to demand the most fundamentalist forms of cultural identification? What are we to say when Muslims demand Sharia Law in Bradford or when Somali migrants in Seattle (or North Africans in Paris) insist that 'circumcising' their daughters is crucial to their identity?

I use these extreme – but quite real – examples to call attention to two significant shortcomings in both the cultural and structural explanations of globalization I mentioned earlier: one of the central shortcomings in these theories is that in their desire to secure the newness of theories of globalization, to posit them as postmodern and postcolonial as it were, many critics and analysts of the phenomenon no longer seem interested in the 'Third World' itself as a source of the cultural energies – and the tragedies – that have brought the new migrants to the West. In insisting on the newness of the global, either as a set of structural patterns determined by the narrative of capital, or as a set of images mediated by the new media, analysts tend to forget that what we are calling the new global culture represents less the transformation of the meaning of the imaginary in the modern world than a reorganization of what Mary Douglas calls 'the stock of knowledge' that helps us mediate or explain social experiences (1995, 13).

In addition, it is easily assumed that globalization is primarily a mode of transformation of cultural or structural relations in the West itself. And yet, global culture is a result of the transformations in both 'First' and 'Third Worlds', and especially a transformation of the institutions of knowledge production, and even the enunciative situations, in both zones. Simply put, what has happened in the aftermath of the crisis of decolonization and the collapse of modern institutions of knowledge production in much of the so-called Third World is that the arena in which the meaning of cultural practices is determined has shifted, as has the speech community in which, to cite Douglas, claims and counterclaims about the meaning of texts are made (1995, 13). The rise of the new globalism, like the denotative shift from 'Third World' to 'Postcolonial', reflects a significant shift in the speech community in which claims about colonialism and nationalism are introduced and discussed.

[. . .]

The last point I want to take up in this essay concerns the privileging of literary texts – the disciplines that teach them – as the exemplars of globalization. For if my discussion so far seems to be caught between the claims of social scientists and literary critics, it is because the two 'guilds' of scholarship have been locked in a surreptitious struggle to map out and redefine globalization. [. . .]

[. . .] Literary scholars, previously marginalized in debates on globalization, development, and modernization because their preoccupations had ostensibly nothing to do with concrete historical or political experiences, could now claim that they were better suited – and trained – to talk about images than social scientists were. Powerful literary traditions – in English and French, for example – were now positioned to claim that, under the guise of Anglophone literature or Francophonie, their projects had always been global. At the bare bottom, postcolonial theory is the assertion of the centrality of the literary in the diagnosis and representation of the social terrain that we have been discussing under the sign of globalization.

But the claim that English literary studies, to use the example I am most familiar with, were global because they originated in the colonial periphery or were an important part of a linguistic commonwealth calls attention to the paradoxical relation between the discipline and its national and colonial origins. From its beginnings in India, Africa, or Scotland, English has been a discipline that has been defined and shadowed by a double paradox, a paradox that has to be located in the history of the English language and the incorporation of English literature itself into the national curriculum. Consider this: of all the European language literary traditions, English literature is the most global; and yet, wherever it has traveled English has been defined in exclusively national, some might say chauvinistic, terms. This is the first paradox. The second paradox is that in the United States and, more recently, in Britain, English departments have come to be perceived as the custodians of globalization in the university; in real terms, however, these institutions tend to consider English literatures other than British and American as secondary to what they consider to be their main task – the teaching of the literature of England (and, sometimes, that of the United States, considered to be an extension of Englishness across the Atlantic). At the same time, however, we cannot underestimate the role of English as the discipline in which many of the major questions regarding globalization [. . .] are formulated. The turn to culture in global studies [. . .] can clearly be attributed to postcolonial scholars such as Edward Said, Bhabha, and Spivak, whose work is located in English. [. . .]

But the rhetoric of globalization inherent in English studies, especially in the aftermath of postcolonial theory, conceals a history and practice that has strongly resisted the expansion of the discipline beyond the boundaries of England. Even when practitioners of English are committed to expanding its horizons, they increasingly seem unable to break out of the organization of the discipline in terms of a set of texts and periods that assume the centrality of England in the business of doing English. One does not need to provide statistics to show that the common periodization of English studies into epochs such as Medieval, Renaissance, Augustan, or Victorian only makes sense if the organization of the discipline is pegged to a certain national history of England. The predominance of this national structure is sometimes easy to ignore, either because certain writers, mostly from minority communities in the metropolitan centers, have been allowed into the canon of Englishness, or because certain spaces have been created for what Spivak has aptly described as the postcolonial ghetto, which is cited as evidence of the new global English studies (2000b, 1). Having one's own ghetto might not be a bad thing after centuries of exclusion, but still we need to keep on recalling that time not so long ago when English departments were considered to be the showcases of national culture and European civilization. [. . .] Before we laud English departments for championing globalization, we need to account for this resistance to the Englishness of the other. We need, in particular, to pose the question of why the national paradigm continues to shape literary studies in the age of globalization.

English studies may have started elsewhere, in Africa, in India, on the Celtic fringe, but as numerous studies have shown, once the discipline became established at the center of the university, and as it began to be celebrated as a field that was central to the life of the modern national subject, its institution of exegesis was wrapped up in some of the most essentialist forms of the national imagination (Baldick 1983; Doyle 1989; Viswanathan 1989; Court 1989; Gikandi 1996; Crawford 1998; Easthope 1999). [. . .] This accounts for the ironic fact that when English spread across the global sphere, it did not travel as a theoretical category that could be transposed and transmuted, but as a social phenomen[on] whose claims would only be translated from one tradition to another in nationalist terms. Thus, when a group of African intellectuals called for the abolition of the English department at the University of Nairobi in 1968, to cite one famous example, their onslaught was directed not at the institution of English itself or how the discipline was taught, but at its inability to be anchored in local traditions and its valorization of alienation rather than local identity. Debates about literature in Africa throughout the 1960s and 1970s were not about the rethinking of the idea of the literary, but attempts to show that African literature in English could make the same exclusive claims that F. R. Leavis had made for English literature in England (Ngugi 1972, 145–50; Sicherman 1995; Gikandi 2000). Now, the Leavises may not have had a direct effect on the transformation of English in the United States, but the Anglo-Saxonism they had inherited from Mathew Arnold was at the very heart of the organization of literary studies in North America from the Yale of the New Critics to the Agrarianism of the Sewanee Review. It is not, hence, an exaggeration to say that the Leavises' influence went beyond the centers where their disciples reigned (the British provincial universities and the colonies) and that it shadowed – and continues to shadow – the study of English literature caught between nationalism and globalization.

[. . .]

. . . [M]y concern here is [. . .] how [Leavis] associated the study of English literature with a particular set of institutions and practices, such as the university and culture, which became, paradoxically, influential in the postcolonial world because of their ability to invoke the national and the universal (or global) in the same discourse. The consequence of this legacy is a startling ambiguity: English literature is simultaneously one of the most universal cultural phenomena, a pantheon that can be traced all the way from the Outer Hebrides of Scotland to Suva in Fiji, but English is also one of the most parochial disciplines, constantly associated with very provincial geographies and concerns. I am interested in how Leavis enabled this paradox and why it continues to plague the discipline today.

One important way of coming to terms with this ambiguity is to recall Perry Anderson's important observation that Leavis's critical oeuvre 'rested on a metaphysics which he could never expound or defend', and that his obsession with the notion of the nation as an 'organic community' reflected his inability to understand literary or cultural difference (1992, 98). From a colonial and postcolonial perspective, however, the enigma of Leavis was precisely that he was able to produce a mode of discourse that was so parochial in its concern with Englishness as a specific British product and still able to exert a lasting influence in colonial and postcolonial worlds where one might have expected all things English to be under nationalist challenge. [. . .] It is my contention that Leavis's appeal in the colonial world, his global aura as it were, depended both on his aphilosophical method (which enabled him to represent the institutions of literature and exegesis as natural and commonsensical) and his refusal to make literary or cultural difference central to his concerns. By talking about English literature as the product of a natural process inherent in the character of the English nation and people, Leavis was clearly an advocate of the mentality of an insular England; but by ignoring difference altogether, he created a grammar, which turned it into a free-floating cultural object. In other words, he made it possible for his postcolonial successors to substitute for England the new nation that had emerged from decolonization – Kenya, Nigeria, Jamaica, or India. [. . .]

[. . .]

In retrospect, the discipline of English literature at the colonial university was an important precursor to the theories of globalization discussed in . . . my essay. Significantly, in Leavis's schema, the universality of the university was intimately connected to what used to be known as literary criticism, for in order to represent the value and meaning of English literature as self-evident, and its attendant moral questions as de facto (as the only questions to consider), Leavis assumed that the values of English literature were 'there', uniform, inherent in our modes of being and unaffected by local circumstances or histories. The implicit claim here was that even students in colonial universities, such as Makerere and Ibadan in Africa, could be trained to read culture and morality in literary texts the same way that these tropes were read at University College, London, the 'mother' institution. In Leavis's discourse on the university, then, English literature was connected, through the institution of criticism, to the idea of a national community; but it was also through criticism, the act of making interpretative and moral judgments, that the mission of English became universal. Leavis's pronouncements on the university thus brought the national and the universal together in unexpected ways: 'The real university is the center of consciousness and human responsibility for the civilized world; it is a creation center of civilization – for the living heritage on which meaning and humane intelligence depend can't, in our time, be maintained without a concentrated creativity somewhere' (1969, 3).

Here, as elsewhere, Leavis took it for granted that values or notions such as consciousness, civilization, and human responsibility were embedded in the character of the English nation and that English literature was a mark of its civilizational drive and achievement. At the same time, however, Leavis's discourse had left itself open to universalism: terms such as *the real university*, *center of consciousness*, and even *civilization* had such a broad meaning that they could easily enter the language of postcolonial nationalism and provide the key terms in the grammar of cultural decolonization. Although Leavis had anchored his terms in an implicit national context, he had generalized them so much that they had become free-floating signifiers. The *real university* could be a university anywhere in the colonial world. More significantly, the idea of the university was simultaneously connected to local and universal concerns. As Bill Readings notes in *The University in Ruins*, while the university might be posited as the safeguard of the state or national cultural interest, it is also mandated to perform an idealistic mission beyond its quotidian function: 'The University . . . is not simply an instrument of state policy; rather, the University must embody thought as action, as striving for an ideal' (1996, 69).

But how is Leavis's idea of a university education, one rooted in English studies, connected to the emergence of the postcolonial theories of globalization that opened my discussion? In two powerful ways: first, the university – and the study of English that was privileged within it – was one of the most powerful instruments of producing elites in both Britain and its (post)colonies. One of the little known sociological facts about the origins of postcolonial literature and theory is that the study of English literature was crucial in establishing relationships between elites functioning at different spheres of social life and in a variety of postcolonial sectors. What do Homi Bhabha and Arjun Appadurai have in common? They share a common

English education at the elite Elphinstone College in Bombay (Bhabha 1995, 245; Appadurai 1996, 2). [. . .] Bhabha, Rushdie, and Zadie Smith read English at Oxford or Cambridge. We can assume that the texts Spivak was reading at the University of Calcutta were not very different from the ones Wole Soyinka was reading at University College, Ibadan. These relationships can be extended to the domain of politics itself: Bhabha and Thabo Mbeki, the South African president, may not appear to have much in common apart from their colonial backgrounds, but they both read English at Sussex, Mbeki as an undergraduate, Bhabha as a graduate student. Ben Mpaka, the president of Tanzania, read English at Makerere University College in the same years as Ngugi wa Thiong'o, the radical Kenyan novelist, and Susie Tharu (née Oomen), the distinguished Indian feminist literary critic. [. . .] Unwittingly, the university in Britain and its colonies had created the structure in which postcoloniality would come to be produced both as an experience and a discourse; and in all these cases the (post)colonial university was committed to the Leavis project in one form or another. [. . .] In these circumstances, what makes Indian worlds accessible to Africans and Britons, and vice versa, more than any real encounters in the cities of the 'First' or 'Third' Worlds, are the texts of Englishness and the experiences embodied in them.

The second point can be made by recalling [. . .] that the new theories and forms of globalization are differentiated from the older sociological ones by the centrality accorded to culture in the analysis of global experiences. It is my contention that the unprecedented valorization of culture in general, and literary culture in particular, in postcolonial theories of globalization, is indebted to the Leavises' project. Like Arnold before him, Leavis established the idea that culture provided a bulwark against materialism in general and industrialization in particular, and that literature was at the heart of what we understood culture to be; where material changes led to ruptures within the presumed organic community of the nation, the poetic tradition represented the 'continuity of cultural consciousness' (1969, 43).

And yet the argument that culture is the symptom of a new global order has to contend with a difficult question embedded in the Leavis project: How could culture, an idea so powerfully embedded in national traditions, be transformed into a transnational category? This question points to another troublesome part of the Leavis legacy: the predication of the act of criticism itself on a consensual community rooted in the organic body of the nation. Let us recall that Leavis was quite consistent in his claim that critical judgments were not predicated on the critic's ability to establish some measure of distance from his or her object of analysis, but to affirm the consensual community that bound texts, cultural traditions, and readers. For Leavis, a proper critical judgment depended on an interrogative – 'This is so, isn't it?' – that was impossible without the concurrence of critics and their interlocutors, both involved in what he called 'a collaborative exchange, a collective and creative interplay of judgments'. (1969, 47) Leavis took it for granted that the writer, the reader, and the critic belonged to what Perry Anderson has aptly called 'a shared, stable system of beliefs and values' (1992, 98).

The important point to underscore, though, is that for Leavis, criticism was not critique: it did not question the norms underlying English literature or the culture of Englishness; it was not concerned with any substantive history, or social epistemology; instead, the task of criticism was to establish a shared body of implicit and unquestionable values as the imperative for literary studies. For this reason, criticism did not have, nor did it need, a theory. On the contrary, it was a creative process that sought to 'establish the poem as something standing in a common world between those discussing, and thus to satisfy our habitual assumption that it does so stand' (Leavis 1969, 48). Leavis was willing to concede that a poem existed for us as private experience, but he was also adamant that its overall meaning depended on its public presence, that the work of art created, or rather was, a moral space 'in which minds can meet, and our business is to establish the poem and meet in it' (1969, 48). But who were we? What made this economy of reading habitual? What was the character of the minds that met in the poem? Leavis took it for granted that the writer, the work, and the critic shared a common Englishness.

We now scoff at this idea of a consensual Englishness. We call attention to the global nature of English literature and even the multiculturalism of England itself. We counter the xenophobia of the last Thatcherites by pointing to the landscape of English writing as a sign of the globalization of English literature; we point out that English language literature, in Britain itself, is likely to be dominated by Anglo-Indian, Anglo-Japanese, Anglo-Chinese, Afro-Scottish, and Afro-Nigerian artists as much as by writers from the proverbial home counties and the Celtic periphery. And yet, the more one listens to this invocation of the new English literature as one of the most powerful signs of global culture, one wonders whether globality has become a supplement, or even alibi, for prior categories of national culture such as Englishness. Is the global culture of professional émigrés the same as that of those who cross national boundaries in dangerous circumstances? What, indeed, is the consensual community shared by these two groups? The questions need to be addressed if postcolonial theories of globalization are to be something more than a passing fad.

Note

1   For an English translation of the original letter, written in French, see Harper's Magazine no. 1794 (November 1999), 22. My thanks to James Ferguson for drawing this letter to my attention.

Chapter 14

Jacques Derrida

GLOBALIZATION, PEACE, AND COSMOPOLITANISM

From *Negotiations: Interventions and Interviews 1971–2001,* ed. and trans. E. Rottenberg, Stanford, CA: Stanford University Press, 2002, pp. 372–86.

[. . .]

[A]LLOW ME TO PROCEED, IN A WAY THAT IS brutally direct, straight to a series of statements. I submit them for discussion less as theses or hypotheses than as professions of faith, in some sense. These quasi professions of faith will be declared through aporias, contradictory and apparently incompatible injunctions, which are (and this is the first point that I bring up for debate), according to me, the only situations in which, forced to obey two apparently antinomical imperatives, I literally do not know what to do, what I would prefer to do, what to privilege, and I must then *take* what is called a *decision* and a *responsibility*, a responsible decision; I must give myself, I must invent for myself a rule of transaction, of compromise, of negotiation that is not programmable by any knowledge, not by science or consciousness. Even if I had at my disposal, or could acquire all knowledge, all possible science or consciousness on this matter – as must in fact be done, this is a duty – an infinite leap still remains before me, because a responsible decision, if it is to be the event of a decision in the face of two contradictory imperatives, cannot simply be dictated, programmed, prescribed by knowledge as such. This is why I am tempted to speak of a *profession of faith*.

Having posed this axiom, let us take the word *mondialisation*, the French word *mondialisation* that should resist, according to me and I will say why, its translation and its alleged English or German equivalents: *globalization* or *Globalisierung*. The term *mondialisation* has become, and the statistics would bear this out, the site of the most symptomatic uses and abuses of our time, especially in the last decade. The inflation, even the rhetorical turgidity that affect the term, and not only in political discourse and the media, often conceal one of the contradictions with which I would like to begin and with regard to which a true cultural critique, the *contract* of a new education or reeducation, is no doubt necessary. This, both against the beatific celebration and the demonization of the phenomenon of the aforementioned *mondialisation*. Celebration and demonization often hide interests and strategies that we must learn to detect.

On the one hand, as is well known, a certain number of unprecedented and irrecusable phenomena justify this concept. The effects of globalization [*mondialisation*] are essentially conditioned by techno-science (a techno-science that is, furthermore, unequally, unfairly distributed in the world in its production and its benefits), and they involve – we know this and I will say it very quickly – the rhythms and the scope of transportation and telecommunication in the electronic age (computerization, E-mail, Internet, etc.), the circulation of persons, commodities, modes of production, and socio-political models on a market that is being opened in a more-or-less regulated way. As for the (altogether relative) opening of borders (which, at the same time, has rarely given rise to so many inhospitable acts of violence, so many prohibitions, so many exclusions, etc.), as for the progress of legislation and especially the practice of international law, as for the limitations or the displacements of sovereignty that the concept of globalization calls forth, globalization depends less than ever on *fact* or techno-scientific knowledge-power [*savoir-pouvoir*] as such. Indeed, it calls for ethical-political decisions and political-economic-military strategies. Here the ideal or euphoric image of globalization as homogenizing opening must be challenged seriously and with unfailing vigilance. Not only because the said homogenization, where it is produced or would be produced, contains in itself both a chance and chance's double – a terrifying risk (too obvious for me to have to spend time on it) – but also because the apparent homogenization often hides old and new inequalities and hegemonies (what I call *homo-hegemonizations*) that we must learn to detect behind their new features – and fight. International institutions – governmental and nongovernmental – are in this regard privileged places, both as revelation, as fields of analysis or experimentation, and as battlefields or as places of palpable confrontation. These are also privileged places for the organization of resistance to these imbalances, the most visible and massive of which are linguistic. These imbalances are all the more difficult to challenge – and this is another contradiction – because, on the one hand, this hegemony is very useful for universal communication (thus equivocal in its effects); and, on the other, because the linguistic-cultural hegemony (obviously I am alluding to the Anglo-American hegemony), which increasingly asserts itself or imposes itself on all modes of techno-scientific exchange, the Web, the Internet, academic research, etc., promotes powers that are either national and sovereign states, or supranational states, this time in the sense of corporations or new figures of the concentration of capital. Since all of this is well known, I will only insist here on the aporetic contradiction in which responsible decisions must be made – and contracts framed. If a linguistic-cultural hegemony (and everything that comes with it: ethical, religious, legal models) is at the same time, as integrating homogenization, the positive condition and democratic pole of a desired globalization, enabling access to a common language, to exchange, to techno-science, and to an economic and social progress for communities, national or not, communities that would not otherwise have access to them and would find themselves, without Anglo-American, deprived of their participation in the global forum, then how does one fight this hegemony without compromising the broadening of exchange and distribution [*partage*]? It is here that a transaction must be sought at every moment, in every singular set of circumstances. It is here that the transaction must be invented, reinvented without prior criteria and without assured norms. One must, and this is the formidable responsibility of the decision, if ever there is one, reinvent the norm itself, the very language of the norm for such a transaction. This inventiveness, this reinvention of the norm, even if it must be inaugural, different, without precedent and without prior guarantee, without available criteria every time, must not for all that yield to relativism, empiricism, pragmatism, or opportunism. It must justify itself by producing its principle of universalization in a universally convincing way, by validating its principle through its very invention. In this way, I am formulating (and I am perfectly aware of it) a task that appears contradictory and *impossible*. Impossible at least for a response that would be instantaneous, simultaneous, immediately coherent, and identical to itself. But I maintain that only the impossible arrives and that there is no event, and thus no irruptive and singular decision except where one does more than deploy the possible, a possible knowledge – where exception is made to the possible.

Instead of pursuing the analysis directly, I will try to illustrate it with an analogy that is not just any analogy, but precisely an analogy of the example of the concepts of world [*monde*] and *mondialisation*. If I maintain the distinction between these concepts and the concepts of *globalization* or *Globalisierung* (and it should be noted that the word *globalization* is itself becoming global to the point of imposing itself more and more, even in France in the rhetoric of politicians and the media), it is because the concept of world gestures toward a history, it has a memory that distinguishes it from that of the globe, of the universe, of Earth, of the *cosmos* even (at least of the cosmos in its pre-Christian meaning, which Saint Paul then christianized precisely to make it say *world* as *fraternal* community of human beings, of fellow creatures, brothers, sons of God and neighbors to one another). For the world begins by designating, and tends to remain, in an Abrahamic tradition (Judeo-Christian-Islamic but predominantly Christian) a particular space-time, a certain oriented history of human brotherhood, of what in a Pauline language – the language that continues to structure and condition the modern concepts of the rights of man or the crime against humanity (horizons of international law in its actual form to which I would like to return, a form that conditions, in principle and by right, the becoming of globalization [*mondialisation*]) – of what in this Pauline language one calls *citizens of the world* (*sympolitai*, fellow citizens [*concitoyens*] of the saints in the house of God), brothers, fellow men, neighbors, insofar as they are creatures and sons of God.

If you grant me, for lack of time, that it is possible in principle to demonstrate the Abrahamic filiation, Christian predominantly or par excellence, of the concept of world and all the ethical-political-juridical concepts that tend to regulate the process of globalization [*mondialisation*], the becoming-world of the world – especially through international law and even international criminal law (in its most interesting, most promising, most turbulent becoming), through the difficulties of international cosmopolitan institutions and even the felicitous crises of national state sovereignty – then responsibility, the most necessary task and the most risky wager would consist in doing two things at once, without giving up either one. On the one hand, it would consist in analyzing rigorously and without complacency all of the genea-logical features that lead the concept of world, the geopolitical axioms and the assumptions of international law, and everything that rules its interpretation, back to its European, Abrahamic, and predominantly Christian, indeed Roman, filiation (with the effects of hegemony implicit and explicit that this inherently involves). On the other hand, it would consist in never giving up – through cultural relativism or a facile critique of Eurocentrism – the universal, universalizing exigency, the properly revolutionary exigency that tends irresistibly to uproot, to de-territorialize, to dehistoricize this filiation, to contest its limits and the effects of its hegemony (all the way to the theological-political concept of sovereignty that is experiencing a sea change in terms of the borders of war and peace and even, at these borders, between a cosmopolitanism that assumes, as does citizenship of the world, the sovereignty of states, and another, democratic International beyond the nation state, even beyond citizenship). Therefore, one must not give up rediscovering, inventing, inventing this time in the sense of inventing as discovering what is already there potentially, namely, in this filiation itself, the principle of its excess, of its bursting outside itself, of its auto-deconstruction. Without ever yielding to empiricist relativism, it is a matter of accounting for what in this genealogy, let us say *European* to go quickly, gets carried away, exceeds itself by exporting itself (even if this exportation did and can still imply an infinite violence, whether we use more or less worn-out words to talk about it – imperialism, colonialism, neo-colonialisms, neo-imperialisms – or modes of domination that are more refined, trickier, more virtual, less identifiable in the future under the names nation-states or national states' gathering).

The task of the philosopher here, such as I see it assigned and implied by the new 'world contract' that we are thinking about, would also be that of whoever tends to assume political or legal responsibilities in this matter: to account for what in this heritage of the concept of the world and in the process of globalization makes possible and necessary – by assuming it, with a profession of faith – an actual universalization, which frees itself of its own roots or historical, geographical, national state limitations at the same moment that, out of faithfulness (and faithful-ness is an act of faith), it implements the best memory of this heritage and fights against the effects of inequality and hegemony, of homo-hegemonization that this same tradition did and can still produce. For it is also from the depths of this heritage that certain themes themselves arise, themes that today, particularly through the mutations of international law and its new concepts – about which I will say a word in a moment – have the potential to universalize and thus to split, or if one prefers, to expropriate the Euro-Christian heritage.

Instead of remaining at this level of abstraction, I would like to indicate, or at least name, the four related examples – thus putting these statements into practice – with which I would have liked to orient the discussion. The titles of these four examples, all of which are linked, would successively be: *work, forgiveness, peace,* and *the death penalty.* The common premises with which I will bring these four themes together in a single problematic are all taken in the process of a globalization that has been accelerated in its rhythm, driven to the point of a true mutation, i.e., of a rupture whose juridical events, which are more than indications here, would be as follows:

1.   The renewed reaffirmation in its many declarations of the constantly enriched 'rights of man'.
2.   The performative production in 1945 of the concept of crime against human-ity, which, together with the war crime, the crime of genocide and the crime of aggression, transformed the global public space and opened the way for international criminal agencies. We can foresee and hope that they will develop irreversibly, thereby limiting national state sovereignties. The four

crimes that I have just listed define the jurisdiction of the International Court of Criminal Law.

3.   Consequently, the putting into question (very unequal, it is true, and indeed problematic, but altogether crucial and irreversible) of the barely secularized theological principle of the sovereignty of nation states.

A few words, thus, on work and then a telegraphic question to begin the discussion about forgiveness, peace, and the death penalty.

1. *Work*. Let us say or make as if the world began where work ended, as if the globalization of the world had both as its horizon and its origin the disappearance of what we call *work*, this old word, painfully charged with so much meaning and history, work, *labor*, *travail*, etc., and which still means actual, effective, and not virtual, work.

When we say *as if*, we are neither in the fiction of a possible future, nor before the resurrection of a historical or mythical past, the past of a revealed origin. The rhetoric of this 'as if' belongs neither to the science fiction of a utopia to come (a world without work, 'in the end without end', *in fine*, *sine fine* of an eternal sabbatical, of a Sabbath without night, as in Augustine's *City of God*); nor does it belong to the poetics of nostalgia that would hark back to a golden age or a paradise on Earth, to the moment in Genesis before sin when the sweat of work had not yet begun to flow, neither from the labor and toil [*la labeur et le labour*] of man nor from the childbirth of women. In these two interpretations of 'as if', science fiction or memory of the immemorial, it would be as if, in effect, the beginnings of the world originally excluded work: work would be not-yet or no-longer. It would be as if, between the concept of world and the concept of work, there were no originary harmony, and thus no given accord or possible synchrony. Original sin would have introduced work into the world, and the end of work would announce the terminal phase of an expiation. One would have to choose between the world and work, whereas, according to common sense, it is hard to imagine a world without work or work that would not be of the world or in the world. The Christian world and the Pauline conversion of the concept of the Greek cosmos introduces – among many other associated meanings – the assignation of expiatory work. The concept of work is burdened with meaning, history, and equivocation; it is difficult to think it beyond good and evil. For, even if it has always been associated at the same time with dignity, life, production, history, goods, and freedom, it nonetheless just as often connotes evil, suffering, penalty, sin, punishment, oppression. No. This 'as if' points in the present to two common places on which to test them: on the one hand, one often speaks about the end of work, and on the other hand, and just as often, of a globalization of the world [*mondialisation du monde*], about a becoming-global of the world [*devenir-mondial du monde*]. And one always associates one with the other. I am borrowing the expression 'end of work' from the title of the well known book by Jeremy Rifkin, *The End of Work: The Decline of the Global Labor Force and the Dawn of the Post-Modern Era*. This book brings together a sort of widespread doxa about a 'third industrial revolution' that, according to him, would be 'a powerful force for good and evil', given that 'new information and telecommunication technologies have the potential to both liberate and destabilize civilization'. I do not know if it is true, as Rifkin says, that we are entering a 'new phase in world history': 'fewer and fewer workers', he says, 'will be needed to produce the goods and services for the global population'. *The End of Work*, he adds, thus naming his book, 'examines the techno-logical innovations and market-directed forces that are moving us to the edge of a near workless world'.

To know if these statements are 'true', one would have to agree on the meaning of each of these words (end, history, world, work, production, goods, etc.). Some-thing serious is indeed happening [*arrive*], is in the process of arriving or is at the point of arriving, to what we call *work*, *tele-work*, *virtual work*, and to what we call *world* – and thus to the being-in-the-world of what is still called *man*. It depends, in large part, on the techno-scientific mutation that, in the cyberworld, in the world of the Internet, of E-mail, and of cellular phones, is affecting tele-work, time, and the virtualization of work; a mutation that, at the same time that it is affecting the communication of knowledge, all forms of making common and all 'community', is also affecting the experience of place, of taking place, of the event and the produc-tion [*œuvre*]: of what arrives.

The problematic of the aforementioned 'end of work' was not absent from certain texts of Marx or Lenin – Lenin, who associated the gradual shortening of the work day to a process that would lead to the complete disappearance of the state. For Rifkin, the third technological revolution inscribes an absolute mutation. The two first revolutions, that of the steam engine, coal burning, steel, and textiles (in the nineteenth century), that of electricity, gasoline, and the automobile (in the twentieth century) did not radically affect the history of work. This is because both isolated a sector that the machine had not penetrated and where human work, non-machinal, nonreplaceable by a machine, was still available. After these two technical revolutions came: ours, the third, that of cyberspace and microcomputing and robotics. Here, it seems, there is no fourth zone in which to put the unemployed to work. A saturation by machines leads to the end of the worker, thus a certain end to work. (End of *der Arbeiter* and his era, as Jünger would say). Rifkin's book leaves room, however, for what it calls the *knowledge sector* in this mutation in progress. In the past, when new technologies replaced workers in different sectors, new spaces emerged to absorb those who had lost their jobs. Today, however, while agriculture, industry, and services send millions of people into unemployment owing to the progress of technology, the only category of worker that is spared is the category of 'knowledge', an elite of industrial innovators, scientists, technicians, computer programmers, teachers, etc. But this remains a narrow space, one that is incapable of absorbing the vast numbers of unemployed. Such would be the dangerous singu-larity of our time.

I am not going to address the objections that one might make to these remarks, neither the objections one might make to the said 'end of work' nor those to the said *globalization* [*mondialisation*]. In both cases, which, furthermore, are closely linked, I would begin by distinguishing – were I to discuss them head-on – between the incontestable mass phenomena registered by these words and the use one makes of these concept-less words. In fact, no one will deny it: something is happening to work in this century, to the reality and to the concept of work – active or actual work. What is happening to work is, in fact, an effect of techno-science, with the virtualization and globalizing dislocation of tele-work. (Even though, as Le Goff has shown, these contradictions concerning the time of work began very early in the Christian Middles Ages.) What is happening [*arrive*] indeed underscores a certain tendency to shorten asymptotically the time of work, as work in real time and localized in the same place as the body of the worker. All of this affects work in its classical forms, those forms we inherit; it affects work through our new experience of borders, of virtual communication, of the speed and range of information. This evolution is moving in the direction of a certain globalization; it is irrecusable and well known. But these phenomenal indices remain partial, heterogeneous, unequal in their development; they call for a fine-tuned analysis and no doubt for new concepts. On the other hand, between these obvious indices and their doxic usage – others would say ideological inflation, the rhetorical and often hazy complacency with which one yields to these words, 'end of work' and 'globalization' – there is a gap. And I think that those who forget this gap should be severely criticized. Because they are then trying to hide or hide from themselves the zones of the world, the populations, nations, groups, classes, individuals who in their massive majority are the excluded victims of this movement of the said 'end of work' and 'globalization'. These victims suffer either because they do not have the work they need or else because they work too much for the salary they receive in exchange for their work on a world market that is so violently non-egalitarian. This capitalistic situation (where capital plays an essential role between the actual and the virtual) is more tragic in absolute numbers than it has ever been in the history of humanity. Humanity has perhaps never been further from the globalizing or globalized homogeneity, from the 'work' and the 'without work' that is often cited. A large part of humanity is 'without work' when it wants to work, more work, and another part has too much work when it wants to have less, or even to put an end to work that is so poorly paid on the market. Any eloquent disquisition on the rights of man that does not take into account this economic inequality is threatened with chatter, formalism, or obscenity (here one would have to speak of GATT, the IMF, the external debt, etc.). This history began a long time ago. Intertwined with it is the real and semantic history of the words *trade* [métier] and *profession*. Rifkin is aware of the tragedy that might be provoked by an 'end of work' that would not have the sabbatical or restful meaning it has in the Augustinian *City of God*. But in his moral and political conclusions, when he comes to define the responsibilities that must be assumed in the face of the 'technological storm clouds on the horizon', in the face of a 'new era of globalization and automation', he rediscovers, and I think that this is neither fortuitous nor acceptable without examination, the Christian language of 'fraternal bonds', of virtues 'not easily reducible to . . . machines', the 'renewed meaning' of life, the 'resurrection' of the service sector, the 'rebirth of the human spirit'; he even imagines new forms of charity, for example, the payment of 'shadow wages' to volunteers, a 'value-added' tax on high-tech products and services 'to be used exclusively to guarantee a social wage for the poor in return for . . . community service', etc.; he then rediscovers, in a way that is a little incantatory, the accents (and more than just the accents) of the discourse that I was talking about earlier when I said that it called for a complex genealogical analysis, but without complacency.

If I had had the time to retrace this genealogy with you, I would certainly have insisted more on the time of work, drawing my inspiration from the work of my colleague Jacques Le Goff. In the chapter 'Time and Work' in *Another Middle Ages* [1999], he shows how, in the fourteenth century, the demands for a lengthening and the demands for a shortening of the work day were already coeval. We have here the premises of a right of work and of a right to work, such as they will later come to be inscribed in the rights of man. The figure of the humanist is a response to the question of work. The humanist is someone who, in the theology of work that governed this period and is certainly not dead today, begins to secularize both the time of work and the use of monastic time [*l'emploi du temps monastique*]. Time, which is no longer simply a gift of God, can be calculated and sold. In the iconography of the fourteenth century, the clock sometimes represents the attribute of the humanist . . . this clock that I am forced to watch over and that strictly watches over the secular worker that I am here. Le Goff shows how the unity of the world of work, faced with the world of prayer and the world of war, did not last very long, if it ever existed. Following the 'contempt for work [*métiers*]', 'a new border of contempt established itself, one that passed right through the middle of the new classes, right through the middle of the work force [*professions*]'. Although he does not distinguish (it seems to me) between 'métier' and 'profession' (as I think should be done), Le Goff also describes the process that, in the twelfth century, gave rise to a 'theology of work' and to the transformation of the tripartite schema (*oratores, bellatores, laboratores*) into 'more complex' schemas, which can be explained by the differentiation of economic and social structures and by a greater division of work.

2. *Forgiveness.* Today there is a globalization, a global dramatization of the scene of repentance and of asking forgiveness. It is conditioned both by the ground swell of our Abrahamic heritage and the new position of international law, and thus the new figure of globalization that has been produced since the last war by the transformed concepts of the rights of man, the new concepts of crime against humanity and genocide, of war and aggression – the chief accusations of these auto-accusations. It is hard to make out the scope of this question. Too often in the world today, especially in political debates that reactivate and displace this notion, one maintains the ambiguity. One often confuses, sometimes in a calculated way, forgiveness with a large number of related themes: excuse, regret, amnesty, prescription, etc., many different themes, some of which have to do with law, with criminal law; forgiveness must remain irreducible to all of them. As mysterious as the concept of forgiveness may be, the scene, the figure, the language with which one tries to accommodate it belong to Abrahamic heritages (Judaism, Christianities, and Islams). Yet, however differentiated and even conflictual this tradition may be, it is both singular and on the way to universalization, precisely through what this theater of forgiveness brings to light. Consequently, the dimension of forgiveness tends to be erased in the course of this globalization and, with it, all measure, all conceptual limit. In all of the scenes of repentance, confession, forgiveness, or excuse that have increasingly appeared on the geopolitical scene since the last war, and in an accelerated way over the last few years, we are seeing not only individuals but whole communities, professional guilds, representatives of ecclesiastical hierarchies, sovereigns, and heads of state ask for 'forgiveness'. They do it in a language that is not always that of the dominant religion in their society (in the case of Japan or Korea, for example). This language thereby becomes the universal idiom of law, politics, economics, and diplomacy: both the cause and the significant symptom of this internationalization. The proliferation of these scenes of repentance and asking 'forgiveness' no doubt signifies, among other things, an *il faut* of anamnesis, an *il faut* without limit: a debt without limit toward the past. Without limit, because this act of memory, which is also the subject of the auto-accusation, of the 'repentance', of the [court] appearance [*comparution*], must be carried beyond both legal and national state authority. Thus, one wonders what is happening when the dimensions are such as these. As for the

reflection elicited by this phenomenon, one path regularly leads back to a series of events without precedent: those events that, after and during the Second World War, made possible, 'authorized' at any rate, with the Nuremberg Trials, the international institution of a legal concept such as 'crime against humanity'. A 'performative' event took place there whose reach is still hard to measure, and yet terms like *crime against humanity* seem so common and intelligible to everyone today. This mutation was itself provoked and legitimated by an international authority at a date, and according to a figure, determined by its history. This history is inseparable from a reaffirmation of the rights of man, of a new Declaration of the Rights of Man, even if it cannot be reduced to it. A sea change of this sort structures the space in which the grand pardon, the great world scene of repentance is being played out – sincerely or not. It often makes one think of a great convulsion. It would be indecent – and needlessly provocative – to say that this convulsion often resembles an irrepressible and very obscure compulsion, ambiguous in its unconscious roots. For it also obeys, fortunately, what one might call a *positive* movement. But it is true – and we should never forget it – that the sham, the forced ritual, sometimes the excess of falsehood in the confession itself, calculation or mimicry, are often there, as well. They corrupt this moving ceremony of guilt from the inside: an entire humanity shaken by the gesture of a unanimous confession! Nothing less than the human race would suddenly come and accuse itself publicly, dramatically, of all the crimes that have indeed been committed by it against itself, 'against humanity'. Were one to take inventory, while asking for forgiveness, of all the past crimes against humanity, there would be no innocent person left on earth. Who, then, would be in the position of judge or arbiter? All humans are the heirs, at least, of people or of events that were marked, in an indelible way, by 'crimes against humanity'. A supplementary but essential paradox: those events of the past, which at times gave rise to organized exterminations, and at other times took the form of great revolutions ('legitimate' and, in any case, still celebrated today by national or universal memory), have allowed for the emergence, and the gradual refinement, of legal pronouncements like the rights of man, the crime against humanity, genocide, the crime of aggression, etc.

Today this convulsion looks like a conversion. An 'objective' conversion and one that tends to exceed all national limits: on the way to globalization. For, if the concept of crime against humanity is the chief accusation of this auto-accusation and of this request for forgiveness; if, furthermore, only a sacredness of the human can, in the last instance, justify this incrimination (no evil, no wrong is worse, according to this logic, than a crime against the humanity of man and against the rights of man); if the sacredness of the human finds its most legible, if not its only source of meaning, in the memory of the religions of the book and in a Jewish, but above all Christian, interpretation of the 'neighbor' or the 'fellow creature'; if, consequently, any crime against humanity touches what is most sacred in the living, and thus already touches the divine in man, some God-become-man or some man-become-God-by-God (the death of man and the death of God would betray the same crime here); then the 'globalization [*mondialisation*]' of forgiveness resembles a huge process in progress, an endless procession of repentants, thus a virtually Christian convulsion-conversion-confession, a 'work' of Christianization that no longer even needs the church or missionaries. This 'work' sometimes looks like atheism, humanism, or triumphant secularization. But the difference is not important. Humanity would be ready as one man to accuse itself of a crime against humanity. To testify on its own behalf against itself, that is, and with good reason, to accuse itself as an other. This is terribly economical.

Whether one sees enormous progress here, a historical rupture, and/or a concept whose limits are still blurry, precarious in its foundations (and one can do both at the same time – this is my *temptation*, if I can still use this word in confessing), one fact remains irrecusable: the concept of crime against humanity governs the whole geopolitics of forgiveness. It gives it its code and its justification. Let us think of the extraordinary Commission for Truth and Reconciliation in South Africa. A unique phenomenon in spite of several South American precedents, particularly in Chil[e]. Well then, what conferred the declared legitimacy on this commission was the definition of apartheid as a crime against humanity by the international community in its UN representation. One could take a hundred other examples, they all return to this reference in the form of a security.

3. *Peace*. Because I will not be able to devote to peace the time necessary for an analysis that would be more appropriate and worthy of this great topic, which is in the contract of this session, I will say just a word that is directly inspired by the title of these large discussions, a new world contract. It seems to me that if there is a lesson to be learned from the most recent phenomena, which one hardly dares to call *wars* anymore (because of the semantic mutations that precisely imply the ambiguous role of the state in such 'interventions') – the aforementioned Gulf War, Rwanda, the Congo, Kosovo, Timor, etc., phenomena all very different in their logic of sovereignties – the lesson is that, late or not, well-run or not, these interventions, in the name of the universal rights of man, with the prospect of judging chiefs of state and military commanders before international criminal courts, have indeed successfully challenged the sacred principle of state sovereignty, but have often done so in disturbing ways. As Arendt notes, only small states ever see their sovereignty contested and disputed by powerful states, even when it is in the name of universal principles. Not only would these powerful states never allow their own sovereignty to be challenged, but, what is more, they orient or preempt the decisions, and sometimes even the deliberations, of the recognized international agencies, in view of their own political-military-economic strategy because they are the only ones who have the economic and techno-military power to implement decisions. A world contract to come would have to acknowledge this fact: as long as these international agencies do not have an autonomy of deliberation, of decision-making, and especially of military intervention, as long as they do not have the force of law it is their mission to represent, well then, all the infractions of sovereignty in the name of the rights of man, which should be just in principle, will be suspect and contaminated by strategies before which vigilance will always remain de rigueur.

4. The serious question of *the death penalty* in the world cannot be dissociated from what I have just said. For, without going through the long abolitionist struggles that have developed over the centuries and even in the United States, one must remember this fact at least: since the last world war, a long series of conventions and international declarations of the rights of man, the right to life and the prohibition, hardly compatible with the death penalty, of cruel treatments (declarations that I do not have the time to cite, but almost all of them emanate from the UN) have created, directly or indirectly, a supra-state pressure to which a great number of democratic countries have been, let us say, sensitive at the moment they abolished the death

penalty. It is always an international and supra-state agency, transcending the sovereignty of the state, that enjoins the states (both the death penalty and the right of pardon have always been the eminent signs of state sovereignty) to abandon the death penalty (seemingly on their own but, in fact, by international obligation). This is obviously the case in Europe, in France for the last twenty years, and in fifty-or-so other countries around the world. One may find, in accordance with certain jurists, that this growing tendency to abolish the death penalty is becoming what in English is called a *customary norm of international law* and in Latin a norm of *jus cogens*. Yet we know that among the countries that resist this tendency, among the nation states that present themselves as great Western democracies in the Christian-European tradition, the United States is today, to the best of my knowledge, the only country that, in the aftermath of the death penalty's turbulent history not only has not abolished the death penalty but makes use of it massively, increasingly, cruelly, and, it must be said, in a way that is discriminatory when it is not blind — as many recent examples have shown. With other international associations, with the International Parliament of Writers, to which I have the honor of belonging (and which will be discussed tomorrow, I think, in connection with refuge-cities and the engagement of UNESCO on their behalf), in the name of these institutions, thus, and in my own name, I ask that the question of the death penalty be inscribed in the form of a solemn appeal in any text about a new 'world contract'. I will spare you my other professions of faith.

Chapter 15

Masao Miyoshi

TURN TO THE PLANET: LITERATURE, DIVERSITY, AND TOTALITY

From *Globalization and the Humanities,* ed. David Leiwei Li, Hong Kong: Hong Kong University Press, 2004, pp. 19–26, 32–35.

Literary studies in 1983

IN 1983, I WAS IN SEOUL TO PRESENT A PAPER. The occasion was a conference on East Asian literature, a topic not too different from the one assigned to me for another event last year in the same city. This seventeen-year interval may not seem to be a long time in a normal phase of history. Between 1715 and 1732, for example, or even between 1918 and 1935, the change was certainly not trifling, but still the sense of continuity was quite strong. The difference between 1983 and 2000, however, is so immense that we can barely grasp the magnitude of the changes and transformations that occurred between these years, and in fact the phrase 'a normal phase of history' is itself beginning to lose meaning. It looks as if we are heading toward a future where the pace of change will accelerate to such an extent that the trace of history may be erased as time hurries along through our everyday life. In this chapter, I'd like to recall the ideas that were crucial, or that I considered crucial at that 1983 conference, and then set those ideas against what seems crucial now and reflect on the intervening events. Such a comparison might also reveal what has survived unchanged and suggest what may remain intact in the future. I will discuss the changes and continuities both inside and outside what has been known as 'literature'.

By the beginning of the 1980s, the impact of Edward Said's *Orientalism,* published in 1978, had spread far beyond its immediate range of the Middle East and colonial history. His Nietzschean and Foucauldian message on the genealogy of the concepts of power and learning had become generalized in the discourse of modern history. As everyone knows, *Orientalism* radically challenged the orthodoxy in disciplines like history, anthropology, geography, and sociology, as well as literary criticism. Many branches of the humanities and social sciences had been formed during the colonial period with unexamined assumptions about the centrality of European and North American civilization, and intellectuals emerging in the just

liberated former colonized world found in Said's criticism something both revolutionary and fundamental for mapping the history and geography of the future.
The term 'Orientalism' was added to the vocabulary of many languages as a name
for the hegemonic ideology of domination. This was to be the beginning of a new
paradigm for equality and the open mind. In the context of the dominant practice of
the Eurocentric formulation of knowledge, however, the anti-Orientalist criticism
was looked on as a disturbing challenge. To the academic establishment, it was a
movement of rebellion and resistance – at least at the initial stage.

The East Asian field (where I have been more than an occasional sojourner) has
long been organized from the colonial perspective, and thus Said's criticism was not
accepted at once, especially by established scholars. Critical categories transferred
from European literature to East Asian literature – without scrutiny as to their
applicability – were still very much in use at the beginning of the 1980s. Genre, form,
structure, periodicity (such as 'modernity' and 'modernization'), intentionality,
affect, authorship, originality, audience, textuality, media, plot, character, tonality,
the idea of 'literature' itself, and many other fundamental literary and cultural
notions – as well as the terms used in describing and analyzing European literature(s)
and culture(s) – were more or less randomly chosen as approximations. Even at the
1983 conference in Seoul, there were sharp divisions and disagreements among the
panelists on the merit of the newly proposed transvaluation.

[. . .]

In 1983 my interest was far more literary than it is now. The problems I saw in
the novel were within a literary context and in literary terms, although these
problems and terms nearly always referred to external historical developments.
I chose prose narrative fiction as the crucial focus of comparison and confrontation
among cultures of the world. Poetry and drama trace back to antiquity everywhere
before diverse economic and industrial developments sundered the world into haves
and have-nots, while the 'novel', or rather prose narrative fiction – of considerable
length, printed and mass-circulated, describing the actions and events of the ordinary
people – emerged after industrialization and colonialism widened the gap between
rich and poor. [. . . .] As I saw it, the prose fiction form reveals this history far more
clearly than do poetry and drama, enabling me to avoid cultural and literary
essentialism. However, if we place the prose narrative forms of various countries
within the one category of the novel, we are likely to overlook different formal
features inscribed by the historical variants in development and power. Difference,
in this view, was the way to illumination.

In the 1983 paper, I discussed the modern Japanese narrative form *shosetsu* as
having features that refuse to be classified under the headings that hold for the
Western novel. Just to take one instance, because of the 'aspect' – the temporal
grammatical category of the Japanese language, where the perfect and imperfect are
used rather than past, present, and future tenses as in English – the narrative
sequence of the *shosetsu* tends to be coeval rather than consequential, discouraging
the causal linking of narrative elements. Here, the preterit or the historical past
tense – 'the ideal instrument for every construction of a world . . . the unreal time
of cosmogonies, myths, History and Novel', according to Roland Barthes – is not
available (1967, 30–31). The *shosetsu* thus tends to be paratactic instead of syntactic,
resulting in weakened and loosened – or freer and open ended – plotting. Similarly,
the absence of Japanese genesis and apocalypse myths has led to the rejection of a

clear beginning and, more important, a clear ending or resolution in Japanese prose narratives. These narratives may often continue on and on, at times refusing the possibility of closure altogether.

This difference between the novel and the *shosetsu* at their high modernist/ modernizing stages – from the late nineteenth century to the mid twentieth – might be explained by the marked residual oral features in the *shosetsu*, even though it is no longer an oral performance but a printed narrative just like any novel. While the modern novel is marked by invention, particularistic landscape, revision, analysis, spatiality, distance, comprehension, expansion, massive length, sculpturesque text-ual autonomy, and depth and interiority in characterization, the oral narrative is characterized by memory, formulas, repetition, display, temporality, proximity and intimacy, insularity, ritualism, episodic brevity and fragmentation, contextual communality, and social roles/relations of characters. Literacy requires the infra-structure of printing, distribution, leisure, and wealth, whereas orality depends on village or other communal space and physical places where the reciter and audience can assemble together. Such intimate sites have either vanished or been replaced by mechanical reproductions, such as radio or television, in the literate industrial societies. Literacy might thus be considered a central cultural marker of capitalist, metropolitan, colonial societies; orality, in contrast, seems tied to agricultural, peripheral, colonized societies.

[. . .]

All this I argued in order to prove that the critical terms that were the products of one form did not fit the other. This, in retrospect, was my attempt to liberate the *shosetsu* and other peripheral narrative forms such as the Chinese, Arab, or Urdu narratives from metropolitan literary domination. I liked to indulge myself by fantasying that, as a written text, the novel – begun in the West nearly simultaneously with the commencement of colonialism – was fit for distribution over great distances and thus particularly suitable, unlike the oral recitation, for the writer in the metropolis to send out to the colonies far away – just like an emissary or a command from the colonial office to viceroys or governors in the far-flung corners of the world. I was convinced that the novel was inescapably colonialist – even with an anti-colonialist theme. However, the oppositional force wished to attribute to the *shosetsu* form had to be considerably curtailed because of Japan's peculiar place in the history of colonialism. It is indisputable, on the one hand, that Japan has been faced with Euro-American hegemony and adventurism since the mid-nineteenth century. Although military occupation was highly unlikely, the economic and political con-tainment of Japan by the US and European powers was as comprehensive as that of any other Asian nation. Even more importantly, Euro-American cultural indifference to Japan was both disturbing and incomprehensible to its intellectuals in the early twentieth century, who were thoroughly familiar with proclamations of Enlighten-ment universalism. By the 1930s, Kuki Shuzo, Tanabe Hajime, Miki Kiyoshi, and other Japanese writers had sought out Heidegger, Husserl, and Jaspers, and when they found that the German philosophers were both ignorant about and indifferent to their country their disappointment was profound. Their construction of a nationalist philosophical system that eventually served as an apologia for Japan's aggression can be traced to such an experience of Eurocentricity. On the other hand, Japan was the first non-Western country to develop modern imperialism. Taking to heart the advice given by Bismarck and other Western leaders, the Japanese oligarchy and militarists quickly employed *real politik* and the instrumentality of colonialism for their own industrial development. After victory against imperial China and Russia around the turn of the century, Japan's swagger over its intra-Asian domination was unmistakable in the *shosetsu* of the time, not only thematically, but also in the narrative forms with which the writers of the time were beginning to experiment.

Said was able to extend the idea of Orientalism to include political oppression and thereby to take an uncompromisingly anti-Orientalist position in dealing with the questions of Palestine and Islamic countries. My own liberationist revisionism concerning the West and the Rest, however, had to be seriously qualified. I had to focus on both the West *and* Japan, that is, on the forces of oppression wherever they may have originated. And the fact that I presented the paper near the former colonial governor's headquarters in Seoul no doubt intensified the need to revise my Saidian anti-Orientalism, without, of course, forgetting Euro-American oppression in the process. All this was eighteen years ago.

Year 2001: discipline on the wane

To switch to the year 2001, the kind of literary exercise I have just described is no longer current in the literary critical scene in the United States and in many other countries. First, the sort of grammatical/formal analysis of literary products seems to interest very few scholars now, according to the programs of conferences and meetings and the books and journals being published. The idea of literature as composed of autonomous formal inventions survives largely within the guarded walls of a few traditionalist enclaves. Gone also is the argument concerning the interrelationships of power among nation-states and national literatures. In fact, the idea of the nation-state is itself very much in decline, not in literary studies alone, of course, but in intellectual discourse as a whole. If colonialism is talked about, it is often in terms of the era after the colonial rule, within the boundary of so-called '*post*colonial' discourse. Colonialism in this view is safely detached from today's state of affairs. Said's name has been replaced by Homi Bhabha's, Stuart Hall's, and Arjun Appadurai's, a changeover signifying the replacement of political economy by culture as a central paradigm. The structure of political-economic oppression is now explained as a hybrid cultural program in which the subalterns powerfully affect the oppressors' culture as they struggle for survival. With this transformation of the political-economical into the cultural, moreover, the suffering of the oppressed is de-emphasized. While colonialism has not as yet been converted into a benign civilizing act, history is certainly now looked upon with more leniency and latitude.

As for the decline in literature in general, one can at once point to the waning of canonic writers and works, established and mainstream scholars, conventional genres, and national literary history. White male masters first began to be replaced by female writers. Nearly at the same time, minority writers – male and female – emerged as a new dominant, but female minority writers took center stage. Over the last decade, fiction as a whole has lost its allure for the general public – except perhaps for pulp romances – and interest in foreign cultures, especially European literatures and languages, has begun to disappear. One of the simplest indicators of this radical change is in the recent figures in enrollment, recruitment, and placement at the undergraduate, graduate, and faculty levels in the humanities. The numbers of those enrolled in Russian, Italian, French, and German literatures and languages are down – conspicuously among undergraduates, but in graduate programs as well. A sharp decline is evident in the interest in literary studies as a whole. Far fewer undergraduates take courses in literature or major in it, which means fewer jobs for PhDs and fewer graduate students and seminars. Among the few enrolled in literature courses are social and natural science majors who want to have some 'fun' in their college life – not a trivial development, since these are likely to be the students who constitute the main clientele of literary studies. There are faculty members, especially in the East Coast colleges, who are still active in specialized research in literary studies, but their classrooms are less crowded now, and fewer copies of their publications circulate.

Even among the disciplines on the wane, however, all is not lost. There are brisk departments, sections, and sectors even amidst the general decline. To begin with the most obvious, 'theories' seem to have supplanted imaginative works such as the novel, poetry, and drama as the objects of study. Students and young scholars are too impatient to read an infinite number of texts that, as they see them, are mere materials for analytic statements. Skipping over novels, poems, plays, or historical documents, young – and older – scholars prefer ready-made summaries, abstractions, and analyses that are presumably provided by theorists as the end products of arduous examinations of primary documents. Novels and poems – at least the bygone works – are no longer being read with unmediated pleasure, an activity which strikes many ambitious scholars as indulgent and inefficient. Theories are to the point and, supposedly, endowed with universal and productive applications. Thus, theories are discussed with enthusiasm. In scholarly publications and graduate seminars, and increasingly also in undergraduate lectures, a knowledge of imaginative texts is no longer presumed, or rather, the students' ignorance is a given. Theories that were born out of a desire for universalism and systematization to redress prejudicial distortion and exclusion are now as commodified as Hollywood films or designer clothes. So what is the theory to theorize? What is the subject?

Today's theories abstract and construct systems of meanings rooted in the interrelationship of social groups: ethnic identities (minoritarian studies such as African-American, Hispanic American, Asian-American, etc.), gender studies (gay, lesbian, queer, and a variety of feminist studies), postcolonial studies (hegemonic/subaltern, diasporan, etc.), local/regional studies, and popular-culture studies, with emphases on the dominated and marginalized. The nation-state is much too totalizing and patriarchal a notion, and in current literary practice it is nearly always divided and subdivided into smaller units. Thus, for instance, the Association of American Studies is no longer about the US as represented by the hegemonic white male elites, that is, 'traditional' history and society; rather it has virtually become a scholarly association devoted to the studies of ethnic minorities, a change suggesting contestations over the subject of history. Under the circumstances, the idea of totality is unsurprisingly taboo, avoided, distrusted, and ignored. Totality and universality, in this view, inevitably suggest repression and exclusion. The new social agenda is to recognize and insist on individual varieties, incommensurable differences. Such a development toward the principle of 'difference', that is, multiculturalism, is no doubt salutary as long as it rejects the logic of concentrated power and authority instanced by univocal pretensions to world hegemony, Eurocentricity,

American imperialism, dictatorship, elitism, racism, patriarchy, and any other totalizing and normalizing institutionality. Multiculturalism is propelled by the democratic impulse for equality and liberation. [. . .]

   [. . .]

Toward an inclusive totality

Global neo-liberalism is powerfully altering fundamental assumptions within literary studies as well. Earlier in the second half of the twentieth century, the logic of difference was a strategy of liberation. The rejection of the nation-state as totalizing similarly implies the existence of more particularistic social units. In an immigrant and multiracial country such as the United States or Australia, multiculturalism is an obvious consensual choice, each group, minority or majority, demanding its own autonomous and independent, that is, incommensurable space. Without doubt, multiculturalism is preferable to the monoculturalist oppression of minorities by the dominant group. The logic of difference, however, paradoxically poses three internal difficulties that are likely to perpetuate a condition of exclusion and neglect for minorities.

   First, insofar as each group's incommensurability means total uniqueness, the affairs of any given group are a matter that does not – or should not – concern the member of any other group. If this principle of noninterference is practiced resolutely, the minority – presumably less resourceful – groups must be left alone to shift for themselves. The majority group then has neither accountability to nor responsibility for the minority groups. Second, the problem of totality does not vanish when a nation is divided into ethnic or gender groups. Each group of course constitutes a totality that is smaller, but nonetheless as controlling and demanding as that of the nation. Consider, for instance, the minority called Asian American? Shouldn't that general and abstract entity be broken down into Chinese-American, Korean-American, Vietnamese-American, and many other sub-groups? And among Chinese-Americans, are the mainland Chinese to be considered in the same category as the Taiwanese? The Hong-Kong Chinese? Overseas Chinese? Chinese Women? Gays? Lesbians? Queers? Where does the logic of difference stop? Doesn't a particular individual remain as unrepresented within such categories as does a citizen of a totalized nation?

   Third, among the three main categories of difference (race, gender, and class), class is distinct from the other two in that class has no reason to retain its identity if liberated, whereas race and gender have no reason to lose theirs. Race and gender can thus be viewed as more 'authentic' identities than class, since class aspires to erase itself. In the identity politics that has consumed literary studies in recent years, this distinction among the three categories is tacitly assumed – with the result that class is seldom mentioned, unlike ethnicity and gender. Quite obviously, the ruling class welcomes this silence. For this reason alone, transnational corporatism has warmly embraced multiculturalism. Diversity at this juncture is a favored public policy, not a subversive program.

   If every literary and cultural system is incommensurable, the idea of 'comparative' literature is an oxymoron. Incomparables cannot be compared. In fact, very little serious work is being done now in the area of comparing national or regional literatures. Such efforts are being supplanted by studies of the inner workings of a culture or literature, which presumably are different from those of another. Power, however, is nearly always introduced as the constitutive factor – effectively casting every ethnic or gender minority in a more or less similar light, the light, for instance, of victimology.

The problem with the logic of difference is not just classificatory. In asserting autonomy and independence, each group rejects commonality with others and demands a certain internal cohesiveness. This need for solidarity is – functionally, at least – as disciplinarian as any national demand for loyalty and patriotism. And where does the authority of each group originate? How is the right to power and representation legitimized? Even parliamentary democracy will have to be rejected here, since elective representation requires the definition of an electorate, a totality. The minority leadership in this sense is likely to be based on self-proclamation, opening a way to opportunism and confusion. If sectionalism and secession are freely allowed, on the other hand, the social structure of a minority group will collapse into atomism. (That literary discourse can also be splintered by a similar kind of factionalism has recently been pointed out by Nina Auerback in 'Acrimony' and K. Anthony Appiah in 'Battle of the Bien-Pensant'.) Such a situation in fact only encourages the usurpation of power by an opportunist within the group who knows how to represent the atomized multiplicity by manipulating sympathy, loyalty, and celebrity. Such a situation also clearly benefits the leaders of the dominant group, who can pursue their own interests with no regard for the minorities, just as they had always done before the days of liberation.

The disintegration of not just comparative literature, but literary studies as a whole, may be already under way. If our fractured groups are engrossed in their self-interests, outsiders have good reason to feel repulsed by them. The general public wants to understand its place in the 'globalized' world, and there is a deep concern with the waste-based economy. And yet those who have traditionally intervened in such issues are preoccupied with their internecine struggles conducted in a language of their own. The public is excluded and unwanted as long as it refuses to learn the jargon of partisans and to become partisan. And as we have already seen, the public seems increasingly to look elsewhere for cultural interpretation and criticism. Literary productions [. . .] are at present still alive, but they are no longer closely connected with the critical and analytic segments of the university.

The global economy, on the other hand, is having a profound impact on today's university, as I have described in 'Ivory Tower in Escrow'. The corporatized university is preoccupied with the market force, most conspicuously around information technology (IT) and bio-engineering. Outside of applied sciences, basic research – now called 'curiosity research' – is visibly being ignored. Technology transfer has become the urgent agenda for administrators and managers of both business and academia. Thus learning is rapidly being transformed into intellectual property, and the free exchange of information into commerce. As 'globalization' thus goes ahead full-speed, literary scholars remain absorbed in joyless self-isolation and futile in-fights. Under such circumstances, literary studies have little chance of competition, or even survival, within the walls of the university itself.

My interest here is, however, not in the recuperation or resuscitation of my professional specialization. Rather, I am concerned with restoring a sense of totality to the academic and intellectual world, both intellectually and politically. By now we know that particularity without totality is nonsense, deadening, and useless. Literary and cultural critics must look out at the world and interconnect all the workings of political economy and artistic and cultural productions. We must keep reminding ourselves that the 'global' economy is not global at all, but an exclusionist economy. We must discover the sense of true totality that includes everyone in the world.

For this purpose, the return to the nation-state probably will not work any more. The old power structure has proven a failure much too often in the past two centuries of its history. Perhaps we need a new organization, one that is truly global and inclusive of all. There is one such core site for organizing such an inclusiveness, though entirely negative at present: the future of the global environment. For the first time in human history, one single commonality involves all those living on the planet: environmental deterioration as a result of the human consumption of natural resources. Whether rich or poor, in the East or the West, progressive or conservative, religious or atheist, none of us can escape from the all-involving process of air pollution, ozone layer depletion, ocean contamination, toxic accumulation, and global warming. Of course, the rich will try to stay as far away as possible from the pollution, but even they cannot remain protected for long. We can start from this realization of total commonality as we map out our world and engage in research and scholarship. Literature and literary studies now have one basis and goal: to nurture our common bonds to the planet – to replace the imaginaries of exclusionist familialism, communitarianism, nationhood, ethnic culture, regionalism, 'globalization', or even humanism, with the ideal of planetarianism. Once we accept this planet-based totality, we might for once agree in humility to devise a way to share with all the rest our only true public space and resources.

What form this research on the preservation of the planet will take is not at all clear now, of course. It must combine environmental engineering with economics, political science, and cultural studies so that scholars in all fields may first work out the idea of an economy that will reduce consumption without cutting employment. The reduction of waste in the First World must be simultaneous with the increase of consumption in much of the Third World. They will have to devise a way to train and integrate the unused labor forces of the Third World to equalize wealth. By far the most difficult task in this project is how to invent a way to persuade, not advertise, culturally as well as politically, that there is no other future for any of us. Either through schools and universities, NGOs, UN-affiliated organizations, media, or residues of the state apparatus, we must curb our material dream and build a future that we will all share with an unprecedented commonality. For such a future we need to reimagine our common and universal culture, as we have never done in human history.

Of course, we may very well fail in this attempt. But if we do, we will not be there to see it. And perhaps we deserve to perish. On the other hand, faced with the fate of universally inescapable destruction and nullification, we may yet finally find a way to confront it together and to find a way to coexist with all others. There is at least that much promise of hope, the only hope we have been allowed to entertain together with everybody else on this planet.

Chapter 16

Emily Apter

'UNTRANSLATABLE' ALGERIA: THE POLITICS OF LINGUICIDE

From *The Translation Zone: A New Comparative Literature* Princeton and Oxford: Princeton University Press, 2006, pp. 97–105.

[. . .]

THE PROBLEM OF TRANSLATION MARKETS and the 'untranslatability' of certain national literatures fits into a larger framework of reflection on literary *mondialisation*, and the future of the 'culture industry' a term borrowed from the *Dialectic of Enlightenment*'s famous fourth chapter, 'Culture Industry, Enlightenment as Mass Deception' (Horkheimer and Adorno 1989). In applying the term 'culture industry', however, one must shift the Horkheimer/Adorno emphasis on the supposedly corrosive influence of mass and popular culture, to a more open-ended inquiry into the conditions of cultural globalization, specifically as they apply to the commodification of foreign authors within a niche market subsuming ethnics, immigrants, elite cosmopolitans, and the formerly colonized in a 'multiculti' hodgepodge. Whereas Adorno, Horkheimer, and the Frankfurt School more generally focused their critique on how emergent capital logics were encoded in mass cultural forms, they paid little attention to questions of translatability across the complex cultural and social terrains of capital. The question of how one achieves a mass cultural object – a cultural object that can be translated across linguistic, cultural, and social contexts – still begs to be answered. When the problem of a globalizing mass culture and public culture is approached from the perspective of translatability, new and important questions of cultural commodification and thus ideology arise. How do some works gain international visibility while others do not?

These questions take on curricular and pedagogical urgency in the context of efforts to globalize the canon. The constraints imposed by what is available in translation become constitutive of a transnational canon, contributing another layer of complexity to the value-laden selection process of authors, and serving as partial explanation for why 'global lit' courses tend to feature similar rosters of non-Western authors (such as Wole Soyinke, Salman Rushdie, Derek Wolcott, Tayeb Salih, Gabriel García Márquez, Nadine Gordimer, Naguib Mahfouz, Assia Djebar, Ben Okri, Arundhati Roy). The most obvious explanation – that these and other writers among the 'happy few' are selected because they are universally acclaimed, excellent writers – obviously fails to account fully for their predominance. The difficulty of book distribution in many economically beleaguered countries remains an insuperable impediment to transnational exchange (a point made by the distinguished author Mongo Beti when he spoke of the dire situation in Cameroon).[1] There are specialized niche markets within the 'global' that contribute to fads and fashions (to wit, the current popularity of Anglo-Indian novelists and Irish playwrights), sorting writers into subcategories such as 'international' (Milan Kundera, Julio Cortázar, Samuel Beckett, Ferdinand Pessoa, Octavio Paz, Orhan Pamuk, Danilo Kiš), 'postcolonial' (Aimé Césaire, Albert Memmi, Anita Desai, Patrick Chamoiseau, Mariama Bâ,), 'multiculti', 'native', or 'minority' (Toni Morrison, Theresa Hak Kyung Cha, Sherman Alexie, Jessica Hagedorn, Gloria Anzaldua, Haruki Murakami, Amitav Ghosh, Colm Tóibín). These labels, though they can help launch or spotlight world-class writers – pulling them out of ethnic area-studies ghettos on the bookstore shelves – also cling like barnacles to their reception and afford constrictive stereotypes of identity. The Australian case is interesting in this regard: a strong, institutionally well-connected Australian poet like John Kinsella fails to warrant inclusion in the global canon even though his poetry uses his native landscape to brilliant effect as the stage for futurist visitations by robots and psychics. Naturalized in the British and American literary market, his writing is not exotic enough, while a poet like Lionel Fogarty – whose dense, compelling verse incorporates Aboriginal language – fails to cross over because it remains too exotic for mainstream taste.

The increased motility of global culture – fostered by an art market system of international galleries, museum shows, and biennials that highlight select 'star' artists all over the world – foretells a time when these labels will become obsolete. Even very locally grounded works are acknowledged to be readily consumable by international media. Web diffusion also contributes to a deregionalization that renders labeling and bracketing within a global frame incoherent. We can already observe a situation in which location has become somewhat meaningless as the work of artists, writers, and thinkers is dispatched simultaneously and instantly to electronic sites, or as artists themselves become conscious of living transiently in one city while exhibiting in others. Producing work directly in a non-native tongue (as in the case of the Haitian novelist Edwige Danticat, who lives in New York and writes in English), many artists seem to bypass the act of translation, subsuming it as a problematic within a larger project of cultural or self-representation. In this picture, 'global' signifies not so much the conglomeration of world cultures arrayed side by side in their difference, but rather a problem-based monocultural aesthetic agenda that elicits transnational engagement.

This drive toward a transnationally translatable monoculture is supported by the fact that linguistic superpowers increasingly call the shots and turn once formidable competitors (European languages) into gladiators fighting among themselves for international market share. In French bookstores, for example, translations or even *un*translated books in English, have acquired more and more space on the shelves. This suggests that France, despite the polemics of its academies, is losing the battle against the encroachment of English, but on a more optimistic note, it indicates a return to cosmopolitan attitudes within French culture, abetted by post-Wall, pro-Europe sentiments and a greater responsiveness to the claims to hospitality, residency, and citizenship by non-nationals in the wake of tragic wars in Africa, the Balkans, and the Middle East. Most cynically perhaps, it implies that France no longer maintains its special hold on the market in 'hot' fiction, philosophy, and theory – a novelty deficit that must be made up domestically by translations. Contemporary American fiction holds sway; the French edition of the latest Russell Banks can be found in the *vitrine* of many bookstores, and it bests British best sellers (though a valiant effort to translate the Edinburgh street slang of Irvine Welsh's *Trainspotting* into French attests to a French interest in Britpack fiction). [. . .]

Like its Anglophone counterparts, French publishing seems to have preserved neocolonial networks of metropole-periphery exchange (even as it fans its reputation as the beacon of world culture for the New Europe). [. . .] But looming on the horizon is a neo-imperialist situation that puts translation, especially from non-Western languages, in an especially precarious state. In this scheme nation-states become obsolete as publishing markets shrink the global literary market using laws of international copyright, regulation, book distribution, and marketing. One can envisage an era in which the appellations of a national literature are headed for extinction. If publishing businesses will have any incentive to preserve the tradition of nationally marked authors within systems of global interstate culture, it will only be because the classificatory device of national literatures enhances the marketability of cultural product. French Lit, British Lit, American Lit and so on, in lending coherence to retail, will survive as mega-units within supermega, transnational corporations, while non-Western cultural identities will be managed as subsidiaries. The 'foreign lit' deemed most susceptible to profit-making will naturally receive preferential treatment.

In this Malthusian scheme, small presses will be increasingly controlled by or located outside the ken of the mega-houses, and writers taken on by these marginal publishers will gain paltry international attention. Publishing will become (indeed has already become) subject to stratified and specialized 'niche' marketing, with strategically targeted communities of readers ghettoized according to nation, class, education, race, and gender. As the division between mass market and high culture erodes in the face of a frenzy for commercial solvency at all levels of the publishing business, the 'niche' of foreign or translated writers turns into a multi-culti hodgepodge – a place in which ethnics, minorities, immigrants, émigrés, elite cosmopolitans, and former colonials are indiscriminately thrown together.

In the marketing of Third World difference, what sells? A writer who appeals to universalism or nonsecular religious philosophy? A dissident author? A subcontinental writer who capitalizes on exoticism or one who explores postcolonial identity? A Pacific Rim writer who reinforces essentialist stereotypes of Asianness, or one who embraces Western literary conceits and avant-gardes? A traditional African writer or an Afro-futurist? Obviously the choices are largely dependent on the whimsy of fashion and politics, but one thing is clear, though the current World Lit market is volatile and unpredictable, an identifiable canon that one might call 'in-translation' (dominated by PEN and UNESCO writers) crowds out competitors that remain stuck in anonymity. [. . .]

We might ask then, to what extent 'foreign' writers of ambition are consciously or unconsciously writing for international markets; building translatability into their textuality. Though the notion of translatability is itself elusive (as Walter Benjamin understood so well when he idiosyncratically assessed what makes a work ripe for translation, its qualities of numinousness, redemptive potential, or 'foreignness', disrupting and estranging the target language), clearly some originals qualify as better candidates for translation than do others (1970, 70).

Though Anglophone publishing statistics reveal a virtual absence of translations on any bestseller lists, PEN estimates that less than 2 percent of literary market share is devoted to works in translation. [. . .] In America, Michael Crichton, John Grisham, Danielle Steele, and Tom Clancey remain the big sellers with movie tie-ins usually a must. The recent boom in Indo-Anglian novels has sent British and American editors scurrying for South Asian talent, though not necessarily on the subcontinent. Despite the fact that India is now the third largest English-language publisher after Britain and the United States, its fiction stars, often specializing in hot themes – 'the partition, the Emergency, identity' – usually prevail on the international circuit only if they have first received backing from publishing houses in Europe and North America (Jaggi 1997).

Occasionally, popular non-Western authors are openly accused of pandering to the interests of commercialized internationalism, as when the scholar Stephen Owen alleged in a now famous article ('What Is World Poetry: The Anxiety of Global Influence') that the poetry of the Chinese writer Bei Dao was often translated because it offered a 'version of Anglo-American or French modernism', embellished with judicious (and always translatable) dollops of 'local color', and marketed to international audiences for its 'cozy ethnicity' (1990). Owen was criticized by Michele Yeh for a 'flawed binarism', while Rey Chow read his implicit nostalgia for China's traditional heritage as perpetuating 'a deeply ingrained Orientalism in the field of East Asian Studies'. (Jones 1994, 171) Summarizing the debate, Andrew F. Jones argued that Owens's detractors ignored his emphasis on the neocolonial dynamics of Third World First World publishing: 'If world literature is envisioned as international traffic', Jones queried, 'are there trade imbalances? Is there exploitation? Do certain nations supply certain kinds of products? Do developing nations supply raw materials to the advanced literary economies of the "First World"? Finally, is it possible to posit a kind of dependency theory inhering in the transnational economy of literary production and trade?' (1994, 181). In addition to a dependency theory of production and trade in cultural capital, Jones also imputes a labor theory of value to the translated text, drawing an analogy between translations and outsourced piecework:

> In rendering a mute text intelligible to his compatriots, the translator single-handedly *creates* the text's 'use-value' for the targeted readership. This 'use-value', of course, is also the basis of the text's 'exchange-value' on the world literary market. The translator, then, 'finishes' the source text in much the same way that an industrial worker in an advanced economy assembles raw materials imported from developing countries into a product to be sold on the open market.
>
> (1994, 182)

The inference to be drawn here is that properly 'finished' translations will aid and abet authors whose eyes are on the prize. And here, it is revealing to take stock rather literally of the wording of international prizes, many of them holdovers from imperial times. The Commonwealth Prize keeps alive a certain idea of the [Q]ueen's

English in lands of the Pacific. The Before Columbus Foundation American Book Awards, 'for literary achievement by people of various ethnic backgrounds' (won recently by Sherman Alexie, *Reservation Blues*; Chita Bannerjee Divakaruni, *Arranged Marriage*; Chang-rae Lee, *Native Speaker*), misleadingly suggests an all-purpose historical watershed applicable to the cultural heritage of Native American, Indian, and Korean peoples. The Kiriyama Pacific Rim Book Prize, whose mission is 'to contribute to greater understanding and increased cooperation among peoples of the nations of the Pacific Rim', bolsters the illusion of regional solidarity among highly disparate languages and cultures. If here the trend is toward simplified territorializations, elsewhere the prizes seem regionally rarefied, as in the Noma Award, which goes 'for Japanese Literature in Translation published in Africa'. The French Prix Méditerranée smacks of the colonial era by harking back to Camus's idealized vision of a common Mediterranean culture untroubled by the gross power imbalance between France and Algeria. Each of these prizes implicitly rewards a kind of writing compatible with the normative baggage of the award.

For Gayatri Chakravorty Spivak, the only way a translator can undermine the neocolonialism of translation-speak is by deploying a technique that she calls 'fraying', a disrupting, yet 'loving' rhetoricity that, instead of trawling for structures of equivalency between original and target, enters into the text's self-staging:

> The task of the translator is to facilitate love between original and its shadow, a love that permits fraying, holds the agency of the translator and the demands of her imagined or actual audience at bay. The politics of the non-European woman's text too often suppresses this possibility because the translator cannot engage with, or cares insufficiently for, the rhetoricity of the original. . . . Without a sense of the rhetoricity of language, a species of neo-colonialist construction of the non-western scene is afoot.
>
> (Spivak 1982, 179)

In the arena of unfrayed, prize-friendly, translation-happy World Lit success stories, Algeria fares poorly. Indeed, Algeria's untranslatability seems to have acquired the status of a given in the global market. Few works by Algerian writers (in French or Arabic) have internationalist distribution or standing; few are available in English translation. A popular anthology boasting a representative potpourri of non-Western authors – Elisabeth Young-Bruehl's *Global Cultures: A Transnational Short Fiction Reader* [1994] – contains not a single entry by an Algerian author. In the French publishing industry, where one expects a stronger ethic of Maghrebian representation, celebrated Algerian writers are frequently confined to a series, only to be routinely featured for a time, and then dropped (as in the case of Nabile Farès, abandoned by Le Seuil). Small presses, such as Sinbad or Marsa, occasionally come to the rescue, but circulation remains marginal. Moreover, when a 'classic' of Algerian fiction finally does make it into English, it is often condescendingly framed. The Braziller edition of Kateb Yacine's *Nedjma* is a case in point; the editors mitigate the Western reader's anticipated hostility to the text by resorting to formulas of cultural essentialism:

> The narrative techniques Kateb Yacine uses are occasionally disconcerting to the western reader. The latter, as a last resort, will take refuge in

the subtleties of comparative literature to exorcise the mystery: apropos of *Nedjma*, some readers will undoubtedly cite Faulkner. It seems to us that the explanation of the novel's singularities are to be found else-where. The narrative's rhythm and construction, if they indisputably owe something to certain western experiments in fiction, result in chief from a purely Arab notion of *man in time*. Western thought moves in *linear* duration, whereas Arab thought develops in a *circular* duration, each turn a *return*, mingling a future and past in the eternity of the moment. This confusion of tenses – which a hasty observer will ascribe to a love of a genius for synthesis – corresponds to so constant a feature of the Arab character, so natural an orientation of Arab thought, that Arab grammar itself is marked by it.

(Editors' preface, Yacine 1961, 6–9. Emphasis in the original)

Part of the problem clearly lies in the West's reactive politicization of all things Arab. Edward Said addressed this dilemma in reviewing the obstacles to his own role as 'broker' for Naguib Mahfouz:

Eight years before Naguib Mahfouz won the Nobel Prize in Literature, a major New York commercial publisher known for his liberal and unpro-vincial views asked me to suggest some Third World novels for transla-tion and inclusion in a series he was planning. The list I gave him was headed by two or three of Mahfouz's works, none of which was then in circulation in the United States. . . . Several weeks after I submitted my list I inquired which novels had been chosen, only to be informed that the Mahfouz translations would not be undertaken. When I asked why, I was given an answer that has haunted me ever since. 'The problem', I was told, 'is that Arabic is a controversial language'.

What, exactly, the publisher meant is still a little vague to me – but that Arabs and their language were somehow not respectable, and con-sequently dangerous, *louche*, unapproachable, was perfectly evident to me then and, alas, now. For of all the major world literatures, Arabic remains relatively unknown and unread in the West, for reasons that are unique, even remarkable, at a time when tastes here for the non-European are more developed than ever before and, even more compelling, con-temporary Arabic literature is at a particularly interesting juncture.

(1995, 97)

Said also charts the extra disadvantage borne by Arabic texts judged translation-resistant because of their rebarbative stylistics. The difficult formalism of Adonis's *An Introduction to Arab Poetics* (Al-Saqi), the Coptic Egyptian author Edwar al-Kharrat's *City of Saffron*, and the Lebanese feminist novelist Hanan al-Shaykh's *Women of Sand and Myrrh* is posed against the content-oriented prose of 'the overexposed and overcited Nawal el-Saadawi' (1995, 101). Thus, formalism emerges as an obstacle to translatability, along with 'subjective geographies' (Aimé Césaire's Martinique or the Peru of Mario Vargas Llosa's *The Green House*).

While stylistic opacity can alienate a mainstream reading public, the 'difficulty' yardstick is not wholly reliable since an aura of arcana can often enhance a book's attractiveness to readers in search of an exoticist *frisson* (in the fin de siècle, writers such as Théophile Gautier, Pierre Loti, and Isabelle Eberhardt discovered the trick of dousing their prose with foreign loan words to impart local color and induce *dépaysment*). More recently, a vogue for intralingual vernaculars and interlingual creoles (replete with glossaries) has made its mark.

Note

1   Mongo Beti, in discussion session during a conference on 'The Chosen Tongue' organized by Maryse Condé and Pierre Force at Columbia University's *Maison Française*, April 7–8, 2000.

PART 3

Literary readings

> I once began collecting, from correspondence in newspapers, and from other public arguments, variations on the phrase 'I see from my Webster' and 'I find from my Oxford English Dictionary'. Usually what was at issue was a difficult term in an argument. [. . .] Of course if we want to be clear about *banxring* or *baobab* or *barilla*, or for that matter, *barbel* or *basilica* or *batik*, or, more obviously, *barber, barley* or *barn*, this kind of definition is effective. But for words of a different kind, especially those that involve ideas and values, it is not only an impossible but an irrelevant procedure.
>
> Raymond Williams *Keywords: A Vocabulary of Culture and Society*

'GLOBALIZATION' WAS NOT ONE OF RAYMOND Williams's original keywords. Although the term had appeared in both *Webster's* and the *Oxford English Dictionary* in the years leading up to the publication of *Keywords* it came into common usage only towards the end of the following decade.[1] Along with terms such as celebrity, diaspora, and queer, globalization entered the vocabularies of literary and cultural studies in the thirty years that lay between the first publication of *Keywords* and the collaborative *New Keywords: A Revised Vocabulary of Culture and Society*, published in 2005, seventeen years after Williams's death (Bennett, Grossberg, et al. 2005, 146). Yet Williams's warning against a reductive or generalized treatment of such central critical concepts remains salutary in a number of different ways. It reminds us of the continuing primacy of cultural forms to political frameworks and of the necessary contingency of any attempt to conceptualize this relationship using only the 'ideas and values' of master phrases. Our epigraph from Willliams also suggests, of course, that it is in our language that we reveal our own position in our global schema.

This part is an attempt to draw out the themes and forms that responses to literary and cultural texts written in English have brought to the globalization debate. It does this in an explicit and implicit matter. Firstly, and most obviously, are the thematic subdivisions employed to organize this third part. These areas – environmentalism, money and markets, technology and cyberculture, migration and labour, worldliness and cosmopolitanisms – indicate some of the keywords employed by literary critics interested in theorizing the effects of globalization. One rationale for prioritizing these particular categories was because they illuminate the ways in which literary studies has been able to supplement, rather than simply implement, the critical vocabularies of globalization. The initial theoretically-led essay in each category has been chosen to highlight what the specific concerns and methodologies of literary studies bring to an analysis of globalization and the wider thematic area under consideration. These categories are necessarily contingent and are not intended to be read as exclusive or comprehensive, as innovative or new, or as entirely discrete from one another. Many of the essays could happily sit in other groupings and they often speak to the lines of interconnections between our thematic categories. We are also aware that the continuing and increasingly rapid development of research in the various fields associated with literature and globalization may come in time to suggest an entirely different set of categories. These themes are, then, intended to indicate some of the ways in which the existing, and internally heterogeneous, critical vocabularies of literary studies have responded to the structural shifts synonymous with globalization, just as they have with a range of other intellectual, political and cultural challenges.

Our first thematic category, 'environmentalism', points to the ways in which literary critics have utilized the field of ecocriticism to further develop a literary analysis of globalization. The very concept of the environment has had a persistently intimate relationship with the globe. A notion of the holistic planet is embedded, as Ursula Heise has noted, in the productive imaginary of the early environmental movement of the late 1960s and early 1970s – from James Lovelock's Gaia hypothesis to Buckminster Fuller's notion of Spaceship Earth. The widely recognized emergence in the early 1990s of a literary ecocriticism that had been developing for over two decades called into being a relatively well-defined field, one that ranged from Biblical allusion through the poetics of Romanticism to the proleptical prose of science fiction (Garrard 2004, 2). Ecocriticism's attention to the discursive construction of the 'natural', the 'human' and the 'civilized' in a range of contexts has similarly required it to develop a complex theoretical vocabulary in which 'cybernetics, evolutionary biology, landscape ecology, risk theory, phenomenology, environmental ethics, feminist theory, ecotheology, anthropology, psychology, science studies, critical race studies, postcolonial theory, environmental history' have 'presented themselves as a corrective or enhancement to literary theory's existing toolkits' (Buell 2005, 10).

Our three selected essays each address the specific importance of the category of the global to ecocriticism, yet they derive their theoretical vocabularies for this pairing from a range of quite different sources. Graham Huggan and Pablo Mukherjee concentrate on the parallels between environmentalism and postcolonialism whereas Ursula Heisse draws explicitly on postmodern notions of deterritorialization and cosmopolitanism. These essays also gesture toward the interdependency of the various thematic categories we have constructed for this final part. Mukherjee is concerned with the politics of migration; Heise and Huggan with the implications of technology and, to a lesser degree, international finance. Most significantly, all three are motivated by the possibility of some kind of 'planetary' consciousness or cosmopolitan citizenship capable of speaking to the increasingly violent 'enforcement of neo-liberal economic and political fundamentalisms'.

Our second theme, 'Money and Markets', explores the contrasting forms and effects of an increasingly deregulated and expanding financial services industry. The ending of the postwar Bretton Woods financial agreement in the early 1970s is frequently taken to be a founding moment for contemporary models of globalization, as it represents the end of the formal international postwar economic consensus, the loss of even a symbolic gold standard, and the cessation of the controls on currency speculation. It was the beginning of what the economist Susan Strange, recalling Maynard Keynes's evocative phrasing, was to dub 'casino capitalism', a global system 'fundamentally out of order' (1986, 170). Yet the 'global financial system' that emerged in the 1980s produced and reinforced extreme international inequalities and was 'global' only in 'that money began to flow more intensively between the three regional blocs of the industrialised world' (Leyshon and Thrift 1997, 201). Literary critics initially addressed the significance of these speculative cultures through exploring what the crisis in representation that the formal abstraction of money seemed to imply that for the authority and significance of mimetic texts (Shell 1982; Rotman 1987; Goux 1994). More recently, literary attention has turned to understanding the implications of speculative capital for a wide range of social relations and the continuing presence of critical alternatives to it (Brantlinger 1996; Woodmanse and Osteen 1999; Cheah 2008).

The first essay in this theme, by Michael Tratner, explores the relationship between these key changes and the emerging languages of critical theory. Tratner takes a usefully contrarian stance regarding these now familiar parallels, insisting on a historically specific reading of the different approaches that the abstractions of finance and those of language require. The following essay, by Tim Woods, explores the varied ways in which Nuruddin Farah's novel *Gifts* reflects on 'giving and receiving, dependence and reciprocity' in the context of 1990s Somalia. Woods' reading of the 'philosophical and anthropological discourses of gift-giving, and the discourse of the politics of Third World aid donorship' prioritizes other economies from those which are described by Tratner. Like the essay by Joseph Medley and Lorrayne A. Carroll under the category of 'Migration and Labour', Woods demonstrates how such economies are either produced by, or co-exist with, globalization, but also how they are dwarfed or neglected by the ominous glamour of the speculative cultures of the official economies. The final essay in this grouping, by Padmaja Challakere, explores the celebratory rhetoric for the neo-liberal marketplace that became part of the descriptions of the fall of the Berlin Wall. Challakere gives a reading of the quixotic and diversionary 'dazzling optimism' of Zadie Smith's *White Teeth* in this context, whilst urging the reader toward texts more capable of analysing the continuing injustices and stark divisions of globalization, of reimagining ' "globality" as the experience of being "haunted" by walls'.

The third theme, 'Technology and Cyber-cultures', examines the ways in which the rapid development of a host of communicative technologies has produced new conceptual, imaginative and affective models for the experience, knowledge and practices of globality. Manuel Castells has convincingly argued that the printed press of Marshall McLuhan's 'Gutenberg Galaxy' has been replaced by an 'internet galaxy' which has radically altered our conceptual categories (2001). Yet the 'digital divide' that emerges when Castells places this technological revolution into its global context disrupts these claims: as he controversially suggests, contemporary 'development without the internet would be like industrialization without electricity' (Castells 2001, 269). Literary and cultural texts have played an important part in imagining both the emancipatory possibilities, and the more ambivalent ironies, of still emergent technologies. Donna Haraway's notion of the cyborg, more recently supplemented by Katherine N. Hayles' accounts of the posthuman, have provided important paradigms for understanding the formative connections between literatures, technologies and subjectivities (Haraway 1990; Hayles 1997).

The subject matter of this third thematic category has led us to expand our narrow prioritizing of literary texts as we explicitly sought readings that engaged with the material practices of technology in varied ways. Rita Raley's opening essay provides a comprehensive overview of the intersections between global capitalism, technology and information in order to theorize the remit and possibilities of the 'Electronic Empire' that has replaced the naturalizing organic metaphors of capital with those of the nonorganic network: 'a loose assemblage of relations characterized by another set of terms: flexibility, functionality, mobility, programmability, and automation'. In the following essay Fredric Jameson adds further complexity to his still expanding account of the aesthetic forms of late capital, in this instance exploring the paradigms and precursors to cyberpunk, 'a kind of laboratory experiment in which the geographic-cultural light spectrum and bandwidths of the new system are registered'. The final essay, by Katrin Sieg, offers a detailed description of the staging in Berlin 2001 of the opera *Indians*, which narrates the 'story of the Indian computer programmer Soraya, who comes to work in Germany to pay off her husband Mahatma's debt'. Sieg's foregrounding of the context, reception, and thematic imagery of this opera offers a rich case study for understanding how cultural texts can actively intervene within the racialized, gendered and sexualized components of a globalized discourse. These essays again demonstrate rich interconnections with the other categories in this part: the force of speculative capital is central to the work of Raley and Jameson and migration and labour are as crucial to Sieg's essay as is technology.

The penultimate thematic category explores the issues of migration and labour. In contemporary literary and cultural studies migration has typically been celebrated for enabling a postmodern hybridity capable of destabilizing fixed ethnic and national identities which are based upon historically enduring geographical origins (Chambers 1993; Bhabha 1994). An emblematic figure for such theories has been Salman Rushdie, whose essays and fiction have offered an extended meditation on the complexities of identification and migration. In his 1982 essay 'Imaginary Homelands', for example, Rushdie compared the process of migration to the notion of 'translation' and argued that if 'something always gets lost in translation . . . something can also be gained'. (1992, 17) However, critics of this portrait of productive ambivalence have argued that it relies upon a socially narrow conception of migration, celebrating the ability of elite migrants to move between locales and ignoring the quite different experience of working-class or subaltern migration in order to paint such movements as paradigmatic (Ahmad 1997, 287–89; Cheah 1997, 172). Despite the narratives of globalization that emphasize the opening of international borders, the recent history of labour migration has actually seen a hardening of national borders, the raising of physical boundaries and a growing reliance upon illegalized migrants as the sources of cheap labour (Castles and Davidson 2000, 56–57). Accordingly, there has been a new emphasis on questions of class (Sivanandan 2001) and a growing attention to the conditions of labour rather than to the questions of identity that might be unsettled by migration (see, for example, Klein 2000; Chow 2002).

Peter J. Kalliney's essay uses M. G. Vassanji's story of generational international migration, *The Gunny Sack,* in order to complicate what he presents as the rigid schema of recent academic accounts of globalization and to 'question the compatibility of postcolonial theory and scholarly accounts of globalization'. Kalliney's essay provides a useful exploration of how the varied and specific histories of migration disrupt some of the common forward and retrospective narratives produced in the name of globalization. The opening essay by Bruce Robbins 'The Sweatshop Sublime', returns to the work of Raymond Williams as Robbins considers the role that literature and culture can play in attempts to make knowledge of a complicity with global inequalities conscious and actionable. The essay by Joseph Medley and Lorrayne A. Carroll reverses the focus of attention on these transactions, as it strives to critique the ways in which the producer rather than the consumer of global commodities has been imaginatively constructed. Medley and Carroll use the fictional writing of Lawrence Chua and the anthropological writing of Aihwa Ong to challenge the flattening hegemonic discourses of development employed by the IMF in South East Asia in the wake of the Financial Crisis of the late 1990s.

The final three essays in the Reader are grouped into the category 'Worldliness and Cosmopolitanisms'. These concepts have been a vital constituent in literary and cultural critics' attempts to problematize the universalizing impetus of hegemonic forms of cosmopolitanism that, as Timothy Brennan has argued, became an alibi through which metropolitan or colonial states 'justified their encroaching power over geopolitically dispersed, and therefore vulnerable, territories' (2001, 659). In this context the language of cosmopolitanism has been used to produce a longer historical and theoretical context for internationalism; to articulate a set of ethical and political imperatives that can be thought of outside the nation state, what Pheng Cheah calls 'cosmopolitics' (1998); and to imagine the possibilities of resistance and alternatives to existing hegemonic discourses. Kwame Anthony Appiah, for example, identifies cosmopolitanism as the essence of ethical humanism and dates it to the Greek philosophies of the Cynics and the Stoics. For him it expresses the twin aspirations of 'shared citizenship' (as an extension of familial ties) and 'the value . . . of particular human lives' which is capable of extending such universal sympathy to culturally diverse groups (2006, xii–xiii). Bruce Robbins, conversely, rejects the term for its implications of a 'detached, individual view of the global' in favour of a 'more collective, engaged, and empowered form of worldliness that is often called internationalism' (Robbins 1999, 14). The possibilities of internationalism can also be used to interrogate the literal ground of globalization: Wai Chee Dimock uses the notion of the 'planetary' in order to theorize supranational relations not of space but of time, 'a duration antedating the birth of any nation and outlasting the demise of all . . . that goes backward (a recursive loop into the past), and it goes forward (a projective arc into the future)' (Dimock 2003, 490–91).

In the first of our three selected essays Sue-Im Lee explores the way in which

Karen Tei Yamashita's novel *Tropic of Orange*, set on the borderlines between North and South America, critiques the imperialist impulse of contemporary globalist rhetoric in which the First World assumes that it can speak for the globe. Lee suggests that Yamashita's novel produces an alternative model of global connectivity capable of expressing 'the transnational, transcontinental nature of human existence' but self-consciously founded on the dialectical relationship between the necessity and the impossibility of such global identities. In the next essay Neville Hoad explores the possibility of queer and African Cosmopolitanisms in the context of the HIV/AIDS pandemic in South Africa. Hoad reads Phaswane Mpe's 2001 novel, *Welcome to Our Hillbrow*, as an elegy, a formal attempt to recognize and incorporate bereavement. By reading this elegiac structure through the queer recuperation of the psychoanalytical category of melancholia, Hoad can suggest that Mpe's novel is able to move 'its protagonists and readers from a xenophobic, exoticizing position' regarding the pandemic to 'the melancholia of a cosmopolitanism that can embrace other people's dead'. The final essay, by Suman Gupta, examines representations of the diverse constituencies of the anti-globalization movement. Analysing fictional accounts by Don De Lillo, Robert Newman and Ian McEwan alongside representations of the 'global' peace and anti-war demonstrations that took place between 2001 and the spring of 2003, Gupta tries to make apparent how the rhetoric of a unified globality has been appropriated in order to mobilize and unite the disparate coalitional bodies that oppose it.

Yet accounting for our five keywords and phrases immediately raises the vexed issue of coverage: these themes, and the different individual emphases that each clearly possesses, also suggest the inevitable omissions and apparent oversights that editorial work of this kind will produce. One founding aspiration is that the apparent narrowness of any specific thematic category in this final part can be read against the broader range of global presences and issues that are included in the collection as a whole. Yet, of course, we are also profoundly aware that significant bodies of work, areas of the world, and political concerns are inadequately represented. Sometimes this is because of our decision to specifically include essays that spoke most productively to our larger theoretical priorities and sometimes it is a consequence of the constraints of such a relatively narrow selection.

Yet some of what we initially felt would be potential omissions were the outcome of research that simply surprised us. Pablo Mukherjee's essay in the first part, for example, begins by stressing the importance of war as a dominant but divisive historical coordinate and ends, conversely, with a celebration of local syncretic religious practices that can demonstrate the 'interconnectedness of everything'. Religion and warfare both play a significant part in many of the narratives and practices of globalization: it is notable that 'military order' is the 'third dimension' of Anthony Giddens' schema for globalization and that Roland Robertson began his seminal enquiry into the nature of globalization through his work on the sociology of religion. Yet despite the evident importance of these themes to contemporary debates about globalization, our research suggested that neither was as prominent in work on contemporary literature and globalization as we had initially expected. Clearly, the critical vocabularies of globalization suggest a number of other potential keywords that could have been used to organize this part of the reader. As potential themes we might have chosen globalization and the body, globalization and cities, globalization and trade, globalization and security, globalization and development, globalization and law. The list of possibilities seems ever growing. We were, however, guided by both the range of the existing criticism and a concern with the particularities of literary criticism as a mode of analysis that focuses upon the contours of language.

This collection is intended as a guide to exploring the nature of literature's contribution to debates about the meaning of globalization. It is certainly not envisaged to be a representative or comprehensive overview of how literature and globalization have been discussed – even if such a thing were possible. The selection of writers discussed in the essays that follow is far from complete and is not intended to suggest anything like a canon. The list of significant novelists, poets and playwrights who can, and have, been productively read through the debates around the meaning of globalization is a long one. It includes, but is not limited to, writers such as Walter Abish, Gloria Anzaldua, Charles Bernstein, Amit Choudhuri, Caryl Churchill, Jeff Derksen, Yan Geling, Rana Dasgupta, Mohsin Hamid, Yu Hua, Kazuo Ishiguro, Hari Kunzru, Jamaica Kincaid, Jhumpa Lahiri, Gabriel García Márquez, Pauline Melville, Bharati Mukherjee, Oonya Kempadoo, Orhan Pamuk, Salman Rushdie, Janice Shinebourne, Leslie Marmon Silko, Lê Thi Diem Thúy.[2] We hope that one valuable by-product of our editorial decisions is that they will stimulate a productive discussion about the alternative themes, texts, and interconnections that the study of literature and globalization presents.

In presenting this Reader as simply an organized offering to a broad and heterogeneous conversation we, of course, acknowledge its limitations. However, more importantly, we also hope to foreground the kinds of connections and discussions we imagine it as fostering. For this reason, we have reproduced the essays in this final part as comparatively full versions because we think that the specific insights into the schemas of globalization studies that literature can offer are best provided by full and detailed readings of literary and cultural texts. In anticipating the kinds of responses that we hope this reader will encourage, we want to open up some of these possibilities by briefly gesturing to the shared concerns and connections that these essays suggest.

The sensitivity to terminology that we ascribe to Williams in our opening to this part is widely shared: one of the most obvious but valuable tendencies of the analyses in these essays is their critical awareness of the construction and performance of the ubiquitously naturalized languages and assumptions of the global. For instance, in Tim Woods' essay, he interprets globalization as an increase in 'western economic and cultural power', but in acknowledging its complexity, he uses Farah to trace how the multifaceted 'lexicon of gift-giving' is linked to ideas of dependence and compliance. Through Farah's novel, Woods shows how the narratives of interdependency that attend globalization can serve to embed existing inequalities of power through a conceptual link between giving and domination. Rita Raley, in a very different context, demonstrates the political implications of the changing discursive and literal forms of the electronic network. Peter Kalliney tries to situate his reading of M. G. Vassanji's *The Gunny Sack* between postcolonial narratives of literary value, based upon 'marginality', and global narratives of the market, founded on the idea of competition. In doing so he is able to reflect upon the staging or positioning of national identity in ways that reflect its complexity. Sue-Im Lee's essay rests upon an examination of the politics of identity contained within the word 'we'. By exploring its link to primordialist ideas of community, she shows how the discourses of global connectivity impose ideas such as universalism and homogeneity onto the model of global capitalism through the languages of intimacy and familiarity.

Such explicitly political readings are entirely in keeping with the aspirations of much critical practice. They respond to a desire for revelation that is the impulse of a good deal of literary criticism. The assumption that literature can make available that which desire, ideology, politics and even language itself has been required to conceal is widely shared: it is apparent in Sigmund Freud's reading of the repressed, Pierre Macherey's sensitivity to textual silences, Homi Bhabha's attention to ambivalence, and Jacques Derrida's privileging of the aporia. The dialectical discourses of globalization, predicated on the fantasy of inclusion that functions to exclude significant swathes of the global population, is clearly available to all of these approaches. It is hardly surprising that the theme of spectrality, of the absent presence, recurs across many of these essays, as a way of recalling the presence of those effectively banished by the triumphant discourses of globalization. It is apparent in Challakere's desire to feel the persistent presence of globalization's 'haunted' walls, in Medley and Carroll's cross-disciplinary metaphor of the 'hungry ghost', and in Hoad's casting of fiction as 'a way of never laying the dead to rest'.

Yet all of these apparently ghostly presences are also importantly real. The ability of literature to defy and complicate the powerful abstractions of globalization is also explored in many of these essays as they undermine the reifying categories of neo-liberalism by bringing back into discourse the sexed, gendered and racial bodies of its actors. This matters in a variety of ways. An attention to gender, race, sexuality and class enables the articulation of a set of pre-existing emancipatory political discourses that are both contextualizing and resistant. Katrin Sieg's attention to the gendered and sexed discourses of migratory labour, like the queer politics invoked by Neville Hoad or the fragile anti-globalization coalitions described by Gupta, suggest the importance of other forms of international connectivity that occur outside the hegemonic discourses of capital. It also matters because the constructed and imagined narratives, experiences and relationships that are explored in these various texts offer important alternative and corrective perspectives on the dominant schemas of globalization. Many of the distinctive techniques of imaginative writing, such as descriptions of setting or characterization, attempt to perform a kind of experiential presence, producing an affective component for the experience of globalization. As Gibson-Graham argue in their contribution in Part 1, the specificity of such situated bodies within the structures that are called to stand for globalization critiques their hegemonic narratives and attests to the existence of the histories, emotions and intimacies that exist outside of its parameters. The specificity and resistance of these narratives also recall Anna Tsing's useful scepticism toward the 'futurist' momentum of globalism, in which a desire to engage with these discourses can be too easily predicated on an unquestioned complicity with their primary assumptions.

Yet, as Peter Kalliney so eloquently reminds us in this part, the production and circulation of literary texts are themselves subject to the economic and cultural forces of knowledge formation that surround the discourses of globalization. Like Apter in Part 2, he reminds us that it is naïve to simply celebrate literature's capacity for critical disinterest. Of course, it is not only the physical text that is bound up with these forces. Bruce Robbins and Katrin Sieg's descriptions of the historically situated reader and viewer demonstrate some of the ways in which the interpretative context of the reader and/or the viewer can be constructed, albeit sometimes very productively, by the ideological and cultural contexts that the text itself appears to be engaging with. It is, finally, important to remember one of the most obvious things of all: that literary texts are themselves important vehicles for all kinds of languages for globalization and these, as Padmaja Challakere's essay makes evident, are as capable of celebrating the possibilities of the neo-liberal market as of critiquing it or exploring imaginative alternatives to it. By way of a conclusion, then, this Reader should serve as an injunction to remember the necessity of critical reading to any engagement with the category of globalization, just as much as with literary texts.

Notes

1   The *Oxford English Dictionary* offers evidence of the word globalization being used as early as the 1960s, but its omission from recent editions of the *Concise Oxford Dictionary* suggests that the widespread use of the term is extremely new (Allen 1990).

2   See, for example George (2001); Robbins (2001); Wallace (2001); Durix (2002); Joseph (2002); Knight (2002); Huk (2003); Connell (2004); Liu (2004); Jay (2005); Annesley (2006); King (2006); Scott (2006); Alfonso-Forero (2007); Bullen and Parsons (2007); Farred (2007); Graham (2007); Brock (2008); Morton (2008); Omaar (2008); Sadowski-Smith (2008); Gray (2009).

I ENVIRONMENTALISM

Chapter 17

Ursula K. Heise

DETERRITORIALIZATION AND ECO-COSMOPOLITANISM

From *Sense of Place and Sense of Planet: The Environmental Imagination of the Global* Oxford: Oxford University Press, 2008, pp. 50–62 and pp. 65–67

IN HIS BY NOW CLASSIC 1984 ESSAY 'Postmodernism, or, The Cultural Logic of Late Capitalism', cultural theorist Fredric Jameson incisively formulated the challenge that globalization poses for individuals' sense of situatedness. This formulation emerges in his architectural analysis of the Bonaventure Hotel in Los Angeles, whose emptiness, symmetry, and camouflaging of spatial boundaries creates what he calls a 'postmodern hyperspace', a space that defies orientation, spatial recognition, and memory. 'This latest mutation of space', Jameson suggests,

> has finally succeeded in transcending the capacities of the individual human body to locate itself, to organize its immediate surroundings perceptually, and cognitively to map its position in a mappable external world. . . . [T]his alarming disjunction point between the body and its built environment . . . can itself stand as the symbol and analogon of that even sharper dilemma which is the incapacity of our minds, at least at present, to map the great global multinational and decentered communicational network in which we find ourselves caught as individual subjects.
>
> (1984, 44)

This difficulty of mapping individual positions in a set of extremely complex global networks also confronts environmentalist discourses of place. [. . .] environmentalism has met this challenge in two ways between the 1960s and the turn of the millennium: first, by creating allegorical visions of the global that over the course of time have shifted from a utopian to a more dystopian emphasis; second, by developing a set of perspectives that share an emphasis on the importance of a 'sense of place', the attachment to or 'reinhabitation' of the local through prolonged

residence, intimate familiarity, affective ties, and ethical commitment. While the
two perspectives are often, implicitly or explicitly, assumed to complement each
other, they are also quite frequently at odds – in part because of the rejection of
abstract and mediated kinds of knowledge that characterizes some versions of
environmentalism, and in part because of the resistance to certain forms of economic globalization over the last decade.

Such problems in rethinking the relation of local inhabitation to global citizenship are by no means limited to environmentalist rhetoric but have surfaced in a
variety of fields from identity politics to globalization theories. [. . .] several waves
of debate about notions involving rootedness in the local or the nation on the one
hand and concepts such as diaspora, nomadism, hybridity, *mestizaje*, borderlands,
and exile on the other have led to an impasse, where advocacies of local and of global
consciousness have achieved equal plausibility when they are formulated at an
abstract theoretical level. It no longer makes sense to rely mechanically on a particular set of terms with the assumption that it always describes the ideologically
preferable perspective: for example, the frequent assumption that hybridity is inherently preferable to claims to cultural authenticity, that an emphasis on migration and
diaspora is superior to one on rootedness or, conversely, that nomadism is destructive while place attachments are not. But acknowledging this impasse does not imply
that such arguments no longer make sense or that they have become superfluous in
specific political and discursive contexts. Environmentalist and ecocritical discourse
in the United States, [. . .] remains constrained in its conceptual scope by an at least
partially essentialist rhetoric of place as well as by its lack of engagement with some
of the insights of cultural theories of globalization. Such an engagement, I would
suggest, might begin with two concepts that have played a central role in globalization theories: deterritorialization and cosmopolitanism.

Deterritorialization in literary and cultural criticism is most centrally associated
with Deleuze and Guattari's attempt philosophically to reconceptualize social,
spatial, and bodily structures outside the classifications, categorizations, and boundaries usually imposed on them. [. . .] But it has also been widely used in anthropo-
logically and sociologically oriented studies of how experiences of place change
under the influence of modernization and globalization processes, as a shorthand for
the way 'locality as a property or diacritic of social life comes under siege in modern
societies' (Appadurai 1996, 179), and it is mainly in this sense that I will use the
term here. More specifically, it refers to the detachment of social and cultural
practices from their ties to place that have been described in detail in theories of
modernization and postmodernization. Sociologist Anthony Giddens, for example,
has examined the 'disembedding' that occurs when modernization processes shift
structures of governance and authority away from villages and counties to more
distant locations and give rise to networks of exchange via symbolic tokens (such as
money), of expertise (such as that which guarantees that buildings are constructed
safely and food does not arrive contaminated at the store), and of social trust in the
legitimation and enforcement procedures of large-scale social communities (1990,
21–36). Expanding this type of analysis to the processes he considers typical of the
postmodernization of the second half of the twentieth century, geographer David
Harvey has similarly pointed to the 'time-space compression' that forces distant
locales closer together and triggers movements of homogenization as well as differentiation of places under the umbrella of global capitalism (Harvey 1990; 1996).

Sociologist Roland Robertson, from a somewhat different theoretical perspective, has introduced the related notion of the 'glocal' to capture 'the extent to which what is called local is in large degree constructed on a trans-or super-local basis. . . . Much of what is often declared to be local is in fact the local expressed in terms of general-ized recipes of locality' (1995, 26). Néstor García Canclini's analysis of different modes of modernization in the developing world also emphasizes deterritorializa-tion as 'the loss of the "natural" relation of culture to geographical and social territories' (1995, 229). While some studies of modernization processes foreground above all increased mobility as the main cause of deterritorialization (Lash and Urry 1994, 252–54), other analyses highlight the ways it transforms the experience of place even and above all for those individuals and communities that stay put. [. . .]

This aspect is addressed in detail by the sociologist John Tomlinson, who emphasizes that while mobility – whether the voluntary one of the leisured traveler or the involuntary one of the migrant worker – forms an important part of the forces that dissociate culture from place, 'the paradigmatic experience of global modernity for most people . . . is that of staying in one place but experiencing the "dis-placement" that global modernity *brings to them*' (1999, 9). This displacement is caused by the availability of internationally produced and distributed consumer products, cultural artifacts, and foods, the presence of media such as radio, televi-sion, and the internet, which bring faraway places and problems into average cit-izens' living-rooms, and the experience of what Tomlinson, following French anthropologist Marc Augé, calls 'nonplaces', locales such as airport terminals, supermarkets, or gas stations that are configured quite similarly across a variety of regions and countries (108–28). Tomlinson is well aware that these elements describe the ordinary life of populations in Europe and North America better than in other parts of the world. Yet he argues that even and perhaps mainly those who live in less privileged regions of the world are also affected by deterritorialization, precisely because processes of exploitation involve them deeply in globalization. Workers in the developing world who are forced to follow the flows of capital experience deterritorialization in this way, as do farmers whose choices of products to cultivate are dictated by the needs of First World markets (136) or whose agricultural success has become dependent on seeds, fertilizers, and pesticides sold by transnational corporations. In urban contexts, in addition, many of the same products (goods, foods, media) that are available in the First World are becoming available across the globe. Therefore, Tomlinson argues,

> what is at stake in experiencing deterritorialized culture is not, crucially, level of affluence, but leading a life which, as a result of the various forces of global modernity, is 'lifted off' its connection with locality. . . . [I]t is possible to argue that some populations in the contemporary Third World may, precisely because of their positioning within the uneven process of globalization, actually have a sharper, more acute experience of deterritorialization than those in the First World.
>
> (137, see also 135)

Tomlinson does not discuss the important dimension of risk as an experience with similar power to transcend geographical, political, and social boundaries [. . .]. Some recent ecological and technological risk scenarios (regional ones such as the nuclear accident at Chernobyl in 1986 or truly global ones such as atmospheric warming and the depletion of the stratospheric ozone layer) affect populations that are geographically, politically, and socially distant from the places where these risks originate. In addition, risks that emanate from political or economic crisis have similar potential to work across national and social borders and affect populations with little control over their causes. They lend additional support to Tomlinson's conclusion that

> globalization promotes much more physical mobility than before, but the key to its cultural impact is in the transformation of localities them-selves. . . . [C]omplex connectivity weakens the ties of culture to place. This is in many ways a troubling phenomenon, involving the simul-taneous penetration of local worlds by distant forces, and the dislodging of everyday meanings from their 'anchors' in the local environment. Embodiment and the forces of material circumstance keep most of us, most of the time, situated, but in places that are changing around us and gradually, subtly, losing their power to define the terms of our existence. This is undoubtedly an uneven and often contradictory business, felt more forcibly in some places than others, and sometimes met by coun-tervailing tendencies to re-establish the power of locality. Nevertheless, deterritorialization is, I believe, the major cultural impact of global connectivity.
>
> (29–30)

Even though deterritorialization thus understood implies profound social and cul-tural upheaval, Tomlinson is at pains to emphasize the ordinariness of many of the daily experiences it involves. Most of the changes they bring are, in his view, quickly assimilated by those who undergo them and become part of what is considered normality (128). Indeed, much of the importance of the deterritorialization process derives from the fact that its effects so quickly come to be accepted as part of individuals' daily routines. Ulrich Beck has described the same process as the 'cos-mopolitization' or 'banal cosmopolitanism' of lifeworlds, which quite often occurs without conscious awareness on the individual's part (2004, 65–67).

Within this theoretical framework, the environmentalist call for a reconnection with the local can be understood as one form of 'reterritorialization', an attempt to realign culture with place. But the framework also shows why this attempt is bound to remain both practically and theoretically problematic. In practical terms, it shows how global connectedness makes an in-depth experience of place more difficult to attain for more people. [. . .] remaining in one place for many decades, taking care of a house or farm, intimately knowing the local environment, cultivating local relationships, being as self-sufficient as possible, resisting new technologies that do not improve human life spiritually as well as materially are options no longer available to many. Deterritorialization implies that the average daily life, in the context of globality, is shaped by structures, processes, and products that originate elsewhere. From the food, clothes, and fuel we buy to the music and films we enjoy, the employer we work for, and the health risks we are exposed to, everyday routines for most people today are inconceivable without global networks of information and exchange. And while it is possible to 'reterritorialize' some of these dimensions by, for example, buying locally grown produce or supporting local artists, a more complete detachment from such networks is surely not within the average citizens' reach. To say this is not in and of itself to question the desirability of reestablishing a sense of place, but it does limit its viability as a model for thinking about the future of significant portions of the population.

Apart from such practical considerations, the concept of deterritorialization also points to a more theoretical problem in environmentalist calls for an ethic based on a sense of place. For it is not just that local places have changed through increased connectivity but also the structures of perception, cognition, and social expectations associated with them. Joshua Meyrowitz, in a seminal study of the impact of television, has shown how basic social parameters, such as the distinction between public and private places and the structures of authority associated with them, are altered by a technological medium that not only broadcasts public events into private living rooms but also gives social groups unprecedented insight into how other groups live and behave. As women see how men act in the absence of women, or the poor observe the lifestyles of the middle and upper classes in abundant visual detail, Meyrowitz shows, social relations themselves change. Structures of authority and of group inclusion and exclusion, as well as social inequalities, come to be perceived and have to be legitimated differently (1985, 69–126, 185–267). Along somewhat different lines, Beck has pointed to changes in the structure of affect and empathy through the embedding of daily life in transnational media networks (2004, 67). Such changes in social relations cannot simply be undone, even in the unlikely event that a majority of the population decided to turn off their television sets permanently. Related arguments surely have to be made for other media and other dimensions of increased global connectedness: once we have to perceive and live in our own places with the expanded awareness of other regions that media such as radio, television, telephony and the internet provide, our relationship to local places changes irreversibly.

The problem with environmentalist advocacies of place, from this perspective, lies in that most of them assume that individuals' existential encounters with nature and engagements with intimately known local places can be recuperated intact from the distortions of modernization. Analyses of media and studies of globalization, by contrast, suggest that the essence of such encounters and engagements itself has changed. Some of these changes may be subtle and for the most part unconscious – the fact that most citizens of Western countries can now compare their own locale with a much greater number of other places they have visited than previous generations, that our perception of the local natural world is inflected by media images of other ecosystems that we may never have seen in person, or that the materials and technologies by means of which we are able to inhabit particular places (from building materials to hiking gear or optical equipment) are fundamentally different. But some dimensions of this change are quite obvious – perhaps most saliently the fact that whatever knowledge inhabitants acquire about a particular place is for the most part inessential for their survival. Unlike tribal peoples, peasants, or hunters in past centuries, whose subsistence depended on their familiarity with the surrounding ecosystems, most citizens of modern societies are free to acquire such knowledge or not, or to learn some parts of it and ignore others. Some distinctly modern forms of intimate acquaintance with nature – highly specialized hobbies such as bird-watching or orchid collecting – depend precisely on their being leisure activities rather than existential necessities; and they are often quite far removed from any genuine ecological understanding, focusing as they do on one particular aspect of ecology rather than its systemic functioning. A sense of place and the knowledge that comes with it, in other words, is something that most people quite rightly perceive as a kind of hobby, something that may be useful and entertaining to acquire but on which basic existence does not depend, however desirable it might be from the viewpoint of the social collective.

This deterritorialization of local knowledge does not necessarily have to be detrimental for an environmentalist perspective, but on the contrary opens up new avenues into ecological consciousness. In a context of rapidly increasing connections around the globe, what is crucial for ecological awareness and environmental ethics is arguably not so much a sense of place as a sense of planet – a sense of how political, economic, technological, social, cultural, and ecological networks shape daily routines. If the concept of deterritorialization foregrounds how cultural practices become detached from place, it also points to how these practices are now imbricated in such larger networks. As a consequence, a wide range of different experiences and practices can serve as the point of departure for understanding these networks – some that are associated with a conventional 'sense of place', others that are unrelated to it. Thomashow rightly points to such a variety of starting points when he argues that observations of local weather or reflections on the migration patterns of birds showing up at a local feeder can lead to an intensified awareness of processes that shape regions far beyond the local (2002, 96–98). Yet he proves in the end unable to break with the conventional assumption that somehow all of them still have to be rooted in local perceptions and experiences. It is true that becoming familiar with local songbirds, for example, might lead one to inquire into their migratory patterns and the conditions of their remote seasonal habitats; or observing damage on local trees might give one the incentive to explore the origin of the acid rain that falls in one's region: familiarity with the local might lead one 'naturally' to the global. But if one grants the usefulness of such an exploration, one would also have to encourage avenues of inquiry into ecological connectedness that do not take their starting point in a familiarity with the local environment. If studying local plants is valuable because it can lead one to questions of global connectivity, so is exploring where the bananas one buys come from and under what conditions they were grown; under what circumstances and with what waste products one's TV set was put together; or how the shipping out of waste from one's own city might affect the community where it will be deposited. All of these inquiries open the local out into a network of ecological links that span a region, a continent, or the world.

Once one pursues such questions, one might also want to value concerns and types of knowledge that are even further removed from the local environment: individuals who have no leisure to pursue local knowledge – immigrants from another country, for example – may know a great deal about the climatological and socioeconomic difficulties of farming in their place of origin; some of those who are more affluent and move often to new places of residence have an acute sense of the consequences of urban sprawl: persons who would not be caught dead in a pair of hiking boots have intensely felt concerns over the impact of air pollution and pesticide use on their health; others are stirred into curiosity and sometimes into action by seeing a documentary about orangutan extinction on television; yet others who spend most of their time in front of a computer screen rather than in protests outside the local nuclear plant turn out to know a great deal about statistical trends in global agricultural production, population growth, or economic development; and some, like the students in Robert Hass's course, may know a great deal about global atmospheric change even though they are unable to identify local plants. If a knowledge of one's local place has value because it is a gateway to understanding global connectedness at various levels, then nonlocal types of knowledge and concern that also facilitate such an understanding should be similarly valuable. The challenge for environmentalist thinking, then, is to shift the core of its cultural imagination from a sense of place to a less territorial and more systemic sense of planet.

Such a reimagination of the global has been in process in many areas of cultural theory, where it has usually been shaped by its opposition to national imaginaries. Throughout the 1980s and 1990s, theorists in anthropology, philosophy, sociology, political science, and literary and cultural studies critically examined concepts of the nation and national identity, highlighting the practices, discourses, and institutions that served to legitimate and make appear natural what most of these approaches cast as highly artificial and historically contingent entities – Anderson's 'imagined communities'. Identities defined by nation or nationalism tended to be viewed as oppressive, while those shaped by hybridity, migration, borderlands, diaspora, nomadism, and exile were valued not only as more politically progressive but also as potential grounds for resistance to national hegemonies, raising 'hopes that transnational mobility and its associated processes have great liberatory potential (perhaps replacing international class struggle in orthodox Marxist thinking). In a sense, the diasporan subject is now vested with the agency formerly sought in the working class and more recently in the subaltern subject' (Ong 1999, 15). Anthropologist James Clifford's influential work *Routes* [1997], among others, expanded this analysis by showing how entire cultures, even native villages conventionally thought to be most clearly place-bound, are diasporic in nature, in that they derive their identity from connections to a variety of places ('routes') rather than their anchoring in just one locale ('roots').

Different types of theoretical projects emerged from this founding critique of nation-based identities. While a great deal of intellectual energy was invested in studies of particular borderlands identities or diasporic communities, other lines of research sought to define forms of belonging that would transcend exclusive commitments to a particular nation, culture, race, or ethnicity in favor of more global modes of awareness and attachment. In this context, scholars across a wide variety of disciplines sought to recuperate and redefine the concept of 'cosmopolitanism' as a way of imagining what such deterritorialized identities might look like. From the mid-1990s on, a profusion of studies revolving around this concept appeared, including work by Appiah [2006] and Nussbaum [and (Cohen 1996)] in philosophy; Clifford [1997] and Ong [1999] in anthropology; Beck [2004], Giddens [1990], Hannerz [1996], Tomlinson [1999] in sociology; Hayden [2005], Held [2002], and McGrew [2002] in political science; and Bhabha [1996], Cheah [and Robbins (1998)], Mignolo [2000], and [Cheah and] Robbins [1998] in literary and cultural studies, among many others. [. . .]

Theories of cosmopolitanism circumscribe a field of reflection rather than a firmly established and shared set of concepts and assumptions. All of them are concerned with the historical, political, and cultural circumstances under which modes of awareness that reach beyond the local and the national emerge and sustain themselves. With the long history of cosmopolitanism in mind – from the Stoics to sixteenth-century Spanish reflections on the nature of indigenous peoples in the new colonies and all the way to Kant – theorists seek to dissociate the term from connotations of European upper-class travel and to redefine it as a way of envisioning contemporary modes of consciousness that might be commensurate with intensified global connectedness. Many foreground a basic sense that nationally and regionally defined identities, far from emerging naturally, are established and maintained by means of complex sets of sociocultural practices, so as to explore how larger-scale affinities have emerged or might do so in the future. But within this general frame-work, theories of cosmopolitanism vary considerably. Many of them include both a descriptive component and a normative one. Descriptively, they seek to capture the ways people live connected to a wide variety of places and spaces that are geo-graphically and often culturally far removed from each other, aiming at many of the processes and phenomena that other researchers have investigated under the label 'deterritorialization'. Normatively, these theories attempt to outline an ideal form of awareness or cultural disposition. This dual orientation has in some ways been detrimental, in that it has led to a neglect of solidly empirical studies aimed at determining under what circumstances, with what subjects, and by what means affective and ethical attachments to the global arise (Skrbis, Kendall, et al. 2004, 119–21, 131–32); yet it has in practice also been productive, making cosmopolitan-ism a concept around which analytical perspectives as well as forward-looking political projects have crystallized.

Theories of cosmopolitanism also differ in other ways. Some of them focus centrally on the experience of the middle classes, sometimes specifically on intellectuals – as in Bruce Robbins's work – while others approach the question of global consciousness from the perspective of formerly colonial, marginalized, or disenfranchised populations and the kind of cosmopolitan awareness that results from international trade, labor migration, political displacement, or exile (for example, in the 'vernacular cosmopolitanisms' of Homi Bhabha or the 'colonial difference' that Walter Mignolo emphasizes).[1] Cosmopolitan perspectives emerge in some approaches as a more or less mechanical consequence of global circumstances and in others as a self-conscious adoption of values (Skrbis, Kendall, et al. 2004, 117); historically as well, cosmopolitanism is sometimes claimed to consist either of practices that have always formed part of even the most locally rooted human cultures or of a project that still awaits realization and is by definition always incomplete. [. . .] Similarly, the questions whether cosmopolitan awareness ultimately rests on a core of shared humanity or an acknowledgement of human difference and whether national and subnational affinities are antagonistic or com-plementary to such an awareness have been matters of controversy, especially in the debate about Martha Nussbaum's well-known essay 'Patriotism and Cosmopolitan-ism'. [. . .] Scholars have also approached the basis for generating and sustaining a cosmopolitan disposition from different angles, with some theorists foregrounding increased knowledge, a kind of transnational cultural literacy, as the foundation and others foregrounding particular forms of affect, while yet others have tended to see it mostly in a framework of ethical questions of responsibility or have investigated what kinds of sociopolitical institutions might further it.

Given this range of approaches, it is unsurprising that critiques of cosmopolitanism have also varied widely, in debates that cannot be unfolded here in detail. [. . .] scholars such as Timothy Brennan, Arif Dirlik, and Karen Caplan have pointed to the continued importance of local, regional, and national claims to identity in the context of political struggles that many of the theorists who advocate various forms of cosmopolitanism would most likely endorse. The significance, for an analysis of environmental discourses, of these debates about local, national, and global modes of belonging lies in the way they highlight how attachments to a particular category or scale of place can shift in value and function when considered in different political contexts. Advocacies of the local can play a useful political and cultural role in one context and become a philosophical as well as a pragmatic stumbling block in another. [. . .] it seems to me imperative to reorient current U.S. environmentalist discourse, ecocriticism included, toward a more nuanced understanding of how both local cultural and ecological systems are imbricated in global ones. This argument for an increased emphasis on a sense of planet, a cognitive understanding and affective attachment to the global, should be understood not as a claim that environmentalism should welcome globalization in every form (there are good reasons to resist some of its dimensions) or as a refusal to acknowledge that appeals to indigenous traditions, local knowledge, or national law are in some cases appropriate and effective strategies. Rather, it is intended as a call to ground any such discourses in a thorough cultural and scientific understanding of the global – that is, an environmentally oriented cosmopolitanism or 'world environmental citizenship', as Patrick Hayden calls it (2005, 121–51).

An indispensable first step in the direction of such an eco-cosmopolitan awareness is the acknowledgment of 'varieties of environmentalism', as Ramachandra Guha and Juan Martínez-Alier have labeled the divergent motivations of efforts for the protection of nature in different regions of the world. Most importantly, Guha and Martínez-Alier distinguish between a First World environmentalism and the 'environmentalism of the poor'. First World environmentalism, they argue, tends to arise from a matrix of what Ronald Inglehart called 'postmaterialist values', that is, a set of cultural values, including the preservation of the natural environment, that move to the forefront once societies have attained a certain level of affluence. In many developing countries, by contrast, poor and sometimes not-so-poor communities struggle for the pursuit of traditional ways of using nature, or simply for control of natural resources that are essential for their survival. Far from any 'postmaterialist' motivation, such fights for the sustainable exploitation of local forests, against the construction of large dams, or against the contamination of groundwater involve the most basic necessities for the survival of the affected communities. Since such struggles tend not to be anchored in any deep-ecological valuation of nature for its own sake, Guha and Martínez-Alier argue, they have often not been recognized as 'environmentalist' by ecologically oriented movements in the industrialized world. Yet they aim at the preservation of natural ecosystems and their sustainable human use in just the same way (1997, 16–21).

Guha and Martínez-Alier admit that the opposition may not be as simple as one between materialist and nonmaterialist struggles for the environment. The fight against pathogenic waste disposals or nuclear armament in developed countries is no less a struggle for survival than that of communities in the developing world for access to crucial resources for their livelihood. In addition, Guha and Martínez-Alier acknowledge that some theorists – Vandana Shiva, for example – have attributed an essentially nonmaterialist approach to nature to some Eastern forms of spirituality as well as to certain indigenous cultures or to women. They therefore end up with a fourfold division between developed and developing countries' and materialist and nonmaterialist environmentalisms (36). Such distinctions provide a first route of access to a broader understanding of what forms the interactions between nature and culture and, more specifically, between different socioeconomic systems, cultures, and natural environments at risk might take. Still, Guha and Martínez-Alier's schema remains strikingly general in its assumptions. It provides no easy way, for example, to account for substantial differences in the cultural perception of genetically modified foods between the United States and western Europe; the deep wariness of nuclear technology that distinguishes German and Japanese culture from the traditional French perception of nuclear plants as icons of progress; the importance of animal rights in British environmentalism, which sets it apart from its continental European counterparts; or representations of nature as rugged and wild in traditional Chinese culture, as opposed to representations of it as constrained, small-scale, and domesticated in Japanese culture, to name just a few examples.[2] What I mean to suggest here is not that varieties of environmentalism necessarily line up with the boundaries of national cultures (though the latter certainly do play an important role in shaping them, as do different indigenous traditions) but that the study of such varieties from an eco-cosmopolitan perspective will need to develop finer-grained distinctions than the very general ones proposed by Guha and Martínez-Alier between First and Third World or materialist and nonmaterialist motivations.

Yet even such an expanded understanding of how different cultures approach nature, which parts they consider most worth preserving, and what they perceive to be the most important dangers threatening it still leaves at least one crucial distinction intact between this kind of eco-cosmopolitan project and the political and cultural theories of cosmopolitanism I have mentioned. The strength of these theories lies in the way they use the cosmopolitan concept to provide a shorthand for a cultural and political understanding that allows individuals to think beyond the boundaries of their own cultures, ethnicities, or nations to a range of other sociocultural frameworks. But whether this understanding is framed as thinking in terms of a shared humanity or in terms of access to and valuation of cultural differences, cosmopolitanism in these discussions is circumscribed by human social experience. Eco-cosmopolitanism, by contrast, reaches toward what some environmental writers and philosophers have called the 'more-than-human world' – the realm of nonhuman species, but also that of connectedness with both animate and inanimate networks of influence and exchange. [. . .] While some environmentalists have claimed that biological diversity is closely associated with cultural diversity (see Nabhan 2002), which might tempt one to conclude that an understanding of other cultures might easily be linked to an interest in the state of other species, the interaction between the two projects is arguably more complex than that. Undoubtedly, environmentalists will encounter scenarios in which the interests of particular human populations cannot be easily lined up with the needs of the non-human environment. Eco-cosmopolitanism will not be able to provide an easy template for making such difficult choices in all cases, but at least it would allow those who are charged with making these choices to base their decisions on a thorough understanding of the cultural as well as the ecological frameworks within which they will play themselves out. In this context, clearly, the question of how the rights (or more generally, the affectedness) of nonhuman parts of the biosphere should be legally, politically, and culturally represented takes on central importance (Stone 1996; Eckersley 2004, 439–32; Murphy 2006); but this question itself needs to be considered from within the different frameworks of cultures that cast their own relationships to other species in quite divergent terms.

Eco-cosmopolitanism, then, is an attempt to envision individuals and groups as part of planetary 'imagined communities' of both human and nonhuman kinds. [. . .] While the cultural mechanisms by means of which allegiance to national communities is generated, legitimated, and maintained have been studied in depth, ecocriticism has only begun to explore the cultural means by which ties to the natural world are produced and perpetuated, and how the perception of such ties fosters or impedes regional, national, and transnational forms of identification. Too often, as I have shown, the temptation on the part of environmentalist writers, philosophers, and cultural critics has been to assume that such ties emerge 'naturally' and spontaneously in the process of inhabiting particular places, while allegiances to larger entities – modern society, the nation-state – have to be created by complex and artificial means. But as analyses of nation-based forms of identity have shown, individuals in certain cultural contexts readily identify themselves as belonging to very large-scale and abstract entities of which they have only partial personal experience, a kind of commitment that place-oriented environmentalists tend to consider highly artificial and arbitrary. As well they should – but not without acknowledging at the same time the possibility that a sense of the local is simply the analogous outcome of a different set of cultural commitments and habits rather than a 'natural' foundation. To call entities such as the nation 'abstract' in this context, at any rate, may well be to misunderstand the work culture accomplishes; arguably, it is precisely through culture that national belonging – just as local belonging – comes to appear concrete, obvious, and woven into the texture of one's own thoughts and feelings [see Ong 1999, 4]. [. . .] The point of an eco-cosmopolitan critical project, therefore, would be to go beyond the aforementioned 'ethic of proximity' so as to investigate by what means individuals and groups in specific cultural contexts have succeeded in envisioning themselves in similarly concrete fashion as part of the global biosphere, or by what means they might be enabled to do so; at the same time, as the work of Vandana Shiva, among others, highlights, such a perspective needs to be attentive to the political frameworks in which communities begin to see themselves as part of a planetary community, and what power struggles such visions might be designed to hide or legitimate.

In this context, 'the issue isn't so much that all places are connected (one of the great clichés of modern environmental studies), as it is understanding which connections are most important', as Thomashow argues (2002, 194). Precisely – but Thomashow is mistaken in concluding that a sense of place will invariably be the privileged cultural means by which such a systemic understanding is achieved. While it can be a helpful tool in some cases and for some people, the focus on the local can also block an understanding of larger salient connections [. . .]. Besides the valuation of physical experience and sensory perception, therefore, an ecocosmopolitan approach should also value the abstract and highly mediated kinds of knowledge and experience that lend equal or greater support to a grasp of biospheric connectedness. McKenzie Wark has made this point forcefully and humorously in an essay that reflects on the enormous role that computer modeling and simulations have played in the scientific description of global ecological processes, as well as on the way these modeling techniques have trickled down to the popular entertainment sphere in the shape of computer games such as SimEarth. The capabilities of such software tools, Wark argues, make it possible for users to understand the consequences of even minor changes in one variable for the system as a whole, and thereby enable an understanding of global ecology that is very difficult to attain through direct observation and lived experience: 'It is only by becoming more abstract, more estranged from nature that I can make the cultural leap to thinking its fragile totality', he concludes (1994a, 127).

Computer images of various types have played an increasingly important role in the cultural imagination of global ecology [. . .]. But they are only a small subset of a much larger array of cultural strategies and devices by means of which Planet Earth has become perceivable and experienceable as a complex set of eco-systems over the last forty years. The task of ecocriticism with a cosmopolitan perspective is to develop an understanding and critique of these mechanisms as they play themselves out in different cultural contexts so as to create a variety of ecological imaginations of the global.

[. . .]

What the analysis of genres such as allegory and collage, and of tropes such as that of the network, suggests is the importance of formal choices in the imagination and representation of the global. Through such choices, existing ideas and ideologies of collectivity and totality, some with very long cultural traditions, are deployed in the attempt to envision global ecological belonging. An awareness of such forms and their cultural background and implications is part and parcel of an environmentally oriented cosmopolitanism that not only seeks to explore how global systems shape local forms of inhabitation but also is aware of how this exploration itself is framed by culturally specific assumptions. [. . .]

John Klima's installation *Earth*, a version of which was exhibited at the 2002 Biennial at the Whitney Museum, takes up the 1960s image of the Blue Planet but inserts it into both new informational systems and networks of different viewers. The installation exists in several different forms – as a stand-alone combination of a computer, monitor, and track-ball input device, as a Java browser module, and as a more complex object with two input stations at the Whitney – a plurality that itself suggests something of the transformability of data into different images that forms the core of Klima's portrayal of the global. The work consists of software that gathers internet data about topography and weather for the Earth and projects them onto a three-dimensional model of the planet, in such a way that the user can zoom in and out of different regions and see them displayed in terms of six different layers of data about the Earth as a whole as well as the specific places the viewer zooms in on. In the stand-alone installation, which is hooked up to the internet, other online viewers are represented by icons of positioning satellites; in an interesting twist, since online users cannot be readily identified in terms of their geographical position, the system has to attempt a good guess at their location in order to represent them in this way. At the Whitney installation, two viewers could use the system simultaneously and see each other's views, which were also being projected on a transparent weather balloon positioned above the computer stations. Through the possibilities of zooming in and out as well as the accessibility of other viewers' perspectives, *Earth* gestures formally toward the kind of ecological cosmopolitanism I have outlined here. Klima's installation generates images that combine different spatial scales into striking visual collages like the one of Patagonia shown here (Figure 17.1). The view of the 'Blue Planet' is here overlaid with detailed, three-dimensional profiles of the local terrain, as well as the regional coast outline and an indicator of the viewer's position. The geometrical, square-by-square representation of the topography contrasts with the jagged coastline as well as with the familiar blue sphere against black space, which here appears at an unusual tilted angle. In its combination of different imaging techniques and scales, the dynamic manipulation of the data by the viewer, and connectedness to both informational and social networks that span the world, *Earth* suggests some of the complexities an eco-cosmopolitan imagination of the global must take into account at the beginning of the third millennium.

Klima's installation uncannily prefigured one of the most recent internet tools to have come into common usage. Google Earth, an application that was originally developed under the name Earth Viewer by Keyhole Inc. and acquired by the search engine company Google in 2004, allows users to travel virtually around the globe, to zoom in and out of different regions and locations, and to display different sets of data about these sites. Like Klima's *Earth*, it builds on data inputs from a variety of sources such as aerial photography, satellite images, and geographic information systems that are projected on to a model of the planet, with some cities and natural sites available for three-dimensional viewing. Because this application is able to display satellite images from around the globe in very high resolution and in

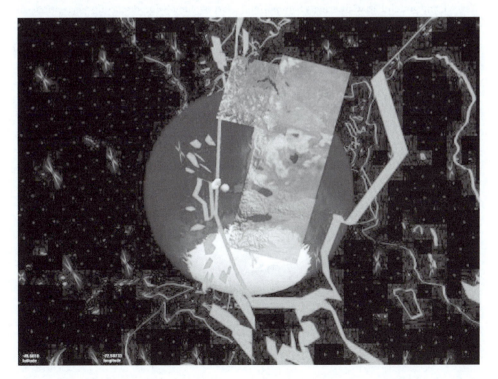

Figure 17.1

close-up, allowing the viewer even to discern structures such as trees and cars in many cases, it has become not only a popular entertainment but also a threat to governments and institutions who would prefer to keep certain parts of their territory shielded from public view. This latest metamorphosis of the Blue Planet image into a searchable and zoomable database in the shape of a virtual globe signals and sums up some of the crucial transformations that have taken place in the imagination of the global since the 1960s. No longer relying on allegorical images of the planet, Google Earth instead instantiates what media theorist Lev Manovich has called the 'database aesthetic' of much new media art, in his view a new aesthetic configuration that is neither narrative nor metaphorical in its basic structure but instead presents infinitely expandable sets of data with the possibility of establishing different sorts of sets and linkages between them (Manovich 2001, 212–43). In its ability to display the whole planet as well as the minute details of particular places in such a way that the user can zoom from one to the other and focus on different types of information, Google Earth's database imaginary may well be the latest and post-postmodernist avatar of modernist collage, which has now turned global, digital, dynamic, and interactive. It also, more metaphorically, points the way to some of the information, as well as formal structures, that eco-cosmopolitanism of the kind I have described here can rely on, and through which it can express itself.

Notes

1   See also Posnock on the question of cosmopolitanism's historical associations with egalitarianism (2000, 803–4).
2   I am grateful to Catherine Diamond and Haruo Shirane for discussing perceptions of nature in Chinese and Japanese culture with me.

Chapter 18

Graham Huggan

'GREENING' POSTCOLONIALISM: ECOCRITICAL PERSPECTIVES

From *MFS Modern Fiction Studies* 50.3: 703–9

[. . .]

THIS ESSAY TAKES ITS CUE FROM [DEANE] Curtin's conviction that global 'ecological citizenship' requires commitments to human, as well as wider ecological justice, engendering the recognition that nature has extrinsic, as well as intrinsic value for us all. As Curtin says, 'the view [held by several prominent radical ecologists] that nature has *only* intrinsic value is strangely anti-ecocentric since it implies that humans are not part of nature' (1999, 189, [brackets by Huggan]). [. . .] It also tries to answer Curtin's call for a carefully case-based, historically contextualized analysis of contemporary social and environmental problems. My analysis weighs the advantages of a pluralistic 'cross-cultural ethical discourse' against the implicit arrogance of First World (neo)liberalism (164) and seeks to add ecocritical perspectives to a number of fundamental postcolonial debates. Among these are what Gayatri Spivak calls the 'worlding' of the Third World (1987), the ambivalent role of the postindependence state in brokering national economic development, and, not least, the value of imaginative writing as a site of discursive resistance to authoritarian attitudes and practices that not only disrupt specific human individuals and societies, but might also be seen as posing a threat to the entire 'ecosphere' and its network of interdependent 'biotic communities' (Naess 1995). [. . .] The essay also gives a recent postcolonial twist, acutely conscious of its cultural location, to the longstanding debate within environmental ethics on the reconcilability or not of (liberal) animal-rights and (radical) ecocentric positions. [. . .] Finally, it offers some thoughts on the cultural construction of the 'ecological subject' (Dobson 1990, 54–55), and on the implications for postcolonial, as well as ecological criticism of entering into the imaginative world – the collective consciousness – of other sentient creatures.

Ecocriticism, at present, is a predominantly white movement, arguably lacking the institutional support-base to engage fully with multicultural and cross-cultural concerns (Glotfelty 1996, xxv; see, however, Buell [1995; 2001]; Murphy [2000];

Slaymaker [2001]). Similarly, ecologically related contributions to postcolonial criticism have tended until fairly recently to focus on the former (also predominantly white) 'settler cultures', taking in such issues as the use of territorial metaphor to reflect changing patterns of land use and spatial perception, the geopolitics of colonial occupation and expansion, the rival claims of Western property rights and Native/indigenous title, destructive encounters between conflicting ecosystems, and the mutual entanglement of biological and cultural factors in providing the ideological basis for imperial rule (Crosby 1986; Carter 1987; Darian-Smith, Gunner, et al. 1996; New 1997). Several of these studies are arguably motivated, at least in part, by a sense of collective historical guilt and vicariously experienced trauma, and are not always sufficiently alert to the temptations of 'imperialist nostalgia' – a closet ideology the practitioners of which are given to mourn what they themselves have helped destroy (Rosaldo 1989, 69–70). [. . .]

It seems useful, in this context, to turn to contributions from non-Western environmental scholars, as well as to case studies from other parts of the world that explore the intersections between postcolonial and ecological concerns. Unsurprisingly, predominantly literary scholars are outflanked here by those working in other – or across other – academic disciplines. Within the vast interdisciplinary field of South Asian studies, for instance, the sociologist Ramachandra Guha's historical account of the Chipko (Himalayan peasant antideforestation) movement in the 1970s (2000), and the ecofeminist-activist Vandana Shiva's analysis of the disastrous consequences of the Green Revolution for subsistence-farming communities in late-twentieth-century Punjab (1991), serve as twin reminders that ecological disruption is coextensive with damage to the social fabric; and that environmental issues cannot be separated from questions of social justice and human rights. In documenting histories from below, both scholars mount an indirect challenge to what Ania Loomba (following Spivak) has called the 'overworlding' of the Third World (1993) – to that well-intentioned, but unmistakably Western-elitist construction of the Third World as a locus of anti-imperialist resistance, the overpowering rhetoric of which risks silencing the very masses on whose behalf it claims to speak (Loomba 1993; see also (Spivak 1987; 2000b; O'Hanlon 2000). [. . .] Yet Guha's and Shiva's primary concern is less with the West or Western imperialism *per se* than with the neocolonialist imperatives of the postindependence Indian state. This 'centralized management system', in pursuing 'a policy of planned destruction of diversity in [both] nature and culture' (Shiva 1991, 12), has actively sought to impose a homogenizing late-capitalist vision of economic progress most obviously beneficial to the nation's ruling elite (Guha 2000, 195–96). The state's coercive allocation and management of natural resources can be seen as a postcolonial version of ecological imperialism in which it becomes clear that 'the forced march to industrialisation' has had disastrous cultural, as well as ecological effects (Guha 2000, 196). For Shiva, there are thus two symbiotically related crises in postcolonial India: an ecological crisis brought about by the use of resource-destructive technological processes and a cultural/ethnic crisis emerging from an erosion of the social structures that make cultural diversity and plurality possible (1991, 12, 235).

Guha and, particularly, Shiva stand behind the work of Arundhati Roy, whose fulminating essays 'The Greater Common Good' (1999) and 'The End of the Imagination' (1998 [1999]), capitalizing on the runaway success of her Booker prizewinning novel *The God of Small Things* (1997), probably represent the most eye-catching ecocritical intervention to date by a recognized postcolonial writer. The essays – first published separately as cover stories for two mainstream English-language Indian magazines, *Outlook* and *Frontline*, and later repackaged for the international mass market as *The Cost of Living* (1999) – are clear attempts to reach out both to a local readership familiar with their controversial issues (the Narmada Valley Project in the first essay, India's decision to go nuclear in the second), and to an international audience possibly unaware of, and probably uninformed on, either issue, but sufficiently attuned to Roy's success to grant her work another look. [. . .] The essays are deliberately designed . . . as a politically motivated publicity venture that, riding on the back of Roy's recently accorded literary celebrity status, seeks to attract and, ideally, convert large numbers of readers both in her home country and elsewhere. Now, it would be easy here to categorize Roy as another media-hungry Indo-Anglian cosmopolitan celebrity (Brennan; Mongia), or to see her as placing a well-timed stake in the latest popular humanitarian cause. Certainly, in the first essay mentioned above (on which I shall concentrate here), Roy takes rhetorical liberties with her disempowered Adivasi subjects, converting them into mythologized victims in her own highly personal moral crusade against the tyrannies of the modern Indian state. And certainly, she is aware throughout the essay of the constitutive, but also distortive, role of the global media in constructing the latest, highly visible human/ecological catastrophe as a newsworthy 'event' (1999, 47, 50, 63; see also Rowell 1996, 282–86). [. . .] But Roy, as in her previous work, is not only interested in manipulating publicity for her own, and other people's, interests, but in showing how publicity – or, in this case, the mediated language of the common good, the *national* interest – achieves its magical effects. Hence the ironic title of her essay, which reflects on the ways in which a centralized state has not only commandeered national assets and resources, but has also sought through media channels to convey the fiction of a carefully monitored 'national progress'. The fiction of 'national progress' demands that government be 'abstracted out of the messy business of politics', thereby releasing it for the utopian task of 'receiving inputs from all parts of society, processing them, and finally allocating the optimal values for the common satisfaction and preservation of society as a whole' (Chatterjee 1986, 160). Technological know-how is an essential instrument of the 'magic of the State' (Taussig 1997). And such expertise, in the hands of the few, requires the self-sacrifice of the many:

> Place all your prayers at the feet of the *sarkar*, the omnipotent and supremely enlightened state, and they will be duly passed on to the body of experts who are planning for the overall progress of the country. If your requests are consistent with the requirements of progress, they will be granted.
>
> (Chatterjee 1986, 160)

These, in Partha Chatterjee's appropriately sardonic terms, are the grounds for Roy's ecological fable of the Narmada Valley Project: the ill-fated postindependence irrigation scheme, affecting hundreds of thousands of lives, that is usually considered to be 'India's Greatest Planned Environmental Disaster' (Roy 1999, 44), and that is sometimes seen, in 'the congealed morass of hope, anger, information, disinformation, political artifice, engineering ambition, disingenuous socialism, radical activism, bureaucratic subterfuge, [and] misinformed emotionalism' that surrounds it (9), as a metonymy for the self-consuming narrative of modern India itself (Preface).

A few facts may be helpful here. India is the third largest dam builder in the world, having built over three thousand big dams in the fifty-odd years since independence (McCully 1996; Roy 1999, Preface). Of these dams, several of the largest and best-known belong to the state-administered Narmada Valley Project, spanning three states (Gujarat, Maharashtra, and Madhya Pradesh) in central India. This hugely ambitious project, first dreamed up more than forty years ago and still – despite massive protests and a legal stay, now lifted, against further construction [. . .] – considered to be a viable proposition, conceives of building '3,200 dams that will reconstitute the Narmada [river] and her forty-one tributaries into a series of step reservoirs – an immense staircase of amenable water'. Two of these dams, the giant Sardar Sarovar in Gujarat and the Narmada Sagar in Madhya Pradesh, will hold 'more water [between them] than any other reservoir on the Indian subcontinent' (Roy 1999, 33, [brackets by Huggan]). The project aims to provide electricity and safe drinking water for millions, while irrigating millions of hectares of infertile farming land. From its inception, however, the project has been fraught with problems, proving in many people's eyes to have been massively misconceived. Hundreds of thousands of local people, mostly Adivasis, have been ousted from their land, with irreparable damage being done to their daily lives, their economic self-sufficiency, and their culture. Evidence suggests that the project may consume more electricity than it produces, and that its state-of-the-art flood-warning and irrigation systems have had a damaging – in some cases, devastating – effect on the very land the dams sought to protect, the very crop-yields they promised to increase. The astronomic cost of the project, heavily subsidized by the World Bank until its forced withdrawal in the early nineties, has helped push 'the country [further] into an economic bondage that it may never overcome' (35). Widespread dissent, mobilized around the powerful Narmada Bachao Andolan (Save the Narmada Movement), has been violently suppressed. All in all, as Andrew Rowell summarizes it, the Narmada Valley Project,

> conceived in the dinosaur development era that deemed megaprojects the panacea for the world's energy problems, has been nothing short of a human and ecological catastrophe, . . . an example of the neglect of local communities' needs and views in the development equation and the state repression against dissent when communities want to have their voices heard.
>
> (1996, 282)

But the story, as Roy knows, is not limited to the facts, depressing though these may be. For the project and, particularly, the big dams at its center have also played a symbolic role in the development of India as a modern nation (McCully 1996, 1; Roy 1999, 15). As Patrick McCully puts it,

> Perhaps more than any other technology, massive dams symbolize the progress of humanity from a life ruled by nature and superstition to one where nature is ruled by science, and superstition vanquished by rationality. They also symbolize the might of the state that built them,

making huge dams a favourite of nation-builders and autocrats. When a dam is given such a powerful symbolic role, its economic and technical rationale and potential negative impacts fade into insignificance in the decision-making process.

(1996, 237)

Big dams, in other words, suggest a potentially deadly alliance between the modernist ideology of technological gigantism and repressively authoritarian politics of state ownership and control (Roy 1999, 91–92). This alliance is further cemented by trans-national commercial interests. The international dam industry, as Roy points out, is

worth $20 billion a year. If you follow the trails of Big Dams the world over, wherever you go – China, Japan, Malaysia, Thailand, Brazil, Guatemala – you'll rub up against the same story, encounter the same actors: the Iron Triangle (damjargon for the nexus between politicians, bureaucrats and dam construction companies), the racketeers who call themselves International Environmental Consultants (who are usually directly employed by dam-builders or their subsidiaries), and more often than not, the friendly neighbourhood World Bank. [. . .]

(35–36)

The national allegory of statist abuse Roy constructs around the Narmada Valley Project thus gradually widens out into an ecological 'war for the rivers and the mountains and the forests of the world' (52). At the same time, the narrative Roy spins out takes on the dimensions both of antistatist fable, quasi-Dickensian in its moral intensity – '[The state is] a giant poverty-producing machine, masterful in its methods of pitting the poor against the very poor' (28, [brackets by Huggan]) – and of cautionary tale on the ecological price to be paid when 'human intelligence . . . outstrips[s] its own instinct for survival', and 'twentieth-century emblems' such as big dams and nuclear bombs become 'malignant indications of a civilisation turning upon itself' (101, [brackets by Huggan]).

If Roy's message is crystal-clear, unashamedly partisan in its intentions, her text remains a curiously unresolved mixture – part hard-headed investigative report, part sentimental political fable,[1] part historically situated postcolonial allegory, part universal Green manifesto and call-to-arms. The different narrative strands cut across and contradict one another. Facts are needed to illustrate the enormity of the story, but its teller also complains of suffocating statistics and the state's own version of 'Fascist Maths' (72). The breathless language of fable is ironized on numerous occasions – 'Nobody knows this, but Kevadia Colony is the key to the World. Go there, and secrets will be revealed to you' (73) – only to be reinstated, writ doubly large, on just as many again:

Who knows . . . what the twenty-first century has in store for us. The dismantling of the Big? Big bombs, big dams, big ideologies, big contra-dictions, big countries, big wars, big heroes, big mistakes. Perhaps it will be the Century of the Small. Perhaps right now, this very minute, there's a small god up in heaven readying herself for us.

(12)

Complex social, political, and ecological systems – as if to counter the technocrat's with the storyteller's magic – are repeatedly reduced to the black-and-white dramatics of the children's morality tale (15, 24, 41). In the end, the standard format of the ecological heroes-and-villains story, however ironically manipulated, proves to be no match for contemporary postcolonial realities. [. . .] Indeed, it raises the question of whom Roy believes herself to be speaking for (Adivasi 'oustees'? The Narmada Bachao Andolan? International environmental activists and 'eco-warriors'? [. . .] The Indian people?) – an open question that blurs the boundaries between the underclass victims of ecological disaster and their privileged supporters (Gadgil and Guha 1995), and that makes Roy vulnerable to the criticism that she is silencing those on whose behalf she wishes to speak. Roy's tirade against the state seems to want to claim a victory for the people (Roy 1999, 48–49). But which people? As other commentators have pointed out, it is already oversimplified to say that the political battle in the Narmada Valley is a basic conflict between 'the state' (in the Blue Corner) and 'the people' (in the Red); there are also numerous conflicts between different sections of the people and different branches of the state, while even within the Narmada resistance movement there are factional splits between different groups, each of which sees itself as acting in the people's interests (Singh 1995, 1; see also Fisher 1995 and Omvedt 1999). Roy's text thus draws attention to at least two different modes of the 'worlding' of the Third World to be found in certain postcolonially inflected forms of environmental protest writing: the first of these launches a rightful attack on a quintessentially neocolonialist 'Iron Triangle' (politicians, bureaucrats, and corporations, with International Aid backing), which has exploited the progressivist ideologies of Third World economic development for its own immediate ends; the second risks amounting to a further subalternization of some of the Third World's poorest people, whose stories are told – in English – so that we privileged First-Worlders, and our Third World middle-class counterparts, might help them 'resist'. 'The Greater Common Good', for all its overdramatized pieties, remains a highly intriguing text – not least because, like the autocannibalizing tiger that provides its first and most arresting image (Roy 1999, Preface), it effectively deconstructs many of its own best arguments by drawing attention to itself as a playful piece of highly literary investigative writing. This raises the larger question of how to harness the resources of aesthetic play to reflect on weighty philosophical/ethical issues, as well as to serve a variety of 'real-world' needs and 'direct' political ends.

Note

1   It is worth noting that while the ninety footnotes to 'The Greater Common Good' are all to nonfictional sources (scientific studies, economic reports, etc.), Roy's essay continually draws attention to itself as a *literary* artifact. Various intertexts come to mind, including Dickens's novels and Swift's satires, but in its combination of righteous indignation and storytelling verve, the essay most recalls the work of Rushdie, particularly the cross-over political allegory/fable/children's-tale-for-adults, itself drawn from multiple sources, that is *Haroun and the Sea of Stories* (1990).

Chapter 19

Pablo Mukherjee

SURFING THE SECOND WAVE: AMITAV GHOSH'S *THE HUNGRY TIDE*

From *New Formations* 59 (2006): 144–57.

> . . . to grasp historical being in its external historical determination, there where it is most historical, as itself natural being, or to grasp nature, there where it apparently resides most profoundly within itself, as historical being.
>
> Theodor W. Adorno

T HE 'NEW WORLD ORDER' PROCLAIMED BY George Bush I more than a decade and a half ago presents us with the deadly spectacle of current and future wars – Afghanistan, the Balkans and Iraq yesterday and today; Iran, Latin America and perhaps China tomorrow. It is also a spectacle where the 'environmental' is increasingly embedded into the social, political and military dimensions of conflict. That 'Palestine' names a series of historic struggles for specific rights over land, water and housing is taken to be common knowledge (Peled 2006; Tilley 2006). [. . .] That 'Iraq' is a short-hand for pre-emptive US attempts to secure energy resources and therefore a position of strength in future bargains for power against rival bidders like China is the stuff of broad-sheet editorials. That the march to the Gulf wars was accompanied by rhetorical drumbeats about Iraq's alleged capacities of degrading the environment of the Gulf area with its chemical/biological weapons merely confirms this entwining (Pelletiere 2001; Rashid 2002; Ali 2004; Coll 2004; Hiro 2005). [. . .] There is nothing startling anymore about Andrew Ross's suggestion that Gulf War 1 was the first explicitly ecological war of our times (Ross 1994, 18–19). The various current and predicted water/minerals/narcotics 'wars' in Africa, Asia, and Latin America seem to be gloomy confirmations of his jeremiad. These analyses and debates about the 'new world order' are further quickened by routine pronouncements about 'global warming' and its possible impact on access to resources, human migration and habitats.

The only surprising thing about this conceptual importance accorded to 'environment' seems to be its relative novelty. Surely, any field purporting to theorise the global conditions of colonialism/imperialism, decolonisation and neo-colonialism (let us agree to call it 'postcolonial studies') cannot but consider the complex interplay of 'environmental' categories such as water, land, energy, habitat, migration, with political or cultural categories such as state, society, conflict, literature, theatre, visual arts. Equally, any field purporting to attach interpretative importance to 'environment' (let us call it eco/environmental studies) must be able to trace the social, historical and material co-ordinates of categories such as forests, rivers, bio-regions and species. The fact that the traffic between postcolonial and eco studies can be chronologically framed within the 'new world order' calls for some periodisation of the two fields.

If we take the number of impressively thick readers or anthologies as an indicator, both 'eco/green' and postcolonial studies are in ruddy institutional health. If these collections can also be seen as chronological markers of a field's maturing, postcolonial and eco studies seem to have developed and entrenched themselves in northern academes around roughly the same historical moment. Four leading eco/green readers appeared between the mid-nineties and 2003 – Glotfelty and Fromm's in 1996; Laurence Coupe's in 2000, Adamson, Evans and Stein's in 2002, and Branch and Slovic's in 2003. Among the truly dizzying numbers of introductions, readers and anthologies of postcolonial criticism and theory are those edited by Mongia (1996), Gandhi (1998), Brydon (2000), Chrisman and Parry (2000), Schwarz and Roy (2000), Young (2001) and (2003), Goldberg and Quayson (2002), Lazarus (2004) and Desai [and Nair] (2005). The contents of these volumes seem to suggest that while *institutionally*, these fields were formed in the mid-to-late 1980[s], their *constitutive* theories and reflective practices were fleshed out largely from the early 1970s onwards.[1] To be more specific, although both postcolonial and eco studies claim an intellectual inheritance of at least two centuries and counting (to Romanticism and various eighteenth- and nineteenth-century anti-colonial struggles), their contemporary lives may be dated roughly from Earth Day in 1970 to the second invasion and occupation of Iraq 2004–5. If it is possible to divide the fields into their 'first' and 'second' wave stages, I will suggest that the breakage between the two was marked by the events of the first Gulf War of 1991.

There have been a number of critics pioneering the tracing of the overlaps between the two fields. SueEllen Campbell has noted the common grounds of 'deep' ecology and post-structuralism (taken to be the dominant theoretical/conceptual source of postcolonialism) – 'both criticize the traditional sense of a separate, independent, authoritative center of value or meaning; both substitute the idea of networks' (Campbell 1996, 131). Dominic Head has detected the specifically shared grounds between postcolonial and environmental theories – 'A position of informed recentring, then, is common to different branches of postmodernism, such as post-colonialism and ecologism' (1998, 28–29). These comments, however, may be most relevant to what may be called the 'first-wave' stages of the fields.

During this 'first-wave' stage spanning the 1970s and 1980s, theorists and critics pioneering postcolonial and eco/environmental methodologies claimed nothing less than a comprehensive critique of European modernity, in particular its core components of capitalism, colonialism/imperialism and patriarchy. They positioned themselves as being integral to the oppositional activism of decolonisation and environmental/green movements. Crucially, both attempted to re-insert the category of the 'world' back into a relation with the 'text' and the 'reader' and articulate a 'new' universality, but *did so only by degrading the social/material as conceptual categories*. As Lawrence Buell points out, 'first-wave' eco-critics 'looked to the movement chiefly as a way of "rescuing" literature from the distantiations of reader from text and text from the world that had been ushered in by the structuralist revolution in critical theory', and yet they tried to do so by privileging the 'wilderness' above the 'social' (2005, 6–31).

Similarly, 'first-wave' postcolonial theorists stressed, above all, the importance of the historical specificity of literature and culture. Yet, frequently, their very notion of 'history' or 'culture' remained textualist/linguistic in conception and their own institutional/material locations undertheorised. This combination produced a number of results – consensus tended to be privileged above conflict as the conceptual paradigm of colonial and post- or neo-colonial conditions, the migrant cosmopolitan rather than the migrant refugee was taken to be the paradigmatic figure of contemporary history, and de-territorialisation was privileged over all types of territorialisations, especially the category of the nation (see San Juan 1998; Lazarus 1999; Hallward 2001; Parry 2004 [. . .]). In short, when 'first-wave' postcolonial and eco theories attempted to relate 'texts' to the 'world', the relative paucity of historico/materialist conceptualisation meant that they often failed to conceptualise the kind of progressive universality to which they aspired. It must also be noted that a strong auto-critical impulse was embedded in the 'first-wave' phase of the theories. The very foundational nomenclatures were subject to severe criticism. Murray Bookchin wrote 'By "environmentalism" I propose to designate a mechanistic, instrumental outlook that sees nature as a passive habitat composed of "objects" such as animals, plants, minerals and the like that must be rendered more serviceable for human use' (1982, 21). Cheryll Glotfelty rejected 'enviro' for being anthropocentric and dualistic. Similarily, Diana Brydon points out that 'as early as 1989, Ketu Katrak was writing about the need to decolonize post-colonial theory' (2000, 8).

However, it was only during the early 1990s that a new sharpness and system becomes evident in this critique of the 'first-wave'. A broadly materialist socio/historical energy re-entered the fields and has since then continued to challenge and reshape the 'first-wave' tendencies. The field of postcolonial theory has been particularly marked by this revision. In addition to Lazarus, Parry, Hallward and San Juan, Anne McClintock has shown the pitfalls of the term 'postcolonial' to be the re-inscription of the very relations of power that it allegedly seeks to disturb. Arif Dirlik has found in the term an expression of the newly found privilege of a certain section of the mobile cosmopolitan elites of the global south [1994]. Aijaz Ahmed has suggested that the re-surfacing of the term 'postcolonial' in literary/cultural studies in the 1980s was simultaneously a suppression/forgetting of its origins in the political discussions of decolonisation (1992) [see Lazarus (1991); McClintock (1992)]. For ecological/environmental theory, the works of Andrew Ross, Michael Bennett [2003], Mike Davis [1990; 2000; 2001; 2006] and Lawrence Buell have been especially influential in mapping out the directions of a social, material and relational understanding of the environment where a position of 'weak' anthropocentrism can be the basis of a progress towards an universality that takes into account the various trajectories of non-European and peripheral modernities. [. . .]

A glance at the publication dates of these 'second-wave' poco/eco critical and theoretical works tells us that the majority, if not all of them were published/anthologised from the 1990 onwards. The historical and material co-ordinates of these works were, and are: the collapse of the Soviet Bloc; the ever-widening and accelerating gap between global wealth and global poverty; a brutal and endemic competition for water and energy resources; the approaching 'tipping point' of global warming; globally dispersed struggles for national independence and local autonomy; US-led wars in the former Yugoslavia and against Iraq, now known as Gulf [W]ar 1 and 2; and militant strikes against 'fixed' US property such as embassies, the Pentagon and the Twin Towers of New York. For postcolonial and eco studies, as with any field of critical theory, it has become imperative to understand, interpret and offer resolutions for this vast range of crises. In effect, the 'unipolar world' and its conflicts, far from signalling the 'end of history', has been the renewed historicisation and materialisation of both 'environment' and 'culture'. Conflict has replaced consensus as the interpretative model for past and present. At the same time, it has become even more urgent to discover alternative concepts of the universal (against pernicious formulae such as 'the free/civilised world' and 'international community' that are routinely put to demagogic use) as resources of hope and struggle. In short, if the period 1989–91 is taken as a point of transition between the 'first' and 'second'-waves of postcolonial/eco studies, then the Gulf War 1 of 1991, with its 'precision bombing', mass displacement of peoples and neo-imperial grabbing of energy resources, set the pattern of events that would call for a reconceptualisation of the fields.

A few salient issues of evolutionary importance now confront postcolonial and eco-studies. The limits of the category of the universal – limits engendered by its eurocentric, imperialist and capitalist co-ordinates – continue to be traced. But the question of retaining a valid concept of the universal that goes beyond these limits – incorporating non-European, anti-imperialist and socialist histories – remains unresolved. The urgency of finding conceptual and practical pathways towards challenging the deadly banality of 'globalisation' is driven home by the daily global events ranging from occupied Iraq to the ravaged rainforests of Brazil. To this end, the practitioners of postcolonial and eco-studies must continue to analyse their own institutional locations; they must analyse a range of discourse and policies that shape the global north-south relations; they must test the feasibility of excavating, representing and locating those severely damaged by globalised disparities; they must re-focus attention on the 'irreducible difference' of the 'local' (Adorno's words); and they must institute solidarity with movements such as Narmada Bachao and Chiapas in India and Mexico to MST in Brazil and the activities of the World Social Forum, as well as the newly-elected left-wing governments of southern states like Bolivia and Venezuela. These latter *political* events and movements are especially relevant, for they open up the possibilities of interrogating and unsettling normative *social* and *cultural* paradigms of 'globalisation' with the velocity of their *historical* force. In doing so, they also question *how* these 'common-sense' understanding[s] of refugees, migrants, terrorists, criminals, the poor and so on are instituted through representative tactics and choices. That is to say, their very existence brings into being a different order of storytelling and perspectives. What do border-crossings look like when the perspectives of the multi-passport holding cosmopolitan migrants are replaced with those of 'illegal' or 'internally displaced' refugees? What kind of histories are written when the 'northern' canons are displaced by paradigms of cultural exchanges within the 'southern' territories? What are the ecologies and environments of these stories and histories? It is with these questions in mind that I turn to Amitav Ghosh's recent novel, *The Hungry Tide* (2004b) [. . .].

Ghosh's work has engaged with issues of migrancy, diaspora, the disruptive and constitutive flows of global colonial and neo-colonial capital – in short, nothing less than the 'ecology' of postcolonialism.[2] In an essay on Ghosh's two early novels, Kavita Daiya finds three core messages in Ghosh's art: '(1) Community, like memory, is transnational; (2) The liminality of inter-national migrants can also be testimonies to the material abjection and psychic violence of globalization that is elided in celebratory discourses; (3) The transitional and translational space occupied by migrants is transnational too: not globalized' (2003, 36–37). It is Daiya's reading of Ghosh's presentation of the tripartite 'transitional', 'transnational' and 'translational' condition of migrancy that I suggest we consider for a moment. Does 'transnational' suggest that all migrants cross borders similarly, with equal kinds of capital and are able to access equal kinds of rights from the multiple states under whose jurisdictions they come? Who retains the interpretative power if their condition is 'translational'? Does the term suggest that the *historical* meaning and condition of the refugee/migrants are forever to be associated with slippages and deferrals that are the hallmarks of the *linguistic* acts of translation? Does 'transnationalism' preclude possibilities of an internationalism that challenges globalisation? Finally, just under what kinds of 'environmental' pressures do people decide to become refugees and migrants? These are some of the questions and problems raised by Daiya's reading of Ghosh, and they take on a special urgency in a global condition that celebrates the border crossing of a minority of cosmopolitan migrants at the cost of a massive degradation of the rights and conditions of a displaced majority. In contrast to Daiya, I will suggest that Ghosh is interested in interrogating the dominant conceptual categories used in reading the conditions of migrancy, such as 'transnational' and 'translational'. Moreover, I think Ghosh's interrogative method suggests the indispensability of environmental categories – land, water, habitats, forests – in any literary, cultural or historical analysis of the conditions of migration.

The Hungry Tide takes a particularly traumatic historical episode in postcolonial India as one of its launching points: the 'Marichjhapi massacres' of January–May 1979, when the communist-led Left Front government of West Bengal ordered the forcible eviction of thousands of Bengali refugees who had settled on the island of Marichjhapi in the tidal mangrove forest areas known as the *Sundarbans*. The government claimed that the refugees had illegally encroached on 'reserved' forest earmarked for a World Wildlife Fund-sponsored tiger protection project. The majority of the Marichjhapi refugees came to West Bengal from Bangladesh in successive waves after the 1971–72 war of independence. As Ross Mallick shows, they lacked the cultural, social and material capital that the earlier Bengali refugees of 1947 possessed. Thus, their plight was easily made into political capital. In opposition, the Left parties had championed the cause of these refugees of 1971–72, but after assuming power as Left Front government in 1978, they abandoned them. When the refugees refused to be deported from the island of Marichjhapi and won a legal battle against the West Bengal government's 'economic blockade', the government hired off-duty policemen and criminal gangs to 'cleanse' the island. Over the three days of May 14–16, 1979, the gangs systematically raped, killed and expelled the refugees.[3]

It is not difficult to enumerate the roots of the Marichjhapi tragedy. First, there is the logic of borders – drawn up, in this case, as a part of the compromise between Indian elites and the British imperial government. These borders of the new postcolonial nation-states enhanced the communalisation of communities, killed millions and made refugees of millions more of people who were now suddenly designated to bear the burden of the mutually exclusive national territories of Pakistan, India and after 1971, Bangladesh. Then, there is also the allied logic of what Bookchin and Ross would call 'environmentalism'. The West Bengal government's criminalisation of the refugees depended on the projection of a scene where they were seen as competing for scarce resources *against* other 'natural' agents like animals, the mangrove forest and so on (Ross 1994, 12–14). The Marichjhapi tragedy also foregrounded the issue of linguistic kinship and the politics of representation. The West Bengal political elites first rallied to support the refugees on the grounds that they could best understand and represent the interests of fellow Bengali-speakers. But it soon became tragically apparent that this elite's claims of representation masked a fundamental conflict of interest which led to the subaltern language of the refugees being ignored, misread and finally suppressed.

A significant amount of Ghosh's creative and critical energies have been devoted to disenchanting the divisive and destructive borders and boundaries propagated by colonial and post-colonial modernity. If one were to trace an arc from the novel *Shadowlines* [1988], to the essays collected in *The Imam and the Indian* [2002], to his recent articles on 'eco-tourism' in the Sundarbans [2004a] and the Asian Tsunami crisis [2005], it seems that he does not believe that any meaningful consideration of the salient contemporary issues can take place without an 'eco' paradigm (see Ghosh 1998, 2002, 2004a). [. . .] It is this paradigm in Ghosh's latest novel that opens up ways for us to reassess some of the central issues faced by 'second-wave' poco/eco theories – how to analyse contemporary postcolonial political crises as being continuous with ecological crises; how to excavate a history of alternative bioregional modernities; how to centre refugee migrants and not 'hybrid cosmopolitanism' as the paradigmatic postcolonial framework in the consideration of what kind of silences are appropriate and what kinds of interpretative powers must be devolved in the communication between global elites and subaltern masses.

Migration and the 'foreign' appear in *HT* [*The Hungry Tide*] as important strategies through which naïve nostalgia about 'roots' is avoided. The novel begins with Kanai watching Piya on a crowded suburban Calcutta railway platform. To Kanai, Piya's androgynous physicality marks her out as an 'exotic foreigner' (*HT* 3). But he himself is the 'one other "outsider" on the platform', and his airlines bag, clothes and sunglasses – the confidence that is contained in his stance – separate him from the locals just as effectively as Piya's broken Bengali and rucksack (*HT* 6). Kanai – the successful entrepreneur who runs a translation bureau for expatriate workers in Delhi – and Piya – the north-American cetologist – embody a metro/cosmopolitan separation from the environs of suburban Calcutta and rural Bengal. But the two protagonists are not the only aliens in the novel – virtually every significant character operates under the sign of migration. Kanai is visiting his recently bereaved aunt, Nilima, to claim some papers his deceased uncle, Nirmal, has left for him. Nilima and Nirmal appear to 'belong' to the *Sundarbans* by virtue of having devoted a large part of their lives working there, but this is an illusion. Nirmal is a refugee from Dhaka, who had arrived in Calcutta during the partition of 1947, and Nilima is a member of a wealthy Calcutta family. Piya is travelling to the *Sundarbans* to track the migratory patterns and habits of the Gangetic River Dolphins. Her investigation brings her to Fokir, the fisherman who appears to be the resident *par excellence*, a man whose intuitive understanding of the flows of the local river and ecosphere never ceases to amaze the widely travelled Piya. Yet, Fokir too, is an 'alien' – son of Kusum, who herself came to the *Sundarbans* as a Bangladeshi refugee, was sold into a Calcutta brothel, and later returned to settle fatefully on the island of Marichjhapi, where she was killed either by the police or thugs hired to evict the refugees. Fokir himself spends as much time as he can on the rivers, fishing with his son Tutul, away from human settlements. His wife Moyna says he feels out of place everywhere (*HT* 133). Mobility, migrancy, uprootedness permeate the world of the novel. Indeed, the very territory the characters gather upon and crisscross, is a mobile one – 'The river's channels are spread across the land like a finemesh net, creating a terrain where the boundaries between land and water are always mutating, always unpredictable . . .' (*HT* 7). It may be populated by them, but the novel's migrants are clearly not all alike. Piya and Kanai begin as the 'new cosmo/metropolitans' – their cultural capital accumulated by access to the global archipelagos of wealth (see Brennan 1997). But by the end, their achieved resident alien status disputes this cosmo/metropolitanism and articulates a new form of belonging – the final chapter's title 'Home: An Epilogue' signalling this transformation. But this distance from the global to the local can only be traversed under the tutelage of the other migrants – whose varying distance and exclusion from the circuits of cosmo/metropolitanism ensures (to varying degrees) their bio-regional and collectivist ethics. If Piya and Kanai are the 'cosmopolitan' elites of the novel, Nilima and Nirmal are their older national(ist) counterparts, while Fokir, Kusum and Moyna form the subaltern tiers of the novel's social map. All are migrants, yet they are differentiated along the axes of class and capital. The new elites, just as the old, must absorb lessons of belonging from their encounters with these subaltern migrants. And what of the subalterns themselves? Is their existence entirely tied to this function of teaching the elites to belong? The novel's deliberately problematic and provocative meditation on language and translation, I think, might be a move to devolve elite representational powers and invite instead rapprochement through reticence. Much of what Kusum, Fokir, Horen say may be incomprehensible to the elites, much of it mistranslated, misunderstood. But they are seldom dismissed, and it is in the novel's refusal to force transparency on to them, in its deference to silences and gaps, that differences are humanised, contacts made, a different idea of the universal glimpsed. This differentiation of the conditions of migrancy is a mark of Ghosh's sensitivity both as a novelist and a critic of globalisation, as it definitively refutes the reflexive privileging of cosmo/metropolitanism that marks much of contemporary analysis.

The elites learn that their imagined liberalism is in fact hobbled by the logic of boundaries that their modernity has bequeathed them. They gradually realise that in order to universalise universalism truly, they need to first cross these boundaries by re-imagining themselves as they appear in the eyes of others. Some of these elites are aware of their bounded condition. They berate those who imagine their solidarity with the subaltern without giving up their elite privileges. Nilima points out the cruel gap between Nirmal and Marichjhapi refugees – whereas the refugees wanted a little land, Nirmal wanted to help them realise their world-historical revolutionary potential (*HT* 119–20). But Nilima too is unable to cross certain lines. She accepts that she will have to refuse any aid to the refugees if she is to stay on the right side of the government and ensure continuous support for her NGO. This is what passes for pragmatism amongst the liberal elites who cannot envisage any meaningful devolution of power. Likewise, Kanai scolds Piya when she automatically reads Fokir as a fellow eco-warrior – intuitively in touch with his habitat and therefore sharing her conservationist ethos (*HT* 268). Piya's misreading is dramatically exposed when Fokir enthusiastically participates in the trapping and burning alive of a tiger, to the nauseous outrage of Piya. She accepts that 'nature' means very different things to her and Fokir, and this difference is constituted through the vastly different kinds of capital and labour they command.

The problem with Piya's environmentalism and Nirmal's would-be Marxism is that in their own ways they remain wedded to idealist notions of 'universal progress' and their ignorance of local ecologies. The historical precedence that Nirmal uses to support the Marichjhapi refugees is an instance of 'benevolent' imperialism. The tidal islands were first settled during the nineteenth-century at the behest of a Scottish businessman – Daniel Hamilton. Hamilton had made his fortune in a shipping business in Calcutta, and then invested it in the re-settling of the islands with regional migrants dispossessed by the circuits of colonial capital. For Nirmal, Hamilton the 'monopolikapitalist' was thus transformed into Hamilton the utopian socialist. It is in his spirit that he wants to support and succour the settlers of Marichjhapi. Revolutionary redemption, for Nirmal, is tied to a vision of enlightened patronage. Hence, over Marichjhapi, he fails to comprehend a 'Marxist' government's betrayal of refugees who embody the principles and dignity of labour. He is unable to factor in various other nodes that form the grid of this particular matrix of power-relations – the high caste/class composition of the 'Marxist' government of West Bengal, the inter-national politics of the formation of the refugee crisis in Bengal, the conflict between the local landed and landless rural 'vote-banks'.

Piya's environmentalism has similar blindspots built into it. Like Nirmal's Daniel Hamilton, a host of benevolent imperialists – William Roxburgh, Edward Blyth, and J. E. Gray ('of *Gray's Anatomy*') – are Piya's intellectual and ideological ancestors. To her, these eighteenth- and nineteenth-century British naturalists, geographers and scientists are very much a part of the heroic narrative of enlightenment – selflessly working in hostile environments for the enlargement of the frontiers of knowledge. But the specificities of colonial and imperial knowledge-gathering are left out of this narrative – how is the classifying of species also a part of the epistemology of imperialism? What lines of power connect naturalists such as Edward Blyth, the dolphins he studies, and the crowd of his Indian helpers? How do the museums and botanical gardens (we recall *Kim*'s *jadoogarh* here) created by these botanists replicate an imperial environment? Piya herself, kitted out with the latest GPS monitor, range-finder, depth sounder and binoculars, literally embodies the panoptical knowledge-machine of colonialism. The resultant gap between her 'environmental' ethos and any properly ecological ethics can be seen in the episode we have already touched upon, when a captured tiger is blinded and then burnt alive by local villagers. Piya cannot understand how Fokir, whom she has imagined as the 'natural man', can participate in the killing of the tiger. Looking at Fokir, Piya can only see unbridgeable difference – 'I know this is what he grew up with. It's just, I thought somehow he'd be different' (*HT* 297).

And yet the novel refuses to validate the reflexive rejection of universalism that has seen the cancer of sectarian violence and religious fundamentalism spread over the body of the postcolonial state. If mistranslation and misreadings secure the distance between the elites and the subalterns, that distance diminishes as the possibilities of readings and translations are also made available. Nirmal, Kanai and Piya are all transformed through their encounters with radically different texts and contexts – songs, folk tales, folk theatre performances, oral historical narratives, and above all, the complex networks of everyday lives that they briefly share with the migrants and refugees. These encounters urge the elites' recognition of the limits of their cultural capital and provide them with glimpses of a universality that accommodates, rather than obliterates differences. Nirmal's diary tracks his transformation and devolution of power in a series of key encounters. One such takes place when it records an incident of cross-reading. Nirmal reads from his copy of Francois Bernier's *Travels* (one of the key early records of modern European encounters with Bengal) to Horen, a boatman. As he reads the accounts of Bernier's having been caught up in a storm three hundred years ago on the very river they are now on, Nirmal assumes that he is enlightening Horen about the presence of the past (*HT* 146–47). To his irritation, however, Horen keeps interrupting the narrative with his own 'text' – his intimate knowledge of the territory that Bernier writes about – establishing a space-time continuum that eludes Nirmal:

> 'Oh!', cried Horen. 'I know where this happened: they must have been at Gerafitola'.
>
> 'Rubbish, Horen', I said. 'How could you know such a thing? This happened over three hundred years ago'.
>
> 'But I've seen it too', Horen protested, 'and it's exactly as you describe . . . I know that place . . . My chhotokaka spent the night there once, and all night long he heard strange voices uttering strange words: it must have been those same ghosts they saw'.
>
> (*HT* 146)

Nirmal intuits that Horen's knowledge is of a different order and form than his, and that he can learn more from people like Horen and Kusum than from Hamilton. This is confirmed in another encounter, as he listens to Horen chant a poem as he performs his *puja* for the local deity – *Bonbibi*. Stunned that a Hindu boatman like Horen is using Islamic invocations and a mixture of Arabic, Persian and Bengali to worship a nominally Hindu goddess like *Bonbibi*, Nirmal is further astonished to see that the prayer is taken from a nineteenth-century pamphlet called *Bon Bibir Karamoti orthat Bon Bibi Johuranama* by a Muslim writer named Abdur Rahaman (*HT* 247).

Nirmal's achievement is that he absorbs these lessons to form the bases of eco-ethics and geo-history that constructively weaken his earlier anthropo- and Eurocentric understanding of 'progress'. The Rilke lines he quotes in his diary track this change – 'some mute animal / raising its calm eyes and seeing through us, / and through us. This is destiny' (*HT* 235); 'Each slow turn of the world carries such disinherited / ones to whom neither the past nor the future belong' (*HT* 165). He learns to imagine himself through the eyes of others – human and non-human. As a result, his very notion of history is expanded, universalised – one might say, naturalised. If he had started from a position of celebrating the benevolent colonisation of Daniel Hamilton, he ends by reciting the story of imperial hubris – the story of the destruction of Port Canning. A would-be model nineteenth-century port named after the then viceroy, Port Canning was an instance of a complete failure of the imperial government to understand or integrate itself with the local eco-system, in this case the cyclonic system of Gangetic Bengal. It was destroyed in the great storm and floods of 1867 and the port project abandoned shortly thereafter. Nearly a century and a half after the Canning fiasco, Marichjhapi too is an incident that measures the ecospheric disturbances created by the hubris of the (now postcolonial) state.

Kanai arrives in the *Sundarbans* to collect Nirmal's diary. As he travels through Nirmal's texts, Kanai too is drawn into the discomfort of abandoning the familiar contours of knowledge and privilege that his job as a translator has brought him. Moyna and Horen point out on separate occasions that it is his misunderstandings and mistranslations that mark him out in that environment. Reading Nirmal's diary, he slowly re-learns the lessons of inhabiting. He remembers a childhood visit to a performance of *Bonbibi Johuranama*, a theatrical version of the very text whose heterogeneity had so jolted Nirmal:

> Kanai had expected to be bored by this rustic entertainment: in Calcutta he was accustomed to going to theatres like the Academy of Fine Arts . . . But much to his surprise, he was utterly absorbed . . . The terror he had felt when the demon charged Dukhey was real and immediate, even though there was nothing convincing about the tiger and it could be plainly seen that the animal was only a man, dressed in a painted sheet and a mask.
>
> (*HT* 105)

It is not its mimetic qualities, but its *location* that provides this theatre with power. Kanai is absorbed, paradoxically, because its universal appeal is born precisely out of its *situatedness* in the local. Like Nirmal, Kanai absorbs these lessons well. Travelling with Piya, Kanai hears the legend of the forest deity chanted by Fokir as he rows Kanai and Piya towards the habitat of the river dolphins. When Piya asks him to translate what Fokir is singing, Kanai refuses to do so. The next day he hands her a packet containing his version of the *Bonbibi Johuranama* with this key preface:

> You asked me what Fokir was singing and I said *I couldn't translate it*: it was too difficult. And this was no more than the truth, for in those words there was a history that is not just his own but also of this place, the tide country . . . it lives in him and in some way, perhaps, it still plays a part in making him the person he is. This is my gift to you . . . *Such flaws as there are in my rendition of it I do not regret, for perhaps they will prevent me from fading from sight as a good translator should: for once, I shall be glad if my imperfections render me visible.*
>
> (*HT* 354, italics [Mukherjee])

Kanai's admission of imperfect and partial translation is more than his declaration of his erotic presence to Piya. It is the moment of his giving up of his claims to power, of putting aside elite liberal claims to the burden of representation, of arriving at Nirmal's realisation that 'everything which existed was interconnected: the trees, the sky, the weather, people, poetry, science, nature' (*HT* 282–83). This realisation of the interconnectedness of everything and all stories, as seen in the circulation of *Bonbibi Johuranama* from Abdur Rahim to Horen, Fokir, Nirmal and Kanai, necessitates an abandoning of hierarchies. It is no accident that Kanai arrives at this renunciation not only after finishing Nirmal's diary, but after a crucial and disturbing encounter with Fokir.

Fokir rows Kanai to *Garjontala*, an island where his mother Kusum used to pray at a Bonbibi shrine and where he says a tiger has been sighted:

> In Kanai's professional life there had been a few instances in which the act of interpretation had given him the momentary sensation of being transported out of his own body and into another . . . But he was not working now and yet it was exactly this feeling that came upon him as he looked at Fokir: It was as though his own vision were being refracted through those opaque, unreadable eyes, and he was seeing not himself, Kanai, but a great host of people – a double for the outside world, someone standing in for the men who had destroyed Fokir's village, burnt his home and killed his mother; he had become a token for a vision of human beings in which a man such as Fokir counted for nothing, a man whose value was less than that of an animal . . . Fokir had brought him here not because he wanted him to die, but because he wanted him to be judged.
>
> (*HT* 327)

This experience of being judged – of seeing himself through other eyes as what he is, a double for murderous agents of the metropoles – is what seals Kanai's re-education. Just as the admission of heterogeneous subaltern texts is also the giving up of the claims of perfect translation, the admission of being the subject to the subaltern gaze(s) is also the giving up of the claims to metropolitan power relations.

Piya too achieves an understanding of the universal by learning to limit and revise her cosmopolitanism. Her childhood rejection of the Bengali language was part of her attempt to be different from her parents: 'she wanted words with the heft of stainless steel, sounds that had been boiled clean, like a surgeon's instruments, tools with nothing attached except meanings that could be looked up in a dictionary – empty of pain and memory and inwardness' (*HT* 94). This desire for an antiseptic, classificatory, limited relationship with the world is the paradigm for her scientific work – her submersion into the process of observing, recording and analysing marine life as data. The world, as far she is concerned, is a 'field' and not a place, and 'it was the exclusion of intimate involvements that made a place into a field and the line between the two was marked by a taboo she could not cross, except at the risk of betraying her vocation' (*HT* 112). If she is to transcend the limits of this cosmopolitanism it is precisely her vocation that she must betray. Piya's transcending of these limits takes place not only through her encounters with the texts of Nirmal, Kanai and the sounds of *Bonbibi Johuaranama*, but through an intimate, material and physical contact with the tide country and with Fokir. Initially, the linguistic, cultural and material gaps between them renders Fokir an inscrutable sign to Piya, a sign she feels she is at liberty to interpret and attach meanings to as she sees fit. It is only in the shock of seeing him exult in the killing of the tiger that she registers that his 'difference' is not of the kind she had supposed. Piya's achievement is the admission of this difference, her surrendering to this intimacy. Before they leave on their final fateful trip down the river, Piya and Fokir sit together on his boat, surrounded by silence and yet connected:

> They sat unmoving, like animals who had been paralysed by the intensity of their awareness of each other. When their eyes met again it was as if he knew at a glance what she was thinking . . . It was as if their shared glimpse of the lunar rainbow had somehow broken something that had existed between them, as if something had ended, leaving behind a pain of a kind that could not be understood because it never had a name.
>
> (*HT* 352–53)

What has ended is the eroticisation and exoticisation of difference and a cosmo-politan dispensation of power. What has replaced it is an acceptance of the specificity of difference, and a realisation of a universal solidarity. The pain is a birth pang as well as one of disenchantment.

In the final section of the novel, Piya and Fokir find themselves caught in a cyclone. The storm and flood wipe out islands. Kanai, Nilima, Moyna survive in the storm shelter built in Nilima's NGO-run hospital. Most of Piya's gadgets are blown away, and she and Fokir tie themselves to a tree to escape a similar fate. There are birds, tired of outpacing the storm, that drop on to them. There is a tiger, swimming across the river and taking refuge on a tree next to them. The wind switches direction:

> Where she had the tree trunk to shelter her before, now there was only Fokir's body . . . Their bodies were so close, so finely merged that she could feel the impact of everything hitting him, she could feel the blows raining down on his back. She could feel the bones of his cheeks as if they had been superimposed upon her own; it was as if the storm had given them what life could not.
>
> (*HT* 390)

The storm's gift is Fokir's death but also the birth in Piya of a sense of place, the final abandoning of the 'field'. In the middle of death, she stumbles onto life.

It is perhaps possible to see the novel as a redemption song for the metro/cosmopolitans – a (painful) celebration of their 'homecoming' and the inception of an ethics of 'belonging'. But I think that Ghosh's novel is primarily engaged in displacing metro/cosmopolitanism with a historically differentiated refugee condi-tion as the paradigm of postcoloniality. It writes a natural history of the migrant refugee and critiques instrumentalist 'environmentalism'. It prioritises subaltern texts and voices in the communicative act and signals the limits of elite capacities of representation and translation. In all this, it responds with critical intelligence to a time when the movement and habitation of both human and non-human beings are being determined by endemic conflict over access to environmental resources and enforcement of neo-liberal economic and political fundamentalisms. It is pre-cisely from works such as these that contemporary postcolonial and eco-theories must derive their conceptual powers.

Notes

1   Diana Brydon suggests that the term 'postcolonial' grew out of the political/economic discussions about decolonisation in the 1970s and accrued a wide range of meanings associated with resisting and understanding both the various forms of colonialism and the problems of 'globalization'. Charlene Spretnek, Glotfelty and Fromm all date the formation of eco-feminism and ecocriticism around the late 1960s to early 1970s. See Spretnak (1990, 5); Glotfelty and Fromm (1996, 1–20,) Brydon 2000 (Vol I, 1–7).

2   For example see, Brinda Bose: 'He is also the one who sees history as that trajectory of events that causes dislocations, disjunctions, movements and migrations, eventually replacing solid markers with shadow lines, destabilizing our notions of the past in the reverberations of the present' (2003, 15).

3   For a detailed study of these and other issues pertaining to the Marichjhapi massacre, see Mallick (1999).

II MONEY AND MARKETS

Chapter 20

Michael Tratner

DERRIDA'S DEBT TO MILTON FRIEDMAN

From *New Literary History* 34 (2003): 791–806

IN THE ESSAY *GIVEN TIME: I. COUNTERFEIT MONEY*, Jacques
Derrida says it is important to trace the literary consequences of certain events in
economic history: 'To study, for example, in so-called modern literature, that is,
contemporaneous with capital – city, *polis*, metropolis – of a state and with a state of
capital, the transformation of money forms (metallic, fiduciary – the bank note – or
scriptual – the bank check), a certain rarification of payments in cash, the recourse
to credit cards, the coded signature, and so forth, in short, a certain dematerialization of money, and therefore of all the scenes that depend on it'. (1992, 110) The
transformation Derrida describes is part of the development of late capitalism;
though his essay analyzes a short story by the nineteenth-century writer Baudelaire,
the transformation away from 'metallic' to 'fiduciary' forms of money officially
occurred in the twentieth century, as did the spread of credit cards and coded
signatures. As the economic historian Randall Hinshaw notes, during the twentieth
century 'commodity money is gradually being displaced by fiduciary money . . . in
1937, gold or commodity money made up about 91% of the world's monetary
reserves . . . this figure had dropped to 49% in mid-1966' (1967, 51). In other
words, fiduciary money became the dominant form of money at just about the time
that Derrida began developing his literary theories.

Derrida seems to define 'fiduciary' money as bank notes and bank checks but
in international exchange the term refers to money backed by reserve positions.
Derrida's awareness of such money may derive from remarkable economic events
during the decade when he was writing his essay. Tracing deconstruction back to the
1970s is a common critical gesture, but only in terms of politics; for example, Tobin
Siebers sees it as a product of cold war suspiciousness; Raman Selden, as the
intellectual follow-up to '60s radicalism; and Barbara Foley, as a development
of liberal pluralism (Siebers 1993, 46–56; Selden 1995, 6; Foley 1985, 113–34).

But consider as well the relevance for deconstruction of the economic transformation that occurred in 1971, when all currencies became fiduciary monies as the mechanisms of international exchange dropped all reference to metals or other 'specie'. Milton Friedman describes the revolutionary nature of this change:

> Until 1971, departures from an international specie standard, at least by major countries, took place infrequently and only at times of crisis. Fisher concluded in 1911 that 'irredeemable paper money has almost invariably proved a curse to the country employing it', . . . The declining importance of the international specie standard and its final termination in 1971 have changed the situation drastically. 'Irredeemable paper money' is no longer an expedient grasped at in times of crisis; it is the normal state of affairs in countries at peace, facing no domestic crises, political or economic, and with governments fully capable of obtaining massive resources through explicit taxes. This is an unprecedented situation. We are in unexplored terrain.
>
> (1987b, 379–81)

The unexplored terrain that emerged in the 1970s is the world of dematerialized currencies that Derrida believes has somehow transformed literature. Lifting the 'curse' on irredeemable monies is tantamount to lifting the curse on signs that operate without reference, a central element of Derrida's linguistic project.

The economic transformation of money in 1971 is in peculiar ways tied to the radical politics of the 1960s, as we can see by noting that in France an important suspension of convertibility of the franc occurred in May, 1968, in direct response to the threat of a General Strike. The radical disruption of the social order that seemed to many linked to the disruptions of deconstruction led to – or was countered by – the ending of 'reference' in that most fundamental 'sign' in the capitalist system, money. Jean Baudrillard recognizes a relationship between the new kind of rebellion of the left in the 1960s, the demise of the gold standard, and deconstruction, though his way of characterizing this complex relationship is to say that the development of an economic system based on what he calls 'uncontrollable play' marked the end of the possibility of 'materialist' contradictions, the end of the Marxist dialectic in which changes in means of production generate changes in the social order, so that a new form of resistance (to signs) was needed. He concludes that at a certain point in history, production was 'elevat[ed] . . . to a total abstraction, . . . to the power of a code, *which no longer even risks being called into question by an abolished referent*' (1975, 129 emphasis Baudrillard). Then in a footnote he explains that, 'economically, this process culminates in the virtual international autonomy of finance capital, in the uncontrollable play of floating capital. Once currencies are extracted from all production cautions, and even from all reference to the gold standard, general equivalence becomes the strategic place of manipulation. Real production is everywhere subordinated to it. This apogee of the system corresponds to the triumph of the code' (129 n. 9).

Baudrillard's comments suggest a peculiar relationship between deconstruction, sixties' radicalism, and the new definitions of money. The end of the gold standard results in uncontrollable play of capital, which sounds like the freeplay that Derrida finds in language. In fact, if we read the new 'definition' of a currency, it seems very much like a Derridean description of the endless 'dissemination without return' of linguistic signifiers – to define one sign is merely to put up other signs, and so on, never reaching any end. The dollar is redefined so that it is no longer a 'silver certificate', a paper referring to physical objects, but rather simply a 'federal reserve note', a note indicating that the Federal Reserve System owes the bearer a dollar. To have a dollar is to be owed a dollar: the sign that represents money actually represents that one has the right to another sign.

After the 1970s, the question of what backs up currencies is no longer answered by an image of a huge stockpile of gold, but rather by a reserve system; internationally, this takes the form of the International Monetary Fund, or IMF, in which countries hold 'reserve positions' or 's.d.r.'s', 'standard drawing rights'; they are granted rights to borrow, and those rights back up their currencies. Internationally, a dollar is now defined as a 'basket' of so many marks plus so many yen, so many pounds, so many of every currency – and similarly a mark is so many dollars plus so many yen, and so on. Defining a currency in terms of a basket of other currencies does rather seem like a system of freeplay of signifiers: searching for the 'meaning' of one monetary sign leads only to an infinite sequence of other signs and ultimately circles back to the same sign. Monetary signifiers are defined in terms of their differences from other signifiers, not in terms of any signified.

Payment across countries is no longer even mythologized as the transfer of objects; indeed payment in effect no longer exists at all; rather, payment has become the transfer of debt from one country to another. If being given an IOU is a way of deferring payment, the current economic system has made such deferrals permanent. The meaning of economic signs no longer derives from reference but rather from a code.

Such changes in economics do not happen all at once and are never complete and uniform across the entire field of economic activity. New economic concepts emerge long before they become orthodoxy, and sometimes such concepts appear first in non-economic texts, as ironic mockery of common practices or descriptions of other social systems or even just imaginary possibilities. In *Given Time*, Derrida in effect retraces the long process of subtle changes in economic notions which led up to the final dematerialization of money in 1971, by citing from texts published near crucial moments in the history of the transformation of money. Derrida focuses particularly on an ironic story by Baudelaire, 'The Counterfeit Coin', published in 1864, and on an account of the economics of 'primitive' societies by Marcel Mauss, *The Gift*, published in 1925. Near each of these publication dates there was a significant change in the way Western governments backed up the money they issued, and elements in these texts reflect those changes. When Baudelaire wrote his story about counterfeit money, there was considerable international anxiety about governments issuing money backed by nothing, particularly the U.S. during the Civil War, which paid its troops with 'Greenbacks' that it printed quite freely. In reaction to this anxiety, the official international gold standard was instituted in 1881. The gradual dematerialization that Derrida wants to trace was the undoing of this international treaty.

Baudelaire may not have paid much attention to international finance, but he was peculiarly sensitive to the issue of spending beyond one's means and going into debt, because early in his life he went though his family fortune so rapidly that his relatives came together in 1844 and put his inheritance under their legal control so he could not spend himself into serious debt (Pia 1961, 33). In effect, when he wrote the story Derrida cites, Baudelaire was suffering under a personal version of the policy that would become international law in 1881: a legal restriction on the ability to spend beyond one's means. Derrida reads into Baudelaire's comments about the possibility of wealth emerging from the circulation of counterfeits a step towards the dematerialization of money that would emerge in the twentieth century. Baudelaire was certainly chafing under his inability to spend beyond his reserves, but to say that he is simply exploring a new economic idea is to ignore the irony of the story, which depends on the reader's familiarity with the nineteenth-century morality of spending only what one had earned. Indeed, Baudelaire's pleasure in telling the tale depends on the sense that circulating a false coin would be considered an evil act, so that the contemplation of the apparently lovely temporary results of such an act could come under the rubric of Baudelaire's general interest in the 'flowers of evil'. The story adopts an ironic stance towards circulating counter-feits, but depends on the anxiety about dematerialization that led to the official gold standard.

Derrida projects quite a bit of later economic history back onto this story, including not only dematerialization but the transformation into a consumerist economy which occurred from around 1880 to around 1920. The first thing Derrida focuses on in the story is that the scene is set outside a tobacco shop. Derrida describes tobacco as 'the object of pure and luxurious consumption . . . an expend-iture at a loss that produces a pleasure . . . tobacco seems to open onto the scene of desire beyond need' (1992, 107). Baudelaire certainly admired lives devoted to consumption, writing extensively about dandies, but he would have thoroughly resisted the notion that such consumption could someday be the norm for everyone; indeed, much of the pleasure of contemplating the dandy is his difference from the average dull, thrifty, bourgeois citizen.

The dandy becomes an important figure in social commentary and literary circles at the end of the nineteenth century, but disappears from discussion early in the twentieth, precisely as consumerism spreads to becoming the basis of economic morality throughout all classes. Lawrence Birken traces this transformation in eco-nomic history in terms rather similar to Derrida's: desire replaces need as the basis of economics (Birken 1988). But this transformation is not the move to some mysterious realm of 'luxurious consumption' as Derrida suggests; rather it is the move to everyday consumerism. One small sign of the move from needs to desires is a change in economic textbooks: in the nineteenth century, every text began with production and with an account of the needs that production hoped to satisfy; in the twentieth, every text begins with demand, with desires.

The moment when consumerism finally replaced productivism as the basis of economics is roughly the moment, 1925, when the other writer Derrida highlights – Marcel Mauss – published his treatise, *The Gift*. The 1920s were a period of rapid transformation of economic morality in which saving became much less important [than] spending, and the average person gained for the first time the ability as a part of normal life to spend more than savings – in other words, to go into debt. This ability came about in reaction to the emergence of the automobile, which led to radical changes in lending laws to allow average persons to buy cars on time. To give a sense of this transformation, the economic historian Martha Olney notes that before 1920, the average American had twice as much in savings as in debt; by 1925, this ratio had been reversed (1991, 47). In other words, 1925 marks the year when average Americans began spending more than they had earned. A similar transformation was occurring all over Europe.

What happened to consumer economics in the 1920s became economic orthodoxy in government policy in the 1930s when the Depression led to the worldwide acceptance of Keynesian policy. It was the Keynesian revolution that eventually made 'consumption the new watchword', according to economic historian Geoffrey Barraclough, and it was Keynes who finally normalized the role of spending more than earnings – deficit spending in governmental policy (1977, 106).

Derrida presents Mauss's gift economy in terms that connect it to the economic transformations of the Keynesian era. Derrida quotes at length a passage from Mauss in which Mauss seems to recognize that the new governmental policies, such as Social Security, are steps towards the kind of gift economy he advocates. The result of such policies, Mauss says, is that 'we will rediscover motives for living and acting that are still prevalent in many societies and classes: the joy of public giving; the delight in generous expenditure on the arts; the pleasure in hospitality and in private and public festival. Social security, the solicitude of the mutuality, of the cooperative, of the professional group, of all those legal entities upon which English law bestows the name of "Friendly Societies" – all are . . . better than the mean life afforded by the daily wage set by management, and even better than capitalist saving' (quoted in Derrida 1992, 65). Mauss implies here that the gift economy which he found in 'primitive' social systems was also emerging in the early twentieth century within capitalist society. Derrida describes Mauss as searching for an alternative economics that is neither 'capitalist mercantilism' nor 'Marxist communism' (1992, 44).

Quite a few economists were searching in the 1920s and '30s for such an alternative, including Keynes, John Hobson, and one C. H. Douglas, who proposed what could be called an entirely 'gift-based' economy. Douglas called his system 'Social Credit', because he advocated replacing money entirely with credit given out by the government, but an unusual kind of credit, because nobody needed to pay it back. He wanted money to be recognized as a free gift from the government, adjusted each year to keep ahead of production so that depressions could not happen. Keynes acknowledged that Douglas was a major influence on his deficit economics, and all the governmental programs such as Social Security and WPA [Works Progress Administration] projects which followed upon Keynesian influences in effect were modified versions of the move toward a gift economy.

Derrida highlights the centrality of credit in Mauss's gift economy, putting in italics Mauss's statement that 'the gift necessarily entails the notion of credit' (1992, 45). Derrida then goes on to make the remarkable claim that credit has the same position in the economic system that *differánce* has in linguistic systems. He says this in an account of Aristotle's distinction between chrematistics and economy. Chrematistics is the system of monetary circulation, a system that Derrida says 'has no limit in principle. Economy, on the other hand, that is, management of the *oikos*, of the home, the family, or the hearth, is limited to the goods necessary to life' (1992, 158).[1] The distinction, Derrida says, depends on the 'limit between the supposed finiteness of need and the presumed infinity of desire, the transcendence of need by desire' (1992, 158). He then writes this sentence: 'As soon as there is monetary sign – and first of all sign – that is, *differánce* and credit, the *oikos* is opened and cannot dominate its limit'. *Differánce* and credit are presented here as two essential features of signs that have the same result: they make it impossible to maintain any limits or to have a closed system; they move one from an economics ruled by needs to one ruled by desires. Derrida's phrasing and his turn to Aristotle imply that credit has been a part of the economic system about as long as there has been money, but I am trying to show that in fact in Western nations credit only becomes a normal and regular part of *oikos*, home or consumer economics, from the 1920s on, bringing into everyday consciousness the notion of desires beyond needs.

After his detailed examination of the ways in which Mauss's gift economy and its notion of credit bears similarity to Derridean linguistic structures, such as *différance*, Derrida's argument takes a rather surprising turn: he goes on to argue that a gift economy could never exist, because in such a world a gift-giver would be expecting a return, and so would not be really giving gifts. To create a gift economy, Derrida says, one has to imagine a 'happy medium' between a 'Shylock' and a 'monk' (1992, 65). In claiming that the gift economy is impossible, Derrida in effect moves beyond Mauss and the 1920s, joining the tide of economic theory of the 1970s, the tide that overthrew the Keynesian orthodoxy. Critics of Keynesian theory argue that Keynesian economics is impossible in very much the same way that Derrida argues that the gift economy is impossible. For example, Robert Lucas and Thomas Sargent, founders of the new Rational Expectations Economics, argue that Keynesian policies of increasing government spending to counter downturns in the economy are impossible because 'countercyclical policy must itself be unforeseeable by private agents . . . while at the same time be systematically related to the state of the economy. Effectiveness, then, rests on the inability of private agents to recognize systematic patterns in monetary and fiscal policy' (1994, 20). In other words, the excess money distributed by the government to counter business cycles must seem an incalculable addition, 'unforeseeable', a pure gift. At the same time, it must be 'systematic', in other words, carefully calculated by government agents. The government has to then act like a Shylock, cannily calculating returns, and at the same time appear to be a monk, giving money away beyond all reason. Lucas and Sargent argue that private agents would always see through the image of monkish generosity to the Shylockian calculation, and so would plan for what is supposed to be unforeseeable generosity, destroying the gift-effect of deficit spending. Derrida's denial of the possibility of the gift economy parallels anti-Keynesian economics of the 1970s, which characterizes deficit spending as merely an illusory gift hiding a form of usury (1992, 42).

Derrida's argument against the possibility of a gift also ends up partly repeating what Baudelaire's narrator says in his story: the man giving away a counterfeit coin to a beggar is trying to please both God and his pocketbook, to give charity and calculate returns at the same time. Edward K. Kaplan describes Baudelaire's story as leading in itself to the conclusion that 'charity is impossible' (1990, 109). So one might think that Derrida, in saying that gift economies are impossible, is returning to the 1860s, not joining in the developments of the 1970s. Actually, the two possibilities can coexist, because the economists who challenged Keynes in the 1970s claimed to be returning to the economic theories of the latter half of the nineteenth century, calling themselves Neoclassical Economists.

Derrida's arguments in *Given Time* come closest to those of one of the most important anti-Keynesians, Milton Friedman. Friedman argues that money plays an important role in the economy precisely because it is a system for distributing signifiers which have no referent. He says that money is 'a social convention that owes its very existence to the mutual acceptance of what from one point of view is a fiction' (Friedman and Schwartz 1963, 696). Sounding very much like a deconstructionist, Friedman goes on to say that money is a 'veil': what it veils most is its own fictionality. Friedman criticizes previous economic theories for believing that the fictionality of money made it irrelevant, that one could always substitute the things actually exchanged in any discussion of what money was doing. Instead, he argues that changes in the sign system itself, in money, are some of the most important determinants of economic events.

Friedman's theories, though developed in the 1950s, remained secondary to Keynesian theories until the 1960s and '70s, when the fictionality of money became much more evident as the value – or the 'meaning' – of monetary signs began fluctuating daily under the influence of rampant inflation. Before the 1970s, certain countries, notably France and the United States, maintained the appearance that monetary signs represented physical realities by holding large quantities of gold to back up monetary reference. Pictures of Fort Knox were circulated as evidence of the backing of the dollar. After the 1970s, the U.S. eliminated its rigid gold price and eliminated its national stockpile. The fictionality of money became an important economic tenet of all governments and a commonplace of newspaper headlines declaring the latest inflation figures. I suggest that the economic developments that made inflation a powerful political buzzword contributed to the plausibility of theories such as Derrida's.

The policies which Friedman advocates bear similarity to some of what Derrida explores in *Given Time*. Though Friedman accepts that deficit spending – governmental gift-giving – is useless, he still has a way to stimulate the economy: by steadily increasing the money supply beyond the limits of what is involved in current exchanges. In other words, he recommends that the government give money away without its having been exchanged for anything, money not backed by anything, a signifier without a signified, very much the same thing which fascinates Derrida. Derrida interprets the counterfeit coin in Baudelaire's story as the insertion of an excess sign into the economic system. He says that the act of passing a counterfeit to a beggar is emblematic of 'what can happen to capital in a capital . . . in the age of value as monetary sign: The circulation of the counterfeit money can engender, even for a "little speculator", the real interest of a true wealth' (1992, 124).

Friedman does not, of course, advocate circulation of counterfeit money, but he does argue vehemently for the government taking very much the role of the man giving away the counterfeit coin: the government should keep expanding the money supply. The government must keep creating fictions, money outside the system of exchange, in order to cause real objects to appear. Monetarist economics uses the circulation of money it has created from nothing to 'engender real wealth'. The results of an expanding money supply are almost magical: 'If any one bank receives an accession to its cash, it can therewith acquire additional noncash assets equal at most to that accession . . . yet if all banks together receive an accession to cash, the banking system can therewith acquire additional assets equal to a multiple of that accession' (1987a, 341). [. . .] Adding to the total supply has effects greater than the apparent added amount of cash: an excess emerges as an effect of the code.

A crucial part of Friedman's theory is the tenet that no person can or should control the excess money added to the total. The process must be completely automatic, never adjusted in reaction to economic events, unlike Keynesian countercyclical stimuli. Friedman joins the Neoclassicists in arguing that economic policies cannot counter cyclical trends. But one can have an automatic excess that keeps changing the money supply in ways that produce a pressure to increase production (he says) and therefore allows growth and keeps the economic engine running.

Derrida describes similarly the necessity of acts outside the circle of exchange – those seemingly impossible gifts – as crucial to keeping the economic engine going: 'The overrunning of the circle by the gift, if there is any, does not lead to a simple, ineffable, exteriority that would be transcendental and without relation. It is this exteriority that sets the circle going, it is this exteriority that puts the economy in motion' (1992, 30). Putting the economy in motion – pressing the throttle of the economic engine – is precisely what a constantly expanding money supply is supposed to do.

The difference between the 1920s logic of Mauss, Douglas, and Keynes that represents government as a gift-giver and the 1970s logic (following Friedman) of automatic increases in the money supply is reflected in intriguing ways in shifts in literature from the 1920s to the 1970s. Both economics and literature change from representing a world in which some important persons can stand apart from the chaos of the world and thereby create order to representing a world in which the system runs automatically, with no individuals shaping it. We can see the literary transformation particularly well by examining writers who represent economic issues or practices in their aesthetic works. In the 1920s, Ezra Pound and William Carlos Williams were followers of C. H. Douglas's Social Credit movement, and wrote long poems, *The Cantos* and *Paterson*, that meditate on the notion of sovereignty, a notion that merges economic and artistic authority. . . . Pound's *Cantos* trace a whole series of powerful governmental leaders (Malatesta, John Adams, various Chinese emperors) who are evaluated in terms of their ability to control the system of finance in their eras; as Pound puts it, 'Sovereignty is in the right over coinage' (Pound 1972) The sovereign must be a genius who can adjust government spending in ways that no one else can anticipate, and so can counter the economic (and mental) cycles that threaten to lead to depressions. The leaders in Pound's poem appear strangely amoral – powerful, glorious, manipulative, and yet generous; they are the combinations of Shylocks and monks that Derrida says are necessary to run gift economies.

In *Paterson*, Williams repeats Pound's credo that 'sovereignty inheres in the POWER to issue money' (Williams, W. C. 1958, 218). His poem also investigates sovereignty by creating enigmatic images of larger-than-life persons: it is based on the conceit that the town of Paterson is somehow the same as a giant man Paterson who is both thoroughly immoral and a potential sexual source of rebirth for the hellish modern world. The poem cites several tracts from followers of Douglas's Social Credit movement, and reaches a climactic demand that the government '[l]et credit / out' from its entrapment in bad fiscal policies because credit is the ' "radiant gist", against all that scants our lives' (183, 186). When credit is 'stalled in money', Williams writes, it 'conceals the generative' and 'thwarts art'; credit as 'gist' is thus a repressed energy, economic, sexual, and artistic, which could erupt if only there were the right sovereign figures (18). Williams also brings himself into the poem: he includes letters that describe (and condemn) his treatment of lovers; and he repeatedly asks himself how he or anyone can solve the poetic – and economic – problems of the modern world. The modernist artist in Williams's poem, as in many early twentieth-century literary works, stands apart from the rest of the world, becoming a figure similar to what Keynesian economics requires: someone who can perform acts which remain incomprehensible to everyone else in order to solve the problem of modern chaos. In T. S. Eliot's terms, the modernist uses art as a way 'of ordering, of giving a shape and a significance to the immense panorama of futility and anarchy which is contemporary history' (1975, 177). In giving shape to what appears chaotic to everyone else, the artist enacts a model of sovereignty.

The rejection of the Keynesian model in the 1970s is basically the rejection of active sovereignty, the rejection of a government that tries to counter the chaos of economic cycles or to create a new shape for history. Anti-Keynesian economists argue, as we saw earlier in the writings of Lucas and Sargent, that no one can act in a countercyclical manner, because the system of cycles will always already have taken into account any leaders' efforts to counter the cycles. The only way that an excess can be found, Friedman argues, is to make that excess as automatic as the system itself. The notion of the impossibility of individual transcendence of the market or the code is reflected in postmodern arts of the 1960s and '70s, whose 'flatness or depthlessness, a new kind of superficiality', according to Fredric Jameson, makes it seem that the 'once-existing centered subject' that remained, however enigmatically hidden, behind modernist works, 'has today in the world of organizational bureaucracy dissolved' (1991, 9, 15).

To give one striking example of the role of economics in postmodern literature, consider *The Crying of Lot 49*, a novel about mysterious signs appearing everywhere and the search for the meaning of them. No one in the novel finds any understandable system of meaning; nonetheless, the book manages to end, and what allows the search to end is one final act: the signs are put on the market. The book ends with its title, with the crying of a lot, the call for bids at an auction, and what is being put on the auction block at the end is a collection of objects marked with the signs everyone has been trying to understand. The novel thus finally turns to the market in order to end its fiction: what stands outside fictional signs and allows them to operate as signs is not reference or meaning but a market for those signs. This is Friedman economics exactly, letting the 'meaning' of the most important signs derive from the market, not from any conscious plans of supposedly sovereign governments, corporations, or individuals.

Derrida's texts are generally treated as emerging out of the worlds of literature and philosophy, not economics. However, by reading back from this essay to earlier ones, we can see that economics has always played a role in Derrida's linguistic analyses. Consider, for example, the essay 'Signature, Event, Context', in which Derrida deconstructs the nineteenth-century writer Condillac's theory of meaning. Throughout this essay, Derrida describes Condillac's theory as one that sets 'production' as the origin of meaning. Condillac's theory is based on 'the simplicity of origin, the continuity of all derivation, of all production' (1988, 4). Similarly, Condillac believes that 'to write is to produce a mark that will constitute a sort of machine which is productive in turn' (1988, 8).

Derrida's challenge to Condillac takes the form of a critique of production. Derrida argues that the meaning or value of a sign does not derive from its production: 'The sign possesses the characteristic of being readable even if the moment of its production is irretrievably lost' (1988, 9). Signs are then 'the nonpre-sent *remainder* of a differential mark cut off from its putative "production" or origin' (1988, 10). This denial of the importance of production as the source of 'meaning' of signs may be a philosophical position, but it seems also to be a corollary to the transformation of the economic system from productivist to consumerist, that transformation which brought credit to seem the basis of the economy. In his critique of Condillac, Derrida brings in several terms to describe what replaces the moment of production as the source of meaning, but in his follow-up article, 'Limited, Inc.', he says that there is really just one structure, the 'parasitic struc-ture', which he has 'tried to analyze everywhere, under the names of writing, mark, step, margin, *differánce*, graft, undecidable, supplement, *pharmakon*, hymen, *parergon*, etc.' (1988, 103). In other words, parasitism, a form of borrowing and indebted-ness, replaces production in Derrida's theory, as it does in the economic history of the twentieth century.

Derrida writes as if what he is doing is simply arguing with Condillac in the ahistorical realm of philosophy, but I suggest rather that he is looking back at the productivist economics of the nineteenth century from the viewpoint of the consumerist economics of the twentieth, when the theory that physical production is the central engine of the economic system no longer holds. Derrida finds in theories of signs a parallel to this economic transformation: production is no longer the source of meaning of signs. Rather, a code produces meaning without distinct acts of production: meanings are then like a stockpile of objects waiting to be used.

Derridean attacks on the connection of meaning to intention or production end up being interpreted as liberalizing gestures, freeing people from the tyranny of the subject. But Derrida's project hardly produces images of freedom; rather the code takes over, creating its automatic effects. Derrida focuses attention on one small sign of the inability of individuals to control even their own possessions: they cannot control their signatures. In *Given Time*, he lists 'coded signatures' as one of the new forms of money. In 'Signature, Event, Context', he presents his deconstruction of the notion of the uniqueness of signatures: 'to be readable, a signature must have a repeatable, iterable, imitable form; it must be able to be detached from the present and singular intention of its production' (1988, 20). Note that once again the key to Derrida's conclusion that signatures are separate from intentions is that they are separated from production. Derrida's deconstruction of signatures marks one of the fundamental features of poststructuralist discourse, the undoing of 'subjects' as the originators and producers of meaning. This alteration in the nature of subjects derives in part from the rejection of production as the source of structural form and value. Without a fundamental concept of production, there is no 'producer' of signs, and hence writers lose their sovereignty over meaning. Nations similarly lost their 'sovereignty' over money as a result of 1970s economics. When currencies are defined entirely by their relations to other currencies (the market and the float), not by seeming reference to objects, the notion of sovereignty changes. Robert Triffin, who proposed the system of defining currencies in terms of baskets of other curren-cies, describes the problem of deciding the 'meaning' of monetary signs – their worth – as precisely a problem of accepting a distinct reduction in sovereignty:

> In a world where countries have become more and more interdependent,
> [there is an] enormous gap between the supranational nature of the

problem with which we dealt and the multiplicity of national currencies, coupled with nationally determined policies which are often inter-nationally incompatible. Yet it is clearly impossible to change overnight these tribal or national systems with which we have been living into a supranational system in which countries are called upon to surrender their precious sovereignty. This is a problem we can only solve gradually – through international, not supranational decisions. What I would insist upon, however, is that in doing this we should not forget that the problem itself is not a national one: it is an international problem.

(Quoted in Hinshaw 1967, 47 [brackets by Tratner])

The 'gap' that Triffin discovers is very much the kind of gap that Derrida repeatedly focuses upon. There is a gap between the meaning of a given monetary sign and the intended meaning that the sovereign issuing nation would like to assign it. Currency gains some part of its meaning or value from the international situation; a daily posting of rates of exchange is like a constantly shifting dictionary. It is the crying of the dollar every day, letting the market shape the code itself into a constantly changing system. Pound's and Williams's belief in sovereignty over coinage falls apart in the 1970s, as it becomes clear that there is no sovereign powerful enough to control the meaning of money.

We could even adapt this economic model into an alternative interpretation of Derrida's account of linguistic signs. Triffin's account suggests that to use a linguistic sign requires not merely an intention on the part of the person using it, but a system of exchange – a market – that determines how others will make use of the sign. One can 'intend' to use a word in a certain way, only to discover that people take the word differently. Linguistic interactions are exchanges partly determining the meanings that words carry, and hence shaping the models upon which individuals build their utterances. The results of utterances shape the 'intentions' that go into further utterances; such results even shape what a person thinks the intentions that supposedly preceded an utterance were. Triffin and Derrida both propose systems that would result in the deconstruction of sovereignty.

In summary, then, I suggest we add to the list of disciplines that have contributed to deconstruction. In *Of Grammatology*, Derrida credits numerous fields, including philosophy (Nietzsche, Heidegger, and Husserl), linguistics (Saussure), ethnography (Lévi-Strauss), and psychology (Freud) (1976). To this list, let's add economics, citing Keynes, who marks the end of production as the basis of economics, but who maintains the belief that individuals in powerful enough positions can still act to counter the effects of the system, and Friedman, who brings in the notion that the sign system operates separate from any individual agency. Historians of theory would probably prefer to cite Marcel Mauss and George Bataille as the ones who led Derrida to the concepts of gifts and of mysterious, uncontrollable economic structures. It is probably true that they figure more consciously in Derrida's own thinking than do Keynes and Friedman. But the emergence of deconstruction and its rapid spread during the 1970s are not merely events in the history of highly intellectual disciplines; they are also events in the broader history shaped by the changes in everyday economics and governmental practices. Keynes and Friedman developed theories which had material consequences; Mauss and Bataille were in effect mythologizing the events going on in mainstream economics.

Mauss and Bataille may seem better predecessors because they were critics of capitalism, as Derrida is, but if mainstream twentieth-century economic practices in effect involve the deconstruction of signs as an everyday part of their functioning, then perhaps deconstruction should not be considered inherently anti-capitalist or even anti-authoritarian. Derridean theorists need to be careful when they generalize that a deconstructive challenge to one form of authority (such as the authority given to production as the source of economic value and the source of linguistic meaning) carries with it a challenge to authority in other realms, or even a challenge to the very idea of authority entirely. Derrida makes such an unwarranted leap when he argues in his essay that the power of a counterfeit coin to generate real wealth is equivalent to a radical disruption of patriarchy: the power of the counterfeit coin in Baudelaire's story, Derrida claims, reveals that 'the phantasm' has 'the power . . . of producing, of engendering, giving, rather than the "True Father" ' (1992, 161). The image of a True Father, Derrida implies, depends on theories of production and human giving as the basis of prosperity, in other words, on outdated economic theories. In noting that the phantasm, the sign, the code, has more power of 'engendering' and of 'giving' than the True Father, Derrida might be tracing not the demise of patriarchy but simply the demise of Keynesian economics and of the liberalism of the 1960s, the demise of the notion that the government can wrap itself in the guise of the True Father and maintain the economic system by appearing to give gifts whenever recession threatens.

By describing the results of the economic transformations he has traced as the end of patriarchy, Derrida's theory implies much more than has happened. The deconstructive revision of money into a system of signifiers in endless freeplay may be a modification of capitalism, one that capitalists and patriarchs opposed for centuries, but it turns out that it is possible to perform such a deconstruction without undoing much of capitalism or patriarchy at all – and Friedman did just that. Twentieth-century economics reveals that non-logocentric sign systems can coexist quite well with capitalism and can even play a crucial role in the functioning of structures of authority, which apparently can operate quite well without invoking any True Fathers at all.

Note

1   For alternative interpretations of the relevance of Aristotle's distinction between *oikos* and chrematistics to twentieth-century economic and literary issues, see . . . Meikle (2000); Seaford (2000).

Chapter 21

Tim Woods

GIVING AND RECEIVING: NURUDIN FARAH'S *GIFTS* OR THE POSTCOLONIAL LOGIC OF THIRD WORLD AID

From *The Journal of Commonwealth Literature* 38 (2003): 91–112

'Then you have learned', Zarathustra interrupted the speaker, 'how it is harder to give well than to take well, and that to give well is an *art* and the ultimate, subtlest master-art of kindness'.

(Friedrich Nietzsche, *Also Sprach Zarathustra*)

I call for an immediate examination of how best to restructure international aid to reduce dependency, promote primary social development objectives such as clean drinking water, basic literacy and health care, and reinforce efforts to make African economies more stable and competitive. . . . Greater aid for infra-structure development in Africa . . . would leave a tangible mark while generating employment, expertise and revenues in Africa itself.

(*The Cause of Conflict and the Promotion of Durable Peace and Sustainable Development in Africa* (Kofi Annan, Secretary General's Report to the United Nations Security Council, 16 April 1998))

IN ADDITION TO ADDRESSES TO THE SECURITY Council of the United Nations, the gift can be located at the centre of current discussions of deconstruction, international politics, gender, ethics, philosophy, anthropology and economics. Nuruddin Farah's *Gifts* (1993) unlocks a wide-ranging critique of the politics of postcolonial autonomy and dependency. *Gifts* has a straightforward plot that focuses on the developing love between the two principal protagonists: Duniya, a middle-aged nurse in Mogadiscio, the capital of Somalia, who is struggling to bring up her teenage son and daughters; and a wealthy friend Bosaaso, who has returned from the United States to offer his services to the Somali government. The head nurse at a maternity hospital in Mogadiscio, Duniya has established a relatively self-sufficient home with her children, the twins Nasiiba and her brother Mataan, and their younger sister Yarey, no small feat for a divorcée in a patriarchal society. Then two unexpected events transform her life. First she accepts an unexpected ride to work from Bosaaso. That evening she receives another 'gift', a newborn baby that her daughter says has been abandoned. Against this background of developing familial relations, Farah's novel is a subtle reflection on giving and receiving, dependence and reciprocity in a starving Somalia seen through the eyes of a single mother, while simultaneously exploring the interrelation of the philosophical and anthropological discourses of gift-giving, and the discourse of the politics of Third World aid donorship. In his bold approach to questions of modern African identity and sexuality in the shifting realities of the Horn of Africa, Farah creates a singular metafictional space where Joseph Conrad collides with spirit-world djinns, where Jungian dreams and local folklore converge with the rattle of modern fax machines and the gunfire of clan violence.

Farah gained an international reputation with his first 'Variations on the Theme of an African Dictatorship' trilogy, for his outspoken critiques of the Somali dictator General Mohammed Siyad Barre who ruled the country during the 1970s and 1980s. *Gifts* was written during the 1980s, against the background of the Ethiopian famine of 1984, and it was published first in Swedish (1990), which was over a year *before* the fall of the Barre regime (in May 1991). Nevertheless, the novel is prophetic, since much of its content focuses upon the Somali war-and-famine crisis of the 1990s, which was the aftermath of Barre's demise. In this respect, the specific context of *Gifts* foreshadows the consequences of Barre's rule – a Mogadiscio plagued by infrastructural chaos, power shortages, and political in-fighting bred by clan-wars in the 1990s (1993, 19 [hereafter cited in the text]). Yet this novel focuses instead on the politics of gift-giving, both in the social context of family relations, as well as in the political context of international aid donorships. *Gifts* demonstrates a subtle understanding of the complex obligations instituted by international charity donors, such as the disarming imposition of a political and economic hierarchy within the context of First World and Third World international relations and a whole set of other vestigial colonial effects. Most chapters of the novel conclude with newspaper or news agency reports concerning international aid to Somalia, such as the donation of milk by the EC (23), Liv Ullmann's tour of the remote famine regions for UNICEF (51–52), or the Italian government's agreement to increase the participation of Italian professors at the National University of Somalia in completing an Italian-Somali dictionary (99–100). Yet in addition to this economic aid on a continental scale, Farah's novel also considers the nature of gift-giving within nations, societies and families and between friends, articulating the various complex dimensions of what constitutes a gift. For example, we are told about Duniya being given in marriage to Zubair ('a gesture of kind violence') in return for a horse (38); and we are told of Nasiiba's donation of blood (27), both of which jar awkwardly with other forms of giving and donation itemized in the newspaper and news agency reports. Does donating one's own blood have the same status as donations of excess butter and milk to a foreign nation experiencing famine, or being given in marriage? Are some gifts hedged round with taboos, mores and inviolabilities? Are all gifts the same? Or are gifts socially contextualized? What gifts are given, or is this also a social question? What makes a gift-giving different from an exchange of commodities?

In exploring the many dimensions of the lexicon of gift-giving – gifts, presents, donations, aid, handouts, contributions, assistance, offerings – Farah acknowledges in the novel's dedication his specific debt to the anthropological studies of Melanesian societies by the pathbreaking anthropologist Marcel Mauss: 'In writing this novel I have incurred many debts, the most important of which is owed to Marcel Mauss, author of *The Gift*, translated into English by I. Cunison [sic]'. Claude Lévi-Strauss regarded Marcel Mauss's study of gift-giving in *The Gift* (1954) as a landmark in anthropological studies that inaugurated a new era for the social sciences. He sees Mauss as the first attempt at a structural anthropology in that the principal import of *The Gift* was to reach beyond empirically observed behaviour and to demonstrate how these unconscious rules of exchange in fact manifest the deeper realities of a society's composition. As far as Mauss is concerned, exchange is at the root of a large number of apparently heterogeneous social activities: where empirical observation sees only giving, receiving, returning, Mauss sees a whole series of social relationships concealed in this process. 'So the whole theory calls for the existence of a structure, only fragments of which are delivered by experience – just its scattered members, or rather its elements' (1987, 46). Mauss perceives the social as a system, among whose parts connections, equivalences and interdependent aspects can be discovered. Parts are construed as transferable, substitutable and comparable. Mauss shows that the act of giving is actually a concatenation of three obligations – giving, receiving and returning. He makes a distinction between gift societies and commodity societies. Gift societies are dominated by kinship relations and groups that define individuals and their relations with and obligations to each other. In transactions in these societies, objects are inalienably associated with the giver, the recipient, and the relationship that defines and binds them. Consequently, objects and people are seen as defined by their locations in a web of social relationships. Another system is the commodity system of the modern West, where people are not defined by kin relationships and groups, but are independent individuals who transact freely with each other. In transactions in these societies, objects are alienated commodities, separate from the giver and the recipient. Consequently, objects and people are defined by their autonomous identities. Gift-giving establishes a relationship of superiority, since a receiver becomes a dependant, for at least as long as he has not 'given back' what he has been given. Gift-giving establishes inequality and difference, which can become a hierarchy. If a hierarchy exists, gift-giving expresses and legitimizes it. Maurice Godelier argues that gift-giving has two opposite movements – solidarity and distancing, sharing and dividing: he states that 'it can be, simultaneously or successively, an act of generosity or of violence', but violence can be disguised as a disinterested gesture, such as sharing (1998, 12).

Farah clearly agrees with Mauss in the importance of understanding the concrete totality of social life, and with his concept of exchange as 'total social phenomena' simultaneously containing legal, social, economic, moral and aesthetic elements. For gift-giving is thoroughly diverse and pervades virtually every aspect of one's daily existence: giving presents, donating to charity, giving advice, offering up a seat, giving a promise, giving one's time. Yet without doubt one of the principal characteristics of the gift is its ambiguity: it can be both valuable and a danger. Farah's novel explores the manner in which a gift shows a number of different facets. On the one hand it is experienced as a refusal of self-interest and of egotistic calculation and an exaltation of generosity. The novel abounds with examples of such altruism, such as Bosaaso's and his friend Dr. Mire's donations of their services to the Somali government free of charge; or a neighbour's offer of home-help in the form of a maid when the foundling arrives at Duniya's home (76); or the hard currency of

American dollars sent to Duniya from Italy by her brother Abshir (82, 180); or the People's Republic of China's donation to the people of Somalia of the Benaadir Maternity Hospital at which Dr. Mire and Duniya work (20) and the contrast between the Chinese doctors and the European doctors:

> The modesty of the Chinese as a donor government was truly exemplary. No pomp, no garlands of see-how-great-we-are. . . . And you would meet the Chinese doctors, who came as part of the gift, as they did their rounds, soft of voice, short of breath when they spoke Somali, humble of gesture. Unlike the Italian and Dutch doctors on secondment from their governments as an overpriced package from the European Community, the Chinese did not own cars.
>
> (20)

On the other hand, the gift never entirely manages to exclude the logic of exchange. In this respect, the novel explores the manner in which the presentation of a gift embeds within it an obligation, either to return the gift, or to be beholden to the donor. For instance, Duniya makes it quite clear to her children that she dislikes the children bringing home 'unauthorised gifts of food, or money, given to them by Uncle so-and-so' (26). Not only do such gifts compromise her role as a parent and make her seem ungenerous, they place her family in a beholden state to her relatives. The giving of gifts, even within a group of intimate and well-known people, still operates with obligations of power, in this case, family power relations: 'Duniya felt uncomfortable eating what was known in their household as "corpse food", a term coined as a result of her saying to her twins that they could consume food gifts only if she, their mother, was dead, not before' (26). As Mauss argued, gifts establish and reinforce kinship relations – are not simply 'pure gifts'. A gift can also be a bribe, which is an impure gift, and indeed one might argue that it is not a gift at all. Duniya never forgets her half-brother Shiriye's 'secret acceptance of bride-gifts from [her first husband] Zubair' (83) in order to buy his agreement for their marriage. Some 'gifts' can 'give away' something, like the husband who 'brings things into our house, good and bad things' (18) and who 'gives' gonorrhoea to his wife, thus 'giving away' his infidelity and endangering her baby's and her health; while other gifts can take on a particularly threatening significance, such as the offer of a lift by a strange man to Duniya, with its concomitant sexual innuendo: 'I'll give you a lift, then reward you with further gifts' (21).

The ambiguity of the gift is most clearly felt by the novel's juxtaposition of different sorts of giving, since this raises questions about the *value* and *source* of a gift. In a complex textual layering, the novel juxtaposes Mataan's fables about the Somali folk-character Juxaa – the morals of which concern the ways in which people are perfectly happy and quite gullible when receiving a gift, but less happy to have it taken away (74), or people's attempts to capitalize on and exploit the gift-giving of someone else (116) – with the difficult passage concerning the 'gift of death', when Bosaaso's ex-wife Yussur, kills her baby and herself: 'The maid told of a flash of insanity brightening Yussur's eyes between her speaking the word "give" and death from the fall' (51). The association of death and a gift here is not to be confused with the Derridean reflection on the denial of history as history of responsibility, the gift's entanglement with the birth of Christianity out of Platonism, and the interconnectedness of religion with secrecy explored in *The Gift of Death* (Derrida 1995). Rather, this is a point of impenetrability into Yussur's mind, who makes an association of giving and birth/death which is obscurely hinted at as a madness. It is another of those moments in the novel where the ambiguity of giving is evident, this time in a painful and dreadful event. This unintelligible quality implicated in some instances of a gift, recurs in the many instances of the novel where chapters and sections begin with dreams, particularly about birds speaking to humans, or doing something for, or to, humans. At one point we see a kestrel giving a woman things in her dream (149), while on other occasions, there are scenes where humans see insects or birds fly into a room, such as Bosaaso seeing a kingfisher fly into Duniya's house (46) and Duniya seeing a dragon-fly (28, 69). The structural repetition of these conscious or unconscious human interactions with nature, pose questions about the significance of these 'meetings'. Are dreams 'gifts' in some sense? Do they 'give' something to people that is part of a cycle of giving, receiving, and returning? What function do the numerous mentions of birds, dragonflies, insects flying into the rooms, play in the novel? Why do these creatures appear to Duniya and Bosaaso? Are they 'gifts' in some sense? What sort of gifts, and from whom, or what? Metaphysical answers to these questions seem to hover in the background, and they are given some affirmation by the way that the novel constantly offers metaphysical alternatives to some of the other imponderable issues in debate. For instance, there is a key discussion between Duniya, Bosaaso and Dr. Mire on the gift of a cultural perspective and how this conflicts or contradicts indigenous concepts. In discussing the emergence of Islamic beliefs in Somali culture, Duniya asks 'What was in it for the Arabs to *give* us their world-view, together of course with an Allah-created cosmos, which contradicted our traditional belief-systems?' (96). Mire and Bosaaso get into a discussion about the differences between Christianity, Islam and Somali beliefs, and Mire concludes that Christianity and Islamic belief embody within them a redemptive gift of an afterlife, which is not available through the definitive ending in Somali belief: 'In the case of the Somali who deifies crows, the answer is clear: Somalis defer to death, crows being associated with the ending of life, a termination of this existence. What the Judaeo-Christian and Islamic systems offer is a forward-looking, reward-offering, life-after-death rationalization, a credo in which you are guaranteed paradisiacal delights after death' (96). In other words, Mire argues that Islamic and Christian belief systems are part of a gift-system, placing its believers in a cycle of giving and receiving, where one invests in activities of worship to be rewarded with the promise of heavenly dividends 'worthy of your trust in a god who gives and takes away life' (97). As Bosaaso comments, 'God gives, man gives' (97). The consequence of such an argument would appear to be that Islamic and Judaeo-Christian societies have a completely different concept of gift structures which ultimately hinge on metaphysical sources and rewards, whereas the Somali gift structure is considerably more materialist. Nevertheless, Duniya clings to a more metaphysical belief system, and 'thought to herself that little is revealed to oneself directly. Revelations are received from out of a mist of doubts, in caves, in the dark, out of a child's mouth, or via the wise utterances of an elderly or mad person' (245). Such epiphanies, which guide and influence Duniya's actions, are 'gifts' in an abstract and intangible sense.

This 'metaphysics' of donorship in Farah's novel, partially evident in his one-word title *Gifts*, might well provoke the question as to whether there is finally any meaningful or useful sense in which subjects as diverse as death, lovers, infidelity and venereal disease can be described, indiscriminately, as 'gifts'. Might Farah be dealing with something imponderable here, or could he be accused legitimately of merely being imprecise? Does not the word 'gifts' (as in his other two novels in this trilogy, *Maps* and *Secrets*, where in the latter, everything, and therefore nothing, is a secret) become a verbal portmanteau in which almost anything can be held? Perhaps we take Farah too much on his own terms and assume as *given* (no pun intended) the mappedness or secrecy of the universe when the terms themselves – their relevance and accuracy – need to be more closely scrutinized.

It might be concluded that Farah appears at times to tread a wavering line between metaphysical and materialist understandings of what constitutes a 'gift'. For against this internal debate about the possible metaphysics of gift structures, the novel does place examples of very specifically materialist and political gifts. As the anthropologist Mary Douglas reminds us, in addition to its structural anthropologist interest, Mauss's *The Gift* is also a book about politics and morality. For Mauss, the theory of the gift is a theory of human solidarity. As Douglas argues, his work fits into the French tradition of the critique of individualism at the heart of English Utilitarianism, or English liberalism, that saw *laissez-faire* economics, social atomization, and the exploitation of the poor under a regime of industrial capitalism as its characteristics. Mauss argues that society's obligations to the worker are never entirely complete. He is a socialist taking a stand against Bolshevism; he contends that the market must be maintained, and he is against *laissez-faire* capitalism, asking the state to intervene and expressing the hope that the rich ought to rediscover the generosity of the ancient Celtic or German nobleman, so that society might not fall prisoner to the 'cold reasoning of the merchant, the banker, and the capitalist' (1954, 75). In this respect, Mauss's book outlines a social-democratic programme before its time, explicitly stating that if western capitalist society is to avoid social and economic hierarchies, it needs to be more equitable in distributing access to the 'common store of wealth'. Steering a middle line between liberalism and Communism, Mauss argues that 'There is no need to seek far for goodness and happiness. It is to be found in the imposed peace, in the rhythm of communal and private labour, in wealth amassed and redistributed, in the mutual respect and reciprocal generosity that education can impart' (81). In this political context, Douglas states in her Foreword to the Routledge edition of *The Gift*, 'Charity is meant to be a free gift, a voluntary, unrequited surrender of resources. Though we laud charity as a Christian virtue we know that it wounds. . . . According to Marcel Mauss that is what is wrong with the free gift. A gift that does nothing to enhance solidarity is a contradiction' (2001, vii). There are no free gifts – gift cycles engage persons in permanent commitments that articulate the dominant institutions. Within the wider context of international aid donorship, gift-giving acts may be perceived of as a structure of delayed colonialism: i.e. the feelings of indebtedness breed feelings of inferiority and vengefulness in the recipient nation. Reminders of the presence of international aid charities in Somali life pervade Farah's novel: Nasiiba wears a T-shirt with a Band-Aid logo on it (32); Mataan is pictured 'wearing a UNICEF T-shirt a few sizes too large for him' (77); while the radio broadcasts 'an item about the Head of State receiving a combined North American and EC delegation visiting to discuss Somalia's foreign-aid requirements' (101); the final family meal takes place in a restaurant called Croce del Sud, a now seedy vestige of 'when the Italians were the master race here. Nor were the waiters allowed to wear shoes' (235). Even when the family go to the airport to welcome Uncle Abshir, and Yarey offers to dress up in white and offer him a bouquet of flowers, Bosaaso remarks upon the vestiges of colonialism in this apparently everyday occurrence: 'this is a very neocolonial trad-ition, inherited along with the idea of flags, a state capital and such paraphernalia'. He goes on to mention the implicit patriarchal power of gifts that is also embodied in it, 'a very male notion in which an innocent young virgin dressed in white is offered to a visiting man who happens to be head of another state. I needn't remind you that in our own tradition a man whose honour is wounded is often rewarded with a maiden as part of the compensation given him' (229). Everyday affairs are constantly seen through the perspective of the metaphor of the politics of gift-aid charity, such as when Bosaaso has a blunt talk with his sister-in-law Waaberi, concerning her excessive expenditure which was driving her back to Bosaaso for further loans: 'This wasn't a story of equals having a show-down, thought Duniya . . . This was more like a donor European or American government having a "frank talk" (the all-purpose phrase which would appear in the official communiqué) with an African country's representatives in which the latter were told that they were being immodest in the number of Mercedes and similar extravagances and in the show-pieces they displayed to the rest of the world' (224).

Despite his significant contribution to the anthropological understanding of giving and receiving, Mauss's theory of gift-giving has two serious flaws. Firstly, in attempting to answer the question of why people reciprocate gifts, Mauss suggests that a spirit or power resides in the thing that compels the recipient to return it. The 'enigma of gift-giving' is ultimately the question as to why one is inspired to give gifts – Mauss believed that things given have a soul that compels them to return to their original owner who gave them away: 'Whatever [the gift] is, food, possessions, women, children or ritual, it retains a magical and religious hold over the recipient. The thing given is not inert. It is alive and often personified, and strives to bring to its original clan and homeland some equivalent to take its place' (1954, 10, [brackets by Woods]). The circulation of gifts is finally explained by this mysterious Maori concept of *hau*, a spiritual power invested in the gift which causes reciprocation. Thus, as Lévi-Strauss pointed out, Mauss adds a religious or metaphysical dimension to exchange, that goes counter to his systematic structuralist approach. Farah's explanation for the circulation of gifts is more materialist than the metaphysical explanation of Mauss and his driving impetus is why people give gifts. What starts the cycle of gift-giving? Mauss failed to ask this question and Farah's novel seems to suggest that the giver is himself bound into a cycle, responding with a counter-presentation – the donor is already implicated as a receiver *before a gift is given*. Mauss fails to recognize that whenever a gift is given, relations of exchange (obliga-tions to give/receive/reciprocate) have already been established. This is the recogni-tion that Duniya articulates to Bosaaso when she first seeks to explain her hesitation in accepting his offer of a lift to work: 'your giving precedes my acceptance or rejection. My accepting your gift of a lift is itself a reciprocal gift' (22). [. . .]

Secondly, it has been pointed out that in most societies there are things that are not subject to exchange. In *The Enigma of the Gift*, Maurice Godelier's analysis of Mauss's work argues that there are some things that must not or cannot be given or sold, for example, sacred objects, knowledge, or rites (1998, 32–36). Together with the anthropologist Annette Weiner's study of 'inalienable possessions' – possessions that are part of a powerful political strategy of 'keeping-while-giving' (1992) – their analysis shifts one's focus from things given to things kept. Godelier's key argument is that there are spheres of sacred things that are not exchanged and there are others that enter into exchanges of gifts or exchange of commodities. And it is this 'keeping-while-giving' structure that preserves differences of identity. There are instances where keeping-while-giving can destroy a person's identity, as it is rumoured that Mataan's woman friend is some rich man's 'kept woman' ([Farah 1993,] 27). Yet despite this patriarchal perversion of gift-giving, the preservation of differences of identity is a key issue in the context of debates about the politics of representation and the subsumption of the 'other' as a gesture of violence. *Gifts* is repeatedly concerned with the hidden ethics of gift-giving, and the manner in which gift-aid charity objectifies the receiver. Theodor Adorno's melancholy dirge hints at a forgotten practice in gift-giving: 'We are forgetting how to give presents' (1978, 42); by which Adorno means a situation where giving is increasingly relegated to bureaucratic charities that facilitate the 'administered beneficence, planned papering-over of society's visible sores' (ibid.), while they often humiliate and objectify the recipients, a situation in which exchange value and anonymity in gift-giving rules. Theodor Adorno argues that modern gift-aid raises the donor into a hierarchical relationship with the recipient. He seeks to counter this, by arguing that generosity can only work if the *otherness* of the other is accepted, that there is no attempt to identify and thereby integrate the other. In seeking undistorted relationships through a transfiguration of giving and receiving, the non-identity of the other person and culture must be respected and preserved. As Romand Coles puts it, Adorno's sense of 'Giving entails an ability to receive the other's specificity, and this receptivity is entwined with an ability to extend ourselves generously toward others and otherness' (1997, 105). As much of Adorno's work has sought to argue, commodity exchange establishes objective quantitative relationships between the objects transacted, while gift exchange ought to establish personal qualitative relationships between the subjects doing the transacting. In the midst of the self-apotheosis of contemporary liberalism, the counter-vision of receptive generosity rooted not in sovereign self-interest but in a non-assimilating openness to others lies at the heart of Adorno's and Levinas's ethics of giving. The import of Adorno's *Minima Moralia* fragment 21 is that ethical relations between people should be animated by receptive generosity and life is not lived if this disappears.

As human history shamefully records, people themselves can be objects for exchange. Women in particular have historically played a significant role in the exchange of gifts, often being the 'gift' or commodity that is exchanged. Women are respected and revered, even feared, in Farah's novels. Ever since the publication of his first book, *From a Crooked Rib* (1970), he has been regarded as a man uniquely gifted at portraying women's perspectives. Farah movingly describes how Somali women derive their identities from their male associations. There are plenty of examples in the novel of misogynist attitudes, such as Bosaaso's embarrassing acquaintance Kaahin, whose bumper sticker reads 'Kaahin: Women's Cain' (155); or Qaasim's indifferent affair with Fariida which resulted in the 'discovery' of Nasiiba's 'foundling' (as it turns out, Nasiiba is actually relieving her friend of the unwanted child); or the reference at one point to Duniya's and Bosaaso's anxiety about possessive behaviour in a relationship, and the manner in which love is a struggle to maintain distinctive differences and close bonds:

Duniya took note of the flourish of pronouns, some inclusive, some exclusive; pronouns dividing the world into separable segments, which they labelled as such. Apparently, the two of them were *we*, the rest of the world *they*. Together, when alone with each other, they in turn fragmented themselves into their respective I's. That is to say, they were like two images reflecting a oneness of souls, more like twin ideas united in their pursuit to be separable and linked at the same time. Is this the definition of love?

(151)

The novel's reflection on the unequal power men have over women is part of the novel's general concern with the symbolically, structurally, and functionally different roles played by women in the ordering of society and the consequences for a society when people are treated as possessions. Mataan at one point raises a discussion about the Islamic concept of *xabs*:

'*Xabs* is interpreted by Islamic scholars as the right of obedience', explained Mataan, 'although the word shares its root with another understood to mean detention. The point is that women aren't permitted to leave their husband's homes without their husbands' prior notification, and any woman who violates this right may be described as rebellious. The home, therefore, the veil and the fact that women can't go out of the house, say, to work in an office or as a nurse in a hospital: these come under *xabs*: the right of obedience. A homeless woman is one who has no husband or a male relation to provide her with shelter'.

(175)

Male power is possessive and acquisitive with a desire to receive a return on one's investments and as Hélène Cixous has argued, this results in an economy that is predicated on the fear of debt, of expropriation, of loss (Cixous and Clément 1986, 80, 87). The gift of shelter is an explicit relationship of gendered power in which a woman is made dependent upon the male authority. Duniya recognizes this structure of power in her society, and manages to get Bosaaso to concede that 'men have assigned to themselves all the sacred, powerful spaces, forbidding women from being visible or present in such places as mosques or at meetings of a council of men reaching decisions which affect the whole community, including women . . . the spaces allotted to women belong to the grey areas of beds, food and the rearing of children' (221). Clearly, women, attempting self-definition, face harsh resistance; Duniya must fight to learn to drive and to swim. She has an allergic reaction to gifts from others, resisting 'all kinds of domination, including that of being given something. As my epitaph I would like to have the following written: "Here lies Duniya who distrusted givers" ' (242). Gifts have always been double-edged swords for her. Her in-laws have given her a home, but require in return that she relinquish her young daughter. In a country defined by grim images telecast by the Western media and by the self-serving aims of the foreign givers, Duniya realizes that no giving was innocent. Even in her own personal life, she has been the object of male offerings, as she is given in marriage by her father to his aged friend Zubair; and after his death, Duniya later gives herself in marriage to the journalist Taariq in exchange for his support for her children. As the novel commences, Duniya is now a single mother who 'thought that marriage was a place she had been to twice already, but love was a palace she hadn't had the opportunity to set foot in before now' (78). Duniya is particularly anxious about maintaining her role as an independent woman, and is thus nervous about the signals she sends out to Bosaaso in accepting his offer of a lift:

> 'Why do you accept lifts from me?' he asked.
> 'That's a foolish question, since your giving precedes my acceptance or rejection. My accepting your gift of a lift is itself a reciprocal gift. So may I ask now why you accept my gift?'
> 'Why are you so hesitant about receiving things from others?'
> 'Because unasked-for generosity has a way of making one feel obliged, trapped in a labyrinth of dependence. You're more knowledge-able about these matters, but haven't we in the Third World lost our self-reliance and pride because of the so-called aid we unquestioningly receive from the so-called First World?'
>
> (22)

Despite juxtaposing the giving and receiving of gifts within the context of inter-national aid and the cycle of collapsing agency and increased dependency in order to articulate her own sense of having been previously trapped twice as the object of exchange in marriage, Duniya is nevertheless attracted to Bosaaso. She wonders whether 'If what she and Bosaaso were doing was the beginning of a long courtship that might eventually lead to such a many-roomed mansion of love . . . could Bosaaso be the conflux of their river of souls, flowing into one another, together, for ever and ever?' (78–79). Their relationship develops gradually and hesitantly, and Bosaaso's presents to the family cause a certain degree of domestic unease as they are rejected. Duniya's relationship with Bosaaso is often couched in the terms of gifts: she recognizes that reliance on Bosaaso's generosity places her in a position of obligation, although it is a reciprocity that respects the other that she wishes to establish as the foundation for her relationship:

> Only, she thought, her reluctance to accept his gifts was making him tense, and this might, in the end, cause a strain on their relationship. But he did not insist that she receive everything he offered. And there were no indications of anxiety in him. In any case, she reasoned to herself, she did accept gifts from him in the form of lifts, in exchange for meals which he ate at her place. Fair was fair, and he was the kind of man who was fair.
>
> (153)

Later, as her relationship with Bosaaso develops more closely and Duniya is learning to drive with him, she wonders whether she is heading into yet another dependent situation: 'Was this going to be another nail hammered into the coffin of her dependence on him? Or was theirs simply another clichéd relationship, so to speak, in which women were the providers of food, shelter, peace at home, and good company in exchange for the man's offer of upward mobility, security and cash?' (156).

we of hybrid necessities, half real, half invented' (135). The consequence of the 'gift' of the foundling to the family, is that it exposes, cements and reinforces the symbolic source of generosity and ethical 'giving' in the novel, the gradually unfolding love between Duniya and Bosaaso. [. . .] The foundling's unexpected death also causes the child to assume symbolic significance, almost achieving mythical status, as Duniya recognizes: 'Everybody had turned the foundling into what they thought they wanted, or lacked. In that case, she said to herself, the Nameless One has not died. He is still living on, in Bosaaso and me' (130).

Farah's examination of gift-giving makes it clear that not all gifts are the same. Some gifts are more sensitive than others – money, food and sex. Gifts have to be socially contextualized since gift-giving is always involved in an increase in symbolic capital, even if it is not looking for material reciprocation. Pierre Bourdieu argues that gift-giving is always part of a political action: giving is taking, gifts are debts. He argues that gifts are part of an increase in 'symbolic capital', where social value is recognized by virtue of its material value having been *mis*recognized. One cannot make useful arguments about the practices of gift-giving if one doesn't recognize that agents in gift-giving do not act as isolated entities, free of historical contexts (Bourdieu 1990, 53–54). Virtue is always a political matter, since people have an interest in disinterestedness and generosity, with virtue always being a political matter that cannot be consigned to the efforts of individuals. Gift-giving is a political question, a question of the *polis*, which addresses fundamental issues of social inter-action between subjects. Taariq's newspaper article entitled 'Giving and Receiving: The Notion of Donations' (194–99), which juxtaposes some of the starker contradictions and ironies of the situation of international aid and African national politics, partly acts as the novel's summation of these issues and makes clear that gift-giving involves an ethical dimension, a dimension of how one treats others.

This ushers in the other discourse under scrutiny in *Gifts*, and that is international relations and the ethics of increasing globalization of western economic and cultural power. Globalization is a complex process that produces new global forms of unevenness, inequality, difference and discrimination. Dependence in an African context is a structural condition affecting many African countries, that is seen both as a constraint and as a resource. It is a constraint because there are economic and political conditions attached to the granting and use of aid; it is a resource because it provides these countries with a financial means that they would otherwise not possess (see Chabal and Daloz 1999 and Pieterse 2001). This pattern of dependence prevents diversification and thereby prolongs economic dependence, and like Duniya's analysis of the trap set up in the cycle of giving and receiving, a vicious circle of economic entrapment occurs. For various reasons, African nations place themselves increasingly in the debt of European countries, a debt which is not merely economic but also cultural and social. It is also a debt that becomes increasingly untenable and leads to the gradual ruination of African economies and cultures. In recognition of this impractical economics, Duniya points out how poverty-stricken people in the streets of Mogadiscio nevertheless wear 'exquisitely tailored clothes', and concludes that 'Both as individuals and as governments, we Somalis, better still, we Africans, tend to live beyond our means' (171). Indeed, African countries have become progressively more and more dependent on the world of aid donors since independences were achieved, and the issue of dependency concerning Africa has been widely debated by political and economic theorists.

Nuruddin Farah's contribution to this debate occurs in a novel that stares the gift-horse squarely in the mouth. Far from welcoming the aid donated to Somalia by various wealthier nations, this novel critically examines the various implications of aid or gift-giving, both in terms of its international politics and in terms of its social implications within a society. Farah's novel is critical of donorship or offerings where an ethical dimension of gift-giving – that harks back to a more altruistic practice of charity – is missing. The novel repeatedly shows how this objectification of the African 'other' is embedded in the practices of foreign aid. Recent poststructuralist analyses of Third World donorship have made similar arguments. For example, Roxanne Doty describes how 'the other' is defined by discourses of foreign aid and development. She examines how these discourses are structured by tropes that are vestigial remnants of colonialism, such as surveillance, aestheticization, classification, naturalization and appropriation. One metaphor in particular recurs with significant frequency – that of parent and child. This patronizing attitude is explicitly embodied in the novel in the figure of Ingrid, a Danish voluntary aid worker in Somalia returning to Copenhagen, who once sold a china tea service to Bosaaso and his wife Yussur. Selling the set ' "dirt cheap", more or less "giving it away" ' (47) for ten US dollars, Ingrid considers it to be a gift. The occasion sparks a 'discussion about the philosophical and cultural aspects of giving and receiving gifts' (47), as Ingrid generalizes about the differences between European and Somali notions of gift-giving. As Yussur says to Ingrid, 'We receive . . . and you give' (48). It becomes clear that Ingrid regards 'you *Apfricans*' as dependants on European largesse, completely misunderstanding the nature of a gift, and ignorant of her racial prejudices: 'Aid is aid, good or bad, whether there are strings attached and whatever its terms of reference. You say one thing but want another, you *Apfricans*. I am fed up listening to this nonsense. Why ask for help if you don't like it? The headlines of your newspapers are full of your government's appeals for more aid, more loans. Nonsense' (48). Ingrid's paradigm for understanding African development is extremely coarse, and her implicit paternalism systematically exculpates Africans for their (mis)deeds on the grounds that the nations' present predicaments are the result of immaturity in political consciousness.

Ingrid's outburst of uncomprehending indignation at the reliance of African nations on European aid betrays exactly Doty's sense that European development has the effect of infantilizing the African 'other'. Doty argues that this metaphor of guardianship and paternalization emerges within the discourses of international aid to Third World countries and reinforces the sense that the western nations are dealing with an 'emerging people or nations' – with the clear implication that the Africans are coming out of darkness, emerging from an uncivilized condition. As a discourse, development constructs the world as an unruly terrain requiring management and intervention. In addition, Doty makes it clear that foreign aid cannot be extricated from a Foucauldian nexus of truth, knowledge and power relations. For she sees foreign aid as part of a Western anthropological project to *know* the mentalities, behaviours and tendencies of those who were impoverished. Aid turns Africans into objects for the application of power rather than subjects experiencing and responding to the exercise of that power. Development thereby becomes the power to transform old worlds and the power to imagine new ones. Similar to Doty, Arturo Escobar argues that the discourse of development can be seen as an apparatus that 'maps people into certain coordinates of control. The aim is not simply to discipline individuals but to transform the conditions under which they live into a productive, normalized social environment: in short, to create modernity' (1995, 156). Escobar argues further that development and aid work are the practical extension of the West attempting to modernize other parts of the world: they are a false 'good conscience' of modernity, an (ir)responsibility. In this respect, Doty argues that international aid operates as a form of epistemological power, as well as an ontological diminution of the 'other'. 'Foreign aid enables the administration of poverty, the surveillance and management of the poor' (1996, 129). Foreign aid is a site for the deployment of disciplinary techniques, and can be said to have been born out of the fears and a sense of social danger incited by poverty and poor. Foreign aid is therefore a practical mechanism that betrays the Western donor countries' concerns about the rise of political extremists in the face of mass need and deprivation. One strand of development aid gifts, then, is rooted in the general normalizing practices of the modern state – the effort to produce and reproduce disciplined citizens and governable subjects. Therefore, resisting development and aid need not necessarily be perceived as the perversion of self-interest brought about by nationalist politics, but a means of possessing one's own space, writing or charting one's own map, taking control over one's own self-fashioning. *Gifts* demonstrates the complexity of social life, the non-childlike behaviour of African peoples, *the perspective of the subjects who are to be developed*. It shows their multifarious daily emotions, human interactions, and social fabrications, in a society deemed in need of development by the First World.

The novel questions this implicit construction of the Third World as underdeveloped, showing it to be a necessary construction at the very core of the First World self-identity. In dissecting the perspectives that construct the opposition between the First and Third Worlds, Farah constantly brings to bear an ironic self-reflexivity. For example, the First World's sense that the Third World is 'elsewhere' is undermined by Bosaaso's information that 'There are more homeless people in the city of New York than there are official residents in Mogadiscio' (174). Taking up the theme of blindness to one's own weaknesses, Nasiiba recounts the story of President Reagan sending tinned milk to Poland after the Chernobyl disaster, which turned out to be bad when opened. In response, the Polish government shipped blankets to New York's homeless, via the White House, and sought to make political capital out of the Americans' patronizing gesture. 'And', as Mataan concludes, 'yet we are under the mistaken impression that being poor, famine-stricken and homeless are phenomena associated with underdevelopment, shortage of hard currency and so on. It's disturbing to think that we, too, will have a million homeless people in our cities if we become technologically advanced' (175). Getting one's own backyard straightened out before one starts to cast aspersions on the untidiness of one's neighbour's yard is at the root of this critique of the First World's warped sense of charity. Bosaaso's African American community worker friend in the United States called Zawadi quotes a variation of an English proverb, 'It is at home that charity is bred like a stallion of Arabian nobility' (147). She refuses to go to Africa with Bosaaso and Mire because she feels that 'there was no point to her coming to Africa to do volunteer work when her home-grown people, the Blacks in the USA, needed her just as desperately. "Besides", she added, "Africa is not ready for my Black American way of life, and I am too old to unlearn all I've learned" ' (147). Zawadi's humility and sensitivity to the power implications of foreign aid and ideas about cultural development lie in stark contrast to the repeated examples of arrogant foreign intervention in Somalia's problems.

Late in the novel, Duniya realizes that her story about her anxiety of receiving gifts in the face of her desire to preserve her integrity and independence, is defined in an epiphanic moment one morning, 'when a story chose to tell itself to her, through her, a story whose clarity was contained in the creative utterance, *Let there be a man*, and there was a story' (245). This story becomes an ethical gift itself, as narratives, stories, tales are forms of 'keeping-while-giving', preserving an identity in their dissemination to others. In this respect, the closing line of the novel, 'The world was an audience, ready to be given Duniya's story from the beginning' (246), is a homage to the gift of love, as Duniya embodies an ethic of gift-giving without interest, a goodness that is without thought of reward or benefit returning to herself. In its discussion of the gift, Farah's novel never strays too far from basic ethical and political issues concerning how humans do and ought to treat one another. *Gifts* is not permeated with the rhetoric of populist resistance evident in Arturo Escobar's analysis of the power of development and the development of power. Unblinkered by any myopia of altruistic idealism, Farah depicts the postcolonial logic of gift-aid to the Third World as a 'something for something' practice, which undermines the ethical integrity of the donor nation on the one hand and the political and cultural autonomy of the recipient nation on the other. If aid is about transformation from the outside (Crush 1995, 1–23), *Gifts* critically scrutinizes the necessity for that transformation, examining the obligations and responsibilities that are exhorted by the donor(s) in their sense of largesse. This is unsurprising since gift-giving places one inescapably within an intersubjective context in contact with others. The logic of the gift is therefore infused with assumptions about our fundamental notions of reciprocity, justice and ethics. While combating the clichés about Somalia offered in the Western media, *Gifts* expands our consciousness of a more politically acceptable framework for responsible and ethical international citizenship in the face of both neo-conservative attacks on the many forms of state social welfare and African governments' confidence in foreign aid which has allowed them to escape with policies that jeopardize the economic well-being of their countries.

Chapter 22

Padmaja Challakere

AESTHETICS OF GLOBALIZATION IN CONTEMPORARY FICTION: THE FUNCTION OF THE FALL OF THE BERLIN WALL...

From *Theory and Event* 10.1 (2007): 1–23 and 32–36

IN RECENT YEARS, THE FALL OF THE BERLIN WALL has had a tremendous rhetorical yield. In the parlance of business and political economy, it is loudly mobilized as cultural currency. This is vividly illustrated in Thomas Friedman's [. . .] fulsome equation between 'democracy and the unleashing of free market global capitalism', and his correlation between 'democratization of finance' and 'the fall of the Berlin Wall' [Friedman 2005]. By Friedman's reckoning, [. . .] 'the second great age of globalization and the second great age of unregulated democracy [read capitalism] began on 11/9 with the collapse of the Berlin Wall'. [Friedman 2005, [brackets by Challakere]] But this equation is also to be glimpsed in contemporary fiction where the symbolism of the fall of the Berlin Wall, already heavy with political and cultural significance, has been recently rejuvenated. Does this mean that a Friedmanian consensus pervades successful contemporary fiction today? [. . .] The cultural preoccupations related to the coming down of the Berlin Wall are revealed in an interview[1] with Nicholas Royle, author of the novel *Counterparts*. Speaking of his interest in the Berlin Wall, Royle has this to say:

> I was particularly drawn to Berlin because of its literal, concrete division. Two halves making a whole, or two entities that were altered doubles of each other? Twins that had been separated and kept in neighboring houses and raised according to different sets of rules as a social experiment?

Royle likens the Berlin Wall to a symptom of incommensurability and sees it as an externalization of already nascent barriers. According to him, the Wall 'makes concrete' an already existing gap in what had been closely correlated and twinned. Wherever walls are put up, they produce interlocked twins who 'had been separated and kept in neighboring houses and raised according to different sets of rules as a social experiment' and in this lies the Wall's dread. The building of the Berlin Wall, as a host of historians have reminded us, was linked to the containment and displacement of Germany's Nazi past into East Berlin. The . . . novel . . . that this essay examine[s] – Zadie Smith's *White Teeth* (2000), [. . .] use[s] the metaphor of 'separated twins' and 'the fall of the Berlin Wall'. However, my argument also speaks in a larger way to the aesthetic codes and values of contemporary fiction. I argue that in its articulation of identity and in its conception of the fall of the Berlin Wall, contemporary fiction mimics rather than resists the metaphorizing mode of neo-liberal capitalism.

John le Carré's *The Spy Who Came in from the Cold* (1965) and the recent film Wolfgang Becker's *Goodbye Lenin* (2000) are paradigmatic popular texts which evoke the memory of the Berlin Wall. The most widely publicized media image related to the coming down of the Berlin Wall is, of course, that of East Berliners 'unpeeling bananas', now famously delivered from the necessity of having to wait in long lines for ordinary necessities. While it is true that East Berlin was 'liberated' into the consumerism of the West, it is also true that this transformation was based on a market economy model of 'what East Berlin must be like' (obviously, like West Berlin). A pliant East German market was thrown open to deregulation; this slide into whole-sale privatization visually embodied in yet another famous image: that of scores of second-hand Mercedes flooding East Germany.

In her essay, 'The Rise of Disaster Capitalism', published in the *Nation* magazine in the wake of the Tsunami disaster, Naomi Klein notes the emergence of 'predatory forms of disaster capitalism that use destruction, desperation, and fear created by military and or natural catastrophe to engage in extreme make-over' and 'push through privatization options for reconstruction of public infrastructure' (2005, 11). Klein explains that such massive social and economic engineering under-girded by World Bank loans are a central feature of the new 'militarization of economy'. Within the logic of this no-holds barred capitalism, military warfare and natural disasters present 'opportunities' [. . .] for the overthrowing of old barriers. All 'barriers' (old infrastructure) are forcibly removed in order to turn space into 'a blank slate on which neoliberals can design their dream economy: fully privatized, foreign-owned, and open for business' (11).

It is familiar by now that the New Economy's glorification of middle class economic autonomy and individual sovereignty is based not only upon the contra-dictory championing of the 'right of capital' and the 'right of person' but also upon a fundamental reversal of public discourse regarding the role of the state. The state's role is now fundamentally 'managerial', and the state reserves the right to act with (rather than upon) the mega-corporations to do 'what it takes' (whether it is conducting military warfare or using public resources or producing propaganda or introducing massive structural adjustment policies on a global scale or applying economic sanctions) to give US-based corporations market dominance.

The rhetorical use of the fall of the Berlin Wall offers a ready template for the articulation of 'a market-based neo-liberal cosmopolitanism', as Peter Gowan terms it. In his essay 'Neoliberal Cosmopolitanism', [. . .] Gowan comments on the emergence of a 'strong ideological current that has gained prominence in the Anglo-American world, running parallel to the discourse of globalization . . . whose theorists are to be found in international relations departments of the Anglophone universities, in offices of the UN Secretariat or in NATO protectorate in Bosnia'

(2001, 79). Gowan notes that the most salient feature of 'neo-cosmopolitanism' is that it completely brackets by off economic inequality as a concern and employs 'financial and market-access pacts over a democratic social polity based on balance of power' as a frame for reading progress (91). This version of cosmopolitanism is compatible with 'market-access agreements' which require that 'economically weak nations open their economies to monetary and financial movements' and to 'structural adjustment policies' to which the employment conditions of their citizens become extremely vulnerable' (91). 'Neo-liberal cosmopolitanism' works within its own set of interpretive assumptions and epistemological conventions which in turn define the limits of its language. The mythos of 'cosmopolitanism' is grounded in the transformation of mobility and consumption patterns of the middle class but it cannot inscribe a position for the working poor. This discursive barrier constitutes the very mythos of 'neoliberal cosmopolitanism'. Instead of cosmopolitanism functioning as a means of understanding the enforcing power of barriers, it has become the mirror of what it describes – the middle class traffic and exchange in and of the self. The most significant form taken by neoliberal cosmopolitanism is its substitution of the language of economic inequality with the language of cultural antagonisms. Neoliberal cosmopolitanism disavows barriers by 'not looking', by resurrecting market rhetoric of 'walls coming down'. To look is to 'be negative'; to become the very obstruction one registers.

The rhetorical use of the fall of the Berlin Wall as a model for a landscape without barriers typifies this. The huge popularity of Thomas Friedman's declarations is, in no small measure, due to the comforting nature of the utopic realm he lays out: 'the fall of the Berlin Wall – no walls – no barriers – democracy of markets – a flat world – all computerized – all digital within the differential unity of a global economy'. As Thomas Frank points out [. . .] what defines the Friedmanian landscape is the non-presence of the worker. Frank's illuminating study of economic restructuring in the 90s shows that within the Friedmanian 'the world-is-flat' culture, the fall of the Berlin Wall is a metaphor for the fall of 'trade unions, labor laws, and public initiatives' which stand in the way of unfettered corporate clout (2000, 26). The ideological work that is done by the rhetoric of the fall of the Wall is that it functions as a kind of *cordon sanitaire*, shielding us from the poor as well as from labor protection legislations of the kind embodied in 'New Deal policies, monetary regulations, anti-trust laws, and environment regulations'. Global market economy's claims [. . .] to smash protectionist 'barriers' and 'level the playing field' [are] directly linked to its ability to wall off issues related to the laboring poor. So it is not surprising that notwithstanding all the talk about globalization eliminating barriers, walls constitute the key setting of our broken present.

[. . .]

Waving the banner of the fall of the Berlin Wall provides a convenient metaphor for human agency while at the same time allowing us to situate the crisis of barriers safely in the past. [. . .] In an age which fetishizes choice, contemporary fiction is driven by a new romantic mythology whose central paradoxical claim is that 'while walls exist, we can walk over them'. This is reflected in contemporary fiction's articulation of a cosmopolitan subjectivity which is 'at home everywhere in the world', and able to contain the force of walls. This essay examines the workings of the metaphor of the fall of the Wall in contemporary fiction to ask what ironies, anxieties, incompatibilities are contained in these literary representations. Such an examination is instructive not only for what it reveals about the key conjunctures between neoliberalism and literary culture but also for what it reveals about the power of the novel to reinforce ideologically dominant values. Reading conflicting figurations of the fall of the Berlin Wall in literature renders visible the discourse surrounding 'globalization'.

While there is nothing new about walls and their fall as subjects and scenes in fiction, the political 'oomph' which shapes the representation of the coming down of the Wall today conceals the violence of walls that are daily going up. If we are to engage with cosmopolitanism outside its neo-liberal form, it is essential to address the recurrent links between the optimistic rhetoric about the fall of the wall, increasing economic inequality and rising poverty. The fall of the Berlin Wall appears in fiction in many contexts and in ways that are unstable and internally contradictory. I begin with a discussion of the representation of the Berlin Wall in [. . .] *The Spy Who Came in from the Cold*. Le Carré's famous spy-thriller opens with the familiar spectacle of an agent who makes it right up to the Berlin Wall but at the very last minute, with only one more remaining checkpoint to clear, he is fatally shot by the agents of the 'Party', the Abteilung in GDR. No escape is possible from this cold. The Berlin Wall figured here as a spectacle underscores the militarism, centralism, and the incarcetary power of the cold-war communist 'zones'. But there is another movement in le Carré's novel which reveals that the frustrated beleaguered hero of le Carré's novel is no James Bond but rather a pawn in the game, betrayed and incarcerated by his self-serving superiors in London. However, a typically cursory reading of le Carré's novel is so completely saturated with cold-war attitudes, that it is difficult to see that le Carré negotiates the divide between 'walled zones' and 'free Western landscape' in a complex way. The underlying thrust of the novel, that spies are as disposable as workers, is barely visible. In this essay, I argue that, from le Carré to Zadie Smith, representation of the fall of the Berlin Wall has become the conduit by which global market capitalism rhetorically transcends itself to become culture.

The successful contemporary novel in its full optimistic mode casts the cosmo-politan subject as an escape artist – a Houdini-figure – who can escape barriers of poverty and racism. But even when walls, barriers, and border zones are, more or less, the focal points of fiction, we see at work a displacement whereby 'the spectacle' of the struggle for agency in the realm of the image takes center stage (Debord 1990). [. . .] In other words, the act of narrating walls paradoxically provokes a narrative that looks away from walls.

[. . .]

At the same time, it is clear that politically and materially, walls are destroying and reorganizing space and affecting human relations with increasing force. Walls allow the occupying authorities to control space with effective ruthlessness, both economically and militarily. In Palestine and Iraq, checkpoints that spring up overnight are daily turning spaces into polarized ghettos and Bantustans on the principle of *apartheid*. While this is most clearly visible in Iraq and in Palestine, it is also visible in the urban ghettos in Detroit and in the French Muslim housing estates of Paris – the *banlieues* – which burnt down in a flame of riots in November 2005. The nature of walls, too, has undergone a massive change. The walls today embody all the contradictions of neoliberal cosmopolitanism. Walls now are as varied and multicultural as culture itself. Walls show the flexibility and variousness of culture and also simultaneously function as active instruments of violence that can wage military war. This is most vividly dramatized in the so-called Security Wall built by Israel on Palestinian nation-territory which, three times higher than the Berlin Wall, is built from specially engineered pre-cast panels which can be rearranged in any way so that it functions as a permeable wall through which Israeli soldiers can travel and shoot. . . .

[. . .]

The complexity that cosmopolitanism discourse seeks lies right here: in the newly flexible 'military tactics' of walling and containment which is effecting a literal (rather than a metaphorical) 'deterritorialization of space' which, for Appadurai, embodies the spirit for globalization [Appadurai 1996]. It is important to recognize that not only culture, but walls today are porous and heterodox. However, military-political authority of the nation-state embodied in these flexible and mobile violent tactics has a way of being avoided, if not altogether disavowed, in cosmopolitan discourse. Porous flexible walls defy both simple description and heavy abstraction, but we find either a ready celebration of escape from walls or a symbolic domestication of walls in current cosmopolitan discourse. It is crucial that an awareness of the economic, political, and social implications of warfare enacted through the violence of walling interrupt the cultural character of cosmopolitan discourse. Walls are being daily erected: whether it is the so-called 'Israeli security fence' or the heavily guarded military installations in Iraq and the Guantanamo Bay detention center or the US senate approved proposal to erect a triple-barrier militarized wall along the US-Mexico border or the economic walls between wealthy western nations and the Least Developed Nations (LDCS) produced by the actions of the WTO. It is only through a recognition of the encoded violence of walls that a politically active and intellectually creative cosmopolitanism can emerge on a world scale. And the defining question is not so much what cosmopolitanism is, but rather what 'do we use cosmopolitanism to do'? The challenge is to forge a cosmopolitanism that can stand up to, what Chomsky [. . .] calls, 'the baleful influence of neoliberalism, structural adjustment, and the Washington consensus' (1993, 326).

Bruce Robbins rejects a complacent emblematic cosmopolitanism [. . .] to argue that an uncritical political optimism about internationalism 'turns out to have unexpected benefits for the world's most powerful nation, which can present itself as just another tiny particular, locked in battle against a totalizing universalism' (1999, 26). Bruce Robbin's [sic] conception of cosmopolitanism affirms the primacy of building a political capacity to 'work vigilantly with the machinery of the nation-state to try to control the predatoriness of global capital' and 'extend citizen rights and entitlements outwards'. This is a significant contribution to the political reconfiguration of cosmopolitanism moving it from an unregulated cultural mode towards a regulatory political citizenship mode. Robbin's [sic] broad configuration, however, raises some concerns, especially when one considers the arguments of the famous Uruguayan writer Eduardo Galeano (Goodman 2006) who points out that 'national sovereignty has become a prerogative of first world nations' and it is really 'first-world nationalism' that is 'masquerading as cosmopolitanism'. Given that first-world nationalism sets itself apart from international law by invoking an enlightened and self-sufficient sovereignty while simultaneously extending its military and economic reach in ever more powerful ways, how can we make sure that 'working with the state' (albeit 'vigilantly') does not get pressed into the service of its unilateralist logic? A politically productive counterfactual cosmopolitanism must resist rather than formulate a rhetorical opposition to the political-cultural systemic authority of the first-world nation-state. An effective cosmopolitanism, by its very nature, cannot come together in any systematic philosophy. To the extent that cosmopolitanism can be said to be systemic, it must emerge from the periphery because it is the failure of the periphery that has created the conditions for US government's unilateral neo-imperial mode. A politically engaged cosmopolitanism must not only reveal and resist the initiatives put forward by the ideologues of the 'war on terror', it must direct our attention to the international human rights charter. The lineaments of such a cosmopolitanism can only move in a direction opposite to the culturally savvy consumption-focused cosmopolitanism laid out by theorists like Arjun Appadurai, Carol Breckenridge, Andrew Ross, and James Clifford. The final paragraphs of this essay suggest another way of contextualizing the relation between cosmopolitanism and responsibility drawn from arguments put forward by Derrida in *The Politics of Friendship* (1997) and Peter Hitchcock in 'Uncanny Marxism: Do Androids dream of Lenin?' [2006] 'A perhaps of democracy', as it is envisioned by Derrida in *The Politics of Friendship*, entails a political framework for which the responsibility of friendship provides a model. Derrida observes that the limitless potential for 'inassurance' in friendship catalyzes a responsibility that allows for the articulation of cosmopolitanism as forgiveness. For Derrida, the discourse of cosmopolitanism is a discourse of 'responsibility with no guarantees'. In thus figuring responsibility as responsiveness to 'inassurance', Derrida rejects 'the conditional tolerance' that shape[s] current projections of cosmopolitanism. The Derridean understanding of cosmopolitanism as 'unconditional hospitality' opens up the possibility of envisioning cosmopolitanism outside the westernized bourgeois mode of cosmopolitanism. I conclude by elaborating Derrida's re-imagination of cosmopolitanism as 'responsibility' in relation to Peter Hitchcock's reflection on 'haunting' to elucidate an argument for understanding cosmopolitanism as 'haunting'. [. . .]

[. . .]

Zadie Smith's *White Teeth* (2000), popular for its comic energy, its Dickensian caricatures and its youth vernacular, is an exemplary successful novel that writes a post-Berlin Wall terrain of human relations. The fictional world of *White Teeth* is trendily multicultural – here we find different ethnic groups speaking the most current street argot; here the possibilities of cultural refashioning are potentially infinite; here ethnic and cultural binaries are playfully unsettled. The novel also grapples with significant historical crises of modernity-colonialism, inequality, war, and the global thrust of capitalism. However, the aesthetic mode in which the novel deals with 'the serious' opens it on to the flatness of TV, where characterization is co-extensive with superficial externalities such as style, looks, dress, and speech modes. *White Teeth* would be more subversive were it not for its investment in essentializing an image-oriented pop culture. The fall of the Berlin Wall emerges here, as in Friedmanian marketspeak, as a *tabula rasa* floating strangely free from its troubled past while at the same time emerging as a symbolic divide erected by people like Samad Iqbal, the novel's much-too-Muslim protagonist.

[. . .]

When we look closely at the institutional and historical reality of walls and their rise in the world, what emerges is that they are less about cultural divisions than about the material and military effects of domination and exploitation. In a talk given at the Institute of Contemporary Arts in March 2006 entitled 'What Happened to the Working Class?' Ferdinand Mount [2006] argues that 'the working-class has all but been erased as a category from political debate' and what has been substituted in its place is a 'knowingness about the language of class' (1). Relatedly, Dominic Head in his essay 'Demise of Class Fiction', notes that 'class is not an issue that has figured very centrally in British fiction over the last 25 years' despite the curbing of union powers, the imposition of strict productivity regimes, and fall in real wages, which have made poverty and economic alienation more urgently fraught than ever before (2006, 230). In *White Teeth*, Smith uses dramatic irony to modernize the free indirect discourse style and the visual effects of Dickens to delineate class frontiers in contemporary multicultural Britain. Smith's modernization of the Dickensian idiom is daring and energetic but also full of contemporary kitsch. Where Dickens's use of working-class language reveals the character's sociological consciousness as produced by class experience, Smith's representation of Jamaican street slang reveals a postmodern *pastiche*, in the manner of TV, moving from the general to the particu- lar. *White Teeth's* mode of doing social history through a pastiche of flat discrete images puts us in mind of Debord's discussion of 'the spectacle'. While there are many truth-baring moments, the incisions made by conflict and violence are avoided, and it is here that this enormously successful novel stages its fidelity to the cheerful optimism of 'neoliberal cosmopolitanism'. In the place of conflict, there is juxtaposition of contrasting images; in the place of dissent, there is consensus achieved through postmodern paradox. While class boundaries and economic disenfranchisement emerge as subjects, they appear flat. As a novel where irony is the master-trope, Smith's *White Teeth* makes us think of Ferdinand Mount's claim that an 'ironic knowingness' about the language of the working class is the new form assumed by the narrative absence of an articulated discourse about class barriers and economic inequality.

I am not suggesting that Zadie Smith's richly particular fictional world bears any easy resemblance to the breezy [Friedmanian] image matrix, nor am I suggesting that Smith's novel flinches from depicting barriers and exploitation. What I am suggesting is that a mythical belief in expanded spatial conditions of 'possibility' pervades the aesthetics of this successful novel. *White Teeth* does manifest a rich 'ironical knowingness' which is seen, for instance, when the novel hints at the interesting link between Samad Iqbal's increasing attachment to Islam and his idealization of his Hindu great grand-father, Mangal Pandey. The dynamism of the narrative here shows that Iqbal's Muslimness is not simply religious-cultural intran- sigence or the refusal of modernity but represents his interesting identification with an ambiguously famous historical figure – the failed Hindu revolutionary. Mangal Pandey, a sepoy in the service of the British East India Company, is famous for firing the first shot of the Indian independence movement in 1857. The irony is that the first shot of 'the Indian Independence movement' was a failed gun-shot that went wide and got Mangal Pandey hanged for sedition, and it was the hanging of Mangal Pandey which gave a revolutionary form to the 1857 movement. Like Mangal Pandey, Samad Iqbal, a waiter in a restaurant in Soho, wants very much to seize the moment against the 'grim tally of bad tips and sleepless nights' serving racist customers. Samad wants to adopt Pandey as the name-of-the-Father but this is a father whose legitimacy is in doubt. History has not been with Mangal Pandey.

Under pressure of the sudden news that their planned mutiny had been leaked to the officers, his gun-shot failed, and the mutiny was suppressed before it could become one. So, Mangal Pandey is and is not (at one and the same time) the name-of-the-father of the Indian independence movement. For Samad, Mangal Pandey is an 'unrecognized hero, tragic hero' (208) through whose failure the Indian independence movement speaks. But the reader has to read against the current of the narrative to see the complexity of the relation between Samad Iqbal and Mangal Pandey because Samad's hero-worship of Mangal Pandey and his embrace of Islam is framed within a generalized postmodern eclecticism. Samad's obsession with Mangal Pandey makes him the butt of jokes at his pub – O'Connell's – although his argumentative earnestness compels the pub owners to put up Pandey's portrait on the wall. Samad Iqbal's Muslimness obtrudes upon the reader as a familiar cliche, as nothing other than churlish 'anti-Westernism'. It is no wonder that this gruff waiter and charmingly out-of-date Bangladeshi parent literally blows up in front of us into a fully morphed 'Muslim fundamentalist' who decides to erect a kind of Berlin Wall between his sons. The suspense that the novel pursues here is rather typical, and the casual reader assents too readily to the opposition set up in the novel, that in contrast with the utopian dismantling of the Berlin Wall in the modern era, 'Berlin Walls' are being rebuilt by people like Samad Iqbal.

Samad Iqbal's intransigence is poised against the trendy charm of his twin boys – Magid and Millat – who, growing up in a suburb of Northwest London, are (whatever else they may be) no Muslim boys. The reader joins the twins in their youthful contempt of Samad's increasingly stark view of the world. As the family watches the fall of the Berlin Wall on TV during a stormy winter night, the news anchor, speaking over the image of the human chain on both sides of the wall, declares that 'the twenty-eight-mile long scar – the ugliest symbol of a divided world, East and West – has no meaning anymore' (200). Samad is unable to see the fall of the Wall as a historical ground for optimism; for this he is mocked by Alsana and the boys. This scene sets the scene for Samad's anxiety about the future of his sons, Magid and Millat, in Britain. Since he can only afford to send one of his sons to Bangladesh, his fatherly responsibility, as he imagines it, is to decide which one of his sons, in his terms, can he lead to the gate in the wall. After watching the fall of the Wall on TV, Samad erects, so-to-speak, a Berlin Wall between his twins but in his imagination he is building a gate for at least one of his sons. [. . .] At the end of the novel, the reader is expected to take comfort in the fact that Samad Iqbal gets his revenge when he finds out that Magid, the son he had sent to Bangladesh, returns to London godless and westernized and with a full purchase on Englishness while Millat, the son who stays behind in London, turns into a Muslim Asian-styled gangster on the outs with Englishness.

Samad realizes that he is too late for Islam in both its cultural and political incarnations, but grasps the salient point that if his sons can grow up with their energies unsaturated by Western popular media, then as a parent he would not have to worry about them in the helpless way in which he now does. But the comic energy of the novel glosses over Samad's complexity and he appears as an unbelieving 'pessimist' – a raving misfit in a purportedly barrier-free world. Samad Iqbal figures as the Wall itself, and the playfulness of the novel is measured in its distance from Samad's embarrassing earnestness and seriousness when he speaks of being descended from the revolutionary hero of India's 'failed Sepoy Mutiny of 1857'.

White Teeth presents ironic energies as the only neccessary aspect of barrier-leaping cosmopolitanism. Considering that social, political, economic walls are going up rather than coming down; considering that 'populist market forces' are conjoined with military operations, what should we make of the excessive optimism about 'deterritorialization of space', an influential term put forward by Arjun Appadurai? Despite its stereotype-busting, the entertaining, readable world of *White Teeth* is upbeat, and this optimism is what accounts for its market success and seductiveness. The denser overtones of the tragic and the serious are avoided. This serving of depth produces a synthetic urban space where democracy is signified through a bright syncretization of different idioms and style. It is worth remembering that Friedman's declarations about democracy are based on just such a conflation of democracy with consumer choice, on 'both Coke and Pepsi being available as choices' to middle class consumers the world over. The blinding sunshine of *White Teeth's* optimism keeps us from noticing that the vision of Bangladesh [. . .] developed in this novel as 'a nation perpetually ravaged by natural disaster, corruption and deplorable human rights' matches rather too neatly the representation of Bangladesh to be found in the brochures of International Banking Institutions, say the *Financial Times*, and *Wall Street Journal* where Bangladesh figures as a 'financially volatile' market that cannot save itself unless it gets firm 'assistance' [. . .] from the World Bank and the IMF.

In an enthusiastic review of *White Teeth*, Jan Lowe in 'No More Lonely Londoners' notes that it is in the field of language and in the robust expression of 'idioms too far to the other side of Standard English on the sliding scale of Standard and Non-Standard that young Londoners speak' that *White Teeth* makes its appearance as a paradigmatically cosmopolitan novel of 'Cool Britannia' (2001, 174). This is visible especially in the novel's fictionalization of the 'Rushdie affair', the richest segment of the text (predictably missing from the TV version sponsored by Mobil Masterpiece Theater), *White Teeth* richly renders the whimsical swagger of the syntax of young Asian-Britons and the relation this bears to racism. Millat, 'son of Samad and Alsana Iqbal' and his 'gang' of Asian friends – Ranil, Hifan, and Rajik – are jauntily setting out to participate in the protest planned in Bradford against Salman Rushdie. The conversation on the bus among these Asian teenagers is about the 'Islam-dissing' author of *Satanic Verses* (although Salman Rushdie is not mentioned by name) carried out in Raggastani style 'a strange mix of Jamaican patois, Bengali, Gujurati, and English' (192):

> 'We have taken it too long in this country. And now we are getting it from our own, man'. Rhas clut! . . . He is a fucking bador, white man's puppet'.
>   'My uncle says he can't even spell', said a furious Hifan, the most honestly religious of the lot. 'And he dares to talk about Allah!'
>   'Allah will fuck him up, yeah?' cried Rajik, the least intelligent, who thought of God as some kind of cross between Monkey-Magic and Bruce Willis. 'He will kick him in the balls. Dirty book'.
>   'You read it?' asked Ranil, as they whizzed past Finsbury Park.
>   There was a general pause.
>   Millat said, 'I haven't exackly read it exackly – but I know all about that shit yeah?'. . . .
>   'So . . . you ain't read it?' asked Ranil nervously.

'Look: you best believe I ain't buying that shit, man. No way, star'.

'Me neither', said Hifan.

'True Star', said Rajik.

'Fucking nastiness', said Ranil.

'Besides', said Millat, with a tone of finality despite his high-rising terminals, 'you don't have to read shit to know that it is blasphemous, you get me?'

(193–94).

There is wonderful wackiness here, one that captures the different styles of teenage swagger in full form. But does Smith's novel perform parody as Linda Hutcheon defines it, as a 'repetition with a critical distance that allows ironic signaling of difference at the heart of similarity', or is irony here replaced with comic-book humor (1994, 185)? It is when Smith's novel is not consciously doing 'cosmopolitanism', that we find the most explosive moments of irony. In other words, the novel is most strongly imbued with cosmopolitanism when it is least aware of it. When Alsana, Millat's mother, gets a glimpse of Millat on TV participating in the Bradford book-burning protest, she is livid with rage. When Millat, the triumphant 16-year-old Raggastani, returns home that evening, he finds 'a bonfire raging in his backyard' (197):

> All his secular stuff – four years' worth of cool, pre- and post-Raggastani, every album, every poster, special-edition T-shirts, club-flyers collected and preserved over two years, beautiful Air Max sneakers, copies 20–75 of 2000 A.D magazine, signed photo of Chuck D, impossibly rare copy of Slick Rick's 'Hey Young World', *The Catcher in the Rye*, his guitar, *The Godfather* I and II, *Mean Streets*, *Rumble Fish*, *Dog Day Afternoon*, and *Shaft in Africa* – all had been placed on the funeral pyre, now a smoldering mold of ashes, which was giving off fumes of plastic and paper, stinging the boy's eyes which were already filled with tears.
>
> (197)

Alsana explains this bonfire to her tearful 16-year-old in this way: 'Either everything is sacred or nothing is' (197). This moment is explosive, a catastrophic moment in an otherwise funny novel. Here, we find the most productive secularizing of the language of faith. Alsana Iqbal uses the unironic language of sacredness to teach her son a lesson about cosmopolitanism, to teach him that 'if he starts burning other people's things, he loses something sacred also'. This moment is explosive, a catastrophic moment in an otherwise funny novel where Alsana teaches her teenager what it means to feel 'not-quite at-home' in the world, as Timothy Brenan has illuminatingly defined cosmopolitanism. This is the moment when the novel seems to break from its trendy knowingness. But such moments are rare.

[. . .]

White Teeth's cosmopolitanism, composed mainly of visual effects, can be said to be fundamentally anti-global in that it is located far away from the realities of the fractured, polarized world in which we live, where global democracy and global environment are under daily threat, and the possibility of a global culture is threatened precisely by the institutions of globalization that are seen as producing global culture: the IMF, the World Bank, and the WTO. It would seem that the Berlin Wall, rather than its fall, (cognitively speaking) serves as a far more accurate metaphor for 'globalization' since, from the perspective of *people's* interests and *people's* rights, globalized corporate power (mediated through structural adjustment policies of world economic institutions such as the World Bank and the IMF) functions like the Berlin Wall. From the perspective of people's rights, globalization constrains, hinders, and blocks rights incompatible with the desires of corporations. But it is only within anti-globalization protests that we find globalization likened to the erection of Berlin Wall. When protestors and activists gathered in Quebec city to protest the Free Trade Agreement of the Americas (FTTA) in April 2001, they invoked the Berlin Wall in their protests to refer not only to 'the 10-foot-high fence some 4 miles long guarded by 7,000 police and 1,200 troops' but to 'the imposition of the GATS principles in the planned Free Trade Areas of the Americas'. These GATS principles 'proposed to the 32 poor nations present that in return for reduction in trade tariffs, the US should have the rights to protect and extend the rights of its capital, including the right to establish operations anywhere', and 'to sue for any potential profits lost because of government policies on the environment' (Cameron 2001). Similarly, in the public protests held on Nov. 9, 2005 in which people in cities across Europe, Canada, the US, Latin America, and Australia joined in solidarity with the Palestinian mobilization against the 'security wall' built by Israel, the 670 mile long wall was likened to the Berlin Wall (Gordon 2003; Makdisi 2005). The dazzling optimism of *White Teeth* is a problem because it directs attention away from where it is most needed: the violence encoded in walls and checkpoints.

[. . .]

The narrative sleight of hand which enables Becker's enormously successful film, *Good-Bye Lenin* (2003), to [convert] the ghost of the Berlin Wall into a visual gain is the subject of Peter Hitchcock's essay. In his essay, 'Uncanny Marxism: Do Androids Dream of a Lenin?' Peter Hitchcock observes that in this film 'the socialist fatherland is regenerated through a pastiche of no-longer available, dreary-sounding commodities: "Spreewald pickles, Mocca Fix, Fillinchean crisp bread, black-and-white TV etc." ' Hitchcock argues that this logic of retrieving, marked by the imperative of technoscience, personifies our commitment to unhaunting. This refusal to be haunted is what allows us to be, as Hitchcock suggests, enticed by 'Lenin simulations sold on eBay'. By this logic, Leninism is not even really scary anymore but just a Gothic image. He laments that the revolutionary impulse today is marked by such an 'instantaneous politics of the automata' that too quickly changes places with the past.

The protagonist of *Good-Bye Lenin*, Alex, works to preserve socialism (as if in brine) in one room within the house for the benefit of his mother who has been in a coma since the Wall collapsed six months ago. The ghost of the Berlin Wall, as Hitchcock argues, is summoned here but it is not present here as 'a specter' that has the power to haunt us. Hitchcock notes that such a canned invocation of the ghost of socialism 'after the fear of the ghost has been banished is rather like playing with the Casper version of the ghost'. In contrast, the 'spectre' that Derrida speaks of in *Spectres of Marx* as haunting Europe presents the challenge of 'a real haunting', and our identity emerges in response to and in necessary relation to the 'ghosts of the workers past', and 'the ghost of what is yet to come, a future ghost, so to speak' (1994, 4).

In response to a literary-critical tradition which inscribes identity within a cultural narrative of the desiring self, Derrida and Hitchcock suggest that the feeling of being haunted by some other identity is vital for 'revolutionary' consciousness. This entails a gaze that will not look away from walls. Contemporary fiction has the power to be haunted by the ghost of walls, past and present. The 'perhaps of democracy', as Derrida evokes it in *Politics of Friendship* is an ethical call to responsibility marked fundamentally by the *instability* of a 'real eventuality':

> There is no more just category for the future than that of the 'perhaps' . . . Such a thought conjoins friendship, the future, and the perhaps to open on to the coming of what comes. . . . The possibilization of the impossible must remain at one and the same time as undecidable – and therefore as decisive – as the future itself. What would a future be, if the decision were able to be programmed, and if the risk, the uncertainty, the unstable certainly, the inassurance of the perhaps were not suspended on it at the opening of what comes, flush with the event, within it, with an open heart
>
> (1997, 29).

Derrida's concern here is to highlight the 'perhaps' which, 'if it were to be accessible in advance . . . would be a poor possible, a future-less possible, a possible already set aside, *life-assured*' (29). The political price to be paid for the downplaying of 'eventuality' and 'haunting' is high. It is worth comparing Derrida's position on 'eventuality' to Vandana Shiva's conception of equality as participation in the struggle against walls. Shiva's description of the Berlin Wall is not framed by the spectacle of the fall of the Wall:

> In 1988, I was in Berlin before the Berlin Wall fell. We were part of the biggest ever mobilization against the World Bank. Addressing a rally of nearly 100,000 people at the Berlin Wall I had said that the Berlin Wall should be dismantled as should the wall between rich and poor the World Bank creates by locking the Third world into debt, privatizing our resources, and transforming our economies into markets for multi-national corporations. I spoke about how the alliance between the World Bank and global corporations was establishing a centrally controlled, authoritarian rule like communism in its control, but different in the objective of profits as the only end of power. As movements we sought and fought for bringing down all walls of power and inequality.

What we need, as Shiva argues, is a cosmopolitanism that 'mobilizes' and participates even at the cost of uncertain recognition [2005]. A productive cosmopolitanism must assume responsibility for the ecological survival of the planet and participate in the razing of the 'walls of power and inequality'. In the pages above, I have argued that cosmopolitan political subjectivity as represented in contemporary fiction is conservative because it is fundamentally spectatorial. Instead of transacting with the claims of neoliberal capitalism in its global guise, contemporary fiction must refuse to narratively reproduce the cozily optimistic allegory of the fall of the Berlin Wall. Rather, contemporary fiction must fundamentally re-imagine 'globality' as the experience of being 'haunted' by walls if it is to become aesthetically and politically dynamic and cosmopolitan.

[. . .]

Note

1   Nicholas Royle was interviewed by Jake Purbright in the *3:AM Magazine*, 2005. The link to this journal can be found on the Nicholas Royle homepage.

III TECHNOLOGY AND CYBER-CULTURES

Chapter 23

Rita Raley

eEMPIRES

From *Cultural Critique* 57.1 (2004): 111, 115–137

I really want it to be called 'UntoCaesar.com'.

Kaleil Isaza Tuzman, Startup.com

It is the *flow* of money, moving quickly and silently to those who are sufficiently wise and creative to establish themselves as players in this new arena.

Steffano Korper and Juanita Ellis,
The E-Commerce Book: Building the E-Empire

e = M-C-M

THE eEMPIRE HAS DEFINITIVELY ENTERED our lexicon, both as concept and as semantic construction, with 'e' continuing to operate as the value-added, universal signifier of the brave new wired world. The signifier 'e', as this essay will demonstrate, cannot be located under one set of stable descriptors. Rather, it must be understood as a fluid and intersecting set of forces, practices, technologies, and events. It is not a singular entity, but comprises communicative networks, electronic commerce, modes of production, and global financial markets. With numerous precursors, most notably associated with Microsoft, the Electronic Empire suggests a triumphant narrative of technology and capitalism. [. . .] However, it goes beyond that to suggest a speculative departure from the material conditions of production and circulation and toward informationalism. Such a speculative departure constitutes the now-dominant mode and stage of capital – a philosophical appraisal anticipated by Marx [. . .] and reanimated by Giovanni Arrighi and Fredric Jameson. The Electronic Empire has different rhetorical registers, ranging from cultural studies to ordinary advertisements. [. . .]

[. . .]

My essay examines the organic paradigm and its relation to various speculative visions of the futures, logic, and possible destruction of capitalist history; of late finance; and of informational capitalism. It reviews the current field of study of technology, information, and global capitalism, and it reviews the idea of the American century – beginning with Henry Luce's manifesto on the rights and responsibilities of America as a new world power – yet it is embedded in both the literal and the metaphoric idea of the network and so looks to the question of new, uncertain, and future reincarnations. In this respect, my essay addresses both the material transformations that the electronic age has brought about and our means of analyzing these transformations.

[. . .]

The grand narrative of this informational society holds that global capitalism is at once facilitator and structural logic, especially as both capital and society have progressed, ascended, or mutated from earlier stages of mercantile capitalism and finance capital. [. . .] Castells, for example, uses the phrase 'informational capitalism' to describe the new 'techno-economic system', the structure of which was ultimately determined by the neoliberalism of the 1980s. [. . .] In contrast to the evolutionary and transformational narrative of the new information economy, Arrighi has articulated a theory of finance capital that holds it to be fundamentally cyclical, and as such, 'a recurrent phenomenon which has marked the capitalist era from its earliest beginnings in late medieval and early modern Europe' (1994, ix). The moment when capital takes flight from production and becomes speculative constitutes its third and final stage. This last and highest stage is recurrent, and the long twentieth century – the title of Arrighi's study – is just one of four systemic cycles of accumulation that he identifies within capital's lifespan. [. . .] So it is that we have the basic operational logic of capital for Arrighi: regeneration, a thesis that comes from his exegesis of Marx.

According to Marx's formula for capital, value had an 'occult' power of self- and automatic expansion, that of being able to augment or 'add value to itself' (Marx 1995, 98). Such a quality of self-reproduction would, in the mid-nineteenth century, almost necessarily be described in quasi-biological terms: so, value 'brings forth living offspring, or, at the least, lays golden eggs' and operates in the guise, mode, and form of money so as to bring about 'its own spontaneous generation' (98). Marx suggests that value, while always linked to material labor, nonetheless postures as capital and commodity and implicitly emerges as auto-generative and 'self-multiplying', as that which lays its own golden eggs (1973, 537). Jameson's amplification of the third stage of Marx's formula, C-M, picks up on this abstraction. In his commentary on the passage from commodity-form to money-form – 'it must spend some time as a cocoon before it can take off as a butterfly' (Marx 1973, 548–49) – and Arrighi's own exegesis of this stage, Jameson notes: 'Capital itself becomes free-floating. It separates from the concrete context of its productive geography. . . . Now, like the butterfly stirring within the chrysalis, it separates itself from that concrete breeding ground and prepares to take flight' (1997, 251).

These biological metaphors for the evolutionary movements of capital are appropriately creative in their vision of birth via metamorphosis and the shedding of a decayed structure, echoing as they do Joseph Schumpeter's famous theory of the birth, regeneration, and essential truth of capital, that of 'creative destruction' (Schumpeter 1950, 83 [. . .]). In concrete terms, creative destruction suggests the dislodging of one product or process by another, such as the replacement of mimeograph machines by photocopiers. For Schumpeter, capital operates according to a biological process of 'industrial mutation', whereby the economic structure 'incessantly revolutionizes . . . *from within*, incessantly destroying the old one, incessantly creating a new one' (1950, 83). But what exactly is the relation between revolution and a biological paradigm? Schumpeter's formulation suggests that a certain degree of destruction is inherent to any systemic change and that there can be no change without energy, but situating capital within a biological paradigm allows him also to speculate both on genesis and its corollary, termination or degeneration. It places him within a dialectical model of growth and decline. [. . .] Linking capital to organic matter lends it continuity and coherence on a path from genesis to decay and eventual death. It further suggests a process of self-reproduction, with capital giving birth to its own offspring, laying its own golden eggs, or decomposing and reorganizing its own larval tissues.

Such a vision of auto-generation reaches an apothesis in Marx's figural reading of commodities and money's power, both of accrual and origination, which is part of the same general formula for capital. 'However scurvy they may look, or however badly they may smell', he writes, commodities 'are in faith and in truth money, inwardly circumcised Jews, and what is more, a wonderful means whereby out of money to make new money' (Marx 1995, 99). [. . .] This is of course value's 'occult' power: literally hidden, concealed, and secret. Circumcision here may serve as an identificatory marker, but an inward circumcision is also suggestive of Schumpeter's mutation 'from within'. By implying that the potential for procreation lies almost exclusively within the system, Marx suggests that capital has the capacity, perhaps the genetic material, both to reproduce and to destroy itself. [. . .] Arrighi performs a similar analysis with his explicative suggestion that capital already has an inherent ' "flexibility" and "eclecticism" ' rather than consisting of 'concrete forms' (1994, 4). Such a critical move assimilates the unpredictability, uncertainty, and indistinctness of the 'afterlife' of the current cycle of capitalist accumulation – the long twentieth century marked by the ascendance of information as a commodity – to the flexibility and mobility of the network.

The impetus of this essay, then, is to situate the Electronic Empire within the network, both as object and facilitator. My starting point is Arrighi's argument that capital is bound to perpetual and cyclical mutation and to regeneration, with capital read as a viral epidemic that is nearly impossible to vaccinate against. But biological and genetic metaphors do not provide a fully adequate lens through which to view the operational logic of the current financial markets or with which to project along a diachronic axis so as to imagine the ends and the futures of capital, U.S. capitalism, and historical epoch. Because it cannot account for the complexity of global, neoliberal capitalism, the organic is a limited and insufficient figure with which to trace a strategic and conceptual break from the rhetoric and paradigms of the American century. The limitations of organic metaphors within economic discourse have also been identified by J. K. Gibson-Graham, who focuses specifically on the representation of the economy as an organic body. In a study of capitalism 'as we know it', Gibson-Graham critiques the dominant articulation of capitalism within the Marxian tradition as unified, singular, and totalizing (1996, 253–65). This tendency to read capitalism as a unified, self-reproducing organism is manifest, Gibson-Graham suggests, in the physiological metaphors used to characterize the economy. [. . .]

Such a reading, in her view, fails to account for capitalism as a 'disaggregated and diverse set of practices unevenly distributed across a varied economic landscape' (117). Reconceptualizing capitalism in terms of heterogeneity, fragmentation, and permeability, rather than organic unity, requires that we recognize noncapitalist economic practices, and it also allows for a more widely integrative notion of revolutionary praxis.

Tariq Ali has suggested that the 'old empires developed organically' [2003]. The Electronic Empire, on the other hand, develops non-organically. Thus, in contrast to the organic figures and evolutionary paradigms so prevalent in current critical theory of capital, information, and Empire, I would like to suggest that the automatism of the network is instead paradigmatic for our period, the speculative stage of finance capital, and thus befits our move into the twenty-first century. Mid-World War II, nearly post-Depression and coterminous with Luce, Schumpeter suggested in *Capitalism, Socialism, and Democracy* (1942) that, when we are dealing with capitalism, 'we are dealing with an organic process' (1950, 83). However, sixty intervening years have brought us to a point whereby we must now consider the process as not inorganic, but nonorganic. The nonorganic is a complex system that has energy, movement, and dynamism. It is not biologically alive, but neither is it an inert, inanimate, material structure: it functions like an organic entity, yet it is not. In order to speak to the Electronic Empire, the apparatus of our time, we need the figure of the network, that which subtends the organic and the nonorganic. The inchoate, indeterminate abyss beyond the long twentieth century may, in my view, best be articulated in terms of the electronic network, that which writes, coordinates, and implements its own rules of operation.

The Electronic Empire

[. . .]

The linking of IT and the new technologies with imperialism and the concept of Empire has given us new historical descriptors, among them the virtual empire, the virtual universal, and my concept of choice, the Electronic Empire, chosen because of its resonance with the electronic network and with computer processes. The electronic, as well, signifies the commodity itself and the means of circulation. It is, in other words, a communicative network. Although organically or biologically based computing developments may eventually make electronics obsolete, in the present moment we can say that electronics, especially microprocessing, has made other technological developments possible (e.g. digital telecommunications, bio-engineering, biotech, materials science) and has historically been not just bound to but also constitutive of the concept of Empire. However, thus far within cultural criticism, information technology has been linked to empire primarily by way of both parallelism and pretext. Debbie Lee and Tim Fulford, for example, analyze the Microsoft-sponsored Web site and adventure magazine, *Mungo Park*, which shares its name with the eighteenth-century Scottish explorer who mapped parts of the interior of Africa during two famous and chronicled expeditions [. . .] (2000, 3–28). They argue that such an instance of naming is not simply fortuitous but rather suggests that the logic of empire and neocolonialism is intrinsic to monopolistic software companies. But this radical extension of the meaning of 'virtual empire', such that it encompasses a British colonial epistemology of science and an American postindustrial, neocolonial epistemology of IT, attenuates the force of the insight, and there are other links one might establish between the electronic and the empire.

The industry understanding of 'eEmpire' suggests a convergence of electronics and commerce, marked by the elimination of geographical boundaries for the client base and global sales and marketing, and by the extension of communication and information networks into what are imagined as highly improbable spaces. Put simply, according to a well-circulated business guide, the Electronic Empire is 'the newest pairing of global business and top-notch technology' (Korper and Ellis 2000, xiii). [. . .] Yet for industry, Electronic Empire is not just the convergence of global business and technology, but also the integration of technologies, whereby various modes of consumption may be synchronized and syncretized into one platform (as in the convergence of e-mail, shopping, entertainment, and information). From the perspective of the mainstream media and much academic writing in the area of communication, cultural, and media studies, the Electronic Empire signifies the control of distribution and of content by a few familiar transnational corporations: Viacom, AOL Time Warner, Sony, Disney, GE, and Seagram, with companies such as Microsoft and Intel controlling the standards, performance, and distribution of digital technologies. [. . .] Oliver Boyd-Barrett has formulated a thesis of media imperialism that calls for the extensive study of the 'colonization of communications space' based on a political concern with U.S. hegemony and ideology, with detailed empirical analyses of generic media imperialism. Such colonization, for Boyd-Barrett and others, differs over temporary and geographic horizons, differs in the intensity of imposition, dependence, and resistance that it generates, and differs according to media forms and governmental regulation. The difference is in degree and kind [Boyd-Barrett 1998].

[. . .]

[. . .] In our current critical and technological moment, and in light of the significant scholarly work on the historical meaning of imperialism, we might say instead that the old imperial paradigm is no longer applicable precisely because that stage of capitalist and territorial accumulation and that episteme (with an attendant understanding of race and nation) has given way and mutated into a 'global net-worked and information society'. In the new mode of Empire, power may be consolidated by transnational corporations, but the logic of power is capitalist and not territorial. [. . .] Finance capital, to return to Jameson, is 'free-floating', mobile, and 'footloose' (Cerny 1994, 337; Jameson 1997, 251). The ascendance of finance over 'real' material goods and the separation of capital from the 'concrete context of its productive geography' facilitates this shift from imperial territory to 'modulating networks of command' (Jameson 1997, 251; Hardt and Negri 2000, xii [. . .]). This understanding of the capitalist logic of power works in concert with many articula-tions of the emergent mode of empire. For example, Guéhenno envisages a future in which 'Rome will no longer be in Rome, and no territorial given, no dominant group, will be able to impose itself. This empire will be neither a supernation nor a universal republic. It will not be governed by an emperor' (1995, 47). Similarly, Thussu notes that the 'virtual empires of the electronic age do not depend on territorial conquest' (1998, 1). However, in his implicit reference to Murdoch as the new emperor, he has recourse to an Enlightenment-era notion of a single controlling human entity: 'the digital globe under construction by Murdoch will lead to empires which have no territories but span the world, with the potential of being more powerful than the territorial-based ones of the past' (6). (Even the 'colonization of communications space' involves a figurative space, territory that is mediatized, dematerialized, commodified, and the province of speculation.) We might go further to observe that the current incarnation of Empire presents us with an interface between the territorial and the nonterritorial. Territories are certainly less materially situated than they are subject to recurrent proclamations of definitive, yet arbitrary, boundaries; thus, on the one hand, there are continual battles for territory (Kashmir, Israel-Palestine). But, Empire depends on entrepreneurial zones and high-tech corridors, which suggests a gridded networking of territory, as with the electronic and physical movement of military bases across national borders.

Within a capitalist logic of power, the nation-state acquires a kind of temporary obsolescence. In spite of one of the more prevalent dramas within the Western imagination, which stages a national contest between American capital and that of the Far East, usually Japan, the new mode of Empire does not maintain the nation-state as either categorical foundation or operational center. [. . .] Michael Hardt, Antonio Negri, and numerous others suggest that it is not simply that the nation-state has lost power and that the United States no longer occupies the center of an imperial order, which is itself defunct, but also that a supranational economic, political, and communicative network has ascended in its place. Hardt and Negri put the point succinctly: '*The United States does not, and indeed no nation-state can today, form the center of an imperialist project.* Imperialism is over' (2000, xiii–xiv). The discourse on financial globalization tends to corroborate this challenge to the power of nation-states and testify to their undermining by financial markets. Philip G. Cerny provides a representative claim: 'financial markets, not states, represent the closest thing to a new hegemony in the contemporary international system' (1994, 339). [. . .]

To go further than the displacement of the nation-state from the position of center requires noting that the very notion of a center has become meaningless. Instead we have nodes within interconnected financial and informational networks – 'centers' for the coordination, standardization, and transmission of payment messages. These centers often battle for control within the network, as with the efforts of Al-Jazeera and CNN to develop competing archives to store and produce the 'truth' of a dominant cultural memory. The network, then, is by nature a counter-network and thereby embodies contradiction, internal contest, and multiplicity. [. . .] For instance, even trans-national corporations maintain nodal centers that often grow in size, importance, and complexity relative to the [corporations'] own rhizomatic development and expansion. In this respect, I find productive the syncretic concept of Empire delineated by Hardt and Negri, which not only 'establishes no territorial center of power and does not rely on fixed boundaries or barriers', but is also 'a *decentered* and *deterritorializing* apparatus of rule that progressively incorporates the entire global realm within its open, expanding frontiers' (xii). [. . .] We have seen other instances of the claim for Empire's decentered and a-territorial quality. What Deleuze and Guattari's paradigm contributes to this analytic is the sense that the new mode and system of Empire has its own forces of operation. Imperial power no longer maintains a positive, 'actual and localizable terrain or center'; rather, it is 'distributed in networks, through mobile and articulated mechanisms of control' (Hardt and Negri 2000, 384). Displacing Caesar and Murdoch from the helm, Empire now operates itself. In terms of practice, then, the Electronic

Empire signifies the convergence of global capitalism and the new technologies and thus the complete imbrication of media and market and control over the content and distributive flows of the communication networks. But the concept of the Electronic Empire is more complexly paradigmatic, encompassing as it does the ascendance of information, the mode and operational logic of the network, and neoliberal global capitalism. It is in fact the paradigmatic concept for the moment beyond or after the American century.

The age of electronic networks

In his wide-ranging study of world-economies, Fernand Braudel meditates upon the periodic movements and conjunctural rhythms of history, contemplates our exist- ence in both the short and the long term, within periods that precede and outlive us, and then asks whether it is 'possible to identify a finite plane or body which, being the site of a movement, fixes its time-span' (1984, 83–85). The question is apposite: can we identify a point of closure, an end, an afterlife – temporal, geographic, psychic, or otherwise – perhaps a post-American century, or a fourth wave? But, what exactly is at an end: is it history; finance capital; 'culture', now ceded to the commercial; the nation; a particular conception of imperialism; the organic body (supplanted or overcoded by biotech); the human; politics (replaced by a categoric- ally different reign of the image and of spectacle); the century of 'total war'; the 'real'; the (old) mass media; or industrial and material productivity (supplanted by information, symbols, and the immaterial)? What indeed will be the replacement mythologies, or will a nonmythology function in that capacity? [. . .]

Is, in other words, the American century, or U.S. hegemony or U.S. capitalism, an infinitely expanding idiom, or has the idiom, and its time, expired, its spectacular and apocalyptic conclusion elegiacally captured on tape on September 11? A different version of this question comes from Arrighi in *The Long Twentieth Century*, in which he addresses the most recent systemic cycle of accumulation, the temporal unit named in the title of the book, and asks whether capitalist history has reached its ends with U.S. capitalism, whether 'the structures of US capitalism constitute the ultimate limit of the six centuries-long process through which capitalist power has attained its present, seemingly all-encompassing scale and scope?' (1994, 19) The answer he gives is no: the ends are more imaginable than realizable, and capitalism will undoubtedly survive in new forms, in new guises. [. . .] Both its own 'spon- taneous generation' and its own destruction are, as Arrighi says elsewhere, coded into capital's 'genes' (1990, 55–56).

Schumpeter's main argument holds that it is the successful and regenerative runs of capitalism, and not its crises and failures, that damage and potentially short- circuit it, much like the successful run of the butterfly, which after all dies shortly after its metamorphosis. The power of this insight notwithstanding, Schumpeter's basic premise about capitalism still holds, even through the doubts of Arrighi and other theorists of late capitalism and economic globalization on the question of its ultimate survival: capitalism 'not only never is but never can be stationary' (1950, 82). Such is the fundamental logic of finance capital, echoed as well in Gertrude Stein's oft-quoted axiom on the durability and perpetuity of money – 'The money is always there but the pockets change' – a sentiment accepted as axiomatic precisely like the fundamental physical law echoed in my first section title (e $= mc^2$). It is not just the pockets that change, however, but also the form, matter, and function of capital, as well as its mode of circulation. This is the crux of the regeneration thesis, both for Marx and for Arrighi, and in a different sense for contemporary CEO-turned-financial-guru Walter Wriston, who suggests that the virtual and immediate changing of pockets in the late twentieth century constitutes a theoretical, essential, and ontological difference, such that money is in fact still here, but now has a qualitatively different power of mutability: 'The increased volition of money gives you a difference in kind – not just degree. It's like a piece of lead: you put it on your desk, it's a paperweight; put it in a gun, it's a bullet' (Marx 1973, 536, 667–68; Wriston quoted in Bass 1996). Although it is not my primary concern here, more substantive academic commentary on the range and targets of these guns is required – on the damage inflicted on 'human material' by the mechanisms of production – and this is largely the province of a recent article by Jerry Harris, who, in the context of an exposé of the operations of informational capitalism, as well as of its comparatively underdocumented material consequences and abuses, hits upon a particularly apt metaphor for the regenerative operation of capital: 'Like a man in a sinking ship looking for a way out, capitalism found in information technology a life boat to a new world of profits' (1998/1999, 34). It would indeed be a ship seeking passage to a 'new world of profits', suggestive as it is of other inaugural moments of Empire and world economy.

If it is the case, as it is also for Arrighi and Jameson, that capital is bound to inevitable regeneration, doomed to repeat and exhaust the three stages of accumulation, production, and speculation (M-C-M), the question before us is what lies beyond the limit of U.S. capitalism and the American century; it is even whether they have in fact reached their limit. One could argue that the recent display of U.S. military power was compensatory and suggests that U.S. economic and cultural hegemony is coming to an end. [. . .] An analysis of this problem, however, must necessarily veer into the imaginative rather than the descriptive, and appropriately enough, into speculation. [. . .] It makes perfect conceptual sense, then, that Arrighi and Beverly Silver together figure the afterlife of U.S. hegemony as 'a yet unknown destination' (1999, 35). Terence Hopkins and Immanuel Wallerstein also comment upon the dynamic and diachronic quality of a historical system, which 'is evolving second by second such that it is never the same at two successive points in time' (1996, 8). Further, they suggest that the 'trends' that disturb the equilibrium of the system eventually destabilize it in a permanent fashion, in effect creating a 'real "crisis", meaning a turning point so decisive that the system comes to an end and is replaced by one or more alternative successor systems' (8). The form and content of this crisis – the disequilibrium and bifurcations of the system – is unpredictable and approximately Borgesian: as Hopkins and Wallerstein note, 'there is always more than one possibility at this point, and there is no way of determining in advance what the outcome(s) will be. All one can do is assess the likelihood that we are approaching a bifurcation (or are already in the midst of one)' (8–9). It is also the case for Arrighi that the futures of world systems should resemble forking paths, that the regeneration of capital comes with an escape clause, a set of parenthetically noted alternative futures (which I will come to) for the histories and futures of capital. Capitalism's futures, in other words, are marked by a significant degree of indeterminacy. Because the outcomes of capitalist history are essentially unknowable, the moment of its end, its futures, the afterlife, and the subsequent cycle of accumulation have all been thought in terms of crisis, turbulence, unpredictability, chaos. [. . .]

For [Hobsbawm] and Wallerstein, this crisis is prefigured in the upheavals of 1989. [. . .] And, though the outcomes of capitalist history are not determinable in advance, for Arrighi, the ends of capitalism are imaginable in bifurcating apocalyptic visions: 'finally, to paraphrase Schumpeter, before humanity chokes (or basks) in the dungeon (or paradise) of a post-capitalist world empire or of a post-capitalist world market society, it may well burn up in the horrors (or glories) of the escalating violence that has accompanied the liquidation of the Cold War world order. In this case, capitalist history would also come to an end but by reverting permanently to the systemic chaos from which it began six hundred years ago and which has been reproduced on an ever-increasing scale with each transition' (Arrighi 1994, 356). For Arrighi, like for Braudel in his meditation on the beginnings of world economies, the ends of capitalism haunt it from its inception in the fourteenth century. Schumpeter's rhetoric of internal mutation is apropos here: capitalism bears within itself the elements of its own destruction and the capacity to bring itself to crisis. Capitalism's dynamic quality and tendency toward destructive biological shifts was, for Schumpeter, understandable in terms of extreme weather phenomenon: creative destruction manifests as a 'perennial gale' (1950, 84, 87). In that he theorized the evolutionary movements of capitalism in terms of cataclysmic discontinuity, then, Schumpeter's organic paradigm was fundamentally unstable. [. . .]

The rhetoric of 'systemic chaos' and of complexity was not available to Schumpeter, but it permeates the discourse on global or neoliberal capitalism. Given the sheer range of disciplinary schema brought to bear on the problem of the 'global', it is not surprising that it lacks a certain semantic and analytic clarity, but the more germane and also ubiquitous models for our historical period, the current cycle of accumulation, the world system, and even global culture comment directly upon this lack of clarity and suggest that the 'global' and the global economy are best understandable in terms of abstraction, elasticity, unknowability, and complexity. [. . .] For example, Bill Maurer draws on the discourse linking economics to computer science and evolutionary biology in order to understand the architectures of offshore finance as 'complex, networked, evolving, and adaptive systems' (1995, 114–15). As another example, Fernando Coronil similarly critiques the new forms of wealth by citing Bankers Trust CEO Charles Sanford's disquisition on 'particle finance', which analogizes the speculative futures of capital to quantum physics and modern biology, with the attendant implication of unpredictability (Sanford 1994; Coronil 2001, 79).

The discourse of complexity theory has also been incorporated into the discourse on Empire, which, for Hardt and Negri, 'cannot be represented by a juridical order, but it nonetheless is an order, an order defined by its virtuality, its dynamism, and its functional inconclusiveness' ([2000], 41). And, for Guéhenno, the age of networks is in fact 'the age of complexity . . . an age of incompletion and disequilibrium' ([1995], 49). Richard Lee also works with the dialectic of order and disequilibrium to outline the conceptual and critical links between computer systems and world systems: 'Since the late 1960s, dynamical-systems research has led to a reconceptualization of the world as one of complexity, determinate but unpredictable: order within chaos (strange attractors); order out of chaos (dissipative structures); visual representation of pathological functions and natural forms exhibiting non-integer dimensions (fractal geometry)' (1996, 197). While a delineation of the analytic conjunctions between scientific paradigms, specifically those related to computer systems, and those of world systems would require a more detailed study, we may say by way of an overview that it seems particularly appropriate that the dynamism and flexibility of world system and network society alike should find its descriptive embodiment in complexity theory: both turn to excess and the remainder, that which cannot be captured by, or forecast within, the system. The global system, in other words, cannot ultimately be contained in, or explained by, discursive structures. Linking system, category, and historical period alike to complexity theory marks a productive and powerful anxiety about both knowing everything and about the unknown. As Castells notes in *The Power of Identity*, 'the turbulence of information flows will keep codes in a constant swirl' – an energy and movement that is nonorganic by interpretation and not by essence (1997, 360).

The Electronic Empire is not particularly locatable or containable, but it nevertheless has effects that can be discerned. It does not easily align with the watchwords, or adjectival buzzwords, of what is called the world economy and cannot as such be integrated, total, systematized, synchronized, compatible, balanced, or complete. Jameson speaks of the contemporary world system in terms of an 'impossible totality' and the only 'dimly perceivable' (1991, 38). The Electronic Empire epitomizes his account of the contemporary world system in this respect, rather than that of Hopkins and Wallerstein, who describe it as 'a single, imperfect, organic whole, each vector quite dependent on the others' ([1996], 2). To go further than the 'dimly perceivable', we have only to posit that the Electronic Empire is not only neither organic nor whole, but arguably not even a system at all. Rather, it is a loose assemblage of relations characterized by another set of terms: flexibility, functionality, mobility, programmability, and automation.

The paradigm for such an assemblage is the network, which involves new geopolitical orderings, a reconfigured sense of center and periphery and an attendant complication of the world-system idea. Networks are by nature connective, suggestive of traceable and identifiable affiliations, alliances, and group politics, and their connective tissues provide a fantasy of community, of sociality, of collectives, of utopias. [. . .] Annelise Riles notes that 'the Network offers a poignant case study of institutionalized utopianism, an ambition for political change through communication and information exchange, of universalism *after* cultural relativism' (2000, 3). The need to reimagine a nontechnicist and nonmercantile internationalism or a philosophical and ethical universalism is not unique to our moment, but the substitutive figure of the network as a complex interconnective system has a particular currency, resonance, and ubiquity within the context of coalition building and the events of September 11 (including the need to fix Al Qaeda as a mappable network), as well as the expansion of mass media and communication, information, and electronic technologies over the course of the last two centuries. [. . .] It follows, then, that Armand Mattelart's *Networking the World* would trace the network back to Henri Saint-Simon and the dawn of the age of modern corporate administration as a way to historicize not just a contemporary figure, but also a contemporary understanding of globalization and global social organization: 'In this project of planetary restructuring, the network, as a model of rationality, became the emblematic figure of the new organization of society' (2000, 15 [. . .]). In a related analysis of the city of London,

Andrew Leyshon and Nigel Thrift employ the figure of the 'actor-network' to describe the constitutive function of communities of everyday social practices associated with finance [1997].

Jameson has followed Ernest Mandel and suggested that the global network is the emblematic figure of late capitalism, that 'the whole new de-centered global network of the third stage of capital itself' constitutes 'a network of power and control even more difficult for our minds and imaginations to grasp'. [. . .] Such a 'great global multinational and decentered communicational network' must for Jameson necessarily involve new spatial and geopolitical arrangements that the individual mind can neither wholly perceive nor wholly chart (1991, 44). The complexity of the networked world system, while allowing for new and recon- figured local connective links, as well as circuits of transmission and exchange, quite simply escapes our totalizing representation and our cognitive reach. [. . .] For Jameson, then, the 'network' is implicitly, as it is explicitly for me, the means to give a provisional, flexible, and paradoxically concrete form to the complexity and abstraction of neoliberal global capitalism. So, too, does it evince the general quality of communications space, which, as Boyd-Barrett notes, is its 'astonishing elasticity' (1998, 163). The network, then, is not static but mobile and highly changeable, of which technical and cultural re-encoding, the disappearance of servers, and the constant change of DNS entries and Web addresses are fitting symptoms.

Thus, in its conceptual and figural manifestation as a network, the Electronic Empire maintains a mutable configuration of command and control; it has 'lost its pivot'; and it is without point of origin and end, even given the frequent and fantastic imagining of its apocalyptic destruction. Situated in its unsituatedness, it is rather 'always in the middle, between things, interbeing, intermezzo' (Deleuze and Guattari 1987, 6, 25). Rather than dichotomies and binary distinctions, then, the network of Empire presents interstices, interconnecting lines, and autonomous flows. The paradigm of 'acentered systems' within *A Thousand Plateaus* is itself paradigmatic: 'finite networks of automata in which communication runs from any neighbor to any other, the stems or channels do not preexist, and all individuals are interchangeable, defined only by their state at a given moment – such that the local operations are coordinated and the final, global result synchronized without a central agency' (17).

Even though the electronic imperial network does not yield to a single, central agency, there are still various forces at work trying to co-opt its movement. Former chair and CEO of Citicorp/Citibank Walter Wriston speaks to the paradox: 'Money goes where it is wanted and stays where it is well treated. . . . This huge pool of money is destabilizing. It can move instantly, and it does. . . . But money really has no volition of its own. It all depends on the people who own it and use it' (Bass [1996]). But the notion that there is a single, central agent, whether nation, subject, or corporation, operating the network of Electronic Empire is contestable. It is, as an asset manager and former International Monetary Fund official notes, 'extremely powerful. Nobody can stand in front of it' (quoted in Collier 1996 [. . .]). Although the instantiation of knowledge and administrative monopolies, the 'expert system', and various control apparatuses indicate the desire and attempt to manage, restrain, and centralize the operations of the network of global capital, it nevertheless remains the case that it is marked by aleatory movement and general unpredict- ability. Further, the network has the capacity to evade its own annihilation in a worldwide systems crash, so that ultimately 'no breakdown, no sabotage is decisive' (Guéhenno 1995, 120 [. . .])

The events of September 11 have been strongly illustrative of this idea. While one might have expected that the leveling of the towers and the bombing of the Pentagon would result in a disruption of the network circuits, precisely the opposite has been the effect. Indeed, the electronic network is not disrupted by but consti-tuted around such events, which it has the capacity to absorb, rework, and replay. This knitting function indicates that the electronic network corresponds to the new mode of Empire, which is, as Hardt and Negri articulate, a 'machine for universal integration' ([2000], 191). Again, however, Empire is less a machine or 'apparatus of rule', which would suggest some kind of human agency or supervisor at the controls, than it is a system (xii [. . .]). This systemic integration is manifest in the set of communication networks that comprise the Electronic Empire, networks that, as I have previously stated, are responsible for the circulation of finance and information in the period of late capitalism.

In either its old or its current manifestation, then, the concept of Empire is an 'indication of the efficiency of communication' (Innis [1950], 9). This insight has a place within Mattelart's rich and essentially axiomatic understanding of communica-tion and information technologies as instrumental facilitator of Empire, economic, and cultural power alike. However, the new system of Empire need not necessarily operate through domination, subjection, and imposition, albeit under the guise of 'free flow', because it now operates through insinuation, which is a modal switch of power and consists of hosts accepting rather than rejecting or being forced to accept. As a counterpoint and strong reminder of the continued material force of the 'old' empire, Arrighi and Silver ask whether globalization and 'the phoenix of high finance . . . can rule the roost without the support of strong states more effectively than it has in the past' ([1999], 10 [. . .]). Mixed metaphor notwithstanding, the use of the phoenix as figure is significant because finance capital is continually imagined as emerging in a new form from the ashes, shell, structure, or chrysalis of the old.

It is these properties of malleability, mutation, and adaptation that will lead Jameson to link capital to a virus in his reading of Arrighi, wherein he describes the movements of late capitalism in similar terms, with metaphors drawn from biology and genetics: 'the system is better seen as a kind of virus (not Arrighi's figure), and its development is something like an epidemic (better still, a rash of epidemics, an epidemic of epidemics)' (1997, 249). In the displacement of capital onto a battle of viruses, or their exponential magnification as epidemic, or better still, a plague, there is an attendant promise that capitalism might indeed carry a fatal disease and bear within itself the elements of its own destruction. Pryke and Allen articulate the potential for disruption in similar terms: monetized time-space is that 'through which "infections" may pass simultaneously' (2000, 270). Indeed, the promise of a future vaccination against this infectious disease and the very idea of biological mechanisms of self-protection and self-preservation serve as a screen for the whole repertoire of tactics Mattelart and others have in mind when they speak of resistance to the forces of global media and capital. But, as Hardt and Negri suggest via their commentary on the viral spread and regeneration of the imperial order, not only is vaccinating against the global network of capital impossible, but transmittal and contamination are inevitable: '*The age of globalization is the age of universal contagion*', they note, and the Empire is formed partly 'on the basis of its capacity to develop itself more deeply, to be reborn, and to extend itself throughout the biopolitical latticework of world society' ([2000], 41).

This, however, is the mode of the network: an autotelic, auto-generative, and autodidactical 'smart' system that drives the global economy and provides its most appropriate figure. Informational capitalism mutates not as an unavoidably communicable virus, but as a nonorganic, electronic network whose operative criterion is performativity. Lyotard notes that the computer 'could become the "dream" instrument for controlling and regulating the market system, extended to include knowledge itself and governed exclusively by the performativity principle. In that case, it would inevitably involve the use of terror' (1984, 67). The electronic network operates according to the Lyotardian technological performative in that its very nature and truth is constituted by its performance and efficiency. [. . .] The networked structure of information and technologies exists in the moment of 'the great unknown' (Arrighi and Silver [1999]), and it is differentiated and defined by its rules of operation. It has its own operating force and thus Lyotard's conception of terror is also a necessary component: the function is that which rules the waves. The general belief at the end of the long twentieth century is that capital itself is given to mutation and flexibility, not to self-destruction, but to autotelic reproduction and regeneration. This is the mode of the network, which is forced to function or else it risks being destroyed. It must perform, not optimally or creatively, but basically. The difference is the nonorganic, networked status of Empire and (late) capital, no longer linked to the organicism of the body – Marx's commodities as 'inwardly circumcised Jews' or Marshall McLuhan's 'nervous system' in a 'global embrace' – but coded in the form of the electronic network. Organicism merely disguises a progressivist narrative, and we can perhaps imagine a conceptual break with Enlightenment paradigms of growth and progress and with nineteenth-century paradigms of degeneration (equally organicist and biological) only in terms of a complex network with unknown effects. But, as this essay has tried to demonstrate, one thing we can say about the nature of the network is that it retains an inherent plasticity and carries along with it the power to reconstitute itself.

Chapter 24

Fredric Jameson

FEAR AND LOATHING
IN GLOBALIZATION

From *New Left Review* 23 (2003): 105–14.

HAS THE AUTHOR OF *NEUROMANCER* REALLY 'changed his style'? Has he even 'stopped' writing Science Fiction, as some old-fashioned critics have put it, thinking thereby to pay him a compliment? Maybe, on the contrary, he is moving closer to the 'cyberpunk' with which he is often associated, but which seems more characteristically developed in the work of his sometime collaborator Bruce Sterling. In any case, the representational apparatus of Science Fiction, having gone through innumerable generations of technological development and well-nigh viral mutation since the onset of that movement, is sending back more reliable information about the contemporary world than an exhausted realism (or an exhausted modernism either).

William Gibson, now the author of *Pattern Recognition* (2003), has certainly more often illustrated that other coinage, 'cyberspace', and its inner network of global communication and information, than the object world of late commodification through which the latest novel carefully gropes its way. [. . .] To be sure, Sterling celebrated the hackers, the heroic pirates of cyberspace, but without Gibson's tragic intensity – portraying them as the oddballs and marginals of the new frontiers to come. The rush and exhilaration of his books, rather alien to the cooler Gibson, has always seemed to me to derive as much from global entrepreneurship, and the excitement of the money to be made, as from paranoia.

But that excitement also expresses the truth of emergent globalization, and Sterling deserves more than a mere paragraph or parenthesis here. The novels are often episodic, but stories like those collected in *A Good Old-fashioned Future* (2001) are authentic artifacts of postmodernity and little masterpieces in their own right, offering a Cook's tour of the new global way-stations and the piquant dissonances between picturesque travellers and the future cities they suddenly find themselves in. Tokyo, to be sure (Tokyo now and forever!), in which a Japanese–American federal prosecutor from Providence, Rhode Island, finds herself entangled in a conspiracy waged through ceramic cats; but also the California of misfit inventors, in which a new process for manufacturing artificial (and aerial) jellyfish threatens to convert all the oil left in the ground in Texas into so much worthless *Urschleim*. Finland then offers an unsurprisingly happy hunting ground for meetings between 60s-style terrorists and the former KGB, along with ruthless young ecological nationalists, veteran industrial spies and an aged Finnish writer of children's books immensely popular in Japan. [. . .]

Meanwhile, Bollywood actors in flight from the Indian tax system have the luck to happen on the biggest mass grave in history, in Bolton, in an England decimated by the plague and now good only for making cheap movies on location; while, in Germany, in Düsseldorf, the new institution of the *Wende* is explored, in which – observed by a 'spex' salesman from Chattanooga – all the destructive collective movements of the time, from football hooligans to anti-modern moral majorities, periodically coincide in a ritual 'turbulence'. Indeed, it is Chattanooga, its burnt-out downtown future megastructure now a rat's nest of squatters, which serves as the stage for a more complex and characteristic encounter: between a de-sexed bicycle repairman (new gender movements have proliferated in this future, including that of Sexual Deliberation, which artificially eradicates the sex drive) and the private police of a long-serving and now senile congressional stalwart, whose artificial identity replacement (the so-called mook) risks being unmasked by an unwanted package in the mail. Finally, classic Science Fiction returns with the discovery in a Central Asian desert, by twenty-first century bounty-hunters, of an enormous artificial underground cavern, in which the Zone (the latest future form of the old East Asian Co-Prosperity Sphere, now run by China) has housed three world-sized human communities as an experiment in testing the viability of 400-year-long space flights. I have only incidentally mentioned some of the wacky SF technology taken for granted in these tales: more significant are the priorities of global cyberpunk, in which technological speculation and fantasy of the old Toffler sort takes second place to the more historically original literary vocation of a mapping of the new geopolitical Imaginary.

Paperback seismographs

This is why such Hunter-Thompsonian global tourism has real epistemological value: cyberpunk constitutes a kind of laboratory experiment in which the geographic-cultural light spectrum and bandwidths of the new system are registered. It is a literature of the stereotypes thrown up by a system in full expansion, which, like the explosion of a nova, sends out a variety of uncharted signals and signs of nascent communities and new and artificially differentiated ethnies. Stereotypes are pre-eminently the vehicle through which we relate to other collectivities; no one has ever confronted another grouping without their mediation. They are allegorical cartoons that no longer convey the racist contempt of the older imperialism and which can often (as Žižek has observed of the ethnic jokes popular in the old Yugoslavia) function as affectionate forms of inclusion and of solidarity.

Indeed, an inspection of this literature already provides a first crude inventory of the new world system: the immense role – and manifest in Gibson's evocations, all the way down to *Pattern Recognition* itself – of Japan as the monitory semiotic combination of First-World science-and-technology with a properly Third-World population explosion. Russia now also looms large, but above all in the form of its various Mafias (from all the former Republics), which remind us of the anarchy and violent crime, as well as of the conspiratorial networks and jobless futures, that lurk just beneath the surface of capitalism. It also offers the more contemporary drama of the breakneck deterioration of a country that had already reached parity with the First World. Europe's image ambiguity – a kind of elegant museum or tourist playground which is also an evolutionary and economic dead end – is instructive; and the absence of Islam is a welcome relief, in a moment in which it is reality, rather than culture or literature, that is acting on the basis of that particular stereotype.

This new geopolitical material marks a significant historical difference between these commercial adventure stories and the equally cynical gonzo journalism of an earlier period; indeed, the affinities and distinctions between the cultural products of the 60s and 70s and those of the 90s and 00s would be well worth exploring further. Equally significant is that these protagonists – busy as they are in locating rare products, securing secret new inventions, outsmarting rivals and trading with the natives – do not particularly need the stimulus of drugs (still a preponderant, one may even say a metaphysical, presence in so recent a world-historical expression as David Foster Wallace's 1996 *Infinite Jest*).

eBay imaginary

But it is by way of its style that we can best measure the new literature on some kind of time-continuum; and here we may finally return to the distinctiveness of *Pattern Recognition*, where this style has reached a kind of classical perfection. I will define it as a kind of hyped-up name-dropping, and the description of the clothes selected by the protagonist (Cayce Pollard) for her first day in London is a reliable indicator:

> a fresh Fruit T-Shirt, her black Buzz Rickson's ma-i, anonymous black skirt from a Tulsa thrift, the black leggings she'd worn for Pilates, black Harajuku schoolgirl shoes. Her purse-analog is an envelope of black East German laminate, purchased on eBay – if not actual Stasi-issue then well in the ballpark.

I have no idea whether all these items actually exist but eBay is certainly the right word for our current collective unconscious, and it is clear that the references 'work', whether or not you know that the product is real or has been made up by Gibson. What is also clear is that the names being dropped are brand names, whose very dynamic conveys both instant obsolescence and the global provenance and neo-exoticism of the world market today in time and space.

A further point is that, little by little, in the current universe, everything is slowly being named; nor does this have anything to do with the older Aristotelian universals in which the idea of a chair subsumes all its individual manifestations. Here the 'high-backed workstation chair' is almost of a different species to the seat in the BA 747 'that makes her think of a little boat, a coracle of Mexcel and teak-finish laminate'. But there are also exercise chairs, called or named 'reformers': 'a very long, very low, vaguely ominous and Weimar-looking piece of spring-loaded furniture', which can also be translated into another language, where it becomes 'a faux-classical Japanese interpretation in black-lacquered wood, upholstered with something that looks like shark-skin'. Each of these items is on its way to the ultimate destination of a name of its own, but not the kind we are familiar with when we speak of a 'Mies chair' or a 'Barcelona chair'. Not the origin, but rather the named image is at stake, so that an 'Andy Warhol electric chair' might be a better reference.

In this postmodern nominalism, however, the name must also express the new, and fashion: what is worn-out, old-fashioned, is only useful as a cultural marker: 'empty chrome stools of the soda-fountain spin-around kind, but very low, fronting on an equally low bar', where it is the 'low', the 'very low' that connotes Japan. And in Moscow the table 'flanked by two enormous, empty wingback armchairs' only stands for backwardness. This is probably why Gibson's Russian episode is less interesting: he brings a residual Cold War mentality to this built space, 'as though everything was designed by someone who'd been looking at a picture of a Western hotel room from the eighties, but without ever having seen even one example of the original'. Current Soviet and Central European nostalgia art (*Ostalgie* in German) is far more vibrant and exciting than this, reflecting on an alternate universe in which a complete set of mass-produced industrial products, from toilet seats to window panes, from shower heads to automobiles, had been invented from scratch, altogether different from the actually existing Western inventory. It is as though the Aztecs had beaten Cortéz and survived to invent their own Aztec radio and television, power-vehicles, film genres and popular culture.

At any rate, the premise here is that Russia has nothing new to offer us in this field (the Sterling aesthetic offers much better chances of appreciating what is genuinely new, world-historically innovative, in Eastern nostalgia art); and the conclusion to be drawn is that name-dropping is also a matter of knowledge, and an encyclopaedic familiarity with the fashions of world space as those flow back into the boutiques or flea markets of the West. What I have called name-dropping is therefore also to be grasped as in-group style: the brand names function as a wink of familiarity to the reader in the know. Even the cynicism (taking the word in Sloterdijk's, rather than in its post-Watergate sense) is a joyous badge of group adherence, the snicker as a form of hearty laughter, class status as a matter of knowing the score rather than of having money and power. In-group style was, I believe, the invention – or better still, the discovery – of Thomas Pynchon, as early as *V* (1963), even though Ian Fleming deserves a reference ('Thank you, Commander Bond', murmurs Cayce, as she pastes a hair across the outside apartment door). But just as we no longer need drugs, so we no longer need Pynchon's staples of paranoia and conspiracy to wrap it all up for us, since global capitalism is there to do it more efficiently; or so we are told.

Birth of an aesthetic?

Nonetheless, *The Crying of Lot 49* remains a fundamental paradigm and, as with Hunter Thompson, the differences are historically very instructive indeed. For the post-horns and the other tell-tale graffiti have here been replaced by something like a 'work of art': the clues point, not to some unimaginable reality in the social world, but to an (as yet) unimaginable aesthetic. It is a question of an unidentified film of some kind which has come to be known, among insiders, as 'the footage', and which shows up in stills and clips in the most unlikely places (billboards, television ads, magazines, the internet), in 'one hundred and thirty-four previously discovered fragments . . . endlessly collated, broken down, reassembled, by whole armies of the most fanatical investigators'. Indeed, as one might expect, a whole new in-group has formed around the mysteries of the footage; we are experiencing, one of the characters observes, the 'birth of a new subculture'. A worldwide confraternity comes into being, committed to this new object and passionately exchanging and arguing contradictory theories about it. The footage thus makes *Pattern Recognition* over into something like Bloch's conception of the novel of the artist, which carries the unknown unrealized work of art inside itself like a black hole, a future indeterminacy suddenly shimmering in the present, the absent Utopian sublime suddenly opening up like a wormhole within the empty everyday:

> Light and shadow. Lovers' cheekbones in the prelude to embrace.
>   Cayce shivers.
>   So long now, and they have not been seen to touch.
>   Around them the absolute blackness is alleviated by texture. Concrete?
>   They are dressed as they have always been dressed, in clothing Cayce has posted on extensively, fascinated by its timelessness, something she knows and understands. The difficulty of that. Hairstyles too.
>   He might be a sailor, stepping onto a submarine in 1914, or a jazz musician entering a club in 1957. There is a lack of evidence, an absence of stylistic cues, that Cayce understands to be utterly masterful. His black coat is usually read as leather, though it might be dull vinyl, or rubber. He has a way of wearing its collar up.
>   The girl wears a longer coat, equally dark but seemingly of fabric, its shoulder-padding the subject of hundreds of posts. The architecture of padding in a woman's coat should yield possible periods, particular decades, but there has been no agreement, only controversy.
>   She is hatless, which has been taken either as the clearest of signs that this is not a period piece, or simply as an indication that she is a free spirit, untrammeled even by the most basic conventions of her day. Her hair has been the subject of similar scrutiny, but nothing has ever been definitively agreed upon.

The problem, for the group forming around this artifact, as indeed for all group formation, is that of the contradiction between universality – in this case the universality of taste as such – and the particularity of this unique value that sets us off from all the others and defines us in our collective specificity. A political sect (as we now seem to call these things) wishes simultaneously to affirm the universal relevance of its strategy and its ultimate aims, and at one and the same time to keep them for itself, to exclude the outsiders and the late-comers and those who can be suspected of insufficient commitment, passion and belief. The deeper anxiety of the practitioners of the footage website and chatroom is, in other words, simply that it will go public: that CNN will get wind of this interesting development; that the footage, or the completed film, the identified and reconstructed work of art, will become, as they say, the patrimony of mankind, or in other words just another commodity. As it turns out, this fear is only too justified, but I omit the details, as I hate people who tell you the ending; except to express my mixed feeling that Pynchon's solution was perhaps the better one, namely to break off *Lot 49* on the threshold of the revelation to come, as Oedipa is on the point of entering the auction room.

After all this, it may come as something of a surprise to learn that the footage is not the central issue of this novel, even though it supplies the narrative framework. Yet it ought already to have been clear that there is a striking and dramatic contradiction between the style, as we have described it, and the footage itself, whose 'absence of stylistic cues' suggests a veritable Barthesian 'white writing'. Indeed, it is rather this very contradiction which is the deeper subject of *Pattern Recognition*, which projects the Utopian anticipation of a new art premised on 'semiotic neutrality', and on the systematic effacement of names, dates, fashions and history itself, within a context irremediably corrupted by all those things. The name-dropping, in-group language of the novel thus revels in everything the footage seeks to neutralize: the work becomes a kind of quicksand, miring us ever more deeply in what we struggle to escape. Yet this is not merely an abstract interpretation, nor even an aesthetic; it is also the existential reality of the protagonist herself, and the source of the 'gift' that informs her profession.

Commodity bulimia

Cayce Pollard's talent, lying as it does halfway between telepathy and old-fashioned aesthetic sensibility, is in fact what suspends Gibson's novel between Science Fiction and realism and lends it its extraordinary resonance. To put it simply (as she does), Cayce's business is to 'hunt "cool" '; or in other words, to wander through the masses of now and future consumers, through the youth crowds, the 'Children's Crusade' that jams Camden High Street on weekends, the teeming multitudes of Roppongi and Shinjuku, the big-city agglomerations of every description all over the world, in order mentally to detect the first stirrings of anything likely to become a trend or a new fashion. She has in fact racked up some impressive achievements, of which my favourite, mildly redolent of DeLillo, is the identification of the first person in the world to wear a baseball cap backwards (he is a Mexican). But these 'futures' are very much a business proposition, and Cayce is something like an industrial spy of times to come. 'I consult on design . . . Manufacturers use me to keep track of street fashion'; these modest formulas are a little too dry, and underplay the sheer physicality of this gift, which allows her to identify a 'pattern' and then to 'point a commodifier at it'.

There is here, no doubt, something of the specialized training of the authenticator of paintings and the collector of antique furniture; but its uncanny temporal direction condemns Cayce irredeemably, and despite her systematically black and styleless outfit, to the larger category of fortune-tellers and soothsayers – and occasionally puts her in real physical danger. This new *métier* thus draws our world insensibly into some Science Fictional future one, at least on the borders, where details fail to coincide. The job of one character is to start rumours; to drop the names of products and cultural items enthusiastically in bars and nightclubs, in order to set in motion what would in Pynchon have been a conspiracy, but here is just another fad or craze.

But Cayce's gift is drawn back into our real (or realistic) world by the body itself; she must pay for it by the nauseas and anxiety attacks, the commodity bulimia which is the inevitable price of her premonitory sensibility – no doubt nourished by obscure traumas, of which the latest is her father's mysterious disappearance in Manhattan on the morning of 9/11. It is as if the other face of the 'coming attraction', its reification and the dead-end product of what was once an active process of consumption and desire itself, were none other than the logo. The mediation between these two extremes of *energeia* and *ergon*, of process and product, lies no doubt in the name itself. I have argued that in the commercial nominalism of the postmodern, everything unique and interesting tends towards the proper name. Indeed, within the brand name the whole contradictory dialectic of universality and particularity is played out as a tug of war between visual recognition and what we may call the work of consumption (as Freud spoke of the work of mourning). And yet, to paraphrase Empson, the name remains, the name remains and kills; and the logo into which the brand name gradually hardens soaks up its toxicity and retains the poison.

Cayce's whole body is a resonator for these omnipresent logos, which are nonetheless louder and more oppressive in certain spaces (and places) than in others. To search for an unusual item in Harvey Nichols, for instance, is a peculiarly perilous activity:

> Down here, next to a display of Tommy Hilfiger, it's all started to go sideways on her, the trademark thing. Less warning aura than usual. Some people ingest a single peanut and their head swells like a basket-ball. When it happens to Cayce, it's her psyche. Tommy Hilfiger does it every time, though she'd thought she was safe now. They said he'd peaked, in New York. Like Benetton, the name would be around, but the real poison, for her, would have been drawn. . . . This stuff is simulacra of simulacra of simulacra. A diluted tincture of Ralph Lauren, who had himself diluted the glory days of Brooks Brothers, who themselves had stepped on the product of Jermyn Street and Savile Row, flavouring their ready-to-wear with liberal lashings of polo knit and regimental stripes. But Tommy surely is the null point, the black hole. There must be some Tommy Hilfiger event horizon, beyond which it is impossible to be more derivative, more removed from the source, more devoid of soul.

These nauseas are part of Cayce's navigational apparatus, and they stretch back to some of the oldest logos still extant, such as her worst nightmare, Bibendum, the Michelin Man, which is like that crack through which the Lacanian Real makes its catastrophic appearance. 'National icons', on the other hand, 'are always neutral for her, with the exception of Nazi Germany's . . . a scary excess of design talent'.

Now it is a little easier to see the deeper meaning of the footage for Cayce: its utter lack of style is an ontological relief, like black-and-white film after the conventional orgies of bad technicolour, like the silence of solitude for the telepath whose mind is jammed with noisy voices all day long. The footage is an epoch of rest, an escape from the noisy commodities themselves, which turn out, as Marx always thought they would, to be living entities preying on the humans who have to coexist with them. Unlike the footage, however, Gibson's novel gives us homeopathy rather than antidote.

It does not seem anticlimactic to return to the future and to everything also auto-referential about this novel, whose main character's name is homonymous with that of the central figure in *Neuromancer*. Indeed, the gender change suggests all kinds of other stereotypical shifts of register, from active to passive for example (from male hacker to female future-shopper). Is it possible, however, that Cayce's premonitions of future novelty can also stand as the allegory of some emergent 'new Gibson novel'? *Pattern Recognition* does seem to constitute a kind of pattern recognition for Gibson, as indeed for Science Fiction generally.

Chapter 25

Katrin Sieg

INDIANS: THE GLOBALIZED WOMAN ON THE COMMUNITY STAGE

From *Theatre Journal* 55 (2003): 291–303 and 309–15.

IN THE SPRING OF 2001, THE OPERA *INDIERINNEN* (*Indians*) premiered on the tiny studio stage of the Neuköllner Oper (Neukölln opera), in a working-class neighborhood in Berlin marked by a high proportion of immigrants. It ran to full houses for a short time and is presently being reworked in the hopes of touring the show. The opera, which features a new libretto set to the music of nineteenth-century German composer Giacomo Meyerbeer, tells the story of the Indian computer programmer Soraya, who comes to work in Germany to pay off her husband Mahatma's debt. She saves enough money to pay for expensive surgery that enables the invalid man to walk again, yet his restored health and sexual potency prompt him to renege on their shared commitment to social equality and put Soraya back in her place: the home. The opera's dramatization of a migrant's story echoed the public debate during the preceding months in Germany, about the introduction of the greencard for Indian computer programmers and other highly-qualified foreigners in high-tech professions. More generally, the show investigated the proposition that women's integration into the global labor force liberates them from the shackles of patriarchal gender arrangements based on unpaid reproductive work and feminine subservience, which neoliberals cite as evidence that globalization knows 'only winners, no losers', increases productivity and affluence around the world, and leads to more democracy and more choice.[1] Its unhappy ending, in turn, raised the question of whether globalization is 'a brakeless train wreaking havoc', ineluctably devaluing labor and diminishing the quality of life for the many while increasing the wealth of the few (Harvey 2000, 68). As theatre is apt to do, *Indians* scales down these large questions to the level of the individual, the globalization woman Soraya. The character's subjective choices, actions, and feelings make the human dimension of abstract relations, processes, and decisions concrete, but her story does not end at the level of individual options and remedies. The way in which *Indians* deftly translates between the systemic/global macroscale, the scale of the accidental and local, and the microscale of the human body, I argue, can offer a model for the multi-tiered operations of feminist politics and cultural production in a global age.

In this article, I would like to do several things: first, I will examine *Indians* in light of the current debates about the gender politics of globalization. I will look at the way the opera stages a feminist critique of the neoliberal emancipation paradigm, which promises the eventual leveling of social inequalities on a global scale, and of the culturalist paradigm, which seeks to preserve cultural differences along with the social inequalities in which they are embedded. I examine how the drama constructs a sexual rhetoric of globalization by juxtaposing the Indian couple's utopian, post-patriarchal love relationship with capitalism's consuming desire for them, and shows up the different terms of participation that the globalized economy offers to the man and the woman in the couple. [. . .] I examine how the opera grapples with the lure of virtual technologies; perched in the altar niche in the couple's home, the young woman's laptop has usurped traditional deities by promising to transcend the constraints of the body and of material place. Soraya's social and geographical mobility, the couple's intercontinental marriage and communication, and Mahatma's injury and restoration are all facilitated by computers. The fantasy that humans' interfacing with computers would solve the problem of the body as experiential matrix and limitation – a vision that imbricates religious disparagements of the flesh, the body's absence from Cartesian formulations of the self, and cybernetic views of materiality as inessential to the emergence and flow of information – is exposed as a betrayal of the struggles of negotiating differences and crafting communities. The pull of the virtual is thus confronted with, and grounded by, the sweating, laboring, mortal bodies on stage. This politics is embedded in the theatre's larger agenda of participating in the construction of cross-cultural, intergenerational, sexually inclusive community in the neighborhood of Neukölln.

Indians installs a feminist perspective at the center of its critique of globalization, examining such issues as the spiraling disparity of capital and labor, the eroticization and naturalization of economic processes, conservatives' appropriation of leftist notions of historical progress, and the impact of modern virtual technologies on the human body and subjectivity through a gendered lens. The opera suggests that globalization needs an asymmetrical gender system and concomitant notions of heterosexual desire, in order to function at full throttle. Likewise, globalization is shown to draw on ethnic cultures and relations forged within imperialist discourses, while purporting to mend the injustices of the past. Most importantly, *Indians* confronts the tendencies toward worldwide webs and technological miniaturization that characterize globalization with an insistent focus on the human body as the fleshly site for future technological interfaces and the measure of economic and cultural developments. Toward that end, the piece brings into play both the virtuosity of *grand opéra* and the modest means of local players.

The erotics of globalization

Mahatma and Soraya, the romantic Indian couple whose story is told in the opera, combat patriarchal traditions, raw economic pressure, and military domination, all of which threaten their hopes for material comforts, social justice, and political autonomy. Their love, based on equality, support, and mutual respect, encodes a positive vision of social relations in a global matrix, a vision that rests on the hope that technological advancement can enhance the quality of human life, that transnational communication and trade can further the exchange of knowledge, and that local injustices can be overcome through universal values and rights. The plot's complications and contrivances, rivaling any nineteenth-century gothic melodrama, continually challenge this utopian vision. Condensing complex transnational relations and historical processes into a series of starkly schematized dramatic interactions, the opera makes palpable the temporal acceleration and spatial compression deemed central to globalization. *Indians* stages the assaults on the couple's self-determination, economic and social opportunity, and dignity as a test of their love and loyalty. It also examines the forces that promise to defend the lovers against the encroachments of the global, especially local cultural tradition and national purity and pride. The couple's longing for each other and for a better world is contrasted with capitalism's desire for them, a desire that is constructed around domination and expropriation. While capitalism wants them both, it accords them unequal places – places traditionally constructed through the sexual division of labor in patriarchal societies but initially suspended in Mahatma and Soraya's marriage. Only under very specific, rather extraordinary conditions, the opera demonstrates, can heterosexual love model a notion of social relations that can integrate individual difference and dependency with equality and consensus. As soon as difference is aligned with a traditional gender hierarchy, other mechanisms of domination kick into gear as well. The exceptional, non-patriarchal structure of their relationship thus makes possible a political vision of globalization that can challenge and transform class oppression and colonial legacies. The eventual alignment of their marriage with traditional (local and transnational) patriarchal discourses through Mahatma's betrayal, in turn, proves the rule that global capitalism is a neocolonial formation that crucially depends on patriarchal inequality and exploitation.

The opera's centering of gender cuts across some of the traditional categories that orient discourses of globalization as leading either to equality, justice, and affluence (the neoliberal view), or to exploitation, inequality, and mass misery (the Marxist view). In the course of a few minutes, the opera sets up this opposition and immediately challenges it. The first act begins on a romantic and festive note, on the occasion of Soraya's graduation from university and return to her husband Mahatma, who works hard to support her studies despite being paralyzed from the waist down. Yet the couple's shared dream of a better life is first disturbed by the remonstrations of the local Guru, a bearded patriarch who objects to women's education, employment, and independence. In addition, their hopes are severely threatened when the international credit shark Kaufland ['the land of buying'] arrives to call in a debt Mahatma had incurred earlier. In order to pay off that debt, Soraya signs a contract to work in Germany. While globalization alters local traditions (as defined by the Guru), the opera does not deplore the loss of 'cultural authenticity' as that concept cloaks women's subservience and dependency. Nor does it portray India's entrance onto the world market naively as liberation from underdevelopment and oppression. When Kaufland auctions off Soraya in the first act, and the local Guru and a German headhunter bid for her while she watches helplessly, the similarity with a slave market highlights the colonial dynamic undergirding the international division of capital and labor today. Working conditions in the German computer lab, Soraya's place of employment in the second act, are also depicted in a critical light.

Moreover, her imprisonment in Kaufland's castle during the last two acts indicates a drastic, indeed catastrophic curtailing of her agency. Yet the opera avoids a deterministic view of globalization as a process whose momentum and direction cannot be controlled. The Guru, the German headhunter, the Pakistani supervisor, her Indian coworkers, and Kaufland all personify different limits to Soraya's self-determination and dignity as a worker, a woman, and an Indian. Her run-ins with these figures, however, take the form of predicaments that she negotiates with varying degrees of agency and choice, rather than being already determined in advance: up to the final scene, Soraya is no victim of globalization.

Language, character portrayal, plot, and set and costume design together evoke the impression that the opera crystallizes, intensifies, and condenses social relations under globalized conditions, using the studio stage like a magnifying-glass. The scaling down of macroscale processes to the microscale of individual bodies allows the opera's producers to shift between a systemic, general analysis of globalization and a particularistic view that allows room for that which is accidental, extraordinary, and idiosyncratic. The result is a decidedly contingent, process-centered, and open-ended notion of globalization that highlights exemplary developments, while also bringing possible alternatives into view. The dialogue is unadorned and straightforward, and the overall impression is one of simplicity. No great skills in subtextual interpretation are needed here, since all characters speak, or sing, their motivations. Characters are not developed for their psychological complexity, but, as in Brechtian play, personify social forces and functions; with the exception of Soraya and Mahatma, names signal social roles. The device of multiple casting (four singers play eleven parts) further undercuts the sense of psychological individuality. Set and costume design, too, simplify and condense social settings and relations. A minimum number of props and imaginative use of lighting transforms the minuscule stage into stylized renditions of an Indian village, a computer lab, and the castle of the capitalist Kaufland. The colors and textures of the costumes emphasize differences and correspondences, contrasting the Indian Guru's earthy-brown garb with Kaufland's metallic, blue suit and Soraya's flowing red-orange sari. The plot's obvious contrivances compress complex sets of circumstances into short stage moments. For instance, the appearance of an American agent with large quantities of high-tech weaponry, who promises to help Mahatma free Soraya from prison, is immediately followed by the revelation that the American is in part responsible for Mahatma's invalid condition, since the bomb that crippled the Indian was intended for the American – throwing a more sinister light upon the latter's offer of military assistance, and embedding their exchange in a broader canvas and longer history of international relations. As the opera progresses, these compressions of transnational relations and temporal processes appear to accelerate. The plot thus makes literal what David Harvey calls the 'time-space compression' he deems typical of globalization (1990, 260–84). As I watched the tiny set, sparkling with glossy, vibrant colors in the sweltering heat of May, squeezed into the sold-out auditorium with other Berliners, I felt myself at once compressed and extended into the intricate webs of transnational finance, economics, and politics.

I regard the opera as a bold and ambitious attempt to give shape to an impossibly entangled and intricate web of relations, motivations, allusions, and passions. *Indians* has the quality of a child's drawing, focusing on a few relationships and compressing them into a story that highlights certain exemplary, interrelated features and processes that scholars associate with globalization. These include the rise of transnational corporations and concomitant weakening of state sovereignty, the dismantling of social nets, the accelerating mobility of corporations and workers, the increasingly international division of labor, and the widening gap between rich and poor. Mahatma's debt to the international man of finance Amor von Kaufland, which sets the plot in motion, points to the economic dependencies suffered by Third World countries as a result of natural or man-made disasters, and the rising power of transnational financial institutions like the World Bank and the International Monetary Fund to shape social relations in these countries. When Kaufland auctions off Soraya to the highest bidder, he curtails (by deferring) her right to accumulate the value of her own labor for her own profit as well as that of her family, community, and nation. Yet Soraya's coerced migration to Germany still enables her to save money and transfer it back to Mahatma, suggesting that the increased, global mobility of capital and labor not only benefits her German employers, who thereby remedy a shortage of qualified, native workers, but also furthers Indian interests. While Mahatma's suffering from Soraya's absence renders tangible the loss represented by the Indian economy's 'brain-drain', his physical restoration and social empowerment in turn illustrate a certain 'brain gain', although that gain is clearly at Soraya's expense. The divergence between the two also brings another issue into focus: Mahatma's disability – he is a paraplegic – and the needs and pressures created by it raise the question of who will care for those who cannot care for themselves in a world shaped only by market forces. The Guru's demand that Soraya assume that responsibility – which would condemn both members of the couple to utter poverty – illustrates not only the indignities caused by the absence of a social net in many countries of the East and the South. His language of feminine duty also resonates with the dismantling of Western welfare systems and the attendant gender-specific distribution of responsibility. Western societies increasingly rely on women's unpaid or underpaid work to compensate for the state's failure to function as an instrument of social justice and wealth-distribution. Certainly, the most important question the opera raises is whether the transnational financial institutions and corporations that are the engines of globalization can assume that function: do the people integrated into the workforce and the nations incorporated into the world-market benefit by way of knowledge transfer, technological advancement, and foreign investment? Will technical know-how and money trickle down for the enrichment of all, as neoliberal theorists proclaim? Whose life does Soraya's migration improve? What is lost in the process?

The opera echoes the hopes and concerns of feminist social scientists, who have analyzed globalization as an open-ended process that is subject to variations, contestations, and the implementation of alternatives. For many western women, the 'de-traditionalizing and denaturalizing of traditional local and national gender orders' that marks globalization provokes anxieties, but also opens up opportunities for a critical reckoning with past practices and assumptions (Lenz, Nickel, and Riegraf 2000, 7 [. . .] [translation Sieg]). The West German state's propagation of a male-breadwinner model, many women hope, will now be tossed on the scrapheap of history. Economist Susan Joekes has voiced one of the most optimistic assessments, contending that no other social group has gained as much from global trade and export as young women, who have attained new degrees of independence and respect (1996, 21). The editors of a recent anthology entitled *Geschlecht – Arbeit – Zukunft*

(*Gender — Work — Future*) sound more cautious when they maintain that 'women are not exclusively losers in this [globalization] process' (Lenz, Nickel, and Riegraf 2000, 9 [translation Sieg]). The World Bank interprets the rising proportion of women (up from 36% to 40% in the last twenty years) in the swelling ranks of the worldwide wage labor force (which doubled to 2.5 billion between 1966 and 1995) as evidence of their improving situation. Feminist critics are less apt to simply equate wage labor with emancipation; nor do they interpret it only in the Marxian terms of economic exploitation and alienation. Many of them regard it as a potential opportunity for more autonomy as well as solidarity among women, and view the degraded working conditions associated with the feminization of labor as a cause for concern and protest (Lenz 2000, 20). From the local level of the Bangladesh textile workers, who push the boundaries of feminine propriety against the familial and religious institutions of social control (Dannecker 2000), to the regional level of women's networks (Ruf 1998; Wichterich 1998), and the global level of feminist human rights activism and networking (e.g., at the 1995 Beijing Women's Confer-ence), scholars and activists have pointed to the ways in which women in Europe as well as in the poor countries of the South have actively and creatively grappled with globalization as a process that is 'politically intended and therefore open to political transformation' (Randeria 1998, 17). Most feminists agree that, as Christa Wich-terich puts it [. . .], 'indeed the restructuring of the labor market and the expansion of consumers' markets offer women new opportunities and individualized options, and call into question traditional gender roles and patriarchal control' (1998, 12). As 'cultural tradition' tends to stand in for a sexual division of labor that shunts women into unpaid or underpaid work and demure acceptance of social inferiority, feminist critics and activists organize the protest against the economic and social effects of globalization less around the preservation of cultural customs than around better working conditions and more autonomy over workers' living situ-ation. This refusal to fetishize local culture sets women apart from those men who, by defending it, cling to patriarchal privileges. These feminists also regard as suspect corporations' motivations for ascribing 'native' cultural traits and habits to local populations, which either make them particularly pliable as workers or herald a process of relentless commodification and cultural appropriation (Klein 1999).

   Soraya, who has enjoyed a university education in informatics, looks like the poster-child for the emancipatory possibilities of globalization. She wholeheartedly embraces the 'new opportunities and individualized options' that open up to her in terms of economic independence and social equality. [. . .] Even migration, which separates her from her home, is portrayed not purely in terms of coercion and loss, but also as a way to recreate that home in a more loving and gratifying way: the advancements of medical technology, the German headhunter tells her, make it possible to restore Mahatma's health (and potency) through neurosurgery, provided she earns enough money. Soraya not only dreams of making a life for herself and her husband that is unconstrained by the traditional sexual division of labor, but also envisions a world in which all women have the opportunity to do so. Romantic choice stands in metonymically for political choices and an expanded horizon of economic and social options. She is supported in her endeavor not only by Mahatma, who encourages her studies and praises her accomplishments, but is also buoyed by the respect and admiration of local women like the innkeeper, who befriends Mahatma in Soraya's absence. The romantic couple thus serves as an icon of consensual, post-patriarchal social relations, economic opportunities, and political autonomy.

While the opera does not characterize the values embodied by the couple as inherently at odds with globalization, it identifies two discourses that do postulate their incommensurability. The opera depicts both the Guru's call to return to local customs and Soraya's Indian coworkers' belligerent nationalism as driven by patri-archal interests, however, and thus challenges these discourses' paternalistic claim to protect the globalized woman. At the local level, the old bearded Guru keeps invoking the grand India of yore, where 'a woman's place was at the hearth, / and man protected her with his sword. / That's the way it always was and should always be' (Siemann [unpublished], 4). The cultural background he conjures up and in which he embeds this vision of patriarchal peace and order invokes India as a splendiferous production at the Bombay opera, whose lush set features a white marble palace, the bamboo huts of a village where a chorus of four hundred enacts scenes from village life, and the snowy peaks of the Himalaya. The India he invokes, replete with the voice of Enrico Caruso emanating from the palace windows, is clearly an orientalist fantasy rather than a memory of indigenous authenticity. Significantly, the Guru's description is punctuated by Kaufland's exclamation 'it's all mine', suggesting a continuity of colonial and neocolonial/global relations of power and cultural ownership. Although the financial means necessary to put on such an extravagant show were and are clearly formidable, the cultural (re) production of Indianness is not therefore immune to interruptions (Soraya's protests), contestations (anticolonial movements), or alternative productions – such as those by the small Neukölln opera. In short, the opera unravels the opposition between global and local, contests the equation of local customs with cultural authenticity, and thereby challenges the Guru's call to preserve a supposedly natural gender order.

The second act, which shows Soraya and male colleagues working in a German computer lab, dramatizes the claims of nationalist rhetoric to protect the purity of Indian culture. When Soraya is sexually harassed by the lecherous supervisor, a Pakistani man, her Indian coworkers, inebriated after an exhausting shift, eventually intervene. Although she is capable of defending herself, the Indian men quickly escalate the confrontation into an assertion of violent, nationalist sentiments. Although she protests against their aggressive assertions of national shame and retaliation, her honor is instrumentalized in a labor dispute augmented by ethnic-national differences, which results in the Indians' murder of the supervisor. Her ability to decide how to fend for her dignity is thus compromised by her class position as an employee and her vulnerability as a woman, but also her nationality. While the opera sympathetically portrays the taxing working conditions endured by the Indians, and explains their aggression as a response to these conditions rather than an inherent national trait, it doesn't heroize their violence as an act of national resistance or revolution. The men's legitimation of violence is too clearly shown to hinge on Soraya's elevation into an allegory of the nation as oppressed and hence in need of protection and revenge, and her simultaneous exclusion from the decision about how to handle and solve the conflict. They quell her calls for a rational, non-violent solution to the dispute. National discourse purports to represent Soraya's needs, but fails to accommodate Soraya's need for representation. In short, the nation and local cultural traditions are characterized as equally inhospitable sites for the empowerment of the globalized woman.

Many mainstream, western texts portray (or fantasize) western culture, ideological values, and social constructions of gender as inherently attractive. By dramatizing the flow of desire from local bodies to global brands, commodities, and
organizations, such texts yoke gender and heterosexuality to socio-economic processes. By cloaking such processes in terms of the organic and natural, they evade
questions as to whose interests drive social transformations, how they are achieved,
and how they may be redirected. Feminist scholars such as Neferti Tadiar, Sue-Ellen
Case [2001], and myself [Sieg 1993] have pointed to the ways in which 'the economies
and political relations of nations are libidinally configured' through such gendered
rhetorics and global sexual fantasies (Tadiar 1993, 183). This sexualized rhetoric
authorizes and mystifies material practices and political processes. On one hand,
Indians counters that mainstream use of sexual tropes by refusing to map the romantic
couple's wish for modern social relations, education, and technology along a Third
World-First World (or East-West) axis. In other words, the opera equates that wish
neither with a flat-out rejection of Indian culture nor with a desire for the West, but
uses it to animate a dynamic account of the local. On the other hand, *Indians*
counters the globalist rhetoric of heterosexuality with a sexual economy of its own,
in which capitalism's rapacious need for labor power is cast in erotic terms.

The love that Amor von Kaufland develops for Soraya, whom he abducts and
imprisons at the end of the second act, reveals much about the fiction of consent that
lies at the bottom of the capitalist vision of the contract between labor and capital,
and at the bottom of the patriarchal vision of marriage. Unlike his namesake from
Roman mythology, Amor von Kaufland is not content to merely stimulate desire
(for things, for a better life) in the romantic couple, but wants to seduce and possess
the woman on whose productive lifeforce he thrives. At the end of the second act,
he abducts Soraya and imprisons her in his castle, and he spends most of the third
act trying to convince Mahatma to abandon and divorce his wife. Kaufland, the
personification of global capitalism, recalls the aristocratic villain of the Bourgeois
Tragedy, who corrupts his bourgeois prey through his unbridled lust. He despoils
not so much Soraya's virtue as her naïve belief that she is a free agent, either as a
worker or a wife. In the final act, when Soraya is discovered chained to the stove, the
opera exposes the falseness of the capitalist myth that every worker is essentially free
to contract out her labor power and reap the benefits of surplus capital through hard
work and frugality. According to David Harvey's explication of Marx and Engel's
Communist Manifesto, the notion of the laborer's accumulation for her- or himself
would make capitalist accumulation and the capitalist mode of production impossible.
'Capital is not a physical thing but a social relation'. It rests on the 'annihilation of
self-earned private property, in other words, the expropriation of the laborer'
(2000, 28). Thus Soraya's futile protest 'but I belong only to myself!' against
Kaufland's auctioning her off in the first act, and against Mahatma's assertion of
patriarchal authority over her at the end, underscores that she does not own herself
but is owned by capital and by patriarchy respectively (Siemann unpublished, 32
[. . .]).

Historically, Harvey argues via Marx, capitalism revealed the falseness of the
myth of possessive individualism in the colonies, where slave labor and raw coercion
forcibly excluded the laborer from control over the means of production, rather
than in the metropolises, where trade unions, political institutions, and a code of law
strengthened the bargaining power of labor. The place where *Indians* exposes the

limits of Soraya's agency as a worker and a wife is Kaufland's castle. Where or what, then, is that castle? The building's geographical location is left unspecified, but the set provides some clues: the walls are constructed of painted, corrugated metal, evoking a generic factory. The machine that is set up in this place is a stove, and Soraya is chained to it while Kaufland watches her from a small window set high into the wall. Conflating the icon of women's traditional unpaid reproductive labor with the setting of industrial production, work here is characterized as unpaid, coerced, and policed. In the castle, the decreasing value and degrading conditions of work appear more crass than in the German computer lab, where workers could comfort each other, steal short moments of rest, use the machines for their own communicative purposes, and resist undue expectations on the part of the supervisor. The referent for Kaufland's castle, I postulate, is the extraterritorial Export Processing Zone (also euphemistically called 'free production zone'), whose number Naomi Klein estimates at close to '1,000, spread through seventy countries and employing roughly 27 million workers. The World Trade Organization estimates that between $200 and $250 billion worth of trade flows through the zones' (1999, 205). In her report about a visit to one such zone, Klein calls it 'a miniature military state inside a democracy' (204). In the opera's aesthetic of compression, the stove connotes the devaluing and feminization of work, the window stands for the surveillance and disciplining of workers, the chain connotes the coercive and violent working conditions, and the unspecified location points to the ubiquity and denationalized status of the EPZs. *Indians*'s sexual rhetoric emphasizes the expropriative thrust of unchecked capitalism, its vampiric hunger for the surplus value it extracts from labor. Kaufland's desperate pursuit of Soraya, in the course of which he drops all pretenses at seduction, reflects the truth that without her, he's nothing. The social relation of capital is interpreted in heterosexual terms, contrasting the (masculine) accumulation of value with the exploitation and feminization of labor. Where, then, is Mahatma located within this sexual economy?

By the phrase 'the feminization of work' sociologists and economists refer not only to the rising proportion of women in the worldwide wage labor force, but to the observation that forms of work previously regarded as typically female – namely unskilled work without any chances of advancement, low-paid work performed in the home, flexible, part-time, and short-term work, non-unionized and otherwise unregulated work, and work in illegal, immigrant, and offshore setting – are seen to increasingly typify the conditions of labor in general (Standing 1989 [. . .]). Male workers are thus feminized as they experience the worsening of conditions of production and the rolling back of hard-won rights and protections for workers even in western industrial countries, where employers regularly complain about the prohibitively high cost of labor to press for a curtailing of workers' rights and a decrease of wages, using the threat to move production toward cheaper locations as a way to blackmail local communities into political cooperation as well as material subsidies and low taxes. Mahatma's castration, his lack of phallic power, suggests that he, like Soraya, is subjected by the feminization of labor in the globalized economy.

Soraya transfers money for expensive neurosurgery to a clinic so that Mahatma's health can be fully restored; his complete regeneration, however, leads Mahatma to renounce the common plight and shared political vision that defines their love relationship. This turn of events also acknowledges that men as a group still enjoy better opportunities within these generally declining conditions than women do, and that they have more to lose than their chains. In the global economy, men continue on average to earn more money even for the same work, they enjoy an advantage in education and professional training, have access to better-qualified jobs, continual qualification and reskilling, and the prospect of promotion and hence upward mobility. Indeed the income disparity between women and men, the main indicator of a gendered power differential, has remained steady at thirty to forty percent (Wichterich 1998, 52). Global capitalism desires all workers, but it doesn't quite position them equally.

At its climax, the opera recapitulates what is at stake in maintaining or abandoning the love relationship. Overjoyed to see her husband enter her prison, the chained Soraya sings of her imminent liberation and a happy future together:

> My heart is ringing with a hopeful dream
> That every woman in these Indian lands
> Will freely choose her place, profession, and her kin
> All of her own volition!
> The two of us together – what a team –
> Will make a child, and build a house, and laugh with friends!
> And years from now, when we are gray and long of tooth
> Remember how with vigor, love, and youth
> We overcame tradition.
>
> [Siemann 31]

But whereas cultural tradition, military might, and economic pressures had earlier failed to persuade Mahatma to either dominate or divorce Soraya, it is apparently his reclaimed masculinity that prompts him to choose the respect of men over his wife's love, and domination over freely chosen dedication. 'You're repeating the muck / from those versions, silly duck / in which I couldn't walk', replies Mahatma, as he refuses Soraya's request to unchain her and join her in building a world based on democratic consensus and political choice. Rather than unchain her, he tells her that she is his property and that he will care for her from now on. Proclaiming that the four things women need are sex, food, jewelry, and a man's orders, the all-male chorus celebrates men's solidarity against women's demands and wiles: patriarchal unity transcends the contest between local customs, national tradition, and global capitalism. His restored lower body allows Mahatma to call on phallic privileges that were out of his reach while he was paralyzed and impotent. The ending, in which male and female life options diverge so starkly, thus ironizes and contests what the feminist spelling of 'IndierInnen' suggests, namely that female *Indians* stand in for the universal. [. . .] In the face of this betrayal, the despairing Soraya pushes a red lighting button on the gas stove, setting off an explosion that destroys everything, leaving spectators with nothing but smoke wafting over the empty stage. This cataclysmic ending, which more than one reviewer described as the detonation of an atom bomb, indicates that the project of justice and equality is a matter of species survival rather than individual happiness.

The final scene stages the convergence of the initially antagonistic discourses of local and national productions of Indianness, and capitalist demands for an ever-expanding workforce. When the Guru, Kaufland, and Mahatma join together to exalt men's beneficent authority over women, and women's prime function of childbearing, they transcend cultural differences between East and West, and between local, national, and transnational imperatives through the conjoining of patriarchal and capitalist motives and dynamics. Although the logic of their victory is persuasive, it is shown to ride only on a few ounces of flesh. Does this ending surrender to essentialist conceptions of patriarchal masculinity lodged in the penis? Conversely, can only men who aren't 'real' men support a feminist agenda? I regard Mahatma's eventual interpellation to patriarchal ideology as plausible, even highly probable, but not unavoidable. The extremely contrived dramatization of his conversion indeed undermines any sense of ineluctable anatomical destiny. To my mind the tenuousness of his immasculation illustrates, most of all, that opportunities for feminist alliances must be seized where and whenever they exist – a project realized by the opera as a whole. Produced by a mixed team in which the libretto (by Holger Siemann), the musical adaptation (by Robert Nassmacher), and the *mise-en-scène* (by Dirk Rave) were created by men, *Indians*, and indeed the larger political agenda of the Neuköllner Oper, contradicts the conclusion that all people with penises are per se indifferent or opposed to notions of gender equality and justice.

[. . .]

Laboring bodies and the pull of transcendence

[. . .]

Indians explores how new virtual technologies construct the live, gendered, ethnically marked body and its social and imaginary possibilities. When Soraya returns from university, carrying her laptop, perches in front of a computer console in a German lab, and is shackled to the stove in Kaufland's castle, her placement and displacement in the physical space of the stage illustrates the transformation of social space and relations, indexing domestic role divisions, neoimperialist migration patterns, and deteriorating class relations. In addition, the story of Mahatma illustrates the literal reconfiguration of the human body through modern technology. First Mahatma's paralysis and sexual dysfunction result from an injury he sustained through a Russian bomb aimed at the American he was carrying. Then, after Soraya electronically transfers money to the online account of a clinic, Mahatma's bodily control and sexual anatomy are surgically restored. Not only is the Indian man's body staged as a literal theatre of war, the jarring shift in his gender identity toward the end of the opera is dramatized as the result of a medical operation. Mahatma's subjectivity, far from being explained in psychological terms, is constituted through his body's transformation by military and medical technology. In stark contrast to Freudian concepts of psychological development and gendered subjectivity, *Indians* presents masculine anatomy and behavior as shaped by military macro-processes and medical micro-processes.

The moment when he regains the use of his limbs clarifies the idea that the human 'meat' [Case 2001, 13] itself has become the site of social transformations formerly represented through the location and movement of bodies on stage, illustrating the difference between old (theatrical) and new (digital) virtual systems: [. . .] after much bellicose marching and singing as preparation for the attack on Kaufland's castle, the men turn to the immobile Mahatma.

Guru: What about you? In the last act you can walk, I know that you always raid the castle with us.

American: How so? Propose! I hear!

Guru: No idea . . . Director? Can I have a script?

A script is handed in, the American takes it, takes a look, holds it the wrong side up, nods wisely, and passes it on. The friend leafs through it.

Guru: Well, here it is: 'Soraya has managed to electronically transfer money for the surgery to the online account of a clinic, and thanks to advanced neurosurgical techniques Mahatma can walk again'.

Mahatma: Oh, Soraya, yours is my life, my love . . . and everything!

American: C'mon, c'mon, up and out of the wheelchair! Let's go.

Mahatma jumps up, still a bit wobbly, but the American's relentless optimism pushes him into line. The three sing again and exit marching.

[Siemann 28]

In this scene, theatre is depicted as being both like and unlike the new virtual (military and medical) technologies: the abruptness with which these technologies can alter individual lives here occasions a comic moment, but it also accelerates (the plot's) progress to the extent of imploding the possibility of dramatic representation. The operation of new communication technology is thus located in a failure of theatrical performance.

The theatrical discourse of embodied signification, so closely tied to the actor's laboring, gesticulating, spitting, sweating body that is, as Herbert Blau put it, dying in front of you, functions as an alternative to virtual discourses that predicate the generation of meaning on the transcendence of the fleshly body and its material location in a geopolitical grid (Blau 1982, 83). The scholarship about computer technology, cyberspace or virtual reality, and informatics has developed this theme during the last decade. Case argues that the digitally created, virtual space that is the world wide web continues in the tradition of the theatre that premised the creation of transcendental meaning on the immobilization of the actor and of action, obeying an impulse that is 'deeply averse to life and the living' (2001, 13). Likewise, Katherine Hayles traces the emergence of scientific and literary discourses that conceptualize consciousness as pure information and fantasize about liberating information from the body, which is viewed as a passive, dispensable, vessel. Tracking how in the course of the cybernetic revolution 'information lost its body', she regards the new virtual technologies and the 'collective hallucination' of cyberspace that William Gibson imagined as the realization of liberal philosophy's long-cherished dream of a consciousness freed from the narrow confines of the body fettered to specific social and geographical coordinates. Like Case, Hayles argues that cyberspace now offers users the tempting promise of finally jettisoning that irksome body, completing the antimaterialist trajectory of the old metaphysics of gender. Both feminist theorists are acutely aware of the stakes of this masculinist dream of disembodiment. While neither of them rejects virtual technology or evidences nostalgia for a pre-cyber world, they interrogate the gendered implications of imagining the mind as disembodied, and aim to retrieve a materialist sense of embodied subjectivity, social relations, knowledge, and critique. 'If my nightmare is a culture inhabited by posthumans who regard their bodies as fashion accessories rather than the ground of being', Hayles writes, 'my dream is a version of the posthuman that embraces the possibilities of information technologies without being seduced by fantasies of unlimited power and disembodied immortality, that recognizes and celebrates finitude as a condition of human being, and that understands human life is embedded in a material world of great complexity, one on which we depend for our continued survival' (1999, 5). Mahatma and Soraya's lifestories are shaped by communicative, military, and medical technologies – they are both posthuman in the sense Hayles describes. The opera dramatizes the social potential lodged in that interface: technology offers a medium of creative social imagination and transformation that changes the way men and women relate to culture, community, nation, and each other. It also grants Mahatma access to a transnational sphere marked by patriarchal bonding across cultural, class, and ethnic differences on the one side, while shackling Soraya's destiny to her anatomy on the other. Her confinement to the crudest coordinates of female existence, the stove and the crib, and his post-op assumption of patriarchal privilege and concomitant unmooring from the constraints of class, ethnicity, and geopolitical location, starkly contrast female and male social experience and subjectivity in the metaphysical terms of immanence and transcendence. The pyrotechnics of the final scene, in which Soraya blows up the stage in despair and protest, brings the old tricks of live theatre to bear on the virtual's pull of transcendence. That ending insists on the laboring, mortal body as the ground and the measure of individual and collective transformation.

Perched at the top of a four-floor walk up with creaking wooden stairs, the small studio theatre is not air-conditioned; the maximum number of narrow chairs has been squeezed into the cramped, sold-out space. It's over thirty degree Celsius, and I think I can smell the sweat on every single actor on the stage. Only the swishing of their brightly-colored saris creates a little bit of a breeze. *Indians* exemplifies the Neukölln opera's project of creating political theatre in a district traditionally characterized by deep ethnic, class, and sexual differences – Neukölln is one of the poorest districts of Berlin, home to a larger than average proportion of Turkish immigrants, unemployed, and gays and lesbians. Although I have no data about the ethnic composition of the audience, the repertoire's themes respond to the neighborhood's rich cultural mix. Gender relations, immigration, economic restructuring, especially unemployment, but also the social changes wrought through communications technology, figure prominently in their librettos. [. . .] These concerns position the institution in the tradition of workers' culture and political entertainment, and connect the analytics of class to those of gender, sexuality, race, and migration.

The first production the Neukölln opera staged after it moved to its current location in 1987 was a Brechtian teaching play, and its approach to musical drama recalls *Threepenny Opera* or *Mahagonny*, rather than franchises à la *Cats* that have sprouted in several German cities during the last decade. It is one of very few theatres in Berlin that seem to weather the current, catastrophic budget crisis caused by the decade-long covert collaboration of corrupt politicians with profit-hungry real estate speculators after the wall came down, which was disclosed in 2001 and forced the city government to step down. In the aftermath of that crisis, many alternative cultural projects have been foundering because they relied so heavily on public subsidies [. . .] – monies that are now almost exclusively reserved for the temples of high culture. The theatre's operating budget derives mainly from ticket sales as well as from a corporate sponsor, and modest public subsidies. In addition, it keeps expenses low by maintaining only a small staff and hiring students or graduates of Berlin's actors' training programs at intern-level wages. Its emphasis on contemporary, topical subjects draws audiences from outside the district; remarkably for a West Berlin house, over one quarter come from the city's Eastern districts. There is an unusually high proportion of younger people (roughly half are under 40), and many who are first-time opera goers, signaling that the concept of a *Volksoper* (people's opera) succeeds in drawing in spectators who otherwise shy away from the institutions of high culture perceived as imposing and/or irrelevant to their concerns. In a time of dwindling public subsidies, when politicians prioritize high culture for funding because it attracts tourists and business travelers, and when privatization fosters commercial franchises such as the high-tech musicals running at the glitzy Potsdamer Platz complex, the Neukölln opera attracts faithful audiences because it neither espouses avantgarde attitudes nor mistakes the popular for the vapid. It puts on shows that confront middle-class spectators with the predicaments of the undereducated and unemployed; native Germans with the aspirations and disappointments of immigrants; and nuclear families with queer desires and sensibilities. In a time of want, fear, and war, it engages in the struggles and pleasures of making a cross-cultural, intergenerational, polysexual community.

Conclusion

My analysis of *Indians* sought to read out from performance into a range of critical discourses about globalization, as well as to identify the ways in which the performance itself constitutes a critical, cultural-political practice. The opera considers the proposition that technological innovation, as well as transnational knowledge transfer and economic relations can emancipate people from local conditions characterized by political oppression, social inequality, and poverty. In particular, it investigates whether Third World women benefit from the capitalist erosion of patriarchal traditions. Within neoliberal arguments the claim to emancipate women can function to mystify an imperialist agenda through a feminist rhetoric of liberation. At the same time, patriarchal traditions are often fetishized as hallmarks of cultural authenticity within the same neoliberal ideology, and feminists have found it important to contest a discourse committed to preserving and exploiting social hierarchies cloaked as cultural particularity. The opera suggests that the convergence of patriarchal and capitalist interests to the detriment of the globalized woman is not unavoidable or irreversible, and stages that convergence while keeping the alternatives to it in view. The social, economic, and cultural dynamics attending globalization are neither contrasted with a nostalgic vision of the good old days, nor are they rejected as inherently or uniformly oppressive. Indeed, the opera stresses throughout the emancipatory potential of technology, trade, and education, recalling socialists' exhilaration about the revolutionary possibilities of new media and technologies in the early twentieth century.

Holger Siemann's topical libretto is set to the music of Giacomo Meyerbeer, a tremendously popular, Jewish composer and director of grand operas in the nineteenth century but nearly forgotten today. The somewhat jarring combination between music and text allows for a comparison between the two historical moments divided by more than a century. Written on the occasion of a vociferous public debate about immigration that centered on the quality of people allowed to work and live in Germany, *Indians* shows the persistence of a certain ethno-nationalist discourse that emerged during Meyerbeer's lifetime and led to his lasting marginalization. At the same time, the opera illustrates how that discourse is no longer the dominant one in the present – which does not necessarily indicate a change for the better, however. It pinpoints a split within socially conservative politics from an exclusionary rhetoric claiming to protect cultural purity, to a demographic-economistic rhetoric advocating selective immigration. Rather than signaling conservatives' move away from right-wing ideology, that shift heralds instead the reorientation of right-wing conservatives from nationalist to globalist imperatives. The opera's tracking of the current permutations of race and cosmo-politanism interrogates facile assumptions of progress, paralleling its dissection of women's ostensible empowerment in the global economy.

Siemann transposes the grand opera's dramaturgy, which pitted man against machine, into the central theme of *Indians*. Yet the downsizing of grand opera to the scale of the studio stage is not so much a technique of miniaturization (characteristic of contemporary technological developments) as it effects a shift of emphasis away from Meyerbeer's deterministic pessimism in the face of industrialization. *Indians* does not share his pessimism; its protagonists show that, theoretically, technology may enhance life as well as justice, consent, equality, and self-determination. The opera's focus on the scale of the individual human body hence insists on the notion of sustainability as anchoring technological and social transformation. Pain, impairment, and death are neither accepted as the collateral damage exacted by the global information revolution (as Kaufland or the American agent may think), nor rejected or miraculously skipped in the posthuman striving toward disembodiment (as Mahatma's quick-time recuperation from his paraplegic state suggests). The promise of information technologies to sublate the inadequacies of the meat is revealed as a betrayal of very particular bodies, a betrayal that perpetuates the familiar metaphysics of gender rather than transcending them. The spatial and financial constraints of the studio theatre, along with the limitations of voices bravely grappling with demanding *belcanto* parts, make palpable the profound material strains as the global, the national, and the local intersects at the site of the actor's body. The poor players strutting the stage in the immigrant neighborhood of Neukölln mediate this production's engagement with momentous questions as part of an ongoing communal project. Their exertions, their pathos, their agony, and their virtuosity are a measure of the superhuman efforts required to keep the posthuman responsive to and responsible for local perspectives and global possibilities, dependence and self-determination, pain and love.

Note

[. . .]

1   [. . .] Peter Sutherland [the director of GATT] [. . .], on the occasion of the founding of the World Trade Organization (quoted in Wichterich 1998, 11).

Chapter 26

Bruce Robbins

THE SWEATSHOP SUBLIME

From *PMLA* 117.1 (January 2002): 84–97

THERE IS A PASSAGE IN DAVID LODGE'S NOVEL *Nice Work* (1988) in which the heroine, a Marxist-Feminist critic who teaches English literature, looks out the window of an airplane and sees the division of labor.

> Factories, shops, offices, schools, beginning the working day. People crammed into rush-hour buses and trains, or sitting at the wheels of their cars in traffic jams, or washing up breakfast things in the kitchens of pebble-dashed semis. All inhabiting their own little worlds, oblivious of how they fitted into the total picture. The housewife, switching on her electric kettle to make another cup of tea, gave no thought to the immense complex of operations that made that simple action possible: the building and maintenance of the power station that produced the electricity, the mining of coal or pumping of oil to fuel the generators, the laying of miles of cable to carry the current to her house, the digging and smelting and milling of ore or bauxite into sheets of steel or aluminum, the cutting and pressing and welding of the metal into the kettle's shell, spout and handle, the assembling of these parts with scores of other components – coils, screws, nuts, bolts, washers, rivets, wires, springs, rubber insulation, plastic trimmings; then the packaging of the kettle, the advertising of the kettle, the marketing of the kettle, to wholesale and retail outlets, the transportation of the kettle to warehouses and shops, the calculation of its price, and the distribution of its added value between all the myriad people and agencies concerned in its production and circulation. The housewife gave no thought to all this as she switched on her kettle.

To contemplate one's kettle and suddenly realize, first, that one is the beneficiary of an unimaginably vast and complex social whole and, second (a point further emphasized elsewhere in the novel), that this means benefiting from the daily labor of the kettle-and electricity-producing workers, much of it unpleasant and under-remunerated, is not entirely outside everyday experience. What seems special about the passage is a third realization: that this moment of consciousness will not be converted into action. The passage concludes:

> What to do with the thought was another question. It was difficult to decide whether the system that produced the kettle was a miracle of human ingenuity and co-operation or a colossal waste of resources, human and natural. Would we all be better off boiling our own water in a pot hung over an open fire? Or was it the facility to do such things at the touch of a button that freed men, and more particularly women, from servile labour and made it possible for them to become literary critics? [. . .] She gave up on the conundrum, and accepted another cup of coffee from the stewardess.
>
> (192–93 [brackets by Robbins])

Let me now juxtapose this passage with a *New Yorker* cartoon by Roz Chast. Its protagonist, 'you', is an unshaven man in pyjamas. 'You' combine Lodge's tea-drinking housewife with his airborne intellectual; your feet are firmly on the ground, indeed you are not yet out your door, yet you do 'give a thought' to the system that provides you with goods and services. It is this thought that we follow. At the top of the cartoon are the words 'One morning, while getting dressed'. From that common point, lines branch off toward boxes containing different possible outcomes. One morning, while getting dressed, you either do or do not examine the label of your shirt. If you do, you either do or do not realize the conditions of life under which this shirt was, or perhaps was not, produced: the pitifully inadequate wages, not to speak of the locked fire exits, the arbitrary harassments and firings, the refusal of genuine union representation, and so on. But whether your thoughts linger or not, whether the shirt turns out to have been made in Mexico or Thailand or the United States, the result is the same as if you had not examined the label. All lines converge in the end on the same box: you put on the shirt and forget about it [Chast 1999].

In Lodge's book and Chast's cartoon, there is a moment of insight accompanied by a surge of power. In thought, at least, you are launched on a one-click leap from the tender, drowsy privacy of early morning at home – the shirt not yet on your back, the first cup of tea just finished – to the outer reaches of a world economic system of notoriously inconceivable magnitude and interdependence, a system that brings goods from the ends of the earth (as Baudelaire put it, with an accuracy that you suddenly recognize) to satisfy your slightest desire. [. . .] Yet at the same time this insight is also strangely powerless. Your sudden, heady access to the global scale is not access to a commensurate power of action *on* the global scale. You have a cup of tea or coffee. You get dressed. Just as suddenly, just as shockingly, you are returned to yourself in all your everyday smallness.

'That in comparison with which everything else is small' is one of Kant's descriptions of the sublime, also defined as 'a feeling of the inadequacy of [the] imagination for presenting the ideas of a whole, wherein the imagination reaches its maximum, and, in striving to surpass it, sinks back into itself, by which, however, a kind of emotional satisfaction is produced' ([1951], 88, 91). Considering how Lodge and Chast play up and down the scales of the immensely large and infinitesimally small, how they combine pleasure with pain in contemplating the obscure infinity of the social whole, and above all the paradox of their making us sense that we possess transcendent powers (albeit powers exercised on our behalf and in this case without our active will) yet finally letting us 'sink back into ourselves', so that we fail to express those powers in any potentially risky, disobedient action, I suggest that we provisionally call this trope, with a certain inevitable discomfort, the sweatshop sublime. [. . .]

The sublime may not seem like the most useful way to pose the question of our responsibilities as citizens faced with the reality of sweatshop labor. A certain useful-ness will I hope become more apparent as I proceed. But the pairing of sweatshops and sublimity is also intended to raise issues of politics and aesthetics, scholarship and commitment, that have become irritatingly familiar of late to progressives working in and around the humanities. Rather than rehearse those issues here, I simply assert, by way of setting an agenda, two propositions that the notion of a sweatshop sublime is meant to suggest. First, literary critics in allegorical airplanes, looking down from above on putatively unconscious housewives – let's say, intel-lectuals contemplating nonintellectuals – are subject to the same dilemma of concern and confusion, action and apathy, as Lodge's heroine. To recognize that this *is* a dilemma means that we should not expect any simple solution to it. And to recog-nize that it is a *shared* dilemma rather than one resulting from the uniqueness of our work ought to help us calibrate more accurately the responsibilities that do and do not attach to that work.

At the same time (my second proposition), the idea that intellectuals do not escape this dilemma is not merely an argument in favor of modestly retracting some of the political expectations we attach to our work. It's also a fact of wider political importance. This is especially true for those of us searching (perhaps immodestly) for political answers that would operate on the same global or international scale as the causes of our ethical and political problems. If internationalism in the desirable sense is ever going to come into existence, if we are ever going to see some organized impulse toward the equalization of life chances between those who make shirts and those who wear them, this change will clearly not happen by means of a sudden mass exercise of Kantian ethics. It will happen as an outgrowth of habitual desires, fears, and anxieties, embarrassed perceptions and guilty pleasures that, though pervaded by thought, do not belong on that level of rigorous conceptual rationality Kant elsewhere demanded. Like the childhood experience of being told to eat an unappetizing food because children in other countries are starving, the experience of sweatshop sublimity is an instance of this illogical but peremptory category. Unpropitious as it may seem, this limited moment of ethically inspired consumer consciousness is just the sort of raw or semiprocessed phenomenological material in which private and public, domestic and international are fused, and it is out of such material that an internationalist antiglobalization politics on a mass scale will have to emerge, if indeed it ever emerges. To put it in other terms, the moment is a rough analogue to what Antonio Gramsci called the 'national-popular': an imperfect and historically determined version of common sense, perhaps only emerging but significant enough to be worth tracking, that links the thoughts and feelings of ordinary people to the fate of others in a larger collectivity ([1971], 421).

To Gramsci this collectivity was the nation. But I see no reason why collectivity formation should stop at the nation's borders, as if fellow feeling found its natural and inevitable telos in nationality. The gradually increasing reservoir of everyday tropes and images that connect our sense of ourselves and our fate with the fates of those who are not our fellow citizens can thus be thought of, I propose, as the international-popular.

It is to be expected that the international-popular will fall well short of any ideal action-oriented solidarity. But it is also to be expected that, under present global conditions, solidarity and even action itself will fall similarly short, will be subject to the same sorts of quasi-sensory, all-too-human interference that we have come to associate with the aesthetic – the illegitimate but seemingly irremediable tyranny of the close over the distant; the analogous perspectivisms of the other senses; the vulnerability to shapeliness, decibel level, boredom, and so on. Thus, sweatshop sublimity offers grounds for anyone interested in defending the significance to society at large of work performed in the domain of the aesthetic – a kind of case that can never rely on the language of the aesthetic alone, that must step outside that language to anchor itself in other interests and concerns.

Now, there are of course things to be done about sweatshops. The literature of groups like the National Labor Committee, the Campaign for Labor Rights, and United Students against Sweatshops abounds in invitations to sudden perception more or less like the cartoon's. For example: 'When you purchase a shirt in Wal-Mart, do you ever imagine young women in Bangladesh forced to work from 7:30 a.m. to 8:00 p.m., seven days a week, paid just 9 cents to 20 cents an hour [. . .]?' But this literature always follows with a section called something like 'What We Can Do', urging readers to write to Wal-Mart with specific and entirely reasonable demands. And it has real grounds to claim, as it does, 'We do have an impact. We do have a voice' (National Labor Committee [1999, brackets by Robbins]). It has helped rally supporters, and it has won a number of small but significant victories. The celebrity of the American television personality Kathie Lee Gifford was successfully used against her, and against the brands she endorsed, to publicize sweatshop abuses in Honduras; many American universities have agreed to new standards concerning how school sweatshirts and other paraphernalia are to be manufactured. If little progress has been made on the crucial questions of wages and the right to unionize, where corporations have been most resistant, it is nonetheless a genuine accomplishment that such groups have brought the beginnings of transparency, monitoring, and accountability to the murky domain of anonymous subcontracting in which the brand-name multinationals have so profitably been hiding out. The antisweatshop movement, increasingly active on United States campuses, was one of the most powerful constituents of the volatile anti-WTO protest mixture in Seattle and since. Moves toward alliance between students and labor unions and between unions and the environmental groups are two of the most promising features of recent international activism against no-holds-barred globalization.

In short, to discover that the sales price of one Disney Pocohantas T-shirt, sold at Wal-Mart for $10.97, amounts to five days' wages for the women who sewed that shirt is not necessarily to be struck down by paralysis and inertia, though it helps if some available mode of action is specified. Even the Chast cartoon, which describes lethargy, might also be interpreted as a provocation intended to shock us out of lethargy. It is not hard to find literary analogues in which economic epiphany leads toward rather than away from action. Many will no doubt remember the passage toward the end of George Eliot's *Middlemarch* in which Dorothea, who has just spent a miserable and sleepless night after finding Will in a compromising position with Rosamond, gets up at dawn and asks herself, 'What should I do – how should I act now, this very day, if I could clutch my own pain, and compel it to silence, and think of those three?'

> It had taken long for her to come to that question, and there was light piercing into the room. She opened her curtains, and looked out towards the bit of road that lay in view, with fields beyond, outside the entrance-gates. On the road there was a man with a bundle on his back and a woman carrying her baby; in the field she could see figures moving – perhaps the shepherd with his dog. Far off in the bending sky was the pearly light; and she felt the largeness of the world and the manifold wakings of men to labour and endurance. She was a part of that involuntary, palpitating life, and could neither look out on it from her luxurious shelter as a mere spectator, nor hide her eyes in selfish complaining.
>
> What she would resolve to do that day did not yet seem quite clear, but something that she could achieve stirred her as with an approaching murmur which would soon gather distinctness. [. . .]
>
> ([1977,] 544)

Dorothea follows through on her resolution to act. Though the sphere of her action is quite limited – it does not include, for example, the people she sees outside her window or the system that sends them into the fields at that hour – her resolution is rewarded with visible results. Like those in the antisweatshop movement, she feels with a jolt her place in the 'involuntary, palpitating' world of labor around her, resolves to do something, and does. With such an example in mind, it's tempting to conclude that the texts by Lodge and Chast represent a moral step backward, a sophisticated evasion of the responsibility for action.

But the sweatshop sublime is not a simple or easily avoidable error. Indeed, appearances to the contrary, it is the mode in which Eliot spends much of her time writing. Dorothea's early-morning revelation, in which everyone else who is awake is going off to work and only she remains behind in her 'luxurious shelter', has been anticipated some chapters earlier by what is surely the novel's most direct reference to the sublime and perhaps also its most sublime moment. 'If we had a keen vision and feeling of all ordinary human life', Eliot writes in a famous sentence, 'it would be like hearing the grass grow and the squirrel's heart beat, and we should die of that roar which lies on the other side of silence' (135).

In the later scene, Dorothea hears the grass grow. She takes in the daily 'labour and endurance' that put the bread on her table but that do not ordinarily attract any notice. From that extraordinary perception, she draws stern, not to say self-punishing, conclusions. The problem is the self-punishment, which is just what the metaphor of hearing the grass grow predicts. Going to see Rosamond is action, but action that displays an altruistic self-effacement so radical as to leave behind almost no self, or no self-interest. To hear the 'roar which lies on the other side of silence' is indeed, from the point of view of an ordinary self, to die. The purely disinterested, selfless self that remains to Dorothea is only too well suited to the metaphor, for it is incapable of forceful action that would change the rules or terms of ordinariness. Forceful, extraordinary action of this sort is rendered irrelevant, if not precluded, by the notion of hearing the grass grow. Asking us to hear the grass grow is not asking us to interfere with it. The only imperative here is to be conscious of what is already happening, to respect what exists. And respect for what exists is a better argument against change than for it. If the division of labor in the early-morning passage is like the grass in the 'hearing the grass grow' passage, and I think it is, then the same moral applies: the only scandal is unconsciousness of the division of labor, not failure to change the division of labor. As Steven Marcus puts it in an essay on Eliot's social theory, 'Society, however errant and unfair some of its arrangements may be, is never a scandal in this way of conceiving things. To say so would be tantamount to saying that human existence itself is a scandal' ([1990,] 204). [. . .]

Among the commonplaces of Eliot criticism that are relevant here are the larger story of Dorothea's abandonment of her heroic, Saint Theresa-like ideal of action; as a partial explanation for this abandonment, her intermittent attraction to the values of the landholding gentry, who owned a good deal of grassland and had famously mixed feelings about plans for modernizing interference with it; and the point Raymond Williams made in *Culture and Society* about Eliot's view of social interdependence:

> Her favorite metaphor for society is a network: a 'tangled skein'; a 'tangled web' [. . .]. 'One fears', she remarked, 'to pull the wrong thread, in the tangled scheme of things'. The caution is reasonable, but the total effect of the image false. For in fact every element in the complicated system is active: the relationships are changing, constantly, and any action – even abstention [. . .] – affects, even if only slightly [. . .] the very nature of the complication.

Eliot fails in her depiction of working people, Williams concludes, because to her 'there seems "no right thread to pull". Almost any kind of social action is ruled out' ([1958a,] 108–9 [brackets by Robbins]).

Lodge's moment of sublimity produces more or less the same effect. In the name of realism, he too chastises and paralyzes his would-be activist heroine. For both novelists, to glimpse even for a moment the unimaginable face of society as a whole is to go through a near-death experience in which the activist self dissolves. Forced to ask, 'Are my hands clean?' – to quote a sweatshop poem by the African American writer Bernice Johnson Reagon – each loses the moral leverage that has helped her challenge the status quo and thus sinks back into the private [Reagon 1988]. Sublimity is not the end of action – Lodge's Robyn, like Dorothea, is successful in her personal mission – but to repeat Williams's judgment, 'any kind of social action is ruled out'.

Yet 'social action' sets a high standard, for the novel and for academic discourse like ours. To say that Eliot rules it out is to imply that it would otherwise be available. Is it available even to so severe a critic of Eliot as Williams – available, that is, while he writes criticism? Francis Mulhern, in a book entitled *Culture/Metaculture*, suggests that Williams's judgment of Eliot can be extended to most if not all of the culture-and-society tradition Williams so influentially assembled, a tradition that has joined Marxists with Romantic reactionaries on the common ground of visions like those of Eliot and Lodge, visions of organic interdependence. For Mulhern, Williams's identification of culture as ordinary, which inaugurates the era of cultural studies, has much the same effect as Eliot's 'hear the grass grow' openness to the ordinary. In Williams's words, 'The arguments which can be grouped under [the heading of culture] do not point to any inevitable action or affiliation' (quoted in Mulhern 2000, 66). Williams stands at the juncture between the older *Kulturkritik* tradition of Thomas Mann, T. S. Eliot, F. R. Leavis, and company, for which culture was extraordinary, a standard cutting against mass society, and cultural studies, for which culture is ordinary, hence not readily separable from the status quo. But this break is not as great as it appears, Mulhern suggests, for both senses of culture are antipolitical. The cultural studies formula 'Everything is political' leaves nothing political in a usefully specifiable sense and thus has the same practical effect as Mann's explicit ideal of the unpolitical man, who is inspired by culture to reject with disgust mass democracy and political instrumentality as such. In other words, Dorothea looking out her window in the morning, hearing the grass grow, sensing the organic interdependency of the division of labor, is a figure for the academic study of culture *tout court*, whether in the older or the present generation. Both versions of literary criticism represent the individual's relation to an obscure, infinite whole that is politically compelling yet seemingly deterred by its premises from resulting in a proper political subject or proper political action. [. . .]

I will not pursue this parallel here, though there is more to be said, for example, about how Dorothea is eventually rewarded for her visit to Rosamond (with the news that Will loves her after all). We humanists too are rewarded for our apparent altruism, with employment that is not high-paying but is relatively stable, unusually autonomous, and unusually gratifying – desirable enough, in short, to make others wonder whether we are quite as disinterested as we pretend. Being apparently outside the division of labor helps us to secure a place in the division of labor. For this reason, inaction should not be seen as a lapse that humanists tumble into in a moment of moral inattention and that can thus be corrected by resonant calls to stand up and grasp once again their designated responsibilities. Inaction, or hesitation when action seems called for, is built into the conceptual structure we inhabit. So, too, therefore, are calls to responsibility, which must be perpetually repeated and must remain perpetually unanswered. One of the strangest things about words like *action* and *activism*, at least as they are currently used in the humanities, is their functional equivalence to apparently distant words like *culture, intellectual*, and *art*, each of which is accorded the privilege of transcending the division of labor. Even when revolutionary action is not meant, *action* is the latest in a series of terms that, for reasons that go back to our disciplinary formation or deformation, we have asked to stand for the magical resolution of social contradictions, for the ideal unities, for the antidotes to the division, fragmentation, reification, and so on that we imagine reigning outside, thereby justifying our disciplinary existence. But if we actually look outside, it is immediately clear that action is no such thing, possesses no such impossible powers, has less to do with art than with politics, politics in the de-idealized, messy sense.

Mulhern accuses the *Kulturkritik* tradition of covert nationalism and cultural studies of incoherent populism. Both charges are reasonable and important, but neither charge can be pinned to the concept of culture. The antisweatshop movement, which does not share our academic dependence on that concept, is saturated with nationalism and populism. How could it not be, given the movement's need to juggle or reconcile the interests of constituencies as different as organized labor, with its history of protectionism, and the so-called constituencies of conscience, with their ethical universalism? This is what politics does. It brings groups together in a common action that will not, cannot, perfectly represent the interests of any of them, that will oppose an antagonist each of them finds scandalous for a slightly different reason – will oppose, in effect, multiple slightly different antagonists.

At the bottom of the *New Yorker* cartoon, three boxes offer three possible facts about the people who made your shirt. In the middle there is an exaggerated clarity: they 'earned three cents an hour'. To the left, however, there is ambiguity: they 'probably have dysentery or diphtheria or worse'. This could be another sign of their misery but could also be a reason for our anxiety and disgust (yuck, germs on my shirt!). And to the right is more ambiguity: they 'hate your stupid Yankee guts'. To which the likely American response is, 'In that case, too bad for them'. In one box we have fear of foreign infection in the AIDS or Ebola style; in the other we have a national circling of the wagons in the presence of hostility judged childish ('stupid Yankee guts'). In other words, two of the three boxes confirm the strong hint of American nationalism suggested above when the cartoon assumes, or assumes its readers will assume, against all the evidence, that a label reading 'Made in USA' guarantees union wages and decent working conditions – in effect, that there are no sweatshops in the United States (a possibility that gets no illustration). Pushing these nationalist buttons no doubt helps Chast prepare for her antiantisweatshop climax. But they are not just her buttons; they are also the antisweatshop movement's buttons.

The history of checking for a 'Made in USA' label has recently been recounted in Dana Frank's book *Buy American: The Untold Story of Economic Nationalism*. Frank opens the book by describing what she calls an 'import panic attack': 'Ms Consumer's epiphany' that 'all the goods she had examined' at the local mall 'were made in China, Japan, or Korea [. . .] she peered at label after label and discovered to her horror that she couldn't find a TV or a VCR or a toaster made in the U.S.A'. What follows is the conclusion that 'because people like herself were buying imports, American workers were losing their jobs' ([1999,] ix [brackets by Robbins]). [. . .] The power of the epiphany, in Frank's analysis, is in direct proportion to the weakness of the logic or rather to the logic's failure to impose an appropriate conclusion, about the causes of the phenomenon or what to do about it. The general reaction in the United States has been to want to buy American, and anti-immigrant racism has never been far away. Epiphanies like these have often led to action, but action of a sublimely confused and nationalist kind, including bashing a Toyota with a sledgehammer and the no less confused act of lobbying Congress to deny normal trade relations to China, thereby claiming a presumptive national virtue for the United States government in the act of refusing it to another government. [. . .] Once you are attuned to the motif of nationalism, examples are all too easy to come by. Randy Shaw, an activist and a historian of activism, entitles his account of the antisweatshop movement *Reclaiming America: Nike, Clean Air, and the New National Activism*. The America Shaw sees the movement trying to reclaim is one that, as recently as the 1970s, was supposedly 'moving toward the equitable society envisioned in the ideals of its founders' ([1999,] 1). If you can believe that, then you will have no trouble referring, with ambiguous restrictiveness, to the new *national* activism.

Yet if we drop the requirement that this activism be genuinely internationalist, then Shaw's patriotism has a certain specifically political astuteness. 'A Disney spokesman named Green, responding to accusations about conditions in a Haitian factory that produces Disney clothes, shot back at a newspaper reporter: [. . .] "With the newsprint you use, do you have any idea of the labor conditions involved to produce it?" ' (Klein [1999,] 188 [brackets by Robbins]). I have little sympathy for Disney or its spokesmen, but the point, however disingenuous, is not irrelevant or uninteresting. How special a case are foreign sweatshops? When Lodge omits the international dimension, talking about the tea kettle but saying nothing about the tea, is he making a significant omission? What precisely is added by the realization that those who work and suffer on Asian tea plantations and in Mexican maquiladoras are not fellow nationals? If the foreignness of the Disney factory in Haiti offers political leverage that is not offered by the production of newsprint, it's in part because of national shame. And there is no national shame without national pride. Can national pride be turned into an ally of internationalism?

Many have suggested before me that national pride can and must and, more generally, that global commitments can emerge more or less organically and continuously only from local, personal, familial commitments. Agreement on this idea is suspiciously easy, yet getting to the next step of the argument – agreeing, say, on a tipping point where continuity switches over into opposition – is much more challenging. Consider, for example, the somewhat risky role in antisweatshop discourse of disease and disgust. People are not worried about the 'moral losses' occasioned by their reliance on paid household help, Barbara Ehrenreich speculates in one of her undercover essays on menial labor, because

> [a]lmost everything we buy, after all, is the product of some other person's suffering and miserably underpaid labor. I clean my own house [. . .] but I can hardly claim purity in any other area of consumption. I buy my jeans at The Gap, which is reputed to subcontract to sweatshops. [. . .] We can try to minimize the pain that goes into feeding, clothing, and otherwise provisioning ourselves – by observing boycotts, checking for a union label, etc. – but there is no way to avoid it altogether without living in the wilderness on berries. So why should housework, among all the goods and services we consume, arouse any special angst? [. . .]

But having paid workers clean one's home does arouse angst, she says, and the reason is that one's home is felt to be different: 'Someone who has no qualms about purchasing rugs woven by child slaves in India or coffee picked by impoverished peasants in Guatemala might still hesitate to tell dinner guests that, surprisingly enough, his or her lovely home doubles as a sweatshop during the day' ([2000,] 69 [brackets by Robbins]). It is not the simple existence of sweatshops but seeing your home as a sweatshop that offers a political hold. The Orwellian disgust that makes something seem actionably political in the household is akin to the disgust that makes us squeamish about something foreign suffusing our shirts, our breakfasts, our most intimate space. It's fine if I know it's happening, as long as it's not happening right here. This is the slogan of the NIMBY movements: not in my backyard. Once you think about it, the disgust is itself a bit disgusting. Yet one asks oneself whether there can be any politics without it – without a provisional reinforcing of borders and hierarchies, privileges and property lines that we know to be more or less illegitimate.

The 'moral challenge', Ehrenreich concludes,

> is to make work visible again: not only the scrubbing and vacuuming but all the hoeing, stacking, hammering, drilling, bending, and lifting that goes into creating and maintaining a livable habitat. In an ever more economically unequal culture, where so many of the affluent devote their lives to such ghostly pursuits as stock-trading, image-making, and opinion-polling, real work – in the old-fashioned sense of labor that engages the hand as well as the eye, that tires the body and directly alters the physical world – tends to vanish from sight.
>
> (70)

Hoeing, stacking, and hammering, like Lodge's list of labors in *Nice Work*, belong to the argument that a 'livable habitat' depends on a great many kinds of work that are normally invisible. But as the culmination of an argument about who cleans the toilets and mops the floors at home, the seemingly innocuous demand to make work visible also makes a riskier suggestion, a suggestion that might paradoxically work against this perception of interdependence. To refuse the division of labor at a point of intimacy is to flirt with refusing the division of labor as such. When Ehrenreich contrasts 'real' work at home with such 'ghostly' sorts of non-manual labor as 'opinion-polling', she inadvertently does just what the ideology of the work ethic does: assuming a criterion of individual self-reliance and self-sufficiency. If it is disgusting to have someone do manual labor in our house, if within our own four walls at least we should be sturdily independent of the work of others, then how can we keep the desire for sturdy independence from spilling over and generalizing itself? Are we prepared to deny our dependence, for example, on such ghostly forms of nonmanual labor as planning rational traffic patterns, collecting opinions on behalf of national health care, or teaching at public universities? The work ethic protects and legitimates the system of individual rewards: it suggests to people, falsely, that they've earned what they receive, that they receive what they receive because of their individual labors. In other words, it blots out the existence of society and the interdependence without which no individual effort could lead to any results, let alone any reward. Whatever else it does, the sweatshop sublime rightly forces on us the knowledge of social interdependence. Ehrenreich, perhaps because she feels the pain of this knowledge more acutely than most, tries to escape it by imagining the home as an enclave of hardworking self-sufficiency. If the home is a pattern – and her essay's arc from housework to manual labor as such suggests exactly that – then the appreciation of 'real' work can easily become (as it so often has in recent public discourse) an argument against the hard-won sense of interdependence, and the ethical conclusions drawn from interdependence, that has made possible voter support for the little we have left of the social welfare state.

In other words, disgust with dependence on the work of other people in the home risks passing over into disgust with dependence on the work of other people in general – a disgust with being part of a highly elaborated division of labor. Yet learning to be part of that division is a precondition for almost any progressive politics, nationally and internationally. And it would seem to demand – on the as yet counterfactual but urgent condition that everyone receive proper wages and benefits – that we unlearn our desire that other people get out of our most intimate space: our shirt, our morning coffee. The social division of labor of course naturalizes and disguises social inequality. But that is not all it does. Not so long ago, poverty was seen as an individual moral failing. More recently, it seemed unnatural and unethical for mothers who had any choice in the matter to put their children in the care of state-sponsored day care centers. To the extent that these beliefs are no longer held and that our society has begun to act on the welfare state's assumption of no-fault poverty, we have taken some deep ethical lessons from the division of labor. Ceasing to be scandalized by paid work in our homes may eventually have to be one of those lessons.

What exactly is the scandal about sweatshops? Naomi Klein, the author of a best-selling book on the antisweatshop movement, *No Logo: Taking Aim at the Brand Bullies*, argues that the key to contemporary injustice is brand names: 'The astronomical growth in the wealth and cultural influence of multinational corporations over the last fifteen years can arguably be traced back to a single, seemingly innocuous idea developed by management theorists in the mid-1980s: that successful corporations must primarily produce brands, as opposed to products' ([1999,] 3). This not unfamiliar but questionable premise allows her to intensify the sense of scandal around the all-too-substantial sweatshop labor that goes into these strangely insubstantial commodities. Such intensity has been a major political resource of the movement; the outrage against transnational corporations is special when they can be presented as a 'global logo web', when there is 'high name-brand recognition' (xviii). Note what assumptions this argument involves. Capitalists are 'abandoning', Klein writes, 'their traditional role as direct, secure employers to pursue their branding dreams' (441). Direct, secure employers? It would be news to workers laid off or fearing layoffs long before the logo takeoff of the 1980s that the 'traditional role' of capitalists was to offer security of employment. It's as if what Engels found in Manchester in 1844 were the good old days. Klein's insistence that the real problem is brands means she has to overvalue the 'old-fashioned idea that a manufacturer is responsible for its own workforce' (187).

This is indeed a very old-fashioned idea. It is old enough to reproduce that 'organic conception, stressing interrelation and interdependence', whose opposition to crude laissez-faire Williams termed 'one of the most important facts about English social thinking in the nineteenth century' (140). It's a bit surprising to find something so close to Eliot's ethic of service and top-down solicitude, to the forthright paternalism of Elizabeth Gaskell's *North and South* (Lodge's model in *Nice Work*), reappearing now in the most up-to-date antisweatshop discourse. But it is not, I think, an absolute mistake. 'As frustrating and irrational as it is', Shaw writes, 'the stance that "all corporations are evil so there's nothing to be done" has been a remarkably effective rationalization for inaction in the face of injustice' ([1999,] 21). This is the commonsense version of 'Everything is political', and it too leaves people thinking, 'In that case, nothing is political, and so why bother?' A relative, compromised criterion will have to be posited according to which some corporations are less evil than others, or else inaction will triumph. The willingness to accept, for rhetorical purposes, the somewhat mythic figure of the responsible employer offering secure employment makes sense as a way of opening up the landscape to action.

This is a backhanded case for the continued political relevance of the culture-and-society tradition, which turns up unexpectedly in the middle of today's timeliest discourse of political action. It is also a case for understanding action in a less theological sense, a sense that is not irreconcilable with the humble acknowledgment that (as novelists like Lodge and Eliot have suggested) those who want to understand the world are not thereby privileged to stand outside and against the division of labor. If action is as politically confused and promiscuous as Mulhern says culture is, then action cannot serve scholars and critics of culture as a repository and arbiter of virtue. And the attempt to make it so serve is politically counterproductive for academics in that the effort can only appear to potential allies as a claim to moral superiority. To call on ourselves to aim our work at action or activism is to imply that we can have the singular good fortune to live, even potentially, a fusion of high moral principles with the universal need to make a living, a fusion that ordinary people hardly dare dream of. Listening in on this call to responsibility, the general population is likely to hear only another form of elitism. When we need allies, and we do need allies – for example, to defend the dignity of our work against its reduction to the logic of the bottom line – we will thus have reason to expect more resentment than solidarity. If action is what we want, then 'Action!' is not the motto we want.

I have been arguing against the sort of self-aggrandizement that often hides out in calls to activist responsibility, not against responsibility itself. In pointing out that moments of insight like ours into the distant workings of the world are more ordinary than we like to think and that the weight of confusions, ambiguities, and other responsibilities that keeps ordinary people from acting on such moments is more characteristic of us than we like to think, I've been trying to give a more modest and more accurate sense, but not a less binding one, of what our responsibilities are. That even action against sweatshops must take place in a muddled zone where it's difficult to distinguish principled internationalism from scary nationalism can stand as one piece of evidence of the need for us scholars and critics not to step out of character. On the contrary, we should take up our responsibilities in the workplace, exercise our most rigorous, academically trained powers of analytic discrimination. As far as action is concerned, there is always the imperative to do some institutional housecleaning – that is, to do what we can to ensure that we do not work in universities, libraries, museums, and other cultural institutions that for many of our colleagues function, as those institutions are under more and more pressure to function, like intellectual sweatshops. [. . .]

I began this essay by speaking about the division of labor and suggesting that the effort to perceive one's place in it offers a contemporary experience of the sublime. The critic most associated with this suggestion is Fredric Jameson. Indeed, Jameson is criticized on just this point by Gayatri Chakravorty Spivak in her *A Critique of Postcolonial Reason*. 'It should [. . .] be clear', Spivak says, 'that Jameson's fable about unrepresentable technology leading to a (generally unsatisfactory) paranoid social practice, a (satisfactory if correctly understood) schizophrenic aesthetic practice, and cognitive (not "moral") political practice, is not a complete rupture with Kant's Analytic of the Sublime' ([2000b,] 325 [brackets by Robbins]). To put this more crudely: in the face of global capital, Jameson fails to imagine any satisfactory politics and offers instead the compensatory satisfactions, such as they are, of cognitive and above all aesthetic practice.

If this is true, there are extenuating circumstances. Among them is the difficulty of arriving at anything like a satisfactory politics under present global conditions – a shared difficulty. When heavy industry moves from Manchester and Milwaukee to Mexico and Malaysia, the map of political possibilities becomes more complicated for Mexicans and Malaysians as well. The complications are different, but people of various nations share the challenge of seeing, speaking, and acting transnationally. Expertise in cognitive and aesthetic practice can properly claim to be of use here, even of significance.

In the final chapter of *Postmodernism; or, The Cultural Logic of Late Capitalism*, Jameson concedes that the word *reification*, understood as 'the transformation of social relations into things', 'probably directs attention in the wrong direction for us today'. He sees more relevance in a second definition of the word:

> 'the effacement of the traces of production' from the object itself, from the commodity thereby produced. This sees the matter from the stand-point of the consumer: it suggest the kind of guilt people are freed from if they are able not to remember the work that went into their toys and furnishings. Indeed, the point of having your own object world, and walls and muffled distance or relative silence all around you, is to forget about all those innumerable others for a while; you don't want to have to think about Third World women every time you pull yourself up to your word processor, or all the other lower-class people with their lower-class lives when you decide to use or consume your other luxury products: it would be like having voices inside your head. [. . .]
>
> ([1991,] 314–15)

The paragraph that immediately follows, however, makes the opposite point and makes it about art: 'The reification of culture itself is evidently a somewhat different matter, since those products are "signed"; nor, in consuming culture, do we particu-larly want, let alone need, to forget the human producer' (315). This frank admission changes everything. If in the case of art we don't need to forget the human producer, if we actively desire to remember the human producer, if we want to see traces of production, indeed will pay good money to have those voices echoing in our heads, then why mightn't we go on to want the same thing with other products as well, products that are not classified as art? The Lodge and Chast texts I've been discussing, taken together with the successes of antisweatshop campaigns based unapologetically in the psychology and ethics of the consumer, offer evidence that consumers don't come in two entirely distinct types, one artistic and the other unartistic – that there exists, in other words, a certain desire to live with voices inside our heads. This desire, not exclusive to intellectuals contemplating works of art, seems to mark a certain political possibility in the humanities. There are certainly less feasible and less consequential goals for humanistic education than the cultivating, augmenting, and channeling of the desire for voices inside our heads. There are also worse ways of thinking about political action in the narrow sense.

Curiously, sublimity and sweatshops turn up together again on the back cover of Spivak's *Critique*, which tells us that the book 'ranges from Kant's analytic of the sublime to child labor in Bangladesh'. This range is not quite so wide as Harvard University Press appears to think, for the discussion of the sublime in chapter 1 and the discussion of child labor in the conclusion are versions of the same argument. Questioning the 'interested use of "child labor" as a way of blocking export from developing countries' ([2000b,] 146), Spivak accuses antisweatshop activists who call for boycotts against the Bangladeshi garment industry of blindly helping to protect northern jobs and markets. 'The transnationally illiterate benevolent feminist of the North supports this [boycotting] wholeheartedly, with "ignorant goodwill"' (416 [brackets by Robbins]). The ignorant goodwill of northern progressives is also the theme of the philosophy chapter, which treats the figure of the aboriginal in Kant. So-called 'New Hollanders' and 'inhabitants of Tierra del Fuego [. . .] bubble up in the cauldron of Kant's contempt', as Spivak nicely puts it, because Kant needs examples of 'man in the raw', man lacking in culture and therefore unable to appreciate the sublime (26, 28n [brackets by Robbins]). Only those lacking in culture will allow Kant to define the process by which culture can manufacture a rational subject, which offers in turn 'a justification for Europe to be the global legislator' (32–33 [brackets by Robbins]). Kant's 'global project for the subject [. . .] of reason' is 'the project of transforming [the New Hollander and the Fuegan] from the raw to the philosophical' (36 [brackets by Robbins]).

According to Spivak, Kant's analytic of the sublime does the same thing that Western human rights discourse does when addressed to Bangladeshi sweatshops: it flattens out the complexity and difference of Third World society to suit a First World standard of ethical rationality. But it is unclear that Kant was always and everywhere committed to that standard. He turns to the aesthetic in his *Critique of Judgment*, as I suggested hastily above, not because he wants to defend rationality but because he can see that the rational community he desires will never come about by means of submission to rationality. People must be induced or cajoled by other means to bind themselves together. They are more likely to do so, he speculated, through their uncoerced and individual yet also universalizing act of appreciating the beautiful than through their rational obedience to the good. In other words, Kant's aesthetics can be read as his political theory, a theory rendered necessary by the political insufficiencies of reason. According to this view, Kant says that political action has to take on the limits and confusions of the aesthetic. For if it does not, if it attempts to embody and enact reason, it risks producing effects that are rationally and ethically undesirable.

This alternative account of Kantian sublimity supports Spivak's argument concerning political action against Asian sweatshops and shows how broadly she agrees with Jameson. What Spivak complains about, in northern antisweatshop campaigns, is the simplification of action whereby 'the only imperative – "What You Can Do in India" – is boycotts and sanctions' ([2000b,] 418n). In calling for resistance to sweatshops accompanied by long-term 'infrastructural followup' (420), Spivak tries, one might say, to theorize a politics in which northerners have to forgo the illusory satisfactions of immediate action in a domain of ostensible political transparency and ethical universality. Like Jameson, she writes in or near the mode of the Kantian sublime. She insists that constraints, obscurities, hesitations, and self-questionings, the inevitable by-products of capitalism in its global mode, must be factored back into the tempting simplicity of action, a simplicity that as she points out has not become less treacherous in the epoch of humanitarian intervention and human rights. This sinking back into ourselves is what politics requires, even and especially on a global scale. Of course, this sinking back also confirms the emotional satisfaction we derive from intellectual work in all its lonely specificity, the slow and patient labor of filling in the steps, analytically and politically, between the perceptual and emotional jolt and the outlet in action that may or may not be found to suit it. If public intellectuals are to pursue something higher than publicity, this continuing communion with privacy is an inescapable part of their task.

Chapter 27

Joseph Medley and Lorrayne A. Carroll

THE HUNGRY GHOST: IMF POLICY, CAPITALIST TRANSFORMATION AND LABORING BODIES IN SOUTHEAST ASIA

From *Postcolonialism Meets Economics,* ed. S. Charusheela and Eiman
Zein-Elabdin New York: Routledge, 2004, pp. 145–64

IMF PRONOUNCEMENTS MADE DURING THE 1997–98 Asian
financial crisis and those addressing its 'aftermath' employ an intriguing and
revelatory rhetoric, one that seeks to reconfigure and at times to obliterate the
meanings of the crisis within a discourse of international economic development.
The language the IMF uses to tell its story of Thai and Malaysian collapse displays
powerful and recurrent tropes of capitalist discipline and triumph, tropes that
appear to erase the deleterious consequences of IMF actions on the populations most
affected by its policies.

These literary figures should be interpreted as part of a 'development' discourse
defined by 'the characteristics and interrelations of . . . three axes':

> The forms of knowledge that refer to it and through which it comes into
> being and is elaborated into objects, concepts, theories, and the like; the
> system of power that regulates its practice; and the forms of subjectivity
> fostered by this discourse, those through which people come to recog-
> nize themselves as developed or underdeveloped.
>
> (Escobar 1995, 10) [. . .]

The last axis – how people come to see themselves and be seen in this context, that
is, how they recognize themselves as participants in a development regime –
depends to a large extent on the narratives that describe the participants and specifies
how they are supposed to act in the 'development' process.

Postcolonial theorists such as Gayatri Spivak ask us to consider these narratives
as formative, disciplinary, and hegemonic. For Spivak, development discourse,
embedded within the broader field of 'the Northwestern European tradition (codename "West")' is predicated on a tale of progress that is initiated and sustained by the

spread of capitalism (1999, 6). Development discourse links this romantic tale of progressive capital with the romantic story of modernization and exhorts 'under-developed' subjects to move towards a liberatory and prosperous future. As Spivak notes, that future is 'unanticipatable', and it appears to be ineluctable: IMF com-muniqués constantly recur to the inexorable nature of capitalist globalization. In IMF logic, once the subjects of this tale come to see themselves as 'underdeveloped', they will take steps to leave their prehistory and approach capitalism and, thus, enter into a new modern 'subjectship' (Spivak 2000, 39). [. . .]

These steps enact the conditions by which capital secures its reproduction in new locales more deeply and intensely. Spivak describes one of these steps in her commentary on 'gender training':

> When international nongovernmental organizations undertake what is now called 'gender training', they are busy with the work of constituting a general gendered will for a globalization where financial capital rather than world trade is the major player.
>
> (ibid., 41)

Such rituals of initiation into capitalism are repeated, with local variation, through-out 'developing' regions. Our reading of the Asian crisis focuses on the intersections of capitalism and gender-formation in the experiences of Thai and Malaysian workers during and after the 1997–98 'crisis'.

We begin with the IMF's story of development that tells us capital will employ workers who seek jobs, will pay them higher wages than they can otherwise earn, and will increase their nation's aggregate income. We retell this story through vivid images that show how capitalist institutions interpellate individual workers into factory regimes that will consume not only their labor, but also their whole being, body and spirit. We also demonstrate how, under the newly structured regimes imposed by the IMF, capitalist use of sex-gendering transforms workers to fit capital's needs. Disciplining female workers to exhibit 'feminine' traits, such as passivity, dependency, and malleability, factory owners seek to construct a general-izable worker, one suited to the conditions of labor in Free Trade Zones (FTZs). The apparently specific 'feminine' thus becomes the universal model of labor. With this gesture, the IMF, and its agents, employ the modernist trope of universal person-hood, a figure – here, a worker – who is thereby flattened, lacking any particularized attributes, save those quite broad qualities that can be read within the field of capital's needs. Thereby, the worker is made 'subject' to capital.

In considering this process, Spivak's theorization of 'subjectship' informs our understanding of the IMF's Asian crisis narrative. People who labor under the conditions produced by the IMF's policies are 'subject to' capital, but they also have recourse to their own 'psychic apparatus' in order to interpret, resist, and counter the conditions that subject them. As Spivak notes, '[subjectship] involves intersub-jective symbolic systems that are the condition and effect of cultural dynamics that also cannot be fully available' (2000, 39). Understanding the constitution of the 'subjectship' of subaltern women and men, then, requires an engagement with these 'intersubjective symbolic systems', that is, it requires an interpretation of the cultural effects, as well as the political and economic ones, that make them subject to capital.

How might any one subject begin this process of interpretation if the symbolic system has already reduced her to a 'worker?' We offer, first, a decoding of the symbolic system that represents women and men in the shapes that capital requires, and then we tell a story of peoples' resistance to this flattening. In our story 'subjectship' vests in figures of subaltern women as they struggle with the conditions set by transnational capital. Through that struggle they express a challenging counter-imagery to the IMF rhetoric that unreservedly praises capital's effects. In IMF rhetoric, transnational capital offers the individual worker a place in modernity's history of progress and 'development'. The individual, in response, offers to give up her body willingly to 'be connected in [her] thinking' with 'the world' (1999, 41). This connection predicates a new form of subjectship in which an array of institutional, discursive, and material effects construct these women as (free) market participants (both as consumers and as workers whose labor is consumed by capital).

However, this formulation suggests a question: if women as workers in 'developing' regions are structured by their new subjectship in capitalism, how do they experience and view their situation? In particular, how might Thai and Malaysian factory workers make meaning within this construction? We offer a series of stories, an assemblage of representations, that challenges the IMF's 'official' version of events. By turning to the fiction of Lawrence Chua and the anthropological work of Aihwa Ong, we suggest a deconstructive and juxtapositional strategy. This strategy draws on our experiences in the academic discourse of the '(codename "West")' to counter hegemonic development discourse while it seeks to avoid 'speaking on behalf of subaltern women' (Sharpe 1993, 18). This '(im)possible' task, as Spivak characterizes it, necessarily becomes for us, and, perhaps, for our readers, a ghost story.

The hungry ghost

> A hungry ghost is a creature with a tiny mouth and an enormous belly, its physique fed by ambition based on craving, worry based on craving, disappointment based on craving.
>
> (Chua 1998, 134–35)

Haunted by the failures of their Asian economic protégés, but even more discomforted, indeed, threatened, by the emergence of external and internal critiques, the IMF seeks to repress a full understanding of its policies' implications. Focusing on the effects of IMF interventions in the Southeast Asian (particularly Thai) economic crash, we find the Fund's effects on Southeast Asia's working people to be a signal instance of the discrepancy between the Fund's stated aims and its real consequences for those least able to protect themselves against IMF decisions and their implementations. In this discrepancy we locate powerful images of the Fund's uncanny, images that the Fund must repress and revise in order to accommodate the story it needs to tell about itself and its accomplishments.[1] Foremost among these haunting images is the figure of the laboring body. This body cannot be described in its particularity by the IMF because to acknowledge it would undermine key elements of capitalism's success story, change its outcome, make visible the exploitation whose nonexistence, 'invisibility', is necessary to secure capitalist profitability.

Each story the IMF tells about development, each call for – and disciplinary practice of – structural readjustment, reiterates a triumphalist tale of capitalism as the source of material well-being and freedom, while it simultaneously banishes images of human suffering that might disrupt or give the lie to their development discourses of capitalist-driven progress.

For the IMF, capitalism, well-being, and freedom completely fill the frame of its portrait of the real – a developing, prosperous Southeast Asia. In order to entice us to believe the Fund's depiction, the Fund's literature invokes what Michel de Certeau calls 'the twofold and strange power of transforming seeing into believing, and of fabricating realities out of appearances' (de Certeau 1984, 186). Nevertheless, the IMF narratives, when recited in dialogue with tales told both by the Fund's boosters and by its critics, display uncanny figures lurking at the edges of the Fund's portrait of Southeast Asia's economic policies and development. Thus, at inopportune moments, ghostly figures of suffering, laboring bodies may float into the frame to contest the adequacy of IMF representations.

Recitations

If, as de Certeau claims, '[O]ur society has become a recited society', then Thomas Friedman's writing functions as, in effect, a textual toady to the IMF recitation, itself a meta-narrative of modernity and progress. De Certeau explains that 'ours' is a 'recited society' 'in three senses: it is defined by *stories* (*recits*, the fables constituted by our advertising and informational media), by *citations* of stories, and by the interminable *recitations* of stories' (de Certeau 1984, 186). In this formulation, Friedman (*New York Times* columnist) is a reciter of IMF stories, deploying anecdotal evidence from the 'man on the street' to proclaim the success of IMF sponsored capitalism. To challenge these 'interminable recitations', we shall turn to Aihwa Ong, who offers a different kind of evidence, not 'man on the street' but 'woman in the factory'.

As de Certeau notes, the transformation and fabrication of the real is produced by powerful institutions such as the IMF, and other texts may recite or, in Ong's case, dispute that representation. But the operation is complicated by

> [A] double reversal. On the one hand, the modern age, which first arose out of a methodic effort of observation and accuracy that struggled against credulity and based itself on a contract between the seen and the real, now transforms this relation and offers to *sight* precisely what must be *believed*. Fiction defines the field, the status, and the object of vision. The media, advertising, and political representations all function in this way.
>
> (ibid.: 186)

This is precisely the realm of the ghost: what the IMF wants people to believe, it makes visible through its stories of the success of free-market capitalist institutions and programs. What it wishes to obscure, it excises from these stories. Many theorists, following Marx, seek to illuminate that obscurity. Spivak, for example, views this aspect of capital.

> in the special sense that although bodyless [capital] must pass through
> unanticipatable moments of embodiment, carry codes with history, slip
> into mental material. . . . It needs spectralization (or quantification, or
> the value form).
>
> (Spivak 2000, 43 [brackets by Medley and Carroll])

Capital needs 'spectralization' so that its representation, the story told about it, can abstract from and conceal some of its effects on workers' bodies. The figure of the ghost is both invited by this need and feared for what its detection might reveal. Hence, in IMF fiction, workers' bodies cannot be shown because those damaged bodies would reveal the diminished, brutalized, and immiserated state caused by capitalist exploitation. Yet this fiction, although coercive and constitutive, is not absolute; its definition can, and should, be challenged by stories that call forth the unspoken and invisible elements of IMF discourse. In presenting these stories, we follow one of the projects of postcolonial theory, the project of 'recovery'. As Leela Gandhi notes,

> [i]f [postcolonial theory's] scholarly task inheres in the carefully
> researched retrieval of historical detail, it has an equally compelling
> political obligation to assist the subjects of postcoloniality to live with
> the gaps and fissures of their condition, and thereby to learn to proceed
> with self-understanding.
>
> (Gandhi 1998, 8 [brackets by Medley and Carroll])

Thus we look to other recitations, fictions, to challenge the dominant narrative fabricated by the IMF.

Lawrence Chua's novel, *Gold By the Inch*, for example, exposes the destructive omissions, the 'gaps and fissures', of IMF representations when his text literally refigures the story of capitalist development. This refiguration emerges through the novel's narrator, whose experiences as a Teochew gay traveling back to visit his families in Thailand and Malaysia anchor a tale of displacement, labor, and exploitation.[2] Throughout the novel, Chua's various representations of third world subalternity make explicit the sexualized consumption fantasies that Western agents of capital bring to these nations.

One notable aspect of Chua's text is its finely rendered description of workers' bodies as they undergo the transformations required of them by capital: bodies that shrink or flatten as they are shaped, literally as well as figuratively, for consumption by transnational capital in its drive for profit. The Malay and Thai workers in his novel are rendered ever more dependent on capitalist employment, the 'hungry ghost', that 'provides their livelihoods' even as it consumes them. In thus making capitalist exploitation visible as a ghost, Chua provides a powerful counter-narrative to IMF fiction, while echoing Marx's centuries-old image of this exploitation in the figure of the vampire.

By referring both to Chua's novel and to Marx's historical critique of capital throughout our reading of IMF literatures, we choose metaphors and rhetorics to contest the IMF's banal and pernicious recitations. We explicitly link the historical tropes of Marx's nineteenth-century critique with contemporary conditions in the post-colonial world in order to disrupt the narrative of progress issued by IMF communications. Our story interjects the missing, the specters the IMF wishes to ignore: the violent vampires and the ghosts seen by violated bodies, which together reveal the exploitative trajectory of IMF policies and capitalist transformation/ deformation.

Recitation I

To discover the 'real' of the IMF, we read its metanarrative, as expressed in the Fund's pronouncements. Michel Camdessus (then Managing Director of the IMF) dramatically stated in a September 1999 address, 'it is the hard, the demanding, task – it is the honor – of the IMF, even if it is not a development institution, to try continuously to help governments, to be responsive to the cries of the poor' (IMF 1999c). In the 'history' that it recites, the Fund seeks to make countries recognize 'the circular relationship between integrity of monetary and financial management, high quality growth, and poverty reduction'. Thus, the Fund's agents state that, in their view, poverty is best reduced first by guaranteeing stable financial returns to investors and then by promoting growth of their enterprises.

While such pronouncements display the premises upon which the IMF operates, they also reveal the Fund's unease. This anxiety arises from the possibility that association of its policies with increasing poverty might create a volatile and antagonistic political environment, one that might threaten its long-term project to open nations to unrestricted penetration by transnational capitalist investment, goods and services, and finance. Therefore, IMF agents 'offer to *sight*' a tale of the ineluctable, liberatory progress that the imposition of free-market capitalism will produce. We turn here to Marx as he described an earlier initiation into capitalist relations:

> Hence the historical movement which changes the producers into wage laborers appears, on the one hand, as their emancipation from serfdom and from the fetters of the guilds, and it is this aspect of the movement that alone exists for our bourgeois historians. But, on the other hand, these newly freed men became sellers of themselves only after they had been robbed of all their own means of production, and all the guarantees of existence afforded by the old feudal arrangements. And this history, the history of their expropriation, is written in the annals of mankind in letters of blood and fire.
>
> (Marx 1977, 875)

Marx's 'letters of blood and fire' powerfully contrast with the bloodless, if succinct, language of the IMF's credo: 'The best route out of poverty is strong, sustainable high-quality growth' (IMF 1999c). In turn, 'high-quality growth', in the Fund's formulation, must be achieved by a variety of linked procedures, and developing nations must follow these prescriptions; as Camdessus proclaimed

> By the early 1980's, much of the world had come to realize that, necessary though it was, macroeconomic stability was not enough. The need to eliminate distortions and inefficiency in markets provided the motivation for a first generation of reforms intended to make markets work more efficiently – pricing, exchange rate and interest rate reforms, tax

and expenditure reforms and the establishment of rudimentary market institutions.

(IMF 1999d)

Although these 'reforms' involved massive restructuring, and, as we shall see, massive human displacement and immiseration, the Fund constructed a fiction of development in which

> Poor countries themselves need to generate high-quality growth . . . We know the ingredients: a stable macroeconomic environment; an open, efficient market economy, a framework that fosters private investment; and, yes, transparency, financial sector soundness, and robust economic institutions. Good governance of course!
>
> (IMF 1999c)

Recitation II

Friedman, in his bestseller *The Lexus and the Olive Tree*, supports and extends the Fund's program for capitalist expansion by striking a different tone. Where the Fund's pious rhetoric masks the exploitation it promotes, Friedman proclaims in language that is brutally direct:

> Analysts have been wondering for a while now whether the turtles who are left behind by globalization or most brutalized by it will develop an alternative ideology to liberal, free-market capitalism. . . . I don't believe there is one that can both truly soften the brutality of capitalism and still produce steadily rising standards of living.
>
> (Friedman 1999, 273)

Moreover, if the IMF story presents a relentlessly disembodied version of economic development and 'high-quality growth', Friedman conjures the body politic of developing nations in order to discipline them to market forces:

> But, in the end, if you want higher standards of living in a world without walls, the free market is the only ideological alternative left. . . . When your country recognizes this fact, when it recognizes the rules of the free market in today's global economy, and decides to abide by them, it puts on what I call 'the Golden Straightjacket'.
>
> (ibid., 86–87)

In the IMF's and in Friedman's constructions of the 'real', there is no alternative to the strictures imposed by implementing the conditions necessary for robust capitalist development. In order to experience freedom, modernity, and prosperity, the 'rules' must be obeyed. The workers whose labor fuels this capitalist development are subsidiary, flattened characters in the larger narrative of profit and expansion; their role is to get a job and to work hard to contribute to 'high-quality growth'. If not, they are merely 'turtles', a term that insultingly reveals the very brutality Friedman wishes to occlude in the rush toward 'growth'.

The IMF narrative of the Asian crisis of 1997–98 reinforces this sense of inevitability: the 'world rules' are those set by international financial institutions; alternative (e.g., socialist or social-democratic, non-Western, non-European) models, alternative 'rules', don't work:

> Let me start with the proposition that the international monetary and financial system may be seen as a global public good. *It is essentially the same system for everyone.* If it works well, all countries have the opportunity to benefit; if it works badly, all are likely to suffer. Hence, all have an interest in reforms that will improve this system for the global public benefit.
>
> (IMF 1999b, italics [Medley and Carrol])

We might consider how well the system works for *everyone* because, ironically, economic success in East and Southeast Asia was apparently a causal factor in Asia's financial crisis. Prior to the onset of the crisis, high profits in the Asian economies attracted enormous, mostly short-term, capital inflows. From 1993 to 1996, Europeans pumped $318 billion, Japanese $260 billion, and the US $46 billion into Asian financial markets in search of quick returns. Thailand received $70 billion to finance long-term, often speculative, building and industrial projects (Sender 1998, 56–59). Initially, this huge influx of money financed rapid and apparently profitable growth. However, world markets, especially in the US, grew more slowly.

Lagging export revenues in Thailand triggered an investment confidence crisis. Considering the concatenation of effects caused by this crisis of confidence, Wiegersma and Medley argue that '[t]he resulting massive outflows of short-term funds meant that despite budget and trade surpluses and low inflation, the affected Asian economies faced domestic credit crises that threatened to produce recessions and destroy otherwise sound businesses' (2000, 134). The apparent 'success' of capital's penetration quickly revealed its downside:

> Foreign capital, regarded as the strategic factor in Thailand's model of development, had turned its back on the country, and with devastating effect. The same global financial markets that had rewarded Thailand with billions of dollars worth of capital when the mood about the country's prospects was upbeat now reacted in herdlike fashion to negative assessments, behaving in a manner that radically worsened the situation, as the baht went on a freefall and the stock market plunged to a record low. As Stanley Fischer, [then] a deputy director of the IMF, was to put it later, after the Thai devaluation triggered the wider Asian financial crisis: 'Markets are not always right. Sometimes inflows are excessive, and sometimes they may be sustained too long. Markets tend to react fast, sometimes excessively'.
>
> (Bello *et al.* 1998, 36)

The agency of the market, its personification, is a long-standing conceit within economic discourse. In Fischer's statement we find a rhetorical shrug of the shoulders in response to this miscalculating 'market' and its errant machinations. Because the 'excessive' behavior of markets spurred the financial crisis in East and Southeast Asia, and because, consequently, the banking systems of these countries were starved of the foreign funds necessary to finance business and trade, the IMF was able to intervene aggressively into the economic affairs of the region. Market 'excess' thus provided the opportunity for profound deregulation of markets. Fischer's characterization of undisciplined 'excess' reveals his endorsement, finally, of the 'free-market' processes that ruined the Thai economy. The 'excess', whose effects on workers Fischer does not address, then seeps back into the IMF repressed, where it awaits another economic collapse to make it visible.

Since the currency, stock, and real estate market collapses made private lenders reluctant to loan money to businesses in the region, the IMF was the only significant source of funds to prevent complete economic collapse. The IMF used its leverage to press economic reform programs on the affected governments, in particular, Thailand. The IMF then explained that '. . . the centerpiece of the Asian programs has been the comprehensive reform of the financial systems' (IMF 1999a). The financial system reforms included closing bankrupt financial institutions, requiring local businesses to accept new (international) business partners in order to reduce debt, and increasing foreign ownership of domestic financial institutions and businesses.

The reforms thus opened the ailing Thai economy to further penetration by foreign capital. In the IMF fable, the abstraction of 'the financial systems' elides both the agents who make the decisions in and for those systems, and the workers whose labor provides the capital that drives them. In 'reforming' the systems, the Thai government abided by IMF prescriptions and hoped for the progress that the fable promises. The accommodation has its costs, but those costs are displaced. As Marx noted,

> Capital, which has such 'good reasons' for denying the sufferings of the legions of workers surrounding it, allows its actual movement to be determined as much and as little by the sight of the coming degradation and the final depopulation of the human race, as by the probable fall of the earth into the sun. In every stock-jobbing swindle everyone knows that some time or other the crash must come, but everyone hopes that it will fall on the head of his neighbour, after he himself has caught the shower of gold and placed it in secure hands . . .
>
> (Marx 1977, 381)

After the crash came, Camdessus hypocritically proclaimed that the Fund could have saved Thailand if only Thailand had implemented what the IMF calls 'second generation reforms', reforms such as 'transparency, good governance, and an emphasis on the quality of fiscal adjustment'. He goes on to lament: 'Alas, the world as a whole could not implement that agenda soon enough to help prevent the succession of crises that began in Thailand in mid-1997' (IMF 1999d). But, according to Walden Bello, Thailand had comported with IMF guidelines, especially the 'liberalization of the financial sector'. Bello argues that 'By the early 1990's . . . strong pressures for deregulation and liberalization were coming from the World Bank and the IMF, as well as from foreign financial institutions . . . which . . . wanted to engage in . . . a domestic market with great potential' (Bello *et al.* 1998, 19). Directly contradicting Camdessus's misrepresentation of Thailand's national failure to comply with IMF demands, Bello *et al.* reveal that by 1997 'the Fund was apparently beginning to rewrite history, saying it had strongly warned the Thai authorities all along about a developing crisis' (45).

As Harvard economist Jeffrey Sachs commented, 'the IMF arrived in Thailand in July with ostentatious declarations that all was wrong and that fundamental surgery was needed' although 'the ink was not even dry on the IMF's 1997 annual report, which gave Thailand and its neighbors high marks on economic management' (quoted in Bello *et al.* 1998: 45). Nobel Prize Winner, former Chief Economist at the World Bank, and famous free-market apostate Joseph Stiglitz confirms in his recent book that 'IMF policies not only exacerbated the downturns but were partially responsible for the onset: excessive rapid financial and capital market liberalization was probably the single most important cause of the crisis' (Stiglitz 2002, 89).

Stiglitz's, Sachs's, and Bello's comments demonstrate that the consequences of capital's penetration are the deeply repressed, uncanny effects that the IMF history wishes to obfuscate. These effects, however, emerge not only in the IMF's haunted stories of 'failed' implementations; they should be read, as well, on and in the bodies of the people whose lives are testimony to the effects of IMF reform programs and the implications of capitalist investment, production, and exploitation.

Recitation III

Lawrence Chua's novel most imaginatively and persuasively rewrites IMF versions of reality by tracing the historical trajectory of this exploitation. For Chua; all these processes, occluded in the IMF fable, work through bodies, displaced and constantly moving:

> Subsistence became poverty, greed became ambition. Your great-grandparents became a resource. They learned to understand their bodies as prospects, dependent on an unquenchable commerce, dominated by foreign desires. Desires that never reach the limits of necessity.
> (Chua 1998: 18)

Chua astutely redeploys Western rhetorics of economic development – especially those imbued with the aura of 'modernity' and 'progress' – as he reveals the initial steps in capitalist exploitation, the dispossession and migration of people caused by the commercialization of agriculture. This process is, in effect, the creation of laboring bodies as commodities. Anthropologist Aihwa Ong's 1987 study of female factory workers in Malaysia resonates with Chua's story; she observes that several of the elements produced by IMF policy imperatives produce shrinking numbers of landholders and farm workers. Ong notes that

> Government statistics show that since 1957, rural Malays have progressively lost their land at the rate of about 10,000 families each year. . . . The centerpiece of this *pembangunan* [development] program was 'export-oriented industrialization' as the combined solution to basic

> problems of landlessness, rural underemployment, and growing political
> disaffection as outmigration by young Malays increased.
>
> (Ong 1987, 143)

Ong argues as well that 'as the father's farm income steadily declines, unemployed brothers accept doles from working sisters, and the household budget derives increasingly from female wages' (108). Both Chua's and Ong's narratives place living bodies at the center of these transformations, and they make specific and visible the consequences of capitalist transformation of agriculture, reallocation of human and natural resources to industry, and IMF disciplinary policies.

Capitalist discipline, as promulgated by the IMF, has a protocol, and each step requires additional transformations of the bodies of workers. Once displaced from village life and farm work, the workers are forced to migrate, looking for a means to survive. Ong and Chua emphasize the ways in which this discipline shapes the prospects and the physical dispositions of the young women forced from their family homes. Ong, for example, notes that 'the recruitment of these women for industrial work was not a problem because of their relative oversupply and the eagerness of peasants, village elders, and local institutions to send otherwise noncash earning village women to the FTZ' (Ong 1987, 153).

The women thus become the providers for two 'hungers': the hunger of the families that can no longer work the land they have lost and the hunger of capital, which requires laboring bodies to produce profits. Chua places this phenomenon in its historical context: 'Perhaps you can trace your origins to this tide: promiscuous migrants crossing rivers of piss and concrete, imported to form an impotent working class. A class outside. A class with no stakes in the land they worked. . . . If people no longer grow rice, they need to buy it. Somebody has to go out and get a job in the new ascendant economy' (Chua 1998, 18). As workers leave the countryside and arrive in the cities, they begin the transformation required to enter directly into capitalist relations. In Thailand, the crowds of displaced workers commenced this transformation the moment they debarked from the trains:

> A very familiar sight during this period was trains coming into Bangkok's Hualumpong train station disgorging hundreds of people fresh from Isan, who were met by labour recruiters or found themselves looking at railway station advertisements promising attractive job placements . . .
> (Bello et al. 1998, 78–9). [. . .]

The employment announcements in Hualumpong Station represent the local version of the IMF fable. As soon as Isan's migrants become Bangkok's workers, they enter into a process that radically redefines their bodies and minds. This transformation marks their physical and spiritual possession by capitalist exploitation, the 'hungry ghost' which will then devour them. As Bello notes 'eleven young workers at the Lamphun industrial estate . . . died suddenly and mysteriously in 1993 and '94, along with two child dependents'. Although the government wished to attribute the deaths to AIDS-related illnesses, it was clear that the deaths resulted from occupational hazards (Bello et al. 1998, 83). These job-induced illnesses produce a haunting image of life mysteriously disappearing without visible or acknowledged cause. The image resonates with the IMF's attempts – here colluded by the Thai government – to deny the effects of rampant capitalist exploitation on the workers' bodies.

Moreover, this 'new ascendant economy' needs not only bodies, but bodies with specific qualities. The process of exploitation intensifies, then, with employment of workers who best satisfy capital's needs. Out of the pool of displaced villagers, one group seems 'ideal'; as Bello *et al.* note,

> Factory owners and management are well aware that the majority of the workers are young, poor, uneducated women from the rural areas of Thailand. They exploit the fact that due to cultural and economic circumstances these young women are more submissive and compliant than men. Studies show that because of their obligations to their families and lack of economic alternatives, poor, uneducated women are more willing to endure poor working conditions, and to do tedious work for lower wages.
>
> (Bello *et al.* 1998, 81–82)

Spivak's discussion of 'gender training' contextualizes and amplifies the phenomenon of the Thai female factory worker. IMF development discourse specifies that in a market economy female workers have a choice. If they really do experience themselves as 'the obviously suffering woman on the factory floor', then, if financial markets are sufficiently liberalized, they can choose, instead, to become 'the female client of microcredit' (Spivak 2000, 41). Thus, 'gender training' teaches women to see themselves as stakeholders with a choice and a voice in the 'free' markets of their rapidly globalizing economies. The gender training tale elides the conditions in which many of the 'trained' women would still find themselves: with no change in the capitalist processes and institutions that constrain their experiences, actions, and choices. Their 'freedom' – here, again, a powerful figure within modernity – figures their entrance into capitalist processes as other-than-worker (but not nearly as a capitalist), a position whose meaning is almost illegible.

With 'gender training', capitalism produces a different kind of worker whose labor is hidden under the guise of a nominal ownership, an ownership whose value to capital is a new form of subjectship. That is, laboring women in the developing countries enter into these more recent manifestations of capitalist processes with a psychic investment in themselves as individuals who can be 'connected in [their] thinking to what [they] perceive to be the great regulative structures of world in history, space in time, and vice versa' (Spivak 2000, 41).

So the conditions for exploitation are constituted by many varied and interlinked cultural, political, and economic processes: these include not only the lost means of support in the agricultural sector and a forced migration to urban areas but also a prevailing social organization of gender that makes young women especially vulnerable. Factory owners recognized these elements and then drew on them to craft a model worker according to their specific job requirements. For example, in Malaysian micromachinery plants,

> management's definition of semiskilled operations as biologically suited to 'the oriental girl' in effect required Malay peasant women to adopt . . . 'feminine' traits. A Malaysian investment brochure provided the

> blurb: 'her hands are small and she works fast with extreme care. Who, therefore, could be better qualified by *nature and inheritance* to contribute to the efficiency of a bench assembly production line than the oriental girl?'
>
> (Ong 1987, 152)

Both financiers and factory owners deployed mutually reinforcing tales to 'offer to *sight*' to the female workers a version of themselves as feminine bodies explicitly aligned with capital's needs. Under such conditions, the female workers must come to see themselves through the mirror of capital's imperatives.

Although these specified 'feminine traits' may never have been part of rural life, some newly 'modernized', urbanized women began to adapt themselves to their new positions by believing in the recast gender roles. As Ong notes, this adaptation was nothing less than 'a reorganization of Malay workers' understanding of socio-cultural change' (ibid., 149). She details the pernicious nexus of certain traditional values – especially, patriarchal values – capitalist imperatives, and almost absolute vulnerability that entraps the women:

> corporations, by reworking indigenous institutions of familial and village cooperation into production relations, have socialized rural Malay women as an industrial labor force in ways which won the approval and implicit cooperation of rural society. Furthermore, the induced docility of factory women sprang from a practical assessment of their insecure position within the labor market and their powerlessness to change it.
>
> (ibid., 187)

The adaptation is complete when the workers internalize the sense that they cannot go home again. Ong describes this step in capitalist transformation by noting that 'Since many can no longer adjust to *kampung* [village] life, factory jobs have become one of the few means of cash earning for female migrants, especially divorcees with children to support' (ibid., 148). As the women adapt their bodies to the rigors of manufacturing work, they become objects open to further transformations.

'*Hantu* are the memories that cannot yet be bought' (Chua 1998, 96)

The IMF's fable, and the disciplines that emerge from it, are the shaping fantasies of international capital, but these fantasies, as we have seen, produce material effects. Workers in Malaysia and Thailand are transformed by capitalist practices enforced by IMF 'reform' programs. In that process of transformation and fabrication, from dispossession to migrancy to refashioning an 'oriental girl' laborer, workers become food for the 'hungry ghost' of transnational capital. But our ghost story of development and discipline produces many specters, some as surprisingly real as any 'real' constructed by IMF recitations. In this tale, the workers counter the conditions of their own exploitation, the ghost that the IMF will not acknowledge, by finding ghosts in the precise location and time of their exploitation. So, Chua writes,

August 10, 1990 – A Penang-based American microelectronics factory had to be shut down for the third day in a row today due to women claiming they were possessed by spirits. . . . It is common belief that the factory is kotor *and supposed to be haunted by a* datuk.

(Chua 1998, 97)

In the newly constituted FTZs where 'the assembly line . . . takes its cue from the souls that feed it', (94) reform and readjustment programs that demand physical and psychological transformations in its workers have uncanny side effects. Factory workers both experience and reimagine these transformations in language and imagery that explains their exploitation and suffering. Ghosts appear, *hantu, datuk,* figures that explain the pain and exhaustion of their daily labor. Because more conventional means of resistance are foreclosed to them by law and custom, the women express themselves through spirit-possession to counter the conditions of their exploitation.

Notably, this expression takes on a collective agency, as when an entire factory shuts down because the workers declare that it is haunted. Spivak reads this phenomenon in gendered terms that clearly apply to the Malaysian workers:

(Women's) resistance of this sort is the irony of globalization. . . . It is the name of the move by which the collectivity of the chorus in Attic comedy moves up, again and again, to interrupt the seemingly coherent dramatic *praxis* . . . to inform the public of a structurally different interpretation of the 'same' action.

(Spivak 2000, 42)

Ong, citing Michael Taussig, argues that 'the *hantu* (evil spirit) . . . becomes "an image which mediates the conflict between [non] capitalist and capitalist modes of objectifying the human condition" ' (1). But, as Spivak's formulation makes clear, the *hantu* is not so much a mediation as a dramatic – and collective – mark of 'subjectship'. The symbolic systems that secure the conditions in the factory – the language of capital, the 'letters of blood and fire' – are recognized in the ferocious imagery of the demonic *hantu,* the imagistic field on which the workers' physical and psychological conflicts play out.

Chua portrays this conflict through the novel's character Martina, who is employed in one of the Penang FTZ electronics factories. Martina's words and experiences dramatize the processes of exploitation and the women's responses to it:

In the networks at Martina's fingertips, everything can now be regulated. Observed and controlled in a way that life in the forest never was . . . *It's not a bad life, you know. I'm earning my keep now. I feel like an adult. But that factory. Something is not right . . . The women say they saw* hantu. . . . A spirit moves easily through the walls, across borders . . . These spirits live in places that mark the boundary between human and natural worlds.

(Chua 1998, 94–95)

The Penang factory workers in Chua's novel account for the 'hungry ghost' that inhabits their bodies, the ghost of capitalist exploitation that feeds off their labor, by naming it 'hantu'. It is this imaging of – this seeing and believing in – exploitation that the IMF seeks to repress, and it is a figure that has haunted capital at least since Marx imagined its parasitic function: 'Capital is dead labour which, vampire-like, lives only by sucking living labour, and lives the more, the more it sucks' (Marx 1977, 342). In the IMF's contorted rhetoric, however, worker exploitation occurs only in the most benighted countries, those not complying with 'the core standards [that] form a set of principles with which most reasonable people would find it easy to agree', as Stanley Fischer states (IMF 1999e).

In his thoroughly Western code of modernity, Fischer rejects what he deems to be irrationality; he might well argue that 'reasonable people' don't believe in ghosts, either. Yet the easy agreement about 'core standards' cannot be found in the factories of the FTZ. There, workers struggle to construct a new version of themselves, as something other than the objects of capital: laboring under conditions over which they have no say, producing products they do not own and cannot use, and suffering for profits they cannot control. Chua aptly depicts the contradictions and confusions that arise from the net of coercion and powerlessness in Martina's eagerness to see herself as a fully rendered human:

> Labor allows her to know herself, to know subjugation and alienation. Without labor, the native is just an unprofitable element in the fabric of the empire. . . . The native becomes neither human nor machine, but both. . . .
>   *– You know, I don't love this job, but that paycheck makes me feel more human.* She sighs.
>   *– But what is human these days, anyway?*
>
> (Chua 1998, 97–98)

That is the question, after all, at the heart of the ghost story. It is by seeing, and then *interpreting* the ghost that the human subject more fully understands the conditions in which she lives and works; if the ghost is nonhuman, she is human. But this is a process that requires more than individuated or atomized expression in order to be critical and valuable. When Chua's Martina relates her paycheck to her humanity, she sees herself as a discrete element, alienated, and alone. Similarly, Ong's reading of spirit possessions, the ghosts in the factories, reiterates this version of the individual worker seeking a moment of transcendence. For Ong 'the *hantu* symbolism, shifting in and out of their consciousness, spoke not of an ideology of class struggle but of the right to be treated *as human beings*. Spirit attacks were indirect retaliations against coercion and demands for justice in personal terms within the industrial milieu' (Ong 1987: 220).

When a worker is transformed by capitalist disciplines, however, the paycheck allows the 'person' to exist only under terms set by capital; the ghosts in the factories are the *field* of exploitation. The means to interpret this ghost, to name and, perhaps, to struggle over its effects, are available in language that is centuries-old, the 'letters of blood and fire', but also in the symbolic systems of cultures that have emerged from colonial into post-colonial organization. For Martina, and for the workers in the FTZs and 'newly ascendant' economies of Southeast Asia, exorcism begins with a collective struggle to recognize their 'subjectship' as the IMF attempts to annihilate it, to refashion it into subjection.

This is the story that the IMF is deathly afraid of, the story that has haunted capitalism from its inception. The Fund enthusiastically recites the most aggressive conditions for capital's profitability but simultaneously refuses to acknowledge the extent to which those conditions promote extreme exploitation without compensating benefits, and consequently, produces extreme suffering of laboring bodies in Asia. In effect, the IMF recites the brutal conditions of nineteenth-century European capitalism and, ironically, resuscitates images invoked by Marx to condemn capital's voracious consumption of worker's bodies to satisfy its lust for profit. Thus, the specter Marx names is now resurrected by the depredation of Asia's laboring bodies and cannot be reinterred by IMF rhetoric alone.

Stanley Fischer, in a rare revelatory statement, noted that 'Globalization can create losers as well as winners. And it is human nature that those who lose will be more vocal than those who gain' (IMF 1999c). In effect, his reply to the 'losers' is that capital really doesn't require worker exploitation: 'So long as competition forces companies to be as efficient as possible, strong labor standards should emerge naturally through enlightened self-interest'. Fischer's invocation of the natural processes of 'enlightened self-interest' barely disguises the fiction at the heart of IMF policies and their implementation. Marx exposed this hypocrisy more than one hundred years ago when he portrayed capitalist exploitation as an inexorable monster, a 'vampire' who will not let go 'while there remains a single muscle, sinew or drop of blood to be exploited' (Marx 1977, 416).

In contemporary Southeast Asia, the West's vampires mutate into *hantu* or *datuk*, figures embodying the culturally specific responses of a different set of workers. These demons devour labor as hungrily and pitilessly as ever Marx's vampires consumed the laboring classes of Europe. Chua's description of one of their victims, 'Ah Mah's ghost' gives the lie to the IMF's modernist, progressivist fable of development while it attests to the validity of Marx's metaphor: 'Undoing the organism. Her body falls away. No more flesh. No more organs. Only a language that is a litany of scars' (Marx 1977, 141) – a powerful language of struggle, of resistance, and of the (im)possible emergence of 'subjectship'.

Notes

1   Maintaining our emphasis on rhetorical figures, we use the concept of the 'uncanny' based on Freud's explanation that the uncanny exerts no influence in fairy tales because readers expect otherworldly events in that genre. However, 'wish-fulfillments, secret powers, omnipotence of thoughts' emerge as uncanny when the writer promises to supply a 'sober truth' and then oversteps it. Significantly, Freud concludes, 'We react to [the writer's] inventions as we would have reacted to real experiences; by the time we have seen through his trick it is already too late and the author has achieved his object. But it must be added that his success is not unalloyed. We retain a feeling of dissatisfaction, a kind of grudge against the attempted deceit' (Freud 1953)

2   Teochew (also Teochiu or Chaozhou) refers to the estimated five million people who are descendants of immigrants from the Chinese province of Guangdong. Thus, Chua's protagonist represents both a contemporary and historical displacement.

Chapter 28

Peter J. Kalliney

EAST AFRICAN LITERATURE AND THE POLITICS OF GLOBAL READING

From *Research in African Literatures* 39.1 (2008): 1–23.

IN *EMPIRE*, **MICHAEL HARDT AND ANTONIO NEGRI** argue that postcolonial theory has reached an impasse because it fails to grasp, much less adequately critique, the emerging system of world sovereignty commonly called globalization. Most accounts of the postcolonial ignore the fact that 'Empire', as they call it, 'is not a weak echo of modern imperialisms but a fundamentally new form of rule'. Because postcolonial theory continues to analyze and contest imperialist forms of power, which have been substantially reconfigured or discarded in our global times, it tends to offer 'a very confused view' of postimperial geopolitics; while its practitioners continue pointing to hybridity as a strategy of resistance, the forces of global power have happily incorporated the celebration of cultural difference into new disciplinary structures. As a consequence, the leading practitioners of post-colonial theory 'remain fixated on attacking an old form of power and propose a strategy of liberation that could be effective only on that old terrain'. It remains a 'very productive tool for rereading history, but it is entirely insufficient for theorizing contemporary global power' (146). In their estimation, postcolonial theory is something from which scholars of globalization can learn, but recent political and economic developments have left postcolonial studies unprepared to assess the political contradictions of our current world.

Postcolonialists have offered a surprisingly muted reply, effectively ceding the discourse of contemporary world politics and culture to critics of globalization. Postcolonialism is rapidly becoming a historical discipline, with many of its prominent figures, far from mounting a counterattack, gladly joining forces with Hardt, Negri, and the growing legion of transnational theorists. Social scientists have been theorizing the declining political and economic sovereignty of the nation-state for almost twenty years, but such thinking has recently become widespread in the humanistic disciplines, too. In literary studies, for example, Amtiva Kumar recently proposed the heuristic 'World Bank Literature' as an alternative, implying that the rubric 'postcolonial' does not sufficiently register the impact of relatively new, supranational organizations such as the World Bank and the International Monetary Fund [Kumar 1999; 2003]. Anthony Appiah, Wai Chee Dimock, Andreas Huyssen, Fredric Jameson, and Gayatri Spivak, in addition to hundreds of less prominent intellectuals in the humanities, have all contributed to ongoing debates about the cultural and philosophical ramifications of globalization.

An important consequence of this transition is the way we now think about the 'history' of globalization as a material process and as a critical practice. Many scholars working on globalization now prefer to think of imperialism as an undeveloped form of economic, political, and juridical power, a kind of immature form of globality. As Immanuel Wallerstein summarizes, from about 1750, there 'began a process of steady incorporation of Africa into the capitalist world-economy whose first stage was that of informal empire and whose second stage was that of colonial rule'. According to Wallerstein, one of the earliest and most influential theorists of globalization, Africa was once outside the world-capitalist system, which originated in Europe and gradually enlarged its sphere of influence through the creation of formal empires. Decolonization in the African continent, however, did not suspend its incorporation in the world-capitalist system, but instead signaled 'the completion of this historic process' whereby the entire globe is brought under one economic regime ([2000,] 62). In this light, nationalist independence move-ments in Africa and the colonized world actually hastened the complete immersion of the continent in the globalized capitalist economy. As Mohammed Bamyeh puts it, '[C]apitalism no longer needs the support and tutelage of an imperialist state' (64). In these accounts and many others, unfettered capitalism (originating in Western Europe and purified by the United States) systematically envelops the entire world, first through direct political domination, but now increasingly through indirect forms of coercion and control. [. . .]

Hardt and Negri have extended this historical narrative by transforming post-colonial theory into an intellectual precursor of sorts, a lower order of analysis that ought to give way to more contemporary and sophisticated accounts of world politics. Postcolonialist interpretations of political inequity, they argue, 'fail to recognize adequately the contemporary object of critique'. Whereas an earlier generation of anticolonial writers, such as Aimé Césaire and Frantz Fanon, provide valuable diagnoses of 'modern' sovereignty during the age of imperialist rule, post-colonial theorists of more recent vintage 'mistake today's real enemy' (137). Thinkers such as Homi Bhabha, and even Edward Said, respond to the now-defunct world of 'modern' sovereignty, a world of Manichean binaries (colonizer v. colon-ized, white v. black) that no longer exists. Though Hardt and Negri freely acknow-ledge their debt to anticolonial thinkers, they are far more suspicious of postcolonial theory's ability to generate accurate accounts of the contemporary environment because its practitioners remain fixated on outdated forms of political organization.

Because the word globalization conjoins several distinct, perhaps incompatible, meanings – the term refers to a 'real', historical process as well as a branch of academic inquiry and critique, especially the critique of global capital – the utility of the term is far from straightforward. The usefulness of the concept is even less transparent in the context of literary studies, where the languages of and literatures written in Arabic, English, French, and Swahili, as Africanists are well aware, have been transnational for quite some time. In this essay, I use M. G. Vassanji's first novel, *The Gunny Sack* (1989), to pose a series of questions about the status of narrative, both fictional and academic, in an age of global cultural production. The novel traces four generations of a South Asian family who migrate from the west coast of India to East Africa in the late-nineteenth century, travel and work throughout Tanzania, the coastal islands, and Kenya during the colonial period, before eventually making their way to North America after Tanzanian independence. The novel's story of international migration allows us to complicate recent academic accounts of globalization and to question the compatibility of postcolonial theory and scholarly accounts of globalization. By considering the implications of recent work on transnationalism for the study of marginalized, hybrid literary traditions, I want to revisit some of the fundamental premises of globalization theory as well as reflect on the cultural conditions in which postcolonial fiction participates in the emerging field of global culture.

Although leading proponents of globalization theory, such as Wallerstein, Saskia Sassen, Anthony King, David Harvey, Anthony Giddens, and Arjun [Appadurai], in addition to Hardt and Negri, represent a wide range of disciplinary concerns, critical approaches, and political commitments, their work can mobilize a surprisingly rigid and teleological historical explanation of globalization.[1] I have already outlined a skeletal version of this narrative: first comes European imperialism, then independence movements and so-called Third World nationalisms, followed by the collapse of the Soviet empire and the creation of truly global economic, political, and cultural systems. At the most basic level, postcolonial scholars should be wary of this narrative of globalization because it privileges the moment of European exploration and imperial conquest as the originary site of a transnational polity. Instead, I will be using *The Gunny Sack* to offer a slightly less schematic account of globalization, to think of Indian Ocean traffic as an alternative, precolonial site of transnational contact. East Africa is an ideal site to perform this kind of cultural scholarship because it is at once historically and manifestly global – it has a long history of trade and migration throughout the Indian Ocean before and during the colonial period – and also marginal within the auspices of North American academy – East Africa is one of the places that literary theory attuned to globalization promises to open up for study.

My point, then, is not to label globalization theorists Eurocentric or sloppy scholars, but to use this as an opportunity to reflect on the ways that we produce, circulate, and attach value to critical models and systems of knowledge. Bringing academic accounts of globalization into dialogue with novels like *The Gunny Sack* may create a space wherein scholars can make transparent their narrative politics. My technique for clearing this space is to reverse the orientation of our reading practices, to use fictional narrative as a tool that can reveal the blind spots of our theoretical apparatus by subjecting this historical narrative to more scrutiny. Offering this engagement with globalization theory from the discursive position of postcolonial studies makes a good deal of sense because one of postcolonial theory's outstanding legacies is a sophisticated understanding of narrative in historical context and as a political instrument.

My key term for critiquing globalization theory's narrative of world history is ambivalence, one of the most useful analytic concepts of postcolonial studies. Globalization theory's understanding of political, economic, and cultural progress is deeply ambivalent about, and even haunted by, its own story of historical evolution. Hardt and Negri's explicit desire to supercede postcolonial theory depends on turning the moment of European imperialism into an immature or nascent form of global sovereignty – a system that leads ineluctably to the world capitalism of today. By ceding a formative place to European imperialism in the narrative of globalization, however, transnational theory has a tendency to grant imperialism a narrative coherence and perdurability it never attained on its own terms. Just as narratives of imperial conquest and domination are always overdetermined by the specter of the colonial subject – often figured as primitive or the pre-modern – so too are globalization's narratives haunted by an immature, imperial system of power. Such narrative gestures, in other words, reduce our ability to imagine contingencies or contemplate scenarios in which European imperialism, and later globalization, do not emerge as preordained winners of various political and cultural contests.

So my first series of questions is premised on reading fiction as a theoretical model and reading theory as a sort of fictional or narrative enterprise. Rather than use globalization theory to interpret *The Gunny Sack* as another example of international contact and exchange, I use this novel to query the assumptions of transnational scholarship. In the second part of this paper, I will reverse the terms of the analysis yet again by thinking about the narrative pleasures made available through postcolonial stories of migration and travel. Like many such novels, *The Gunny Sack* is a tale of dispossession, marginality, hybridity, and mobility, all of which now form important tropes in the postcolonial cultural imagination. Similar in technique to texts like Tayeb Salih's *Season of Migration to the North*, Salman Rushdie's *The Satanic Verses*, or, more recently, Zadie Smith's *White Teeth*, *The Gunny Sack* tries to imagine political subjectivity through narratives in and of transit. Although these novels recognize the traumas associated with migrations, both voluntary and forced, they also try to recuperate a sense of agency in the experience of cultural dislocation. The parameters of *The Gunny Sack*'s narrative are determined by a productive ambivalence towards mobility and migration: the text is simultaneously invested in recording a communal history of loss, trauma, and dispossession, yet it is also careful to resist the allure of simple nostalgia steeped in nationalist tropes.

These are exactly the kinds of narratives that scholars interested in both postcolonial and postnational literatures now put in high esteem. We might say that the novel becomes legible in the field of postcolonial studies by announcing its cultural portability and rehearsing the relative political subordination of its subjects in our current geopolitical climate. The novel becomes a locus of scholarly and pedagogical utility precisely through its circulation in global systems of reading and instruction that privilege narratives of migration, international transit, and marginality. In short, this text provides an opportunity to think about why we value these types of narratives: what sorts of needs do they satisfy, what pleasures do they make available to their audiences, and what kinds of knowledge do they help produce? The conjunction of globalization theory and postcolonial literary studies gives us special occasion to consider how we evaluate and appropriate narratives of physical displacement and cultural crossing. Because the most useful strains of globalization theory offer a critical vocabulary for considering systems of power and domination in our current geopolitical climate, its engagement with and critique of postcolonial studies may provide a language whereby literary scholars can be more self-reflexive about our research and teaching interests. Transnational theory, in other words, should allow postcolonial studies to do more than continue its calls for the inclusion of more noncanonical texts in our syllabi: ideally, it should allow us to situate our own intellectual communities and institutions in this new system of world power.

1

Before discussing the relationship between postcolonial studies and globalization theory, it might be useful to describe the novel in greater detail. The text's narrative device is very sophisticated, constructing a series of frames out of which it offers a fragmented, multilayered, asynchronous collection of stories about the Asian community in East Africa. The novel is set in the 1970s. The narrator has fled from Tanzania several years after independence, the text representing his attempt to recover the buried history of his family and the Asian community in East Africa. The narrator begins his composition after the death of his grand aunt, who bequeaths him an old gunny sack. The modest suitcase holds an assortment of trinkets from three continents and four generations. The objects themselves have little material value – cheap bead necklaces, broken rosaries, torn, faded photographs, account ledgers, a bloodstained muslin shirt, and an incense holder clamor for attention as the hapless narrator sifts through the bag's contents – but they acquire symbolic significance as he uses them as an occasion for the production of familial and communal history. Each object helps the narrator uncover a fragment of the family's murky past: the ledger book explains some of his ancestors' shady business deals, the broken rosaries recall the prayers and thanks for safe passage along the family's many journeys, while the bloodstained shirt prompts the narrator to recount the tale of his great-grandfather's violent murder.

Set predominantly in colonial East Africa, the text goes to some lengths to portray the region as an exhilarating and painful 'contact zone' for a wide range of people, languages, religions, ideas, and objects. Zanzibar functions as East Africa's New York City, a nodal point for trade and commerce, the place where dispossessed immigrants can make themselves anew. The narrator's great-grandfather, eager to make his fortune and forget his past by emigrating from India, unceremoniously drops his family name upon arriving in Africa, thereby erasing information about his village of origin and his social status. He immediately visits the local *mukhi* (community leader, with both religious and secular responsibilities), who finds him a place to live and gives him credit to begin work as a small-time trader. He acquires gum copal from the indigenous population, bartering with cloth, beads, wire, or the occasional gun, turning a small profit by reselling his acquisitions to larger Asian wholesalers.

This pattern of movement and commercial activity was being repeated all over East Africa during the precolonial and early colonial era. Before the arrival of the British and Germans in the late 1880s, there were thousands of Swahili, Omani, and South Asian merchants, financiers, and planters doing a brisk business along the east coast of Africa. Mainland Africa, the Arabian Peninsula, the west coast of India, and the Indian Ocean islands were part of a complex web of commerce and migration throughout the nineteenth century [. . .]. Like the mercantilist triangle trade in the Atlantic, the Indian Ocean was a site of robust international commerce that, unlike its more renowned counterpart, was less directly connected with Euro-imperial systems of authority. As the novel makes abundantly clear, such systems of trade were far from equitable, based largely on human trafficking, plantation slavery, and widespread violence. Entrepreneurial merchants – Arab, Asian, and Swahili – engaged highly disciplined, organized expeditions of porters to trek hundreds of miles to the interior to acquire slaves, gum, copra, rare skins, and ivory.

While slaves, indentured servants, porters, and sailors provided the bulk of physical labor for the Indian Ocean trade, it was the highly mobile Asian population who helped finance trading ventures as well as manage the extensive traffic in goods, people, and knowledge. Asian merchants, traders, and financiers were able to capitalize on their willingness to travel and their extremely portable commercial skills. They were also able to mobilize vast familial, communal, and religious networks to their advantage, creating significant trading leverage by combining their technical acumen with a truly global set of relationships. As *The Gunny Sack*'s narrator suggests, there has always been a *mukhi* to help newcomers get established wherever there existed a small community of Muslim South Asians: London, Singapore, Toronto, Port of Spain, and Dar es Salaam are part of an elaborate trading diaspora (10). But with this description, Vassanji also subtly reminds us that East Africa's Asians cannot be excused from the region's history of exploitation, and their later cooperation with British imperialism, simply because they were more involved in mercantile rather than political activities. Throughout the nineteenth century, the growing Asian population helped reconfigure East Africa's economy on the basis of travel and barter along the extensive caravan routes that went deep into the Congo and the Great Lakes region. The island of Zanzibar, and to a lesser extent, the coastal cities of Mombasa, Tanga, Bagamoyo, and Dar es Salaam, became the commercial center of this system of global exchange. Cloth, guns, agricultural equipment and skills, vehicles, labor, commercial and financial techniques, capital, language, and religious practices were all imported to the area in large quantities, while a comparable volume of raw materials, agricultural products, labor, and ideas were exported in return, with most of this traffic channeled through Zanzibar and the other coastal trading outposts.

It is worth emphasizing that this system of economic and cultural exchange began and flourished at least a century before the Germans and British brought European imperialism to the region. When Europeans did establish hegemony in East Africa, it was not the colonial authorities who brought new techniques of global commerce to the area, but the reverse. It was the Germans and British, in fact, who learned something about transnational exchange and governance by attempting to observe, control, and redirect the Indian Ocean trade routes. Moreover, they immediately placed Asians in the civil service and used them as labor recruiters and business liaisons. This was not simply because the colonial authorities needed a proverbial middle-man – the Germans were highly suspicious of placing British subjects in positions of authority – but also because Asians had more skills and knowledge about how to conduct business in the region. They had more practical information and resources at their disposal, and they also possessed various commercial skills which were otherwise in short supply. It was Africans, Arabs, and Asians, in other words, who were teaching the new imperialist powers something about the region's potential in the global marketplace. Historical evidence suggests that the new European powers had only limited success in their efforts to harness Indian Ocean trade. The British, for instance, never established effective trading connections with East Africa directly, relying instead on the less efficient

Zanzibar-Bombay-London route. The Germans, meanwhile, were so fixated on coastal plantations (most of which failed) that they virtually ignored other commercial opportunities. [. . .]

In an effort to capture the cultural diversity and incredible physical mobility of the intrepid Asian community in East Africa, *The Gunny Sack* offers a narrative of perpetual motion. Both political regimes and the family are in a state of constant transition, with the clan embarking on a series of regional and international migrations, sometimes to exploit business opportunities, sometimes to resolve family conflicts. For a novel that records the traumatic experiences of Asians in East Africa, culminating in their dispersion into the global diaspora, this novel is very unusual in that it reserves little nostalgia for either India or East Africa as a place of origin. Furthermore, the narrative makes a conscious effort not to insulate the story of East Africa's Asians from their participation in the region's history of violence and exploitation. The narrator is himself a descendant of a mixed union – his great-grandfather, before his legal marriage to an Indian woman, had a son with an indigenous woman – and our storyteller improbably elects to name himself after his mixed-race grandfather when he enrolls in school. As a young man, on national service in the wake of independence, he meets his one true love, Amina, who is black. Predictably, but not without regrets on both sides, the relationship falls apart rather quickly. Despite Tanzania's official doctrine of multiracial cooperation under Nyerere, their partnership dissolves under intense pressure from family and friends, both Indian and indigenous.

True to the novel's title, this is a narrative of packing and unpacking, of making do in situations that offer few easy choices. The gunny sack becomes a signpost for the family's resourcefulness, and really their participation in transnational systems of migration. They supplement the paucity of their material possessions and financial resources with technical knowledge, cultural capital, and sheer pluck – in other words, commercial skills and collective stories of transit are part of the luggage they take with them from place to place. The community's itinerant condition is a source of considerable sorrow and frustration, but it is also a point of pride, a mark of their ability to survive and even thrive in circumstances that would destroy a less hearty, tenacious group.[2]

Although the novel refuses to construct a stable essence at the heart of this community's narrative of displacement, it is equally sanguine about the costs associated with continual migration. The gunny sack is a reminder of the community's tenacity, but it is also a record of pain that most of the family hope to leave behind in Africa. When a cousin gives the narrator the gunny, he leaves it with a stern warning: 'It's brought nothing but bad luck, they say. They [the family] want you to burn it, once and for all to bury the past' (5). Admittedly, the painful memories it contains allow the narrator, a lonely refugee, to connect his wandering with the complicated itineraries of his predecessors. By the end of the novel, however, the narrator agrees that the family has too often used travel to avoid facing up to its problems:

> [T]he running must stop now [. . .]. The cycle of escape and rebirth, uprooting and regeneration, must cease in me. [. . .] Perhaps here lies redemption, a faith in the future, even if it means for now to embrace the banal present, to pick up the pieces of our wounded selves, [. . .]

because from our wounded selves flowers still grow. We had our dreams,
[. . .] we dreamt the world, which was large and beautiful and exciting,
and it came to us this world, even though it was more than we bargained
for, it came in large soaking waves and wrecked us, but we are thankful,
for to have dreamt was enough.

(268–69 [brackets by Kalliney])

The family's relative success as immigrants has proved both a curse and a blessing.
Each new destination offers the promise of stability, growth, and prosperity, and
most importantly, the hope of renewal. But each physical dislocation leaves a scar, a
psychological trauma that can be healed, but not erased, through a retelling of the
family archive. As a result, the novel retains a strong sense of ambivalence throughout, coupling each moment of celebration with a memory of past disappointments
and each instance of despair with a reminder of past resurrections.

Ironically, it is the memory of an earlier global condition that gives the narrator
the strength and the knowledge to cope with his own and the community's most
recent journeys. When the narrator claims that it was enough to have 'dreamt the
world', he does not refer simply to the contemporary global situation, marked
by political turbulence and mass emigration, but to the quite different history of
transnationalism in the Indian Ocean. Those first migrations, we realize, were
largely voluntary for the East African Asians; the most recent travels are the result of
expulsions and hasty, forced departures. His family archive and his collection of
narratives about the transnational communities throughout the Indian Ocean form a
cultural resource out of which the narrator tries to make sense of his most recent
migration to North America. The novel rejects more conventional styles of nostalgia, which often privilege a place or a moment as an ideal which has been
subsequently corrupted or destroyed, usually by forces beyond its own control. In
fact, this novel does precisely the opposite: when it celebrates the past, it goes out of
its way to emphasize the South Asian community's diasporic hybridity rather than
invoke myths of pure, unadulterated origins.[3] *The Gunny Sack*'s moments of nostalgia
invoke a previous global moment in which the exchange of language, religion, ideas,
and material goods was subtended by its own set of contradictions, but was relatively
free from direct Euro-imperial control.

Rather than imagine East Africa or India as a place of stable, nostalgic origins,
the novel treats East Africa as a site of memory, a node of material, social, and
cultural traffic. What is important is not the place itself in some abstract or reductive
way, but its ability to function as a medium of exchange and a point through which
a wide range of people, goods, and knowledge could circulate. The novel is a
profound attempt to demonstrate how our current global imagination is indebted to
and embedded in earlier, marginalized legacies of transnational exchange and transit.
It offers a subtle reminder that European imperialism and capitalism impose their
own set of spatial limits – boundaries that may inhibit both conquerors and con-
quered, albeit in different ways. Frederick Cooper, one of the few postcolonial
scholars to critique the academic discourse of globalization on these historical
grounds, offers exactly this observation when he reminds us that '[c]olonial conquests
imposed territorial borders on long-distance trading networks within Africa and
monopolies on what was then a growing external trade, damaging or destroying
more articulated trading systems crossing the Indian Ocean and the Sahara desert

and along the West African coast' ([2001], 205, [brackets by Kalliney]). Cooper's insight is not simply that people in Africa were sophisticated traders, like their European counterparts. His perspective reminds us that the historical narratives attached to the current discourse of globalization tend to deemphasize European imperialism's internal and external limits: the places it could and could not conquer, the practices it could and could not assimilate, the possibilities it could and could not imagine.

The Gunny Sack also rejects the premise that colonialism was the first stage in creating our global consciousness. If anything, imperialism absorbed and then suppressed this alternative historical narrative of transnationalism, and it was imperialism, too, that created the political conditions responsible for the exodus of Asians from East Africa. I am here suggesting that postcolonial scholars should be suspicious of teleological narratives of globalization because they do not have the historical complexity that postcolonial theory has been championing for the last twenty years. We should not read imperialism as a lower stage or first step in globalization's evolutionary ladder; imperialism, in the context of the Indian Ocean, is something that disrupted the types of 'development' implied by many historical narratives of transnationalism. To return to Cooper's critique, much transnational theory does not allow us to 'watch history unfold over time, producing dead ends as well as pathways leading somewhere, creating conditions and contingencies in which actors make decisions, mobilized other people, and took actions which both opened up and constrained future possibilities' ([2001], 205). The novel's recovery of this other global history is a rejection not only of imperial narratives of conquest, but also of current narratives of globalization that rely on imperial systems of historical knowledge.[4] Foregrounding contingencies and conflicts in the history of empires, past and present, may better equip us for understanding the contemporary world and the range of responses at our disposal.

When globalization theorists, such as Hardt and Negri, criticize postcolonial theory for its strategic celebration of cultural hybridity and of the transgressive or disruptive potential of postcolonial migrations – when they argue, for instance, that multinational capital has now outflanked such theoretical interventions, becoming highly mobile and disaggregated itself – their critique overlooks the fact that the best discussions of cultural hybridity in postcolonial studies are underwritten by an explication of narrative ambivalence. The argument that the experience of imperialism or colonialism gets articulated primarily as a contradictory, ambivalent condition – a situation born of conflict – is one of the foundations of postcolonial theory. To cite a few prominent examples: in *Orientalism*, for instance, Edward Said contends that imperial structures of authority are premised on a hierarchical, but also deeply interdependent, set of relations between European imperialists and their colonial counterparts. The object of his analysis, moreover, is not simply a system of power, but the set of representational strategies inseparable from the functions of rule. The consolidation of such political power, in other words, cannot be separated from the narrative transactions that support and contest its application. Gayatri Spivak's *Critique of Postcolonial Reason*, with its analysis of the 'native informant' and its plea for 'transnational literacy' alluding to globalization itself, begins with the premise that postcoloniality is an 'impure', hybrid system of thought. Recent debates about Englishness and metropolitan responses to imperialism, likewise, tend to emphasize the contradictory role of overseas expansion in the discourse of

metropolitan identity, arguing that a simultaneous, paradoxical embrace and dis-
avowal of imperialism has been at the heart of narratives about the meaning of
English national culture (see Gikandi 1996; Baucom 1999; or Esty 2004).

As *The Gunny Sack* and other migration tales suggest, ambivalence is an
indispensable analytic concept for theorizing the politics of narrative in postcolonial
texts. The postcolonial discussion of cultural hybridity is not only useful for its
ability to complicate the rigid distinctions between metropole and colony, center
and periphery, but also for its ability to decipher the political utility of narrating
collective trauma and displacement. More than a naive celebration of hybridity
for its liberatory potential – which Hardt and Negri (as well as others) rightly
criticize for its latent elitism – postcolonial discussions of this nature are valuable
as reading strategies, as ways to understand the investments and anxieties of specific narrative constructions. Globalization theory, despite offering a sophisticated
grammar for diagramming world systems of power, has yet to develop a compelling
set of new hermeneutic principles designed to interpret the political imagination of
narrative.[5] By contrast, this recognition of ambivalence as a constitutive narrative
condition of so many imperial and postcolonial texts – fictional, historical, and even
archival – is one of the enduring qualities of postcolonial theory.

Globalization theory, it is important to note, is itself quite ambivalent – often in
highly productive, provocative ways – toward the object of its own critical practice.
Should we celebrate the imminent demise of the nation-state, or is the new regime
of world power simply a more insidious form of juridical and economic control?
Are national or regional political structures something in which we can seek refuge
from the tyranny of the global, or is the national a type of repression best left
behind? This debate, which has adherents on both sides, reflects anxieties about
globalization's narrative of historical progress. Just as discursive constructions of
imperial power tend to betray significant ambivalences toward their putative objectives, so too is globalization's narrative of history conditioned by a kind of reflexive
consideration of its other, figured as the systems of culture and politics we have
reportedly left behind (consigning the imperial and national as nascent articulations
of globality). As a theoretical engagement with imperialism and nationalism, then,
postcolonial studies figures as a primitive haunting that globalization hopes to banish
through a series of argumentative exorcisms.

This ambivalent repudiation of postcolonial theory as an inadequate, but
instructive, diagnosis of the contemporary world is not a bad thing in and of itself.
My contention, rather, is that globalization theory thereby grants imperialism a
degree of consistency and integrity that it may not, in fact, have earned on its
own terms. For students of literature, this retroactive attribution of coherence to
narratives of imperialism has serious consequences for the way we read texts as well
as situate them in an historical context of political struggle. This is not to say that
imperialism was not effective as a means of political rule and material exploitation.
But some of its most debilitating, interesting weaknesses, or contradictions, emerge
in its histories, archives, and narratives. Compromising this ability to read texts
contrapuntally is one of the consequences of accepting globalization theory's
implicit narrative of world history.

2

To this point in the essay, I have been reading *The Gunny Sack* as a kind of theoretical enterprise that offers us provocative insights into the cross-currents and counter-narratives of globalization. I have been arguing that practitioners of postcolonial studies should think twice before fully embracing the historical narratives upon which some transnational theory is built. The point is worth arguing, if only because many of the leading practitioners of postcolonial theory have yet to voice such critiques. By the same token, I do not want to dismiss recent work on globalization out of hand: there is a great deal that globalization theory can offer postcolonial studies. So in the second part of my paper, I want to reverse the terms of my analysis. If I have been offering a critique of transnational theory from the perspective of a more historically attentive postcolonial studies, I now want to think about the ways in which the study of transnational systems can challenge the working assumptions of literary and postcolonial studies.

To date, literary studies has used globalization theory primarily to bolster calls for an expansion of the canon, with the particular aim of making our syllabi more representative of other cultural traditions, especially those of non-Western provenance.[6] But this project, in spirit, is a continuation of the work done from the 1970s onwards by scholars associated with the new social movements: African-American, Native-American, Latino, Queer, and other cultural studies programs emphasizing minoritarian politics and traditions. As a provocative account of world systems of political power and cultural production, globalization theory may be most instructive for literary studies when we engage it to theorize how our own intellectual and institutional commitments inform our hermeneutic and pedagogical practices. The fact that calls to make higher education more culturally representative have come just as globalization entered a new, accelerated phase should prompt us to ask if there is a relationship between the two. Rather than adapt globalization theory to make a stronger case for the inclusion of more minority texts we might be better served by using it to analyze why such calls to make our work more representative seem particularly urgent at the present moment and why they continue to encounter resistance in some quarters. As I will argue, perhaps postcolonial studies is divided by its own set of internal contradictions and ambivalences. More specifically, I want to consider the impact of this novel on the field and how postcolonial studies, which has its own blind spots and hierarchies, has mobilized texts like *The Gunny Sack*. What do texts like this offer – why might they be valuable in the classroom and as objects of research? Towards the conclusion of this essay, I will consider the question of why this text has been marginalized even within the field of postcolonial studies: what aporias does the field have, and what might this tell us about how the discipline is organized?

Two aspects of globalization theory will be particularly relevant to the rest of my discussion. First, a working knowledge of transnational theory may help readers decipher *The Gunny Sack*'s representations of migration and displacement. Following the work of Arjun Appadurai, May Joseph, and others, I want to suggest that the novel's trajectory traces postnational circuits of desire – encapsulated by the novel's concluding reflection that it was enough 'to have dreamt the world'. More precisely, the text implies that postcolonial reading strategies, especially those that over-emphasize the prescriptive nature of the colonizer/colonized relationship, may be unable to fully account for the narrative's complex affiliations which stretch well beyond national boundaries. Stories of migration, particularly those that run outside the more familiar, two-way channels of imperial exchange, may force us to expand the scope of postcolonial theory. Second, a consideration of the global market for literary texts – and the transnational circulation of cultural capital – may help clarify how *The Gunny Sack* makes meaning in a global cultural context. Conventional literary historical categories – such as the division between British and American literatures – as well as the umbrella term postcolonial literature may be equally unsuited to the task of situating the pedagogical project of cultural inclusiveness. Or to state the matter more polemically, postcolonial studies – precisely because many of its practitioners are concerned with challenging established hierarchies within Anglo-American literary culture – may not offer us the best tools for decoding the narrative politics of novels such as *The Gunny Sack*.

I will start by mentioning two seemingly trivial facts about the text. First, this book has been out of print for several years in the United States and most of the world, although it was recently reissued in Canada (the significance of which I discuss below). Frustrating as it may be, this is a perennial problem for teachers in the US wishing to incorporate African fiction into their syllabi. And this is not an issue only with some of the comparatively lesser-known texts such as *The Gunny Sack*; it hampers plans to teach writers such as Ngugi wa Thiong'o and Wole Soyinka, figures with a truly international profile. Things are not likely to improve soon, either: *The Gunny Sack* was first issued under the imprint of Heinemann's renowned African Writers Series, which has now folded. The second incidental piece of information appears on the cover of the original paperback edition of the novel [. . .]. In the top corner, Heinemann calls the novel 'Africa's answer to *Midnight's Children*'. In certain respects, this is a very accurate, pithy description of the novel that puts it in excellent company; *The Gunny Sack*'s concern with a newly-independent Tanzania invites thematic comparisons to Salman Rushdie's novel, one of the most acclaimed texts of the emerging postcolonial canon. This particular marketing blurb, however, speaks volumes to the text's relative subordination in the field of postcolonial studies. For the moment, though, I want to consider briefly the qualities that make *The Gunny Sack* a potentially attractive text for scholars working on issues related to globalization, postcoloniality, migration, and diaspora.

Borrowing a phrase from Barbara Herrnstein Smith, the novel, like most post-colonial texts, participates in a 'double discourse of value', alluding to the particular set of contradictory cultural expectations many of us place on minority literatures. My adaptation of the phrase represents an attempt to describe the intellectual utility of postcolonial texts, or the way that such fiction circulates and is mobilized within the North American system of higher education. Like most postcolonial texts that make their way onto university syllabi, *The Gunny Sack* possesses at least two distinct qualities that are, under certain conditions, incompatible. It has an aesthetic and a political value. Its aesthetic value is fairly conventional and open to wide interpret-ation; the novel is something of a complicated narrative and cultural puzzle, and in this respect resembles many canonical texts. [. . .] The novel's political value, on the other hand, is loosely compatible with the rise of postcolonial studies, multicultural literature, and the recent institutional trend towards the instruction of diversity. The narrative's investment in miscegenation and migration make it a likely candidate to appeal to teachers interested in stretching the cultural horizons of the English curriculum. Most importantly, these two forms of intellectual value, despite their articulation through single texts, are relatively autonomous. When they come into conflict – as they do in the case of this novel – it gives us the opportunity to consider the ideological disjunctions between the global market for cultural products and the North American discourse of academic progressivism.

The Gunny Sack's aesthetic qualities are embodied most clearly in the text's elegant narrative system. The modest suitcase, a trenchant symbol of the family's continuous migration, contains the detritus of four generations of transit, displacement, and new beginnings. Opening the old gunny, tied with a frayed length of sisal, reveals an assortment of dusty, broken trinkets, portable mementoes hastily amassed in preparation of another unexpected departure. Sitting alone in his dank basement apartment in New York, the narrator plays Prince Shehriyar to the gunny's Sheherezade: he calls the bag a 'seductive companion, [. . .] postponing her eventual demise [by] spinning out yarns, telling tales that have no beginning or end, keeping me awake night after night' (5) [brackets by Kalliney]. The novel's patchwork style does a wonderful job of capturing the ephemeral, unstable conditions so typical of this migrant community's experience. It is, like the Asians in East Africa, a narrative-in-transit, struggling to retain links to the past and make plans for the future in an unsure present. The narrative creates this sense of perpetual motion through an assortment of disorienting spatial and temporal dislocations, moving from Muscat in 1885 to Voi in 1923 to Dar es Salaam in 1962 to New York in the present all within the space of a few pages.

As a result, many unsuspecting or untrained readers might find this particular novel somewhat unsatisfying. It is, in a word, demanding – it has a large, confusing cast of characters, many with several names, and it incorporates phrases in Swahili, Cutchi-Gujarati, and Arabic. In addition to these linguistic and technical obstacles, the narrative's self-consciously difficult formal economy makes this a fairly inaccessible novel (like the vast majority of twentieth-century novels on university syllabi). Finally, the history with which it is intertwined – that of East African Asians – is quite marginal within most North American readers' frame of reference. For these reasons, this novel and others like it are great texts to teach and upon which to build a research agenda. For many academics, there is a tangible pleasure in the difficult, the inaccessible, and the obscure. In other words, we tend to privilege, or ascribe aesthetic value to, texts that require extratextual criticism, interpretation, and other kinds of scholarly intervention. This type of value, moreover, is hardly unique to postcolonial texts. Though more comfortably canonical texts such as *The Canterbury Tales*, *Paradise Lost*, and *Ulysses* are all important and difficult for different reasons, their axes of hermeneutic intransigence – fundamental linguistic barriers, cultural inscrutability, historical distance, and sophisticated types of formal innovation – are in many ways identical to those presented by Vassanji's text. In its capacity to serve as a marker of aesthetic value, *The Gunny Sack* is little different from other kinds of texts that we commonly employ in the classroom. We might say that the novel is consistent with modernist discourses of aesthetic value.

But politically progressive scholars often become interested in minority literatures because they also have the ability to function as sites of political value. Such political expectations, moreover, tend to function as rejections of or challenges to this system of modernist exegesis. I am interested in how the novel turns a piece of luggage, the sign of a destitute, dispossessed migrant who hastily throws together the family's most portable possessions, into a novel, which becomes a signpost for articulating political allegiances. Throughout the text, the narrator repeatedly comments on the insignificance of the objects that comprise the family archive. There is an inverse relationship, it seems, between the material value of the objects in the gunny and the value of the gunny sack when it becomes a cultural object. The novel becomes a potential holder of cultural and instructional value, in part, by attesting to the dire material circumstances of its characters and their political marginality in a global context. The novel's title and its cover, which promotes it as 'Africa's answer to *Midnight's Children*', also suggest that it acquires value by opening up a little-known corner of the world. This is not to argue that the novel's virtues as art are completely negated in this transaction – comparing it to Rushdie's novel also makes a claim about the aesthetic quality of the novel – but merely to acknowledge how this aesthetic value is supplemented by the text's relative novelty in the global literary marketplace.

Stuart Hall has observed that the emergence of minoritarian cultural formations is a direct consequence of transnational cultural systems that have come into being during the era of decolonization. The contemporary world order in arts and letters has been marked by a 'profound cultural revolution [. . .] as a consequence of the margins coming into representation – in art, in painting, in film, in music, in literature, in the modern arts everywhere, in politics, and in social life generally'. As he argues, the new prominence of 'hitherto excluded' groups has involved a transformation of the cultural and political arenas simultaneously: artistic production by and global exposure of nonmetropolitan artists have increased just as colonial movements challenged European imperialism. Moreover, this cultural development represents a paradox: '[M]arginality has become a powerful space. [. . .] In the contemporary arts, I would go so far as to say that, increasingly, anybody who cares for what is creatively emergent in the modern arts will find that it has something to do with the languages of the margin' ([1991,] 34, [brackets by Kalliney]). The terms of this paradox, in which the politically marginal becomes part of a cultural dominant (or more precisely, a site of symbolic prestige), point to the difficulties of interpreting the political function of works of art in a postcolonial age. It is possible to read the modern arts trading in 'the languages of the margins' as responsible for opening a counterhegemonic space, but it is equally apparent that such works circulate in a system of cultural production that celebrates them for those putatively counterhegemonic traits. To return to the arguments of Hardt and Negri, the seemingly perverse logic of this situation implies that global capital has indeed outflanked and defanged postcolonial theory – at least in the world of high culture. The international marketplace, far from treating minoritarian art as a threat, flourishes by promoting cultural objects from the margins.

Anxiety that postcolonialism would become depoliticized by serving as a catch-all repository of marginality dates back to the early 1990s at least. In 'Woman Skin Deep', one of the canonical essays of postcolonial studies, Sara Suleri expresses concern that the term postcolonial was losing its historical specificity (as well as its political import) by serving as a vague signifier for marginality of any kind. The relative success and academic popularity of postcolonial theory allowed it to become 'more of an abstraction available for figurative deployment in any strategic redefinition of marginality'. The costs of such metaphorical flexibility, of course, could be measured in the erosion of postcolonialism's specificity, or the loss of 'any locality for cultural thickness' ([1992,] 759). When applied to literary studies, the concept of globalization is in danger of becoming an analogous signpost, a vague demand to include more minority texts without fully examining the way we pose the questions or making clear our investments in such an agenda. Without seriously questioning why minoritarian politics and literary rehearsals of otherness are important for our research and our teaching, such demands to globalize literary studies have the distinct possibility of reinforcing, rather than dismantling, the kinds of cultural biases we hope they will redress.

In debates about canon reform and cultural exclusion in the academy, converting narratives of marginality and displacement into objects of cultural value has been loosely aligned with a progressive institutional politics. Advocates of canon reform, for the most part, have not argued that we need to include any or all previously excluded texts, but that we ought to admit more texts representative of politically and culturally marginalized groups. Rather than interrogate our traditional (and too often, vaguely-conceived) expectations of aesthetic importance, we have simply heaped equally vague political demands upon the texts we hope will satisfy our multicultural requirements. This has created a double discourse of value for postcolonial literature. The field of postcolonial studies, in other words, is structured by its own ambivalences, or haunted by its own primitive reading strategies, otherwise known as the types of close reading designed to work with high modernism. Postcolonial texts simultaneously serve as bearers of an older, more traditional concept of cultural capital – suggestive of their uniqueness and quality as aesthetic objects – and also as bearers [of] a wider, corporate interest in our current reading climate. Simply making the canon more culturally representative by adding more subfields of study to English departments has proved an ineffective means of disrupting the proper functioning of those institutions; as we know from the work of Gerald Graff, John Guillory, and others, departments and canons are designed to accommodate diverse, even antithetical, interests without any serious loss of integrity.

This double discourse of value has put postcolonial fiction, and other so-called minority literatures, in a delicate position within the space of the academy. On one hand, these texts clamor for recognition like any other. We weigh their literary merits and aesthetic value as we would with any piece of literature. But in addition to that, we have placed an extra political expectation on minority literatures. Guillory, in *Cultural Capital*, makes exactly this point when he suggests that 'the project of legitimizing noncanonical works in the university produces an irresolvable contradiction between the presentation of these works as equals in cultural value to canonical works, and at the same time as the embodiment of countercultural values [which by] their very definition are interpreted to delegitimize the cultural values embodied in canonical works' ([1993,] 47). In a novel like *The Gunny Sack*, this results in an overt and perpetual staging of marginality. In part, the text attempts to secure a certain level of cultural importance by continually adverting its minoritarian concerns, circulating as a cultural tribute to stories of displacement, marginalization, and oppression. The novel effectively makes a bid to express cultural and political value by marking itself as a minority text. This leaves postcolonial literature in an unusual, paradoxical situation: texts like *The Gunny Sack* can enter the cultural center – what we typically call the canon – only by staging relative subordination in a wider geopolitical context. This double discourse of value puts minority literatures in a game they can never hope to win: in order to gain entry into the cultural center, they must incessantly rehearse conditions of subordination and exclusion. The expectation that minority literatures perform an oppositional politics not only puts the texts themselves, but also their teachers, in an equivocal position.

Given this situation, which tends to ghettoize postcolonial and other minority literatures, there is still no clear reason why a novel like *The Gunny Sack* could not become at least a minor luminary in the field of postcolonial studies. It is, after all, a travel narrative, now one of the elite subfields in postcolonial scholarship. It also foregrounds questions of hybridity and cultural mixing throughout, which are some of the key theoretical preoccupations of postcolonial studies during the last decade or so. Nevertheless, this novel remains fairly marginal even within this more restricted field of inquiry. The text and author's hybrid identity, I suspect, complicates matters. Most scholars and journalists claim Vassanji, who lives in Canada and is very active in the Canadian literary scene, either as a Canadian writer or as a member of the South Asian diaspora, and much more rarely as an African novelist.[7] He has won several awards; this novel was a Commonwealth Writers' Prize-winner for African fiction. It was published by Heinemann in their African Writers Series (once the leading brand name in postcolonial writing), and as it says on the original back cover, the novel is 'deeply committed to both the traditions and future of contemporary Africa'. Subsequently, however, all of his awards have been for Canadian and South Asian writers (including Canada's prestigious Giller Prize, a feat he has accomplished twice). So his hybridity as a writer, or his ability to move and speak across national and cultural boundaries, affords his work a great deal of mobility and flexibility. The result, however, is that his value as a novelist of East Africa ends up being suppressed, while his identity as a Canadian or a South Asian postcolonial writer gets enhanced.

This problem speaks to the more general subordination of Africa, and particularly East Africa, in both the global culture industry and also postcolonial studies in the North American academy. For better or worse, scholarship on South Asia has figured very prominently in postcolonial work. This situation has produced a wealth of groundbreaking scholarship, and I am not interested in arguing for the existence of a conspiracy to exclude work on Africa in general, or East Africa in particular, from the field. But I do believe that postcolonial studies could benefit from being more aware of the ways that it mobilizes texts and authorizes readings. Of the few scholars who work on Vassanji and *The Gunny Sack*, most read his text as part of the South Asian diaspora rather than as an African novel. In effect, the novel's marginality and the author's mobility allow the text to serve almost like a free-floating signifier, with most professional readers situating him in a Canadian or diasporic context. Some of this work is indeed very illuminating, but it also has a tendency to elide the novel's specific connection with East African politics and instead put it in a more geographically and culturally indistinct position. If it gets cited at all, scholars mobilize it to think about hybridity and travel as a general symptom of the postcolonial (or now, increasingly global) situation. The book's cover says it all: texts like *The Gunny Sack*, otherwise good candidates for a niche in university syllabi, are always trying to match the success of a markedly South Asian text, making the cynical wonder if the novel might have secured more course adoptions if it had been packaged accordingly. Novels such as *The Gunny Sack* are continually staging their marginality not only within the global consciousness, but also within the more limited field of postcolonial studies.

My interest in transnational theory, then, is twofold. Recent work on globalization is valuable because it diagnoses, critiques, and even resists the logic of global
capitalism. This has particular salience for scholars of East African culture, which is
one of the most politically, economically, and culturally marginalized regions of the
world. But it is also my hope that transnational theory can open up a productive
dialogue with postcolonial studies, breathing new life into a field that is, by now,
fairly established in the academy. In particular, globalization theory in conjunction
with postcolonial studies can allow us to reflect more seriously on the ways we
circulate texts and authorize readings in our teaching and our scholarship. My point,
to put it somewhat reductively, is that we need to resist the temptation to blame it
all on the workings of global capital: the marginalization of African literatures is
effected under the auspices of postcolonial studies as well, which has its own aporias
and institutional investments. In other words, texts such as *The Gunny Sack* are
diminutive players in the fiercely competitive arena of global culture, but also within
the more restricted field of postcolonial studies, which sometimes positions itself as
the antidote to such hierarchies. Furthermore, it is not my ultimate goal to make
more room for African literature on university syllabi, although this would be nice.
Simply adding more components to the curriculum does not address the kind of
structural blind spots that I have been discussing. What is required is more dialogue
not only between disciplines, but also between fields within literature departments.
It is only through such kinds of debate that we are forced to justify our choices and
make transparent our investments in particular texts and critical strategies. And a
discussion about globalization, perhaps, is a useful place to begin. At the very least, it
constitutes a field of inquiry that seeks to analyze the conditions under which we all
now labor – the conditions that frame the texts we assign, how we teach them, and
how we describe our own role in that process.

Notes

1   For a much more detailed and polemical critique of Wallerstein and other world-system
     or globalization theorists as Eurocentric, see the introduction and conclusion of Andre
     Gunder Frank's *ReOrient*. I am less concerned with the supposed Eurocentrism of
     globalization theory than I am with its debatable historical foundations – premises that
     may lead us to inadequate understandings of the present, too.
2   Asians were not the only groups for whom mobility was a condition of work: the indigenous
     population, many of whom were engaged as porters, were incredibly mobile laborers
     before and during the colonial periods. See Sunseri (2002).
3   The novel's themes of hybridity and miscegenation are most evident in its portrayal of
     religion (its fictional 'Shamsi' community practices a syncretic Muslim/Hindu faith) and
     its documentation of the family genealogy (the narrator consciously emphasizes his mixed
     ancestry).
4   See also Vassanji's later novel, *The Book of Secrets* (1996), which offers a fictional reading of
     a British colonial administrator's diary.
5   Appadurai's *Modernity at Large* [1996] is the obvious exception to this characterization of
     globalization theory.
6   See in particular Gunn, *PMLA*'s special issue, *Globalizing Literary Studies* (2001).
7   Vassanji himself, it should be noted, though claiming Canadian citizenship, goes out of his
     way to neither affirm nor deny allegiance to any particular nation-state: 'I feel as much
     African as Asian, and I have lived in the United States as well as Canada; labels based on
     nationality are a convenience and always slippery' (qtd. in Gale, *Contemporary Authors*,
     entry on Vassanji).

V WORLDLINESS AND COSMOPOLITANISMS

Chapter 29

Sue-Im Lee

'WE ARE NOT THE WORLD': GLOBAL VILLAGE, UNIVERSALISM, AND KAREN TEI YAMASHITA'S *TROPIC OF ORANGE*

From *Modern Fiction Studies* 53.3 (2007): 501–27.

IN KAREN TEI YAMASHITA'S POLITICAL realist-fantastic novel, *Tropic of Orange* (1997), Third World[1] labor confronts First World industry in a professional wrestling match. The champion of the Third World is a five-hundred-year-old messianic man called Arcangel, who fights under the name of El Gran Mojado (colloquially translated, 'The Great Wetback'). The champion of the First World is NAFTA, alternately called 'SUPERNAFTA' or 'SUPERSCUMNAFTA'. The representatives of the two hemispheres face each other in a Los Angeles stadium, amid all the pomp and screaming splendor of a televised pro-wrestling match. As the champions strut around the ring in the prematch show of self-promotion, Arcangel declares:

> *I do not defend my title for the*
> *rainbow of children of the world.*
> *This is not a benefit for UNESCO.*
> *We are not the world.*
> *This is not a rock concert.*
>   (259) [. . .]

When Arcangel mocks the popular slogans with which the First World describes a global community, he expands his challenge beyond his immediate opponent, the economic and political policies of NAFTA. He denounces the very notion of a collective, singular subject position that stands as the 'we' in the 'We are the world'. Sung by the biggest American pop stars of the mid-1980s who called themselves

'Band Aid', 'We are the World: U. S. A. for Africa' was a worldwide phenomenon in 1985, and the title came to function as the popular slogan for global interconnectedness and oneness. The best encapsulation of the globalist 'we' is, of course, the concept of the 'global village'. Since Marshall McLuhan famously used the term in the 1960s to foreshadow a new world order, one in which the electronic communications medium overcomes and diminishes the physical and temporal distance that separates the world's inhabitants, 'global village' has been the dominant term for expressing a global coexistence altered by transnational commerce, migration, and culture. More importantly, 'global village' translates that altered material condition into a hitherto unrealized condition of proximity, intimacy, and interrelatedness, the ultimate basis for a singular, collective 'we'.

Arcangel's critical role must be understood in light of the unmistakable authority that Yamashita endows him. Arcangel is a prophet and a messiah who masquerades as a bawdy performance artist and street vagrant. He travels throughout South America and Mexico singing 'political poetry' (148), recounting the southern continent's history of exploitation at the hands of Europeans. He literally bears, on his body, the scars of slavery and colonialism, and is the self-identified voice and the consciousness of the colonized and of the Third World.[2] So when Arcangel rebuts the global village sentiments, he is not specifically deriding the First World's philanthropic enterprise at large but the facility with which the globalist 'we' circulates in the First World's political, economic, and cultural discourse. The globalist 'we', indeed, is a central protagonist in the First World's discourses of politics, commerce, and culture, crucial to its narrative of 'progress' and 'development'. It underwrites trade policies like NAFTA (that free trade and trade increases will benefit all of 'us') is also a highly marketable – indeed, invaluable – concept in the First World's culture industry ('we are the world'). However, Yamashita offers more than a critique of the First World's unilateral 'we' in *Tropic*. The novel also argues the need to conceive of a new collective subject positioning that can express the accelerated movement of capital and humans traversing the world. Set in Mexico and Los Angeles, the novel highlights the transnational crisscrossing of labor, goods, resources, languages, and cultures in the late twentieth century, and its characters, whose formally disparate lives, separated by oceans and continents, are brought into hitherto unknown proximity and interconnectedness with each other.

This essay delineates the two dueling tensions in the novel's exploration of the globalist 'we', and examines those tensions in relation to contemporary debates on universalism. The globalist 'we' under critique, I argue, is fundamentally a universalist 'we', and *Tropic*'s denunciation of the global village celebration is an indictment of the imperialist nature of the few who presume to speak for all, whose particularity presumes the status of the universal. In *Tropic*, the First World's deployment of a global intimacy and shared fate is the latest rendition of imperialist – that is, unidirectional – universalism. In its stead, the novel postulates another model of global collectivity, a different rationale for a globalist 'we' that can express the transnational, transcontinental nature of human existence without imperialist dimensions. Simultaneously, this new model of global collectivity bears the seeds of its own negation, demonstrating the fragility, and indeed, the impossibility, of achieving an absolute universalism. *Tropic*'s dueling tension, in essence, simultaneously declares that 'We are not the world' and that 'We are the world'. This essay unfurls the theoretical and philosophical implications of these contradictory declarations through recent poststructuralist recuperations of universalism.

To begin with, it is crucial to note that the subject under indictment is not globalization per se, but a particular view of globalization – the view that globalization results in the economic, political, and cultural intimacy and shared fate of a primordialist village.[3] A Japanese American writer whose years spent in Brazil, Japan, and the US reflect a thoroughly transnational imagination, Yamashita's novels have consistently attempted to read the momentous and minute changes affecting individual lives as a result of globalization. Indeed, Yamashita's novels are deeply immersed in the phenomena of globalization: the high-speed information, media, and transportation technologies; the transnational modes of production and consumption; the accelerated flow of people, capital, goods, information, and entertainment; all of which result in the shift in the human experience of space, distance, and time. [. . .] Globalization as a force of deterritorialization is a constant interest in all of Yamashita's novels, as she explores the unmooring of fixed ethnic, national, and geographical identities and of established categories by which humans are organized and distinguished. Indeed, contesting the discourse of purity (of blood, race, ethnic, nation, or culture), Yamashita's novels explore and celebrate the porous categories of identities emerging from the phenomena of globalization. Conversely, her novels explore the ways in which the unmooring of identities and affiliations translate into formations of *new* moorings. The altered condition of coexistence presents a pressing challenge: on what basis, through what rationale, may a globalist 'we' be conceptualized?

Nowhere does this challenge press more imperatively than in *Tropic*, in which the geography of the globe literally shifts. The Tropic of Cancer, the imaginary line that divides the globe into two hemispheres, becomes attached to a magical orange growing in Mazatlan, Mexico. In the hands of Arcangel, the orange – and the Tropic of Cancer – moves northward to Los Angeles. Accompanying Arcangel and the Tropic of Cancer are Mexicans seeking work in the US, traveling toward, as they sarcastically call it, their 'manifest destiny' (132). Allegorical of labor's movement from the south to the north, from the Third World to the First World, the shift literally destabilizes the topography of the land. Yamashita's choice of Los Angeles as the ultimate site of confrontation speaks to the city's synecdochical role in the contemporary imagination as the epicenter of global confluence, or, some would say, global conflagration. Yamashita uses the city to explore the novel's pressing challenge – what is the role of the universal in the various conceptualizations of a globalist 'we'?

Tropic's project, then, has much in common with recent reconsiderations of universalism. Aggressively countering the delusional 'we' at the heart of unidirectional deployments of universalism (such as Eurocentricism, colonialism, imperialism, racialism, nationalism, sexism, paternalism, heterosexism, and more) has been central to the anticolonialist, antiracialist, antisexist scholarship of the late twentieth century. Generally traced back to Descartes and the ascendancy of the Enlightenment through thinkers like Rousseau and Montesquieu, the history of universalism is a history of a tool of oppression – the discursive and material coerciveness of a few who presume to speak for all. What complicates this rendition of universalism, however, is the pivotal place that universalism occupies in progressive political movements. Ernesto Laclau encapsulates the paradoxical role of universalism succinctly: 'without a universalism of sorts – the idea of human rights, for instance – a truly democratic society is impossible' ([1996], 122). Recent recuperation of universalism starts from precisely this oppressive/progressive function of universalism, and Laclau is representative of the poststructuralist attempt at recuperating universalism principally through the discourse of human rights and progressive politics. [. . .] As the poststructuralist recuperation argues for the perennial relevance of universalism without relying on foundational tenets (claims about the essence of 'human nature'), it distinguishes itself from the rationalist defense of universalism, best represented by Habermasian use of rationality as the foundational feature of humans and the speech act. [. . .] A recent consideration of universalism's paradoxical function is best represented in *Contingency, Hegemony, Universality*, in which Judith Butler, Laclau, and Slavoj Žižek exchange a series of essays on universalism. Despite their many differences, the three thinkers are bound in the assertion that universalism is a concept that supersedes any particular instantiation, 'a process or condition irreducible to any of its determinate modes of appearance' ([2000,] 3).

The poststructuralist revitalization of universalism, then, crucially renders a dialectic tension within the concept – as a concept constitutive of any discussion of human rights, justice, equality, and dignity, yet whose particular instantiations invariably fall short of the expansive promise held therein. A model of universalism as the site of an impossible/necessary dialectic, I suggest, is crucial in understanding projects like Yamashita's, which reject the unidirectional, imperialist deployments of universalism without rejecting the concept itself. Not only does the novel sit at the nexus of current discussions of universalism, it postulates its own model of universalism that I call a romantic universalism. As the novel's final answer to the challenge of a globalist 'we', romantic universalism richly illuminates the transformative power of universalism in serving the political needs of those rendered invisible in the great material divide of globalization. Furthermore, through the modality of the romantic, the novel enriches our understanding universalism's impossible and ideal dimensions.

In the transnational, transgeographical flow of people, labor, capital, and culture, Yamashita suggests that a coming together is inexorable. The task of conceiving a new singular collective 'we' and of conceiving a new use for universalism becomes not a matter of choice, then, but a pressing task. Hence, *Tropic* does more than contribute to the impressive body of scholarship that looks critically at the global village celebration. It pushes beyond the critique to attempt a nonimperialist, nonparticular, absolutely total universalism.

The overworked village

As Benedict Anderson put it, 'all communities larger than primordial villages of face-to-face contact (and perhaps even these) are imagined communities. Communities are to be distinguished, not by their falsity/genuineness, but by the style in which they are imagined' ([1991,] 6). The concept of the global village surely requires a stretch of the imagination. The conjoining of two vastly different scales of human coexistence demonstrates the domesticating work performed by the smaller scale of the 'village' in defusing the threat posed by the immense scale of the 'global'. The 'village' is not just a denotation of a smaller scale of coexistence however. It simultaneously connotes a particular relationality at work. Just as the village is a scale of coexistence that is always already in the past – the primordial aspect that Anderson identifies – it suggests a simpler and more immediate relationality of person to person contact.

The global village concept is perhaps the ultimate fetishization of the village's primordial aspect. This fetishization is explicit in Marshall McLuhan's formulation of the global village [when] he writes: '[T]he electro-magnetic discoveries have recreated the simultaneous "field" in all human affairs so that the human family now exists under the conditions of a "global village". We live in a single constructed space resonant with tribal drums' ([1962,] 31). McLuhan's global village discourse fundamentally appeals to primordialism (human family, tribal drums) in translating high-speed electronic medium into a *social* relationality of intimacy, cooperativeness, and familiarity: 'electric speed [brings together] all social and political functions in a sudden implosion', and 'the electronically contracted globe is no more than a village' ([1964,] 20). As Andreas Huyssen notes, the 'constant sliding of categories in McLuhan from the technological to the social and vice versa' reveals a mix of technological and theological discourse. 'Rather than offering a media theory McLuhan offers a media theology', in which a high-speed electronic medium, such as television, 'retribalizes the world' ([1998,] 12). [. . .] Gayatri Spivak, discussing McLuhan's *The Global Village*, casts a more political condemnation: 'global village' is an 'appropriation of the rural'. The concept of global village, built on the '[e]lectronification of biodiversity . . . is colonialism's newest trick' ([1998,] 330).

Tropic mulls over precisely this unidirectional logic of the globalist 'we' by sharply delineating the material inequalities that obstruct the binding of the First World and Third World into one subject position. In its depiction of Los Angeles, too, the novel focuses on extremely disparate socioeconomic positions and emphasizes the growing fissures that run through the global village discourse. There is an illegal immigrant couple, Bobby and Rafaela, and a white-collar professional couple, Gabriel and Emi. Revealing the highly uneven benefits of globalization in First World's major metropolis, Manzanar and Buzzworm represent the mass of urban homeless. The novel's fragmented form also dramatizes the fracture in the First World's use of global village universalism. Yamashita begins the book with a 'HyperContexts', a diagram that shows, in one glance, the division of the narrative into the seven days of the week, with each chapter attending to one day in the life of one of the seven major characters. This disjunctive organization leads to an atomistic sense of each character's life, as each chapter seems to stand on its own with little continuity from the other. Always, there is a sense of impending doom, as various human and natural catastrophes, such as illegal human organ harvesting and sales, cocaine-injected oranges, and major freeway pileups and explosions affect the lives of the characters. All the while, the Tropic of Cancer steadily moves northward, unsettling all rules of space and time.

Within this instability and chaos, Yamashita posits her challenge to the global village universalism. In an emblematic scene, Gabriel and Emi are dining in an upscale Japanese restaurant in Los Angeles. Emi, a Japanese American TV producer who delights in spoofing any orthodoxy, including that of political correctness, is speculating on the racial make-up of another diner sitting at a distance. A nearby diner takes umbrage at Emi's speculations. Identified only as 'a white woman', she remonstrates Emi on the importance of cultural diversity: 'I happen to adore the Japanese culture. What can I say? I adore different cultures. I've traveled all over the world. I love living in LA because I can find anything in the world to eat, right here. It's such a meeting place for all sorts of people. A true celebration of an international world' (129). Her model of global village follows an entirely consumerist logic. Contact is entirely reduced to consumption. If you can eat 'their' food, travel and sight 'them', then you have made contact. As she reifies difference into food matter, she also exemplifies a view of globalization as an exchange in free-floating 'cultures' without any material referents or consequences. Further continuing the capitalist logic in which the more choices the consumer has, the healthier the overall state of economy, in the white woman's rationale, the greater the number of different cultures' foods available, the 'truer' the celebration of an international world. This unidentified white woman stands as the synecdoche of the First World's imperialist assumption of globalist 'we', and Yamashita's mockery turns unabashedly didactic. In the hands of Emi, the protagonist that Yamashita identifies as approximating her mouthpiece, the white woman's consumerist celebration of a global village and her fetishizing of different cultures are shown to be indefensible, even to herself (Yamashita 2005). [. . .]

So who is in this overworked global village? The village is occupied by First World consumers who rationalize their privileged mobility and consumption as responsible acts of global citizens. These First World 'villagers', oblivious to their own role in the relations of power, project the consensual participation of *other* fellow villagers, those of 'different cultures'. Thus, '[a]s "universal", the dominant erases the contingencies of time and space, history and location, and with the same gesture elides its operations of domination, projecting instead the appearance of being democratic' (Palumbo-Liu 1995, 188). As 'my' consumption becomes 'our' celebration, the slippage of the subject in the First World's global village universalism demonstrates its unidirectional and imperialist nature. Ernesto Laclau's discussion of nineteenth-century European imperialism highlights the enormity of the slippage. In the work of imperialism, European culture of the nineteenth century circulated as 'a particular one, and at the same time the expression . . . of universal human essence', and in the simultaneity of this circulation, the particularity of European culture takes on the ontological status of universality itself: 'The crucial issue here is that there was no intellectual means of distinguishing between European particularism and the universal functions that it was supposed to incarnate, given that European universalism had constructed its identity precisely through the cancellation of the logic of incarnation and, as a result, through the universalization of its own particularism' (1996, 24). Likewise, the white woman's privileged mobility and consumption circulates as evidence and criteria of global village universalism. In constituting a 'we' out of 'my' experience, the woman's global village universalism performs a unidirectional conscription: she speaks for the millions and billions of others in prescribing the supposed unity and the intimacy.

Precisely this global village universalism is contested in the novel's focus on the disenfranchised and uncounted subjects. Bobby's and Rafaela's struggles are representative of first generation immigrants', especially of illegal immigrants', experience. Bobby is a Chinese Singaporean who entered the US as a boy, posing as a Vietnamese war refugee. Through years of low-wage physical labor, he achieves economic security, owning his own business of an office cleaning service. He marries Rafaela, a Mexican, during a trip to Tijuana, and they set up a home in a Los Angeles suburb. For all intents and purposes, Bobby and Rafaela exemplify the immigrant success story: they are small business owners, they own property, their house is filled with appliance and goods, and Bobby supports his family in Singapore as well as sends his younger brother to college in the US. Bobby's and Rafaela's visibility – as people of color and as immigrant success stories – are crucial to the global village discourse of Los Angeles as the true celebration of an international world.

However, what Bobby and Rafaela experience most deeply is not their economic comfort but their social invisibility, a pervasive sense of disaffiliation from the larger city. Their work, representative of the army of office cleaners whose nighttime work remains unseen by the white-collar workers, is symptomatic of the invisible nature of cheap, immigrant labor. Bobby recalls: 'Ever since he's been here, never stopped working. Always working. Washing dishes. Chopping vegetables. Cleaning floors. Cooking hamburgers. Painting walls. Laying bricks. Cutting hedges. Mowing lawn. Digging ditches. Sweeping trash. . . . Keeping up' (79). Indeed, Bobby exemplifies an immigrant model whose only sense of affiliation to his larger community is economical – as a laborer and a consumer. He lives under a perennial sense of anxiety – terror that his illegal immigration status will be prosecuted, that all his economic achievements will be taken away, and that his family's welfare will be threatened. [. . .] Bobby's only way to keep terror at bay is to purchase appliances, gadgets, and furniture, affirming to himself that a good American is a consuming American. While Bobby lives to work and to buy, Rafaela seeks an inclusion in the larger social, economic, and political structure. She attends community college; she learns, and feels deeply about, the causes of labor activism. Bobby actively discourages and ridicules Rafaela's growing political awareness, keeping to his policy of keeping his mouth shut and keeping his head down. Rafaela, in turn, feels stifled in Bobby's atomistic vision of life to be lived: 'She didn't want any of this [Bobby's purchases]. She wanted more' (80). Rafaela finally leaves Bobby, fleeing to her hometown in Mexico with their child.

In the two representative immigrants of Los Angeles, then, Yamashita throws a discord in the celebratory vision of Los Angeles as a model of the global village. While these two might be the ideal candidates of Los Angeles's 'international world' in the eyes of the white woman in the sushi restaurant, Bobby's and Rafaela's terror and alienation make a mockery of any unified claims of Los Angeles as the ideal amalgam of difference. Yamashita further compounds the delusory nature of a unified, globalist 'we' by highlighting the homeless population of Los Angeles. Buzzworm, an African American Vietnam War veteran, is a self-elect, one-man champion for the homeless. He walks the streets everyday armed with nothing but a card that reads 'Angel of Mercy', providing medical, housing, and legal assistance. Through his eyes, Yamashita relays the fleet of marginalized and uncounted segments of the homeless population who live on the street – teenagers, elderly, veterans, families, children, people with mental problems, drug addicts, criminals, and youth gangs. Los Angeles, through Buzzworm's eyes, is a den of social injustice and economic iniquity. Speaking of Los Angeles's insatiable car culture in which cars are better housed than homeless people, he remarks: 'All these people living in their cars. The cars living in garages. The garages living inside guarded walls. You dump the people outta cars, and you left with things living inside things. Meantime people going through the garbage at McDonald's looking for a crust of bread and leftover fries' (43). Buzzworm's encounters with the people who eat, sleep, and live in the street indict the great discrepancy of welfare in Los Angeles, and challenge . . . any conception of unity in the global village pretensions of Los Angeles.

In a spreading arc of criticism, Yamashita extends her critique of global village universalism beyond Los Angeles, extending it to Mexico, the novel's prototypical example of the Third World labor. Arcangel's political poetry, which Yamashita sets apart in italicized style, functions as the testimony of the indigenous, the displaced, the exterminated, the poor, and the workers. Identifying himself simply as a 'messenger' (199), he travels through Mexico, reciting his poetry. In a striking food scene, Arcangel offers a counterpoint to the scene in the Los Angeles sushi restaurant. On his northbound travel toward Los Angeles, Arcangel is eating lunch at a roadside tavern called 'Misery and Hunger' (130). As his waiter cites a long list of American beers that the tavern offers, Arcangel asks:

> 'You don't think it strange?. . . . All American beers. But we are in Mexico, are we not? Where are the Mexican beers?'
> 'Perhaps you would prefer Coca-cola or Pepsi?'
> 'Perhaps I would like a hamburger, Fritos, and catsup'.
> 'It is our special today'.
> It was true. Arcangel looked around at all the hungry and miserable people in the cantina – all eating hamburgers, Fritos, catsup, and drinking American beers. Only he, who had asked the cook for the favor of cooking his raw cactus leaves, ate nopales.
>
> (131)

The vastly different significance given to the food of 'different cultures' highlights the role of geopolitical context in the fetishization of the other. The transmogrification of the other into consumable goods only makes sense within the capitalist consumer logic – that the wealth of consumer choices indicates the health of the overall system. While the availability of tacos and fajitas in Los Angeles would be another evidence of the health of the global village, in this Mexican tavern, the flow of American fast food staples is no cause to claim an access to the other. Quite the contrary, the omnipresence of American fast food and the dominance of American brands are reminders of the rift that make the globalist 'we' impossible.

As Arcangel heads north, he also indicts the globalist 'we' as the central protagonist in the First World's economic discourse of universal progress. Yamashita employs dramaturgical strategies, staging Arcangel's protest principally through a highly stylized back-and-forth dialogue. It is in one such exchange that Arcangel announces his role as the champion of the Mexican/Third World labor against the US/First World industry. The crowd asks:

> 'El Gran Mojado, what are you doing here?' someone in the crowd wanted to know.
> 'Fool. He is going north, of course'. Everyone knew his story. His manifest destiny.
> 'Ah', said El Gran Mojado, lifting a can of Budweiser, 'But for the moment the North has come South'.

'Haven't you heard? It's because of SUPERNAFTA!' someone shouted.

'While you are busy going north, he's here kicking ass. And he's saying we are North, too!'

Another said, 'It's all hot air what he says. What's the good of being North when it feels, looks, tastes, smells, shits South?'

'That's right! If Martians landed here, they would know. They would swim nude in Apaculpo, buy sombreros, ride burros, take pictures of the pyramids, build a maquiladora, hire us, and leave'.

'El Gran Mojado! Stay here and save us!'

(132)

The crowd dramatizes what postcolonial critics have long voiced – that the great narrative of development and progress underwriting the First World's global economic policies must be understood in direct continuation with imperialism. Spivak argues the very concept of globe as a singular, integrated unit serves the interests of First World industry: 'Globality is invoked in the interest of the financialization of the globe, or globalization' (330). In the celebratory discourse of globalization, '[T]he great narrative of Development is not dead' (332).

The unidentified voices of Arcangel's chorus coalesce into one indictment: that the globalist 'we' as the central protagonist of universal progress is once again the particular (the interest of the First World) serving as the universal (the interest of all). Trade-led models of progress, which measures progress by the volume of trades between nations, tout the 'universal progress' that will benefit all of 'us'. [. . .] When restrictions and barriers to trade are removed, the rise in trade of labor, services, goods, and raw resources will lead 'the South' to be like 'the North', until the geographical distinction is no longer synonymous with 'the Third World' and 'the First World'. Instead, Arcangel and the crowd decry, the 'North has come South'. As the dominance of American fast foods and brands at the roadside tavern demonstrates, the South has become another marketplace for the North's goods. The South functions as a source of raw material, of low-wage work force who earn a fraction of what their counterparts earn in the North, who work without health care and environmental and legal protection, whose small businesses and farms cannot compete with the massive dominance of US products in the domestic market. While the great narrative of universal progress promises to unsettle the Third World/First World designations, Arcangel's chorus argues NAFTA to be yet another example of a zero-sum game. That the benefit of trade-led 'progress' goes to a select few and not to all is the requisite condition of the game itself. As Arcangel later pronounces, the narrative of universal progress is a 'myth of the first world' (259).

Recuperating the universal

Counterbalancing the novel's strong denunciation of global village universalism is an equally strong acknowledgement that coming-together of the South and the North is inexorable. I use the rather awkward phrase 'coming-together' to describe the complex nature of this encounter – the confrontational nature of as well as the inevitability of the relationship. As Yamashita makes explicit, the wrestling match of

'The Great Wetback' and 'SUPERSCUMNAFTA' is the Third World's refutation of the global village universalism. But the destabilization of the Tropic of Cancer is also a dramatization of the thorough interdependence that binds the North and the South. Symbolic of the millions of human migration, Arcangel's travel northward takes place in a bus filled with Mexicans seeking work in the North. In tandem with 'the rising tide of that migration from the South' (240) is the 'waves of flowing paper money: pesos and dollars and reals, all floating across effortlessly – a graceful movement of free capital, at least 45 billion dollars of it, carried across by hidden and cheap labor' (200). The interdependence is certainly no guarantor of equitable relationship, as Yamashita amply demonstrates. But a confrontation between two interdependent parties, whose fates and interests are interwoven, results in a par-ticularly nuanced conflict. The coming-together becomes the literal dramatization of coexistence and of the inevitability of the singular plural 'we'. As Los Angeles becomes the site of inexorable coming-together – of bodies, labor, capital, and geography – the question becomes: in a novel filled with indictments of false univer-salisms, can a singular plural 'we' be formulated without the unidirectional imposition of intimacy and collectivity? [. . .]

Yamashita offers her answer in the character of Manzanar, a homeless man who stands atop LA's freeway bypasses and 'conducts' the traffic. In the mold of the messianic figure who disowns a life of comfort for a penurious one of serving others, Manzanar is a surgeon who leaves his family and profession to pronounce the absolute interconnectedness of humans. A Japanese American, his name stands as a quiet protest and reminder of the internment of Japanese Americans during World War Two. A homeless man, his visibility poses a resistance against the public policy of enforced invisibility for the homeless. However, as he stands atop freeway bypasses, Manzanar functions as the symbolic nodal point in which *all* of humanity, in a spiral of ever-increasing scope, is joined. It is significant that Buzzworm, the street-wise activist for the homeless, calls Manzanar the 'ultimate romantic' (235). Buzzworm's description encompasses the spectrum of meanings in the word 'romantic' – unrealistic, hopelessly idealistic, and even mad, as it represents a vision endorsed by no one else.

My argument is that Manzanar's romantic universalism richly illuminates the modality of the ideal and the impossible in the poststructuralist recuperation of universalism. In reviving universalism as an antifoundational, nonnormative force of political necessity, the ideal and the impossible dimension are crucial – universalism as an ideal that cannot be achieved and as a perennial ingredient in all human struggles for hegemony.[4] Indeed, the ideal dimension of universalism is the constitutive feature in Etienne Balibar's 'Ambiguous Universalism'. While there are numerous, specific manifestations of universalism, the liberatory potential of universalism rests on the fact that 'universality also exists *as an ideal*, in the form of absolute or infinite claims which are symbolically raised against the limits of any institution' ([1995,] 63–64). This 'symbolic' or 'ideal universalism' exists in 'all the idealistic philosophies which view the course of history as a general process of emancipation' (72).[5] Thus ideal universalism stands as the core principle behind any institutional practice of human equality, liberty, and rights. Concomitantly, the principle of ideal universalism is repeatedly contradicted in the actual practices of, say, the church or the state. Hence ideal universalism stands as the immortal promise, an irrepressible principle that is revived again and again in different situations but is continuously displaced in history.

In order to fully appreciate the absolute nature of Manzanar's romantic universalism, we must also attend to the modality of the 'impossible' that sits at the heart of the poststructuralist dialectic model. The impossible and the ideal are related concepts, of course, since the ideal may be defined as that achievement which is equal in its impossibility as in its necessity. Although Butler, Laclau, and Žižek, in *Contingency, Hegemony, Universality*, employ different metaphors to describe that impossibility of absolute universalism, they are joined in their argument that universalism remains of perennial relevance in any and all political struggles for rights. Laclau's metaphor of the 'void' or the 'empty place' plays a pivotal role in their discussion of universalism as a constitutive feature in any struggle for hegemony:

> From a theoretical point of view, the very notion of particularity presupposes that of totality . . . politically speaking, the right of particular groups of agents – ethnic, national or sexual minorities, for instance – can be formulated only as *universal* rights. *The universal is an empty place, a void which can be filled only by the particular, but which, through its very emptiness, produces a series of crucial effects in the structuration / destructuration of social relations*. It is in this sense that it is both an impossible and necessary object.
>
> ([2000,] 58)

As specific groups seeking hegemony formulate their political claims as universal rights, they ceaselessly and variously fill the empty space with the particular. In this dialectic relationship, the universal is never completely filled. Inasmuch as it manifests itself only through the particular instantiations, the universal will only manifest itself through the particular. As Laclau repeatedly argues, exclusion and antagonism are crucial in struggles for hegemony; indeed, they are foundational features of a democratic society. Individual groups' use of universalism, as in a particular group's claim of and for rights, is fundamentally the exercise of a few speaking for some rather than for others. Hence, actual manifestations of universalism are always necessarily incomplete, inasmuch as they are never completely devoid of the particular that requires exclusion and antagonism. '[T]he complex dialectic between particularity and universality, between ontic content and ontological dimension, structures social reality itself' ([2000,] 58).

In Butler's and Žižek's revitalization of the concept, too, the political necessity of universalism is paralleled by its fundamental incompleteness. Rather than Laclau's 'empty place' metaphor that may suggest the universal to be a static category 'filled' by 'political content', Butler opts for the figurative concept of 'non-place': 'The universal announces, as it were, its "non-place", its fundamentally temporal modality, precisely when challenges to its existing formulation emerge from those who are not covered by it, who have no entitlement to occupy the place of the "who", but nevertheless demand that the universal as such ought to be inclusive of them' ([2000,] 39). Žižek, in turn, theorizes the conceptual permanence of the universal through the concept of 'ingativity'. When considered in the 'Hegelian determinate negation', the deficiency between the actuality and the notion can be explained by the fact that 'a particular formation [for instance, of the State] never coincides with its (universal) notion' (1999, 177). Thus universalism's perennial political relevance emerges from the *impossibility* of its completion (Butler, Laclau, et al. 2000, 110).

[. . .] Through these various – but interrelated – metaphors, poststructuralist recovery of universalism posits universalism's incompleteness as the constant feature in any specific application of the concept.

The absolute nature of Manzanar's romantic universalism, then, attains a greater significance against this poststructuralist backdrop. Manzanar personifies the impossibility of universalism – an instantiation of universalism that is absolutely full because there is no exclusion or antagonism. Relatedly, romantic universalism enacts the ideal dimension of universality – an achievement whose impossibility renders it an imaginary thing, an achievement that stands as a standard of perfection inspiring imitation. Manzanar alone supersedes the paradox of urban coexistence – the dense, physical proximity counterbalanced by the atomistic nature of the population's movements and the division of spaces by race and class. The richest example of this proximity/atomistic paradox may be the automobile culture of Los Angeles, the millions who hurtle alongside each other, each in his own home away from home. While LA's freeways have long occupied the contemporary imagination as the ills of chaotic urban living, in Manzanar's eyes, the freeway is the most vital organ of the human cohabitation. 'The freeway was a great root system, an organic living entity. It was nothing more than a great writhing concrete dinosaur and nothing less than the greatest orchestra on Earth' (37). Manzanar sees the artificial construct in the same realm as the elemental structures of nature, and through the language of elemental organism, describes the interconnected nature of urban existence.

Likewise, he alone sees the infrastructure that contains the urban mass of Los Angeles, the artesian rivers and the faults that run underground, as well as the human-made grid of civil utilities like the pipelines, the tunnels, waterways, pipes, electric currents, telephone cables, cable TV, fiber optics, computer networks, and many more. '*There are maps and there are maps and there are maps.* The uncanny thing was that he could see all of them at once, filter some, pick them out like transparent windows and place them even delicately and consecutively in a complex grid of pattern, spatial discernment, body politic' (56). To Manzanar, such an 'inanimate grid structure' (238) is a physical reminder that we occupy a single structure of existence and that the wires, pipes, cables, and freeways are all evidence of our bounded-ness, our interconnectedness to each other in the making of a single organism. [. . .]

As Manzanar envisions the population as a single totality, the rationale for his universalism is as banal as observing that we share the same power and phone company and as profound as observing that we exist in the one and the same here and now. Put another way, Manzanar's romantic universalism is one that draws the most profound conclusions from the most banal observations. Yamashita repeatedly endorses this transformative process in the narrative, continuing and sharing Manzanar's language of organicity that finds a single symphony out of atomistic disorder.

> And perhaps they [freeway drivers] thought themselves disconnected from a sooty homeless man on an overpass. Perhaps and perhaps not. And yet, standing there, he bore and raised each note, joined them, united families, created a community, a great society, an entire civilization of sound. The great flow of humanity ran below and beyond his feet

in every direction, pumping and pulsating, that blood connection, the
great heartbeat of a great city.

(35)

Indeed, Manzanar's romantic universalism is foundational to a greater vision – a
single totality that encompasses not only the geographical span of Los Angeles, but
of countries, continents, and oceans. His vision extends to 'the great Pacific stretching along its great rim, brimming over long coastal shores from one hemisphere to
the other' (170). He also . . . foreshadows the inexorable coming-together of the
North and the South, the joining of the two hemispheres: 'he knew the entire event
was being moved, stretched. And he was quite sure that the direction was south'
(123). In the scope and reach of Manzanar's romantic universalism, Yamashita offers
her own dramatization of the globe as a village – the globe as a single totality, whose
disparate parts are interconnected into a single organism.

What distinguishes this model from the other universals that abound in the
novel? First, this global village is not an instance of the particular 'making empire
out of its local meaning' (Butler, Laclau, et al. 2000, 31). In constituting a 'we' out
of 'my' experience, the white woman's global village universalism performs a
unidirectional conscription: she speaks for the millions and billions of others in
prescribing the supposed unity and the intimacy. The singular 'we' that results is an
unidirectional affection and affectation. In contrast, the crowds that accompany
Arcangel's Third World labor 'we', and the cacophony of unidentified voices that
join Buzzworm's urban homeless 'we', characterize these deployments of universalism as reciprocal ones. There is no slippage between 'my' and 'we', as Arcangel and
Buzzworm speak as the particular subject positions they represent.

But it is also important to distinguish Manzanar's romantic universalism from
Arcangel's and Buzzworm's particular deployment of universalism. As Laclau
argued most forcefully, antagonism and exclusion are not unique features of
imperialism and Eurocentricism: in the dialectic logic of universal/particular, *all*
instantiations of universalism (claims of specific marginalized groups, such as of
Third World labor or of the homeless) are incomplete inasmuch as they are claims
of the particular. Thus universalism of the Third World labor 'we' or the homeless
'we' observe the fundamental contradiction in the idea of universalism and the
political application of universalism – what Žižek calls the 'split' grounded '*already
on the level of the notion*' (1999, 177). Only Manzanar's romantic universalism
supersedes that negativity, as it postulates a 'we' that is absolutely inclusive because
there is no criterion for inclusion, which is the same thing as saying that there is no
possibility of exclusion. Romantic universalism's 'we' is a unity of a limitless
nature, whose absolute lack of particularity completely fills the 'empty space' or
the 'non-space' of universalism. Romantic universalism becomes the very horizon
of universalism.

In its absolute inclusiveness, romantic universalism fulfils another ideal dimension of universalism: a logic of 'we' that does not exert a normalizing function. As
Balibar identified in his model of fictional universalism, exemplified by institutions
such as the church or the state, the governing function of fictional universalism is
also the function of normalization. The dilemma that Balibar poses is: what deployment of universalism can avoid being a normative force? Through romantic universalism, *Tropic* offers an answer: when the participation in the universalism is entirely

voluntary and reciprocal. In addition to bringing people to tears (235), Manzanar's conducting begets other believers, inspiring them to start conducting themselves. A spontaneous uprising of romantic universalism grabs hold of Los Angeles. As Arcangel and the Tropic of Cancer approach the city, causing geography to literally shift and streets to expand and distort, Manzanar notes a different kind of organization to the city: 'Little by little, Manzanar began to sense a new kind of grid, this one defined not by inanimate structures or other living things but by himself and others like him. He found himself at the heart of an expanding symphony of which he was not the only conductor'. As the entire city of Los Angeles become self-inspired conductors, Manzanar's romantic universalism generates a 'we' greater in scope than Arcangel's 'crowd' or Buzzworm's homeless. Indeed, each of the conductors begins to personify, as Manzanar had done, the immensity of humanity as a single totality. Manzanar notes that 'the tenor of this music was a very different sort, at times a kind of choral babel. . . . The entire City of Angels seemed to have opened its singular voice to herald a naked old man [Arcangel] and a little boy [Bobby and Rafaela's son] with an orange followed by a motley parade approaching from the south' (238).

That the romantic universalists' conducting heralds the arrival of Arcangel and the Third World labor underscores the transformative power of universalism. Literally dramatizing the perennial relevance of universalism in the particular claims of specific groups, Manzanar's all-inclusive, all-voluntary universalism becomes foundational to the march of Third World labor and later, of Buzzworm's vision for the homeless. When Arcangel finally confronts SUPERNAFTA in the wrestling ring, his address to the crowd, like his earlier addresses to the crowd in Mexico, becomes an emblematic Third World labor's protest against the First World's myth of universal progress:

> You who live in the declining and abandoned places
> of great cities, called barrios, ghettos, and favelas. . . .
> The myth of the first world is that
> development is wealth and technology progress.
> It is all rubbish.
> It means that you are no longer human beings
> but only labor.

> (258–59)

As Arcangel protests a reality in which they are 'no longer human beings', the formation of Third World labor as historical actors and their claim for human rights take place on Manzanar's romantic universalism. As the crowd breaks into cheers and tears, their solidity is:

> accompanied by a choral symphony that came from outside the auditorium and slowly swelled to fill it by the people themselves. Everyone knew the music and the words in their own language, knew the alto, bass, and soprano parts, knew it as if from some uncanny place in their inner ears, as if they had sung it all their lives. Some people jumped up to conduct entire sections of the auditorium.

> (260)

Illustrative of the complex nature of coming-together, the confrontation of Arcangel and SUPERNAFTA does not result in a single winner. Each vanquishes the other in the ring, while the mythical manner of Arcangel's death by conflagration fore-shadows his eventual rise again. What remains the greatest achievement of the confrontation, however, is the symbolic oneness of the South and the North joined in conducting. For a brief moment, Los Angeles enacts a model of global village universalism that is absolutely all-inclusive, all-voluntary, and all-reciprocal, and Manzanar can finally 'let his arms drop. There was no need to conduct the music anymore. The entire city had sprouted grassroots conductors of every sort' (254).

Like the spontaneous 'chorus' (238) and 'symphony' (265) that frame the coalition of Arcangel's Third World universalism, Manzanar's romantic universalism underwrites Buzzworm's particular universalism for the homeless. The literal geo-graphical shift of the globe causes a meltdown of LA freeways, and chaos abounds between drivers who abandon their cars, the homeless who move in, and the law enforcement officers who combat them. The upheaval comes to an inevitable con-clusion – a shootout between the law enforcement and the homeless – and the homeless are massacred in great numbers. As Buzzworm considers the blight and the reconstruction work that await him, his vision is profoundly altered by Manzanar's vision. Buzzworm separates himself from his main source of connection to the world, the radio. The radio, he notes, is always singing 'one big love song. I love you. You love me. I love myself. We love us. We love the world. We love God. We love ourselves but hate some of you. I hate myself but would love you if. You screwed me and I'm learning to love me or that other one'. Instead of the facile cult of love that characterizes popular music, Buzzworm opts for what he calls a 'mythic reality', a term he hears on the radio before he makes his final disconnection. A mythic reality takes place when 'everyone gets plugged into a myth and builds a reality around it. Or was it the other way around? Everybody gets plugged into a reality and builds a myth around it. He didn't know which. Things would be what he and everybody else chose to do and make of it. It wasn't gonna be something imagined'. A mythic reality differs from the cult of love in its constructivist dimension – one remains fully conscious of the fact that one *chooses* the myth that best accompanies one's desired reality. 'Unplugged and timeless, thinking like this was scary, Buzzworm gritted his teeth. Took a deep breath. Manzanar's symphony swelled against his diaphragm, reverberated through his veteran bones. Solar-powered, he could not run out of time' (265).

Conclusion: a global village through romantic universalism

In romantic universalism's all-inclusive, all-voluntary, and non-normative 'we', Yamashita offers an answer to the challenge: how to build a collective subject positioning in the face of seemingly irresolvable discrepancy and fissures. The white woman's celebration of the 'international world', emblematic of the stance that globalization results in 'our' unity and intimacy, is an instance of some speaking for all. In the unidirectional manner of this exercise, the discrepancies and fissures that contest that single subject positioning are simply ignored. In contrast, in Arcangel's and Buzzworm's deployments of universalism, they speak as the particular sub-ject positions they represent. Through the dramaturgical use of 'crowds' (132) to represent the Third World labor and the urban homeless, in which the voices merge between the chosen speaker and the 'crowd', Yamashita emphasizes the active, reciprocal nature of these singular collective formations.

Romantic universalism affects all of these instantiations of universalism in unique ways. As the most expansive and nondiscriminatory instance of 'we', it highlights the unidirectional and imperialist nature of the First World's global village universalism. In lending its transformative power to Third World labor 'we' and the homeless 'we', romantic universalism also proves its perennial relevance to all political struggles. In romantic universalism's absolute nature, then, Yamashita offers one answer to the impossible/necessary dialectic in the poststructuralist recuperation of universalism. The impossible/necessary dialectic may be superseded, romantic universalism suggests, in an instance of universalism that includes all of humanity. When an instance of universalism has absolutely no remnant of the particular, it becomes that empty place, the ever-receding horizon of the ideal itself.

Romantic universalism, however, must not be simply understood as the solution that rescues the concept from the dialectic tension. The absolute nature of romantic universalism invokes its own set of inquiries. First, what is the political utility of a universalism that is all-inclusive? What is the progressive, emancipatory aim of a collectivity that claims to speak for all? How does it specifically challenge fictional universalisms – the normative, governing forces of institutions such as the state or the church? Second, when the emblematic moment of romantic universalism is the Third World and the First World joined in song, just how much can romantic universalism distinguish itself from the cult of love that rules the radio airwaves?

The answer to both inquiries, I suggest, returns us to the impossible/necessary dialectic. In presenting us with the seemingly impossible feat – an absolute 'we' – romantic universalism also presents us with the fact that the idea of universalism itself – the empty space – does not serve specific political needs *except* as it serves particular instantiations. The only satisfactory way of asserting the political utility of romantic universalism – and to distinguish it from the 'We are the World' variety – lies in assessing its specific manifestations – the 'we' of the homeless, or the 'we' of the Third World labor. Assessing the transformative power of romantic universalism within particular instantiations is the only means of identifying its political utility. Like Manzanar's conducting that encompasses all revolutions, both individual and collective, romantic universalism transforms individual protests (of Third World labor, of the homeless) into historical forces and into historical actors pursuing the ideal of human rights.

In returning to the particular dimension of universalism, the novel's conclusion encounters the dialectic bind. Rather than being a solution that overcomes the impossible/necessary dialectic, then, romantic universalism adds great nuance to the ideal of universalism propelling the dialectic. Through her use of the fantastic genre in representing romantic universalism, Yamashita renders a greater complexity to the theoretical conception of the 'empty place', 'non-place', or 'negativity' at the heart of universalism. A globe that literally shifts its spatial perimeters, the city and the continent that joins in song: the fact that envisioning an absolute universalism requires the mode of the fantastic enriches our understanding of the impossible (improbable, unrealistic, unrealizable) nature of an all-inclusive 'we'. Furthermore, Yamashita's use of the fantastic to actualize the ideal of universalism enhances our understanding of the romantic (imaginary, unreal, extravagantly fanciful) dimension of universalism. Indeed, the ideal of universalism can be profound and facile at once, and Yamashita richly illustrates these modalities through her use of the fantastic genre.

What, then, of the global village? *Tropic* amasses the spectrum of needs and uses fulfilled by universalism, from the unidirectional imperialist, consumerist kind, to the particular groups' struggle for hegemony, and to the absolute horizon of the concept. As the novel concludes with a vision of an absolutely total global village, the modality of the romantic directly colors the terms under which we can conceive of the globe as a village. That is: to transport the kind of relationality, intimacy, and shared fate of the primordialist village onto the globe can be simultaneously a profound and trite act. The distinction can only emerge from the ways in which the ideal of universalism serves particular instantiations of universalism. That is, how does the ideal serve specific subject positions' claims for universal human rights? As Yamashita deploys the most expansive 'we' as the foundation for the political articulations of Third World labor and the urban homeless, she unmistakably asserts the work of the romantic universalism – the transformative power of its imaginary and unrealistic vision, as well as its inspirational power as the ringing reminder of the ever-luring horizon of universal human rights.

Notes

[. . .]

1   'Third World' is a phrase that *Tropic of Orange* uses quite explicitly to challenge the celebratory discourse of globalization [. . .] to directly refute the view that globalization will remove the economic and geopolitical disparity between the 'First World' and the 'Third World'.

2   Yamashita identifies him as 'a literary interpretation of [Guillermo Gomez-Pena]. Arcangel's performance is grotesque, freakish, yet Christ-like, accounting for 500 years of history in the Americas' (Yamashita 2005, par 16.).

3   Yamashita's novels reflect a far-ranging understanding of globalization as 'processes of change which underpin a transformation in the organization of human affairs by linking together and expanding human activity across regions and continents' (Held, McGrew, et al. 1999, 15). As *Tropic* emphatically targets the First World's deployment of the 'globe' as a 'village', the novel joins critical examinations of the First World's celebration of globalization. See Buell (1994); Appadurai (1996); Jameson and Miyoshi (1998); Falk (1999); Tomlinson (1999); Weinbaum and Edwards (2000); Eriksen (2001).

4   It is important that 'hegemony' in this discussion be understood not as the negative force wielded by a few to oppress the many, but as in . . . [Laclau and Mouffe (1985)], as the contingent articulation by different subject positions that take place in the field of limitless, differential relations that is the social. Hence, rather than being the political logic/attribute of a specific social sector or identities, hegemony is the articulation of power for which *all* subject positions strive.

5   Baliber distinguishes 'ideal' universality from 'real' and 'fictional' universality. 'Real universality', describing the actual condition of increased interdependency of individuals, invokes the shift in the human experience of time, space, and distance brought about by globalization. Like the coming-together in *Tropic*, then, 'real universality' renders ' "humankind" a single web of interrelations' for the first time in history (1995, 56). [. . .]

Chapter 30

Neville Hoad

AN ELEGY FOR AFRICAN COSMOPOLITANISM: PHASWANE MPE'S *WELCOME TO OUR HILLBROW*

From *African Intimacies: Race, Homosexuality, and Globalization* Minnesota: University of Minnesota Press, 2007, pp. 113–27

Johannesburg is Monte Carlo on top of Sodom and Gomorrah.

Winston Churchill

MY CHAPTER TITLE APPEARS TO CONTAIN a contradiction: African cosmopolitanism. *African* is a word that designates a geographic, if not racial, specificity. In contrast, *cosmopolitanism* aspires to a worldliness unbound by either geography or race and suggests that multiple specificities exist. [. . .] I think this contradiction is shared by Phaswane Mpe's novel, *Welcome to Our Hillbrow* [2001]. It further mobilizes us to imagine a cosmopolitanism in Africa, in Hillbrow, an inner-city neighborhood in Johannesburg, as well as a cosmopolitanism that is African in the world of postapartheid South Africa.

Hillbrow, as its name suggests, straddles a ridge immediately to the northeast of Johannesburg's central business district. It is (and has been for some time) the most densely populated area of South Africa, if not the entire continent. In the white apartheid-era popular imagination, it was the destination of every teenage runaway, a lively haven of drugs, dreams, and discos. Initially home to succeeding waves of white European immigrants, its high-rise buildings and abundant restaurants and shops offered its inhabitants an experience of urbanity, unlike that to be found in the wealthy sprawl of the suburbs to the north or the impoverished sprawl of Soweto to the city's southwest. Hillbrow was one of the first areas of Johannesburg to 'go gray', before the repeal of the Group Areas Act, and was the only constituency ever to send a gay representative to the whites-only parliament in the apartheid era. It continues to enjoy a lively street life, coupled with a high crime rate, and is considered a no-go zone for respectable white people and tourists. In the late 1990s, it also became the home of waves of often illegal immigrants from elsewhere in Africa.

Who is the 'our' of our Hillbrow? Both the potential expansiveness of the 'our' and the geographic place to which we are being welcomed (Hillbrow) work against the elite overtones of the cosmopolitan to invoke the lineaments of an insurgent and rooted, yet open, cosmopolitanism. Hillbrow is, and historically has been, a new and often transitory home for many different kinds of people. It has had its capacity to extend a welcome tested under a variety of political and social conditions, where civility based on notions of cultural, racial, or national sameness cannot take root. Instead, as this chapter argues, different kinds of connections – new forms of intimacy, some of them impersonal or transpersonal – between people/s need to be imagined.

Strictly speaking, the novel is an elegy or a eulogy. Its opening words are: 'If you were still alive, Refentse, child of Tiragalong . . .' (Mpe 2001, 1) (the narrator uses the second-person mode of address with intermittent invocations of Refentse's name throughout). In the last section, the subject of the elegiac address shifts to Refentse's first girlfriend, Refilwe. I hope the 'for' in my chapter title will be double-edged, simultaneously suggesting that African cosmopolitanism is the dead subject of the elegy and that the elegy is a poetic gift or an argument for an African cosmopolitanism that is very much alive.

What is an elegy but an invitation to join the speaker/writer in her mourning? Likewise, what is mourning but a way of incorporating the loved and lost object in order to be able to continue in the face of its passing, rather than be crippled by its loss? These are the terms in which we, the readers, are welcomed to Hillbrow. By setting Mpe's novel in dialogue with scholarly attempts to reanimate certain strands of psychoanalysis in the face of the devastation of the U.S. AIDS crisis of the 1980s and 1990s, this essay further invokes a queer cosmopolitanism. Douglas Crimp reminded activists that mourning needed to be added to militancy in his 1989 essay 'Mourning and Militancy' (Crimp 1989, 107).

Subsequent queer scholars of color like José Esteban Muñoz and David Eng also have made powerful arguments for the further depathologizing of melancholia in the face of so much premature death. Muñoz argues that melancholia can be 'a mechanism that helps us (re)construct identity and take our dead with us to the various battles we must wage in their names – and in our names' (Muñoz 1999). David Eng and Shinhee Han suggest that melancholia marks a nascent ethical and political attempt to keep the loved object, or (in the case of the racialized immigrant, the lost homeland, culture, or symbolic order) a refusal to consign it, and the many possibilities it may contain for political and subjective agency, to oblivion. Melancholia for these thinkers asserts a refusal to move on, a psychological keeping alive of the dead against the imperative of mourning (Eng and Han 2002).[1] The cosmopolitanism brought about by using these queer theorists to illuminate Mpe's novel needs to be forcefully separated from the imperialist fantasy of my Churchillian epigraph, largely through the imagining of shared suffering.

In this chapter, I will suggest that Mpe's novel performs a melancholic response for its readers in the face of the deaths it describes, and that this melancholia is envisaged as useful for a storytelling that perhaps could mobilize militancy. Fiction self-consciously becomes, for *Welcome to Our Hillbrow*, a way of never laying the dead to rest. The novel works equally hard to distinguish the melancholic work of fiction from other projects that strive to keep the dead alive – most notably the abundant witchcraft practices and allegations that have become a feature of social life in the new South Africa (see Comaroff and Comaroff 2002). Whether the continued attachment to the dead in the form of melancholia can be mobilized by the living in the interests of their own survival is a question that the sublimating, aestheticizing end of the novel may beg.

Although the novel's real interest lies in its remarkable, subtle shifts in the narrative voice as it imagines the audience as cosmopolitan Africans through the mediating magic of reading and in its meditations on questions of belonging and migration, loss and responsibility, sexuality and death, a brief narrative summary may be useful in orienting the reader to the world of our Hillbrow. In six chapters, revealingly entitled 'Hillbrow: The Map', 'Notes from Heaven', 'The Journey from Alexandra', 'Refilwe', 'Refilwe on the Move', and 'The Returnee', our nameless narrator recounts the sexual misadventures of a group of mildly incestuous young friends from Tiragalong as they live, study, and work in and out of Hillbrow.

Refentse is in love with Lerato, who cheats on him with his friend Sammy. Refentse had previously cheated on Lerato with Sammy's girlfriend, Bohlale. Refilwe is a former girlfriend of Refentse's from Tiragalong, who dislikes Lerato and spreads rumors that she is the daughter of a foreigner. Refentse commits suicide. Refentse's mother, back in Tiragalong, is accused of witchcraft when she attempts to keep her son away from Lerato and is consequently murdered. Once in heaven, Refentse watches a film that reveals that Lerato is the daughter of Piet, father of Tshepo, a beloved Tiragalong friend of Refentse. Piet is also killed as a consequence of witchcraft allegations in Alexandra. Refilwe goes to study in Oxford. She then falls in love with a Nigerian man, who resembles Refentse; discovers that she is HIV positive; and comes home to die. Underlying the melodrama of this narrative are the pressing preoccupations of contemporary South Africa – xenophobia, AIDS, witchcraft, crime, urbanization, democracy – all presented in the lives and stories of the denizens of our Hillbrow.

The affect world of the cosmopolitan

In an extended essay on Freud's *Moses and Monotheism* (1939), Edward Said, shortly before he died, makes the argument that identity, whether national, cultural, religious, or communal, is always unresolved, and that the claim that Moses was an Egyptian does this work for Jewish identity in the thought of Freud. Said further claims that the personal experience of the foreign element at the core of identity is 'a necessary psychological experience'.

> . . . identity cannot be thought or worked through itself alone; it cannot constitute or even imagine itself without that radical originary break or flaw which will not be repressed, because Moses was Egyptian, and therefore always stood outside the identity inside which so many have stood, and suffered, and later, perhaps, even triumphed. The strength of this thought is, I believe, that it can be articulated in and speak to other besieged identities as well – not through dispensing palliatives such as tolerance and compassion but, rather, by attending to it as a troubling, disabling, destabilizing secular wound – the essence of the cosmopolitan, from which there can be no recovery, no state of resolved or Stoic calm, and no utopian reconciliation even within itself.
>
> (Said 2002, 54)

Mpe's novel works through the problem of contemporary (South) African identity in ways that reveal it to risk 'the essence of the cosmopolitan', keeping the ongoing historical wounds of rapid urbanization, xenophobia, resurgent witchcraft, and the HIV/AIDS pandemic open, and exposing the fantasy of coherent national and/or communal identities as false palliatives. I argue that the novel's deployment of a narrative structure of affect, which is close to Freudian conceptions of melancholia, allows it to perform the important ethical and cultural work of the cosmopolitan. Said's Freud offers the cosmopolitan experience as one of continual loss of identity by hanging on to the originary break in identity, as well as an ethical transvaluation of this loss by an insistent reminding that the self/other relations are structured not only in antagonistic reaction formation, but that the self is indebted to the other in more proximate and intimate ways. The cosmopolitan experience may bear some relation to a depathologized melancholia that seeks to refigure identity and sociality.

However, the novel implies that 'the cosmopolitan' is not an individual or even an attribute of an individual. Instead it is something like a structure of feeling, a web of relations between the living and the dead, the rural and the urban, the healthy and the sick, the kinsman and the stranger, Africans and the world.

The multiplicity and indivisibility of place or no safe place

The difficulties of a democratic South Africa negotiating its relation to its apartheid past is evident in a range of South African public fora, most famously the Truth and Reconciliation Commission hearings. The HIV/AIDS pandemic's impact on the renegotiation of South African identity and its place in the world are best encapsulated in a scandalous image, found on posters and t-shirts in HIV/AIDS activist circles. Among the most iconic images of South African's liberation struggle is a photograph by Sam Nzima. In it, the body of Hector Petersen, one of the youngest schoolchildren shot and killed by the police in the Soweto riots of 1976, is being carried by one of his schoolmates. This famous image has acquired a second iconic life in the context of HIV/AIDS by having the caption 'Who is killing South Africans now?' appended to it. This appropriation and recirculation of the image marks an assertion of horrifying continuity in a national narrative of rupture, liberation, and transformation. In the words of the South African satirist Pieter-Dirk Uys: 'In the old South Africa, we killed people, now we are just letting them die'.[2]

Mpe's novel, while never making so strong an accusation, reveals a similar contestation of the new national story. Like the reconstituted image of Hector Petersen, it invites consideration of the political work of reconfiguring the meanings of the death of young black South Africans. The novel opens by recalling a celebration of a victory by the South African national soccer team (affectionately known as *Bafana Bafana*, 'the boys, the boys' in Zulu) gone wrong. In the late 1990s, the successes and tribulations of national sporting teams were often charged with carrying the optimism and ebullience of the freshly democratic nation entering the world community of nations.

> You would remember the last occasion in 1995, when Bafana Bafana won against Ivory Coast, and in their jubilation, people in Hillbrow hurled bottles of all sorts from their flat balconies. A few bold souls, boasting a range of driving skills, swung and spun their cars in the streets, making

U-turns and circles all over the road. You would recall the child, possibly seven years old or so, who got hit by a car. Her midair screams still ring in your memory. When she hit the concrete pavements of Hillbrow, her screams died with her. . . . *Shosholoza* . . . drowned the choking sobs of the deceased child's mother.

(Mpe 2001, 1–2)

The spectacle of the street celebrations exemplifies the exhilaration of the Hillbrowans reveling in their new nation, but the costs of this exuberance are poignantly noted in the child's death. The tragic irony of her death is highlighted by the subsequent scene in which the sound of the crowd singing 'Shosholoza' (a popular freedom song in the days of the anti-apartheid struggle) drowns out the sobs of the bereaved mother. This opening vignette prepares the reader for the many ways in which popular patriotism, in itself a cause for celebration, will repay its constituents with death by homicide (accidental or otherwise), AIDS, and xenophobia over the course of the novel.

This use of celebratory patriotic song in the context of national sporting triumphs as the soundtrack for scenes of violence and danger is not an isolated incident. Later, we are offered this description of a carjacking in the adjacent predominantly white suburb of Parktown:

All the time you and your friends were lying there, flat on your stomachs, people were jubilantly singing Amabokoboko ayaphumelela . . . in the streets because the South African rugby team, the Springboks, had just won the World Cup.

(22)

Our protagonists are not only ambiguously situated in relation to the emergent nation at large, figured in terms of these sporting triumphs, but also in relation to the most significant geographic counter to Hillbrow, which is Tiragalong, a rural town outside Polokwane (formerly Pietersburg) in Limpopo province. The 'migrant grapevine of Tiragalong' competes with our narrator in interpreting the novel's central events, though ultimately the intimate web of connections between city and countryside reveal this to be a false opposition. The attempt to work through the thematics of urban migration marks the novel's sustained and self-conscious dialogue with its long tradition in South African letters. Refenste's story is in many ways a classic version of the *Jim comes to Jo'burg*[3] genre: a young man from the countryside is destroyed by the evils of city life and city women. The narrator writes: 'The lure of the monster was, however, hard to resist; Hillbrow had swallowed a number of the children of Tiragalong, who had thought the city of Gold was full of career opportunities for them'. (Mpe 2001, 3)

Mpe's profound ambivalence about city life places his novel in the legacy of memoirs like Bloke Modisane's *Blame Me on History* ([1963]) [. . .] and Ezekiel Mphahlele's *Down Second Avenue* (1959), [. . .] and against the pastoral terror and loathing of Johannesburg in a novel like Alan Paton's *Cry, the Beloved Country* (1948). [. . .] The novel's narrator, self-consciously staging himself as a writer, is explicit about inserting his narrative into the history of South African letters, reanimating a range of living and dead writers. The narrator refers to a range of other writers and novels – J. M. Coetzee's *Waiting for the Barbarians* (1980), Herman Charles Bosman's Oom Schalk Lourens short stories, Nadine Gordimer's *Six Feet of the Country* (1956), Zakes Mda's *Ways of Dying* ([1997]) – in direct and oblique ways as he describes Refentse and Refilwe's attempt to narrate their experiences.

However, Mpe's elegy, while engaging questions of exile, criminality, and suicide, does not envisage any of the earlier literary outcomes as a stopping point for his narrative. Two strategies emerge that may explain the novel's avoidance of these literary historical outcomes. One is an assertion of moral equivalence between city and countryside:

> You, Refenste, child of Tiragalong (and as you insisted in the days before your death, also of Hillbrow) never shared such sentiments. It was your opinion that the moral decay of Hillbrow, so often talked about, was in fact no worse than that of Tiragalong.
>
> (Mpe 2001, 17)

The second narrative strategy is an insistence on the back and forth connections between Tiragalong and Hillbrow:

> You discovered on arriving in Hillbrow, that to be drawn away from Tiragalong also went hand-in-hand with a loss of interest in Hillbrow. Because Tiragalong was in Hillbrow. You always took Tiragalong with you in your consciousness whenever you came to Hillbrow or any other place. In the same way, you carried Hillbrow with you always.
>
> (6)

These back-and-forth connections take a number of forms, both intimate ones, like the psychological form of personal experience described previously and read in terms of melancholic refusal to give up the lost object, and significant historical ones. What the Tiragalong gossip migrants, in their continued attempts to blame the HIV virus on foreigners and loose women, fail to realize is that they themselves are most likely key participants in the disease's spread. This is not to render them responsible. Much recent social science work reveals that systems of migrant labor, instituted over the course of the twentieth century, have produced norms and forms of transactional sex, family life, and gendered attitudes that have proved conducive to the spread of HIV (see Campbell 2003). Tiragalong, as much as it wishes to deny it, is very much part of the set of problems that it wishes to confine to places like Hillbrow.

Tiragalong and Hillbrow are further linked through the circulation of images in the mass media. Little boys in Tiragalong learn the styles of masculine modernity from images of Hillbrow gangsters, thus subverting any notion of the countryside as an uncontaminated place for the reproduction of social norms and values – in a word, tradition:

> Heroes of grimy courage and exceptionally vicious greed were followed by the voracious camera lenses of modern technology, and the little boys of Tiragalong emulated their TV heroes, driving their cars made of wire with wheels of tennis balls.
>
> (Mpe 2001, 5)

The novel also makes it clear that Hillbrow is not just a place of danger and excitement for the new arrivals from Tiragalong but also a place of domestic comfort and ease:

> The following day you woke up, washed yourself thoroughly; quite a treat. Water being such a scarce resource in Tiragalong, you only used to take a proper bath once a week. Sure there were taps at most street corners in Tiragalong. But the water taps were often as dry as a desert. So here you received a treat; warm, hot and cold water right in the flat.
>
> (10)

Hillbrow here enables the respectable forms of embodiment of Tiragalong, urbanity as hygiene rather than depravity. Refentse carries Tiragalong into Hillbrow in multiple ways. He is told by his cousin: 'Hey you! You do not go around greeting every fool in Hillbrow. He looks harmless. But not all people who greet you in Hillbrow are innocent well-wishers'. (12) We see here that Hillbrow offers possibilities for different kinds of relationship to oneself and to strangers. It offers something that Tiragalong appears not to: that is, the possibility of what Lauren Berlant calls 'stranger intimacy', also known as citizenship (see Berlant 1997). Tiragalong manners resignify the city's possibilities. The streets, filled as they are with strangers, exceed or refute kinship as the primary explanation of social connection:

> It was during your second month as a lecturer that you saw your friend from the shelter being wheeled away in a wheelbarrow in the direction of Hillbrow hospital in Klein Street. He did not say Aibo! This time. This pained you. In the five years that you had known him, you had become friends without ever saying anything to each other, except for the mutually warm greetings.
>
> (Mpe 2001, 16)

Here we see some of the risks and dangers of loving strangers. Civility, even (and perhaps especially) under very difficult conditions, becomes a kind of performative social reproduction in the face of the failure of the historically besieged forms of family and kinship, but . . . it is also materially vulnerable. The prostitution in Hillbrow, which the novel repeatedly gestures to as a reality on the ground and as an important phobic component of the Tiragalong popular imagination, may give us a debased form of the ethical problem of loving strangers in somewhat literal ways. However, prostitution is described in ways that suggest new possibilities for collectivities robust enough to cope with the questions of human differences and commonalities that the xenophobic denizens of Tiragalong/Hillbrow can only pose in divisive moralizing terms.

Refentse learns many things from these forms of sociality in Hillbrow (and alongside him, the reader, through the second-person mode of address): 'You had learnt that you were as vulnerable as the drunks and womanizers that you used to criticize for their carelessness: as vulnerable as the prostitutes populating Quartz and other streets, pasted against the walls of the concrete towers of Hillbrow'. (59) A recognition of shared vulnerability to both desire and illness makes the differences between the imagined custodians of virtue and the profligate victims of the city immaterial. The novel frequently describes sex — whether commercial sex between strangers or romantic sex between characters given psychological interiority — in the impersonal and transpersonal language of body parts or bodily fluids (semen, penises, anuses, blood, sweat). This apparent self- and social alienation may have the opposite effect in the sense that the frailty of the flesh becomes universal and the cultural, national, moral, and gendered differences needed to police reader[s'] sympathy may fall away.

This sense of a shared, almost transcendant vulnerability of the body as a ground for both community and intimacy is seen as something that needs to be continually renarrated and redescribed, avoiding any essence of the human, while perhaps allowing for a reader's voyeurism to turn ethical:

> Euphemism, Xenophobia, Prejudice. AIDS. You wrote your story to think through all these issues, child of Tiragalong and Hillbrow. But your story was neither long nor sophisticated enough. You realized when it was published that it would never be sufficient. You became keenly aware that no matter what other stories you might write, none of them would ever be sufficient to answer such imponderables. . . . There would always be another story of love, betrayal, friendship, joy and pain to add to your narrative granary. There would always be the need to revise, reinforce, contradict. For every new personal experience adds to our knowledge of life and living, death and dying. Every act of listening, seeing, smelling, feeling, tasting is a reconfiguring of the story of our lives.
>
> (61)

I would add reading and writing to the previous list of human activities. Our narrator addresses Refentse in heaven: 'You did not own life when you were alive. Now that you are alive in a different realm, you know for sure that you do not own life'. (67) Yet neither God nor the devil nor the ancestors own life. It appears that the ever-expanding promiscuous web of connections that is Tiragalong, that is Hillbrow, that is the world, that is heaven, constitute life and death. The novel's humanism broaches the possibility of an African universalism.

The increasingly global embrace of the 'welcome' in the novel's title is visible in both political and intimate registers. The narrator directly accuses the corrupt policeman cousin of Refentse:

> Many of the makwerekwere, you accuse of this and that are no different to us sojourners, here in search of green pastures. . . . You would want to add that some makwerekwere were fleeing their war-torn countries to seek sanctuary here in our country in the same way that many South Africans were forced into exile in Zambia, Zaire, Nigeria and other African and non-African countries during the Apartheid era.
>
> (18–19)

The opposition between the foreign and the local is confounded by ethical obligations of reciprocity produced by the history of the South African liberation struggle. More subtly, we see in the likening of both local men and *makwerekwere* to spreading pumpkin plants an assertion of Ubuntu, or African humanity, between the stranger/ foreigner and us. We first encounter the simile xenophobically:

> And then makwerekwere stretching their legs and spreading like pump-
> kin plants filling every corner of our city and turning each patch into a
> Hillbrow coming to take our jobs in the new democratic rainbowism of
> African Renaissance.
>
> (26)

The same simile is invoked again when Refentse's mother meets Lerato in heaven and recognizes her as not the daughter of a foreigner but of the brother of the beloved Tshepo: 'If we met in Tiragalong or in its neighbouring villages, I would have said that indeed, men do spread like pumpkin plants' (70). The *makwerekwere* have simply become men in their shared likeness to the cultivated wildness of the spreading pumpkin plant putting down its roots in response to the stimulus of the sun and water, thriving both against and for the gardener's will.

This commonality is restated explicitly in terms of Refilwe's experiences in England:

> Our Heathrow strongly reminded Refilwe of our Hillbrow and the
> xenophobia it engendered. She learnt there, at our Heathrow, that
> there was another word for foreigners that was not very different from
> Makwerekwere or Mapolantane. Except that it was a much more widely
> used term: Africans.
>
> (102)

In a political register, historical experience can produce collectivity either through reciprocity of exchange or through shared oppression. If all people are *makwerekwere* somewhere, what happens to the central difference for the Tiragalong gossips? It is perhaps in the dream sequence in which Refilwe falls in love with the young Nigerian at Oxford that the stranger/kinsman dichotomy is resolved. Refilwe coun-ters the xenophobia of contemporary urban South Africa embodied in characters like Refentse's cousin by simultaneously recognizing the familiarity and the strange-ness of both exile and her new love interest.

> The stranger-who-was-not-a-stranger teased her quite often that night.
> He came carrying the taste that stood the test of time [advertising logo
> for Castle Lager] in his hands, despite the fact that one hardly ever saw
> any South African brew in our Jude the Obscure [Refilwe's Oxford pub
> hangout]. He visited her in dreams that substituted Vicker's Place
> [Refilwe's Hillbrow flat] for Morrell Hall [Refilwe's Oxford dorm].
> [brackets by Hoad]

He is a stranger who is not a stranger, who comes bearing gifts from home – the wistfully ironic 'taste that stood the test of time'. He allows her, in her dreams, to substitute Hillbrow and Oxford – not make the one become the other, but allow the places to be interchangeable, to allow the dislocations of self-imposed exile to become expansive.

Their union is doomed. Shortly after getting together, they discover they are both HIV-positive and return to their respective national homelands to die. However, the novel refuses the conventions of what might be termed (inter)national romance. A union between a Nigerian and a South African is not allowed to solve the problems of xenophobia, AIDS, witchcraft, and sexual shame that lie at the novel's center. The fantasy that exile might also be something of a solution is quickly dismissed. This penultimate gesture of the novel recognizes that the complex and overdetermined sociopolitical realities of contemporary urban South Africa are irretrievable for genres of romantic allegory. Refilwe's death takes us back to the opening death of the young girl on the streets of Hillbrow and is resonant of the title: *Welcome to Our Hillbrow*. The terms of this welcome become clear: to be embraced by the hospitality of the cosmopolitan, we need to accept the invitation to share the work of mourning, or perhaps more accurately we are encouraged to inhabit the novel's melancholia.

AIDS, mourning, politics

Welcome to Our Hillbrow suggests a vibrant interconnectedness between urban and rural worlds, home and exile for negotiating this entity I am calling African cosmopolitanism. As a route to the imagining of collectivity across difference, this cosmopolitanism has two dark undersides – witchcraft and the AIDS pandemic – which paradoxically may also be its conditions.

The novel's narrative strategies mimic its descriptions of both the disease and witchcraft in interesting ways, with important differences. Writing, like witchcraft, is imagined as having animating and healing powers. The narrative voice shows us a movie in heaven and can move with surprising grace between the worlds of the living and the dead. Yet writing, unlike witchcraft, seeks to keep the dead alive in the memories of the living, and more particularly in the endlessly revisable stories that the living can tell about the dead. The novel subtly but sustainedly reminds us that reading and writing are a kind of world-making magic.

Acknowledging a unifying and arbitrary vulnerability to HIV/AIDS becomes the condition of welcome to our Hillbrow. To engage in love, and sex, and to be desiring subjects is to share in this vulnerability. The novel is clear that the virus respects neither national boundaries nor even the integrity of discrete individual bodies. Questions of origins and certainties of identity can offer no protection. While certain protagonists in the novel, particularly Refentse's corrupt policeman cousin, provide the familiar 'AIDS is the wages of sinning by other people' argument, the novel shows that everyone can be affected.[4] The novel both presents and debunks all phobic folk narratives, which seek inoculation from the disease through the assertion of identity-based virtue and sin:

> . . . certain newspaper articles attributed the source of the virus that causes AIDS to a species called the Green Monkey, which people in some parts of West Africa were said to eat as meat, thereby contracting the disease. Migrants (who were Tiragalong's authoritative grapevine on all important issues) deduced from such media reports that AIDS's travel route into Johannesburg was through Makwerekwere; and Hillbrow was

the sanctuary in which Makwerekwere basked. There were others who
went even further, saying that AIDS was caused by the bizarre sexual
behaviour of the Hillbrowans. How could any man have sex with another
man. . . . Surely, this large group argued, it was the shit that the greedy
and careless penises sucked out of the equally eager anuses, that could
only lead to such dreadful illnesses?

(Mpe 2001, 4)

The Tiragalong migrants, themselves displaced people of a sort, would like to claim
safety from HIV/AIDS in that they are not green monkey eaters from West Africa,
nor homosexuals who have anal sex. Yet, the people who die in the novel are the
young, educated respectable people from Tiragalong. The previous passage is further
noteworthy for the description of sex in terms of part-objects – body parts that are
unruly and have a life of their own that are not subject to rule by will. The novel is
not willing to deny the humanity of desire, as doing so would risk embracing the
migrants' hypocrisy that the narrative voice is at pains to escape. Yet Tiragalong
and its values, no matter the critical distance taken by the protagonists, remain part
of home.

The narrator tells us of the protagonist of Refentse's short story:

But then she discovered like you did Refentse, that a conscious decision
to desert home is a difficult one to sustain. Because home always travels
with you, with your consciousness as its vehicle. So her second resolution was to pour all her grief and alienation into the world of storytelling. You had her write a novel about Hillbrow, xenophobia and AIDS and
the prejudices of rural lives.

(55)

Writing allows for Refentse to work through these questions of identity and morality in ways that further complicate their connection. The protagonist of Refentse's
story is a woman and is in this important respect very different from himself.
However, she too is a writer pouring all her grief and alienation into 'the world of
storytelling'. Like him, unlike him, she mimes his vulnerabilities and enacts his
imagined solutions. Home is not reducible to identification with place or people but
becomes the telling and retelling of stories of loved and lost people.

The kind of home that the narrator has Refenste imagine for his protagonist
shares attributes with the structure of Freudian melancholia. However, great care
must be taken in making this analogy, since the narrative voice is not marked by
despair or self-loathing (the affective markers of the melancholic). It appears that the
loved objects, Refentse and Refilwe, are not given up. Instead, they have become
part of the fabric of this narrative voice, and both they and the novel's readers can be
hailed as 'Child of our World and other Worlds' (124). The novel suggests that
melancholia, which is always an implicitly pathological structuring of relation
between subject and lost objects in psychoanalysis, can also be an ethical relation.

The final paragraphs of the novel reveal a sense that Hillbrow is a global place,
that the problems of xenophobia, AIDS, and premature death that can be found
there circulate between Tiragalong, Hillbrow, Alexandra, Oxford, Lagos, and
heaven and earth. Furthermore, the work of mourning needs to be reconfigured.

Normal mourning overcomes the loss of the object. . . . Each single one of the memories and situations of expectancy which demonstrate the libido's attachment to the lost object is met by the verdict of reality that the object no longer exists; and the ego, confronted as it were with the question whether it shall share this fate, is persuaded by the sum of the narcissistic satisfactions it derives by being alive to sever its attachment to the object that has been abolished.

(Freud, Strachey, et al. 1995, 255)

The narrator is unable to forget Refilwe or Refentse or to sever his attachment to them. His act of writing could be seen as analogous to the Freudian ego here, marking persuasion 'by the sum of narcissistic satisfactions that it is alive'. However, instead of helping to sever the attachment, the act of writing and the understanding of writing as endlessly revisable helps keep the lost objects alive with and within him.

How, in Muñoz's words, can the writing protagonists of the novel take 'their/ our dead with us to the various battles we must wage in their names – and in our names' (1999, 74)? I think Mpe's novel can move its protagonists and readers from a xenophobic, exoticizing position in relation to the African HIV/AIDS pandemic to the melancholia of a cosmopolitanism that can embrace other people's dead. How this translates into political work is a question that may require yet another archive. To complete another circle here, we may need melancholia *and* mourning, as well as militancy.

Notes

1   Freud himself defines mourning as follows: 'Mourning is regularly the reaction to the loss of a loved person, or to the loss of some abstraction which has taken the place of one, such as one's country, liberty, an ideal and so on' (Freud, Strachey et al. 1995, 243). [. . .]
2   Cited in Campbell (2003, 188).
3   *Jim Comes to Jo'burg* is a 1951 film that dramatizes the pleasures and dangers of urban living.
4   'I was interested in looking at that part of sexuality that people don't stigmatise, the sexuality of people who are supposed to be educated and respectable'. (Mpe quoted in Tait 2001, 9).

Chapter 31

Suman Gupta

MOVEMENTS AND PROTESTS

From *Globalization and Literature* Cambridge: Polity, 2009, pp. 13–31

Plucking a theme

AS IT STANDS NOW, 'GLOBALIZATION' IS one of those extra-ordinarily protean terms of our time which seems to be relevant, and is increasingly accepted as meaningful, everywhere. In it the absolute embrace of the core word, the 'globe' itself, struggles against the modification of the suffix, the process marked by '-ization'. A wide variety of possibilities slip through that slight disjuncture between the absolute and the potential: the possibility of active globe-making, discernment of a global teleology, mediation between the bits (the local) and the whole of the globe, reference to systems that span the globe, the ambition of constructing global concepts, the desire of tapping into the material (resources, labour, markets) of the globe, etc. These possibilities do not necessarily sit together comfortably, and yet they are contained in the fertile suggestiveness of the term. Arguably, the term's protean nuances are represented and given flesh in literature most self-consciously where it has everyday currency, in contexts which constantly present themselves as centres of globalizing processes. Contemporary North American and British literature therefore often describe various strands of everyday and social life that are symptomatic of globalization. These often deal with protagonists and events caught in the machine of multinational business, located in the confronta-tion of global political forces from above and below, placed in the cosmopolitan spaces of global cities or moving fluidly across national and cultural boundaries, etc. Such themes are naturally intermeshed with each other to convey something of a process that is ultimately uncontainable in any single narrative or descriptive effort. These literary works also register the enormity and flux of globalization within their forms, and in the deliberateness of their use and recording of language. To come to grips with literary *representation* (expression) of globalization [. . .] a focus on some contemporary North American and British literary works seems apt. The diffuse relationship between literary representation and a globalizing social world argues for a more or less arbitrary foothold to begin contemplation: a focus on any relevant theme could be expected to unravel into others under the purview of globalization, and into the disposition of literary form and language. To set this part off therefore a theme is plucked out: the literary representation of global movements from above and below, pro- and anti-globalization. Others are drawn out from that as we proceed.

Anti-globalization protests

Consider the following fictional description of an anti-globalization protest:

> Someone flung a trash can at the rear window. Kinski flinched but barely. To the immediate west, just across Broadway, the protesters created barricades of burning tires. All along there'd seemed a scheme, a destination. Police fired rubber bullets through the smoke, which began to drift high above the billboards. Other police stood a few feet away, helping Eric's security detail protect the car. He didn't know how he felt about this.
> 'How will we know when the global era officially ends?'
> He waited.
> 'When stretch limousines begin to disappear from the streets of Manhattan'.
>
> (DeLillo 2003, 91)

The scene is from Don DeLillo's *Cosmopolis*, set in one April day of 2000, when billionaire financial speculator Eric Packer plays havoc with the world markets in his stretch limousine, which is equipped with internet screens for tracking world markets and phones for trading, as he goes around Manhattan and runs into a violent anti-globalization protest. Eric appears to represent free market capitalism. With him is his 'chief of theory' Vija Kinski, whose function seems to be to theorize (conveniently for the reader) the contemporary world without understanding either the technology or the economics of Eric's operation. The question and answer in the quotation are both Kinski's. Her theorizing up until this point had been confined to how digitized and speeded-up information transfers in the interests of free market capitalism have captured the contemporary world. On encountering the protest, Kinski naturally gives it a concordant theoretical turn, arguing that such protests are a necessary part of, and almost in continuity with, free market capitalism:

> 'They are working with you, these people. They are acting on your terms', she said. 'And if they kill you, it's only because you permit it, in your sweet sufferance, as a way to re-emphasize the idea we all live under'.
> 'What idea?'
> [. . .]
> 'Destruction', she said.
> [. . .]
> 'The urge to destroy is a creative urge'.
> 'This is also the hallmark of capitalist thought. Enforced destruction.

Old industries have to be harshly eliminated. New markets have to be forcibly claimed. Old markets have to be re-exploited. Destroy the past, make the future'.

(DeLillo 2003, 92–93 [brackets by Gupta])

As she proceeds with this line of thinking, the protesters are described as engaged in a quite extraordinarily reckless and desperate series of actions, which the police fail to contain with their considerably less reckless methods. In the midst of that Eric spies the defining slogan of the protest:

The top tier of the electronic display across the avenue showed this message now:
A SPECTER IS HAUNTING THE WORLD – THE SPECTER OF CAPITALISM.
He recognized the variation on the famous first sentence of *The Communist Manifesto* in which Europe is haunted by the spectre of communism, circa 1850.
They were confused and wrongheaded. But his respect for the protesters' ingenuity grew more certain.

(DeLillo 2003, 96)

As Eric watches the spectacle he feels exhilarated, and continues trading on the phone. The protest ends with a protester attempting self-immolation. The sight of the burning man impresses Eric, and it crosses his mind that: 'Kinski had been wrong. The market was not total. It could not claim this man or assimilate his act' (ibid., 99–100), though Kinski then observes that the protester had copied images of Vietnamese monks self-immolating, it wasn't an original gesture.

An interesting set of juxtapositions are at work here. Eric's mobile office with its global reach, the site where precisely the kind of 'enforced destruction' that Kinski attributes to 'capitalist thought' occurs, is juxtaposed *against* the destructive action of the anti-globalization protest. Kinsky mediates as the theorist of globalization, in command of those generalizing academic discourses where globalization is apprehended and conceptualized. That the theorist of globalization is in the representative capitalist's protection and pay suggests complicity between globalization theory and capitalist practice. This is immediately evidenced by the lines of co-optation and continuity that Kinski draws between the destructiveness of 'capitalist thought' and the destructiveness of anti-capitalist action, and in the suggestion that the protests inspire Eric and are within his control. The polarized opposition between thought and action is, however, set to slip out of that view of co-optation and continuity. Eric thinks, his various subordinates think, Kinski thinks that the paraphernalia of financial trading somehow conquer reality and enable the sway of speculation (in both senses). When the contemplative movement of Eric's world-embracing capsule in Manhattan hits upon the reckless abandoned desperate activity of the protest, the polarized opposition between thought and action is jarringly reinserted. If there is a pattern or strategy in the protests it is for Eric and Kinski to contemplate and for the protesters to spontaneously enact. Insofar as the protesters express a point of view, it always appears to be a derivative one: the deliberate and indicative misquotation of *The Communist Manifesto*, a reenactment of a famous image of protest as martyrdom. This derivativeness itself conveys a kind of world-embracing quality or global consciousness too, but only insofar as Kinski or Eric can contemptuously ('they were confused and wrongheaded') discern it. The slippage of the polarized opposition between thought and action from a view of capitalist co-optation and continuity is most cogently conveyed in Eric's misgivings that the act of self-immolation has somehow eluded or defeated the totality of markets.

It doesn't take a veteran of anti-globalization protests to recognize that this description is of a strangely and exaggeratedly violent and destructive affair. It is more a protest of the imagination than based on any recognizable reality. This perception fits the contrived character of the situation itself, the neatness of the juxtaposition of Eric's limo with theorist inside against the raging protests without, the formal structures of the plot which seem to collude in the construction of these juxtapositions. In fact, it seems plausible that this imaginary protest is a product of the literary mode, and comes with licence of a fictionalizing arrangement where situations are posed against each other, and downplayed or played up, for maximum effect. Some sense of literary appositeness underlies the description of this protest. The ideological import of this description is not to be discerned simply by focusing on the scene I have picked on, but against the novel as a whole. The protest scene is a highlight in the simmering and occasionally explosive violence that stretches across the novel. The abstract violence of Eric's sheer power (a kind of, often literally, sexual drive) dovetails into the evidence of real violence which surrounds him, which he is aware of, and which he even enjoys as spectacle. He watches pictures of two assassinations on his screens in the limo: of Arthur Rapp, managing director of the International Monetary Fund, and of Nikolai Kaganovich, 'owner of Russia's largest media conglomerate' and Eric's friend. He is also being stalked by a real assassin, Richard Sheets alias Benno Levin, who ultimately kills him. In the course of the day he is attacked by a fake assassin, 'André Petrescu, the pastry assassin, a man who stalked corporate directors, military commanders, soccer stars and politicians' (DeLillo 2003, 142). In the scheme of the novel the visceral violence of the anti-globalization protesters appears in the middle as an intensification and widening (to the masses) of the different strands of violence that knit the plot together.

At different points of the novel this sort of real violence is presented as a concretization of the abstract violence of global capitalism itself. As observed above, this occurs in Kinski's theorizations, and, more importantly, towards the end of the novel when Eric himself disintegrates into real violence. He murders, quite gratuitously, his chief of security Torval, and in his final moments, as he faces his murderer, he shoots himself in the hand:

> He pressed the muzzle of his gun, Eric did, against the palm of his left hand. He tried to think clearly. He thought of his chief of security flat on the asphalt, a second yet left in his life. He thought of others down the years, hazy and nameless. He felt an enormous remorseful awareness. It moved through him, called guilt, and strange how soft the trigger felt against his finger.
>
> (DeLillo 2003, 196)

But Eric's own descent into physical violence is rather different from the violence of the protest. In shooting his bodyguard he effectively removes his own armour, in shooting himself he finally removes that capacity that made him a success, 'the predatory impulse, the sense of large excitation that drove him through the days, the sheer and reeling need to be' (ibid., 209). Eric's violence is directed against what he stands for. It becomes parcel of the violence that is described through the novel, in assassinations of capitalists, in the shattering violence of the anti-globalization protesters. Eric is the opposite of Bateman in Brett Easton Ellis's novel *American Psycho* (1991), the 1980s Wall Street banker in Manhattan who spends his time in conspicuous consumption and fantasies (perhaps realities) of serial killing. In the millennial moment where DeLillo sets *Cosmopolis*, Eric seems to move against the grain of Ellis's portrayal of capitalist psychopathology; Eric's violence is directed against himself and what he stands for just as the protesters' violence is. DeLillo's novel presents a world in the grip of an abstractly destructive and dehumanizing global capitalism which even incorporates its opponents. But its main agents appear to be peculiarly vulnerable and mortal, and its ostensible opponents – the anti-globalization activists and protesters – seem to have a near monopoly on real violence. The imaginary anti-globalization protests described in the novel are a deliberately exaggerated and manipulative envisioning of this idea. DeLillo's fictional ploys may leave his ideological take on globalization processes and free market capitalism hazy, and may deliberately evade theoretical academic pinning down, but are used to present a relatively clear placement of anti-globalization protests. They are a co-opted product of and in continuity with what they oppose, and have a near monopoly on real violence. Even the state's violence (through the police), traditionally regarded (by Weber's celebrated definition) as exercised through its monopoly on force, wanes in significance before the protesters' sweeping destructiveness. The police shoot their rubber bullets uselessly over the billboards.

That the anti-globalization protest in DeLillo's *Cosmopolis* belongs to the sphere of the imaginary, is constructed according to the exigencies of fictional structure, is sufficiently clear within that novel. Its character as an anti-globalization (or, for that matter, anti-capitalist) protest makes immediate sense only within that artificial structure of the novel; its relationship to real protests and public gestures which are sometimes contentiously dubbed 'anti-globalization' in the mass media is equally immediately distant. In the latter, protesters are typically far from being conceptually derivative or agents of physical action and typically identify [. . .] with 'social movements' or 'globalization from below'. A fictional account of such real-world protest, carefully constructed to convey a sense of historical and contextualizable reality, could be usefully considered alongside *Cosmopolis*, and the obvious candidate is Robert Newman's *The Fountain at the Centre of the World* (2003).

Newman's *The Fountain* presents, as its climax, a day-by-day description of the celebrated protests organized in Seattle during the WTO meeting in December 1999. In the course of the novel, as the fictional characters traverse internal and international boundaries across Britain, Mexico and the United States, to converge in Seattle in December 1999, numerous factual (or sometimes factual-sounding) details are thrown in. Details of the South American disease *chagas*, the nuances of VNRs or video news records, the dangers of working in a Componentes Mecánicos factory in Mexico, the political and economic situation in Mexico, proceedings in Global Power Forum summits, the legal meaning of a private corporation, how to make a fertilizer bomb (this, though convincingly technical sounding, is actually unworkable), 1989 statements by Secretary of State Madeleine Albright, etc., are woven seamlessly into the plot. These factual details work alongside and within the fiction, which involves the central character Chano Salgado, who is on the run from the Mexican police for bombing a multinational company's toxic waste plant, his brother and powerful international corporate PR guru Evan Hatch, from whom he was parted in childhood, and his long lost son Daniel. Just as DeLillo juxtaposes the protesters, the powerful financial speculator, and the globalization theorist within a single space, so Newman engineers meetings and partings between the brothers as representatives of diametrically opposed ideological positions. But these contrivances coalesce with details which serve to convey a concrete historical context that is documented and verifiable. The 1999 Seattle protests are presented within that frame.

Since a specific historical event is now at issue, some registering of discussions of social movements and protests similar to the 1999 Seattle one (visibly and effectively staged since at meetings of transnational economic and military alignments such as the World Bank, IMF, WTO, NAFTA, and G8 – Montreal 2000, Genoa 2001, Davos 2001, Calgary and Ottawa 2002, Cancun 2003, etc.) is called for. So, a brief digression from *The Fountain*, outlining the key ideas relevant here follows; I return to the novel below.

Discussions of social movements and protests have broadly centred on the following perceptions. First, the increasing frequency and visibility of such protests are merely the tip of the iceberg – symptoms or surface manifestations of a larger and deeper phenomenon. These represent the convergence of a range of identity-based or local issue-based activities and gestures (addressing poverty, localized oppressions, culture-specific disaffections, the operations of corporations/states on specific ecosystems, etc.) within the global South or East; left- and right-oriented marginal political factions with specific agendas (ending Third World debt and mistreatment of migrants, protecting the environment or animal rights, extending Christian charity, etc.) in the global North or West; and locally as well as transnationally active NGOs. The global scale of the phenomenon merits attention. Behind such moments of convergence lie an enormous variety of protest activities dispersed among interest groups in a large number of locations. Second, these moments of convergence present an opportunity to announce some degree of commonality of objective and purpose in them, or perhaps to generate such commonality of purpose among them. These very divergent interests can be presented as aligned in a specific direction through the adoption of an inclusive terminology, as in 'social movement', 'globalization from below' and 'movement of movements'. Third, though the impetus of such protests is provided by the moments of convergence of diverse interests, the fact still remains that these are momentary convergences involving provisional pacts that retain their diverse and fragmentary character at all times. To retain the promise of the convergence, and yet at the same time not disturb the diversity of interest groups entering provisional pacts, is a tricky business. This is to a great extent a matter of presentation, and may involve disposing different kinds of interests into a finite number of structurally related categories (such as identity-based, issue-based and region-based), presenting the different interests as aligned with a finite number of ideological positions (radical, liberal, moderate), or presenting the diverse kinds of protests and activities involved as falling into a limited number of types (direct action against transnational/state/corporate entities, reform of existing state and transnational entities, NGO-based facilitations, enabling communal autonomy). Fourth, the balance between convergence and divergence in social move-ments is necessarily a kind of mirror-image of that which such social movements seem to oppose, and in fact a great deal of transfer or co-opting of the norms avowed by globalization champions is unproblematically possible. Thus, for instance, social movements often seem to enter into some sort of competition with establishment alignments in claiming democratic legitimacy. In their book *Globalization/Anti-Globalization* (2002), Held and McGrew are therefore understandably able to see little contradiction between the promise of democratization through globalization processes and that through anti-globalization movements. However, social move-ments and protests do demand change of the establishment in clearly enunciated, and often radical, ways. Callinicos's *An Anti-Capitalist Manifesto* (2003), for example, presents a clear exposition of the kind of radical changes that may be demanded. Fifth, and finally, combining ideas of radical change with existing understandings of social movements does recall transformative agendas rooted in the history of Marxism and the international working-class movement. To a certain extent, social movements are conceptualized both as replacing and correcting the problems in that history and as retaining the spirit of the historical working-class movement against the exploitations of industrial, agrarian and colonial capitalism and with universal human interests at stake. DeLillo's linking of anti-globalization protests with *The Communist Manifesto* gestures towards this.

Newman's *The Fountain* actually represents various levels of local disenchant-ment and rousing of protest which are brought to converge in the great 1999 Seattle anti-WTO protest. The main protagonist, Chano Salgado, who gradually comes to represent the spirit of the Seattle protest, is introduced as follows:

> But what can a protest march achieve? asked Chano Salgado.
>
> We have to do something, right? replied Oscar, his forearm flat on the table like the shadow on a sundial pointing at Chano. The others at El Café Fuente were all looking at Chano too. Yes, they'd known him a long time – but a long time ago. Did they still?
>
> Of course you have to act, Chano replied, but we need to find, well, some other way, a new way.
>
> (Newman 2003, 9)

In this instance the proposed march is against a toxic-waste plant constructed by a multinational water corporation that is pumping up to 60,000 gallons of water a day and depleting the local water resources. The alternative way that is later suggested to him by his friend Ayo, and that Chano reluctantly accepts, is bombing the toxic-waste plant. Chano can make bombs – he has a past as a student activist, his wife Marisa was killed while attending a strike meeting at a Ford *maquilla* (border factory), and he had spent time in prison. The end result is that Chano successfully bombs the plant, but his own house unfortunately explodes too, and he has to go on the run. Chano's friend Yolanda, to pick up another thread, worked in the Components Mecánicos – 'subsidiary of a famous US make of car' (ibid., 61) – *maquilla*, where she, like many of her co-workers, was gradually poisoned by the chemicals that she had to deal with without protection. As a result her son was born with a fatal disease, Sturge–Weber Syndrome. Yolanda and fellow sufferer Elena discuss the different options for seeking redress here – Elena is in favour of raising consciousness through the media and taking legal action; Yolanda wants to organize a different sort of more inclusive protest (Elena speaks first in the quotation, contemplating a series of legal actions around the world):

> Ah, but if the company lose in *China*. Ah! You see, what then? Now they have nowhere left to go until they find little green women in space. What then?
>
> El-e-na! Look around! Then there's another hundred companies here meanwhile all doing the same thing or something else like it, and another and another, streets and streets of them in Matamoros, Reynosa, Juarez, Nogales.
>
> So, we do nothing?
>
> [. . .]
>
> Let's do something else. An occupation, *protesta*, *manifestación*, a general *maquilladora* strike, yes – but not the courts. *Their* courts.
>
> (Newman 2003, 63 [brackets by Gupta])

The description of these local disenchantments (and the complicities of the agents of injustice with larger multinational corporations and international alignments) and the formation of the desire for a new kind of more inclusive and wide-scale protest lead first to the description of a protest march, a *manifestación*, in the town of Calderon. The novel then sweeps towards the 1999 Seattle protests, mentioning some of the other such local disaffections and search for redress that get incorporated, thus creating, in its build up towards the climax, a sense of the enormous diversity of interests and gestures that converge in the 'movement of movements' concretized at Seattle.

There are other ways in which *The Fountain* coheres with discussions of real social movements and their convergence in 'anti-globalization' protests. For instance, the ostensible mirroring of apparently similar democratic norms on both sides of the globalization alignments, from above and from below, and yet the ineradicable difference between them, are registered neatly in the novel. This occurs by setting up a confrontation of and intellectual engagement between the brothers – between Chano, the representative of oppositional social movements, and Evan, the representative of establishment global capitalism – in a hotel in Seattle. Consider, for instance, the following bit of their exchange:

> You're right. We're not clever enough, said Chano. None of us. That's why it's impossible for one human or a few humans to lead lots of other people. *Only* the people can run their own lives. One leader makes everyone else less human. Chano found that there was something about talking to his younger brother which lent him fluency and clarity. He was surer of certain beliefs than he'd thought, not in the sense of being sure those beliefs were right, but of being sure they were his. [. . .]
>
> [. . .]
>
> Well, said Evan, I don't see the masses out on the streets calling for the revolution that you want. I see them buying Air Nikes, queuing for the multiplex and buying free-trade coffee with Big Mac and fries.
>
> (Newman 2003, 191 [brackets by Gupta])

The difference between Chano's progressive idealism and Evan's cynical realism is clear, but in a way it is borne on the reader that there is a certain common ground – the two are looking at the screen of people (the *demos* in democracy) from opposite sides. To put it as a crude and simplistic opposition: Chano wishes to give people what they deserve to have, some kind of self-possession, while Evan wishes to give people what they appear to want to have, to fulfil the desire for possessions and pleasure. The accord underlying the indelible discord, and vice versa, between the two brothers' ideological positions is underlined by the mutually enhanced clarity of conviction that they feel in this exchange.

Ultimately, though, the literary form of the novel proves to be particularly conducive to conveying the complexity of Seattle-like mass protest as a convergence of diverse social movements (local to global) because, as observed above, the momentary unity in diversity is to a significant extent a matter of presentation, a kind of linguistic performance as much as the performance of a material gesture and an image. The studied discussion of this depends on the suggestiveness of apt phrases, such as 'movement of movements', and an accounting of particularities which is always open-ended, whereas the fictional representation can be impressionistic and connected and whole at the same time. The sweep of disaffection and the will to protest for change that is captured in *The Fountain* by focusing on the specifics of a small Mexican town, Tonalacapan, and then building from there to the *manifestación* in Calderon, and from there finally to the WTO protests, conveys impressionistically but comprehensively something of the structure of social movements and convergences – in ways that are difficult to achieve in a theoretical or academic or journalistic exposition. This is demonstrated briefly in the description of the Calderon *manifestación* (Newman 2003, 123–25, 130–33), but that remains incomplete as the military move in to arrest Chano's son to entrap Chano. It is shown on a grand scale in the day-by-day account of the Seattle protests (occupying all of part 4, entitled 'The Battle of Seattle', chapters covering 30 November to 3 December 1999, pp. 245–311). The fluid and often truncated narrative here slips from protagonist to protagonist, from group to group, from action to action, weaving disparate scenes and conversations and events into a fictionally and realistically coherent whole.

Interestingly, what comes across powerfully in this attempt to give literary form to a (well-conceptualized) reality of global scale, focalized into a convergent period of protest, is in fact exactly the opposite of what is conveyed in DeLillo's anti-globalization protest of the imagination in *Cosmopolis*. If in the latter violence was somehow, obviously implausibly, concentrated on the protesters and activists, so that the anti-globalization activists seem to have a near monopoly on real violence, in *The Fountain* that monopoly is clearly the establishment's. It is in the hands of the US police and military, as the shields and agents of the most obvious global capitalist alignment, the WTO. *The Fountain* describes in visceral detail all the modes of crowd control and dispersal – concussion grenades, tear gas shells, CN gas shells, rubber bullets, arrests and beatings, cordons – unleashed by the police and paramilitary forces in Seattle against a non-violent mass. The effects of being tear-gassed on the first day of the protests set the tone:

> Tear gas seared his skin, scorching every pore and blood vessel. He
> screamed out. Acid hooks pulled at the roots of his tongue, burning his

throat and mouth. Screams broke all around him, bodies were heaving and tipping this way and that. He tore off his molten goggles and thrashed around on his back, legs lashing out. The pain grew worse by the breath. (Like missing the moment you snatch your scalded hand away from a pan. Instead the hand stays there, only it's your whole body, and the burning gas is everywhere.) Lava dribbled down his chin. He grabbed at his scalded eyes with scalding hands. He whimpered in terror and panic and tried to breathe but seized up, convulsed in a paroxysm of strangled airless panic.

(Newman 2003, 254–55)

In the midst of a steady proliferation of such violence as the protest grows, Chano is described as symbolizing the spirit of the protest. Though protesters are subjected to these painful measures with ever-increasing intensity, they remain stolidly and non-violently resistant – their spirit immured and toughened by their sense of injustice and oppression. Chano significantly discovers that he has grown resistant to the effects of tear gas through prolonged chemical poisoning, and is able to move through it unaffected: 'Alone among the fifty thousand protesters Chano's long years of marination in sodium metabisulphite had rendered him immune to tear gas. [. . .] Now and then he coughed in the gas and his eyes stang a little, but only as much as someone standing downwind of a bonfire' (Newman 2003, 259 [brackets by Gupta]).

Peace movements

The literary representation of anti-globalization movements/social movements is one among many threads that could characterize discussions of globalization. What such representations arguably convey is a sense of a coherent and dynamic social awareness that, while clearly located and contextualized, is not contained by immediate locations and contexts. In other words, a sort of social awareness is conveyed that understands its location and context in terms of world-embracing systems or global interconnectedness. This apprehension of interconnectedness has various levels – political, economic, communicative, organizational, etc. – which are naturally within the ken of literature, and must in some sense reconstitute ideas about literariness. Literary treatment of such a global social awareness is not seen simply in the meaningful event or gesture, such as a particularly large-scale or effective protest. The global social awareness in question, while effectively concretized and concentrated in such events, is ultimately dispersed in the everyday life of people. At any rate, some such dispersal of a global social awareness in the interstices of everyday life is often assumed and discerned by globalization theorists and registered in literary works – in, for instance, the contemporary British and North American literature to which this chapter is devoted.

By way of maintaining continuity with the discussion in this chapter so far, the dispersal of a global social awareness can be traced in literary representations that deliberately delve behind such significant events as large-scale international protests. Perhaps the most globally effective protests in recent years, certainly in terms of scale and organization, have been not so much the December 1999 Seattle kind of 'anti-globalization' protest as the anti-war protests or peace marches after the Islamist terrorist attacks in New York and Washington of 11 September 2001 and the military actions against Afghanistan (immediately after) and Iraq (in 2003) that followed. In various ways the post 9/11 context has given globalization both from above and from below an edge that is distinct from perceptions in 1999 or 2000, which the novels by DeLillo and Newman cited here addressed. In terms of protest movements, some of the largest international mobilizations were evidenced during and following the US–UK led attack on Iraq, which was undertaken without United Nations sanction and on the unproven allegation that Iraq was harbouring weapons of mass destruction that were dangerous to international security, and which was later touted as a war for international democracy against tyranny. This military attack deposed the Saddam Hussein-led Baathist government in Iraq and unleashed a protracted period of internecine violence and instability in that country.

Of the many peace marches and anti-war protests that took place in this period the most memorable and enormous were undoubtedly those organized worldwide on 15 and 16 February 2003 (see Gupta 2006, chapter 12), when the impending attack on Iraq was widely regarded as inevitable. Over that weekend it was estimated that more than 600 cities and towns around the world had witnessed protest marches (Conradi 2003), with about 30 million persons participating. A more cautious estimate later suggested that, for 15 February alone, 12 million worldwide, with 6 million in Europe, joined anti-war marches. All the newspaper and broadcast reports on these noted at the time that the largest rallies took place within those Western European countries whose governments were pushing for military action in Iraq most single-mindedly – particularly in London, Rome, Barcelona and Madrid. It was reported that the London rally of 15 February 2003 had (according to police estimates) 500,000 to 750,000 protesters or (according to organizers' estimates) between 1.5 to 2 million. The consensus now appears to be that there were at least 1 million protesters marching in London that day. According to a brief survey of protests in The Guardian (Chrisafis, Fickling, et al. 2003), rallies in Barcelona and Madrid were estimated as bringing together 1 million people, campaigners in Rome claimed 3 million people had converged (though police put the figure at 650,000), and organizers in New York counted 400,000 demonstrators marching in defiance of a court order. Though estimates of figures differed widely between police and organizer sources, it is generally accepted that these were the largest international protests ever seen. However, they had little effect on the plan for invading Iraq, which was initiated by US President George Bush on 19 March 2003.

Worth noting here is the difference of such international protest gestures from the anti-globalization or social movement protests, which reflect in effect another turn to the globalization/anti-globalization opposition. If anything, the peace protests brought together an even more diverse set of interests under the banner of a strongly defined anti-war objective. They were addressed not directly to an abstract system of global economic alignments and regulations but to a specific and contingent series of events that could be related to those; however, they also had an independent moral impetus. The main organizing groups, though aligned broadly with the left, clearly incorporated a wide ideological spectrum. Writing about the British Stop the War Coalition (STWC), a report in The Guardian (Vidal 2003) observed: 'More than 450 organisations, including such disparate groups as Greenpeace, Americans against the War and Britons versus Bush – a group of Bedford cabdrivers – have joined 11 political parties including SNP, the Liberal Democrats,

Plaid Cymru and the Greens, and affiliated themselves to the STWC'. It was also observed that there were separate anti-war groups that had come together outside the STWC because of the predominantly left make-up of its steering group, such as Our World Our Say (which registered its protest by placing advertisements in major national dailies). The International ANSWER (Act Now to Stop War and End Racism), United for Peace and Justice and the Not in Our Name project, the main protest organizations based primarily in the United States, listed on their websites a range of endorsements from representatives of groups that embraced positions far outside the remit of left associations. A *New York Times* report (Clemetson 2003) mentioned a number of groups with no specific ideological position other than a humanitarian one (such as Win Without War and September Eleventh Families for Peace), church-based groups, and even Republican and business associations (Business Leaders for Sensible Priorities) coming together with an anti-war agenda.

Unsurprisingly the anti-war protests in the context of the 2003 attack on Iraq have been drawn into literary representation, but often interestingly not so much to present them directly (as in *Cosmopolis* or *The Fountain*) as to register the more dispersed and fraught global social awareness that enabled them. One example can serve to demonstrate the literary treatment of this: British novelist Ian McEwan's *Saturday* (2006), which follows the movements and thoughts of a London surgeon with the protests in the background [. . .]

McEwan's *Saturday* describes an eventful day, 15 February 2003, in the life of a London neurosurgeon Henry Perowne, through his eyes and thoughts. The novel begins with Perowne rising at dawn and witnessing from his window a plane crashing, then details his interactions with his immediate family and colleagues, his memories, his social and philosophical attitudes, and his professional activities, and is gradually structured around two events – an encounter with a gang of aggressive youths after a slight car accident and the reappearance of this gang at his home to wreck an evening family get-together. Perowne obviously belongs to the affluent professional middle class, lives in an up-market house in central London and drives an expensive car, and his view of the world and life – effectively conveyed through a sort of stream of consciousness (rather more formally and linguistically orthodox and less immediate than James Joyce's or Virginia Woolf's stream of consciousness novels) – is circumscribed by his circumstances. The two encounters with the gang of youths, particularly their leader Baxter, turn out to be encounters across a class chasm, infused with the desire and aggression that the less solvent Baxter feels towards Perowne and his family. Baxter's disadvantages are underlined by his having inherited a genetically transmitted disease, which Perowne discerns in their first meeting (thus establishing a kind of authority). The novel ends with Perowne, the authority figure and devoted family man, overcoming Baxter, and then, as healer and humanist, saving his life by performing surgery on him (though unable to cure him of his fatal inherited disease).

The reader is tempted to read this sequence of events, especially the well-heeled London surgeon's overcoming and patching up of the diseased and disadvantaged criminal, as somehow related to the larger conflict that occupies the background – the invasion of Iraq by US–UK led forces on the pretext of overcoming tyranny and a threat to world peace, and the global protests against that. There is no attempt whatever in the novel to labour any such association – merely the juxtaposition of Perowne's experiences against the most momentous anti-war protest march in history as an intimation. An association is also suggested through the occasional foregrounding of Perowne's thoughts on the matter of impending war, inevitably lurking in his mind as on everyone's mind in London at the time, as he passes the anti-war march that takes over the city that day or as he debates the issue with his anti-war daughter. But mostly his preoccupation with the pros and cons of the coming war are in an almost subliminal stratum of his consciousness: he finds himself thinking of Saddam Hussein as he watches his sleeping wife, for instance. Despite qualms about the motives of the drive for war, Perowne is not against it. On the contrary, and largely due to a personal encounter with a professor who was tortured in Iraq, he rather thinks it might lead to desirable outcomes, albeit in a conflicted fashion. While watching the protesters from his car he lists in his mind all their arguments against war and recognizes their veracity, and yet 'can't feel, as the marchers themselves probably can, that they have an exclusive hold on moral discernment' (McEwan 2006, 73). Or, as he later explains in an argument with his daughter: 'No rational person is for war. But in five years we might not regret it. I'd love to see the end of Saddam. You're right, it could be a disaster. But it could be the end of a disaster and the beginning of something better. It's all about outcomes, and no one knows what they'll be. That's why I can't imagine marching in the streets' (ibid., 187). But more than these explicit positions it is in his passing reflections on the protesters themselves – redolent with Perowne's sense of individual scepticism against their collective certainty – that conveys his position:

> There are ragged practice chants which at first he can't make out. Tumty tumty tum. Don't attack Iraq. Placards not yet on duty are held at a slope, at rakish angles over shoulders. Not in my name goes past a dozen times. Its cloying self-regard suggests a bright new world of protest, with the fussy consumers of shampoos and soft drinks demanding to feel good, or nice. Henry prefers the languid, Down With this Sort of Thing. A placard of one of the organising groups goes by – the British Association of Muslims. Henry remembers that outfit well. It explained recently in its newspaper that apostasy from Islam was an offence punishable by death. Behind comes a banner proclaiming the Swaffham Women's Choir, and then, Jews Against the War.
>
> (McEwan 2006, 71–72)

Perowne's view of the myriad of protesters is reductively contained (or conveniently selected by the author) in his two substantive observations there. He disparagingly associates the protesters as a whole, on the basis of misreading one of their slogans, with moral self-regard and self-gratifying consumption. And he homes in on the co-sponsoring group, the Muslim Association of Britain (MAB), whose conservative Islamic ideology and alleged links to the Egyptian Muslim Brotherhood were hotly debated by alignments within the anti-war coalition itself (the statement referred to here appeared in an article published in the MAB newspaper *Inspire* in 2002) – without any reference to the other sponsors (the Stop the War Alliance, incorporating an enormous number of differently located interest groups, and the Campaign for Nuclear Disarmament or CND) or the varied ideological interests which converged in the anti-war protest.

By sieving the protest, while keeping it tellingly in the background, through Perowne's overarching consciousness and suggestively juxtaposing it on the surgeon's carefully close-up humaneness and humanity, it could be argued, the book itself is positioned ideologically vis-à-vis the anti-war protests and the invasion of Iraq. But, equally, it may be argued that any reader's determination to find a position in this regard for the book, the novel's invitation to the reader to do so, itself makes a point. The book demonstrates deliberately how deeply embedded the matter of this war and these protests were in the routine consciousness of people in London (and presumably elsewhere), how enmeshed in the domestic, personal, everyday preoccupations of people such as Perowne (and others, presumably both all the protesters and all those who didn't protest). At the same time, a reader's interest in determining where the novel comes from in this regard, a reader's suspecting that every aspect of Perowne's day may be inextricably interlinked in a grand design (at least a fictional design) with the enormity of events and protests which, ultimately, spin out across the globe, draws that reader into a similarly engaged social-intermeshed-with-personal consciousness. It involves them in the complicity of taking the fictional Perowne and his attitudes to be as real as themselves and their own. The novel presents and plays upon, seemingly, a sort of global social awareness and mixes it up with individual private lives by evoking 15 February 2003 as a backdrop.

[. . .]

. . . *Saturday* [. . .] appear[s] to convey, in the context of disquiet about the Iraq war in 2003, a sense of a continuum between global politics and oppositional movements, their immediate collective manifestations in local contexts (in specific images of protest marches, for instance), and individual preoccupations with/engagements in these within the flow of ordinary individual lives. The central protagonists are not involved in immediate strife, and nor are their thoughts guided entirely by narrow self-interest or entirely circumscribed by their own national or cultural allegiances. The everyday lives of the central protagonists, their personal and professional concerns, are impinged upon by those larger events and oppositions in a more or less continuous fashion, as a continuous prickle to emotion and intellect. It is this intermeshing between the macro- and micro-levels of awareness which gives weight to the collective materialization of these anti-war protests and gestures towards the ubiquity of a global social awareness (especially since most readers would know that the specific protest described is but one amidst a global phenomenon).

The . . . novel . . . present[s] this global social awareness as naturally and obviously given: there already, but heightened and crystallized by the pressures of the Iraq war period. [It] do[es] not attempt to analyse or highlight the means through which this consciousness has come about or how it is fed. But the primary means are written as incidental and unquestioned facts of contemporary living: the presence of distant realities as selectively presented realities, but immediate, even personal and visceral, through mass media. [. . .]

[. . .]

[. . .] That these media are a key battle-ground both for establishment forces of globalization from above and for dissenting and oppositional global social movements from below is a well-recognized and much researched area. To a great extent global fissures and tensions are fought in specific living quarters in the contemporary world. This feature of the current world is not merely reflected in the kind of global social awareness remarked in the literary works discussed above; it also impinges upon the conception of literature and literary form [. . .]

Bibliography

Abu-Manneh, B. (2003). 'Editorial: The Illusions of Empire'. *Interventions: International Journal of Postcolonial Studies* 5(2): 159–76.

Adams, W. M. and M. Mulligan, Eds. (2002). *Decolonizing Nature: Strategies for Conservation in a Post-Colonial Era*. London, Earthscan.

Adamson, J., M. M. Evans, et al., Eds. (2002). *The Environmental Justice Reader: Politics, Poetics, and Pedagogy*. Tucson, University of Arizona Press.

Adorno, T. (1978). *Minima Moralia*. London, Verso.

'After GATT Pique, Pix Pax Promoted'. (1994). *Daily Variety*. 8 June: 1, 16.

Ahmad, A. (1987). 'Jameson's Rhetoric of Otherness and the "National Allegory"'. *Social Text* 17: 3–25.

—— (1992). *In Theory: Nations, Classes, Literatures*. London, Verso.

—— (1997). 'The Politics of Literary Postcoloniality'. *Contemporary Postcolonial Theory: A Reader*. Ed. P. Mongia. London, Arnold: 276–93.

Albrow, M. (1996). *The Global Age: State and Society Beyond Modernity*. Cambridge, Polity Press.

Alfonso-Forero, A. M. (2007). 'Immigrant Motherhood and Transnationality in Jhumpa Lahiri's Fiction'. *Literature Compass* 4(3): 851–61.

Ali, T. (2003). 'Globalization: For Whom? By Whom'? Plenary Presentation. Towards a Critical Globalization Studies Conference, University of California, Santa Barbara, 1–4 May.

—— (2004). *Bush in Babylon: The Recolonisation of Iraq*. London, Verso.

Allen, R. (1995). *The Arabic Novel: An Historical and Critical Introduction*. Syracuse, NY, Syracuse University Press.

Allen, R. E., Ed. (1990). *The Concise Oxford Dictionary*. Oxford, Clarendon Press.

Altvater, E. (1993). *The Future of the Market: An Essay on the Regulation of Money and Nature after the Collapse of 'Actually Existing Socialism'*. London, Verso.

Amin, S. (1980). *Class and Nation: Historically and in the Current Crisis*. New York, Monthly Review Press.

Anderson, B. (1991). *Imagined Communities: Reflections on the Origin and Spread of Nations*. London, Verso.

Anderson, P. (1992). *English Questions*. London, Verso.

Annesley, J. (2006). *Fictions of Globalization: Consumption, the Market and the Contemporary American Novel. Continuum Literary Studies*. London, Continuum.

Appadurai, A. (1986). 'Introduction: Commodities and the Politics of Value'. *The Social Life of Things*. Ed. A. Appadurai. Cambridge, Cambridge University Press: 3–63.

—— (1990). 'Disjuncture and Difference in the Global Cultural Economy'. *Public Culture* 2(2): 1–24.

—— (1996). *Modernity at Large: Cultural Dimensions of Globalization. Public Worlds*. Minneapolis, University of Minnesota Press.

Appiah, A. (2006). *Cosmopolitanism: Ethics in a World of Strangers*. New York, W. W. Norton.

Appiah, A. K. (2000). 'Battle of the Bien-Pensant'. *New York Review of Books*. 27 April: 42–44.

Arnold, D. and R. Guha, Eds. (1995). *Nature, Culture, Imperialism: Essays on the Environmental History of South Asia*. Oxford, Oxford University Press.

Arrighi, G. (1990). 'Marxist Century – American Century: The Making and Remaking of the World Labor Movement'. *Transforming the Revolution, 1990*. Ed. S. Amin. New York, Monthly Review Press: 54–95.

—— (1994). *The Long Twentieth Century: Money, Power and the Origin of Our Times*. London, Verso.

Arrighi, G. and B. J. Silver (1999). *Chaos and Governance in the Modern World System*. Minneapolis: University of Minnesota Press.

Ashcroft, B., G. Griffiths, et al. (2002). *The Empire Writes Back: Theory and Practice in Post-Colonial Literatures*. London, Routledge.

Auerback, N. (2000). 'Acrimony'. *London Review of Books*. 6 July: 6–8.

Baldick, C. (1983). *The Social Mission of English Criticism, 1848–1932*. Oxford, Oxford University Press.

Balibar, E. (1995). 'Ambiguous Universality'. *Differences* 7(1): 48–74.

Balladur, E. (1993). 'Entrevista a Edouard Balladur, Primer Ministro Francés. ¿Qué es lo que quiere eu . . . la desaparición del cine europeo'? *El Nacional*. Mexico. 23 October: 27.

Bamyeh, M. A. (2000). *The Ends of Globalization*. Minneapolis, University of Minnesota Press.

Barber, K. (1987). 'Popular Arts in Africa'. *African Studies Review* 30(3): 1–78.

Barraclough, G. (1977). 'The Keynesian Era in Perspective: Essays on the Disintegration of the Keynesian Political Economy'. *The End of the Keynesian Era*. Ed. R. Skidelsky. Basingstoke, Macmillan.

Barthes, R. (1967). *Writing Degree Zero*. Trans. A. Lavers and C. Smith. New York, Hill and Wang.

Baruah, S. (1986). 'Immigration, Ethnic Conflict and Political Turmoil: Assam, 1979–85'. *Asian Survey* 26(11 November): 1184–1206.

Bass, T. A. (1996). 'The Future of Money'. *Wired* 4(10): www.wired.com/wired/archive/4.10/wriston.html.

Baucom, I. (1999). *Out of Place: Englishness, Empire, and the Locations of Identity*. Princeton, NJ, Princeton University Press.

Baudrillard, J. (1975). *The Mirror of Production*. Trans. M. Poster. St. Louis, MO, Telos Press.

—— (1986). *L'amérique*. Paris, B. Grasset.

—— (1988). *America*. London, Verso.

Bauman, Z. (1998). *Globalization: The Human Consequences*. Cambridge, Polity Press.

—— (2002). *Society under Siege*. Cambridge, Polity Press.

Beck, U. (2004). *Der kosmopolitische Blick oder: Krieg ist frieden*. Frankfurt, Suhrkamp.

Becker, W. (2003). *Goodbye Lenin!* Bavaria Film. Germany.

Behdad, A. (2006). 'On Globalization Again'. *Postcolonial Studies and Beyond*. Eds. A. Loomba, S. Kaul and M. Bunzi. Durham, NC, Duke University Press: 62–79.

Bello, W., S. Cunningham, and Li Kheng Poh (1998). *A Siamese Tragedy: Development and Disintegration in Modern Thailand*. London, Zed.

Benjamin, W. (1970). *Illuminations*. Ed. H. Arendt. Trans. H. Zohn. London, Wm Collins Sons and Co.

Bennett, M. (2003). 'From Wide Open Spaces to Metropolitan Places: The Urban Challenge to Ecocriticism'. *The Isle Reader: Ecocriticism, 1993–2003*. Eds. M. P. Branch and S. Slovic. Athens, GA, University of Georgia Press: 297–312.

Bennett, T., L. Grossberg, et al. (2005). *New Keywords: A Revised Vocabulary of Culture and Society*. Malden, MA, Blackwell.

Berlant, L. (1997). *The Queen of America Goes to Washington City: Essays on Sex and Citizenship*. Durham, NC; London, Duke University Press.

Berman, M. (1983). *All that Is Solid Melts into Air: The Experience of Modernity*. London, Verso.

Bernstein, N. (2000). 'Widest Income Gap Is Found in New York'. *New York Times*. Online edition. 19 January.

Beti, M. (2000). In a discussion session during a conference on 'The Chosen Tongue' organized by Maryse Condé and Pierre Force at Columbia University's Maison Française, April 7–8.

Bhabha, H. K. (1991). 'Caliban Speaks to Prospero: Cultural Identity and the Crisis of Representation'. *Critical Fictions: The Politics of Imaginative Writing*. Ed. P. Mariani. Seattle, WA, Bay Press: 62–65.

—— (1994). *The Location of Culture*. London, Routledge.

—— (1995). 'Postcolonial Critic: Homi Bhabha Interviewed by David Bennett and Terry Collits'. *Literary India: Comparative Studies in Aesthetics, Colonialism, and Culture*. Eds. P. C. Hogan and L. Pandit. Albany, NY, SUNY Press: 237–53.

—— (1996). 'Unsatisfied: Notes on Vernacular Cosmopolitanism'. *Text and Nation: Cross-Disciplinary Essays on Cultural and National Identities*. Eds. L. Garcia-Moreno and P. C. Pfeiffer. Columbia, SC, Camden House: 191–207.

Bird, J. (1993). *The Changing Worlds of Geography: A Critical Guide to Concepts and Methods*. Oxford, Clarendon.

Birken, L. (1988). *Consuming Desire: Sexual Science and the Emergence of a Culture of Abundance, 1871–1914*. Ithaca, NY, Cornell University Press.

Blair, T. (2005). 'BBC News: Full Text of Tony Blair's Speech'. Retrieved 13 February 2010 from http://news.bbc.co.uk/1/hi/uk_politics/4287370.stm.

Blau, H. (1982). *Take up the Bodies*. Urbana, University of Illinois Press.

Bloch, M. (1928). 'Pour une histoire comparée des sociétés européennes'. *Revue de synthèse historique* 46(136–38): 15–50.

Bluestone, B. and B. Harrison (1982). *The Deindustrialization of America: Plant Closings, Community Abandonment, and the Dismantling of Basic Industry*. New York, Basic Books.

Bookchin, M. (1982). *The Ecology of Freedom: The Emergence and Dissolution of Hierarchy*. Palo Alto, CA, Cheshire Books.

Bose, B., Ed. (2003). *Amitav Ghosh: Critical Perspectives*. Delhi, Pencraft International.

Bourdieu, P. (1990). *The Logic of Practice*. Trans. R. Nice. Cambridge, Polity.

Bourricaud, F. (1987). 'Modernity, "Universal Reference" and the Process of Modernization'. *Patterns of Modernity*. Ed. S. N. Eisenstadt. *Beyond the West*. 2. London, Pinter.

Boyd-Barrett, O. (1998). 'Media Imperialism Reformulated'. *Electronic Empires: Global Media and Local Resistance*. Ed. D. Thussu. London, Arnold: 157–76.

Boyer, M. C. (1988). 'The Return of Aesthetics to City Planning'. *Society* 25(4): 49–56.

Branch, M. P. and S. Slovic, Eds. (2003). *The Isle Reader: Ecocriticism, 1993–2003*. Athens, GA, University of Georgia Press.

Brantlinger, P. (1996). *Fictions of State: Culture and Credit in Britain 1694–1994*.

Braudel, F. (1984). *The Perspective of the World*. Trans. S. Reynolds. London, Collins.

Brennan, T. (1997). *At Home in the World: Cosmopolitanism Now*. Cambridge, MA, Harvard University Press.

—— (2001). 'Cosmo-Theory'. *The South Atlantic Quarterly* 100(3): 659–91.

Brock, R. (2008). 'An "Onerous Citizenship": Globalization, Cultural Flows and the HIV/AIDS Pandemic in Hari Kunzru's < I > Transmission < /I >'. *Journal of Postcolonial Writing* 44(4): 379–90.

Brydon, D. (2000). *Postcolonialism: Critical Concepts in Literary and Cultural Studies*. London, Routledge.

Buell, F. (1994). *National Culture and the New Global System*. Baltimore, Johns Hopkins University Press.

—— (1998). 'Nationalist Postnationalism: Globalist Discourse in Contemporary American Culture'. *American Quarterly* 50(3): 548–91.

Buell, L. (1995). *The Environmental Imagination: Thoreau, Nature Writing, and the Formation of American Culture*. Cambridge, MA, Harvard University Press.

—— (2001). *Writing for an Endangered World: Literature, Culture, and Environment in the U.S. and Beyond*. Cambridge, MA, Harvard University Press.

—— (2005). *The Future of Environmental Criticism: Environmental Crisis and Literary Imagination*. Oxford, Blackwell Publishing.

Bullen, E. and E. Parsons (2007). 'Dystopian Visions of Global Capitalism: Philip Reeve's "Mortal Engines" and M. T. Anderson's "Feed" '. *Children's Literature in Education* 38(2): 127–39.

Butler, J., E. Laclau, et al. (2000). *Contingency, Hegemony, Universality: Contemporary Dialogues on the Left*. London, Verso.

Callinicos, A. (2003). *An Anti-Capitalist Manifesto*. Cambridge, Polity.

Cameron, A. and R. Palan (2004). *The Imagined Economies of Globalization*. London, Sage.

Cameron, D. (2001). 'Ten Reasons for Canadians to Join with Other Citizens and Protest the Free Trade Area of the Americas Meetings in Quebec City'. *Counterpunch* Retrieved 11 January 2010 from www.counterpunch.org/ftaaprotest.html.

Campbell, C. (2003). *'Letting Them Die': Why HIV/AIDS Prevention Programmes Fail*. Bloomington, Indiana University Press.

Campbell, S. (1996). 'The Land and Language of Desire: Where Deep Ecology and Poststructuralism Meet'. *The Ecocriticism Reader: Landmarks in Literary Ecology*. Eds. C. Glotfelty and H. Fromm. Athens, GA, University of Georgia Press: 124–36.

Carafiol, P. C. (1991). *The American Ideal: Literary History as a Worldly Activity*. New York; Oxford, Oxford University Press.

Carter, P. (1987). *The Road to Botany Bay: An Essay in Spatial History*. London, Faber.

Case, S.-E. (2001). 'Cyberbodies auf der transnationalen Bühne'. *Die Philosophin: Forum für feministische Theorie und Philosophie* 24: 10–27.

Cassirer, E. (1955). *The Philosophy of Symbolic Forms*. Yale, CT, Yale University Press.

Castells, M. (1997). *The Power of Identity*. Oxford, Blackwell.

—— (2001). *The Internet Galaxy: Reflections on the Internet, Business, and Society*. Oxford, Oxford University Press.

Castles, S. and A. Davidson (2000). *Citizenship and Migration: Globalization and the Politics of Belonging*. Basingstoke, Macmillan.

Castoriadis, C. (1998). *The Imaginary Institution of Society*. Trans. K. Blamey. Cambridge, MA, MIT Press.

Cerny, P. (1993). 'The Deregulation and Re-Regulation of Financial Markets in a More Open World'. *Finance and World Politics*. Ed. P. Cerny. Aldershot, Edward Elgar: 51–85.

Cerny, P. G. (1994). 'The Dynamics of Financial Globalization: Technology, Market Structure, and Policy Response'. *Policy Sciences* 27: 319–42.

Césaire, A. (1972). *Discourse on Colonialism*. Trans. J. Pinkham. New York.

Chabal, P. and J.-P. Daloz (1999). *Africa Works: Disorder as Political Instrument*. Oxford, International African Institute in association with James Currey.

Chakrabarty, D. (2000). *Provincializing Europe: Postcolonial Thought and Historical Difference*. Princeton, NJ, Princeton University Press.

Chambers, I. (1987). 'Maps for the Metropolis: A Possible Guide to the Present'. *Cultural Studies* 1(1): 1–22.

—— (1993). *Migrancy, Culture, Identity*. London, Routledge.

Chartrand, H. H. (1999). 'Copyright an the New World Economic Order'. Retrieved 21 January 2009 from www.intelproplaw.com/Copyright/Forum/msg/498.shtml.

Chase-Dunn, C. (1989). *Global Formation: Structures of the World Economy*. Oxford, Basil Blackwell.

Chast, R. (1999). 'Cartoon'. *New Yorker*. 29 November: 88.

Chatterjee, P. (1986). *Nationalist Thought and the Colonial World: A Derivative Discourse?* London, Zed Books.

Cheah, P. (1997). 'Given Culture: Rethinking Cosmopolitical Freedom in Transnationalism'. *boundary 2* 24(2): 157.

—— (1998). 'Introduction Part II: The Cosmopolitical-Today'. *Cosmopolitics: Thinking and Feeling Beyond the Nation*. Eds. P. Cheah and B. Robbins. Minneapolis, University of Minnesota Press: 20–41.

—— (2008). 'Crises of Money'. *positions: east asia cultures critique* 16(1): 189–219.

Cheah, P. and B. Robbins (1998). *Cosmopolitics: Thinking and Feeling Beyond the Nation*. Minneapolis, University of Minnesota Press.

Chomsky, N. (1993). *Radical Priorities*. Ed. C. P. Otero. New York, Vintage.

—— (1998). 'Free Trade and Free Market: Pretense and Practice'. *The Cultures of Globalization*. Eds. F. Jameson and M. Miyoshi. Durham, NC, Duke University Press: 356–70.

—— . (2006). 'Globalization: Noam Chomsky Interviewed by Maria Ahmed'. *Global Agenda*. Retrieved 29 September 2009 from www.chomsky.info/interviews/2006----.htm.

Chow, R. (2002). *The Protestant Ethnic and the Spirit of Capitalism*. New York, Colombia University Press.

Chrisafis, A., D. Fickling, et al. (2003). 'Millions Worldwide Rally for Peace: Huge Turn-out at 600 Marches from Berlin to Baghdad'. *The Guardian*. London. 17 February.

Chrisman, L. and B. Parry (2000). *Postcolonial Theory and Criticism*. Cambridge, D. S. Brewer.

Chua, L. (1998). *Gold by the Inch*. New York, Grove Press.

Cixous, H. (1980). 'The Laugh of the Medusa'. *New French Feminisms*. Eds. I. Courtivron and E. Marks. Amherst, University of Massachusetts Press.

Cixous, H. and C. Clément (1986). *The Newly Born Woman*. Trans. B. Wing. Minneapolis, University of Minnesota Press.

Clemetson, L. (2003). 'Protest Groups Using Updated Tactics to Spread Antiwar Message'. *New York Times*. New York. 15 January.

Clifford, J. (1997). *Routes: Travel and Translation in the Late Twentieth Century*. Cambridge, MA, Harvard University Press.

Coetzee, J. M. (1980). *Waiting for the Barbarians*. Harmondsworth, Penguin, 1982.

Cohen, S. and L. Taylor (1978). *Escape Attempts: The Theory and Practice of Resistance to Everyday Life*. Harmondsworth, Penguin.

Colebrook, C. (1998). *New Literary Histories: New Historicism and Contemporary Criticism*. Manchester, Manchester University Press.

Coles, R. (1997). *Rethinking Generosity: Critical Theory and the Politics of Caritas*. Ithaca, NY, Cornell University Press.

Coll, S. (2004). *Ghost Wars: The Secret History of the CIA, Afghanistan, and Bin Laden, from the Soviet Invasion to September 10, 2001*. New York, Penguin.

Collier, R. (1996). 'Bullish Investors Pouring Billions Back into Mexico'. *San Francisco Chronicle*. 5 July: A-1.

Collins, J., K. Gibson, C. Alcorso, S. Castles, and D. Tait. (1995) *A Shopful of Dreams: Ethnic Small Business and Restructuring in Australia*. Sydney: Pluto Press.

Colquhoun, A. (1985). 'On Modern and Post-Modern Space'. *Architecture, Criticism, Ideology*. Ed. J. Ockman. Princeton, NJ, Princeton Architectural Press: 103–17.

Comaroff, J. and J. Comaroff (2002). 'Alien-Nation: Zombies, Immigrants, and Millennial Capitalism'. *South Atlantic Quarterly* 101(4): 779–805.

Conley, V. A. (1991). *Hélène Cixous: Writing the Feminine*. Lincoln, NE, University of Nebraska Press.

Connell, L. (2004). 'Global Narratives: Globalisation and Literary Studies'. *Critical Survey* 16(2): 78–95.

Conradi, P. (2003). 'Demos Follow Sun around the Globe'. *The Times*. London. 16 February: 2.

Cook, D., Ed. (1965). *Origin East Africa: A Makerere Anthology*. London, Heinemann Educational.

Cooper, F. (2001). 'What Is the Concept of Globalization Good For? An African Historian's Perspective'. *African Affairs* 100(399): 189–213.

Cooppan, V. (2006). 'Ruins of Empire: The National and Global Politics of America's Return to Rome'. *Postcolonial Studies and Beyond*. Eds. A. Loomba, S. Kaul and M. Bunzi. Durham, NC, Duke University Press: 80–100.

Coronil, F. (2001). 'Toward a Critique of Globalcentrism: Speculations on Capitalism's Nature'. *Millennial Capitalism and the Culture of Neoliberalism*. Eds. J. Comaroff and J. L. Comaroff. Durham, NC, Duke University Pres: 63–87.

Coupe, L. (2000). *The Green Studies Reader: From Romanticism to Ecocriticism*. London, Routledge.

Court, F. E. (1989). *Institutionalizing English Literature: The Culture and Politics of Literary Study, 1750–1900*. Stanford, CA, Stanford University Press.

Crang, M. and N. J. Thrift, Eds. (2000). *Thinking Space*. London, Routledge.

Crawford, R., Ed. (1998). *The Scottish Invention of English Literature*. Cambridge, Cambridge University Press.

Crimp, D. (1989). 'Mourning and Militancy'. *October* 51(Winter): 3–18.

Crosby, A. W. (1986). *Ecological Imperialism: The Biological Expansion of Europe, 900–1900*. Cambridge, Cambridge University Press.

Crush, J. (1995). *Power of Development*. London, Routledge.

Cruz, A. and M. F. Manalansan, Eds. (2002). *Queer Globalization : Citizenship and the Afterlife of Colonialism*. New York; London, New York University Press.

Curtin, D. W. (1999). *Chinnagounder's Challenge: The Question of Ecological Citizenship*. Bloomington, IN, Indiana University Press.

Daiya, K. (2003). ' "No Home but in Memory": Migrant Bodies and Belongings, Globalization and Nationalism in *The Circle of Reason* and *The Shadow Lines*'. *Amitav Ghosh: Critical Perspectives*. Ed. B. Bose. Delhi, Pencraft International.

Dallmayr, F. (2005). 'Empire or Cosmopolis? Civilization at the Crossroads'. *Globalizations* 2(1): 14–30.

Daly, G. (1991). 'The Discursive Construction of Economic Space: Logics of Organization and Disorganization'. *Economy and Society* 20(1): 79–102.

Dannecker, P. (2000). 'Globalisierung und "Migration" von Produktions-und Geschlechterstrukturen: Fabrikarbeiterinnen in Bangladesch'. *Geschlecht-Arbeit-Zukunft*. Eds. I. Lenz, H. M. Nickel and B. Riegraf. Münster, Westfälisches Dampfboot: 49–74.

Darian-Smith, K., E. Gunner, et al., Eds. (1996). *Text, Theory, Space: Land, Literature and History in South Africa and Australia*. London, Routledge.

Davis, M. (1990). *City of Quartz: Excavating the Future in Los Angeles*. London, Verso.

—— (2000). *Ecology of Fear: Los Angeles and the Imagination of Disaster*. London, Picador.

—— (2001). *Late Victorian Holocausts*. London, Verso.

—— (2006). *Planet of Slums*. London, Verso.

Dayal, S. and M. S. Murphy, Eds. (2007). *Global Babel: Questions of Discourse and Communication in a Time of Globalization*. Newcastle upon Tyne, Cambridge Scholars Publishing.

de Certeau, M. (1984). *The Practice of Everyday Life*. Berkeley, CA, University of California Press.

De Landa, M. (1991). *War in the Age of Intelligent Machines*. New York, Zone.

Debord, G. (1983). *Society of the Spectacle*. Detroit, Black and Red.

—— (1990). *Comments on the Society of the Spectacle*. London, Verso.

Delanty, G. (2000). *Modernity and Postmodernity: Knowledge, Power and the Self*. London, Sage.

—— (2001). 'Nationalism: Between Nation and State'. *Handbook of Social Theory*. Eds. G. Ritzer and B. Smart. London, Sage: 472–84.

Deleuze, G. and F. L. Guattari (1977). *Anti-Oedipus: Capitalism and Schizophrenia*. Trans. R. Hurley, M. Seem and H. R. Lane. New York, Viking Press.

Deleuze, G. and F. L. Guattari (1987). *A Thousand Plateaus: Capitalism and Schizophrenia*. Trans. B. Massumi. Minneapolis, MN, University of Minnesota Press.

DeLillo, D. (2003). *Cosmopolis*. London, QPD.

Derian, J. D., Ed. (1998). *The Virilio Reader*. Oxford Blackwell.

Derrida, J. (1976). *Of Grammatology*. Trans. G. C. Spivak. Baltimore, Johns Hopkins University Press.

—— (1988). *Limited, Inc*. Trans. S. Weber and J. Mehlman. Evanston, IL, Northwestern University Press.

—— (1992). *Given Time: I. Counterfeit Money*. Trans. P. Kamuf. Chicago, IL, University of Chicago Press.

—— (1994). *Specters of Marx: The State of the Debt, the Work of Mourning, and the New International*. Trans. P. Kamuf. New York; London, Routledge.

—— (1995). *The Gift of Death*. Chicago, IL, University of Chicago Press.

—— (1997). *Politics of Friendship*. Trans. G. Collins. London, Verso.

Desai, G. G. and S. Nair, Eds. (2005). *Postcolonialisms: An Anthology of Cultural Theory and Criticism*. Oxford, Berg.

Deshpande, S. and A. Kurtz (1994). 'Trade Tales'. *Mediations* 18(1): 22–52.

Dicken, P. (1986). *Global Shift: Industrial Change in a Turbulent World*. London, Harper & Row.

Dicken, P., J. Peck, et al. (1997). 'Unpacking the Global'. *Geographies of Economies*. Eds. R. Lee and J. Wills. London, Arnold: 158–66.

Dillon, J. (1993). 'Intellectual Property'. *Canadian Forum* 71(816): 11–12.

Dimock, W. C. (2003). 'Planetary Time and Global Translation: "Context" in Literary Studies'. *Common Knowledge* 9(3): 488–507.

—— (2006). *Through Other Continents: American Literature across Deep Time*. Princeton, NJ, Princeton University Press.

Dirks, N. (1990). 'History as a Sign of the Modern'. *Public Culture* 2(2): 25–32.

Dirlik, A. (1994). 'The Postcolonial Aura: Third World Criticism in the Age of Global Capitalism'. *Critical Inquiry* 20(2): 328–56.

—— (2002). 'Rethinking Colonialism: Globalization, Postcolonialism, and the Nation'. *Interventions: International Journal of Postcolonial Studies* 4(3): 428–48.

Dobson, A. (1990). *Green Political Thought: An Introduction*. London, Unwin Hyman.

Dobson, J. (1993). 'TNCs and the Corruption of GATT: Free Trade Versus Fair Trade'. *Journal of Business Ethics* 12(7): 573–78.

Dominguez, V. R. (1992). 'Invoking Culture: The Messy Side of "Cultural Politics" '. *South Atlantic Quarterly* 91(1): 19–42.

Doty, R. (1996). *Imperial Encounters: The Politics of Representation in North–South Relations*. Minneapolis, University of Minnesota Press.

Douglas, M. (1995). 'Forgotten Knowledge'. *Shifting Contexts: Transformations in Anthropological Knowledge*. Ed. M. Strathern. London, Routledge: 13–29.

Doyle, B. (1989). *English and Englishness*. London, Routledge.

Dumont, L. (1983). *Essais sur l'individualisme*. Paris, Editions du Seuil.

Durix, J.-P., Ed. (2002). *The Global and the Particular in the English Speaking World*. Dijon, France, Editions Universitaires de Dijon.

Durkheim, E. (1984). *The Division of Labor in Society*. New York, Free Press.

Eagleton, T. (1983). *Literary Theory: An Introduction*. Oxford, Basil Blackwell.

—— (1989). *Raymond Williams: Critical Perspectives*. Cambridge, Polity.

Easthope, A. (1999). *Englishness and National Culture*. London, Routledge.

Eckersley, R. (2004). *The Green State: Rethinking Democracy and Sovereignty*. Cambridge, MA, MIT Press.

Ehrenreich, B. (2000). 'Maid to Order'. *Harper's* April: 59–70.

Eliot, G. (1977). *Middlemarch*. New York, W. W. Norton.

Eliot, T. S. (1975). *Selected Prose of T. S. Eliot*. Ed. F. Kermode. London, Faber.

Emerson, R. (1964). *Self-Determination Revisited in the Era of Decolonization*. Cambridge, MA, Center for International Affairs, Harvard University

Eng, D. L. and S. Han (2002). 'A Dialogue on Racial Melancholia'. *Loss: The Politics of Mourning*. Eds. D. L. Eng and D. Kazanjian. Berkeley, University of California Press: 324–71.

Eriksen, T. H. (2001). *Tyranny of the Moment: Fast and Slow Time in the Information Age*. London, Pluto.

Escobar, A. (1995). *Encountering Development: The Making and Unmaking of the Third World*. Princeton, NJ, Princeton University Press.

Esty, J. (2004). *A Shrinking Island: Modernism and National Culture in England*. Princeton, NJ, Princeton University Press.

Even-Zohar, I. (1990). 'Laws of Literary Interference'. *Poetics Today* 11(1): 53–72.

Evin, A. O. (1983). *Origins and Development of the Turkish Novel*. Minneapolis, MN, Bibliotheca Islamica.

Faison, S. (1995a) 'China Closes a Disk Factory as Sanctions Deadline Nears'. *New York Times*. 26 February: 6.

—— (1995b) 'Razors, Soap, Cornflakes: Pirating Spreads to China'. *New York Times*. 17 February: D1, D2.

Falk, R. (1999). *Predatory Globalization*. Cambridge, Polity.

Farah, N. (1990). *Gåvor*. Stockholm, Bonnier.

—— (1993). *Gifts*. Harmondsworth, Penguin.

Farred, G. (2007). ' "to Dig a Well with a Needle": Orhan Pamuk's Poem of Comparative Globalization'. *The Global South* 1(2): 81–99

Featherstone, M. (1990). 'Global Culture: An Introduction'. *Global Culture: Nationalism, Globalization and Modernity*. Ed. M. Featherstone. *A Theory, Culture and Society Special Issue*. London, Sage Publiations: 1–14.

Feld, S. (1988). 'Notes on World Beat'. *Public Culture* 1(1): 31–37.

Fisher, W. F. (1995). *Toward Sustainable Development? Struggling over India's Narmada River*. Armonk, NY, M. E. Sharpe.

Foley, B. (1985). 'The Politics of Deconstruction'. *Rhetoric and Form: Deconstruction at Yale*. Eds. R. C. Davis and R. Schleifer. Norman, OK, University of Oklahoma Press.

Foucault, M. (1984). *The Foucault Reader*. Ed. P. Rabinow. Harmondsworth, Penguin Books.

Franco, J. (1969). *An Introduction to Spanish-American Literature*. Cambridge, Cambridge University Press.

Frank, A. G. (1998). *Reorient: Global Economy in the Asian Age*. Berkeley, CA, University of California Press.

Frank, D. (1999). *Buy American: The Untold Story of Economic Nationalism*. Boston, Beacon.

Frank, T. (2000). *One Market under God: Extreme Capitalism, Market Populism and the End of Economic Democracy*. New York, Doubleday.

Freud, S. (1916). *Mourning and Melancholia*. London, The Hogarth Press.

—— (1953). 'The Uncanny'. Retrieved 28 August 2002 from www.engl.virginia.edu/ ~enec981/Group/chris.uncanny.html.

Freud, S., J. Strachey, et al. (1995). *The Standard Edition of the Complete Psychological Works of Sigmund Freud*. London, Hogarth Press and the Institute of Psycho-analysis.

Frieden, K. (1995). *Classic Yiddish Fiction*. Albany, NY, State University of New York Press.

Friedman, M. (1987a). 'A Monetary History of the United States: A Summing Up'. *The Essence of Friedman*. Ed. K. R. Leube. Stanford, Hoover Institution Press.

—— (1987b). 'Notes on the Quantity Theory of Money'. *The Essence of Friedman*. Ed. K. R. Leube. Stanford, Hoover Institution Press.

Friedman, M. and A. J. Schwartz (1963). *A Monetary History of the United States*. Princeton, NJ, Princeton University Press.

Friedman, S. S. (1998). *Mappings: Feminism and the Cultural Geographies of Encounter*. Princeton, NJ, Princeton University Press.

Friedman, T. (1999). *The Lexus and the Olive Tree*. New York, NY, Farrar, Straus and Giroux.

Friedman, T. L. (2005). *The World Is Flat: A Brief History of the Globalized World in the Twenty-First Century*. London, Allen Lane.

Fujimura, J. (1988). 'The Molecular Biological Bandwagon in Cancer Research: Where Social Worlds Meet'. *Social Problems* 35(3): 261–84.

Gadgil, M. and R. Guha, Eds. (1995). *Ecology and Equity: The Use and Abuse of Nature in Contemporary India*. London, Routledge.

Gandhi, L. (1998). *Postcolonial Theory: A Critical Introduction*. Edinburgh, Edinburgh University Press.

Gans, E. (1985). *The End of Culture: Toward a Generative Anthropology*. Berkeley, University of California Press.

Garb, Y. (1990). 'Perspective or Escape? Ecofeminist Musings on Contemporary Earth Imagery'. *Reweaving the World: The Emergence of Ecofeminism*. *I*. Eds. I. Diamond and G. Orenstein. San Francisco, CA, Sierra Club Books: 264–308.

García Canclini, N. (1982). *Los culturas populares en el capitalismo*. Havana, Casa de las Américas.

—— (1995). *Hybrid Cultures: Strategies for Entering and Leaving Modernity*. Trans. C. L. Chiappari and S. L. López. Minneapolis, MN, University of Minnesota Press.

Garnham, N. (1987). 'Concepts of Culture: Public Policy and the Cultural Industries'. *Cultural Studies* 1(1): 23–37.

Garrard, G. (2004). *Ecocriticism*. *The New Critical Idiom*. London, Routledge.

Gasperetti, D. W. (1998). *The Rise of the Russian Novel: Carnival, Stylization, and Mockery of the West*. DeKalb IL, Northern Illinois University Press.

Geertz, C. (1986). 'The Uses of Diversity'. *Michigan Quarterly* 25(1): 105–23.

George, O. (2001). 'Alice Walker's Africa: Globalization and the Province of Fiction'. *Comparative Literature* 53(4): 354–72.

George, R. M. (1996). *The Politics of Home: Postcolonial Relocations and Twentieth-Century Fiction*. Cambridge, Cambridge University Press.

Ghosh, A. (1988). *The Shadowlines*. London, Bloomsbury.

—— (2002). *The Imam and the Indian*. New Delhi, Ravi Dayal.

—— (2004a). 'Folly in the Sudarbans'. Retrieved 8 January 2010 from www.amitavghosh.com/essays/essayfull.php?essayNo = 57.

—— (2004b). *The Hungry Tide*. New York, Houghton Mifflin.

—— (2005). 'The Tsunami of December 2004'. Retrieved 8 January 2010 from www.amitavghosh.com/essays/essayfull.php?essayNo = 60.

Gibson, W. (2003). *Pattern Recognition*. New York, Putnam.

Gibson-Graham, J. K. (1996). *The End of Capitalism (as We Knew It)*. Oxford, Blackwell.

Giddens, A. (1985). *Nation-State and Violence. A Contemporary Critique of Historical Materialism*. Cambridge, Polity.

—— (1990). *The Consequences of Modernity*. Cambridge, Polity.

—— (1998). *The Third Way: The Renewal of Social Democracy*. Cambridge, Polity Press.

Gikandi, S. (1996). *Maps of Englishness: Writing Identity in the Culture of Colonialism*. New York, Columbia University Press.

—— (2000). *Ngugi Wa Thiong'o*. Cambridge, Cambridge University Press.

Gilroy, P. (1993). *The Black Atlantic: Modernity and Double Consciousness*. London, Verso.

Glotfelty, C. (1996). 'Introduction: Literary Studies in an Age of Environmental Crisis'. *The Ecocriticism Reader: Landmarks in Literary Ecology*. Eds. C. Glotfelty and H. Fromm. Athens, GA, University of Georgia Press: xv–xxxvii.

Glotfelty, C. and H. Fromm, Eds. (1996). *The Ecocriticism Reader: Landmarks in Literary Ecology*. Athens, GA, University of Georgia Press.

Godelier, M. (1998). *The Enigma of the Gift*. Trans. N. Scott. Cambridge, Polity Press.

Gole, N. (2000) 'Snapshots of Islamic Modernities'. *Daedelus* 129: 114.

Goldberg, D. T. and A. Quayson, Eds. (2002). *Relocating Postcolonialism*. Oxford, Blackwell.

Goodman, A. (2006). ' "Voices of Time": Legendary Uruguayan Writer Eduardo Galeano on Immigration, Latin America, Iraq, Writing – and Soccer'. Retrieved 11 January 2010 from www.democracynow.org/2006/5/19/voices_of_time_legendary_uruguayan_writer.

Goodman, N. (1976). *Languages of Art: An Approach to a Theory of Symbols*. Indianapolis, IN, Hackett.

—— (1978). *Ways of Worldmaking*. Hassocks, The Harverster Press.

Gopal, P. and N. Lazarus (2006). 'Editorial'. *New Formations* 59: 7–9.

Gordimer, N. (1956). *Six Feet of the Country: Short Stories*. London, Victor Gollancz.

Gordon, N. (2003). 'Silence in the Face of Israeli Apatheid: Captives Behind Sharon's Wall'. *Counterpunch*. Retrieved 11 January 2010 from www.counterpunch.org/gordon11062003.html.

Goux, J.-J. (1994). *The Coiners of Language*. Norman, OK, University of Oklahoma Press.

—— (1999). 'Cash, Check, or Charge'? *The New Economic Criticism: Studies at the Intersection of Literature and Economics*. Ed. M. W. a. M. Osteen. London, Routledge.

Gowan, P. (2001). 'Neoliberal Cosmopolitanism'. *New Left Review* 11: 79–93.

Graff, G. (1987). *Professing Literature: An Institutional History*. Chicago, IL, University of Chicago Press.

Graham, S. (2007). 'Memory, Memorialization, and the Transformation of Johannesburg: Ivan Vladislavić's the Restless Supermarket and Propaganda by Monuments'. *MFS Modern Fiction Studies* 53(1): 70–97.

Gramsci, A. (1971). *Selections from the Prison Notebooks of Antonio Gramsci*. Trans. Q. Hoare and G. N. Smith. New York, International.

Gray, J. (2004). 'From the Great Transformation to the Global Free Market'. *The Globalization Reader*. Eds. F. J. Lechner and J. Boli. Oxford, Blackwell Publishing: 22–29.

Gray, R. (2009). 'Open Doors, Closed Minds: American Prose Writing at a Time of Crisis'. *American Literary History* 21(1): 128–51.

Gregory, D. and J. Urry, Eds. (1985). *Social Relations and Spatial Structures*. London, Macmillan.

Grosz, E. (1994). *Volatile Bodies: Toward a Corporeal Feminism*. Bloomington, Indiana University Press.

Guehenno, J.-M. (1995). *The End of the Nation-State*. Trans. V. Elliott. Minneapolis, MN, University of Minnesota Press.

Guha, R. (2000). *The Unquiet Woods: Ecological Change and Peasant Resistance in the Himalaya*. Berkeley, CA, University of California Press.

Guha, R. and J. Martínez-Alier, Eds. (1997). *Varieties of Environmentalism: Essays North and South*. London, Earthscan.

Guillory, J. (1993). *Cultural Capital: The Problem of Literary Canon Formation*. Chicago, IL; London, University of Chicago Press.

Gunn, G. (2001). 'Globalizing Literary Studies. Special Issue'. *PMLA* 116(1): 1–272.

Gupta, A. and J. Ferguson (1992). 'Beyond "Culture": Space, Identity, and the Politics of Difference'. *Cultural Anthropology* 7(1): 6–23.

Gupta, S. (2006). *The Theory and Reality of Democracy: A Case Study*. London, Continuum.

Haas, P. (1992). 'Introduction: Epistemic Communities and International Policy Coordination'. *International Organization* 46(1): 1–35.

Hall, S. (1991). 'The Local and the Global: Globalization and Ethnicity'. *Culture, Globalization, and the World-System*. Ed. A. King. London, Macmillan: 19–39.

Hallward, P. (2001). *Absolutely Postcolonial: Writing between the Singular and the Specific*. Manchester, Manchester University Press.

Hamelink, C. J. (1983). *Cultural Autonomy in Global Communications: Planning National Information Policy*. New York, Longman.

Handler, R. (1988). *Nationalism and the Politics of Culture in Quebec*. Madison, WI, University of Wisconsin Press.

Hankiss, E. (2001). *Fears and Symbols: An Introduction to the Study of Western Civilization*. Budapest; New York: Central European University Press.

Hannerz, U. (1987). 'The World in Creolization'. *Africa* 57(4): 546–59.

—— (1989). 'Notes on the Global Ecumene'. *Public Culture* 1(2): 66–75.

—— (1996). *Transnational Connections: Culture, People, Places*. London, Routledge.

Haraway, D. (1990). 'A Manifesto for Cyborgs'. *Feminism/Postmodernism*. Ed. L. Nicholson. London; New York, Routledge: 190–235.

Hardt, M. and A. Negri (2000). *Empire*. Cambridge, MA, Harvard University Press.

Harris, J. (1998/1999). 'Globalisation and the Technological Transformation of Capitalism'. *Race and Class* 40(2/3): 21–35.

Harrison, B. and B. Bluestone (1988). *The Great U-Turn: Corporate Restructuring and the Polarization of America*. New York, Basic Books.

Harvey, D. (1990). *The Condition of Postmodernity: An Enquiry into the Origins of Cultural Change*. Oxford, Blackwell.

—— (1996). *Justice, Nature and the Geography of Difference*. Oxford, Blackwell.

—— (2000). *Spaces of Hope*. Berkeley, University of California Press.

Hayden, P. (2005). *Cosmopolitan Global Politics*. Aldershot, Ashgate.

Hayles, K. N. (1997). *How We Became Posthuman: Virtual Bodies in Cybernetics, Literature, and Informatics*. Chicago, University of Chicago Press.

Head, D. (1998). 'The (Im)Possibility of Ecocriticism'. *Writing the Environment: Ecocriticism and Literature*. Eds. R. Kerridge and N. Sammells. London, Zed: 27–39.

—— (2006). 'The Demise of Class'. *Concise Companion to Contemporary British Fiction*. Ed. J. English. Oxford, Blackwell: 229–47.

Hechter, M. (1975). *Internal Colonialism: The Celtic Fringe in British National Development, 1536–1966*. Berkeley, CA, University of California Press.

Held, D. (2002). 'Cosmopolitanism: Ideas, Realities and Deficits'. *Governing Globalization:*

Power, Authority and Global. Eds. D. Held and A. McGrew. Cambridge, Blackwell: 305–24.

Held, D., A. G. McGrew, et al. (1999). *Global Transformations: Politics, Economics and Culture*. Cambridge, Polity.

Held, D. and A. G. McGrew (2002). *Globalization/Anti-Globalization*. Cambridge, Polity.

Helleiner, E. (1993). 'When Finance Was the Servant: International Capital Movements in the Bretton Woods Order'. *Finance and World Politics*. Ed. P. Cerny. Aldershot, Edward Elgar: 20–48.

Herzfeld, M. (1982). *Ours Once More: Folklore, Ideology and the Making of Modern Greece*. Austin, TX, Texas University Press.

Hinshaw, R., Ed. (1967). *Monetary Reform and the Price of Gold*. Baltimore, MD, Johns Hopkins Press.

Hiro, D. (2005). *Secrets and Lies: The True Story of the Iraq War*. London, Politico's.

Hirst, P. and G. Thompson (1999). *Globalization in Question: The International Economy and the Possibilities of Governance*. Cambridge, Polity.

Hitchock, P. (2006). 'Uncanny Marxism: Do Androids Dream of Lenin'? Paper presented at 'Spaces of Dissent: The Borders of Transnational Dreams'. 8th Annual Conference of the Marxist Reading Group, University of Florida, March 29–April 2.

Hobsbawm, E. (1994). *The Age of Extremes: A History of the World, 1914–1991*. New York, Vintage.

Hobsbawm, E. and T. Ranger, Eds. (1983). *The Invention of Tradition*. Cambridge, Cambridge University Press.

Hoogvelt, A. (2006). 'Globalization and Post-Modern Imperialism'. *Globalizations* 3(2): 159–74.

Hopkins, T. K. and I. Wallerstein (1996). *The Age of Transition: Trajectory of the World-System:1945–2025*. London, Zed Books.

Horkheimer, M. and T. W. Adorno (1989). *Dialectic of Enlightenment*. Trans. J. Cumming. New York, Continuum.

Huk, R., Ed. (2003). *Assembling Alternatives: Reading Postmodern Poetries Transnationally*. Middletown, CT, Wesleyan University Press.

Huntington, S. P. (1993). 'The Clash of Civilizations'. *Foreign Affairs* 72(3): 22–49.

—— (1996a). *The Clash of Civilizations and the Remaking of World Order*. New York, Simon & Schuster.

—— (1996b). 'The West: Unique, Not Universal'. *Foreign Affairs* 75(6): 28–46.

Hutcheon, L. (1994). *Irony's Edge: The Theory and Politics of Irony*. London; New York, Routledge.

Huyssen, A. (1998). 'In the Shadow of McLuhan: Jean Baudrillard's Theory of Simulation'. *Assemblage* 10: 7–17.

IMF (1999a). ' "The IMF's Response to the Asian Crisis." Fact Sheet, January 17, 1999'. Retrieved 28 August 2002 from www.imf.org.

—— (1999b). ' "International and Financial Monetary Stability: A Global Public Good." Address by Michel Camdessus, May 28, 1999'. Retrieved 28 August 2002 from www.imf.org.

—— (1999c). 'Address by Michel Camdessus to the Board of Governors of the Fund, September 28'. Retrieved 28 August 2002 from www.imf.org.

—— (1999d). ' "Second Generation Reforms: Reflections and New Challenges."

Address by Michel Camdessus, November 8, 1999'. Retrieved 28 August 2002 from www.imf..org.

——— (1999e). ' "Global Markets and the Global Village in the 21st Century: Are International Organizations Prepared for the Challenge?" Address by Stanley Fischer, November 19, 1999'. Retrieved 28 August 2002 from www.imf.org.

Innis, H. A. (1950). *Empire and Communications*. Oxford, Clarendon Press.

Irele, A. (1990). *The African Experience in Literature and Ideology*. Bloomington, IN, Indiana University Press.

Ivy, M. (1988). 'Tradition and Difference in the Japanese Mass Media'. *Public Culture* 1(1): 21–29.

Iyer, P. (1988). *Video Night in Kathmandu*. New York, Knopf.

Jaggi, M. (1997). 'Stars Are in the West'. *Guardian Weekly*. 28 August: 28.

Jameson, F. (1984). 'Postmodernism, or the Cultural Logic of Late Capitalism'. *New Left Review* 146: 53–92.

——— (1986). 'Third-World Literature in the Era of Multinational Capitalism'. *Social Text* 15: 65–88.

——— (1988). 'Cognitive Mapping'. *Marxism and the Interpretation of Culture*. Eds. C. Nelson and L. Grossberg. Urbana, IL, University of Illinois Press: 347–60.

——— (1991). *Postmodernism or, the Cultural Logic of Late Capitalism*. New York, Verso.

——— (1997). 'Culture and Finance Capital'. *Critical Inquiry* 24(Autumn): 246–65.

——— (1998). 'Notes on Globalization as a Philosophical Issue'. *The Cultures of Globalization*. Eds. F. Jameson and M. Miyoshi. Durham, NC, Duke University Press: 54–77.

Jameson, F. and M. Miyoshi, Eds. (1998). *The Cultures of Globalization*. Durham, NC, Duke University Press.

Jaspers, K. (1953). *The Origin and Role of History*. New Haven, CT, Yale University Press.

Jay, G. (1991). 'The End of "American" Literature: Toward a Multicultural Practice'. *College English* 53(3): 264–81.

Jay, P. (1998). 'The Myth of "America" and the Politics of Location: Modernity, Border Studies, and the Literature of the Americas'. *Arizona Quarterly* 54(2): 165–92.

——— (2005). 'The Post-Post Colonial Condition: Globalization and Historical Allegory in Mohsin Hamid's *Moth Smoke*'. *ARIEL* 36(1–2): 51–71.

Jencks, C. A. (1984). *The Language of Post-Modern Architecture*. London, Academy Editions.

Joekes, S. (1996). *Women and Trade: European Strategies for an International Agenda*. Brussels, WIDE.

Jones, A. F. (1994). 'Chinese Literature in the "World" Literary Economy'. *Modern Chinese Literature* 8(1–2): 171–90.

Joseph, B. (2002). 'Gendering Time in Globalization: The Belatedness of the Other Woman and Jamaica Kincaid's *Lucy*'. *Tulsa Studies in Women's Literature* 21(1): 67–83.

Kane, J. (1996). *Savages*. New York, Vintage.

Kant, I. (1951). *Critique of Judgment*. Trans. J. H. Bernard. London, Collier-Macmillan.

Kaplan, E. K. (1990). *Baudelaire's Prose Poems: The Esthetic, the Ethical and the Religious in the Parisian Prowler*. Athens, GA, University of Georgia Press.

Kaplinsky, R. (2005). *Globalization, Poverty and Inequality: Between a Rock and a Hard Place*. Cambridge, Polity Press.

Katz-Fishman, W. and J. Scott. (1994). 'The High Tech Revolution and the Permanent Poverty Economy: Educating and Organizing for a New Society'. Retrieved 27 July 1994 from igc.econ.poverty.

Kavolis, V. (1986). 'Civilization Paradigms in Current Sociology: Dumont vs. Eisenstadt'. *Current Perspectives in Social Theory* 7: 125–40.

Kearney, M. (1995). 'The Local and the Global: The Anthropology of Globalization and Transnationalism'. *Annual Review of Anthropology* 24: 547–65.

Keck, M. and K. Sikkink (1998). *Activists Beyond Borders*. Ithaca, NY, Cornell University Press.

Keil, R. (1998). 'Globalization Makes States: Perspectives of Local Governance in the Age of the World City'. *Review of International Political Economy* 5(4): 616–46

Kenyatta, J. ([1938] 1962). *Facing Mount Kenya: The Traditional Life of the Gikuyu*. New York.

Kiely, R. (2005). 'Capitalist Expansion and the Imperialism–Globalization Debate: Contemporary Marxist Explanations'. *Journal of International Relations and Development* 8(1): 27–57.

King, B. (2006). 'To Be or Not to Be Diasporic – Alas, Poor India!, I Knew Her'. *Journal of Postcolonial Writing* 42(2): 139–54.

Kirby, K. M. (1996). *Indifferent Boundaries: Spatial Concepts of Human Subjectivity* London: Guilford Press.

Klein, N. (1999). *No Logo: Taking Aim at the Brand Bullies*. New York, Picador USA.

—— (2000). *No Logo: No Space, No Choice, No Jobs, Taking Aim at the Brand Bullies*. London, Flamingo.

—— (2005). 'The Rise of Disaster Capitalism'. *The Nation*. 2 May.

Knight, D. S. (2002). 'Capitalist and Enlightenment Values in 1990s Chinese Fiction: The Case of Yu Huas Blood Seller'. *Textual Practice* 16: 547–68.

Kohn, H. (1971). 'Nationalism and Internationalism'. *History and the Idea of Mankind*. Ed. W. W. Wagar. Albuquerque, NM, University of New Mexico Press: 119–34.

Kojin, K. (1993). *Origins of Modern Japanese Literature*. Ed. F. Jameson. Durham, NC, Duke University Press.

Korper, S., and Juanita Ellis (2000). *The E-Commerce Book: Building the E-Empire*. San Diego, CA, Academic Press.

Koselleck, R. (1985). *Futures Past: On the Semantics of Historical Time*. Trans. K. Tribe. Cambridge, MA, MIT Press.

Kramer, A. E. (2005). 'Mapmakers and Mythmakers: Russian Disinformation Practices Obscure Even Today's Oilfields'. *New York Times*. 1 December.

Krasicki, I. (1992). *The Adventures of Mr. Nicholas Wisdom by Thomas H. Hoisington*. Trans. H. Goscilo. Evanston, IL, Northwestern University Press.

Krishnaswamy, R. and J. C. Hawley, Eds. (2008). *The Postcolonial and the Global*. Minneapolis, MN, University of Minnesota Press.

Kuhn, T. (1962). *The Structure of Scientific Revolutions*. Chicago, IL, University of Chicago Press.

Kumar, A. (1999). 'World Bank Literature: A New Name for Postcolonial Studies'. *College Literature* 26(3): 195–204.

—— , Ed. (2003). *World Bank Literature*. Minneapolis, MN, University of Minnesota Press.

Laclau, E. (1996). *Emancipation(s)*. London, Verso.

Laclau, E. and C. Mouffe (1985). *Hegemony and Socialist Strategy: Towards a Radical Democratic Politics*. London, Verso.

Lakoff, G. and M. Johnson (1980). *Metaphors We Live By*. Chicago, IL; London, University of Chicago Press.

Lash, S. and J. Urry (1987). *The End of Organized Capitalism*. Madison, WI, University of Wisconsin Press.

—— (1994). *Economies of Signs and Space*. London, Sage.

Lazarus, N. (1991). 'Doubting the New World Order: Marxism and Postmodernist Social Theory'. *differences: A Journal of Feminist Cultural Studies* 3(3): 94–138.

—— (1999). *Nationalism and Cultural Practice in the Postcolonial World*. Cambridge, Cambridge University Press.

——, Ed. (2004). *The Cambridge Companion to Postcolonial Literary Studies*. Cambridge, Cambridge University Press.

—— (2006). 'Postcolonial Studies after the Invasion of Iraq'. *New Formations* 59: 10–22.

Le Carre, J. (1965). *The Spy Who Came in from the Cold*. London, Pan Books.

Le Goff, J. (1999). *Un autre Moyen Âge*. Paris, Gallimard.

Leavis, F. R. (1969). *English Literature in Our Time and the University*. London, Chatto & Windus.

Lee, D. and T. Fulford (2000). 'Virtual Empires'. *Cultural Critique* 44(Winter): 3–28.

Lee, R. (1996). 'Structures of Knowledge'. *The Age of Transition: Trajectory of the World-System, 1945–2025*. Eds. T. Hopkins and I. Wallerstein. London, Zed Books: 178–206.

Lefebvre, H. (1991). *The Production of Space*. Trans. D. Nicholson-Smith. Oxford, Basil Blackwell.

Lenz, I. (2000). 'Globalisierung, Geschlecht, Gestaltung'? *Geschlecht-Arbeit-Zukunft*. Eds. I. Lenz, H. M. Nickel and B. Riegraf. Münster, Westfälisches Dampfboot.

Lenz, I., H. M. Nickel, and B. Riegraf, Eds. (2000). *Geschlecht-Arbeit-Zukunft*. Münster, Westfälisches Dampfboot.

Levenson, J. (1968). *Confucian China and Its Modern Fate*. Berkeley, CA, University of California Press.

Lévi-Strauss, C. (1987). *Introduction to the Work of Marcel Mauss*. London, Routledge and Kegan Paul.

Leyshon, A. and N. J. Thrift (1997). *Money / Space: Geographies of Monetary Transformation*. London, Routledge.

Lipietz, A. (1985). *The Enchanted World: Inflation, Credit and the World Crisis*. London, Verso.

Ma, Liquin, (1985). 'Lun shuli yanjiude Zhongguohua' ('Sinicization of research in alienation'). Trans. Y. Cia and X. Xiao. Taibei: 191–212.

Liu, K. (2004). *Globalization and Cultural Trends in China*. Honolulu, University of Hawaii Press.

Lodge, D. (1988). *Nice Work*. Harmondsworth, Penguin.

Loomba, A. (1993). 'Overworlding the Third World'. *Colonial Discourse and Post-Colonial Theory: A Reader*. Eds. P. Williams and L. Chrisman. Hemel Hempstead, Harvester Wheatsheaf: 305–23.

Loomba, A., S. Kaul, et al., Eds. (2005). *Postcolonial Studies and Beyond*. Durham, NC, Duke University Press.

Lowe, J. (2001). 'No More Lonely Londoners'. *Small Axe* 5(1): 166–80.

Lucas Jr., R. E. and T. J. Sargent (1994). 'After Keynesian Macroeconomics'. *The Rational Expectations Revolution: Readings from the Front Line*. Ed. P. J. Miller. Cambridge, MA, MIT Press.

Lyotard, J. F. (1984). *The Postmodern Condition*. Manchester, Manchester University Press.

Makdisi, S. (2005). 'An Iron Wall of Colonization: Fantasies and Realities about the

Prospects for Peace between Israelis and Palestinians'. *Counterpunch*. Retrieved 11 January 2010 from www.counterpunch.org/makdisi01262005.html.

Mallick, R. (1999). 'Refugee Resettlement in Forest Reserves: West Bengal Policy Reversal and the Marichjhapi Massacre'. *The Journal of Asian Studies* 58(1): 104–25.

Mandel, E. (1978). *Late Capitalism*. London, Verso.

Manovich, L. (2001). *The Language of New Media*. Cambridge, MA, MIT Press.

Marcus, G. (1995). 'Ethnography in/of the World System: The Emergence of Multi-Sited Ethnography'. *Annual Review of Anthropology* 24: 95–117.

Marcus, J. (2004). 'BBC World Service | The Age of Empire'. Retrieved 15 September 2009 from www.bbc.co.uk/worldservice/specials/1020_ageofempire/index.shtml.

Marcus, S. (1990). 'Literature and Social Theory: Starting in with George Eliot'. *Representations: Essays on Literature and Society*. New York, Columbia University Press: 183–213.

—— (1992). 'Fighting Bodies, Fighting Words: A Theory and Politics of Rape Prevention'. *Feminists Theorize the Political*. Eds. J. Butler and J. Scott. London, Routledge.

Mariani, P. (1991). *Critical Fictions: The Politics of Imaginative Writing*. Seattle, WA, Bay Press.

Marsh, N. (2007). *Money, Finance, and Speculation in Recent British Fiction*. London, Continuum.

Martí-López, E. (1996). 'La orfandad de la novela española: política editorial y creación literaria a mediados del siglo XIX'. *Bulletin Hispanique* 98(2): 347–62.

Martin, R. and B. Rowthorn, Eds. (1986). *The Geography of De-Industrialisation*. London, Macmillan.

Marx, K. (1973). *Grundrisse*. Trans. M. Nicolaus. New York, Penguin Books.

—— (1977). *Capital, Vol 1*. New York, Vintage.

——, Ed. (1995). *Capital: An Abridged Edition*. Ed. D. McLellan. New York, Oxford University Press.

Mattelart, A. (1983). *Transnationals and the Third World: The Struggle for Culture*. South Hadley, MA, Bergin & Garvey.

Mattelart, A. (2000). *Networking the World, 1794–2000*. Trans. Liz Carey-Libbrecht and James A. Cohen. Minneapolis, University of Minnesota Press.

Mattelart, A., and Seth Siegelaub Ed. (1979). *Communication and Class Struggle, Vol. 1, Capitalism, Imperialism*. New York, International General.

Maurer, B. (1995). 'Complex Subjects: Offshore Finance, Complexity Theory, and the Dispersion of the Modern'. *Socialist Review* 25(3&4): 114–45.

Mauss, M. (1954). *The Gift: Forms and Functions of Exchange in Archaic Societies*. Trans. I. Cunnison. London, Cohen & West.

—— (2001). *The Gift*. Ed. M. Douglas. London, Routledge.

McClintock, A. (1992). 'The Angel of Progress: Pitfalls of the Term "Post-Colonialism" '. *Social Text* 31/32: 84–98.

McCully, P. (1996). *Silenced Rivers: The Ecology and Politics of Large Dams*. London, Zed Books.

McEwan, I. (2006). *Saturday*. London, Vintage.

McGrew, A. (2002). 'Liberal Internationalism: Between Realism and Cosmopolitanism'. *Governing Globalization: Power, Authority and Global Governance*. Eds. D. Held and A. McGrew. Oxford, Blackwell: 267–89.

McHale, B. (1987). *Postmodernist Fiction*. London, Methuen.

McKenna, B. (1995). 'Road Shows in the Information Highway: Intellectual Property Rights Take on New Definitions in a Time of Technological Transformation'. *On Campus* 14(8): 8–9,13.

McLuhan, M. (1962). *The Gutenberg Galaxy: The Making of Typographic Man*. Toronto, University of Toronto Press.

—— (1964). *Understanding Media: The Extensions of Man*. New York, McGraw-Hill.

McQueen, H. (1988). 'The Australian Stamp: Image, Design and Ideology'. *Arena* 84: 78–96.

Mda, Z. (1997). *Ways of Dying*. Cape Town, Oxford University Press.

Meikle, S. (2000). 'Quality and Quantity in Economics: The Metaphysical Construction of the Economic Realm'. *New Literary History* 31(2): 247–68.

Meyer, J. W. (1987). 'Self and Life Course: Institutionalization and Its Effects'. *Institutional Structure: Constituting State, Society, and the Individual*. Eds. G. M. Thomas, J. W. Meyer, F. O. Ramirez and J. Boli. Newbury Park, CA, Sage: 242–60.

Meyrowitz, J. (1985). *No Sense of Place: The Impact of Electronic Media on Social Behavior*. Oxford, Oxford University Press.

Mignolo, W. (2000). 'The Many Faces of Cosmo-Polis: Border Thinking and Critical Cosmopolitanism'. *Public Culture* 12(3): 721–48.

Miller, J. H. (1999). *Black Holes*. Stanford, CA, Stanford University Press.

Mink, L. O. (1974). 'History and Fiction as Modes of Comprehension'. *New Directions in Literary History*. Ed. R. Cohen. London, Routledge & Kegan Paul.

Mintz, S. (1998). 'The Localization of Anthropological Practice: From Area Studies to Transnationalism'. *Critique of Anthropology* 18(2): 117–33.

Miyoshi, M. (1974). *Accomplices of Silence: The Modern Japanese Novel*. Berkeley, CA, University of California Press.

—— (1993). 'A Borderless World? From Colonialism to Transnationalism and the Decline of the Nation State'. *Critical Inquiry* 19: 726–51.

—— (2000). 'Ivory Tower in Escrow'. *boundary 2* 27(1): 7–50.

Modisane, B. (1963). *Blame Me on History*. Harmondsworth, Penguin.

Mohammadi, A., Ed. (2002). *Islam Encountering Globalization*. Abingdon, Routledge-Curzon.

Monbiot, G. (2003). *The Age of Consent: A Manifesto for a New World Order*. London, Flamingo.

Mongia, P., Ed. (1997). *Postcolonial Theory: A Reader*. London, Arnold.

Moosa, M. (1997). *The Origins of Modern Arabic Fiction*. Boulder, CO, Lynne Rienner.

Moretti, F. (1996). *Modern Epic: The World-System from Goethe to García Márquez*. London, Verso.

—— (1998). *Atlas of the European Novel, 1800–1900*. London, Verso.

Morgenthau, H. J. (1960). *Politics among Nations*. New York, Knopf.

Morton, S. (2008). ' "There Were Collisions and Explosions. The World Was No Longer Calm." Terror and Precarious Life in Salman Rushdie's *Shalimar the Clown*'. *Textual Practice* 22(2): 337–55.

Motion Picture Association of America (1999). 'Statement of Jack Valenti, Chairman and Ceo, Mpa, before the Committee on Ways and Means Subcommittee on Trade Regarding U. S.–China Trade Relations and the Possible Accession of China to the WTO'. Press Release. 8 June.

—— (2002). 'Study Shows Copyright Industries as Largest Contributor to the U.S. Economy'. Copyright Press Releases. 22 April.

Mount, F. (2006). 'What Happened to the Working Class'. London: ICA, 15 March.

Mpe, P. (2001). *Welcome to Our Hillbrow*. Scottsville, University of KwaZulu-Natal Press.

Mphahlele, E. (1959). *Down Second Avenue*. London, Faber and Faber.

Mukherjee, M. (1985). *Realism and Reality: The Novel and Society in India*. Oxford, Oxford University Press.

Mulhern, F. (2000). *Culture/Metaculture*. London, Routledge.

Muñoz, J. E. (1999). *Disidentifications: Queers of Color and the Performance of Politics*. Minneapolis, MN, University of Minnesota Press.

Murphy, P. D. (2000). *Farther Afield in the Study of Nature-Oriented Literature*. Charlottesville, VA, University Press of Virginia.

—— (2006). 'Grounding Anotherness and Answerability through Allonational Ecoliterature Formations'. *Nature in Literary and Cultural Studies: Transatlantic Conversations on Ecocriticism*. Eds. C. Gersdorf and S. Mayer. Amsterdam, Rodopi: 417–34.

Nabhan, G. (2002). *Coming Home to Eat: The Pleasures and Politics of Local Foods*. New York, W. W. Norton.

Naess, A. (1995). 'The Third World, Wilderness, and Deep Ecology'. *Deep Ecology for the Twenty-First Century*. Ed. G. Sessions. Boston, MA, Shambala: 397–407.

Nandy, A. (1989). 'The Political Culture of the Indian State'. *Daedelus* 118(4): 1–26.

National Labor Committee (1999). 'Wal-Mart's Shirts of Misery'. 16 July 2001 www.nlcnet.org/WALMART/bangwal.html.

New, W. H. (1997). *Land Sliding: Imagining Space, Presence, and Power in Canadian Writing*. Toronto, University of Toronto Press.

Newman, R. (2003). *The Fountain at the Centre of the World*. London, Verso.

Ngugi, J. T. o. (1968). *The Black Hermit*. Nairobi, Heinemann Educational Books.

—— (1972). *Homecoming: Essays on African and Caribbean Literature, Culture and Politics*. London, Heinemann.

Nicoll, F. (1989). 'My Trip to Alice'. *Criticism, Heresy and Interpretation* 3: 21–32.

Nordau, M. (1968 [1892]). *Degeneration*. New York, Fertig.

North American Free Trade Agreement between the Government of the United States of America, the Government of Canada and the Government of the United Mexican States (1993). Washington, DC, Government Printing Office.

Nussbaum, M. C. and J. Cohen (1996). *For Love of Country: Debating the Limits of Patriotism*. Boston, MA, Beacon Press.

O'Brien, S. and I. Szeman (2001). 'Introduction: The Globalization of Fiction/the Fiction of Globalization'. *South Atlantic Quarterly* 100(3): 603–26.

O'Hanlon, R. (2000). 'Recovering the Subject: Subaltern Studies and Histories of Resistance in Colonial South Asia'. *Mapping Subaltern Studies and the Postcolonial*. Ed. V. Chaturvedi. London, Verso: 72–115.

Obiechina, E. (1975). *Culture, Tradition and Society in the West African Novel*. Cambridge, Cambridge University Press.

Ohmae, K. (1990). *The Borderless World: Power and Strategy in the Interlinked World Economy*. London, Fontana.

Olney, M. L. (1991). *Buy Now, Pay Later: Advertising, Credit, and Consumer Durables in the 1920s*. Chapel Hill, NC, University of North Carolina Press.

Omaar, H. (2008). 'Playing Indian / Disintegrating Irishness: Globalization and Cross-Cultural Identity in Paul Muldoon's "Madoc: A Mystery" '. *Contemporary Literature* 49(2): 232–62.

Omvedt, G. (1999). 'An Open Letter to Arundhati Roy: The Friends of River Narmada'. Retrieved 21 June 2004 from www.narmada.org/debates/gail/gail.open. letter.html.

Ong, A. (1987). *Spirits of Resistance and Capitalist Discipline: Factory Women in Malaysia*. Albany, NY, State University of New York Pres.

—— (1997). 'Chinese Modernities: Narratives of Nation and of Capitalism'. *The Cultural Politics of Modern Chinese Transnationalism*. Eds. A. Ong and D. Nonini. New York, Routledge: 171–202.

—— (1999). *Flexible Citizenship: The Cultural Logics of Transnationality*. Durham, NC, Duke University Press.

Ortiz, R. (1988). *A Moderna Tradição Brasileira*. São Paulo, Brasinliense.

Osteen, M. W. a. M. (1999). 'Taking Account of the New Economic Criticism: An Historical Introduction'. *The New Economic Criticism: Studies at the Intersection of Literature and Economics*. Ed. M. W. a. M. Osteen. London, Routledge.

Owen, S. (1990). 'What Is World Poetry: The Anxiety of Global Influence'. *The New Republic*. 19 November: 28–32.

Palumbo-Liu, D. (1995). 'Universalism and Minority Culture'. *Differences* 7(1): 188–208.

Paolini, A. (1995). 'The Place of Africa in Discourses about the Postcolonial, the Global, and the Modern'. *New Formations* 31(Summer): 83–106.

Parla, J. (forthcoming). Desiring Tellers, Fugitive Tales: Don Quixote Rides Again, This Time in Istanbul.

Parry, B. (2004). *Postcolonial Studies: A Materialist Critique*. London, Routledge.

Pasha, M. K. (2004). 'Globalization, Islam and Resistance'. *The Globalization Reader*. Eds. F. J. Lechner and J. Boli. Malden, MA, Blackwell.

Paton, A. (1948). *Cry, the Beloved Country*. London, Jonathan Cape

Peck, J. (1998). 'From Federal Welfare to Local Workfare? Remaking Canada's Work–Welfare Regime'. *An Unruly World? Geography, Globalization and Governance*. Eds. A. Herod, G. Ó. Tuathail and S. M. Roberts. London, Routledge: 95–115.

Peled, Y. (2006). 'Zionist Realities'. *New Left Review* 38 21–36;.

Pelletiere, S. C. (2001). *Iraq and the International Oil System: Why America Went to War in the Gulf*. Westport, CN, Praeger.

Pepper, D. (1993). *Eco-Socialism: From Deep Ecology to Social Justice*. London, Routledge.

Pérez de Cuéllar, J. (1996). 'President's Foreword'. *Our Creative Diversity: World Commission on Culture and Development*. Paris, UNESCO.

Pia, P. (1961). *Baudelaire*. Trans. P. Gregory. New York, Grove Press.

Pieterse, J. N. (1998). 'Hybrid Modernities: Mélange Modernities in Asia'. *Sociological Analysis* 1(3): 75–86.

—— (2001). *Development Theory: Deconstructions/Reconstructions*. London, Sage.

Platz, N. (1998). 'Literature and Ecology: A Brief Agenda for Exploring the Green Dimension in Canadian Literature'. *Informal Empire? Cultural Relations between Canada, the United States and Europe*. Eds. P. Easingwood, K. Gross and H. Lutz. Kiel, I & F Verlag: 229–53.

—— (2000). 'Greening the New Literatures in English: A Plea for Ecocriticism'. *Anglistentag 1999 Mainz Proceedings*. Eds. B. Reitz and S. Rieuwerts. Trier, Wissenschaftlicher Verlag Trier: 313–26.

Plotinus (1956). *Enneads*. Trans. S. MacKenna. London, Faber and Faber.

Pollack, D. (1986). *The Fracture of Meaning: Japan's Synthesis of China from the Eighth through the Eighteenth Centuries*. Princeton, NJ, Princeton University Press.

Pollock, S. I., H. K. Bhabha, et al. (2000). 'Introduction'. *Public Culture* 12(3): 577–89.

Porte, J., Ed. (1983). *Ralph Waldo Emerson: Essays and Lectures*. Cambridge, MA, The Press Syndicate of the University of Cambridge.

Porter, C. (1994). 'What We Know That We Don't Know: Remapping American Literary Studies'. *American Literary History* 6(3): 467–526.

Posnock, R. (2000). 'The Dream of Deracination: The Uses of Cosmopolitanism'. *American Literary History* 12(4): 802–18.

Poulantzas, N. (1978). *State, Power, Socialism*. Trans. P. Camiller. London, NLB.

Pound, E. (1972). *The Cantos of Ezra Pound*. New York, New Directions.

Powell, C. S. (1995). 'The Rights Stuff: Buying and Selling Art in a Digital World'. *Scientific American* 272(1): 30–31.

Pramoedya, Ananta Toer (1996). *Child of All Nations*. Trans. M. Lane. New York, Penguin.

Pred, A. and M. Watts (1992). *Reworking Modernity: Capitalism and Symbolic Discontent*. New Brunswick, NJ, Rutgers University Press.

Pryke, M. and J. Allen (2000). 'Monetized Time-Space: Derivatives – Money's "New Imaginary" '? *Economy and Society* 29(2): 264–84.

Quayson, A. (1997). *Strategic Transformations in Nigerian Writing: Orality and History in the Work of Rev. Samuel Johnson, Amos Tutuola, Wole Soyinka and Ben Okri*. Bloomington, IN, Indiana University Press.

Randeria, S. (1998). 'Globalisierung und Geschlechterfrage: zur Einführung'. *Globalisierung aus Frauensicht: Bilanzen und Visionen*. Eds. R. Klingebiel and S. Randeria. Bonn, Dietz.

Rashid, A. (2002). *Taliban: Islam, Oil and the New Great Game in Central Asia*. London, I. B. Tauris.

Readings, B. (1996). *The University in Ruins*. Cambridge, MA, Harvard University Press.

Reagon, B. J. (1988). *Are My Hands Clean?*. Performance by Sweet Honey in the Rock. Live at Carnegie Hall. Flying Fish, 1988.

Ricoeur, P. (1981). *Hermeneutics and the Human Sciences: Essays on Language, Action and Interpretation*. Trans. J. B. Thompson. Cambridge, Cambridge University Press.

Rifkin, J. (2000). *The End of Work: The Decline of the Global Work-Force and the Dawn of the Post-Market Era*. London, Penguin.

Riles, A. (2000). *The Network Inside Out*. Ann Arbor, MI, University of Michigan Press.

Robbins, B. (1999). *Feeling Global: Internationalism in Distress*. New York, New York University Press.

—— (2001). 'Very Busy Just Now: Globalization and Harriedness in Ishiguro's "The Unconsoled" '. *Comparative Literature* 53(4): 426–41.

Robertson, R. (1990). 'Mapping the Global Condition: Globalization as the Central Concept'. *Global Culture: Nationalism, Globalization and Modernity*. Ed. M. Featherstone. *A Theory, Culture and Society Special Issue*. London, Sage Publiations: 15–30.

—— (1992). *Globalization: Social Theory and Global Culture*. London, Sage Publications.

—— (1995). 'Glocalization: Time-Space and Homogeneity-Heterogeneity'. *Global Modernities*. Eds. M. Featherstone, S. Lash and R. Robertson. London, Sage Publications: 25–44.

Rochberg-Halton, E. (1986). *Meaning and Modernity: Social Theory in the Pragmatic Attitude*. Chicago, IL, University of Chicago Press.

Roht-Arriaza, N. (1996). 'Of Seeds and Shamans: The Appropriation of the Scientific and Technical Knowledge of Indigenous and Local Communities'. *Michigan Journal of International Law* 17: 919–65.

Rosaldo, R. (1989). *Culture and Truth: Remaking of Social Analysis*. Boston, MA, Beacon Press.

Rosenberg, J. (2002). *The Follies of Globalization Theory*. London, Verso.

Ross, A. (1994). *The Chicago Gangster Theory of Life: Nature's Debt to Society*. London, Verso.

Ross, K. (1988). *The Emergence of Social Space: Rimbaud and the Paris Commune*. Basingstoke, Macmillan.

—— (1995). *Fast Cars, Clean Bodies: Decolonization and the Reordering of French Culture*. Cambridge, MA, MIT Press.

Rotman, B. (1987). *Signifying Nothing: The Semiotics of Zero*. London, Macmillan.

Rouse, R. (1991). 'Mexican Migration and the Social Space of Postmodernism'. *Diaspora* 1(1): 8–23.

Rowell, A. (1996). *Green Backlash: Global Subversion of the Environmental Movement*. London, Routledge.

Roy, A. (1997). *The God of Small Things*. London, Flamingo.

—— (1999 [1998]). 'The End of the Imagination'. *The Cost of Living: The Greater Common Good and the End of the Imagination*. London, Flamingo.

—— (1999). 'The Greater Common Good'. *The Cost of Living: The Greater Common Good and the End of the Imagination*. London, Flamingo.

—— (1999). *The Cost of Living: The Greater Common Good and the End of the Imagination*. London, Flamingo.

Royle, N. (1996). *Counterparts*. Clarkson, GA, White Wolf Publications.

Ruf, A. (1998). 'Frauennezwerke im Spannungsfeld von Globalisierung und Vielfalt'. *Globalisierung aus Frauensicht: Bilanzen und Visionen*. Eds. R. Klingebiel and S. Randeria. Bonn, Dietz: 66–85.

Rushdie, S. (1990). *Haroun and the Sea of Stories*. London, Granta.

—— (1992). *Imaginary Homelands: Essays and Criticism 1981–1991*. London, Granta Books.

Sadowski-Smith, C. (2008). *Border Fictions: Globalization, Empire, and Writing at the Boundaries of the United States*. Charlottesville, VA, University of Virginia Press.

Said, E. (1995). 'Embargoed Literature'. *Between Languages and Cultures: Translation and Cross-Cultural Texts*. Eds. A. Dingwaney and C. Maier. Pittsburgh, PA, University of Pittsburgh Press: 97–102.

—— (2002). *Freud and the Non-European*. London, Verso.

Said, E. W. (1978). *Orientalism*. London, Penguin Books.

—— (1985). *Beginnings: Intention and Method*. New York, Columbia University Press.

—— (1993). *Culture and Imperialism*. London, Vintage.

Saint Augustine (1972). *The City of God*. Trans. H. Bettenson. Harmondsworth, Penguin.

Sakai, N. (1989). 'Modernity and Its Critique: The Problem of Universalism and Particularism'. *Postmodernism and Japan*. Eds. M. Miyoshi and H. D. Harootunian. Durham, NC, Duke University Press: 93–142.

San Juan, E. (1998). *Beyond Postcolonial Theory*. Basingstoke, Macmillan.

Sanford, C. (1994). 'Financial Markets in 2020'. *Proceedings of Federal Reserve Bank of Kansas City Economic Symposium*: 1–10.

Sanger, D. E. (1995). 'U.S. Threatens $2.8 Billion of Tariffs on China Exports'. *New York Times*. 1 January: 14.

Santos, M. I. (1994). 'El sistema literario: teoría empírica y teoría de los polisistemas'. *Avances en teoría de la literatura*. Ed. D. Villanueva. Santiago de Compostela, Universidad de Santiago de Compostela: 309–56.

Sassen, S. (1988). *The Mobility of Labor and Capital: A Study in International Investment and Labor Flow*. Cambridge, Cambridge University Press.

—— (1996). *Losing Control? Sovereignty in an Age of Globalization. University Seminars/ Leonard Hastings Schoff Memorial Lectures*. New York, Columbia University Press.

—— (1998). *Globalization and Its Discontents*. New York, The New Press.

—— (2000). *Cities in a World Economy*. Thousand Oaks, CA, Pine Forge Press.

—— (2002). *Global Networks, Linked Cities*. New York; London, Routledge.

Saul, J. S. (2003). 'Globalization, Imperialism, Development: False Binaries and Radical Resolutions'. *Socialist Register 2004: The New Imperial Challenge*. Eds. L. Panitch and C. Leys. London, The Merlin Press: 220–44.

Saussy, H., Ed. (2006). *Comparative Literature in an Age of Globalization*. Baltimore, MD, Johns Hopkins University Press.

Sawer, P. (2008) 'Gordon Brown Warns on Global Financial Crisis'. *Daily Telegraph*. London. 5 April.

Schama, S. (1991). 'Homelands'. *Social Research* 58(1): 11–30.

Schiller, H. I. (1976). *Communication and Cultural Domination*. White Plains, NY, International Arts and Sciences.

Schiller, N. G., L. Basch, et al., Eds. (1992). *Towards a Transnational Perspective on Migration: Race, Class, Ethnicity, and Nationalism Reconsidered*. New York, New York Academy of Sciences.

Schumpeter, J. A. (1950). *Capitalism, Socialism, and Democracy*. New York, Harper & Row.

Schwarz, H. and S. Roy, Eds. (2000). *A Companion to Postcolonial Studies*. Malden, MA, Blackwell.

Schwarz, R. (1992). *Misplaced Ideas: Essays on Brazilian Culture*. London, Verso.

Scioliono, E. (1995). 'President Imposes Trade Sanctions on Chinese Goods: A Trade Tie That Binds'. *New York Times*. 5 February: 1, 12.

Scott, H. (2006). *Caribbean Women Writers and Globalization: Fictions of Independence*. Aldershot, Ashgate.

Seaford, R. (2000). 'Aristotelian Economics and Athenian Tragedy'. *New Literary History* 31(2): 269–76.

Sedgwick, E. K. (1993). *Tendencies*. Durham, NC, Duke University Press.

Selden, R., Ed. (1995). *The Cambridge History of Literary Criticism*. Cambridge, Cambridge University Press.

Sender, H. (1998). 'Money Isn't Everything'. *Far Eastern Economic Review* 161(7): 56–59.

Shapiro, M. J. (1997). *Violent Cartographies: Mapping Cultures of War*. Minneapolis, MN, University of Minnesota Press.

—— (1999). *Cinematic Political Thought: Narrating Race, Nation and Gender*. Edinburgh, Edinburgh University Press.

Sharpe, J. (1993). *Allegories of Empire: The Figure of Woman in the Colonial Text*. Minneapolis, MN, University of Minnesota Press.

Shaw, R. (1999). *Reclaiming America: Nike, Clean Air, and the New National Activism*. Berkeley, CA, University of California Press.

Shell, M. (1982). *Money, Language and Thought*. Baltimore, MD, Johns Hopkins University Press.

Shiva, V. (1991). *The Violence of the Green Revolution: Third World Agriculture, Ecology and Politics*. London, Zed.

—— (2005). 'The Polarised World of Globalization – a Response to Friedman's

Flat Earth Hypothesis'. *Z-NET*. Retrieved 11 January 2010 from www. tamilnation.org/oneworld/shiva.htm.

Sicherman, C. (1995). 'Ngugi's Colonial Education: "The Subversion . . . of the African Mind" '. *African Studies Review* 38(3): 11–41.

Siebers, T. (1993). *Cold War Criticism and the Politics of Skepticism*. Oxford, Oxford University Press.

Sieg, K. (1993). 'The Revolution Has Been Televised: Reconfiguring History and Identity in Post-Wall Germany'. *Theatre Journal* 45(1): 35–48.

Siemann, H. (unpublished). *IndierInnen*.

Singh, S. (1995). 'Introduction'. *The Dam and the Nation: Displacement and Resettlement in the Narmada Valley*. Eds. J. Drèze, M. Samson and S. Singh. Delhi, Oxford University Press: 1–25.

Sivanandan, A. (2001). 'Poverty Is the New Black'. *Race & Class* 43(1): 1–5.

Skrbis, Z., G. Kendall, et al. (2004). 'Locating Cosmopolitanism: Between Humanist Ideal and Grounded Social Category'. *Theory Culture Society* 21(6): 115–36.

Slaymaker, W. (2001). 'Ecoing the Other(s): The Call of Global Green and Black African Responses'. *PMLA* 116(1): 129–44.

Sluyter, A. (2002). *Colonialism and Landscape: Postcolonial Theory and Applications*. Lanham, MD, Rowman & Littlefield Publishers.

Smith, A. D. (1979). *Nationalism in the Twentieth Century*. New York, New York University Press.

Smith, P. (1988). 'Visiting the Banana Republic'. *Universal Abandon: The Politics of Postmodernism*. Ed. A. Ross. Minneapolis, University of Minnesota Press.

Smith, Z. (2000). *White Teeth*. London, Hamish Hamilton.

Soja, E. W. (1988). *Postmodern Geographies: The Reassertion of Space in Critical Social Theory*. London, Verso.

Sommer, D. (1991). *Foundational Fictions: The National Romances of Latin America*. Berkeley, CA, University of California Press.

Spivak, G. C. (1982). 'The Politics of Translation'. *Destabilizing Theory*. Eds. M. Barrett and A. Phillips. Cambridge, Polity Press: 177–200.

—— (1987). *In Other Worlds: Essays in Cultural Politics*. London, Methuen.

—— (1993). 'Reading the Satanic Verses'. *Outside in the Reading Machine*. New York, Routledge.

—— (1998). 'Cultural Talks in the Hot Peace: Revisiting The "Global Village" '. *Cosmopolitics: Thinking and Feeling Beyond the Nation*. Eds. P. Cheah and B. Robbins. Minneapolis, MN, University of Minnesota Press: 329–48.

—— (1999). *A Critique of Postcolonial Reason: Toward a History of the Vanishing Present*. Cambridge, MA, Harvard University Press.

—— (2000). 'Other Things Are Never Equal: A Speech'. *Rethinking Marxism* 12(4): 37–45.

—— (2003). *Death of a Discipline*. New York, Columbia University Press.

—— (2006). 'World Systems and the Creole'. *Narrative* 14(1): 102–12.

Spretnak, C. (1990). 'Our Roots and Flowering'. *Reweaving the World: The Emergence of Ecofeminism*. Eds. I. Diamond and G. F. Orenstein. San Franciso, CA, Sierra Club Books: 3–14.

Standing, G. (1989). 'Global Feminization through Flexible Labor'. *World Development* 17(7): 1077–95.

Sterling, B. (2001). *A Good Old-Fashioned Future*. London, Millennium.

Stiglitz, J. E. (2002). *Globalization and Its Discontents*. New York, W. W. Norton.

Stone, C. D. (1996). *Should Trees Have Standing? And Other Essays on Law, Morals, and the Environment*. Dobbs Ferry, NY, Oceana Publications.

Strange, S. (1986). *Casino Capitalism*. Oxford, Basil Blackwell.

Suleri, S. (1992). 'Woman Skin Deep: Feminism and the Postcolonial Condition'. *Critical Inquiry* 18(4): 756–69.

Sunseri, T. R. (2002). *Vilimani: Labor Migration and Rural Change in Early Colonial Tanzania*. Portsmouth, NH, Heinemann.

Tadiar, N. X. M. (1993). 'Sexual Economies in the Asia-Pacific Community'. *What Is in a Rim? Critical Perspectives on the Pacific Region Idea*. Ed. A. Dirlik. Boulder, CO, Westview Press.

Tait, L. (2001). 'Welcome to Our Literature'. *The Sunday Times*. London. September.

Taussig, M. T. (1997). *The Magic of the State*. London, Routledge.

Taylor, P. and F. Buttel (1992). 'How Do We Know We Have Global Environmental Problems? Science and the Globalization of Environmental Discourse'. *Geoforum* 23(3): 405–16.

The Economist (2007). 'Robert Peel: Father of Globalisation'. *The Economist*. 30 June: 97.

Thomashow, M. (2002). *Bringing the Biosphere Home: Learning to Perceive Global Environmental Change*. Cambridge, MA, MIT Press.

Thrift, N. (1996). *Spatial Formations*. London, Sage.

Thussu, D., Ed. (1998). *Electronic Empires: Global Media and Local Resistance*. London, Arnold.

Tilley, V. (2006). 'The Secular Solution'. *New Left Review* 38: 37–57.

Tomlinson, J. (1999). *Globalization and Culture*. Cambridge, Polity.

Toschi, L. (1989). 'Alle origini della narrativa di romanzo in Italia'. *Il viaggio del narrare*. Ed. M. Saltafuso. Florence, La Giuntina.

Tratner, M. (2001). *Deficits and Desires: Economics and Sexuality in Twentieth-Century Literature*. Stanford, CA, Stanford University Press.

Tsing, A. (1999). *Notes on Culture and Natural Resource Management*. Berkeley Workshop on Environmental Politics, Working Paper WP 99–4, Institute of International Studies, University of California at Berkeley.

—— (2000). 'Inside the Economy of Appearances'. *Public Culture* 12(1): 115–44.

Vassanji, M. G. (1989). *The Gunny Sack*. Oxford, Heinemann.

—— (1996). *The Book of Secrets*. New York, Picador.

Vidal, J. (2003). 'They Stood up to Be Counted – and Found Nobody Could Agree on Totals'. *The Guardian*. London. 17 February.

Virilio, P. (1980). *Esthétique de la disparition*. Paris, Balland.

—— (1986). *Speed and Politics: An Essay on Dromology*. Trans. M. Polizzotti. New York, Semiotexte.

—— (1997). *Open Sky*. London, Verso.

Viswanathan, G. (1989). *Masks of Conquest: Literary Study and British Rule in India*. London, Faber and Faber.

Waldinger, Roger D. (1986). *Through the Eye of the Needle: Immigrants and Enterprise in New York's Garment Trades*. New York: New York University Press.

Wallace, M. (2001). ' "Venerated Emblems": Delillo's *Underworld* and the History-Commodity'. *Critique* 42(4): 367–83.

Wallerstein, I. (1974). *The Modern World-System*. New York, Academic Press.

—— (1984). *The Politics of the World-Economy*. Cambridge, Cambridge University Press.

—— (2000). *The Essential Wallerstein*. New York, The New Press.

Wang, D. D.-w. (1997). *Fin-de-siècle Splendor: Repressed Modernities of Late Qing Fiction, 1849–1911*. Stanford, CA, California University Press.

Wark, M. (1994a). 'Third Nature'. *Cultural Studies* 8(1): 115–32.

—— (1994b). *Virtual Geography: Living with Global Media Events*. Bloomington, IN, University of Indiana Press.

Warner, M. (1990). *The Letters of the Republic: Publication and the Public Sphere in Eighteenth-Century America*. Cambridge, MA; London, Harvard University Press.

Weber, M. (1949). *The Methodology of the Social Sciences*. New York, Free Press.

Weinbaum, A. E. and B. H. Edwards (2000). 'On Critical Globality'. *ARIEL* 31(1–2): 255–74.

Weiner, A. B. (1992). *Inalienable Possessions: The Paradox of Keeping-While-Giving*. Berkeley, CA, University of California Press.

Wellman, L. (1999). 'The Effects of the Internet on Copyright and Intellectual Property: New Legal Issues for Publisher in the Electronic Marketplace'. Retrieved 30 August 1999 from www.office.com/global/0,2724,63–286_I,FF.html.

White, H. (1999). *Figural Realism: Studies in the Mimesis Effect*. Baltimore, MD, Johns Hopkins University Press.

Wichterich, C. (1998). *Die globalisierte Frau: Berichte aus der Zukunft der Ungleichheit*. Hamburg, Rowohlt.

Wiegersma, N. and J. Medley (2000). *US Economic Development Policies toward the Pacific Rim: Successes and Failures of US Aid*. New York, St. Martin's Press.

Williams, P. and L. Chrisman, Eds. (1993). *Colonial Discourse and Post-Colonial Theory: A Reader*. Hemel Hempstead, Harvester Wheatsheaf.

Williams, R. (1958). *Culture and Society, 1780–1950*. London, Chatto.

—— (1973). *The Country and the City*. London, Chatto and Windus.

—— (1976). *Keywords: A Vocabulary of Culture and Society*. London, Fontana.

Williams, W. C. (1958). *Paterson, Book Five*. New York, New Directions.

Wilson, R. and W. Dissanayake (1996). 'Introduction: Tracking the Global/Local'. *Global/Local: Cultural Production and the Transnational Imaginary*. Eds. R. Wilson and W. Dissanayake. Durham, NC, Durham: Duke University Press: 1–18.

Wolf, E. R. (1982). *Europe and the People without History*. Berkeley, CA; London, University of California Press.

Woodmanse, M. and M. Osteen (1999). *The New Economic Criticism: Studies at the Intersection of Literature and Economics*. London, Routledge.

World Bank (2000). *Global Economic Prospects and the Developing Countries*. Washington, DC, World Bank.

Wren, R. M. (1990). *Those Magical Years: The Making of Nigerian Literature at Ibadan, 1948–1966*. Boulder, CO, Lynne Rienner.

Yacine, K. (1961). *Nedjma*. Trans. R. Howard. New York, George Braziller.

Yamashita, K. T. (1997). *Tropic of Orange: A Novel*. Minneapolis, MI, Coffee House Press.

—— (2005). 'An Interview with Karen Tei Yamashita: With Jean Vengua Gier and Carla Alicia Tejeda'. *Jouvert* 2(2).

Yijie, T. (2000). 'Zai Jingji Quanqiuhua Xingshi Xiade Zhonghua Wenhua Dingwei (The Establishment of Chinese Culture in the Age of Economic Globalization) [Trans. Dirlik]'. *Zhongguo wenhua yanjiu (Chinese Culture Research)*. Trans. Dirlik. 30.

Yoshimoto, M. (1989). 'The Postmodern and Mass Images in Japan'. *Public Culture* 1(2): 8–25.

Young-Bruehl, E., Ed. (1994). *Global Cultures: A Transnational Short Fiction Reader*. Hanover, NH, University Press of New England.

Young, R. J. C. (1999). ' "Dangerous and Wrong": Shell, Intervention and the Politics of Transnational Companies'. *Interventions: International Journal of Postcolonial Studies* 1(3): 439 – 64.

—— (2001). *Postcolonialism: An Historical Introduction*. Oxford, Blackwell.

—— (2003). *Postcolonial Theory: A Very Short Introduction*. Oxford, Oxford University Press.

Yúdice, G. (1999). 'La industria de la música en el marco de la integración Américana Latina–Estado Unidos'. *Integración económica e industrias culturales en América Latina*. Eds. N. Garcia Canclini and C. Moneta. Mexico City, Grijalbo.

Zhao, H. Y. H. (1995). *The Uneasy Narrator: Chinese Fiction from the Traditional to the Modern*. Oxford, Oxford University Press.

Žižek, S. (1999). *The Ticklish Subject: The Absent Centre of Political Ontology*. London, Verso.

Zukin, S. (1993). *Landscapes of Power: From Detroit to Disney World*. Berkeley, CA, University of California Press.

Index

Related titles from Routledge

The Routledge Concise History of Southeast Asian Writing in English
Rajeev S. Patke and Philip Holden

The Routledge Concise History of Southeast Asian Writing in English traces the development of literature in the region within its historical and cultural contexts. This volume explores creative writing in English across different genres and media, establishing connections from the colonial activity of the early modern period through to contemporary writing across Southeast Asia, focusing especially on the Philippines, Malaysia, Singapore and Hong Kong.

In this critical guide, Rajeev S. Patke and Philip Holden:

- interweave text and context through the history of creative writing in the region
- examine language use and variation, making use of illuminating examples from speech, poetry and fictional prose
- trace the impact of historical, political and cultural events
- engage with current debates on national consciousness, globalization, modernity and postmodernism
- provide useful features including a glossary, further reading section and chapter summaries.

Direct and clearly written, this concise history guides readers through key topics while presenting a unique, original synthesis of history and practice in Southeast Asian writing in English. It is the ideal starting point for students and all those seeking a better understanding of Southeast Asian literatures and cultures.

ISBN13: 978–0–415–43568–0 (hbk)
ISBN13: 978–0–415–43569–7 (pbk)
ISBN13: 978–0–203–87403–5 (ebk)

Available at all good bookshops
For ordering and further information please visit:
www.routledgeliterature.com

Related titles from Routledge

Fifty Key Literary Theorists
Richard J. Lane

What is it that defines literary theory? Richard J. Lane explores fifty influential figures who have shaped this field over the last century. In one volume, theorists from a multitude of disciplines are brought together in order to explore literary theory in all its diversity, covering feminism to postcolonialism, postmodernism to psychoanalysis.

Each entry deals with key concepts and ideas that have informed literary studies in the twentieth and twenty-first centuries. Included in this comprehensive guide are entries on:

- Roland Barthes
- Judith Butler
- Jacques Derrida
- Sigmund Freud
- Edward W. Said

An essential resource for all students of literature, *Fifty Key Literary Theorists* explores the gamut of critical debate, offering both an excellent introduction to and a comprehensive overview of modern literary theorists.

ISBN 13: 978–0–415–33847–9 (hbk)
ISBN 13: 978–0–415–33848–6 (pbk)
ISBN 13: 978–0–203–44142–8 (ebk)

Available at all good bookshops
For ordering and further information please visit:
www.routledge.com

Related titles from Routledge

Literary Theory: The Basics
Third Edition
Hans Bertens

With a new introduction and fully updated pointers to further reading, this third edition of Hans Bertens' bestselling book is a must-have guide to the world of literary theory.

Exploring a broad range of topics from Marxist and feminist criticism to post-modernism and new historicism it includes new coverage of:

- the latest developments in post-colonial and cultural theory
- literature and sexuality
- the latest schools of thought, including eco-criticism and post-humanism
- the future of literary theory and criticism.

Literary Theory: The Basics is an essential purchase for anyone who wants to know what literary theory is and where it is going.

ISBN 13: 978– 0–415–39670–7 (hbk)
ISBN 13: 978– 0–415–39671–4 (pbk)

Available at all good bookshops
For ordering and further information please visit:
www.routledgeliterature.com

Related titles from Routledge

Orality and Literacy
Second Edition
Walter J. Ong

'No comparable work on this important subject exists. Thanks to the lucidity of its style and presentation of complex thought, this is a work that will be accessible and useful ... it will be the standard introduction to this topic for some years to come' – *Choice*

This classic work explores the vast differences between oral and literate cultures offering a very clear account of the intellectual, literary and social effects of writing, print and electronic technology.

In the course of his study, Walter J. Ong offers fascinating insights into oral genres across the globe and through time, and examines the rise of abstract philosophical and scientific thinking. He considers the impact of orality-literacy studies not only on literary criticism and theory but on our very understanding of what it is to be a human being, conscious of self and other.

This is a book no reader, writer or speaker should be without.

ISBN13: 978–0–415–28128–7 (hbk)
ISBN13: 978–0–415–28129–4 (pbk)
ISBN13: 978–0–203–42625–8 (ebk)

Available at all good bookshops
For ordering and further information please visit:
www.routledgeliterature.com

Related titles from Routledge

Postcolonial Ecocriticism
Literature, Animals, Environment
Graham Huggan and Helen Tiffin

In *Postcolonial Ecocriticism*, Graham Huggan and Helen Tiffin examine relationships between humans, animals and the environment in postcolonial texts. Divided into two sections that consider the postcolonial first from an environmental and then a zoocritical perspective, the book looks at:

- narratives of development in postcolonial writing;
- entitlement and belonging in the pastoral genre;
- colonialist 'asset stripping' and the Christian mission;
- the politics of eating and representations of cannibalism;
- animality and spirituality;
- sentimentality and anthropomorphism;
- the place of the human and the animal in a 'posthuman' world.

Making use of the work of authors as diverse as J.M. Coetzee, Joseph Conrad, Daniel Defoe, Jamaica Kincaid and V.S. Naipaul, the authors argue that human liberation will never be fully achieved without challenging how human societies have constructed themselves in hierarchical relation to other human and nonhuman communities, and without imagining new ways in which these ecologically connected groupings can be creatively transformed.

ISBN13: 978–0–415–34457–9 (hbk)
ISBN13: 978–0–415–34458–6 (pbk)
ISBN13: 978–0–203–49817–0 (ebk)

Available at all good bookshops
For ordering and further information please visit:
www.routledgeliterature.com

Related titles from Routledge

The Post-Colonial Studies Reader
Second edition
Graham Huggan and Helen Tiffin

In *Postcolonial Ecocriticism*, Graham Huggan and Helen Tiffin examine relationships between humans, animals and the environment in postcolonial texts. Divided into two sections that consider the postcolonial first from an environmental and then a zoocritical perspective, the book looks at:

- narratives of development in postcolonial writing;

- entitlement and belonging in the pastoral genre;

- colonialist 'asset stripping' and the Christian mission;

- the politics of eating and representations of cannibalism;

- animality and spirituality;

- sentimentality and anthropomorphism;

- the place of the human and the animal in a 'posthuman' world.

Making use of the work of authors as diverse as J.M. Coetzee, Joseph Conrad, Daniel Defoe, Jamaica Kincaid and V.S. Naipaul, the authors argue that human liberation will never be fully achieved without challenging how human societies have constructed themselves in hierarchical relation to other human and nonhuman communities, and without imagining new ways in which these ecologically connected groupings can be creatively transformed.

ISBN13: 978–0–415–34457–9 (hbk)
ISBN13: 978–0–415–34458–6 (pbk)
ISBN13: 978–0–203–49817–0 (ebk)

Available at all good bookshops
For ordering and further information please visit:
www.routledge.com

ROUTLEDGE RESEARCH IN POSTCOLONIAL LITERATURES

Edited in collaboration with the Centre for Colonial and Postcolonial Studies, University of Kent at Canterbury, this series presents a wide range of research into postcolonial literatures by specialists in the field. Volumes will concentrate on writers and writing originating in previously (or presently) colonized areas, and will include material from non-anglophone as well as anglophone colonies and literatures.
Series editors: Donna Landry and Caroline Rooney

Available in this series:

For further information on individual books in the series, visit: www.routledgeliterature.com